Working-Class Formation

Working-Class Formation

Nineteenth-Century Patterns in Western
Europe and the United States

EDITED BY

Ira Katznelson and Aristide R. Zolberg

PRINCETON UNIVERSITY PRESS

Copyright © 1986 by Princeton University Press
Published by Princeton University Press, 41 William Street, Princeton,
New Jersey 08540
In the United Kingdom: Princeton University Press, Guildford, Surrey

Library of Congress Cataloging in Publication Data will be found on the last printed
page of this book

ISBN 0-691-05485-1   ISBN 0-691-10207-4 (pbk.)

Publication of this book has been aided by the Whitney Darrow Fund
of Princeton University Press

This book has been composed in Linotron Times Roman type

Clothbound editions of Princeton University Press books are printed on acid-free
paper, and binding materials are chosen for strength and durability. Paperbacks,
although satisfactory for personal collections, are not usually suitable for library
rebinding
Printed in the United States of America by Princeton University Press
Princeton, New Jersey

Contents

Preface

Most edited collections either are the products of scholarly conferences or are compilations by editors of essays written by authors who do not gather face to face. In contrast, *Working-Class Formation* is the result of a collaborative process marked by systematic and intensive interaction between the authors.

In 1978, when they were colleagues at the University of Chicago, Ira Katznelson and Aristide Zolberg initiated the project that has resulted in this volume. With the aim of generating studies of working-class formation that would be free of teleology and sociological abstraction and that could overcome the fragmentation of ad hoc case studies, they enlisted the colleagues whose work appears below (and Rudolph Braun, an initial member of the group).

The Council for European Studies provided funds to allow the constitution of a Research Planning Group (a category the Council had established with the assistance of the German Marshall Fund and the Rockefeller Foundation). A small grant, in this case funded by the Rockefeller Foundation, enabled the full group to gather twice for intensive face-to-face discussion: at the University of Chicago in late 1979 to work out a shared agenda for the individual essays and, two years later, at Reid Hall in Paris, where early drafts of the papers were discussed.

Ira Katznelson circulated a discussion paper in advance of the first meeting. It suggested a preliminary framework for the comparative study of working classes at the early moments of their formation. Many of the arguments in that essay did not survive collegial critique; its core, however, which proposed that discussion of the topic often fails to distinguish between aspects of class and class analysis, did remain a central element of the collective project. It argued that "class" as a term is too frequently used in a congested way, encompassing meanings and questions that need to be separated from each other. The paper suggested, as does chapter one below, that we think of class as a concept with four connected layers of structure, ways of life, dispositions, and collective action.

The circulation of this essay and the discussion that followed provided a common framework for the authors working on France, Germany, and the United States. Their papers were completed for the second meeting, where the drafts were held up to collective examination and criticism.

The core essays in this book are revised versions of these papers, which were rewritten extensively after the session at Reid Hall.

A conference in May 1983 held under the auspices of the Centre d'Etudes Nord-Américaines of the Ecole des Hautes Etudes en Sciences Sociales in Paris gave the editors the opportunity to expose their interpretive, synthetic essays to collegial critique. They also received a helpful reading of their chapters from Ross Thomson. Finally, the exceptionally sympathetic readings given to the draft volume by Ronald Aminzade and Sean Wilentz, who served as readers for Princeton University Press, stimulated all the authors to revise their essays one last time.

The result is the book in your hands. Along the way, we were fortunate to have the very helpful participation of Rudolph Braun at our Chicago meeting and of Pierre Birnbaum and Marianne Debouzy at our Paris meeting. In addition, some of the authors presented drafts of their papers at a number of academic meetings, including the Conference of Europeanists, the Social Science History Association, and the American Political Science Association, where they received very useful reactions and comments.

These acknowledgments do not exhaust our debts. Marion Kaplan and Ioannis Sinanoglou of the Council for European Studies gave us indispensable help. Sanford Thatcher is one of the best editors of social science anywhere. Elizabeth Gretz has improved the manuscript in numerous ways. We are proud to have worked with them and with their colleagues at Princeton University Press.

Introduction

1 Working-Class Formation: Constructing Cases and Comparisons

• Ira Katznelson

As anyone familiar with the history of economic thought will immediately recognize, practically all the economists of the nineteenth century and many of the twentieth have believed uncritically that all that is needed to explain a given historical development is to indicate conditioning or causal factors, such as an increase in population on the supply of capital. But this is sufficient only in the rarest of cases. As a rule, no factor acts in a uniquely determined way and, whenever it does not, the necessity arises of going into the details of its *modus operandi*, into the mechanisms through which it acts. Examples will illustrate this. Sometimes an increase in population actually has no other effect than that predicted by classical theory—a fall in per capita income; but, at other times, it may have an energizing effect that induces new developments with the result that per capita real income rises. Or a protective duty may have no other effect than to increase the price of the protected commodity and, in consequence, its output; but it may also induce a complete reorganization of the protected industry which eventually results in an increase in output so great as to reduce the price below its initial level.

What has not adequately been appreciated among theorists is the distinction between different kinds of reaction to changes in 'condition.'—*Joseph Schumpeter*[1]

This book is about different kinds of reaction to proletarianization in nineteenth-century France, Germany, and the United States. It seeks to explain variations in the formation of working classes in these countries at the moment when class emerged as a way of organizing, thinking about, and acting on society; and it asks how initial patterns of sentiment, behavior, and organization shaped class relations later in the century.

In his recent essay, "The Making of the Working Class 1870-1914," Eric Hobsbawm, by nearly cloning the title of Edward Thompson's *The Making of the English Working Class*, raises an important issue of periodization. By the 1830s, at the close of Thompson's study, England

---

[1] Joseph Schumpeter, "The Creative Response in Economic History," *The Journal of Economic History* 7 (Nov. 1947):149-50. Studies of such "different kinds of reaction" are deeply indebted to the seminal article by Val Lorwin, "Working-Class Politics and Economic Development in Western Europe," *American Historical Review* 63 (Jan. 1958).

had not only a language of trade but one of class. The meaning of such terms as manufacturer and craftsman now had altered to refer to industrial capitalists and wage workers. Industrial and political struggles were conducted by social classes about issues of class. Yet, as Hobsbawm points out, the working class at this moment was very different from the proletariat of semiskilled employees of large factories who lived in homogeneous working-class neighborhoods a half-century later.[2]

This volume spans these two moments. It chronicles and accounts for different patterns of working-class formation in the decades when both more and more positions in the social structure and more and more people in France, Germany, and the United States became proletarian in the full sense of lacking ownership or control over the means of production and over the labor power of other workers, and when national labor mar-

---

[2] Eric Hobsbawm, "The Making of the Working Class 1870-1914," in Hobsbawm, *Worlds of Labour: Further Studies in the History of Labour* (London: Weidenfeld and Nicolson, 1984). The starkness of the contrast stressed by Hobsbawm may also be seen in a comparison, for example, of the reality and analysis discussed in Craig Calhoun, *The Question of Class Struggle: Social Foundations of Popular Radicalism during the Industrial Revolution* (Chicago: University of Chicago Press, 1982) and in Patrick Joyce, *Work, Society and Politics: The Culture of the Factory in Later Victorian England* (London: Methuen, 1982). Analyses of the transition from the first to the second moment of English working-class formation have proved difficult and elusive. For two thoughtful treatments, see Trygve Tholfsen, *Working Class Radicalism in Mid-Victorian England* (New York: Columbia University Press, 1977); and Dennis Smith, *Conflict and Compromise: Class Formation in English Society—A Comparative Study of Birmingham and Sheffield* (London: Routledge and Kegan Paul, 1982).

It should be acknowledged that this essay and this volume suffer on the whole from a lack of consideration of the significance of family and gender relations at this moment of transition. Men and women did not experience this transformation in the same way. There were sex-specific engagements with the changing means of production, with levels of consumption, with the social organization of residence communities, and with the most visible institutions of working-class assertiveness. It remains all too true that the discussions that follow in this volume are principally about men in the working class. This emphasis is regrettable for many reasons, not least because it precludes a careful examination of the role of the family in class formation. Michael Hanagan, for one, is exploring in his current research the extent to which cross-trade affiliations based on a common class identity emerged in French cities in part because various members of working-class families worked in different parts of the wage-labor economy and thus brought diverse class experiences home with them, where their commonalities could be explored and understood. Some feminist theorists have stressed that the failure to confront gender relations may produce distorted portraits of bases of exploitation. Thus, for example, Nancy Folbre has written in a memorandum for a New School for Social Research seminar on class formation (Fall 1984), "Why is the possibility of exploitation within the home so seldom raised? Partly, I think, because such possibilities deflect our attention from the logic of capital to the logic of patriarchy. Partly because historians, like economists, tend to think that patriarchy has no historical logic. Partly because it's just plain difficult to figure out, logic or no logic." Also see Christopher Middleton, "Patriarchal Exploitation and the Rise of English Capitalism," in Eva Garmarnikow et al., *Gender, Class and Work* (London: Heinemann, 1983).

kets came to enmesh the great majority of wage workers.[3] Working-class people had to make sense of these massive changes in the economy and in society during this long and fundamental period in order to be able to act on them. How they did so, and how to think about how they did so, are the subjects of this book.

I

The analysis of social class raises issues that are among the most contested in modern social theory and social science. The starting point for the historians and political scientists who have contributed to this book is the importance of proletarianization as a key theme of modernity, and the pivotal significance of class for understanding ties between the states, economies, and civil societies of the countries studied. Indeed, it is this very centrality that has made class a contested term and has made the working class the repository, sometimes exaggerated, of very great hopes and fears.

These themes are not new. Their broadly understood significance has helped divide recent discourse in the social and political sciences between those who see the "end of class" and those who do not. But there is little quarrel on either side of this divide with the importance of the formation and reformation of social classes as central objects of scholarly and political concern. The issue is not whether to study class formation, but how.

The contributors came together initially because of a shared unease with many discussions of class formation, even those by scholars who recognize the pivotal place of social classes in the history of modern western societies. We are particularly unsettled by an excessive preoccupation with "objective" classifications of class structures as *the* master tool for understanding class formation.[4] We agree with Erik Olin Wright's obser-

---

[3] This familiar formulation does not engage important questions such as whether exploitative relationships between owners and nonowners of the means of production, organizational domination within systems of production, or work for unevenly distributed wages constitute the key markers of class in capitalist societies. An exceptionally illuminating and provocative attempt to examine these issues and to develop a framework for the analysis of class structure in feudal, capitalist, and postcapitalist societies is Erik Olin Wright, *Classes* (London: New Left Books, 1985).

[4] When we set out to write this book, the work of Nicos Poulantzas had succeeded in opening a fertile debate about how to do better in mapping social classes, their relations, and variations in specific class structures than standard two-class Marxist models (which were unable to grapple with the massive growth of middle classes) and Weberian models based solely on the distribution of money or authority. What this debate undertheorized was how to think about the linkages between specific class structures, on the one hand, and thought, culture, and action, on the other. If social classes are objectively defined locations in the class structure and if people are thus bearers of class relations, they are

vation that theories of social conflict and social change are "radically incomplete . . . without a rigorous account of the structure of class relations,"[5] and we acknowledge that such work has an important place in charting alterations over time in the ways class structures have been shaped by capitalist development, even where class has not been the articulated subject of consciousness and conflict. Further, class as a position within the structure of production exerts a "determining" effect on culture and collective action in no more, but also in no less, than the sense of Raymond Williams's definition of determination as "not just the setting of limits" but "also the exertion of pressures."[6]

Nevertheless, even in some of the most creative and important work on the classification of social classes, we observe that class ideas, organizations, and activity tend to be inferred from class structure. The essentialist assumption that classes "in themselves" will, indeed must, act "for themselves" at some moment is rarely stated in such a direct, old-fashioned way, but it continues more loosely and implicitly to underpin much of the theoretical debate about class classifications.[7]

In the most extreme formulation of such theoretical work, class for-

---

reduced, in Gordon Marshall's words, to "the status of simple executants of strategies imposed on them by the system." The debate Poulantzas stimulated about class structure did not overcome this elision. "The concrete activities of real people or of groups of people and, more importantly, how they themselves define these activities are nowhere to be found." To take this position, however, does not need to disparage, as Marshall does, work on class structure in favor of an action-oriented perspective. Rather the challenge is to specify how connections can be made between these levels of reality and analysis in actual historical situations. Gordon Marshall, "Some Remarks on the Study of Working Class Consciousness," *Politics and Society* 12, no. 3 (1983):274-75; Nicos Poulantzas, *Political Power and Social Class* (London: New Left Books, 1973) and especially his *Classes in Contemporary Capitalism* (London: New Left Books, 1975).

Since Descartes, at least, issues of structure and agency and the closely associated question of methodological individualism have been central concerns of philosophers and social scientists. Some recent and illuminating considerations include Anthony Giddens, *Central Problems in Social Theory: Action, Structure and Contradiction in Social Analysis* (Berkeley: University of California Press, 1979); Steven Lukes, "Power and Structure," and "Methodological Individualism Reconsidered," in Lukes, *Essays in Social Theory* (London: Macmillan, 1977); Raymond Boudon, *The Uses of Structuralism* (London: Heinemann, 1971); Jeffrey C. Alexander, *Positivism, Presuppositions, and Current Controversies* (Berkeley: University of California Press, 1982); and Adam Przeworski, "The Ethical Materialism of John Roemer," *Politics and Society* 11, no. 3 (1982).

[5] Erik Olin Wright, "Varieties of Marxist Conceptions of Class Structure," *Politics and Society* 9, no. 3 (1980):333, n. 1.

[6] Raymond Williams, *Marxism and Literature* (New York: Oxford University Press, 1977), p. 85.

[7] More precisely, why do such debates matter for studies of class consciousness and behavior? They do matter, of course, for other significant questions concerning economic development, demographic and family patterns, and social theory.

mation is given a definition condensed by the term "revolutionary consciousness,"[8] in which class formation is seen as an all-or-nothing matter. Workers either are prepared and able to overturn capitalism or they are not. If we were to stick with this dichotomy we would repeatedly be compelled to explain our theoretical disappointments, because there has never been a working class with revolutionary consciousness in the fullest and most demanding sense of the term.

The political deformations of such a world view, distinguishing as it does between correct and incorrect ways of acting, are manifest in our time. The analytical deformations, however, concern us here. By making class formation the logical outcome of class structure and by avoiding a direct engagement with the actual lives of working people in favor of taking only ultimate societal transformations seriously, class formation is reduced to a formula.

Such a perspective has been associated most commonly with some strains of Marxism, but this form of its argument has been adopted in mirror image by those political sociologists and "post-Marxists" who argue that the erosion of traditional workplaces and communities in the immediate past significantly reduces the possibility that people will think and act in class-based ways. These approaches also conflate class structures, world views, and organizational activities as if the first *necessarily* entails the others.[9]

---

[8] This kind of formulation is found on both sides of the divide Gouldner draws between scientific and critical Marxism; in, say, Lukacs as much as in Lenin. See Alvin Gouldner, *The Two Marxisms: Contradictions and Anomalies in the Development of Theory* (New York: Seabury Press, 1980). The opposite of "revolutionary consciousness" is "false consciousness," a problematic fraught with immense and familiar analytical and political difficulties. These constructs coexist uneasily with concrete historical analysis, as the strains in John Foster's important work illustrate. See his *Class Struggle and the Industrial Revolution: Early Industrial Capitalism in Three English Towns* (New York: St. Martin's Press, 1974). On this subject Charles Tilly has observed: "Revolutionary class consciousness is to labor history as frictionless motion is to elementary mechanics: Neither has ever existed, but both underlie vast theoretical constructions and wide-ranging empirical inquiries. Physicists, however, have the good sense not to waste their time looking for frictionless motion or, worse yet, striving to prove that it fails to characterize one real situation or another. Labor historians (at least those of modern England) generally lack that good sense" (Tilly, review of Robert Glen, *Urban Workers in the Early Industrial Revolution* [London: Croom Helm, 1984], in *Labor History*, forthcoming).

[9] Such a position has underpinned the work of Daniel Bell, for example. See his *The End of Ideology: On the Exhaustion of Political Ideas in the Fifties* (New York: Free Press, 1962), and *The Coming of Post-Industrial Society: A Venture in Social Forecasting* (New York: Basic Books, 1973). A recent quite concrete discussion of this formulation has concerned the political analysis of Eric Hobsbawm. See his title essay and the commentaries in Eric Hobsbawm et al., *The March of Labour Halted?* (London: Verso Books, 1981). A strongly argued essay on the contingent ties between class structure and

The most withering recent critique of such analytical and historical reductionism has come from the pen of Thompson. His "Poverty of Theory" declares war on the view, stated in *Reading Capital* by Etienne Balibar, that "classes are *functions of the process of production as a whole. They are not its subjects, on the contrary, they are determined by its form.*"[10] Thompson comments:

> The subject (or agent) of history disappears once again. Process, for the *n*th time, is re-ified. And since classes are "functions of the process of production" (a process into which, it seems, no human agency could possibly enter), the way is thrown open once again to all the rubbish of deducing classes, class fractions, class ideologies ("true" and "false") from their imaginary positioning—above, below, interpellatory, vestigial, slantwise—within a mode of production . . . and this mode of production is conceived of as *something other than* its eventuation in historical process, and within "the ensemble of social relations," although in fact it exists only as a construction within a metaphysical oration.[11]

Instead, Thompson forcefully argues a position with which, put at this general level, we cannot but agree:

> Class formations . . . arise at the intersection of determination and self-activity: the working class "made itself as much as it was made." We cannot put "class" here and "class consciousness" there, as two separate entities, the one sequential upon the other, since both must be taken together—the experience of determination, and the "handling" of this in conscious ways. Nor can we deduce class from a static "section" (since it is a *becoming* over time), nor as a function of a mode of production, since class formations and class consciousness (while subject to determinate pressures) eventuate in an open-ended process of *relationship*—of struggle with other classes—over time.[12]

This perspective neatly captures an important impulse of the second main current of scholarship on working-class formation: the great outpouring of historical studies written about western working classes since the 1960s, for which *The Making of the English Working Class* set the standard and the key themes of research. This corpus attempts "to

---

political action is James Cronin, "Politics, Class Structure, and the Enduring Weakness of British Social Democracy," *Journal of Social History* 16, no. 3 (Spring 1983). For a fuller explication, see his *Labour and Society in Britain, 1918-1979* (London: Batsford Academic and Educational Books, 1984).

[10] Etienne Balibar, "The Basic Concepts of Historical Materialism," in *Reading Capital*, ed. Louis Althusser and Etienne Balibar (London: New Left Books, 1972), p. 267. Emphasis in original.

[11] E. P. Thompson, "The Poverty of Theory," in Thompson, *The Poverty of Theory and Other Essays* (London: Merlin Press, 1978), p. 299. Emphasis in original.

[12] Ibid., p. 298. Emphasis in original.

recover past struggles in order to create a politics for the present."[13] Centering on the category of experience, social historians have carefully reconstructed the world views and patterns of life of working people. They have rescued working classes from the conservative historiographical claim (in G. M. Young's words) that "history is the conversation of people who counted."[14] In so doing, the new social history has moved studies of the working class to the center of historical concern.

Such scholarship has also argued for a number of key propositions. Working-class formation as a process is not identical from country to country (or from place to place within countries). The histories of national working classes are composed not only of workplace relationships, trade unions, or the visible leadership of workers' movements and organizations. Inherited, preindustrial, precapitalist traditions count. Nonclass patterns of social division also affect class formation. Class, society, and politics cannot be conflated; their relationships are contingent. Class dispositions and behaviors are not fixed by interests but shaped by relationships. Sean Wilentz has summarized the most important impulses of this "new social history":

In place of a static, instrumentalist economic determinism, they have treated class as a dynamic social relation, a form of social domination, determined largely by changing relations of production but shaped by cultural and political factors (including ethnicity and religion) without any apparent logic of economic interest. They take for granted the inescapable fact that class relations order power and social relationships; they have examined the numerous conflicts and accommodations that give rise to and accompany these relations as a complex series of social encounters, fusing culture and politics as well as economics. In short, they insist that the history of class relations cannot be deduced by some "economic" or sociological calculus and imposed on the past; nor can it be ignored if it does not appear just as the historian thinks it should, either in or out of politics. It must be examined as part of a human achievement in which men and women struggle to comprehend the social relations into which they were born (or entered involuntarily) and in which, by the collective exercise of power, they sustain or challenge those relations in every phase of social life.[15]

Given our agreement with these orientations and propositions and our great debt to this tradition of historical scholarship with which we iden-

[13] Richard Johnson, Gregor McLennan, Bill Schwartz, and David Sutton, eds., *Making Histories: Studies in History Writing and Politics* (Minneapolis: University of Minnesota Press, 1982), p. 9.

[14] G. M. Young, *Victorian England: Portrait of an Age* (London: Oxford University Press, 1978), p. 18.

[15] Sean Wilentz, *Chants Democratic: New York City and the Rise of the American Working Class, 1790-1850* (New York: Oxford University Press, 1984), p. 10.

tify, it may seem churlish to say that this book was prompted, in part, by vexation with some of the tradition's key tendencies. In particular, the formulation proposed by Thompson and adopted without much discussion or reflection by the new social history that class formation lies at the junction of determination and consciousness has made it possible to use the term as a convenient label for an unsorted kitbag of findings. It has also substituted for a direct confrontation with important issues of class conceptualization and comparative analysis.[16]

One result has been rather ironic. Because historical facts can only be made to appear within the framework of a conceptual perspective (even if it is only implicit), the new working-class history has adopted a weak version of the structural "class in itself–for itself" model of class formation as a hidden and unexamined functioning tool to order the multitude of facts generated by the study of working-class activity and culture.

Such, for example, is the case in studies of working-class formation in England, both in the scholarship of Thompson, whose "Poverty of Theory" mocks the essentialism of the Althusserians, and as an aspect of some "labour aristocracy" accounts of the gradualist political impulses of the proletariat.

The English case, of course, is the best-researched and most familiar instance of nineteenth-century working-class formation—for just this reason this volume places its empirical emphases elsewhere. Historians of English working-class formation have posed two principal questions: how did class, rather than other bases of solidarity, become the basis of working people's dispositions and activity; and why did this working class show a preference for reformist rather than more militant or revolutionary forms of political action?[17]

The Making of the English Working Class addresses the first of these questions. In spite of its author's antitheoretical predilections (or, per-

---

[16] The most developed recent considerations of these issues have been written by practitioners of comparative and historical sociology. See Philip Abrams, *Historical Sociology* (Ithaca: Cornell University Press, 1982), which contains a sympathetic critical appreciation of Marxist approaches to the study of class formation; Charles Tilly, *Big Structures, Large Processes, Huge Comparisons* (New York: Russell Sage Foundation, 1985); and Theda Skocpol, ed., *Vision and Method in Historical Sociology* (New York: Cambridge University Press, 1984). Evidence that my lament about the unreflective character of the new social history may become obsolete can be found in essays by Geoff Eley ("Combining Two Histories: The SPD and the German Working Class before 1914") and David Hunt ("Working People of France and Their Historians") in *Radical History Review*, nos. 28-30 (Sept. 1984).

[17] I treat these issues at greater length in Ira Katznelson, "Working Class Formation and the State: Nineteenth-Century England in American Perspective," in *Bringing the State Back In*, ed. Peter Evans, Dietrich Rueschemeyer, and Theda Skocpol (New York: Cambridge University Press, 1985).

haps, because of them), the book quietly fuses essentialist and historicist perspectives. Without arguing the point, Thompson's logic of presentation seems to assume that once a working class is "made" by the impact of external conditions, people sharing a fate will "make themselves" into a class capable of affecting history.

The book's single-country focus allows Thompson to avoid the question of whether the movement from the experience of class society to class dispositions and activity is necessary, likely, or entirely contingent; nor does the work present an ordered causal account of the process that produces such an outcome. Indeed the absence of comparison and the focus on England make it easy to adopt a weak but still teleological version of the "class in itself–for itself" model. As Gareth Stedman-Jones points out, in England "equations between social and political forces have been only too easy to make because much of modern English political history has generally been thought to coincide with class alignments, and because, at the level of everyday speech, one of the peculiarities of England has been the pervasiveness of the employment of diverse forms of class vocabulary."[18]

Although Thompson's approach "fits" the English case, it inhibits comparative analysis because it takes for granted that which elsewhere must be explained. One unfortunate aspect of the new social history is that Thompson's genius and the scope of his achievement have prompted attempts at imitation even in settings where class formation cannot be understood if class remains an unexamined term.

The second question, concerning militancy, has frequently been addressed by some variant of the "labor aristocracy" approach.[19] As in the work of Thompson, working-class formation is defined, by statement or by implication, as the emergence of a relatively cohesive working class, self-conscious of its position in the social structure and willing and capable of acting to affect it. The absence of such collective formations is treated as a deviation either from what theory predicts or from what his-

[18] Gareth Stedman-Jones, *Languages of Class: Studies in English Working Class History, 1832-1982* (New York: Cambridge University Press, 1983), p. 2. For critiques of Thompson's work, see Gregor McLennan, "E. P. Thompson and the Discipline of Historical Context," in Johnson et al., eds., *Making Histories*; Bryan D. Palmer, *The Making of E. P. Thompson: Marxism, Humanism and History* (Toronto: New Hogtown Press, 1981); and Perry Anderson, *Arguments within English Marxism* (London: New Left Books, 1980).

[19] Rooted in an article by Engels ("England in 1845 and 1885," in *On Britain*, ed. Karl Marx and Friedrich Engels (Moscow: International Publishers, 1934) and in Lenin's treatment of imperialism, the concept of a labor aristocracy was introduced into contemporary historical scholarship by Eric Hobsbawm ("The Labour Aristocracy," in Hobsbawm, *Labouring Men* (London: Weidenfeld and Nicolson, 1964). He reviews the debates about this approach and revisits the concept in his *Worlds of Labour*.

tory in the French or German, or more broadly, the Continental experience seems to have decreed as a norm. This abnormality is explained by special factors that impede the expected outcome. A "theoretical alibi" must be found for the working class.[20]

There is a massive literature about the concept and empirical grounding of the labor aristocracy. Scholarly journals are full of debates about whether a term referring to such a plethora of issues—wage levels, regularity of work, membership in trade unions, styles of life, norms and values, neighborhood segregation, and political party leadership—can bear the weight; about whether the term clearly refers to a particular set of workers; about whether it makes sense a priori to assert the significance of a particular segment of the working class; and about the linkage between the structural position of the "aristocrats" and their political conservatism.[21] Our concern here is much less with these discussions than with the assumption that the more militant or revolutionary working class that did not exist is the more "natural" one, and hence that social theory and history must search for the causes of failure to meet a set of unrealized expectations.

Students of class formation, especially those whose work has been informed by the Marxist tradition, have tended to polarize into the camps of theory and history, identified in recent years with the names Althusser and Thompson. This polarization has obscured the obvious, that theory is arid if not historically grounded, and that history, even if dedicated to discovering "facts" alone, cannot be recovered without theory. When Thompson has been faced with principled theoretical rejections of history he has reacted by defending history as such, irrespective of the conceptual lenses historians have worn when making sense of what they have seen.[22] Because he cannot justify straightforward empiricism, Thompson tells us that the place of theory is to develop models of the logic of a situation as a benchmark to assess deviations. But how should such mod-

[20] Geoff Eley and Keith Nield, "Why Does Social History Ignore Politics?" *Social History* 5 (May 1980):260-61.

[21] For a selection of these discussions, see Henry Pelling, "The Concept of the Labour Aristocracy," in Pelling, *Popular Politics and Society in Late Victorian Britain* (London: Macmillan, 1968); R. Q. Gray, "Styles of Life, the 'Labour Aristocracy' and Class Relations in Nineteenth Century Edinburgh," *International Review of Social History* 18, part 3 (1973); H. F. Moorhouse, "The Marxist Theory of the Labour Aristocracy," *Social History* 3 (Jan. 1978); H. F. Moorhouse, "The Significance of the Labour Aristocracy," *Social History* 6 (May 1981); Alastair Reid, "Politics and Economics in the Formation of the British Working Class: A Response to H. F. Moorhouse," *Social History* 3 (Oct. 1978); and Foster, *Class Struggle*.

[22] Thompson, "The Poverty of Theory," especially section vii.

els be developed? How can we avoid the unacceptable antinomy of theory and history?

What do we want from a theory of class formation? We need theory to help us make sense of a series of comparative and historical puzzles about similarities and variations in the dynamics and character of class relations in different societies, and to provide us with the tools to ask systematic questions about historical variation and their causes. Theory, in short, should help us build on the insights of the best recent historical scholarship on class formation, while overcoming the tendency toward theoretically underspecified treatments of class and comparison, by identifying the events and actions in history we should strive to explain; by providing grounded vocabularies to reconstruct these cases analytically; by suggesting possible causal explanations; and by facilitating reconstructions and accounts that would have been meaningful to the actors themselves. Theory helps select, describe, explain, and interpret.[23]

What kind of history, guided by such theory, should we be doing? In the pages below the invocation of Charles Tilly that we discover how concrete "huge comparisons" help us understand such basic large-scale processes as proletarianization and class formation is generally followed. But we can take steps toward such grand comparison only by first constructing our cases to make macrohistorical comparisons possible.[24]

II

If theory cannot be avoided even when arid approaches to abstraction are rejected and if working-class historiography of the most fertile kind remains rooted in a set of unexamined essentialist assumptions, is it possible to do better in relating theory and history in the study of class formation?

The concept "class" provides the obvious starting point. As a term, "class" has been used too often in a congested way, encompassing mean-

---

[23] A stimulating discussion may be found in W. G. Runciman, *A Treatise on Social Theory*, vol. 1: *The Methodology of Social Theory* (New York: Cambridge University Press, 1983). See also Hugh Stretton, *The Political Sciences: General Principles of Selection in Social Science and History* (London: Routledge and Kegan Paul, 1969).

[24] Tilly, *Big Structures*; Theda Skocpol and Margaret Somers, "The Uses of Comparative History in Macrosocial Inquiry," *Comparative Studies in Society and History* 22, no. 2 (1980). Any such construction of cases much face up to Albert Hirschman's question: "But after so many failed prophecies, is it not in the interest of social science to embrace complexity, be it at some sacrifice of its claim to predictive power?" (Hirschman, "Rival Interpretations of Market Society: Civilizing, Destructive, or Feeble?" *Journal of Economic Literature* 20 [Dec. 1982]; 1483).

ings and questions that badly need to be distinguished from each other. I suggest that class in capitalist societies be thought of as a concept with four connected layers of theory and history: those of structure, ways of life, dispositions, and collective action.

"It is not against a body of uninterpreted data, radically thinned descriptions that we must measure the cogency of our explications," Clifford Geertz has written, "but against the power of the scientific imagination to bring us into touch with the lives of strangers. It is not worth it, as Thoreau said, to go round the world to count the cats in Zanzibar."[25] The extensive literature on working-class formation has succeeded in achieving much more than counting cats in Zanzibar, but it has not always known how to identify a particular kind of cat or to make crisp distinctions between types. As a contribution to social theory, the effort to distinguish between levels of class is an attempt to provide tools to construct cases of class formation systematically in order to promote comparative historical analysis.

As a concept, class has soaked up so much meaning that it has become bulky to use. Because it is often employed without a clearly specified definition, debates about class often become conversations in which people talk past each other because they are talking about different dimensions of class. Without clear analytical distinctions between levels or layers of class, it is hard to improve on the "class in itself–for itself" model. With the specification of different levels it becomes possible to construct the various cases of class formation in their own terms and to explore the competing capacities of various macrohypotheses about linkages between the levels. Above all, the distinctions that follow are meant to be aids to concrete description and explanation.

The *first* level is the structure of capitalist economic development, whose main elements include an economy based on privately owned autonomous firms that seek to make profit-maximizing decisions. These enterprises employ labor for a wage and sell what they produce in the market. This process of economic development contains some elements shared by all capitalist societies and others that are distinctive to each. As Karl Polanyi pointed out, this "great transformation" entailed the commodification of money, land, and labor. Capitalism is unthinkable without proletarianization; and, as Marx observed as the centerpiece of his political economy, capitalism is impossible without a quite specific mechanism of exploitation.

Because these key properties are shared by all capitalisms, it is appro-

---

[25] Clifford Geertz, *The Interpretation of Cultures* (New York: Basic Books, 1973), p. 16.

priate at this first level of class analysis to propose such distinctions as collective capital and collective labor, and productive and unproductive labor. And it is at this level that the heuristic model building Marx did in his mature works of political economy must test its mettle against other competing accounts.

Structural analyses of capitalism at this level use class analytically as a construct that is "experience-distant" (that is, as a concept employed by specialists to further scientific, philosophical, or practical aims). Used in this way as a tool to analyze the "motion" of capitalist development, class has no direct or unmediated phenomenological referents.

But economic development, of course, occurs not just in theory or in capitalism in general, but in real places at actual times. If capitalism is structured everywhere in coherent ways, it is also structured in different particular manners. Each specific national history of capitalist development is shaped by the shared impulses and boundaries of all capitalisms; but each national economy is shaped not only by these tendencies. Family patterns, demography, cultural traditions, inherited practices, state organization and policies, geopolitics, and other factors help determine the specific empirical contours of macroscopic economic development at this first level of class.

Even as we pay attention to these variations, however (as, for example, Aristide Zolberg does in the concluding essay of this book), at this level of economic structure class remains an experience-distant analytical concept, needed to describe and explain what happened because class is a constitutive element of any capitalist structure. Distinctive national histories of capitalist economic development perforce are structural histories of class formation in the sense of Charles Tilly's "thin" definition in his treatment of the demographic origins of the European proletariat: "people who work for wages, using means of production over whose disposition they have little or no control."[26] Proletarianization at this level provides a necessary, indeed the necessary condition for class formation in the more thickly textured senses of ways of life, dispositions, or patterns of collective action. But even when we take variations in macrolevel economic development into account it is not a sufficient condition. It is impossible to infer ways of life, dispositions, or collective action directly from analyses of class at the first level.

Nevertheless, broad patterns of economic development are of central importance in shaping patterns of life and social relations in specific capitalist societies. This *second* level, determined in part by the structure of

[26] Charles Tilly, "Demographic Origins of the European Proletariat," in *Proletarianization and Family Life*, ed. David Levine (New York: Academic Press, 1984), p. 1.

capitalist development, refers to the social organization of society lived by actual people in real social formations. For this reason, theories that deal with this level of class must be "experience-near."

Because this second level includes such economic phenomena as workplace social relations and labor markets, it is tempting to collapse the first two levels of class into the single category of the "economy." Such a conflation, however, eliminates in one stroke a series of important questions about the connections between key aspects of capitalist accumulation and national economic histories on one side and the organization of labor markets and workplaces on the other. As any student of capitalist industrialization knows, the growth and expansion of capitalism has proved capable of fostering many different kinds of workplaces and work. This is a theme to which the essays below return as they search for the implications of variations in capitalist development and in the social organization of work for the content and forms of class formation in different societies.

Although the second level of class includes work settings and labor markets (here classes can be stacked up and counted according to criteria that distinguish between various active members of the labor force),[27] it is not coextensive with these social relationships. The level of ways of life refers to how actual capitalist societies develop at work *and* away from it.

One of the hallmarks of industrial capitalist societies is that they tend to foster ways of life that differentiate between the location and social organization of these two realms. Over time, this distinction is expressed in the social geography of industrial cities. Work leaves the home. Cross-class households break up. Whole regions of cities come to be defined as areas of residence or of production. Further, residential communities segregate by the class position of their residents (in both the Marxist sense of location in a system of production and the Weberian sense of capacity to consume goods and services in the marketplace). With these separations between work and home and between the social classes in space, class relations are lived and experienced not only at work but also off work in residence communities.

The first two levels of class are closely related, of course, in that it is something of a conceit to separate too starkly the structure of capitalist accumulation and the self-sustaining development of the economy at the first level from how such broad patterns of economic development exist

---

[27] For an extended theoretically informed empirical analysis along such lines, see Erik Olin Wright, *Class Structure and Income Determination* (New York: Academic Press, 1979).

for working people where they labor and where they live at the second level. Moreover, if we understand that neither level of social relations is purely economic, then it makes sense to see the second level as an attribute of the first. But however closely connected, they are separate nonetheless, and many debates, such as the one between Erik Olin Wright and Nicos Poulantzas about mappings of class, suffer from the failure to make this distinction.[28]

At the first two levels of class it is appropriate to construct classifications of class relations, and the literature of social science is full of them. At both levels class is defined, from an orthodox Marxist position, as G. A. Cohen writes, solely "with reference to the position of its members in the economic structure, their effective rights and duties within it. A person's class is established by nothing but his objective place in the network of ownership relations, however difficult it may be to identify such places neatly." Even if the criteria used in such definitions are expanded to other bases of class relations and to patterns of class embedded in residence communities, Cohen is right to stress that at these levels of analysis a person's "consciousness, culture, and politics do not enter the *definition* of his class position. . . . Not even his behavior is an essential part of it."[29] Yet by themselves no such schemata, however compelling, can tell us how class exists distinct from other bases of solidarity and action in specific societies at specific times. This level of analysis may tell us how workers exist and live in certain circumstances, but not how they will think or act in those experienced circumstances.

At a *third* level social classes are not heuristic or analytical constructs nor do they consist of members of this or that cell of a typology. At this level, classes are formed groups, sharing dispositions. Such cognitive constructs map the terrain of lived experience and define the boundaries between the probable and improbable. Note that I am deliberately avoiding the term "class consciousness" in order to make clear my rejection of any notion of degrees of consciousness, with the highest corresponding to the "real" interests of the working class. Further, the scheme of four levels of class does not imply a series of necessary stages or a natural progression (after all, ways of life are not independent of thought or action).

[28] Theoretical discussions of the base-superstructure metaphor within Marxism also suffer from a collapse of these two levels into the "economy." A brilliant attempt at "bringing workers back in" at the point of production through an analysis of the labor process, which succeeds in overcoming the theoretical problems I have alluded to—albeit a treatment rather different in emphasis than that of this essay and book—is Michael Burawoy, *The Politics of Production: Factory Regimes under Capitalism and Socialism* (London: Verso Books, 1985).

[29] G. A. Cohen, *Karl Marx's Theory of History: A Defence* (Princeton: Princeton University Press, 1978), p. 73.

It is, rather, a classification that aims to promote the development of theory free from developmental assumptions.

I take it that the third level of class is what Thompson means when he writes:

Class is a social and cultural formation (often finding institutional expression) which cannot be defined abstractly, or in isolation, but only in terms of relationship with other classes; and, ultimately, the definition can only be made in the medium of *time*—that is, action and reaction, change and conflict. When we speak of *a* class we are thinking of a very loosely-defined body of people who share the same congeries of interests, social experiences, traditions, and value-system, who have a *disposition* to *behave* as a class, to define themselves in their actions and in their consciousness in relation to other groups of people in class ways.[30]

This suggestive formulation condenses a number of significant issues. To say that people share dispositions can mean that they have come to share understandings of the social system or that they have come to share values of justice and goodness. These two kinds of disposition are at least partially independent. Further, whether they are class dispositions is a contingent matter. Members of a class may share dispositions of either kind, but they need not necessarily be class based analytically or normatively. Further, either knowledge- or norm-based dispositions may view the current situation as the outcome of circumstances that cannot be altered or as posing the possibility of something better.

Much of the variation between the French, American, and German cases consists of variations in the ways working people, confronting changes in the conditions of life at the second level of class, mapped and interpreted these changes at the level of dispositions. Most new social history joins the story of class formation here, studying situations from the point of view of a specific working class in a specific place at a specific time. It is at this level that a Geertzian cultural analysis of the ways people construct meaning to make their way through the experienced world is most compelling,[31] especially because shared dispositions are interactive. They are formed by the manner in which people interact with each other. Thus dispositions are transindividual, not merely opinions or views of individual actors. They constitute cultural configurations within

[30] E. P. Thompson, "The Peculiarities of the English," in *Socialist Register 1965*, ed. Ralph Miliband and John Saville (London: Merlin Press, 1966), p. 357. Emphasis in original.

[31] Geertz, *Interpretation*; Paul Rabinow and William M. Sullivan, eds., *Interpretive Social Science: A Reader* (Berkeley: University of California Press, 1979). In Geertz's work there is some ambiguity about whether he wishes to claim that culture is the encompassing concept or whether culture is a distinctive mapping of society.

which people act. In Bernard Cohn's terms, "there can be no practical realities without the symbolic coding of them as *practical*. . . . People cannot act as maximizers—either out of self interest or out of deep psychological conditionings— . . . without the preexistence of meaning in cultural terms."[32]

The third level of class, that of dispositions, is not coextensive with class structures and class-based ways of life; nor, however, do dispositions simply mirror reality. Rather, they are plausible and meaningful responses to the circumstances workers find themselves in.

A number of important recent discussions in philosophy concern the issue of "correspondence." Analytical philosophers, much like some orthodox Marxists, have taken very seriously the idea that for something to be "right" it must correspond to something "real." Some efforts have recently been made, especially by Hilary Putnam and Neison Goodman, to transcend this assumption of correspondence. Putnam proposes that the key issue is "how can language or thought connect up to what is outside the mind"; and Goodman insists that "philosophy must take into account all the ways and means of worldmaking." But though such worlds are made, they are not constructed from scratch. Meaning is the result of the interaction between the world and human efforts to signify it.[33] If the construction of meaning is not entirely an open or contingent matter, what are the causes of the construction of different kinds of meaning systems about class? I will return to this question shortly.

Thompson follows his discussion of class dispositions by adding, "but class itself is not a thing, it is a happening."[34] Here he moves much too quickly from this third level of class to a *fourth*, collective action. Groups of people sharing motivational constructs ("disposition to behave") may or may not act collectively to transform disposition to behavior. Even where workers have close contact at work and in their residential communities; even if this interaction promotes strong collective identities; and even if these workers share common systems of meaning that incline

---

[32] Bernard S. Cohn, "History and Anthropology: The State of Play," *Comparative Studies in Society and History* 22 (Apr. 1980). Emphasis in original. William Roseberry puts the point this way: "People do not simply act in terms of objective limits or positions but also in terms of apparently subjective evaluations of limits, positions, and possibilities. As they do so, the 'subjective' becomes 'objective'; culture becomes material. Action is, in short, meaningful, as Weber long ago insisted" (William Roseberry, "Why Should Marxists Take Culture Seriously?" paper presented at the Annual Meeting of the American Anthropological Society, Nov. 1984).

[33] Hilary Putnam, "After Ayer, After Empiricism," and Nelson Goodman, "Notes on the Well Made World," *Partisan Review* 51, no. 2 (1984). The references are to pp. 270 and 284.

[34] Thompson, "Peculiarities," p. 357.

them to act in class ways, they may not necessarily act together to produce collective action. For this reason it is useful to distinguish between class at the third level and at the fourth, which refers to classes that are organized and that act through movements and organizations to affect society and the position of the class within it. This kind of behavior is self-conscious and refers to activity that is more than just the common but unself-conscious shared behavior of members of a class. After all, members of categorical classes must immanently share certain behaviors, but they do not necessarily act consciously and collectively in pursuit of common goals.

The "class in itself–for itself" formulation makes thinking about the links between the social organization of class, class dispositions, and collective action superfluous. But in fact class conflict of any particular kind is not necessarily entailed in the class organization of patterns of social life, nor even in the development of groups of people inclined to act in class ways. The one broad exception to this general rule of contingency is the development of trade unions to fight for better wages and working conditions at the place of work. Although here too there are wide variations between the experiences of different working classes, there are no examples of national histories of class formation utterly lacking in the effort to create trade unions.

There are always impediments to collective action,[35] to those occasions when "sets of people commit pooled resources, including their own efforts, to common ends." A key feature of the historical study of class must consist "of discovering which sets of people, which resources, which common ends, and which forms of commitment were involved in different places and times. Did the configurations change systematically with the advances of capitalism and large organizations?"[36] Both the content and the form of collective action are highly variable, and this variation demands explanation.

Class, Thompson suggestively points out, is a "junction term," which lies at the intersection of structure and process, social being and social consciousness. Structural change gives rise to changed experience: that

[35] The best-known treatment of these impediments is Mancur Olson, *The Logic of Collective Action* (Cambridge: Harvard University Press, 1965). See also Russell Hardin, *Collective Action* (Baltimore: Johns Hopkins University Press, 1982). For a stunning treatment of related issues of strategy and rationality, see Jon Elster, *Ulysses and the Sirens: Studies in Rationality and Irrationality* (New York: Cambridge University Press, 1979).

[36] Charles Tilly, "Introduction," in *Class Conflict and Collective Action*, ed. Louise A. Tilly and Charles Tilly (Beverly Hills, Calif.: Sage Publications, 1981). Also see the discussion of collective action in his *From Mobilization to Revolution* (Reading, Mass.: Addison-Wesley, 1978).

is, both to a set of subjective perceptions of objectively ordered realities and to a more active process of learning, possibly leading to action to modify the objective realities. I have already noted that Thompson, in my view, makes the movement from class structure to class action too certain a passage, but this teleological element can be extruded from his formulation.

The distinctions drawn here between the four levels of class may be read as an elaboration of Thompson's insight that class is a junction term. They allow us to specify more precisely the points of connection *between* the structure of class relations at the macroeconomic level; the lived experience of class in the workplace and in the residence community; groups of people disposed to act in class ways; and class-based collective action. These points of contact specify the possibility of alternative kinds of relationships between the levels, a problem best approached by asking what we mean by class formation after moving beyond "class in itself–for itself" formulations.

It is possible, of course, to continue to define class formation in terms of specific outcomes, rather than to leave open the content of class formation. We might say that class formation has occurred only when class exists at all four levels of structure, patterns of life, dispositions, and action simultaneously. This would have a number of advantages. It would turn our attention to the links between class levels, and it would treat class formation as only one of a number of possible outcomes. It would dispose of the Hobson's choice between structuralist formulations that claim, at least implicitly, that experience is ideology, and culturalist stances fashionable in much current linguistic and semiotic theory in which class society is said to exist only when it is signified.

But despite these advantages, such a definition would be unsatisfactory. An outcome approach hinging on the appearance of class at each of the four levels without specifying the components of class and the range of both class and nonclass possibilities at each of the levels too starkly posits a dichotomous outcome (and in this way resembles the tradition of "revolutionary consciousness"): class either exists or does not as the basis of social solidarity and action. This distinction does not appear to be terribly helpful in explicating the puzzles posed by our three cases. Further, such an approach fails to answer the question, class formation with respect to what content?

Class formation may be thought of more fully and more variably as concerned with the conditional (but not random) process of connection between the four levels of class. The specification of four levels of class allows us to keep the advantages of defining class formation in terms of outcomes while providing a more elaborated and variable object of comparative historical analysis. The content of each of the four levels of necessity will vary from society to society; no level need be understood or analyzed exclusively in class terms; and the connections between the levels are problematical and conditional.

Questions about the content of each level and about the connections between the levels of class constitute the very heart of the analysis of class formation. A precise (but not too narrow) charting of class formation, based on a contingent but not undetermined approach to the relationship between these levels, and the attempt to develop macrocausal hypotheses about variations in class formation are the interrelated tasks that follow from this approach.

Although their analytical emphases differ and the range of questions they ask is very broad, the essays that make up the main part of this book are constructed to permit such systematic comparisons. The essays treat comparable periods. They use the typology of levels of class in the double sense of identifying the aspects of each case that need to be constructed and identifying the relevant theoretical issues at each level. And they try to account for variations in patterns of class formation by looking at common sources for the construction of hypotheses and explanation. In short, read alone or together, the essays respect the distinctiveness of each case while recognizing that, together, they compose a family.

III

Working classes of the early to mid-nineteenth century in each of the countries studied here had to make sense of and deal with a cluster of fundamental changes in the organization of production, conditions of work, community organization, and politics. These basic alterations in the structure and conditions of life were so massive and multifaceted in character that they invariably provoked basic changes in language, consciousness, and institutions—in short, in the symbolic and organizational aspects of culture. If we are prepared to see culture as "webs of significance" spun by people in society and if, in consequence, culture demands interpretation, these webs were spun by working people suspended between very hard and jagged economic, social, and political rocks.[37]

The broad outlines of these changes were shared across political

[37] See the section on culture in Raymond Williams, *Politics and Letters: Interviews with New Left Review* (London: New Left Books, 1979) and Raymond Williams, *Culture* (London: Fontana Books, 1981) for discussions that locate cultural forms in material context much more explicitly than Geertz, who defines culture in semiotic terms: "Believing that . . . man is an animal suspended in webs of significance he himself has spun, I take culture to be those webs, and the analysis of it to be therefore not an experimental science in search of law but an interpretive one in search of meaning" (Geertz, *Interpretation*, p. 5).

boundaries. Skilled artisan production based on traditions and obligations centuries old was disrupted irretrievably. New kinds of social relationships of production, new forms of exploitation, and new dimensions to the process of proletarianization ushered in vigorous defenses of the old order as well as new thoughts and deeds concerning the conditions of workers within the new order.

Working people, for the first time, altered their vocabularies and world views to speak and think of themselves as workers, rather than just as members of this or that trade. They generalized the sense of solidarity of trade beyond specific and segmented crafts. The timing of this transformation is rather similar in the three countries we consider: in the early 1830s in France and the United States, and in the late 1840s in Germany. But the extent and content of this new collective awareness varied considerably. This diversity, at class levels three and four, is the principal object of our analysis of working-class formation.

Perhaps it is obvious that the study of these variations assumes a shared backdrop of capitalist development and its partner, proletarianization. Because there was a rough similarity in these features of change across national boundaries it should come as no surprise that workers responded to their new conditions in commensurable ways. In France, the United States, and Germany (and in other societies undergoing substantively similar economic change), artisans played the key role in developing a response to proletarianization; workers sought to organize to affect their workplace conditions both within and outside the law; they formed a variety of self-help organizations such as insurance and friendly societies; and some workers tried to find political redress on a class basis. Inevitably, these efforts were informed by broadly comparable preindustrial traditions and cultural resources. Class behavior and organization had a contingent but not unbounded or entirely open relationship to changes in the structure of society and the ways of life these alterations made possible. The authors of the essays below not only agree on this general formulation of the conditional relationship between the levels of class within limits but attempt more specified causal accounts.

It may also be obvious that if this book sought principally to explain these shared features of working-class formation, the essays would have paid even more attention than they do both to broad structural economic changes and to more fine-grained alterations in workplaces and labor markets. Their main aim, however, is to explain differences in spite of similarities. Hence the case studies invariably are drawn to extra-economic factors of explanation, such as those concerning space, religion, and, above all, the organization of the state and its public policies. But each essay looks first to economic factors in order to see how far such factors take us in constructing satisfactory explanations of class formation before moving on to these other bases of explanation. The concluding essay, moreover, is an attempt to tie together the various insights on how shifts in the organization of capitalism helped cause different patterns of class formation to develop.

Because our primary emphasis is on explaining "different kinds of reaction," it is important to specify the particular foci to which we pay attention in order to construct each case in a manner suitable for systematic comparison. How should we order our questions about class formation to make meaningful comparative study possible? In saying that class formation is our object of analysis and that the term refers to the junctions between the various levels of class, how can it be more precisely specified?

Instead of asking whether class formation occurred—a question that assumes a standard of a formed working class that can be "more" or "less" achieved—we inquire about the terms and content of class formation with respect to a quite specific, but deliberately open, object of analysis: the ways the newly emerging working classes expressed their claims to their employers and to the state. This focus does not assume a priori that any particular outcome is natural or likely. Rather, by self-consciously eschewing such an assumption at the start we have tried to arrive at a portrait of similarities and variations by looking at our three historical cases through the same lenses.

In constructing our objects of analysis at the third and fourth levels of class, we ask: What rhetoric did workers use in presenting their demands to employers and the state? What forms of organization were used to make their claims? What was the character of the relationship between the two sets of claims in rhetorical and organizational terms? Did such rhetorics and organizational forms embody a unity of dispositions and action about the social relations of work and the residence community or did they embody divisions, expressed in dichotomous politics of work and off-work? To what extent did workers, in placing their demands before their employers and the state, interpret their concerns in terms of the division between capital and labor? How attractive were various radical, socialist, and, in the middle and later years of the period, Marxist perspectives? To what extent did workers regard themselves as part of national groups or movements? How did workers, in making demands, reveal the outer limits of the working class? And if there were dominant national patterns, what were the secondary ones? In no case was there only a single outcome of class formation that encompassed artisans, marginal workers like those in construction, and people who worked in the new, large-scale industrialized plants.

Consider some of the more obvious comparative puzzles suggested by these questions when the French, American, and German cases are examined.

The French working class reacted to challenges to traditional norms and ways of life by organizing political action that transcended inherited boundaries of the trade. The vertical linkage of master and workers weakened and the horizontal ties joining workers together regardless of trade strengthened. Utilizing a radical republican discourse fused to the language of socialism, workers resisted at the microlevel of the village and the workshop and, in the 1830s but especially in 1848, in a national workers' movement that was underpinned organizationally by workers' corporate associations. At these moments there was a remarkable unity to the targets of working-class mobilization—both employers and the state—and to the rhetoric of the working-class movement.

This unity, grounded in a cross-trade, yet trade-based, socialism, did not survive the second half of the century. Rather, as key characteristics of industrialization altered (many aspects of the economy came more and more to resemble their English, American, and German counterparts; handweaving, for example, began to decline in favor of factory-based mechanical weaving), and as important rules concerning the law of trade unions and the franchise changed, working-class organization based in the factories became increasingly important. Workers came to see themselves as victims of the misfortunes of capitalist development and to view employers as their principal enemy. Strikes emerged as the central form of collective action (buttressed by an elaborated ideology of the general strike).

This nonreformist syndicalist impulse was far broader than the organized labor movement, which, in comparative terms, was rather puny. Further, even the organized trade union movement developed apart from working-class party politics. French electoral socialism and French workplace organizations found themselves on quite separate tracks of activity and mobilization, roughly paralleling the development of distinctive identities of citizen and worker.

A split between the politics of work and off-work characterized the American pattern of class formation, just as it did the French. But this resemblance is only partial. The syndicalism and socialism characteristic of the French experience provide only footnotes to the American case. There, the developing pattern of dispositions and action divided a reformist, procapitalist craft-based trade union movement from urban, cross-class political machines. For both the dominant unions and the political parties revolutionary impulses did not overwhelm allegiance to electoral politics and orderly wage bargaining.

No single clear direction to working-class sentiments or organizational activity emerged in the United States before the Civil War. Mass political action included the short-lived Workingmen's parties of the late 1820s and early 1830s, which sought to articulate a class-based republican response to the degradation of artisan life; a nativist response in the mid-1830s and early 1840s, which interpreted these changes in cultural, ethnic, and religious terms; various labor movement attempts to secure a shorter workday, free public schooling, and democratic political reforms; militant strikes; and cross-class collaborative party politics.

This variety of political forms crystallized after the Civil War into a distinctive, recognizable, and clearly institutionalized system of class dispositions and organizations. Martin Shefter summarizes these developments in his essay below:

Differences between the interests, values, and behavioral dispositions of workers and employers sparked conflicts during the post–Civil War years that at times approached full-scale class warfare. The labor union and the political machine institutionalized an accommodation between these warring forces. By no means did the emergence of these organizations put an end to such conflicts. Nonetheless, the institutionalization of the trade union and the political machine established the characteristic manner in which class conflicts in the United States could be channelled and thereby contained.

These two predominant organizations crystallized a division between the politics of work and off-work. Although they often pressed policy demands on the state in addition to the demands they made to employers, American unions were, on the whole, disconnected from partisan electoral activity. Their domain came to be restricted largely to the workplace and to political demands that directly affected work or their right to organize.[38] In reciprocal fashion, public officials tolerated strikes only when they were limited to workplace concerns, and the trade unions increasingly diminished the scope of their activity to bread-and-butter unionism.

The political machine, in turn, was a trans-class institution, which mobilized supporters where they lived on the basis of territorial and ethnic identities. Political mobilization based on the neighborhood (here, class and ethnicity intertwined) and on demands for city services provided the basis for an accommodation between the working classes and the political and economic order. Led by professional politicians, these

---

[38] This is an argument I develop in my *City Trenches: Urban Politics and the Patterning of Class in the United States* (New York: Pantheon Books, 1981), especially chap. 3. See also Amy Bridges, *A City in the Republic: Antebellum New York and the Origins of Machine Politics* (New York: Cambridge University Press, 1984).

organizations downplayed class and class conflict in the interest of a politics of patronage and distribution. Even where union leaders sought to organize third parties to fight for social change, they virtually always did so in alliance with middle-class reformers, under the banner of middle-class slogans and ideas. Such trade unionists frequently became detached from the rank and file.

All in all, the central hallmark of nineteenth-century class formation in the United States was the development, in the words of Shefter's essay, of "a division between the organizations through which workers pursued their interests at the workplace, on the one hand, and in the realm of politics, on the other." By 1860, the dominant forms of working-class collective action had been established clearly: votes for Republicans or Democrats, and trade union mobilization.

Even the role of American socialists was divided in this way, in spite of the holistic interpretation of capitalist development that the various strains of socialist ideology promoted. Many socialists (including Samuel Gompers!) were absorbed into the trade union movement and became leading promoters of a vigorous bread-and-butter craft unionism. Others sought to build socialist parties. When the conditions of work permitted close relationships between work and home, as in the garment industry at the turn of the century, and where there was a large concentration of new immigrants who brought a socialist political culture with them, as in the case of Lower East Side Jews in New York City, efforts to create electoral alternatives to the Democrats and Republicans succeeded. But in the more typical cases, where these conditions did not obtain, socialist electoral efforts failed.

The case of German working-class formation provides a stark contrast. Whereas American workers did not create a class-specific labor, socialist, or social democratic political party, their German counterparts produced Europe's largest parliamentary and Marxist mass political party. While American workers fashioned trade unions quite apart from party politics, German trade unions by the late nineteenth century were to a significant degree integrated with the Social Democratic party structure. And while American workers understood their interests to be in opposition to employers at the same time that they thought of themselves as citizens in a state they could directly influence, the German working class's central antagonist was an authoritarian and repressive state. Too, American political parties and trade unions were secular in character; in Germany the Catholic Church created a network of working-class institutions that provided an alternative to the social democratic unions and party.

The German case, in short, is the one that came closest in consciousness and organization to the classic Marxist model. Although artisans rather than factory workers provided the impetus and leadership for working-class collective action in 1848 and after, the craft characteristics, language, and world views of *Handwerk* organizations played less of a role than elsewhere in shaping the patterns of "modern" working-class formation. Compared to their American, French, and English counterparts, German trade unions were less likely to build barriers between different crafts, less likely to insist on guild-type labor controls, less likely to fight for traditional patterns of artisan rights and practices, and, overall, less likely to insist on distinctions between skilled and unskilled workers.

The same emphasis on the "arbeiter" class as a whole can be found in the very early creation, in the 1860s and 1870s, of an independent political party that used the term in its title. After a period of division caused by a split between socialist and liberal tendencies within the Allgemeiner Deutscher Arbeiterverein, they united again in 1875 to oppose the Bismarckian state and its relationship to the working class. By the 1890s Marxist language provided tools of analysis and debate for both the trade unions and the party as they confronted employers and the state.

Nineteenth-century patterns of working-class formation in France, the United States, and Germany thus differed sharply:

First, artisan values, culture, organization, and leadership were key elements in French class formation. The crafts provided the foundation of French industrialization. When new forms of work and exploitation challenged craft prerogatives, artisans succeeded in melding workers together to resist across trade lines. Later in the century, when factory industrialization posed new challenges, the traditions of independent artisans helped shape the development of fiercely independent forms of resistance at the workplace.

In contrast, the political orientations of American artisans (represented in the various workingmen's and nativist parties) and their anticapitalist labor organizations (particularly the urban craft unions of the 1830s and 1850s) did not succeed in informing the dominant machine politics and pro-system unions of the post–Civil War working class. American artisans failed to transfer their leadership, their language, or their orientations to the new proletariat.

The German situation differed from both the French and the American. There, Jürgen Kocka shows, domestic workers contributed more to the emergence of the early labor movement than many historians have acknowledged, and journeymen, who worked for small employers and who were transformed in the mid-century decades into something like modern wage workers, provided the primary initial support for the growth of the new trade unions and an independent labor party.

But in Germany the issue was less that of artisan traditions continuing to shape working-class dispositions, organizations, and action, as in France, or of the failure to link up traditional perspectives to new patterns of working-class activity, as in the United States. Rather, what is striking is the great extent to which artisan organizations and perspectives were assimilated into new and striking modern class rhetoric and organized mobilizations.

Second, the degree to which demands presented to employers and to the state took a linked or a divided form also varied in each of our cases. William Sewell describes a French working class at mid-century whose republican socialism provided the basis for a holistic class consciousness; but by late in the century, the politics of work and off-work had diverged significantly. Such a split, Amy Bridges and Martin Shefter show, was already in place by the American Civil War, and it remained a hallmark of class formation in the United States. In Germany, however, there was a great unity, in both the social democratic and Catholic movements, between the rhetoric, organizations, and demands at work and away from it.

Third, the working classes of the three countries developed quite different orientations toward integration with their respective states and societies and in the concomitant levels of militancy that they exhibited in their patterns of collective action. The oppositional stance of the French working class at mid-century gave way to a more mixed pattern, in which as workers they maintained their militant rejectionism but as citizens became more integrated in electoral, socialist politics. American workers were incorporated on a reformist and nonmilitant basis in both realms; and German workers in neither.

Fourth, in all three countries workers had a mix of local and national affiliations. Germany and the United States stood at opposite poles of such a continuum. In America, the federalism of the regime, the sheer size of the country, and the organization of political parties tended to make national organizations difficult to sustain; in Germany effective centralized party and union organizations of workers were in place by the end of the nineteenth century. The French pattern oscillated between these two poles and throughout the century showed a very mixed picture of national and local linkages.

Fifth, there were likewise important differences among the cases in the relative importance of socialist and Marxist appeals. A republican and so-called utopian socialism shaped working-class formation in France, and Marxism was central to the German experience. In the United States, however, socialism provided only a minor rhetorical voice among many competitors.

Sixth and finally, the French, American, and German cases differ in the extent to which there was a hiatus between early and late nineteenth-century patterns of class formation. The theme of a gap between the experience of the first and the second industrial revolutions has been central to English historiography, where the years between the collapse of Chartism and the rise of the new unionism remain a great puzzle. In this respect none of our cases poses the problem in quite the same way. Although there were important differences in France between the situation of 1848 and that of five decades later, there was no single break. Instead, as discussed below, there was a complicated history of change in France that was intimately connected with changes in political regimes, franchise rules, and labor law. In Germany before 1848, and in the United States before the Civil War, there were multifaceted and conflicting tendencies. But the dominant pattern in each case remained ascendant and became more clear in the second half of the century.

IV

This book is organized in two ways: by country and by time (some of the essays stress the formative moments of class formation, and others analyze aspects of continuity and change in the latter part of the nineteenth century).

Generally speaking, the hypotheses developed to explain each country's exceptional history of class formation come in three broad clusters. One set is economy-centered, concerned with the internal analysis of capitalist and class development. What are the effects of variations in the basic dynamics of economic change and patterns of work and labor markets on the histories of western working classes? More precisely, what is the effect of factors such as the character and timing of economic developments, variations of labor-market conditions, and the organization of work in accounting for variations in class formation? Although the essays place most of their stress elsewhere, the contributors share the view that it is important to exhaust the explanatory power of these factors before constructing hypotheses based on others.

A second cluster is society-centered. It looks outside the processes of capitalist development and proletarianization for sources of variation in the linkages between the levels of class. The role of religion, for example, looms large in the German case. Demographic trends are another factor, considered both in terms of natural population growth and population movements. Variations in spatial configurations within cities and in the balance between city and countryside are the other sources of society-centered hypotheses.

The third and most important macrocausal focus is the state. Under this rubric a number of important issues are considered. These include the formation of the nation-state; the impact of the French Revolution, in fact or by example; the extent and character of state bureaucratization; the capacity of the state to tax, conscript, repress, and make public policy authoritatively; constitutional questions such as federalism and the organization of the regime; citizenship and the franchise; and the content of various public policies such as labor law. The state appears in these analyses both as an actor, the degree of whose autonomy varies considerably, and as a shaper of the motives, interests, strategies, and activities of other actors.[39]

The dividing lines between economy-, society-, and state-centered explanations necessarily blur. Some aspects of demography, for example, are integral to the timing and pace of economic development and to such matters as the crowding of labor markets and the spatial organization of cities. Further, virtually all factors based in the economy and society are deeply intertwined with the one most stressed here, the state.

Each of the essays, of course, develops its own specific causal analysis. The threads of their analyses, however, may be drawn together in order to present composite summaries of the arguments.

It has long been commonplace for studies of French capitalism to take note of its retarded character. But as Sewell observes at the very outset of his essay, this characterization is usually misleading. France *was* transformed by industrial capitalism of a very distinctive kind, although unlike England, the United States, or Germany, French industrialization did not produce a rapid, almost discontinuous, ruralization of the countryside and urbanization of capitalist production. Nor did French industrialization cause a sudden growth in the size of the factory proletariat or an uprooted urbanized mass. Rather, French industrialization developed in small and medium-sized enterprises. Older forms of craft production were reorganized but not eliminated or superceded by massive factories.

These new patterns of accumulation, authority, exploitation, and sometimes technology went hand in hand with an unusually dense and complicated set of relationships between places of work and residence. In her essay below, Michelle Perrot points out that, in an inversion of the

---

[39] For a discussion of state analysis stressing these issues, see Theda Skocpol, "Bringing the State Back In," in Evans, Rueschemeyer, and Skocpol, *Bringing the State Back In.* Alan Dawley has observed that most analyses of the state are primitive with respect to issues of class formation; and that treatments of class formation in the United States are especially deficient in this regard. See his "E. P. Thompson and the Peculiarities of the Americans," *Radical History Review* 19 (Winter 1978-79).

American situation, where "integration into the local community and into the state occurs by way of the place of residence, locus of family life and of consumption, while 'class consciousness' is forged in the workplace—the large modern factory," in France the popular autonomy of the village or city neighborhood provided the shelter necessary for the potent reproduction of solidaristic class traditions.[40]

Social geography and dispersed, small-scale, incremental industrialization went hand in hand. Consider the case of handweaving, as discussed by Sewell, Perrot, and Alain Cottereau. Unlike England, where mechanical looms replaced handlooms very precipitously, handweaving actually increased in France in the first seven decades of the century. Indeed, the very success of the British textile industry and its comparative advantage in the production of low-cost goods forced the French into the production of luxury goods. During this period the nature of handweaving changed: there was an intensification of work, leading to a significant increase in productivity and, with a decline in piece rates, a significant increase in exploitation. Because the key instrument of production remained the handloom, the worker's house fused the functions of residence and work, and the house itself was, in Perrot's language, "an instrument of production, a bit of capital, a guarantee of independence." Workers not only resisted the introduction of new technologies (and the intensification of exploitation with old technologies) but also resisted the impending split between work and home.

Not all crafts permitted such a total identity between work and home. But these relationships remained more closely linked in France than in the other countries considered here as a result of the tempo and nature of industrialization. Thus the more typical small family workshop remained embedded in the artisan neighborhood; even when factories and workshops were clearly demarcated from the home they were located in close enough proximity to allow workers to take mid-day dinner at home.

Sewell is wrong to conclude from the evidence that "issues of urban space are far less important for the history of class formation in France than in Britain" because the separation of work and home was retarded in France. Rather, as his own work demonstrates, the issue is not one of a single objective patterning of space across national cases, but of the importance of the particular national situation for the shaping of a distinctive history of class formation. All of the essays on France stress that

---

[40] One of the few instances of a systematic linkage between spatial development and class formation is Richard Dennis's synthetic work, *English Industrial Cities of the Nineteenth Century: A Social Geography* (London: Cambridge University Press, 1984).

the neighborhood surrounding work areas provided the working class with the social and political space in which to resist economic change and to forge political responses to shifts in its condition. The more stark spatial separation of factory areas from very large and class-specific residential neighborhoods, common in the United States and Germany after mid-century, was much more of a twentieth-century development in France. One important result of this there was the "relative continuity in the urban experience of workers" that Sewell notes.

Sewell, Cottereau, and Perrot argue that both the slow tempo and the spatial features of capitalist development in France were the consequence in part of deeply embedded artisan traditions that were mobilized to resist technological and social incursions on the household economy in the interest of "productivist" ideologies and practices. These organized traditions transcended class lines in preindustrial France. As customary practices were challenged and sometimes shattered by the introduction of a liberal economy and the concurrent rescinding of customary social and moral codes concerning work, the craft traditions provided a basis for resistance to capitalist control and changes in the organization of labor.

The capacity to resist surely was shaped by these factors, but not by them alone. The very low fertility rates throughout the nineteenth century produced a persistent labor shortage. The Catholic Church, which in Germany channelled Catholic workers away from secular labor organizations, remained committed in France to rural patron-client relationships. For the most part it withdrew from challenging working-class efforts to contest capitalist industralization. Mid-century socialists and late-century syndicalism did not have Catholic competition.

It would be much too bland to say that the capacity of the French working class was also affected by state-centered factors. The quite remarkable shifts from an artisan work force under the Old Regime, for whose members the corporate organization of the trade, across class lines, was the pivot of social life, to the class-specific, cross-trade, militant, socialist, working class of the February revolution in 1848 is inexplicable without a consideration of the role and legacy of the French Revolution. Similarly, French class formation in the second half of the nineteenth century cannot be explained without an understanding of the fundamental influence of various regime changes and political struggles, and of the ebb and flow of political, organizational, and civil rights.

The centrality of the state extends to the economic and societal factors already noted. The density and texture of artisan traditions may have provided the basis for a powerful resistance to the new economic order.

But it was the French Revolution that simultaneously reshaped the basic rules of economic activity and provided for a new language of class based on rights, contracts, and law.

The Revolution replaced corporate rights with individual ones and in so doing made a liberal economy based on free labor markets possible.[41] Before the Revolution, corporate regulations restrained masters who wanted to intensify exploitation and create new divisions of labor. Although the pace of transformation was relatively slow and continuous, the direction of economic change was clear. In Sewell's words, "The socially controlled trade community of the Old Regime corporation was gradually being transformed, by the combined action of a new legal system and an expanding market economy, into an anarchic collection of individualized entrepreneurs and laborers."

Class is discursive. The Revolution fundamentally altered the ways workers conceived and talked of class. It created new categories of citizen and rights; it made concrete new versions of contract and sovereignty; and it spawned new vocabularies of political justification. Throughout the century, Perrot observes, workers created scenarios of the French Revolution with "happy endings." Under the impact of important regime changes—the Restoration, 1830, 1848, and so forth—a remarkable fusion of class and political language became a constitutive element of class formation. When joined to the new socialist discourse of the 1830s and 1840s, French working-class language proved capable of animating collective action both in the workplace and in political life.

The relationship of workers to the state oscillated with the complicated, stochastic history of constitutional change, and shifts in franchise regulations, the law of trade unions, and other organizational rights. These oscillations made the state an ambivalent phenomenon, more "them" than "us," for the working class.

The shifting character of regimes and policy, together with the state's consistent organizational centrality and strong presence in every sphere of civil society, help explain why the working class in the second half of the century maintained its militancy but, at the same time, fragmented its organizational life and its patterns of action between a syndicalist labor movement and quite separate political parties contesting elections.

The experience of the Second Republic, for example, made it clear that workers were a distinct minority within the electorate and made many

[41] For discussions, see Ronald Aminzade, *Class, Politics, and Early Industrial Capitalism: A Study of Mid-Nineteenth-Century Toulouse, France* (Albany: State University of New York Press, 1981); and William H. Sewell, Jr., *Work and Revolution in France: The Language of Labor from the Old Regime to 1848* (New York: Cambridge University Press, 1980).

workers skeptical of political action. These political limits reinforced inclinations toward direct action at the place of work. Indeed, throughout the century there was an ebb and flow of political and civil rights; at the same time, organizational rights were retarded. This combination, Cottereau stresses, helped promote a split between work and off-work forms of collective action. At the same time, it made struggles in both spheres militant to the extent that the state came to be defined as the target of mobilizations on behalf of political and organizational rights.

Compared to the French, American industrialization was more swift, more factory-based, and more urban. Within the span of one generation in the decades preceding the Civil War there was a fundamental disorganization of artisan production, supplanted by the dichotomy of capital and wage labor. Amy Bridges estimates that in the late 1820s roughly half the working class was engaged in craft work still organized along traditional lines. This proportion had diminished to only one in five by 1860.[42] The pace of change was dizzying. Cities and the enterprises in them grew rapidly in size. The division of labor grew more intense. Apprenticeship degenerated. As work was subdivided the jobs of journeymen became fragmented. More and more work came to be subcontracted, and was performed by "outwork" laborers.

The experience of the various urban crafts differed, of course, but common themes united these histories. The most important was the basic shift in the social relations of work that occurred once tasks performed by artisans were divided between a minority of relatively well paid journeymen and a large majority of wage laborers. In the years before the Civil War mass factory production had yet to become the dominant form. Rather, the artisan workshop continued to be the main locus of production, but one that had been radically changed in size, in the nature of work and authority patterns, in skill levels, and in its dynamics of exploitation.[43] These shifts in production took the same trajectory as the French, but they were more rapid and more discontinuous.

The divided and relatively domesticated features of American class formation appear as puzzles against this history of economic development. By the magnitude of the assault on artisan independence and customary rights and by the concentration of workers in large workplaces, long thought to be a condition promoting class consciousness, American industrialization appears from one angle to have established felicitous conditions for a radical working-class movement. Further, as Bridges points out, against the classic treatments of Louis Hartz and Daniel

[42] In addition to Bridges's essay below, see also Wilentz, *Chants Democratic*.
[43] The fullest discussions are in Bridges, *Republic*, and Wilentz, *Chants Democratic*.

Boorstin, American republican artisan traditions and culture differed little from their counterparts in England or France in their fierce insistence on values like independence, liberty, and productive labor. They also shared with their French counterparts a revolutionary language of rights.

But, as we know, the American pattern of class formation proved to be very different. Key sets of difference, concerning space, demography, and the state, helped shape a working class with a divided politics of work and off-work, one that was well integrated into the political regime.

Far more so than in France, configurations of urban space altered dramatically in the United States. The walking city of neighborhoods devoted to both production and home life did not survive urban growth and industrial change. The social geography of large American cities changed in fundamental ways. By the Civil War, the majority of workers no longer labored in their homes or in immediate proximity to them. Rather, they lived in increasingly well defined, class-specific communities that contained a plethora of institutions—gangs, fire companies, self-help insurance societies, saloons and clubs—that divided the organizational and social lives of workers from nonworkers. Even more, they provided bases for subtle variations within the working class, as different workers with different market positions came to live in different areas of the city. These were defined by income, skill level, and, increasingly, by ethnicity.[44]

These divisions by themselves were necessary but not sufficient to produce a divided pattern of class formation. In fact, there was a remarkable similarity between the social geography of mid-nineteenth-century English and American cities.[45] As the English case makes clear, such spatial demarcations are not incompatible with the emergence of class as a category of disposition and action spanning the divide between work and off-work. But if by themselves spatial demarcations do not produce dichotomous working-class politics, they clearly make such a pattern possible. Nevertheless, an explanation for the American outcome remains to be identified.

Like their English and French counterparts, American artisans did produce anticapitalist political visions, and they did build labor organizations that resembled social movements. What distinguished American craft workers, however, was their incapacity to transfer their leadership, their language, or their orientation to the new proletariat. To be sure,

[44] See Katznelson, *City Trenches*; also relevant is David Scobey, "Boycotting the Politics Factory: Labor Radicalism and the New York City Mayoral Election of 1886," *Radical History Review*, nos. 28-30 (Sept. 1984).

[45] See Katznelson, "Working Class Formation."

there were instances when radical artisans did instruct and lead the new working class. But the discontinuities, concretized in many settings by different partisan loyalties, as much more impressive in a comparative context. It is this failure of transmission that opened the way to the separate and reformist politics of craft labor and political party machines.

How is the hiatus between traditional artisan perspectives and those of the modern proletariat to be explained? Bridges offers two principal hypotheses in her essay. The first is demographic. As a result of massive immigration from Germany and especially from Ireland and as a consequence of a clear cultural division of labor at the workplace, "in the most literal ways the American working classes did not have artisan origins."[46] Most workers of the 1850s had been born outside the United States. The persistent importance of artisan traditions stressed in the essays on France thus could not easily find a counterpart in the United States.

This point, obvious once made, turns Hartz's argument about the absence of a feudal tradition in America on its side, if not on its head. The importance of the liberal tradition in America could not have had its imputed effect by an easy intergenerational transfer of values. Indeed, the societies from which most American proletarians came did have a feudal tradition. Rather, if the liberal tradition had an effect it was that of facilitating the very early introduction of suffrage for adult white males. This constitutional feature of the American regime is the centerpiece of the accounts of Bridges and Shefter.

Bridges proposes an especially interesting formulation of the importance of the franchise. She writes,

I am not saying here, as Reinhard Bendix did, that workers in the United States were less angry about industrialization than voters elsewhere because they had the vote as "compensation." Nor am I saying, with Alan Dawley and Paul Faler, that the vote offered a "ritual" of democracy that made politics a safety valve for working-class discontent. I am arguing that when workers had political goals (e.g., laws limiting the workday or the abolition of contract labor), were entitled to vote, and were an urban minority, they were inevitably drawn into electoral politics and party politics—and those practices just as inevitably shaped their consciousness and their culture. (Footnotes omitted)

This point is a telling one, but it is incomplete. The issue is not only whether workers were necessarily absorbed under these conditions into

[46] For a detailed and thoughtful treatment of the development of craft labor markets and a distinctively American accommodation between wage labor and employers, see Robert Jackson, *The Formation of Craft Labor Markets* (New York: Academic Press, 1984).

electoral politics as a means to pursue their working-class goals in a mass franchise democracy. The fact that the demand for the vote did not have to be a central feature of working-class politics meant, first, that the state was not defined as "them" and thus was not a target of constitutionally oriented collective action; second, that the regime had a high degree of legitimacy based on shared citizenship; and, third, that working-class politics could more easily fragment between proletarian-employer conflict at the workplace and a politics organized by cross-class political parties away from work.

Additional features of state structure and public policy also affected the formation of the American working class. As Shefter stresses, the American state is decentralized and fragmented. Because the central state was relatively underdeveloped,[47] it did not present a concrete target for attention or attack. Rather, government was experienced as both nearby and accessible; it was made even more so by the close interpenetration of local political parties and bureaucracies. Workers were thus mobilized through the country's political institutions, not against them.

This incorporation was reinforced by the early access workers had to mass public education. In the United States workers did not have to fight on a class basis either for inclusion in the system or for control as citizens over its direction.[48]

Even state repression was "soft." Although American trade unions faced the same common law as their English counterparts, proscriptions against combinations were usually rendered moot by sympathetic working-class juries and by judges who feared the wrath of working-class citizens.[49] Local police forces and penal institutions were controlled at the city level by ward politicians, that is, by people who were familiar, reachable, and malleable. "Workers in the United States," Shefter concludes, ". . . did not find themselves subjugated by an official, and officious, class. This in conjunction with the relatively narrow domain of government in the United States during the late nineteenth century meant that on the whole whatever oppression or exploitation American workers experienced was not oppression by the State."

Not so in Germany. There, an exceptionally clear antagonism between the working class and the state developed as a result of simultaneous and discontinuous experiences of industrialization and state building.

---

[47] An influential discussion is Stephen Skowronek, *Building a New American State: The Expansion of National Administrative Capacities, 1877-1920* (New York: Cambridge University Press, 1982).

[48] These questions are discussed at length in Ira Katznelson and Margaret Weir, *Schooling for All: Class, Race, and the Decline of the Democratic Ideal* (New York: Basic Books, 1985).

[49] For discussions, see Wilentz, *Chants Democratic*, and Katznelson, *City Trenches*.

Capitalist accumulation in Germany entailed an even more stark rupture between artisan and factory production than in the United States. By 1800, as Kocka observes in his essay, guild protections had weakened and markets had been better integrated than in France before the Revolution. By the beginning of the nineteenth century, virtually half of all production was accounted for by the putting-out system and only just more than half by the traditional artisan system of masters, journeymen, and apprentices. Although this situation was the result of changes that took place over centuries, the emergence of industrial capitalism was compressed in the four decades from the middle 1830s to the middle 1870s. Production centralized in the crafts. Journeymen increased in number relative to masters. The number of factory workers rapidly increased and cottage workers declined sharply in number.

Although the category of journeymen remained by far the largest in the labor force, its content altered radically. All over Germany journeymen lost traditional corporate privileges and became wage workers governed by labor contracts. For masters, many corporate privileges survived well into the industrial revolution of mid-century, but for journeymen they did not. As the division between masters and journeymen deepened, the latter were cut adrift from the old order and became directly subject to the vicissitudes of the new. Many of their traditional prerogatives were suppressed by state intervention. "Generally speaking," Kocka notes below, "the state was present in the everyday life and experiences of German journeymen to an extent that would have surprised their counterparts in England and the United States, perhaps also in France."

This positioning of journeymen, together with the fact that they possessed important organizational resources, helps explain why they were the leading supporters of the early labor movement in Germany; and it helps begin to account for one of the central puzzles of German class formation. If slow, incremental small-scale industrialization in France established conditions for class consciousness and militancy, and if a more rapid and discontinuous industrialization contributed to the American divided and reformist outcome, then how was it that a rapid and discontinuous industrialization in Germany produced such a "classically Marxist" pattern of dispositions and collective action? The puzzle deepens when we acknowledge that German urbanization was much more like the American than the French, in that in the big cities of northern Germany, Saxony, and the Rhineland, the separation of work and home and residential segregation by class took forms much more like those of American cities than of French. Moreover, why in Germany did socialism prove so attractive to political activists, when in the United States it was a secondary phenomenon?

Kocka's and Mary Nolan's explanations of the connections between the different levels of class in Germany focus to a small degree on demographic factors, but principally emphasize the strong impact of the state and its policies.

Population growth was striking, unlike France and like the United States. But whereas population and labor-force growth in America depended in no small part on immigrants (many of whom came from Germany) and where, as a result, there was a rupture between many of those who were artisans and others who were proletarians, in Germany these were the same people: artisans became proletarians. Positions in the economy did not keep pace with population growth. Many journeymen were displaced, experienced great misery, and were compelled to migrate from the countryside to the fast-growing cities or overseas. Cottage workers, including handloom weavers, experienced a similar fate due to competition from British and domestic textile factories.

But if these population and employment trends contributed to German class formation, it was the very special and intense role of the state that provided the fulcrum. Capitalist industrialization, authoritarian state building, and conflicts about rights to political participation and to collective organization were dealt with at the same time in Germany, initially between 1848 and 1870. This compression, Kocka argues, left little room for liberal alternatives to socialist and Marxist practice. German liberals had been weak before 1848 because of the strength of bureaucratic government, and they were weaker still after 1848 and 1849. In Prussia, they proved a weak counterforce to Bismarck in the 1860s. On the other side, a developed set of labor institutions already existed when the franchise was introduced in 1867. By the time political competition was organized in this way, German society was already marked by a modern class structure, developed working-class dispositions, and a significant working-class capacity for collective action. Thus, very much unlike the United States, political incorporation of the working class could not take place effectively on liberal terms. And unlike France, socialism was not well integrated into a quasi-legitimate republican tradition. Rather, Marxism faced Catholicism as the contender for mapping and acting on the situation of the working class.

It was the state too that had the leading role to play in stimulating close ties between the trade unions and the Social Democrats in Germany. Rather than a division occurring on a reformist basis, as in the United States, or in militant terms, as in France, there was a remarkable centralization and coordination of working-class activity across the work–off work divide. The proscription of the SPD in 1878 played a critical role in this development, because after the party was outlawed the trade unions became its major organizational vehicle.

The legal situation of the party changed, of course, but the legacy of this moment of enforced collaboration between unions and party remained. The precarious and oscillating legal situation of the party reinforced what Vernon Lidtke has called its "ambivalent parliamentarism" and its focus in the neighborhoods and at the workplace on building a supportive working-class culture and community, openly where possible and covertly where necessary.[50] By the 1880s Marxism had become the linguistic centerpiece of these efforts. The Catholic Church aside, there were no competitors. Working-class debates in Germany took place within the embrace of Marxism, rather than between Marxist and other alternatives.

[50] Vernon Lidtke, *The Outlawed Party* (Princeton: Princeton University Press, 1966).

Part One

France

2 Artisans, Factory Workers, and the Formation of the French Working Class, 1789-1848 • *William H. Sewell, Jr.*

Viewed from the standpoint of Britain, the history of French working-class formation is paradoxical. Britain was the homeland of the industrial revolution; the French economy remained predominantly rural and artisanal until the twentieth century. Yet the French were the unquestioned leaders in the development of socialism and working-class consciousness. Most of the great early socialist theorists, with the exception of Robert Owen, were French: "Gracchus" Babeuf, Claude-Henri de Saint-Simon, Charles Fourier, Louis Auguste Blanqui, Pierre-Joseph Proudhon, Louis Blanc. It was also in France, in the revolution of 1848, that socialism first became a mass movement. Given the usual understanding of class consciousness as the product of a burgeoning industrial economy, the precociousness of French working-class consciousness is downright embarrassing. The embarrassment, however, is founded on a set of misunderstandings, both of the nature of French industrial capitalism and of the relationship between class consciousness and the development of factory industry. Although France did not experience a British-style "industrial revolution," French society was nevertheless transformed by industrial capitalism in the nineteenth century. And although French industrialization did not spawn a huge mass of factory workers, it did produce an abundance of discontented artisans who were the mainstay of the early working-class movement, not only in France but in all the early industrial countries.

I. *French Industrialization*

The key characteristics of French industrialization were a very gradual and early start, continued predominance of handicraft production, relatively slow growth of factory industry, and low rates of population growth. This peculiar pattern left its marks on the French working-class movement.

France never experienced a "take off" of the sort hypothesized by W. W. Rostow—a sudden spurt of output that begins sustained industrial growth. According to J. Marczewski, French industrial production began its upward movement as early as the 1750s, before the beginning of the British "industrial revolution," and rose gradually but steadily thereafter.[1] This expansion took place both in rural industries, especially cotton, linen, and woolen textiles, and in urban industry, where luxury goods were very prominent. The increased productivity that resulted from mechanization and the application of steam power was, hence, not at the origin of modern French industrial growth, but was added to an already expanding base of handicraft industrial production.

Much of the industrial growth of the nineteenth century continued to be in handicrafts. Although the British captured the bulk of the world market for iron and inexpensive cotton and woolen textiles, the French continued to dominate the market for certain luxury goods. The silks of Lyon, the silk ribbons and trimmings of Saint-Etienne, the porcelains of Limoges, and the innumerable luxury products of Paris were among the most important and most rapidly growing industries in nineteenth-century France. What the Parliament of Paris said of French crafts in the eighteenth century remained true in the nineteenth: "Our merchandise . . . is sought after all over Europe for its taste, its beauty, its finesse, its solidity, the correctness of its design, the perfection of its execution, the quality of its raw materials."[2] Rather than competing directly with British factory-made goods, France continued to exploit its comparative advantage in high-quality products that required highly skilled workmanship. In fact, even the French factory industries that were most successful on the international market—the cottons of Mulhouse and the woolens of Roubaix—specialized in the finest grades of cloth.[3] In addition to craft industries producing for the international market, craft industries supplying the wants of the domestic population continued to thrive. As in all other countries during the first half of the nineteenth century, factory industry was quite limited in scope, and housing, clothing, food, and most other consumer goods continued to be produced by hand.

The classic innovations of the British industrial revolution were adopted later and on a much smaller scale in France than in Britain. In the case of textiles, the British advantage in all but the highest quality goods was so pronounced that most French markets were limited to producing mainly for the internal French market. A large number of textile factories were erected in Rouen, Elbeuf, Lille, Tourcoing, Roubaix, Mul-

---

[1] J. Marczewski, "The Take-Off and French Experience," in *The Economics of Take-Off into Sustained Growth*, ed. W. W. Rostow (London: Macmillan, 1963). Rostow's hypothesis was originally set forth in *The Stages of Economic Growth: A Non-Communist Manifesto* (Cambridge: Cambridge University Press, 1961).

[2] Jules Flammermont, ed., *Remonstrances du Parlement de Paris au XVIIIe siècle*, vol. 3 (Paris, 1898), p. 347.

[3] M. Lévy-Leboyer, "Le processus d'industrialisation: Le cas de l'Angleterre et de la France," *Revue historique* 230 (1968):281-98.

house, Reims, Saint-Quentin, and other cities, and cotton manufacture was one of the most rapidly growing industries in the country. But in comparison with Lancashire, Glasgow, or the West Riding of Yorkshire, French centers were distinctly second-rate. Mining and metallurgy in France was restricted by relatively poor coal resources (the rich deposits of the Pas-de-Calais were unknown until the late nineteenth century) and by the distance of ore deposits from coal deposits. Mining and metallurgy were important nodes of industrial growth for France, but they were hardly comparable to British and (later) German counterparts. It was the relatively slow growth of the French factory sector that caused J. H. Clapham to wonder whether France ever had a real "industrial revolution,"[4] and led the following generation of economic historians of France to write endlessly about the "stagnation" or "retardation" of the French economy in the nineteenth century.[5] But more recent quantitative studies have demonstrated that the concern about "retardation" was misplaced. French output per capita grew at essentially the same rate as British output per capita until World War I, and beyond. The shape of economic growth in France was very different from that in Britain, with French agriculture and handicraft industry playing a more important role, but the economy's overall performance was no less impressive.[6]

One reason that French industrialization differed in form was the low rate of French population growth. French birth rates had already begun

[4] J. H. Clapham, *The Economic Development of France and Germany, 1815-1914*, 4th ed. (Cambridge: Cambridge University Press, 1936), p. 53.

[5] See, e.g., S. B. Clough, "Retardative Factors in French Economic Development in the Nineteenth and Twentieth Centuries," *Journal of Economic History* 6 (1946), suppl.: 91-210; Clough, "Retardative Factors in French Economic Growth at the End of the Ancien Régime and during the French Revolutionary and Napoleonic Periods," in *Studies in Economics and Economic History: Essays in Honor of Harold F. Williamson*, ed. M. Kooy (Durham: Duke University Press, 1972); David S. Landes, "French Entrepreneurship and Industrial Growth in the Nineteenth Century," *Journal of Economic History* 9 (1949):45-61; Landes, "French Business and the Businessman: A Social and Cultural Analysis," in *Modern France: Problems of the Third and Fourth Republics*, ed. Edward Mead Earle (Princeton: Princeton University Press, 1951); Landes, "New Model Entrepreneurship in France and Problems of Historical Explanation," *Explorations in Entrepreneurial History* 1 (1963):56-57; R. E. Cameron, "Profit, croissance et stagnation en France au XIXe siècle," *Economie appliquée* 10 (1957):409-444; Cameron, "Economic Growth and Stagnation in Modern France, 1815-1914," *Journal of Modern History* 20 (1958):1-13; Tom Kemp, "Structural Factors in the Retardation of French Economic Growth," *Kyklos* 15 (1962):325-50; and C. P. Kindleberger, *The Economic Growth of France and Britain, 1851-1950* (Cambridge: Harvard University Press, 1964).

[6] The best statements of this thesis are Lévy-Leboyer, "Le processus d'industrialisation"; Richard Roehl, "French Industrialization: A Reconsideration," *Explorations in Economic History* 13 (1976):233-81; and Patrick O'Brien and Caglar Keyder, *Economic Growth in Britain and France 1780-1914: Two Paths to the Twentieth Century* (London: George Allen and Unwin, 1978).

to fall by the late eighteenth century, and during the entire nineteenth century France's population increased by less than 50 percent. Britain's population, in contrast, grew by 350 percent in the nineteenth century and would have grown even more had it not been for massive emigration. With the population expanding only moderately, it was possible to sustain impressive rates of growth in per capita income in France without the extraordinary growth of factory industry that occurred in Britain. Britain's very rapid population growth contributed to massive urbanization (the extra hands could not be accommodated in agriculture) and thereby created a more unified and mobile market both for labor and for the type of commodities that factories produce. In France, a much higher proportion of the population was composed of peasants who were only partially engaged in the cash nexus, and the national territory remained divided into only partially integrated regional markets—both for commodities and for labor. These circumstances placed limitations on the possibilities for factory production in France and made it economically rational for a large part of the nation's capital to be invested in agriculture and in handicraft industry. To an earlier generation of economic historians, this French pattern of low population growth and the continued predominance of agriculture and handicrafts appeared stagnant. It is now clear that it was simply an alternative form of industrialization, one that led to rising per capita incomes and eventually to "high mass consumption" as ineluctably as an industrial revolution in the British style.

This French pattern of industrialization had two important consequences for the formation of the French working class. The first was a relative continuity in the urban experience of workers. Owing to low overall rates of population increase, French cities grew much less rapidly during the early stages of industrialization than British, German, or American cities. Between 1800 and 1850 only one of the ten largest cities in France (the Mediterranean port city of Toulon) had doubled in population; in Britain all of the ten largest cities had doubled or more than doubled in population in the same years. Leeds and Birmingham, in fact, had more than tripled, Manchester, Liverpool, and Glasgow had more than quadrupled, and Bradford had multiplied eightfold. British cities were also strikingly different in kind from French cities.[7] Only four of the twenty-five largest cities in France in 1851 (Rouen, Lille, Saint-Etienne,

---

[7] For French cities, see Charles Pouthas, *La population française pendant la première moitié du XIXe siècle* (Paris: Presses Universitaires de France, 1956), p. 98. The British figures are from B. R. Mitchell and Phyllis Deane, *Abstract of British Historical Statistics* (Cambridge: Cambridge University Press, 1962), pp. 24-27.

and Reims) were significant centers of factory industry, and only Saint-Etienne, which grew from a village in the eighteenth century to a city of 56,000 by 1851, had not been an important center of commerce, administration, and handicrafts long before the industrial revolution. In Britain, six of the top ten cities in 1851 were centers of factory industry: Glasgow, Manchester, Birmingham, Leeds, Sheffield, and Bradford. Three of these, Manchester, Birmingham, and Bradford, had been mere villages in the early eighteenth century. A majority of the great cities of nine-teenth-century Britain were essentially creations of the industrial revo-lution and factory industry, and their urban form and culture reflected this fact. In France nearly all the important cities had long and proud urban traditions, and most of them grew gradually enough that they retained much of their traditional spatial and cultural form through the nineteenth century. With some important exceptions, the class segrega-tion and radical separation of home and work that occurred in the new factory towns of Britain was far less pronounced in French cities. To be sure, such textile towns as Roubaix, Tourcoing, and Mulhouse resembled British textile towns very closely—except that they were much smaller. And in Lyon, the precocious labor movement of the silk workers in the 1830s was based, to a significant extent, on the development of the highly segregated Croix Rousse industrial suburb. However, far from signifying a separation of home and work, the industrial suburbs of Lyon were pop-ulated almost exclusively by domestic weavers who worked with their families and occasional journeymen at the command of wealthy putting-out silk merchants.[8] But in spite of exceptions, it is true that the vast majority of French workers continued to live in mixed centers of admin-istration, commerce, and industry. For this reason, issues of urban space are far less important for the history of class formation in France than in Britain.

The second important consequence of the French pattern of industrial-ization for French class formation was that artisans rather than factory workers long remained the overwhelming majority of French industrial workers. Even as late as 1876, the industrial population employed in small-scale industry was twice that in large-scale industry.[9] Even in Brit-ain, artisans outnumbered factory workers until past the middle of the century and were disproportionately represented in working-class politi-

[8] See Robert Bezucha, *The Lyon Uprising of 1834: Social and Political Conflict in a Nineteenth-Century City* (Cambridge: Harvard University Press, 1974).

[9] Thimor J. Markovitch, "Le revenu industriel et artisanal sous la Monarchie de Juillet et le Second Empire," *Cahiers de l'Institut de Science Economique Appliquée*, series AF, 4 (1967):87.

cal activity. But in France the imbalance was far more pronounced. Down to the Commune of 1871, the history of working-class protest in France was essentially the history of artisan protest. The conventional assumption that the class-conscious workers' movement was a product of the factory is even less tenable for France than for other early industrial countries. An account of French working-class formation, therefore, must give special attention to the specific experiences of artisans.

II. *Artisans, Textile Workers, and the Dynamics of Industrial Capitalism*

The fact that artisan industry survived in France well into the twentieth century by no means implies that it was untouched by the development of industrial capitalism. In fact, capitalism began to transform crafts long before the introduction of English technological innovations in the late eighteenth and early nineteenth centuries. The first handicrafts to feel its effects were woolen and linen textiles. Initially these were urban industries, and as such they were governed by the same kinds of guilds that regulated all other urban crafts. As a longtime staple of interregional and international commerce, the textile industries were subjected to the dynamics of capitalist development very early. By the sixteenth and seventeenth centuries, the merchant capitalists who dominated the textile industry began to put out spinning and weaving operations to rural families who worked in their own cottages and who usually combined these industrial activities with cultivation of a tiny plot of ground. Rural putting-out textile industry was introduced as a means of circumventing the urban guilds' high labor costs, restrictive practices, and insistence on high quality. Not only would rural weavers accept lower pay than urban guild weavers (as part-time agriculturalists they could afford to work for less) but they were willing to fabricate the lighter, lower quality, cheaper cloths that constituted the main growth sector of the textile trade.[10]

The putting-out textile industry—in which manufacture was rural and domestic, but coordination and control was in the hands of urban capitalists who operated in an inter-regional or international market—was the most advanced sector of the capitalist economy in the seventeenth

[10] The classic study of rural textile workers is Pierre Goubert, *Beauvais et le Beauvaisis de 1600 à 1730, contribution à l'histoire sociale de la France au XVIIe siècle* (Paris: S.E.V.P.E.N., 1960). See also Franklin F. Mendels, "Proto-industrialization: The First Phase of the Process of Industrialization," *Journal of Economic History* 32 (1972):241-61; and a special issue of *Revue du Nord* 61 (Jan.-Mar. 1979) entitled *Aux origines de la révolution industrielle: Industrie rurale et fabriques.*

and eighteenth centuries. When cotton manufacture was introduced in the eighteenth century, it followed the same putting-out pattern already established by woolens and linens. The introduction of spinning and weaving factories in the first half of the nineteenth century and the consequent re-urbanization of the textile industry marked not the beginning of industrial capitalism in France, but the arrival of a new stage in the exploitation of an industry that had already been capitalist for at least two centuries.

The history of the textile trades was unique in the seventeenth and eighteenth centuries. In most other crafts, manufacture continued to be carried out in cities under the more-or-less detailed supervision of guilds. It was not until the abolition of guilds in the French Revolution and the quickened expansion of national and world markets in the first half of the nineteenth century that industrial capitalism began to have pervasive effects on a broad range of artisan trades. Considered abstractly, capitalism had a uniform dynamic, the same in the nineteenth-century urban artisan trades as in the rural putting-out textile industry of the seventeenth and eighteenth centuries or in the new textile factories of the nineteenth. Systems of production were reorganized to turn out a larger quantity of standardized, usually lower quality goods at a lower cost by a less-skilled labor force, in order to take advantage of expanding market opportunities. But in terms of concrete experiences, what happened to nineteenth-century urban artisans was quite distinct from what happened to textile workers, either in the seventeenth and eighteenth centuries or in the nineteenth.

Scholars have commonly considered nineteenth-century urban crafts to be "traditional," mainly because few of them were affected by important technological changes until near the end of the century. Recent research, however, has revealed a profusion of new exploitative practices that transformed many handicraft trades even without the introduction of new machinery. Entrepreneurs in such diverse industries as garment making, jewelry, furniture, building, and shoemaking responded to rising demand for their products by turning away from the older practice of making items to order for their clients and instead specializing in standardized, ready-to-use items that could be mass produced and sold at a lower price. Such entrepreneurs thoroughly reorganized existing patterns of production, increasing the division of labor, introducing various subcontracting schemes, diluting workers' skills, or putting out some phase of manufacture to women and children who worked in their own rooms or garrets. These practices not only lowered the earnings and reduced the autonomy of workers in the reorganized branch of the trade, but reduced wages for workers who remained in the traditional branch. Exploitation, recent studies make clear, could be as intense in handicraft industries as in factories in the first half of the nineteenth century.[11]

This finding is of major significance for any attempt to understand the predominance of artisans in the early working-class movement, since it implies that artisans had as much reason to protest as factory workers. But it goes only halfway. It helps to explain why artisans' rates of participation in protest movements were as high as those of factory workers, but not why they were vastly higher. To explain this disparity, we must widen our inquiry beyond the question of exploitation to explore the ways that different types of workers understood and acted on their workplace experiences.

A useful starting point is the classical Marxist account of the development of class consciousness among factory workers. Marx pointed not only to the intensity of exploitation in the factory but to the increasingly socialized process of production. Gathered together under one roof and constrained to cooperate with other workers in a complex process of production, factory workers would be made aware of the commonality of their interests as wage workers and thereby encouraged to act together on those interests. The problem with this explanation is its excessively literal materialism. Marx assumed that a consciousness of commonality depended on the workers' sheer physical proximity, on their visible and palpable interconnections on the factory floor. In fact, development of collective consciousness is less a matter of recognizing palpable facts than of constructing interpretive webs that give certain facts a special salience. The fact that workers are crowded together into factories does not lead automatically to a recognition of common interests and a feeling of soli-

[11] See Christopher H. Johnson, "Economic Change and Artisan Discontent: The Tailors' History, 1800-1848," in *Revolution and Reaction: 1848 and the Second French Republic*, ed. Roger Price (London: Croom Helm, 1975), pp. 87-114; Johnson, *Utopian Communism in France: Cabet and the Icarians, 1839-1851* (Ithaca: Cornell University Press, 1974), esp. pp. 177-82; Johnson, "Communism and the Working Class before Marx: The Icarian Experience," *American Historical Review* 76 (June 1971):657-67; Bernard H. Moss, *The Origins of the French Labor Movement: The Socialism of Skilled Workers, 1830-1914* (Berkeley: University of California Press, 1976), esp. ch. 1; Ronald Aminzade, "The Transformation of Social Solidarities in Nineteenth-Century Toulouse," in *Consciousness and Class Experience in Nineteenth-Century Europe*, ed. John M. Merriman (New York: Holmes and Meier, 1979), pp. 85-105; Aminzade, *Class, Politics, and Early Industrial Capitalism: A Study of Mid-Nineteenth-Century Toulouse, France* (Albany: State University of New York Press, 1981), ch. 2; Alain Cottereau's introduction to the reprint of Denis Poulot, *Question sociale: Le sublime, ou le travailleur comme il est en 1870, et ce qu'il peut être* (1870; repr. Paris: François Maspéro, 1980), esp. pp. 63-81; and Alain Faure's introduction to Agricol Perdiguier, *Mémoires d'un compagnon* (Paris: François Maspéro, 1980), pp. 21-22. The classic discussion of this problem is E. P. Thompson's analysis of London artisans in *The Making of the English Working Class* (London: Victor Gollancz, 1963), ch. 8.

darity, nor does the fact that workers labor in scattered workshops nec-essarily inhibit such a recognition; it all depends on how they understand their work and their relations to one another. But if Marx was wrong to think that the physical arrangement of work would be the crucial factor leading workers to understand that their labor was social, he was cer-tainly right to point out that some such understanding was a necessary condition for collective action and consciousness.

The crucial difference between artisans and factory workers was in the way they understood their labor; the artisans' proclivity for class-con-scious action was largely a consequence of a social understanding of their labor that derived from the corporate or guild system of the medieval and early modern cities. In contrast, the relative quiescence of factory work-ers—at least of factory workers in the textile industry—grew out of a less social, more individualized conception of the relations of production. These different understandings of labor arose from the distinct histories of capitalism in the textile industry and the urban crafts. The growth of a rural, domestic, putting-out organization of the textile industry created a new labor force whose self-conception was not significantly influenced by urban corporate institutions. In urban crafts, corporate institutions and traditions constituted the major framework of productive relations until—and in some respects beyond—the French Revolution. Class con-sciousness emerged in France as a transformation of the artisans' cor-porate understanding of labor under the twin impact of capitalist devel-opment and revolutionary politics. The impact of industrial capitalism on the artisan trades has already been outlined. To discover how artisans became conscious of themselves as members of a working class, we must examine their corporate cultural and institutional heritage, and then determine how this heritage was transformed into a class-conscious work-ers' movement during the revolutionary political upheavals of the nine-teenth century.

III. *The Corporate Understanding of Labor*

Virtually all the urban skilled trades of Old Regime France were orga-nized in corporations of some kind. These corporations were chartered by royal or municipal authority and were empowered to regulate the prac-tice of a trade in a given city. Their powers included: a local monopoly (only members of the corporation could practice the trade within its juris-diction); quality control (the corporation's statutes specified the types and quality of goods that could be manufactured and sold); control over train-ing (no one could work as a journeyman or be accepted as a master unless he had passed a proper apprenticeship); limitation on entry (the statutes limited the number of apprentices—usually to one per master—and gave the existing body of masters the power to decide who would be accepted as new masters); and disciplinary authority (the corporation's officers were empowered to inspect shops, to oversee the application of regulations, and to impose penalties on those who committed infractions). In the prerevolutionary corporation, labor was nothing if not social. The trade was not composed of individual masters who, as absolute private proprietors of their capital, organized production as they saw fit. They were not, in other words, individualistic "petty bourgeois" of the nineteenth-century type. Nor were workers free to work for whoever offered them the most favorable conditions. Rather, both masters and workers were subjected to the collective discipline of the corporation, which regulated everyone and everything in the trade—ostensibly for the good of the trade as a whole and for the good of society at large. The production and sale of goods in the urban skilled trades of Old Regime France was organized by the corporation—a collective body—rather than by individuals connected only by market relations.[12]

Relations of production in the artisan trades were social not only in an institutional but in a moral sense. Corporations, in addition to being units of regulation and discipline, were also units of pervasive solidarity. This element of moral solidarity was signified, for example, by the fact that masters swore a solemn oath of loyalty to the corporation upon their elevation to the mastership. But the moral community of the trade was manifested above all in the corporation's religious life. The corporation was coextensive with a confraternity established under the protection of the traditional patron saint of the trade. All members of the trade were therefore expected to venerate the same saint and to celebrate his or her festival in common with a mass, a procession, and a banquet. The confraternity also organized distribution of mutual aid. Every member paid monthly dues to a common treasury—to which were added any fines assessed by the corporation's officers—and benefits were paid to members

[12] The standard works are Emile Coornaert, *Les corporations en France avant 1789* (Paris: Gallimard, 1941); Etienne Martin Saint-Léon, *Histoire des corporations de métiers, depuis leurs origines jusqu'à leur suppression en 1791*, 2d ed. (Paris: F. Alcan, 1909); Henri Hauser, *Ouvriers du temps passé* (*XVᵉ-XVIᵉ siècles*) (Paris: F. Alcan, 1899); François Olivier-Martin, *L'organisation corporative de la France d'ancien régime* (Paris: Recueil Sirey, 1938); and E. Levasseur, *Histoire des classes ouvrières en France depuis la conquête de Jules César jusqu'à la Révolution*, 2 vols. (Paris: Guillaumin, 1859), republished as *Histoire des classes ouvrières et de l'industrie en France avant 1789*, 2 vols. (Paris: A. Rousseau, 1900). See also William H. Sewell, Jr., *Work and Revolution in France: The Language of Labor from the Old Regime to 1848* (New York: Cambridge University Press, 1980), pp. 25-32.

who were sick or had fallen on hard times, or to their widows and orphans. In addition, the confraternity provided a proper funeral for departed members. The corporation was, in short, a moral community whose members were bound to one another "in sickness and in health, 'till death do us part."[13]

This does not mean that life in the urban trades was characterized by brotherly love and perfect harmony. Like any human community, trades were riven by innumerable jealousies, quarrels, intrigues, and enmities. Above all, they were split by struggles between masters and journeymen. Journeymen were generally excluded from the annual assembly at which the masters discussed the trade's problems and elected officers, and they usually were excluded from the benefits of the confraternity as well. Legally, journeymen were considered to be under the paternal authority of masters, much like children, servants, and wives. But journeymen frequently organized illegal corporate brotherhoods of their own, challenging the masters' authority, establishing their own parallel systems of mutual aid, claiming a right—like that of the masters' corporations—to regulate the trade for the common good, and attempting to maintain good wages and working conditions by carrying out strikes or by gaining control of job placement. The most powerful of these journeymen's brotherhoods were organized into national federations called "compagnonnage" (from *compagnon*, which in French means both "journeyman" and "companion"). These brotherhoods maintained rooming houses for itinerant journeymen making their "tour de France" and had an astonishingly elaborate ritual life. Trade "communities" sometimes resembled battlegrounds between rival masters' and journeymens' organizations. Yet the notion that the trade was a community was honored even in these struggles. Both masters and workers claimed to be acting on behalf of the trade as a whole, not for the interests of journeymen or of masters. Here it is significant that the journeymen's brotherhoods invariably chose the same patron saint as the masters'.[14]

Relations between masters and journeymen in a given trade were often

[13] Sewell, *Work and Revolution*, pp. 32-37.

[14] On journeymen's brotherhoods see Germain Martin, *Les associations ouvrières au XVIIIᵉ siècle (1700-1792)* (Paris: A. Rousseau, 1900); Hauser, *Ouvriers du temps passé*; Steven Kaplan, "Réflexions sur la police du monde du travail, 1700-1815," *Revue historique* 261 (Jan.-Mar. 1979). The standard works on compagnonnage are Emile Coornaert, *Les compagnonnages en France du moyen âge à nos jours* (Paris: Editions ouvrières, 1966); Etienne Martin Saint-Léon, *Le compagnonnage* (Paris: Armand Colin, 1901). For an account of the symbols and rituals of compagnonnage, see Cynthia Truant, "Compagnonnage: Symbolic Action and the Defense of Workers' Rights in France, 1700-1848" (Ph.D. diss., University of Chicago, 1978). See also Sewell, *Work and Revolution*, ch. 3.

tense or bitter, but the tensions and bitterness were founded on a sense
of permanent membership in a common community. One might make an
analogy with family quarrels that set brother against brother or son
against father. Such an analogy has much to recommend it, since family
metaphors (paternal authority, fraternity, etc.) played an important role
in corporate language. Sixteenth-century printers' journeymen studied by
Natalie Davis stated the ideal explicitly at one point during their protracted struggles with the masters: "The Masters and Journeymen are or
ought to be only one body together, like a family and a fraternity."[15] The
analogy with family quarrels is also appropriate in another sense, for just
as sons could expect to succeed their fathers as they grew to adulthood,
so journeymen expected eventually to become masters. In some trades a
rising scale of operations might render this expectation illusory, and
many journeymen were in fact condemned to remain journeymen for life.
But disputes between masters and journeymen were often generational
quarrels as much as quarrels between lifetime classes.

   In summary, urban artisans of the Old Regime understood their labor
as social, both in the sense that it was and ought to be given shape by
collective regulations of the corporation and in the sense that men working in the same trade formed a solidary moral community. This understanding of labor as social was not, however, class conscious. In the first
place, it included both wage workers and employers in a single—if often
contested—trade community. Second, it did not extend community feelings or community regulations beyond the boundaries of the trade. Those
who worked in different trades were regarded with indifference at best,
and all too often with hostility. The masters' corporations were engaged
in constant legal battles with corporations in rival trades, and journeymen
of different trades commonly engaged in violent brawls with each other.
The sense that all wage workers were brothers, members of a single solidary class, was utterly absent in the artisan trades of the Old Regime. It
was only in the new society created by the French Revolution that class
consciousness could emerge.

   The French Revolution effected a far-reaching transformation of the
social order. In terms of political theory, at least, France was transformed
from a society composed of privileged corporate bodies linked by their
common subordination to the crown into a collection of individual citizens, joined together by a social contract that was founded on their natural rights and that guaranteed their equality before the law. In carrying

[15] Natalie Zemon Davis, "A Trade Union in Sixteenth-Century France," *Economic
History Review*, 2d. ser., 19 (Apr. 1966):53.

out this transformation, the revolutionaries swept away the artisans' privileged corporations, leaving each artisan legally free to carry on his trade
according to his own inclinations, capacities, and interests. The regime
of corporate regulation was replaced by a regime of "industrial liberty."
At the same time, private property was exalted to the status of a "natural, inalienable, and sacred right" by the Declaration of the Rights of
Man and Citizen, and in practice the revolutionary and Napoleonic legal
reforms freed the property of artisan masters, as of all other proprietors,
from any collectively imposed constraints.

These changes did not immediately turn the corporately minded master artisans of the Old Regime into petty-capitalist individualists who
henceforth engaged in a ruthless and single-minded pursuit of their own
interests. Most probably continued to operate very much as before the
Revolution, following the customary practices of the trade and basing
their decisions on what they regarded as the good of the trade as well as
on their own self-interest. But the legal framework in which they operated was now drastically different. Even before the Revolution, many
masters were tempted by the steadily expanding economy of the later
eighteenth century to experiment with some of the new ways of organizing production discussed above—taking advantage of economies of scale
and cutting labor costs in order to produce a larger quantity of standardized products that could be sold below the going price. Although such
practices had been introduced in some trades, they continually ran afoul
of corporate regulations. But after the Revolution, these "abuses"
became perfectly legal exercises of the entrepreneur's "industrial liberty," his right to dispose of his property as he saw fit. Consequently, even
though most masters in the handicraft sector continued to operate in traditional ways, it was now virtually impossible to stop a more aggressive
minority from introducing innovations that cut costs and intensified the
exploitation of labor. This had two important results. First, it tended to
reduce wages and cause deteriorating working conditions even among
employees of masters who did not innovate. Second, within the trade, it
caused an increasing heterogeneity of working conditions, of wages, of
quality and price of product, and of employer/employee relations. The
socially controlled trade community of the Old Regime corporation was
gradually being transformed, by the combined action of a new legal system and an expanding market economy, into an anarchic collection of
individualized entrepreneurs and laborers.

Not surprisingly, these changes in the handicraft trades quickly gave
rise to attempts to reunite the trade community and to restore some measure of corporate control over the productive process. But these attempts

were undertaken primarily by workers, not masters. The power of the masters' corporations had rested on their legal privileges, and when these were abolished in the French Revolution, masters' corporations were effectively destroyed. But the legal prohibitions had very little effect on the alternative corporations of the journeymen, because these had always been illegal and were already accustomed to a clandestine existence. Moreover, although masters were increasingly disunited by the changes that were overtaking their trades, the workers were generally united in their opposition to the new exploitative practices. The result, especially after 1815, when the Restoration of the Bourbons tempered the severity of the Napoleonic police apparatus, was a flowering of workers' corporations that attempted to impose far-reaching controls over working conditions in their trades. By the late 1820s, virtually all the skilled trades in the major cities of France had some kind of corporate workers' organization that was actively resisting exploitative practices.[16]

Yet as widespread as the corporate workers' movement of the 1820s may have been, it did not signify the formation of a self-conscious working class. Workers in different trades maintained the traditional attitudes of indifference or hostility toward workers in other trades. And although the workers' corporations could be quite militant in their stance toward masters in labor disputes, they posed no articulate alternative to the existing property system that ensured the masters' continued power. The corporate workers' movement of the Restoration did differ in important respects from the corporate system of the Old Regime. It was dominated by workers rather than by masters, and it was in opposition to rather than in harmony with the law and the principles enforced by public authority. But it retained the essential Old Regime vision of the trade as an exclusive solidary community, and assumed that the masters would continue to collect their profits and exercise day-to-day authority in the workshops. The workers' movement of the Restoration retained the forms, language, and vision of the Old Regime journeymen's corporations with only minor changes. This idiom provided the workers with a solid organizational foundation from which to press their claims, but it also limited the kinds of claims the workers could make. It was only when the idiom of the workers' movement was expanded to take in the forms, the language, and the vision of the French Revolution that the corporate workers' movement could begin to become class conscious.

[16] Sewell, *Work and Revolution*, ch. 8. For an excellent collection of contemporary documents, see Georges Bourgin and Hubert Bourgin, eds., *Les patrons, les ouvriers, et l'état: Le régime de l'industrie en France de 1814 à 1830*, 3 vols. (Paris: A. Picard, 1912-41).

IV. *Revolutionary Political Discourse and the Emergence of Class Consciousness*

The French Revolution's transformation of the institutional structure of society was accompanied by the development of a new political language or discourse that set the terms in which public claims of all sorts could be couched—a language of individual citizens, natural rights, popular sovereignty, and the social contract. During the course of the revolutionary and Napoleonic era this discourse developed many variations. Revolutionary language could soon be spoken with a distinct Jacobin, moderate, sans-culotte, Thermidorian, or Napoleonic accent, and it could be used to justify either repression and maintenance of order or struggle and insurrection. It became, in short, a complex and fully articulated linguistic world, complete with standard rhetorical figures, characteristic debates and dilemmas, silences, and unquestioned assumptions.

The Restoration in 1814 sharply changed public discourse. Respect for tradition and authority, horror of revolution, and religious piety became the order of the day. Yet the return of the Bourbon monarchy could not restore prerevolutionary political conditions. Louis XVIII claimed to be monarch by divine right rather than by the will of the nation, but he prudently decreed a constitution—a "Charter," as he called it—that included a wide range of "liberal" guarantees and established a representative form of government. Moreover, the alternative political discourse of the revolutionary era thrived in the opposition, both in the parliamentary opposition of the liberal constitutional monarchists and in the extraparliamentary opposition of radical journalists and republican conspirators. In 1830, when Louis XVIII's successor, the inflexible Charles X, attempted to suppress the liberties guaranteed in the Charter, the result was a popular insurrection, the overthrow of the Bourbons, and the establishment of a more liberal Orleanist monarchy. The Orleanist regime restored revolutionary language, though of a moderate and liberal sort, to the center of political life. It was in the social and political struggles following the July 1830 revolution—in a political atmosphere replete with talk of liberty—that the artisans of Paris, Lyon, and other French cities transformed their corporate understanding of labor into class consciousness.

In the days following the July revolution, Parisian workers, who had been the shock troops of the insurrection, quite naturally expected sympathetic treatment from officials of the new regime. But these initial expectations soon evaporated when Orleanist officials dismissed workers' demands for controls on their trades as assaults on the "liberty of industry." The workers, shocked and hurt by these rebuffs, responded by developing a new political and organizational language that met the regime on its own chosen terrain: the discourse of liberty. In doing so, the workers embraced, but also modified and elaborated, the liberal language of the French Revolution. Class consciousness, in other words, was a transformed version of liberal revolutionary discourse. The workers' new political language was worked out on many levels simultaneously: in newspapers and pamphlets, in newly formed political organizations, in the statutes and practices of workers' corporations, and in strikes and direct actions against the masters or political authorities. The workers' movement that developed class-conscious discourse stretched over a turbulent period of some three and a half years, from the July revolution of 1830 to the unsuccessful Lyonnais and Parisian insurrections of April 1834. Because this movement was complex and multifaceted, any summary description of its discursive practice is bound to oversimplify and distort; nevertheless, some crucial features can be identified.[17]

An articulate minority of workers quickly appropriated revolutionary language, modifying it to highlight the moral and political standing of workers. One example was the appropriation of an argument the Abbé Sieyès had introduced in *What Is the Third Estate?* The Third Estate, he claimed, was the entire nation because it performed all the useful work of society, while the nobility "is foreign to the nation because of its idleness."[18] Sieyès, of course, conceived of useful work as including all the tasks and occupations carried out by the Third Estate. The workers in the early 1830s took one more step and declared that manual labor alone supported all of society. It followed that workers, because they did all of society's useful labor, were in fact the sovereign people. The bourgeoisie, which did not labor, was in effect a new aristocracy. Working-class authors fortified this conclusion by changing the usage of a cluster of important revolutionary words: "aristocrat," "privilege," "servitude," and "emancipation," among others. Bourgeois were dubbed "new aristocrats," who used their "privilege" of property ownership to keep workers in "servitude" as industrial "serfs" or "slaves." This turned the bourgeois constitutional government based on a property franchise into an

---

[17] See Sewell, *Work and Revolution*, ch. 9; Octave Festy, *Le mouvement ouvrier au début de la monarchie de Juillet (1830-1834)* (Paris: Domat Montchrestien, 1944; new ed., Paris: Editions Anthropos, 1969); Bezucha, *The Lyon Uprising of 1834*; Alain Faure, "Mouvements populaires et mouvement ouvrier à Paris," *Le mouvement social* 88 (July-Sept. 1974):51-92.

[18] Emmanuel Joseph Sieyès, *Qu'est-ce que le Tiers Etat?* intro. and notes by Roberto Zapperi (Geneva: Droz, 1970), p. 125.

oppressive "feudal" tyranny, and justified the workers' efforts to gain their "emancipation"—by revolution, if necessary.[19]

The great problem posed by the workers' adoption of revolutionary language was that it initially gave the workers no way of justifying their essentially corporate demands. According to revolutionary discourse, society was composed of free individual citizens, not suprapersonal corporate bodies, and attempts to impose collective regulations on a trade therefore appeared as an infringement of the liberty of the individual. The workers solved this problem during the course of 1831, 1832, and 1833 by elaborating the idea of "association," which became the key slogan of the workers' movement in these years. The right of association had not been stressed much during the French Revolution, since eliminating all intermediary bodies between the individual and the state had been one of the Revolution's primary tasks. Yet the citizens' right to associate freely with one another was an inseparable part of the "liberté" proclaimed in 1789 and revived so conspicuously in 1830. If the state itself was conceived of as a society, as an association formed by the free and equal citizens of the nation and united by bonds of fraternity, it is hardly surprising that citizens should wish to construct more limited associations along the same lines. This was precisely what the workers did in the early 1830s. They rechristened their corporate organizations with such names as "Philanthropic Society," "Society of Perfect Accord," "Society of Fraternal Amity," and "Association of Brothers of Concord,"[20] and turned them into democratic voluntary associations based on secular humanitarianism rather than exclusive corporations whose solidarity was based on the religious idiom of the Old Regime. When workers' organizations became associations, the regulations they proposed became not an assault on freedom of industry but an expression of the associated free wills of the producers, much as laws of a nation were an expression of the general will. In this way their claims for collective regulation were made compatible with revolutionary discourse.

The idea of association was also developed in another distinct direction: it was in the early 1830s that workers and socialists developed the idea of producers' associations or producers' cooperatives. The basic concept, which was proposed as early as October of 1830 by the working-class newspaper L'Artisan and later worked out more systematically by the socialist theorist Philippe Buchez, was for workers to establish "associa-

---

[19] An excellent collection of working-class writings from this period is Alain Faure and Jacques Rancière, eds., La parole ouvrière (Paris: Union Générale d'Editions, 1976).

[20] Festy, Le mouvement ouvrier, pp. 138, 254-56, 294.

tive" workshops in which they would be joint owners of the means of production. These workshops were to be capitalized initially by regular weekly contributions from the associates and would eventually expand to include the whole industry, absorbing masters and workers alike into a unified trade community in which private property would be abolished.[21] The notion of producers' associations was predicated on an ambiguity in liberal discourse. If citizens possessed the right to associate freely, they could use this right to create voluntary organizations intended to overcome the egoistic individualism and anarchy of the current liberal system. By purely peaceful and legal means, workers might eventually hope to supplant private property with associative property, thereby transforming the whole of society.

The final innovation of these years was the extension of the idiom of association to encompass not merely the workers of a given trade, but workers of all trades. It was in the form of an "association of all trades" that a solidary, unified working class first made its appearance in France. This development took place in 1833, when the long economic depression that followed the revolution of 1830 finally gave way to a sustained boom. The workers responded to the favorable economic circumstances with a gigantic wave of strikes that crested in the fall of 1833.[22] These strikes were organized and coordinated by the workers' refurbished corporate trade associations, or "philanthropic societies." They were an attempt to establish, by direct action, the unity and collective control over the trade implied by the term "association." In the course of these strikes, workers sometimes also established associations in the other sense—producers' cooperatives. Although the idea of producers' associations was largely borrowed from the utopian discourse of Buchez and his followers, it was applied in a thoroughly practical fashion. The main function of producers' associations set up in the fall of 1833 was to strengthen the workers' hand in strikes by providing jobs while the masters' shops were shut down—not, for the time being, to supplant the masters permanently.[23] In other words, the second meaning of association—producers' cooperatives—was encompassed by and subordinated to the first—corporate associations established to impose collective controls over the trade.

One of the most notable features of the strikes of the fall of 1833 was an unprecedented cooperation between trades. Striking workers in one trade would appeal to other trades and receive moral and material sup-

---

[21] *L'Artisan*, September 26, 1830; Armand Cuvillier, *P.-J.-B. Buchez et les origines du socialisme chrétien* (Paris: Presses Universitaires de France, 1948).

[22] J. P. Aguet, *Les grèves sous la monarchie de juillet (1830-1847): Contribution à l'étude du mouvement ouvrier français* (Geneva: Droz, 1954).

[23] Faure, "Mouvements populaires et mouvement ouvrier," pp. 88-89.

port, which would be reciprocated if and when the second trade went on strike. There was a widespread feeling that, as the stonecutters of Lyon put it, "we are no longer in a time when our industries engage in mutual insults and violence; we have at last recognized that our interests are the same, that, far from hating one another, we should love one another."[24] In the enthusiasm of a strike movement animated by associations, it suddenly became clear to many workers that the spirit of association should be expanded to encompass all workers, and that this could be accomplished by associating their single-trade societies in a grand "association of all the trades."[25] The workers of Lyon stated the basic idea: "If all the fraternities would join hands to support each other," they could "succeed in forming the bonds of the confraternity of proletarians."[26] The creation of a class-conscious proletariat, this language implies, was a generalization, a projection to a higher level, of the loyalties that workers in a given trade had long felt for each other. But it was not until workers' corporations were themselves seen as free associations of productive laboring citizens, rather than as distinct corporations devoted to the perfection of a particular craft, that the wider fraternity of all workers became thinkable.

One final feature of the strike movement of 1833 should be noted. In Paris, and to a lesser extent in some of the provincial cities, the strikers were aided by the revolutionary republican Society of the Rights of Man. Initially a small but militant bourgeois republican sect, the society began to recruit working-class members in 1832 and had come to contain a majority of workers by the fall of 1833, including leaders of some of the most important "philanthropic societies." At the same time, the society modified its originally purely political republicanism to embrace various vaguely socialist proposals for economic reform. This new interest in economic and social questions was given practical expression in the help the society extended to the workers in their strikes. Thus, the fall of 1833 saw not only the creation of a new and powerful sense of class consciousness among artisans working in different trades, but also the first steps toward a political alliance between radical republicanism and socialism.[27]

On the level of institution building, the workers' movement of the early 1830s can count few lasting achievements. Once the strike wave had run its course, the government countered with overwhelming force. In the

---

[24] Quoted in Festy, *Le mouvement ouvrier*, p. 181.
[25] This is the title of a pamphlet written by the shoemaker Efrahem in 1833 (*De l'association des ouvriers de tous les corps d'état*). It is reprinted in Faure and Rancière, *La parole ouvrière*, pp. 159-68.
[26] Quoted in Festy, *Le mouvement ouvrier*, pp. 181, 294.
[27] Faure, "Mouvements populaires et mouvement ouvrier," pp. 79-92.

spring of 1834 it enacted a new law sharply restricting the right of association—outlawing both the Society of the Rights of Man and most of
the organizations the workers had constructed. The workers of Lyon
responded with a massive insurrection, which was followed by a smaller
rising in Paris.[28] These unsuccessful risings broke the élan of the workers'
movement and government repression soon drove its remnants underground. Yet the transformations of the early 1830s created the intellectual, linguistic, and organizational space on which the subsequent workers' movement was built. These transformations established for the first
time a class-conscious discourse and institutional practice that was further elaborated by workers over the following decades.

The repression of 1834 quieted the workers' movement for the next
five years. But in 1839 and 1840, something of the agitation of the early
1830s returned. There was an abortive rising in Paris in 1839 and a huge
wave of strikes the following year. Cabet's *Voyage en Icarie*, Louis
Blanc's *Organisation du travail*, and Proudhon's *Qu'est-ce que la propriété?* appeared within a few months of each other in 1839 and 1840.
The publication of these works led to an explosion of socialist writings.
From 1840 on, socialist ideas became a palpable presence in French public discourse, in the press, on the street, in workshops, and in working-
class bars and cafés.

As the February revolution of 1848 was to demonstrate, socialism had
won a large following among the working class by the late 1840s. In part
this was a matter of workers becoming militants of one or another of the
socialist schools. Above all in Paris, but also in some of the major provincial cities, significant numbers of workers became followers of the Saint-
Simonians, the Fourierists, Buchez, or especially of Etienne Cabet, who
was by far the most successful at proselytizing among workers.[29] But as
important as the socialist schools were in developing and broadcasting
socialist ideas, they could never have made socialism the mass movement
it became in 1848. The socialist schools had two crucial weaknesses.
First, they were sectarian and dogmatic, more worried about being theoretically correct than about attracting a broad audience. Second, they
rejected political action as a means of constructing socialism, relying
instead on some combination of moral persuasion and working-class self-
help. This meant that they could never enlist the large number of politically aware French workers who adhered to the revolutionary tradition
of popular political action.

[28] On Lyon, see Bezucha, *The Lyon Uprising of 1834*.
[29] On the followers of Cabet, see Johnson, *Utopian Communism*. For a fascinating analysis of the intellectual life of working-class socialists in the 1830s and 1840s, see Jacques
Rancière, *La nuit des prolétaires: Archives du rêve ouvrier* (Paris: Fayard, 1981).

The really massive development of socialism among the working class took place outside the distinct socialist schools and was the consequence of an appropriation, rather than an abandonment, of the revolutionary political tradition. It was, in a sense, a continuation of the work begun by the Society of the Rights of Man in 1832 and 1833. The creation of an explicitly republican socialism is associated above all with the name of Louis Blanc, or, in a more insurrectionary mood, with Blanqui.[30] It was, however, very much a collective development, a broad and loosely articulated collaboration between left-wing republicans, workers, and socialist theorists. Blanc's influential journal *La Réforme* was the communication center of this emerging political and intellectual project, but it was also carried on in other journals, in books, in republican societies, and in cafés and workshops all over the country. Republican socialism was based on two essential ideas. First, socialism was a necessary completion of the French Revolution. The legal and political freedoms gained in the first French Revolution must now be completed by social and economic reforms that would free workers from the tyranny of wealth and egoism and establish a real as well as a formal liberty and equality. And second, this could not be achieved without a political revolution and the establishment of a democratic and republican form of government. By the late 1840s this republican socialism had captured the left wing of the republican movement, and in doing so it had also become the creed of politically conscious workers who would never have embraced the apolitical socialism of the schools. In fact, by 1848 there was no significant nonsocialist radical alternative competing for workers' political allegiance; any bourgeois republican who wished to cultivate a working-class following had no choice but to endorse at least a vaguely socialist program.[31]

How thoroughly things had changed since 1830 was made clear in 1848. Whereas the July revolution of 1830 had caught the workers unaware and incapable of articulating an independent program until it was too late, the February revolution of 1848 immediately provoked a massive class-conscious workers' movement, not only in Paris, but in cities throughout France. From the beginning, the workers of Paris pushed the revolution to the left, forcing the provisional government to proclaim a republic on February 24, to proclaim the "right to labor" and the establishment of National Workshops on February 25, and to set up the

[30] See Leo O. Loubère, *Louis Blanc: His Life and His Contributions to the Rise of French Jacobin Socialism* (Evanston, Ill.: Northwestern University Press, 1961) and Alan B. Spitzer, *The Revolutionary Theories of Louis Auguste Blanqui* (New York: Columbia University Press, 1957).

[31] For a discussion of the rise of republican socialism in Toulouse, see Aminzade, *Class, Politics, and Early Industrial Capitalism*, pp. 126-48.

famous Luxembourg Commission on February 28. The commission was
headed by Louis Blanc and included delegates from all the trades of
Paris; it was to formulate legislation that would accomplish the "organization of labor." The commission was an officially sanctioned "association of all the trades," and it formed the center of the revolutionary
workers' movement of 1848. It not only provided workers with a public
forum and a recognized place in the affairs of the republic, but also
required them to form unified trade organizations that could elect and
instruct delegates to the commission. It was above all in these revitalized
corporate trade associations that the workers sketched out their alternative socialist version of the new republic in the brief revolutionary spring
of 1848.[32]

The workers' corporate associations of 1848 were little republics,
formed in virtually all trades of the capital, based on universal suffrage
of the trade, led by elected officers and delegates, and regulated by written constitutions, frequently prefaced by miniature declarations of rights.
Their ends were at once economic, social, and political. Economically, the
workers' associations asserted control over all aspects of production and
exchange. The workers negotiated conventions with masters that fixed
uniform wages, hours, and conditions of work for the entire trade. These
conventions were often signed in solemn ceremonies before the Luxembourg Commission. The conventions with the masters reestablished practical collective regulation over the trades in the short run; at the same
time workers launched schemes for associated production that were
intended eventually to solve problems permanently by turning private
property into associated property. Socially, the workers' associations
extended the usual provisions for mutual aid—for the sick and injured,
for widows and orphans, for workers on strike and for funerals. It was in
politics that the workers' associations of 1848 moved furthest beyond
their predecessors of the 1830s. In 1848 workers' associations became
political actors. They functioned as units, for example, in the numerous
great mass demonstrations of the spring and in the electoral campaign of
April. But they also saw their political role as extending much further.
They envisioned that the Luxembourg Commission, which they dubbed
the "Estates General of Labor," would become a second National
Assembly, representing the trade associations that organized and performed all the nation's labor and that maintained fraternal republican
solidarity through mutual aid. Workers' associations, in other words,

---

[32] On the workers' movement of 1848, see Rémi Gossez, *Les ouvriers de Paris*, bk. 1,
L'organisation, 1848-1851, vol. 24 of the *Bibliothèque de la Révolution de 1848* (La
Roche-sur-Yon: Imprimerie Centrale de l'Ouest, 1967) and Sewell, *Work and Revolu-
tion*, ch. 11.

were to become the constituent units of a new "democratic and social republic" based on the sovereignty of labor.

This vision, which was projected in both the theory and the practice of the workers' movement that grew up around the Luxembourg Commission, was doomed to failure. The victory of conservatives in the elections of April, the abortive workers' *Putsch* of May 15, and finally the bloody repression of the June workers' uprising destroyed the commission and many of the workers' associations it represented. But the workers' movement of the spring of 1848, which in turn was based on the organizational and conceptual breakthroughs made in the early 1830s, set the pattern for the French working-class and socialist movement through and beyond the Commune. The French workers' long-lived ideal of what Bernard Moss has dubbed a "federalist trade socialism" grew out of the corporate heritage of the urban skilled trades, as transformed by the revolutionary upheavals of the 1830s and 1848.[33]

V. *Factory Workers*

The agitation of the early 1830s and 1848 was not without effect on workers in the new cotton, woolen, and linen factories. The new political language created by the artisans in the 1830s and brought to fruition in 1848 certainly intended to include factory workers as a part of the oppressed working class that was held in servitude by the bourgeoisie. But textile workers remained at the margins of the workers' movement. The movement of the thirties was concentrated in two cities—Paris and Lyon—both of which had overwhelmingly artisanal labor forces. And even in the more widespread agitation of 1848, the northern and eastern textile centers were of distinctly secondary importance. Moreover, a close reading of the textile workers' actions in these cases when they did act indicates a consciousness quite different from that of the artisans.

This is especially clear in the case of strikes, or concerted work stoppages. Most strikes in the artisan trades were carefully planned and well-organized affairs, in which the workers clearly perceived their efforts as bringing economic pressure on the masters to induce them to accept certain regulations over the trade—often higher wage rates, but also revision of piece-rate schedules, changes in hiring practices, shorter hours, restrictions on forming apprentices, and so forth. Most strikes of textile factory operatives were spontaneous, poorly organized, and of very short duration.[34] As William Reddy has shown, they do not seem to have been

[33] Moss, *Origins of the French Labor Movement*, p. 3.
[34] Peter N. Stearns, "Patterns of Industrial Strike Activity in France during the July Monarchy," *American Historical Review* 70 (Jan. 1965):371-94.

attempts to put concerted pressure on mill owners in order to bargain more effectively, but expressions of anger and solidarity in the face of some perceived injustice.[35] Typically workers in one factory would react with outrage at an action by the owner, abandon their machines, and form a crowd outside the factory gates. They would then march about from factory to factory, attempting to get others to join them. After some hours (in rare cases a few days) of marching through the streets with drums and banners, the national guard or the troops would break up the crowd, the workers would scatter, and work would resume as usual the following morning. The point of factory operatives' work stoppages— Reddy doubts whether "strike" is really an appropriate label—can hardly have been to put economic pressure on the owners. If that was intended, why would workers return to their jobs as soon as their crowds were dispersed? Instead they seem to have been visibly displaying their unanimous outrage by demonstrations, which were more like public warnings to the owners—"we can be pushed only so far!"—than concerted attempts to win specific concessions. The forms these work stoppages took differ sharply from the more disciplined and less expressive strikes of the artisans and seem to have been based more on the models of grain riots and village festivals than on strikes in the skilled urban trades. The very different character of their work stoppages demonstrates that artisans and textile factory operatives lived in distinct worlds in the 1830s and 1840s. It was not until the last quarter of the nineteenth century that they were genuinely merged into a common labor movement.

This separation of textile operatives' and artisans' worlds dates back to the growth of putting-out textile industry in the seventeenth and eighteenth centuries. The relations of production that grew up in putting-out industry were very different from those in the urban crafts. The country weavers and spinners sometimes became dependent on a given merchant—usually by going into debt to him—but they were nevertheless free and independent agents whose links with the merchant were not wage relations but relations of buying and selling. In principle, the merchant sold the raw materials to the spinner or weaver, who then sold them back to the merchant as finished products at a higher price. Spinners and weavers could, and sometimes did, switch from one putter-out to another, or even buy their raw materials and sell their products on the open market. The units of production in putting-out industry were independent

[35] William M. Reddy, "Skeins, Scales, Discounts, Steam and Other Objects of Crowd Justice in Early French Textile Mills," *Comparative Studies in Society and History* 21 (Apr. 1979):204-213 and Reddy, *The Rise of Market Culture: The Textile Trade and French Society, 1750-1900* (Cambridge: Cambridge University Press, 1984), pp. 113-37, 185-204.

rural families, linked together in a series of overlapping commercial networks. These families were tied to other textile producing families as members of common communities of residence but, in sharp contrast to urban crafts, there was little sense of loyalty to a trade community transcending family and residential community lines.

The growth of factory production in the textile industry took place in the same districts where rural industry had already been established. As far as we can tell, the men and women who took jobs in the new mills were often recruited from rural textile-producing families.[36] The conventional picture of early textile factories, one that derives mainly from nineteenth-century bourgeois observers, is of highly disciplined industrial armies working under detailed and exacting regulations, subject to the constant gaze of overlookers and to the no less dictatorial rhythms of the machinery. But the more that we learn about the internal organization of the early mills, thanks above all to the detailed and sensitive researches of William Reddy, the more unrealistic this conventional portrait appears.[37] Two considerations will demonstrate its inaccuracy. First, far from being reduced to an atomized mass and subjected to the abstract discipline of machines and detailed factory regulations, most factory work seems to have taken place in *family* units, under the discipline of parents, aunts, and uncles. It took a team of workers, usually composed of an adult male and several children, to operate a spinning machine or loom, and these teams were commonly, perhaps usually, family units of some kind. In other words, the formerly independent rural-dwelling weaver who received raw materials from the merchant and worked them up on his own loom with the assistance of his family now agreed to operate a mill owner's spinning machine or loom in an urban factory, but still as a *père de famille*, assisted by his children and sometimes by his wife— with, of course, the occasional niece, nephew, or child of a friend.[38]

Second, relations between factory owners and workers continued to be cast in a commercial idiom. The *père de famille* who took charge of a spinning machine or loom was given a certain amount of raw material to be worked up. At the end of the week the bobbins of yarn or bolts of cloth were checked for quality and measured, and the spinner or weaver was paid for his product according to a schedule of prices. What he received was not a wage for his labor, but a price for the stuff he and his team

---

[36] William M. Reddy, "Family and Factory: French Linen Weavers in the Belle Epoque," *The Journal of Social History* 8 (Winter 1975):104 and Reddy, "The Textile Trade and the Language of the Crowd at Rouen, 1752-1871," *Past and Present* 74 (Feb. 1977):78.

[37] Reddy, *The Rise of Market Culture*.

[38] Reddy, "Family and Factory," pp. 102-112; "The Textile Trade," pp. 78-81; *The Rise of Market Culture*, pp. 163-65.

produced. The spinner or weaver then paid his own assistants whatever had been agreed upon or, if these were family members, he kept the whole of the weekly payment for the family's expenses.[39] The extent to which work relations within the factory remained essentially commercial is made especially clear by certain details of payment practices. In the woolen and linen spinning factories of Lille and Roubaix, the mill owners, after weighing and evaluating their workers' weekly product, deducted certain "discounts" from the price that the worker was paid. These "discounts" were charges for the heat, lighting, and steam power that the mill owner furnished to the workers. The charge for steam was initially set at nine francs a week, the amount that spinners had to pay a laborer to turn the winches on jennies before steam power was introduced. The charges for heat and light compensated for expenses that the workers would have had to bear under the domestic putting-out system. Far from seeming an unjust imposition, these discounts were initially accepted by the workers; they made perfect sense within the commercial idiom of buying and selling that governed the internal relations of their industry.[40]

In short, rather than a super-exploited and atomized mass whose prior attachments to family and community were dissolved in the factory and who were thereby prepared for the lesson of solidarity inscribed in the material conditions of factory life, workers in the early textile factories continued to experience their work as independent family units enmeshed in a network of commercial relations. Descended from semipeasant domestic weavers and spinners, removed from the influence of the corporate values and organizational forms that pervaded the urban skilled trades, they did not share the artisans' deeply social, corporate sense of the trade and of work in general as a locus of moral community. Hence they understood only dimly the artisans' message of association and brotherhood of all workers; although the artisans believed their message to be valid universally, the corporate idiom in which it was cast meant that it in fact appealed mainly to other artisans. It was only in the second great burst of socialist ferment and organization, in the decades following the Commune, that factory workers and artisans were integrated into a common class-conscious labor movement.

[39] Reddy, "Objects of Crowd Justice," pp. 207-209.
[40] Ibid., pp. 207-208 and Reddy, *The Rise of Market Culture*, pp. 211-13.

3 On the Formation of the French Working Class • *Michelle Perrot*

Whether we mean by "working class" a labor force, a stratum sharing a relatively unified way of life, a social category acknowledging itself as such in its cultural expression, or even a set of social or political organizations that claim to represent the interests of labor, the process of class formation is always and everywhere difficult. In no way does it resemble a victory march. To become "working class" is not an end in itself for the individuals who compose it and who, quite often, would rather not belong to it. This class is like a nation: a unifying, uniformizing whole, which requires that internal differences be shed; it arises via the destruction of groups who owed their vitality in the social struggle to their particularistic consciousness. Resting on a pile of ruins, it sometimes appears bloodless.

That is why this essay is in no way meant as an ode to the dawning of the only possible source of social salvation. Inevitable, necessary in a given historical moment within the nation-state configuration, the working class is not intrinsically superior to what came before and cannot set itself up as a judge of the past. The history of workers should not be judged by their standards alone. Shunning teleological visions of the subject, we shall reject in advance notions of archaism or modernity, of forward or backward movement along some "progressive" front. It is not our business to drag journeymen or members of mutual aid societies, machine breakers or members of cooperatives, or members of some alleged "labor aristocracy" before a class tribunal. Nor do we assume some qualitative hierarchy of forms of struggle, within which, because of its stability, the union is superior to the fleeting strike, which itself is of higher merit than violent rebellion. That is why the notion of "levels," sometimes used here for comparative purposes, should not mislead us: it is a classificatory scheme rather than a scale of values, and does not constitute a series of stages implying a developmental morphology.

Although the process of working-class formation in France was generally slow and difficult, it was so to a varying extent in relation to the several "levels." In one sense, the sociocultural consciousness of an identity *qua* workers, nurtured in the womb of the "Fourth Estate," emerged

THIS ESSAY was translated from the French by Aristide R. Zolberg.

very precociously, despite the extraordinary diversity of economic structures and the reluctance of workers to identify themselves with a unitary
political organization. This is but one of the distinctive characteristics of
the French working class that will be considered here, without pretending
to present the overall history of its formative process.

I. *Popular Resistance to Industrialization*

Industrialization is not merely a matter of establishing factories, introducing machines, or modifying the composition of the national product.
It entails an entire education of producers, both entrepreneurs and workers, and the assumption of new values, of a different vision of time and
things. In France, this transformation ran into many obstacles. It is a
commonplace to emphasize the slowness of the process—"a landslide
with little uprooting," in the words of Pierre Caspard—and the low
degree of industrial concentration.[1] Several indicators on the eve of the
second industrialization are illustrative of the situation: in 1911, 55 percent of the population was rural; in the 1906 census, France's 11 million
blue-collar workers constituted 32 percent of all wage earners and 16
percent of the gainfully employed; 60 percent of them worked at home
or in firms with fewer than ten employees, and only 25 percent in firms
of over one hundred (against 36 percent in Germany).

Among the factors hampering industrialization and especially industrial concentration, the first was an unanticipated consequence of the
French Revolution: the maintenance and consolidation of small and middle-sized peasant enterprises, sufficiently adaptable to survive the challenge of successive crises. Their continued existence, in combination with
the low birth rate, offset rural exodus.[2] A second factor is the persistence
of small artisanal and commercial enterprises—the workshop and the
store[3]—constantly reinvigorated by the practice of industrial subcontracting, which was grafted onto technological change.

One should also take into consideration the lasting power of aristocratic values among all social milieus, bourgeois or popular, expressed
among other things by a tendency to depreciate work. Always ready to
praise idleness, the French populace has a taste for games and wasteful-

---

[1] Pierre Caspard, "La manufacture au village: Cortaillod," special issue of *Le mouvement social* (Oct.-Dec. 1976) on *Naissance de la classe ouvrière en France.*

[2] Maurice Agulhon, *Histoire de la France rurale*, vol. 3 (Paris: Seuil, 1976).

[3] *L'atelier et la boutique*, special issue of *Le mouvement social*, no. 108 (1979);
M. Lévy-Leboyer, "Le patronat français a-t-il été malthusien?" *Le mouvement social*
(July-Sept. 1974).

ness that has been deplored by employers and economists alike.[4] The former are particularly outraged by "Holy Monday," the workers' practice
of taking a day off, which, according to Bergery, an industrial manager
who graduated from the Ecole Polytechnique, cost industry two million
francs a week around 1830.[5] The criticisms of Jean-Baptiste Say against
lotteries, which wreak havoc with savings, and against free theater, which
disorganizes the workday, parallel those of the Saint-Simonians concerning the abuses of Carnaval.[6] The Saint-Simonians we are speaking of
here are the theorists; as for Saint-Simonian workers, whose words and
networks have been evoked by Jacques Rancière, they did not identify
with any trade whatsoever; work, the only available way to make a living,
was for them an imposition, a beast that devoured their time and
strength, and that it was proper to fight off. "To brutalize oneself as little
as possible," was their motto. Rancière rejects, for these workers, the
myth of the craftsman proud of his beautiful masterwork.[7] Describing
Parisian workers under the Second Empire, Anthine Corbon, a frequent
contributor to the newspaper L'Atelier (The Workshop)—whose motto
was "He who does not work does not deserve to eat"—denounced the
prejudice according to which "the obligation of working in order to live
is a mark of inborn inferiority that cannot be overcome. In reality, this
prejudice is merely a hidden expression of the doctrine of Fall and Expia-
tion."[8] As late as 1913, Anatole Weber, author of the voluminous work
Aid to the Poor, defined work as "painful effort for pay" and remarked
"to enjoy is to destroy, to work is to suffer."[9] Should one see in this language the dominance of a Latin and Catholic vision, in contrast to the
puritanical ethic analyzed by Max Weber? Representations of work in
nineteenth-century France constitute a broad field of barely explored
anthropological investigation.[10] In any case, this negative vision weighs

[4] Paul Lafargue, Le droit à la paresse, réfutation du "droit au travail" de 1848 (Paris:
Oriol, 1883; reissued, Paris: Maspéro, 1969, with a preface by M. Dommanget).
[5] Claude-Lucien Bergery, Economie industrielle ou science de l'industrie (Metz: Thiel,
1829-1831), p. 52; see also M. Perrot, "Travailler et produire: Claude-Lucien Bergery et
les débuts du management en France," in Mélanges d'histoire sociale offerts à Jean Maitron (Paris: Editions ouvrières, 1976).
[6] Jean-Baptiste Say, Olbie ou essai sur les moyens de réformer les moeurs d'une
nation, An VIII, in Oeuvres diverses (1848), p. 585.
[7] Le producteur, vol. 2 (1826), pp. 330ff (critique of Carnaval and proposals for a hol-
iday to honor inventors); Jacques Rancière, La nuit des prolétaires: Archives du rêve
ouvrier (Paris: Fayard, 1981).
[8] Anthine Corbon, Le secret du peuple de Paris (Paris: Pagnerre, 1863), p. 74.
[9] Anatole Weber, Essai sur le problème de la misère (Paris: Rivière, 1913), p. 481.
[10] The Lévi-Strauss seminar at the Collège de France, led by Maurice Godelier, was
devoted in 1980-1981 to representations of work in various types of society. "Represen-

heavily against the launching of an industrial society founded on calculation, anticipation, accumulation, and rationalization of time and space.
By the same token, it interferes with the formation of a class consciousness celebrating "producers." But, more concretely, who resists, against
what, and how?

Who Resists? Let us establish first that it is less a matter of resisting
industrialization, properly speaking, than industrial concentration.
Industrialization, which was welcomed or even sought after for the additional income it provided—in Colbert's time, the cottage labor of the
lacemakers enabled peasants of the Alençon region to pay their taxes[11]—
was feared when it entailed uprooting, the destruction of a daily way of
life. The nucleus of this resistance was the defense of the household economy and its subtle equilibrium, perfected over several generations. The
household was the basic community, founded on a pooling of the complementary contributions of each of its members, whose roles and tasks
it governed, at the level of the couple as well as at the level of the parent-
child relationships. This type of economy prevailed just as much in rural
industry—particularly within the textile sector—as among the "technical
endogamies" constituted by certain highly localized urban trades (silkweavers of Lyon, ribbon makers of Saint-Etienne, glaziers of Givors,
cabinetmakers of the Faubourg Saint-Antoine in Paris), founded on
three elements: family, trade, and territory. Attempting to maintain its
autonomy and shrouding itself in secrecy, the household economy paced
its activities according to its needs, thereby opposing itself to the wishes
of employers who, after a period of cooperation, turned against it in order
to subject it to market forces. Mechanization, concentration, and segmentation of the labor force were the principal means of destroying this
obstruction that constituted, in some sense, a brake on economic growth.
Such was the backdrop to industrialization, a very complex story of
which merely a few examples are given here.

In the Country: Home Weavers. Although home weaving is generally
associated with "proto-industrialization," the term was no longer appropriate in the nineteenth century, when a full-fledged industrial activity

---

tation of Work in France (Place, Practice, Organization, and Meaning)" was also the
theme of a conference at Cornell University, April 1983.
   [11] E. Levasseur, *Histoire des classes ouvrières en France depuis la conquête de Jules
César jusqu'à la révolution,* vol. 1 (Paris: Guillaumin, 1859), pp. 203ff.

had developed: specialized, commercialized, and integrated into a complex production process.[12] The specific nature of the French case stems from the belated character of mechanization. Although spinning was mechanized in the late eighteenth and early nineteenth centuries, as of the mid-nineteenth weaving remained largely manual; around 1860, France numbered 200,000 handlooms against 80,000 mechanical ones, whereas in England, there remained only 3,000 handweavers (against 250,000 in 1810). Weavers, whose task occurred between spinning and mechanical finishing, occupied a key economic position, a fact that accounted for their relatively high salaries and extreme freedom. They formed a highly distinctive milieu, characterized by a solid family structure and a high degree of endogamy, together with high fertility, as children constituted a useful productive force very early on.[13] The milieu was also marked by an idiosyncratic culture, a mix of oral traditions and material drawn from almanacs, peddlers' pamphlets, and ballads.[14] Their own masters with respect to the pace of production, weavers sought to maintain a moderate rate, preferring leisure to additional income. Louis Reybaud wrote of them: "Living from little and working only to meet their needs, these people took on tasks that did not exceed their strength and reflected their tastes. It was like a golden age, which accorded well with a certain indolence of behavior."[15] They abstained from work on Monday, frequented taverns, and bought from peddlers, but did not indulge in excessive expenditure. Assured of steady work, they saved very little, detaching themselves in this regard from the rural world in which they were rooted but from which they were ever more sharply differentiated. But this does not mean that they became full-fledged proletarians; they remained deeply attached to the soil, to their native village, and to their home, which, designed as it was to house looms, amounted to a sort of capital, a form of investment through which weavers owned at least some part of the means of production. In fact they displayed considerable ingenuity to preserve this intermediate status, combining ever-renewed agricultural and industrial resources and, later on, putting the factory to

[12] Among the enormous literature on proto-industrialization, see especially: J. Thirsk and F. Mendels, "Proto-industrialization: The First Phase of the Industrialization Process," *Journal of Economic History* 42 (March 1972); and H. Medick, "The Proto-Industrial Family Economy," *Social History* 3 (1976).

[13] Martine Segalen, *Nuptialité et alliance: Le choix du conjoint dans une commune de l'Eure* (Paris: Larose, 1972).

[14] Audiganne, *Les populations ouvrières et les industries de la France*, vol. 1 (Paris: Capelle, 1860), p. 98 (on the weavers' culture).

[15] Louis Reybaud, *Le coton* (Paris: Michel Lévy, 1863), p. 156.

use on behalf of their survival. This is the case, for example, with the weavers of Picardy described by A. Demangeon.[16]

These socioeconomic reasons undoubtedly accounted for the strength of their resistance. We can tentatively add another, related to gender. Mechanization of spinning was accepted because it brought about the constitution of a masculine craft: in the emerging factories, male spinners, bosses of teams often made up of families, replaced the female operators of spinning wheels or *jeannettes* (the usual French word for "jenny") found in the country. The reverse was true in weaving: the male weaver, head of a family, was also the master of the heavy and bulky rural loom, whose manipulation justified the use of masculine strength. Under these conditions, mechanization dissolved and feminized the craft, indicating a loss of status of the sort often dubbed "dequalification."[17]

It is understandable, under these circumstances, why weavers adamantly resisted mechanization, a resistance that was passive, disguised, and often verged on sabotage. Consider the case of Alsace in the 1820s, at the time of the introduction of the first mechanical looms: no violence, "there was merely inertia. The threads kept breaking, and the machines stopped without anyone being able to tell whether the men or the machines were to blame."[18] In this region, however, dynamic employers were able to use another type of manpower by resorting to foreign immigration and by creating a web of welfare institutions. Resistance was more effective in the north, in both Picardy and Flanders. "The testimony of manufacturers is nearly unanimous on this point," reported Reybaud on the basis of a survey conducted around 1860: "They say that the workers, formed from childhood on to handwork, resist the use of mechanical means with all their power. They are less afraid of a lowering of wages than of a revolution in procedures. They insist that this is the dominant sentiment among the 200,000 handweavers in our northern provinces."[19] The stubbornness of workers was such that it often forced manufacturers to give up, or even to step backwards. For example, around 1818 there was an attempt to mechanize and concentrate the shawlweaving industry of Picardy, involving the use of the Jacquard loom and the organization of large workshops; but the ill will and absenteeism of workers caused a

---

[16] A. Demangeon, *La Picardie* (Paris: Colin, 1905).

[17] Hélène Robert, *Mécanisation et travail féminin* (3d cycle thesis, Department of Economics, University of Paris I, 1980).

[18] Reybaud, *Le coton*, p. 50.

[19] Ibid., p. 157.

number of firms to go bankrupt, and in 1832 there was a return to the old technology and its family-based organization.[20]

However, if "golden age" there was—clearly we must be skeptical of these retrospective mythologies that have been exploded by English historians as well—it did not last very long. From the 1830s on, a very bitter struggle was under way between hand and mechanical weaving. This involves a complex history, yet to be written. Although reduced to a defensive stance, the weavers stonewalled, preferring lower wages to factory life: "They consented to the biggest wage cuts rather than to change the locale of their work. The reason they are attached to it is that they carry out their work *under their own roof*, beside their relatives and also more or less when they feel like it. They have an insuperable horror of the barracks-room called 'common workshop,' and would rather give up their trade altogether than submit to factory enrollment."[21] However, the weavers were finally defeated by a succession of economic crises: 1846-1848, the depression of the 1860s triggered by free-trade treaties, and especially the Great Depression of 1882-1890, which generated a "deindustrialization of the countryside," analyzed by Gabriel Désert for Lower Normandy and by Yves Lequin for the Lyon region.[22] As it was, the deindustrialization of Normandy took place simultaneously with the disappearance of handlooms, the decline of female industries such as lace, which had played a key role in the mobilization of women and children into the labor market from the eighteenth century on, and the closing of small rural factories scattered alongside the rivers. In the Department of Calvados alone, "within the space of half a century, the employment provided by the textile industries and their related branches was reduced by three-fourths, amounting to an absolute loss of 50,000 jobs. . . . On the eve of World War I, there are only 893 textile workers left in 724 rural municipalities, as against 1,071 in the seven most industrialized towns."[23] The same evolution took place in Upper Normandy, where rural weaving disappeared completely from the region and from Elbeuf and Louviers, as well as in Champagne and in the Cambrai region. A few small islands

---

[20] *Les ouvriers des Deux-Mondes*, vol. 1, 1857: *Monographie de l'ouvrier tisseur en châles de Gentilly* (Paris: Firmin-Didot, 1857), p. 343.

[21] Reybaud, *Le coton*, p. 222. Emphasis added.

[22] C. E. Labrousse, ed., *Aspects de la crise et de la dépression de l'économie française au milieu du 19ème siècle* (La Roche-sur-Yon: Société de 1848, 1956); Gabriel Désert, *Les paysans du Calvados, 1815-1895* (Lille: Université de Lille 3, service des thèses, 1975), esp. pp. 684ff; Yves Lequin, *Les ouvriers de la région lyonnaise, 1848-1914* (Lyon: Presses de l'Université de Lyon, 1977).

[23] Désert, *Les paysans du Calvados*, esp. pp. 684ff.

survived until 1914 in the latter around Avesnes-les-Aubert, and down to the present in provinces that did not experience urbanization, such as Maine, where the system based on the family-craft-territory triad has resisted with unusual success all attempts to destroy its autonomy.[24] Moreover, the lengthy agony of home weaving was marked by final jolts such as the strikes of 1886-1888 in the Choletais, of 1888-1889 in the Lyonnais, and the Cambrésis riots of 1889, all noteworthy because the organization of the movements involved was founded on traditional sociability.[25]

The end of rural weaving was translated into migrations, toward the city rather than toward the factory, as resistance continued at the individual level where workers refused to become classic proletarians. In Lower Normandy, according to Désert, women became domestic servants and men went into the building trades, preferring the free atmosphere of the yards. In the north, things were undoubtedly different; many home weavers (*tisserands*) were forced to become loom operatives (*tisseurs*) in factories where, at the end of the nineteenth century, their turbulence turned Roubaix into the strike capital of France. The same occurred in Roanne or in Reims. The case of these workers raises, in a crucial manner, the problem of the transformation of the isolated worker into a member of a mass, into factory workers deprived not merely of their wage autonomy—the home weavers had lost this long ago—but of their autonomy with respect to space.[26]

In the Country: The Difficult Birth of Miners. In her classic monograph on the miners of Carmaux, Rolande Trempé has shown, on the basis of the unusually rich archives of certain firms, the extreme difficulty of assembling a stable, regular, and full-time body of manpower for the mines.[27] From the vantage point of the rural populations concerned, attached to their soil, mining appeared as "the last of the trades," to be used as a source of supplementary income and to be abandoned as soon as possible. Love of the miner's trade is a myth, largely concocted in the

[24] Michèle Colin et al., *Feux et lieux: Histoire d'une famille et d'un pays face à la société industrielle* (Paris: Galilée, 1980); see also M. Colin et al., "Travail, famille, territoire" in *Ethnologie française*, n.s., 12, no. 2 (1982). For a remarkable autobiographical account of the vestiges of the domestic system, see Serge Grafteaux, *Mémé Santerre* (Paris: Marabout, 1975; New York: Schocken, 1985).

[25] M. Perrot, *Les ouvriers en grève, 1871-1890*, vol. 1 (Paris: Mouton, 1974), p. 352.

[26] The control of pieces and of raw materials was much less rigorous in the domestic system; the stealing of raw materials was one of the reasons invoked for concentrating production.

[27] Rolande Trempé, *Les mineurs de Carmaux (1848-1914)* (Paris: Editions ouvrières, 1971), see esp. vol. 1, ch. 2, "Du paysan-mineur à l'ouvrier-mineur."

twentieth century to meet the needs of national industry. Resistance to mining is manifested by seasonal absenteeism to participate in regional grain, grape, or potato harvests; by a preference for loose schedules allowing for coming and going; and by a high and persistent turnover that personnel records sometimes enable us to measure with precision. In Carmaux in 1911, for example, it was necessary to hire thirty people to obtain a single miner![28] People entered the mines as soon as there was an agricultural crisis; but when other job possibilities arose, including railroad construction, the young disappeared.

Trempé has also demonstrated the diversity of means resorted to by employers to assemble a competent body of manpower: payment by the job; reorganization of tasks around the hewer, whom management sought to transform into a genuinely responsible profession (in this they failed, because workers refused this promotion, which was full of catches); and development of techniques for descending into and lighting the mines, which fit into the overall rationalization of mining but which at the same time facilitated control of work performance. Around 1870, elevators replaced ladders and imposed fixed schedules for descent and ascent; individual safety lamps were labeled with the name of each miner and thus clearly revealed who was absent. Sixty years of daily struggle were needed in Carmaux to transform peasant-miners into miner-peasants, and then into just plain miners.

The case of Carmaux is exemplary. It was manpower problems of this sort that prompted the creation of mining communities at the end of the Second Empire. The companies developed a genuine housing policy designed to settle workers in one spot, to ensure intergenerational continuity, and to reconstitute, for their own benefit, those selfsame "technical endogamies" that, elsewhere, were being destroyed as obstacles to industrialization. Such efforts to control the reproduction of manpower bear witness to the difficulties of recruiting it in the first place.[29]

In the Urban Sector: The Resistance of Skilled Workers. Artisans resisted industrialization not as a matter of principle—on the contrary, as men of the Enlightenment, many were inclined to admire the "progress" of machines—but insofar as it entailed proletarianization, that is to say,

[28] Rolande Trempé, "Pour une meilleure connaissance de la classe ouvrière: L'utilisation des archives d'entreprise—le fichier du personnel," in *Mélanges d'histoire sociale offerts à Jean Maitron.*
[29] Lion Murard and Patrick Zylberman, *Le petit travailleur infatigable: Ville-usine, habitat et intimité—Les cités minières au 19ème siècle*, published by the journal *Recherches* (Paris: CERFI, 1976); Royden Harrison, ed., *Independent Collier: The Coal-Miner as Archetypal Proletarian Reconsidered* (London: Harvester Press, 1978).

dispossession of the means of production, loss of autonomy. There are numerous examples. Sometimes entire professions sought to preserve their status, defending their corporate structures even in the absence of corporations as Sewell indicates; sometimes, within the framework of manufactures and factories, certain occupations entrenched themselves behind their level of "qualification." Tailors, cabinetmakers, shoemakers, glaziers, printers, papermakers, cloth shearers, Lyon silkweavers, puddlers, dryers, and others thus raised the barrier of ancient practices, adapted to new circumstances, against attempts by management to rationalize production.[30]

Consider the unruly papermakers. Solidly organized under the Ancien Régime, they obeyed neither the Le Chapelier Law against "combinations in restraint of trade" nor the similar law of 6 Fructidor, Year IV, which was aimed at them more specifically. They continued to impose all sorts of obligations on manufacturers, including local and familial recruitment, beds to be reserved for traveling journeymen, and payment by the month (including holidays!). They obliged delinquents, employers as well as workers, to pay fines into a common fund that they later "ate" (sic) in the course of joyous libations that shocked Restoration philanthropists, keener on saving than on feasting. Deciding to keep the best of the day for themselves, in the Puy-de-Dôme they went to the workshops from midnight to noon, working by candlelight.[31] The employers, concerned with increasing paper production in response to a soaring demand that was stimulated by the growing market for books and by the dawn of a penny press, undertook to subject these workers to regular work conditions. To this effect, they organized large factories, equipped with welfare institutions, fully controlled by management, such as those of the Montgolfier in Annonay (Ardèche) from which not a word was heard half a century later.[32]

The case of the wool shearers—of Sedan and Vienne—is particularly interesting because it shows how a combination of mechanization and

---

[30] Studies of occupational groups are very useful in this respect. See, for example, Christopher Johnson, "Economic Change and Artisan Discontent: The Tailors' History, 1800-1848," in *Revolution and Reaction: 1848 and the Second French Republic*, ed. Roger Price (London: Croom Helm, 1975); M. Aksashi, "Les ouvriers tailleurs parisiens, 1815-1870" (3d cycle thesis, Paris VII, 1979); E. Hobsbawm and J. Scott, "Political Shoemakers," *Past and Present*, no. 89 (Nov. 1980):86-114; J. Scott, *The Glassworkers of Carmaux, 1848-1914* (Cambridge: Harvard University Press, 1974). This is an area in need of further research.

[31] Georges Bourgin and Hubert Bourgin, eds., *Les patrons, les ouvriers, et l'état. Le régime de l'industrie en France de 1814 à 1830*, 3 vols. (Paris: A. Picard, 1912-41). See vol. 2, p. 159, and vol. 3, pp. 114-20.

[32] Lequin, *Les ouvriers*, vol. 2, pp. 113ff: "Les silences de l'usine."

state intervention broke the resistance of workers. The "shearmen," pug-
nacious in England as well, possessed a power founded on their abilities:
"their art is a difficult one." Knowing themselves to be irreplaceable, they
exercised control over wages, apprenticeship—reserved for their own
children—and pace of production, which they maintained at a moderate
level allowing for leisure. Remarkably organized, in Sedan they designated a commissioner or "orator" for each workshop, paid by a monthly
withholding from their wages, and they quarantined recalcitrant workshops, a practice known as *cloque* (blister). They were thus able to maintain the upper hand, going so far as to oppose themselves to the First
Consul, Napoleon Bonaparte, in the course of his visit to Sedan. It was
from this experience that Napoleon conceived the idea of the *livret* (mandatory work record) to police workers. The manufacturers would have
liked to replace the men with the "English machines," the Douglas shearers; but they dared not, fearing a workers' insurrection. They eventually
did so with the help of the minister of interior, a committed industrialist.[33]
During the Restoration, the introduction of the "Great Shearer"—thus
personified, the Douglas machine took on the air of a fantastic beast—
provoked great troubles in the south. As in the cases already mentioned,
its purpose was to break the resistance of the shearers and of their family
teams by gathering within the confines of a single factory the old shearing
tables hitherto scattered amidst a plethora of small, rudimentary
workshops.[34]

    All of this sheds light on the function—or at least one of the func-
tions—of mechanization and confirms, with respect to the French case,
the validity of the hypotheses set forth by Stephen Marglin concerning
English industry.[35] Mechanization took place not merely because of technical or economic necessities but because of conflicts of authority. The
machine was a weapon of war directed against nuclei of resistance composed of skilled workers. It facilitated their elimination and the acquisi-
tion by employers of control over the entire productive process. Mechanization entailed the destruction of domestic workshops, whose
impenetrability constituted an obstacle to employer scrutiny, and the
erection in its stead of the factory, spatial setting of a new discipline.
Much as the Taylor system would eventually foster Ford's assembly line,

[33] On this subject, see M. Perrot, "Les ouvriers et les machines en France dans la première moitié du 19ème siècle," in *Le Soldat du Travail*, ed. Lion Murard and Patrick
Zylberman (special issue of *Recherches*, Sept. 1978).
[34] Ibid.
[35] Stephen Marglin, "Origines et fonctions de la parcellisation des tâches: A quoi ser-
vent les patrons?" in *Critique de la division du travail*, ed. A. Gorz (Paris: Seuil, 1973).

so the machine implies the factory. Technology and the organization of work are indeed linked, but in a manner mediated by social structure.

The resistance of craftsmen rested on three main elements: (1) knowledge, that is, ways of doing (handling, examining, etc.), including as well ways of saying things, concrete and empirical information, protected by secrecy and transmitted on the job, within the framework of everyday workshop gestures. Apprenticeship was a genuine initiation rite whose significance largely exceeded the technical level, and which schooling killed off; (2) the family, guardian of traditions but especially a means of transmitting the knowledge that ensured one's standing. Acquaintanceship, friendship, love, marriage—all took place within the framework of the trade, which delineated the emotional and cultural horizon. The significance of this was demonstrated for the Lyonnais in the 1880s, before it was destroyed by the Great Depression, which upset existing ways of life;[36] (3) a system of wages that was very distant from the hourly wage of the factory workers, wavering between subcontracting and piecework. This accounts for the importance of the *tarif* (piece-rate schedule), at the heart of the great Lyon conflicts of 1832 and of numerous strikes throughout the first half of the nineteenth century. To secure the guarantee of a written schedule, signed by the employer, was a recurrent demand. We find here at the same time a quasi-religious respect for the written word and a modern notion of contract. Such procedures indicate to what extent the craftsman still escaped the wage worker's condition, maintaining a certain degree of control over his remuneration.

We are also better able to understand the meaning of "the craft"; not a spontaneous reality, but on the contrary, an elaborate system in defense of a status, of dearly conquered advantages, justified on the basis of competence, protected by the double secret of knowledge and of family; not an immediate given of the economy, but a sociocultural construct whose ideological representations were ever more strengthened as pressures to dislocate the trade became more severe. Glorification of the craftsman, of the "beautiful masterwork," of the workshop with its "dear colleagues" engaged in refined politeness moved to the fore contemporaneously with the rise of the great factories: it was a way of resisting the facelessness of the mass worker.

The trades had a tough skin, as does manual labor; they experienced perennial revival within the interstices of large-scale industry by way of the practice of subcontracting.[37] As late as the turn of the century, there

[36] Lequin, *Les ouvriers*, vol. 1, ch. 5, pp. 205-238, "La naissance et le métier."
[37] Raphael Samuel, "Steam Power and Hand Technology in Mid-Victorian Britain," *History Workshop*, no. 3 (1977).

could be found in France, notably in Paris and the big cities, workshops where large areas of freedom survived, to the amazement of foreign observers; and it is possible that some of these are perhaps still with us today. In 1907, the leather-dressers of Gentilly (near Paris) walked out of their workshops because employers sought to impose fixed work schedules; in the same year, the nailmakers of Revin (Ardennes) struck for over 100 days against a regulation that fixed arrivals and departures and prohibited workers from going out to "refresh themselves" in the neighborhood tavern.[38] Such workshops were usually nests of anarcho-syndicalism. In the same vein, the "technical endogamies" often associated with the trades also displayed a surprising adaptability. They endured by means of successive reconversions, and anthropologists have observed them in operation in contemporary southeastern France, a land of workshops.[39]

Autonomy of the mode of production and autonomy of daily life were the poles of a resistance that was rooted in the persistence of the household economy, in the strength of the trades. An examination of the relationships between residence and workplace will reveal another dimension of these problems.

II. *Residence and Workplace*

An important recent achievement in this field is the growing awareness of space as a strategic element in games of power, as a stake in social struggles, which sociologists, architects, and historians have gained in the wake of Michel Foucault. The thesis of Ira Katznelson is particularly worthy of attention: the separation between residence and workplace provides one of the keys for understanding the formation of the modern working class and types of union organization, notably in the United States. In this perspective, integration into the local community and into the state occurs by way of the place of residence, locus of family life and of consumption, while "class consciousness" is forged in the workplace—the large modern factory.

But for the period with which we are concerned—the first industrial

[38] The leather-dressers of Gentilly "began their week or their day whenever they felt like it, brought drinks into the factory and played cards if they wished, without tolerating the least remark" (Office du Travail, *Statistique des grèves*, 1907). On the situation and the strike of Revin nailmakers, see Thierry Baudoin, "Grèves ouvrières et luttes urbaines" (3d cycle thesis, Paris VIII, 1978).

[39] Jacques Vallerant is studying these "technical endogamies" of southeastern France. See his "Savoir-faire et identité sociale," *Ethnologie française*, n.s., 12, no. 2 (Apr.–June 1982). He chose three urban examples: the knifemakers of Thiers, Lyon weavers, and glovemakers of Grenoble.

revolution, dominated by the textile sector—it seems to me that the proposition should be reversed. Because the family remained the principal center of decision making, the family residence, and more broadly the local community—the village or urban neighborhood—formed the basis of a popular autonomy rooted in the structures and networks of this community.[40] It was often in order to overcome its inertia or its overt resistance that employers seeking to recruit a docile work force set out to organize manufacturing plants and factories.[41] Moreover, in order to carry out their plans, they avoided cities, with their rebellious craftsmen who knew how to defend their wages, preferring the countryside, or at the least rural periphery of great centers. Accordingly, in France the first industrialization, cast within the framework of paternalism—a mode of social relationships encountered in many periods, but nevertheless characteristic of the first age of industrial discipline—was more rural than urban.[42] Let us remember, however, that besides relatively enclosed spaces such as houses, workshops, and factories, there were also yards— open and mobile workplaces, where there probably arose other types of wage relations, whose influence on working-class formation remains to be specified.

Community and Territory: The Power of Localism. The domestic system obviously constituted an extreme case of total fusion of residence and workplace, in which the modalities of work dictated their law to housing arrangements. Weavers required cool, spacious places, in contact with the street: they often found these in cellars, which constituted a traditional part of the house in northern and western France. But in Lyon, silkweavers lived and worked in the upper stories, with high windows dictated by the size of their looms as well as by the lighting requirements of extremely detailed silk patterns. These arrangements gave the houses of the Croix Rousse their very special appearance. One of the tasks of industrial archaeology is to inventory these various forms of housing.

Under these conditions, one's home was an instrument of production,

---

[40] See the pioneer works of Maurice Agulhon, focusing especially on political transformations: *La République au village* (Paris: Plon, 1970). The genre has been renewed by a number of recent American works: e.g., Tamara K. Hareven, *Amoskeag: Life and Work in an American Factory-City in New England* (London: Methuen, 1979); Michael P. Hanagan, *The Logic of Solidarity: Artisans and Industrial Workers in Three French Towns, 1871-1914* (Urbana: University of Illinois Press, 1980).

[41] See Bergery, *Economie industrielle*, on advice for the establishment of a manufactory.

[42] M. Perrot, "The Three Ages of Industrial Discipline in Nineteenth-Century France," in *Consciousness and Class Experience in Nineteenth-Century Europe*, ed. John M. Merriman (New York: Holmes and Meier, 1979).

a bit of capital, a guarantee of independence. Hence the resistance to displacement that Reybaud observed throughout northern France, without understanding the reasons for it. In Amiens, Saint-Quentin, and Lille, weavers, dyers, and finishers, who lived in the lower city, obstinately refused the healthier housing they were offered elsewhere. "All efforts to attract them to healthier, airier, better built neighborhoods were in vain; they resisted moving." In Amiens, "the workers remained where they were, in the Saint-Leu and Saint-Germain parishes, and displayed nothing but indifference toward the new quarters, probably because they were advertised as having been built for them." In Lille, the situation was even worse: "It was necessary to resort to violence to empty those cesspools [the cellars], and to reduce their number from thousands to mere hundreds. But as the police closed off the cellars, where did the workers seek refuge? In horrible streets which are no better, and which are called *courettes* [little courtyards]."[43] Did the weavers display a perverse taste for promiscuity and garbage? Reybaud and his contemporaries were not far from thinking this was the case, viewing workers as wild beasts that loved their den. But reality was very different. Because of their location in the center of the city, near the street, the cellars were convenient; the weavers therefore saw little advantage in moving to the periphery, in climbing up to the lofts they were being offered. They opposed this process of "haussmanization," this urban renewal, all the more because it was contemporaneous with the mechanization of weaving. Along with their habitat, it was their mode of existence, their very identity that was at stake.

More generally, workers were suspicious of the increased control implied by any rationalization, whether of the city or of the factory. In 1848, the Paris insurgents destroyed lampposts, symbols of the eye of the police. Around 1890-1900, according to labor inspectors, workers were cool toward using Usine Nouvelle (New Factory) architecture. Today, the former inhabitants of *bidonvilles* (shantytowns), relocated in properly built transitional facilities, yearn for the freedom and conviviality of their precarious housing.[44] In all these instances, the problem is that of spatial independence.

A second case is that of the small family workshop, distinct from the worker's residence, but located so close to it that there was free circulation from one to the other, interpenetration of family and work and of trade and neighborhood. In this setting, for example, were the ceramic

[43] Reybaud, *Le coton*, p. 227.
[44] Colette Pétonnet, *On est tous dans le brouillard: Ethnologie des banlieues* (Paris: Galilée, 1979).

workers of Nevers, described by Toytot around 1860.[45] They were recruited almost exclusively within families that had worked within the industry for two hundred years or more. "They rarely inspire in their children a taste for another, more lucrative occupation. . . . Gathered in a single neighborhood, near the plants, in the part of the city they have always occupied, the ceramic workers all know one another and live in good fellowship." Married women, employed as their husbands' helpers, had a key to the workshop and entered it as they pleased. Against this, unmarried female laborers worked in the courtyard; "they get and deserve little respect. Mixed up with the men, whose work they share in the courtyards, the workshops, near the ovens, they easily lose all modesty . . ."; the ceramic workers took care to keep their daughters out of it. The pace of life was set by family festivities, particularly burials; for a colleague's funeral, the workshops were closed for several days. But twenty years later, everything had changed: a new regulation set the hours of arrival and departure and prohibited the presence of wives, whose key was taken away. Further, the ceramic workers left the old quarters on the edge of the Loire and went to live far from the plants. By the end of the nineteenth century, the workshop was a regulated, masculine place, clearly separated from domestic space. This is a typical evolution that can be found in many other occupations: in the foundries, for example, whose familial character down to the middle of the nineteenth century is suggested by numerous engravings.

A third type of situation is one in which the workshop, the plant, the factory, were clearly distinct places, but were located within the village or the working-class neighborhood. Generally speaking, the workers went home at noon to take their meal. This lengthy dinner pause (as it was called) was sacred; to reduce its duration could provoke riots. The following took place in Houlme, near Rouen, in 1825: after Levasseur, owner of the spinning mill, reduced the pause from one hour to half an hour—probably in order to force employees to eat a bite on the premises to avoid time loss due to comings and goings—the workers went on strike and brought into it the entire village community, which engaged in a three-day confrontation with the forces of law and order. There were a number of victims, including a gendarme, and a hundred arrests; there followed a trial in criminal court and a death sentence; meant to stand as an example, the public execution was surrounded with a solemn rigamarole.[46] Another, less tragic example: in 1888, nine hundred miners of the Gard (mines of Rochesadoule and Martinet) went on strike because they were

[45] E. de Toytot, "Faïenciers de Nevers" (1864 and 1885), in Les ouvriers des deux-mondes, ed. Société d'économie sociale, new series, 4th issue (Paris: Firmin-Didot, 1886).
[46] Bourgin and Bourgin, Les patrons, les ouvriers, et l'état, vol. 3, pp. 49-56.

made to bring a meal basket and eat on the premises; after parading their containers from one end of the village to the other, they burned them in a symbolic auto-da-fé, shouting "Down with the basket!"[47] These examples show how workers defended their way of life and resisted incarceration in the factories. The right to a mid-day meal at home, in the peasant manner, was for them inalienable.

In fact, the more important right was not "to stay at home" but to go out into the street, into the neighborhood. Workers' housing at this time was worse than mediocre, particularly for those who migrated to the cities; yet the workers had few demands in this respect. But they had definite views concerning urban space: the right to cross the city freely, to use the commons (I purposely use the old peasant term here), to be at the heart of the city—these were their major aspirations.[48] The working-class neighborhood, with its shops, taverns, dance halls, wash-houses, yards, vacant lots, formed the setting of everyday life, of sociability. Is a meeting called for? Let's go to the tavern. . . . And for a larger one, let's hire the dance hall. . . .

Moreover, the neighborhood did not shape social life by its topography alone, but also by the structure constituted by its shopkeepers, who were genuine "sociocultural mediators."[49] Maurice Agulhon has shown their contribution to the penetration of republican ideas in the towns of the Var.[50] In the Gard, socialism penetrated along the same paths. In Bessèges, where particularly well kept police files have enabled a precise analysis of protests in 1887, artisans and shopkeepers accounted for 33 percent of the militants; the Workmen's Circle was founded by the public scribe–grocer Jourdan and other retailers such as the shoemaker Dumas, the watchmaker Bracourt, and the candymaker Manifacier.[51] The shops, vending stands, and taverns, genuine reading rooms that broadcasted the popular press were the clubs, the nerve centers of a protest action that, going considerably beyond wages, was concerned with municipal freedoms, another episode in a secular struggle for autonomy and freedom.

When a symbiosis such as this occurred between neighborhood and trade or occupation, labor conflicts and strikes took on the character of a local struggle. They entailed the formation of a coalition against the

[47] M. Perrot, Les ouvriers en grève, vol. 1, p. 291.

[48] M. Perrot, "Les ouvriers, l'habitat et la ville au 19ème siècle" in La question du logement et le mouvement ouvrier français, ed. J. P. Flamand (Paris: La Villette, 1981).

[49] Following the expression of Michel Vovelle at a conference on this theme, Aix-en-Provence, 1979.

[50] M. Agulhon, La République au village; also his Une ville ouvrière au temps du socialisme utopique: Toulon (1815-1851) (Paris: Mouton, 1970).

[51] M. Perrot, "Archives policières et militants ouvriers sous la Troisième République. Un exemple: Le Gard," Revue d'histoire économique et sociale (Apr.-June 1959).

employer or the authorities around the hard nucleus of the workers themselves, including their families and small businessmen, particularly when
the company store sought to monopolize the consumer market. Certain
mining strikes, particularly in the 1880s, involved issues of concern to the
municipality as a whole. In the demonstrations, the entire family group
came into play, with women and children at the head of the marches,
carrying flags or reenacting the motions of Charivari (shivaree). Labor
demonstrations, such as those of the First of May, were expressed in the
ritual form of popular festivities.

The people were the matrix of a world of workers who demanded a
right to the city and to the street, rather than the right to occupy
factories.[52]

The Factory as a Place. In contrast with the neighborhood and the street,
the plant or the factory was the territory of the masters, successors of the
monastery (sometimes quite literally: many manufacturing plants were
established in old monasteries sold as national property during the Revolution) or of the castle. A common theme of working-class discourse was
indeed that a "new feudalism" had replaced the old. The factory was a
place of discipline, whose law one was obliged to accept in order to secure
work; work regulations were never negotiated, but imposed one-sidedly
by employers.

Let us note, however, that the images and sentiments inspired by the
factory were not solely negative. It was often accepted or even sought
after as a source of wages; it kept workers warm in the winter (for this
reason, Roubaix weavers seldom struck in January); it provided fellowship. We are but too familiar with the nostalgia triggered off in our own
day by a factory about to shut down not to be able to conceive of the
possibility of positive images. For the young apprentice Norbert Truquin,
accustomed to the blows of his masters, the Picard wool spinning mill
where he began work around 1846 looked like a lesser evil, even as an
improvement. The pace of work was relatively relaxed, supervision was
light, and sociability highly developed. There were good moments of
laughter around characters who told stories. Above all, he met a certain
Constant, a follower of Cabet, whom many mocked, but who initiated
him to Icarian communism.[53] No matter that Truquin did not adopt this
doctrine, which he found overly authoritarian; what is important is that

---

[52] A special issue of *Le mouvement social* (118, no. 1 [Jan.-Mar. 1982]) was recently
devoted to the notion of "working-class neighborhood." See also Gérard Jacquemet,
Belleville au 19ème siècle (Paris: Ecole des Hautes Etudes, 1982).

[53] Norbert Truquin, *Mémoires et aventures d'un prolétaire à travers la Révolution*
(Paris: Maspéro, 1977), p. 70: "In the factories, the workshops are heated, sufficiently
aired and well lit; order and cleanliness prevail; the worker leads a social life. . . ."

he encountered a form of working-class consciousness. By exploding the often tyrannical confines of the family and the local community, the factory acted as a crucible. It brought about encounters that shaped the paths of individuals and the networks by which a class comes into being.

However, in the first moments of industrialization, the factory was neither a crucible of consciousness nor an epicenter of rebellion. Often borrowed, its material shape—architectural as well as functional—was slow to emerge. Recent works have established a belated rationalization of French interior factory space.[54] The ordering of this space was determined by the flow of goods and of men; but this factory was obviously much less constraining than the sequence of mechanical operations associated with automobile construction. From a formal point of view, the factory is first of all an enclosed space: walls, a gate—a door, a doorkeeper—these are constraining elements since they impose fixed schedules, a surveillance of access that is often resented. "You had to get up very early in order to enter the factory on the dot of a quarter to five," writes Truquin; "the least lateness implied a fine, and a third time around, you were fired with a bad certificate that made it impossible to find work in the region."[55] The factory meant discipline.

But the "paternalist" factory was, in addition, a system for integrating manpower; it was founded on the exploitation of family work power, transported into the walls of the factory, with the father's responsibilities often reinforced. The prime example is that of the spinning mills, where the father crew chief was assisted by his wife and especially his children, on whose behalf he received a family wage. A second element of the system pertained to residence: the owner lived on the premises, and his house was often right next door to the factory. Finally, social relationships were modeled on the family, as reflected in language (the *patron*—employer— was the *père*—father—of the workers) as well as in institutions. This system, more or less complete, dominated the first stage of industrialization. It was victorious in the great factories: Schneider in Le Creusot, the glassworks of Baccarat, Michelin, de Wendel in Lorraine, Menier in Noisiel (near Paris), Montgolfier in Ardèche were the prototypes. In exchange for complete submissiveness, these institutions provided regular work, a certain degree of protection, for a stable nucleus of workers. There is something feudal about this system, which, when the advantages disappeared, transformed itself into the most comprehensive system of exploitation. By means of assimilation or of fear, it often resulted in the formation of an integrated body of manpower, whose docility goes a long

[54] Particularly P. Ngo, "Usine, espace de travail et architecture industrielle: Essai de généalogie" (3d cycle thesis, Université de Provence, 1980).

[55] Truquin, *Mémoires*, p. 70.

way toward explaining the frequent silence of factories in the early stages of industrialization. Even later on, the calm atmosphere of large factories stood in sharp contrast to the agitation of middle-sized ones. In the period under consideration, a high concentration of workers by no means determined a high frequency of strikes.

For the factory to become the center of rebellion, it was necessary for wages to become the sole source of income, for ties to the soil and to the "father" to be torn asunder. As a matter of fact, the crisis of paternalism often erupted as a consequence of the physical withdrawal of the owner. Subsequent management by underlings, who always sought shelter behind distant high authority—most of the time, in Paris—fostered a sense of anonymity. In the 1880s, when the Roubaix textile-mill owners left the factory neighborhood to live in the "palaces" of Paris Boulevard, workers gave vent to their hatred. We encounter here, from the side of the employers, the psychological importance of the residence factor.

With the waning of paternalism, the factory revealed its other face: that of the industrial "penal colony," where the "convicts" labor under the surveillance of the "guards." Fourier was probably the first to use this terminology, but it came into general usage in the years 1860-1880.[56] In the first half of the century, the workers objected particularly to the "English" factories, mechanized, rationalized, and as a matter of fact often managed by foreigners; in the second, the factories became ordinary targets of violence. But it should be emphasized that this violence originated on the outside, because a strike was a get-away, a mass exit toward the open, the village, the street, the community restored. While on strike, the factory was deserted; it was never occupied. If ever attacked, it was from the outside, expressing an extraterritorial relationship. A classical gesture: to break factory windows with stones. There was even greater violence at the level of speech: there was talk of burning it down—"to burn the factories" was a great working-class dream—of blowing it up with dynamite, but never of running it.

Changes began to emerge between 1900 and 1914, notably around the great factories devoted to mechanical construction, especially automobiles. Workspace became the object of a rationalization that, in France, was only exceptionally governed by Taylorism, but was nonetheless very important.[57] The space-time nexus of the factory and the labor of workers were subjected to increased control. At one blow, the factory and its

---

[56] M. Perrot, *Les ouvriers en grève*, vol. 1, pp. 295ff, and "The Three Ages of Industrial Discipline."

[57] Yves Cohen, "Ernest Mattern, les automobiles Peugeot et le pays de Montbéliard industriel avant et pendant la guerre de 1914-1918: Sur une pratique d'organisateur" (3d cycle thesis, Besançon, 1981).

space, as well as the organization of work, were propelled to the center of the struggle as its major stakes. In reaction to this, workers demanded a share in the control of work itself. The Federation of Metallurgists, for example, devised a comprehensive project involving shop delegates working in liaison with union delegates, issued from the factory's basic work groups. In the "New Factory," a new form of unionism emerged between 1900 and 1914 that placed the firm at the center of its concerns.[58] Membership in a firm—Renault, Berliet, Peugeot—was soon to become more important than craft. Life came to be organized around a threefold division of space—the home, the factory, and the town—and its concomitant threefold division of time—"eight hours of work, eight hours of sleep, eight hours of leisure."

The occupation of factories in 1936 implied an entirely different relationship not merely to the instrument of work, but also to space. Dispersed with respect to residence, the workers were reunited daily in the factory, which became the locus of their collective existence; dislocated with respect to their crafts, they were reunited in the firm, which became the locus of their convergence, and thereby all at once the epicenter of the labor movement. But this history, which is still to be written, was linked to the second industrial revolution.

The Contribution of the Yard. In addition to these enclosed spaces, the open—and in some sense more abstract—space of the construction yard played a role that deserves separate consideration. This role was first of all economic, so important indeed that it is possible for this period to speak of "building cycles," that is, economic cycles based on the activity of the building industry. This is captured as well by the old popular saying, "when construction is going well, everything is going well." Surges of construction were related to the creation of infrastructure—railroads, for example, together with the development of cities ("haussmanization" did not take place in Paris alone, but in most large cities).

At the social level, the yards displayed a number of noteworthy characteristics: temporary and mobile, they forged a masculine workforce and absorbed a large, more or less floating population that originated in rural areas—the yard, like the factory, was a source of supplementary income for the local peasantry—and, to an ever greater extent in the second half of the nineteenth century, in foreign countries.[59] They were often zones of turbulence and conflicts, in which xenophobia played a significant role.

---

[58] Patrick Friedenson, "France, Etats-Unis: Genèse de l'Usine Nouvelle," in *Le Soldat du Travail*, ed. Murard and Zylberman (*Recherches*, Sept. 1978).

[59] In the first half of the nineteenth century, the presence of women is often reported in construction yards.

In periods of depression, French workers went after foreigners, genuine scapegoats whom they accused of stealing the bread of natives. The Great Depression at the end of the nineteenth century was marked by numerous events of this sort.[60]

Because in the sphere of public works, local communities and the state play the part of employers, construction yards also engendered new bargaining practices, implying a different relationship between workers and public authorities. Thus in Paris, at the end of the century, the services of the Prefecture of the Seine established a fixed schedule of "series prices," that is, an official wage rate for each occupational category. Although these prices were advisory only and not mandatory, workers relied on them to demand wage increases or to oppose cuts. This adumbrates the coming of collective bargaining in a domain where freedom by and large had prevailed.

Pioneers in this regard, construction workers led the way in yet another manner: the degree of activity of the yards and the situation of the hiring market at the time of the active spring season fostered among them an acute awareness of the state of the business cycle. The visibility of the market enabled them to launch successful strikes, a fact that in turn endowed them with considerable prestige and influence; many other occupational groups were inspired by their organizational example and followed their lead.[61]

Thus, in the yards, there came into being another type of worker behavior, or even consciousness, less rooted in a particular locality, cast in a broader frame: the market, the state, or even Europe as a whole became generally viewed as a threat. The contribution of the construction workers to the labor movement was thus considerable and stands out in sharp relief: one of the iconographic representations of the worker, on the eve of World War I, was the outdoor laborer whose powerful muscles expressed the masculine strength that would make the Revolution.[62] Heirs of the old *compagnonnage*, the traditional journeyman system whose forms of struggle they passed on, the construction workers were in some respects also the sentries of the new working-class world.

III. *The Formation of a Collective Identity*

Slowly but surely, the ranks of those enumerated as "workers" grew throughout the nineteenth century, as indicated by a steady increase of

[60] M. Perrot, *Les ouvriers en grève*, vol. 1, pp. 164ff, on xenophobic movements.
[61] Ibid., pp. 377ff.
[62] E. J. Hobsbawm, "Sexe, Symboles, Vêtements et Socialisme," *Actes de la recherche en sciences sociales*, no. 23 (Oct. 1978).

the secondary sector's share of the gainfully employed population. But if it is possible to measure the overall increase, it is almost impossible to reconstruct its component flows—entries into and departures from the ranks of workers, their mobility, and the transmission of status from one generation to another. We can sometimes observe how the "technical endogamies" of the trades were made and unmade; but these formed only one part of the working class, and probably a declining one. Were there generations of workers and, if so, of what order of magnitude? What was their role in the constitution of a memory, or at least of a "habitus," as P. Bourdieu would call it? Or on the contrary, is the working class merely an empty receptacle through which individuals come and go, as Schumpeter suggested? What relationships can we establish among individuals, groups, and classes? Class *in itself* is difficult to grasp.

What is there to say about class *for itself*? When and how did the individual worker of the nineteenth century come to see himself as belonging to a larger whole? How did he conceive of this whole over time and space? And how can historians grasp this? How far should we generalize the views of a handful, expressed exclusively in the written word? The methodological problems involved are frightful, and I do not believe that they have been truly resolved.

However, there exists, at least among historians, a fairly high degree of agreement to the effect that, at least in the French case, "class consciousness" has been largely independent of economic structures, and that the expression of a class consciousness arose precociously in that country, as early as the first half of the nineteenth century. The role of urban artisans and of mutual aid societies—whose influence has been unduly minimized in the literature—was fundamental here, and the impact of political factors and events, more particularly of the revolutions of 1830 and 1848, was decisive. This historiographic stance is not entirely new. The work of historians of the 1930s such as Octave Festy, Edouard Dolléans, or Fernand Rudé, to mention only a few names, already pointed in this direction, and the famous course taught by Ernest Labrousse at the Sorbonne in 1948-1949 on the labor movement in France and England stopped, as a matter of fact, in 1848. More recently, the works of R. Gossez and J. Rougerie have insisted on the place of artisans and on the lasting character of *sans-culottisme* in the revolutions of the nineteenth century. This is a powerful political tradition which can still be seen at work today, even if it sometimes is experienced as an archaic obstacle in the way of understanding the problems of the modern world. A source of both strength and weakness, this political culture exists, and one cannot understand anything about French social movements if one does not take it into account.

Nevertheless, the work of British historians like E. P. Thompson and Eric Hobsbawm has reopened the question of the role of the artisans. Charles Tilly and his students and collaborators have done the same concerning the decisive role of political factors in relation to class formation; the analyses of William Sewell rightly emphasize this as well.[63] The writings of Jacques Rancière, A. Faure, and Alain Cottereau also invite us to reexamine the experiences of workers in the "first nineteenth century" from a different perspective and with new questions in mind.[64]

I agree with these analyses, but my purpose here differs slightly—it is to deal with the second half of the nineteenth century. At this time, and especially in the last third, there seemed to emerge out of a broadly drawn popular representation of the world a more focused one, associated more specifically with workers and within which economic factors became more prominent. This working class defined itself by its enemies, its limits, its consciousness of a shared "fate" and a shared exploitation, its vision of the future. All of this, often voiced by militants who were both mediators and spokesmen, was crystallized in words and images, a language that became an instance of reality, a referent that in turn structured the imagination. The media, whether or not they were the working class's own, broadcast and amplified this representation of the world. With respect to this process, it is by no means certain that economic factors were determinative; it is evident, in particular, that the Great Depression of the 1880s produced ambivalent and contradictory effects. The political situation was probably more important: the founding of the Republic eliminated a major preliminary political objective and established new rules of the social game. Since much remains to be done in this field, the following remarks should be taken as an essay in the literal sense, a tentative account.

Concerning Some Previous Forms. To think of themselves as an entity, workers had at their disposal existing categories that in some sense served as a matrix. We should examine the influence of religious models, how one moved from the "poor" to the worker (the modern poor), from brotherhood to solidarity; how Christian eschatology fashioned revolutionary messianism, so lively at the end of the nineteenth century, with its vision

---

[63] In addition to his contribution to this volume, see William H. Sewell, Jr., "Conscience de classe sous la Monarchie de Juillet," *Annales E-S-C* (July-Aug. 1981).

[64] Rancière, *La nuit des prolétaires*; A. Faure and J. Rancière, eds., *La parole ouvrière* (Paris: Union Générale d'Editions, 1976); A. Cottereau, introduction to the reprint of Denis Poulot, *Question sociale: Le sublime* (1870; repr., Paris: François Maspéro, 1980); and the journal *Révoltes logiques*.

of the Great Evening and the Promised Land. Religious rituals shaped workers' demonstrations, whose marches initially still bore a strong resemblance to the processions of yesteryear.

Originating in the Ancien Régime, the notions of order, estate, and corps were quite hardy, as Sewell has shown. For example, Fourth Estate was a common term by which the "people" referred to itself at least until the 1880s.[65] This term deserves our attention: it implies at the same time the idea of a split and of a succession. The Third Estate was the bourgeoisie, which benefited from an unfinished revolution; this had to be continued to bring about the coming of the Fourth. The workers were constantly reenacting the French Revolution, but with another ending—a happy one: the abolition of classes, equality finally realized—yet within a state that remained by and large unaltered. Another legacy of the French Revolution was the idea of federation: "We must federate ourselves," said the workers when they spoke of organizing at the national level. To federate: that is to say, to unite disparate groups and associations into comprehensive bodies coordinated on behalf of common objectives. This distant evocation of a party was quite opposed to the modern conception: the latter knows only individuals, whereas a federation entailed mediation by way of groups.

In the Eyes of Others. We know that the notion of class was of bourgeois origin. It made its appearance in the last third of the eighteenth century from the pen of writers who, observing the society of their time, were struck with the inadequacy of a categorization by orders and sought other taxonomies.[66] Does it follow that workers were perceived as a class by the ruling classes before they viewed themselves as such? That remains to be seen.[67] In any case, as shown by Louis Chevalier, words and notions such as "proletariat," "dangerous classes," haunted the discourse and imagination of the first half of the nineteenth century.[68] These terrifying, negative, savage visions often forced workers to situate themselves in relation to them, either to make them their own, or more commonly, to distinguish themselves from them. Workers sometimes emphasized negative traits, declaring themselves to be *lundistes* (Monday absenteeists), drunks, fighters, dirty talkers; in this regard, *ouvriérisme* is akin to *négri-*

---

[65] *Le quatrième état* was the title of the Toulouse labor party's newspaper in 1883-1884 (51 issues published).

[66] J.-C. Perrot, "Rapports sociaux et villes au 18e siècle," *Annales E-S-C* (1974).

[67] William H. Sewell, Jr., disagrees: see his "Conscience de classe."

[68] Louis Chevalier, *Classes laborieuses et classes dangereuses à Paris dans la première moitié du 19e siècle* (Paris: Plon, 1958).

tude.[69] Alternatively, when they were said to be dirty, they emphasized cleanliness; when called ignorant, they insisted on their love of books and of the Enlightenment; when declared coarse, they prided themselves in their elegance and took care of their appearance. The image they wished to give of themselves was constructed reactively. Jacques Rancière has stressed the fundamental importance of the outlook of the Other and has shown how it became one of the sources of discourse on "the dignity of workers": "This outlook justifies not merely the power of the dominant class, but it contributes to constitution of the dominated class as such. Because it is not the mechanical necessity of the mode of production that reduces the working class to its inferior place. It is the judgment of the dominant class. . . . The working class is first of all a caste, constituted like any caste, by a decision of the masters."[70] The call for moral propriety, the claim to culture, the affirmation of "the capacity of workers," all were cast in this perspective. It was necessary to give a positive image of oneself against those who denied it; identity formed itself in this tension, in this relationship to the adversary.

Consciousness of a Common Fate. The consciousness of workers was first of all an awareness of misfortune. Workers had taken the place of paupers; they were defined by their material, intellectual, emotional, moral misery—by their lack of everything. They were hungry and cold; they lacked bread and clothing; they were without shelter, without family, without culture. Their progeny were doomed to abandonment and death; the charity ward awaited the old. The consciousness of social inequality in the face of death is a key idea that physicians and hygienists (such as Louis-René Villermé) developed from the beginning of the century. Rickets was the characteristic illness of the proletariat, a miserable race; the misfortune of workers was a demographic, biological fact. To be a worker was in some sense a curse, the horror of which was exceeded only by the curse of being a female worker—"blasphemous word," exclaims Michelet. This sentiment of a collective misfortune endowed the discourse of workers with a miserabilist tone that has lasted for a long time and has been, moreover, largely independent of individual condition. The metalworkers of the Tours region interviewed by Patrice Augerau today do not voice any personal complaints; but they consider themselves privileged, and believe class truth to consist of misery and exploitation.[71] Over

[69] Jeffrey Kaplow, "La fin de la Saint-Lundi, Le Paris populaire au 19ᵉ siècle," *Temps libre*, no. 2 (Summer 1981).

[70] Rancière, *La nuit des prolétaires*, p. 270.

[71] Patrice Augereau, "Les évènements dans la mémoire des ouvriers" (3d cycle thesis, Nantes, 1981).

time, successive elements contributed to the making of a heroic mural of the condition of the working class, a construct that should not be taken as a report of its real and concrete condition.

Another major dimension was the consciousness of being a victim. In his daily life, the worker was emptied of his blood, as if sucked dry by a vampire. But to his daily sacrifice must be added the great massacres in the course of which masses of workers were murdered. Armed repression, revolutionary events, the "great days" that ended in the death of workers, acted in this respect as catalysts. The days of June 1848, the shootings at La Ricamarie and Aubin in 1869, the Bloody Week of the Commune with its 30,000 killed, the shootings at Fourmies (1891) and Draveil-Vigneux (1907)—the latter two more horrendous because they were the acts of a Republican regime—delineated the bloody path of the workers' consciousness. In the same manner in tsarist Russia, the killings of 1905 and the Kolyma massacre of 1911 had a decisive effect on the crystallization of a working class.[72] Those who shot were the army, the state's army, Authority's army: we grasp here the full impact of political givens. The workers became red: red from the blood that binds their class.[73]

The blood of workers flowed together with the sweat made to pour by the exploitation to which they were subjected. Even if the economic dimension was not the most important factor in shaping class consciousness, the idea that the worker was not paid a just price for his work appeared very early on. In the nineteenth century, work became an abstract notion, a quantity that could be measured by the rate of wages, which emerged very early at the heart of demands. It is in order to increase or defend their earnings that workers coalesced; questions of the duration of work or of discipline only came afterwards. To negotiate a piecework schedule, to obtain an increase in the price of a day or an hour, were central concerns. This consciousness of wages was monetized and quantified; even when they did not know how to read, workers knew how to count. One is struck, in reading their autobiographies, with their precise memory for wages; in the very typical memoirs of Truquin, notes to this effect occur on nearly every page.[74] This has been observed in more recent surveys as well: the memory of work is anchored in the remembrance of earnings and paydays, the highlights of working-class life. Let us not forget that wages were also a source of autonomy for workers, who were thereby radically differentiated from the rest of the popular classes—peasants, domestic servants, or even artisans. The wage nexus

[72] As shown in the forthcoming work of L. Haimson.
[73] The diversity of nineteenth-century obsessions concerning blood is considered in a special issue of *Romantisme*, no. 31 (1981).
[74] Truquin, *Mémoires*, pp. 82-85, 96, 203, etc.

influenced their vision of time, of work, of life, and of themselves. Wage earning has long remained synonymous of working class.

Work and Production as Class Sacraments. As laborers and producers, workers opposed themselves to *rentiers*, to the idle and the useless. Work is hard and painful. It is a physical act that involves the entire body, and first of all the hands, symbol of the class: the seals of most unions depict a pair of clasped hands. Work implies physical movement, muscular effort, simultaneously to bear and to transform. Real work, male work, is carried out on hard materials that resist these efforts and that must be overcome. "To the man, wood and metals; to the woman, family and cloth," wrote a worker delegate to the World's Fair of 1867 in a striking summary of the sexual division of roles and tasks. The male worker had a certain contempt for sewing, women's work; in textile factories, he could conceive only of exercising supervisory functions. Moreover, soft materials allowed themselves to be mechanized much more easily. And if it was glorious to manufacture machines, to rule over them, it was degrading to serve them. The pre-Taylor metallurgist was "the lord of workers."

By producing material objects, this labor adds something to the wealth of the world; it is concrete, visible, useful—the only really useful thing there is. The arms of manual workers suffice to make the world go round, and the world would die should they stop. The idea of a revolution by way of the general strike is founded on this quite restrictive *ouvriérisme*, which delineates class boundaries as well.

Class Boundaries. Excluded from the working class were, to be sure, domestic servants and, more broadly speaking, people involved in services. Tied as they were to masters, they retained an element of servility, or personal allegiance to the rich, to the bourgeois. Thus drivers and particularly private coachmen—things were somewhat different for drivers of public conveyances—did not have the sympathy of the working class, which did not consider them as its own, even when they went on strike, which occurred every time there was a world's fair.[75] Given the feminization of domestic service, the condition of servants suffered in addition because of the discredit attached to all that is feminine. Housework has no recognized value. Moreover, at the beginning of the twentieth century,

[75] On Paris coachmen, see the book by Nicolas Papayanis (Paris: Sycomore, forthcoming).

there was a shortage of servant girls.[76] Peasants used to place their daughters as domestics; but workers became more and more reluctant to do so, and the women themselves preferred to become workers. The recognition of class boundaries by women was another indicator of their crystallization.

In the same manner, workers criticized white-collar employees in both the public and private sectors, whom they mocked and held in contempt as useless, good-for-nothing parasites. "Bureaucrats," *ronds-de-cuir* (pen-pushers), do not rank high in French opinion. Intellectuals evoke suspicion as well. It is by no means certain that the workers of the 1890s loved books to the same extent as the working-class followers of Saint-Simon, mad for the written word, studied by Jacques Rancière. This suspicion redounded on "politicians," even on the left, and accounts in part for the distance workers maintained from socialist parties, their refusal to allow themselves to be led by "pontificating bigwigs." The very concept of direct-action syndicalism implies a certain degree of anti-intellectualism.

One could describe many other boundaries: in relation to foremen, "watchdogs" of the employer and automatically excluded from unions; in relation to foreigners, seen as competitors, particularly in times of depression, but also rejected as different in the eyes of a working-class consciousness that likes to define itself as national.

In closing, I would stress the importance of a masculine consciousness, which made its appearance as a dimension of class at the beginning of the twentieth century. This was in keeping with the system of representations and values of workers, with the distribution of tasks and sexual roles. Syndicalism organized by taking over on its own behalf the bourgeois definition of public space as masculine space. This state of affairs was expressed at the level of symbols, as Hobsbawm has shown.[77] The symbols of the Republic were feminine: she is Marianne. Maurice Agulhon has attempted to explain why and how she embodies the Republic.[78] The symbols of the working class, however, became more and more masculine: it has been represented by the barrel-chested male worker with broad shoulders, swollen biceps, and powerful muscles. The ideas of manual labor and production we have spoken of are obviously at the center of this identification, which is of course by no means specifically French. On the contrary, one still finds many women in French working-class

[76] Anne-Martin Fugier, *La place des bonnes: La domesticité féminine à Paris en 1900* (Paris: Grasset, 1979).

[77] E. J. Hobsbawm, "Sexe, Symboles," n. 64.

[78] Maurice Agulhon, *Marianne au combat: L'imagerie et la symbolique républicaines de 1789 à 1880* (Paris: Flammarion, 1979). Vol. 2 is forthcoming.

imagery, for example to represent the General Strike: in northern France, in 1906, it consisted of a savage Eve, naked and wrapped in her long hair. Nevertheless, the waning of feminine images is a noteworthy trend.

The Principal Enemy: Employers. In the course of the latter third of the nineteenth century, paternalism as a type of social relationship showed numerous signs of losing its stamina.[79] At the end of the Second Empire and even more after the Commune, the term *patrons* came to be laden with hostile meaning. They became the "them," "those Gentlemen," outsiders, strangers, antagonists. Workers' discourse formulated different types of representations with respect to employers that I have attempted to analyze elsewhere.[80] Broadly speaking, we can distinguish three series of images: (a) the bosses, new lords, despots and tyrants were *oppressors* with arbitrary power; (b) these bourgeois were lazy *pleasure-seekers*, incapable, "fat-bellied and glutted." In the then-current iconography, the employer was represented as obese, with a cigar in his mouth, his watch chain spread over a hanging belly; very often, as well, he had a hooked nose: he was a "Jew," another synonym for "boss," whose god was Rothschild;[81] (b) employers were capitalists, exploiters, thieves and vampires who lived off the sweat and the blood of the people, whom they transformed into unproductive gold. These "millionaires" (a term often used as well) were not so much industrialists as greedy financiers, speculators, stock-market manipulators. They did not invest in their enterprise, which they did not seek to modernize. Metalworkers, notably, complained of their bosses' ignorance of technical progress, their lateness in mechanizing. These vanguard workers demanded, in the name of their ability and their knowledge, the right of job control within the factory.[82] We find ourselves very far from the cottage weavers who fought to stay at home. With the advent of the *métallos* (workers in metallurgical factories), the center of the struggle has begun to shift.

Labor newspapers, with rubrics such as "The Review of Penal Colonies" (penal colony = factory), gave full rein to these representations. But it was particularly on the occasion of strikes, the major events in the labor struggle of these times, that the fundamental antagonisms were

[79] M. Perrot, "The Three Ages."

[80] M. Perrot, "Le regard de l'Autre: Comment les ouvriers français voyaient leurs patrons," in *Le Patronat de la Seconde Industrialisation*, ed. M. Lévy-Leboyer, "Cahiers du mouvement social" (Paris: Editions ouvrières, 1979).

[81] Zeev Sternhell provides an analysis of the bases of this popular anti-Semitism in *La droite révolutionnaire (1885-1914): Les origines françaises du fascisme* (Paris: Seuil, 1978).

[82] P. Fridenson, "France, Etats-Unis."

tested and put forward. The identification of employers as the principal enemy, to a greater extent than any other factor, contributed to the forging of class unity.

IV. *Into a New Century*

What was the situation of the French working class at the beginning of the twentieth century?

We must remember, first of all, the role of the great economic depression of 1882-1890, which washed away the remainders of the "domestic system" (in rural weaving, for example), closed down numerous small rural factories, shifted the regional distribution of industry toward northern and eastern France and, finally, provoked important urban migrations. This is a prelude to the "second industrial revolution"—involving metallurgy, the automobile, the internal combustion engine—which is marked by a vigorous spurt of economic growth, in which economists detect the roots of French modernity. Between 1905 and 1910, the annual rate of growth of industrial production was 4.58 percent, highest of the century.[83] Prices and profits increased, together with an acceleration of production and exchanges and a development of the tertiary sector.

Even if this transformation was tempered in France by the maintenance of a strong agricultural sector and the resistance afforded by small farms, by the persistence of petty artisanal and commercial enterprises, and by the weight of the textile sector, it was nonetheless considerable. The working class was expanding: between 1906 and 1911, it may have grown by 1.3 million. Because of declining demography, even within a working class that long remained quite fertile these new workers were recruited mainly among women, who constituted 37 percent of the gainfully employed population in 1906—a rate that would be exceeded only during the First World War, and would subsequently decline—and among immigrants. The latter numbered 1,159,000 in 1911, or 2.86 percent of the total population, and from 8 to 10 percent of the working-class population, with particularly strong sectoral concentrations in the north and the south. Employer strategies for renewing their manpower reserves ran, of course, into the resistance of workers, concerned with competition; but this resistance sometimes was directed against the women and immigrants themselves, a source of tensions and conflicts that left organized labor without effective weapons, despite a real effort on the

[83] On all these subjects, see C. E. Labrousse and F. Braudel, eds., *Histoire économique et sociale de la France*, vol. 4, pt. 1 (Paris: Presses Universitaires, 1979), esp. pp. 527ff.

the part of the CGT (Conféderation Générale du Travail), at least toward women, in 1912-1913. With respect to immigrants, we see here the beginnings of the formation of a subproletariat that is more difficult to integrate and that adumbrates the whole issue of relationships between proletarians of developed and underdeveloped countries.

New patterns emerged as well concerning habitat, that is, residence and workplace. On the one hand, the period marked the birth of the suburbs, which played a fundamental role in the development of the new proletariat. These suburbs of the great cities (especially Paris and Lyon), where the new factories were located—the great metal or chemical works, and soon automobile plants as well—drew the uprooted of all kinds, provincial or foreign. But these suburbs developed more structure and organization than was once thought, and they gradually integrated the newcomers into social and political life. For example, in Saint-Denis—the leading working-class suburb of northern Paris—around 1906-1910 the Bretons, who came from hungry Brittany without much of a political consciousness, began turning toward the left—toward socialism.[84] The suburbs became the "red belt of Paris," which they were to remain for half a century, from the 1920s to the 1970s. In this case, residence did not contribute to the assimilation of workers into the consumer society, because these suburbs were not exclusively residential and domestic as in America. Work and residence remained inextricably linked: the factory colonized the neighborhood, or rather created it altogether. The French working-class suburb was not a void, but a place of fairly dense sociability that deserves to be studied as an original political phenomenon. However, in 1914, it was barely beginning.

With the return of growth, rationalization is the order of the day: produce, gain time, save manpower. The Taylor system, introduced at the beginning of the twentieth century in a few large firms of Lyon (Berliet), Saint-Nazaire (Penhoët), Douai (Arbel), and especially Paris (where the Renault automobile factories opened in 1912) affected very few people directly—hardly more than 1 percent of workers. But it was merely the most visible part of a multifaceted reorganization of the firm, social and technical, spatial and financial. The new industrial architecture strove to achieve an arrangement of space allowing for a smoother flow of products, a more logical sequencing of operations to avoid loss of time, and better lighting. As noted before, however, a better-lit factory was a better-controlled factory. This reorganization of space was accompanied by

[84] J. P. Brunet's remarks in *Jaurès et la classe ouvrière*, ed. M. Rebérioux, "Cahiers du mouvement social" (Paris: Editions ouvrières, 1981), p. 202. This work is fundamental for what follows, and I shall refer to it frequently.

the development of a wage system more suited to the regulation of time and productivity: as a solution to the crisis of piecework, management devised an hourly rate with bonuses.

Concurrently, discipline became more severe. Regulations, imposed by the employer on the newly hired worker, were ever more detailed and lengthy; hygiene and security measures were added to all the others. Many small workshops, which had preserved large areas of freedom, were subjected to more rigorous schedules, with strict control over comings and goings. This fostered the growth of conflicts related to industrial discipline, very acute in the early part of the century, and of demands for job control on the part of the most highly skilled workers.[85] There was indeed a great contrast between the achievement of political democracy and the lack of economic democracy, the perpetuation of factory despotism. Despite a few exceptions, to be found among a handful of large firms concerned with social peace, on the eve of the war French employers adamantly maintained their "divine right" over their employees.

This situation explains in part the importance of the theme of authority in the doctrine of direct-action syndicalism. But this also preoccupied Jean Jaurès, who forcefully denounced the contrast between economics and politics, as well as men such as Alexandre Millerand, René Viviani, and Albert Thomas who sought to establish an industrial democracy founded on the recognition of social partnership and the establishment of a genuine labor contract. The idea of "workers' commissions," of "factory councils" that might negotiate with employers, got under way; but employers stiffened their stance, multiplying lockouts and dismissals. The issue of union authority within the firm was moving to the fore when war struck.

And what about the standard of living? Jeopardized by unemployment and rising prices, the purchasing power of workers remained mediocre. Seasonal fluctuations in employment were reduced somewhat and the troughs of the business cycle were not as deep as in the Great Depression; nevertheless, there was a high level of permanent unemployment, evaluated at 300,000-400,000 in 1910, a normal year. Job insecurity remained one of the great plagues of the workers' condition, a major risk of which, by the way, the state became aware. In 1910, an International Conference on Unemployment took place in Paris; its organizer was Léon Bourgeois, developer of "solidarism"—the social philosophy of the Third

[85] In addition to the study of P. Fridenson cited above in note 58, see J. P. de Gaudemar, *L'ordre et la production: Naissance et formes de la discipline d'usine* (Paris: Dunod, 1982), and the special issue of *Le mouvement social* entitled *L'espace de l'usine* (no. 125, Oct.-Dec. 1983).

Republic. The idea that employment must be managed, which would become central in the thought of Keynes, was in the making.

Wages fell between 1900 and 1905, then rose sharply between 1905 and 1913. But the gain was largely offset by a strong increase in the cost of living, steady since 1905 and rapid and brutal in 1911-1912, when Europe as a whole experienced a large-scale inflationary crisis. In France, this triggered massive demonstrations, which were severely repressed, causing a number of deaths. Overall, however, purchasing power rose significantly from 1900 to 1909, truly a Belle Epoque for employed workers. Let us note that these happy years were also the climax of direct-action syndicalism, a time of labor innovation and offensive. Real wages then declined, and even money wages were sharply reduced from 1909 to 1913, with great disparities according to regions and occupations; construction and especially the textile sector, which were experiencing a structural crisis, were the most severely affected.

With respect to consumption, food continued to absorb from 60 to 70 percent of expenditures. Although hunger had been defeated and bread was no longer a problem, meat, whose cost had risen steadily since 1880, remained an element differentiating between standards of living. Against this, the continuing decline of industrial prices and a better distribution system provided access to clothing, especially shoes, and even to watches. All sorts of aspirations crystallize around clothing, which is laden with symbols; it was the most rapidly expanding item within the working-class budget. By contrast, housing remained extremely deficient: in 1906, barely 20 percent of workers' dwelling units were provided with individual toilets. In Paris, 26 percent of the units recorded at this time consisted of only one room and 30 percent of two; hence the movement of workers toward the outskirts of the city and the suburbs. Between 1900 and 1914, Paris and Lyon both ceased to be working-class cities.

Under these conditions, saving was impossible. The concentration of wealth probably increased in the early years of the century. Although there are few studies of the subject, all indicators point to a very low degree of upward mobility, perhaps even a blockage of the popular classes and particularly of blue-collar workers.[86] The escape paths were narrow, with three major possibilities: the tertiary sector of public employment, which provided security, retirement, and perhaps dignity as well and within which new links were being forged with the state; shop-keeping, a source of great envy but also very chancy; and the practice of

---

[86] A. Daumard, *Les fortunes françaises au 19ᵉ siècle* (Paris: Mouton, 1973); F. P. Codaccioni, *De l'inégalité sociale dans une grande ville industrielle: Le drame de Lille de 1850 à 1914* (Lille: Presses Universitaires, 1976).

subcontracting, an adjunct to the development of new industries. Together, they provided for some circulation in this rather rigid society.

There was a considerable contrast between a working class that was more and more literate, educated, and increasingly a consumer of the written word, and the low degree of upward mobility it faced.[87] The Belle Epoque (1900-1914) worker undoubtedly yearned for education and dreamt of social mobility for his children, who had become fewer and concomitantly more precious. However, to an ever greater extent, mobility could take place only within the wage labor market itself. The blockage of individual mobility undoubtedly fostered the formative of a collective consciousness; but political factors made an equally significant contribution of their own, and determined some of the characteristic traits of the French working-class model.

V. *Political Syndicalism at the Beginning of the Twentieth Century*

In truth, this model provides singular contrasts between a relatively strong consciousness of identity; a minoritarian syndicalism, endowed with a striking and often attractive ideology but organizationally very weak; and finally, a very low degree of political integration—even in relation to the socialist movement—with, however, a reinforcement of this integration on the eve of the war.

Consciousness of Identity. A strong working-class consciousness rested on the alliance of a popular culture, understood in the broad sense of the term and of which family and neighborhood were fundamental components, with a sentiment of identity of which we have analyzed a few aspects. Let us remember its major characteristics: the sense of being manual workers; of being exploited by employers who, in the popular mind, have replaced feudalism; a lively attachment to freedom, which formed the basis of the sans-culotte spirit as well as of direct-action syndicalism; extreme suspicion toward all forms of authority, toward those who are referred to as "them," ranging from the state to the workshop and even including unions, whenever the "little leaders" take advantage of their functions to act like big shots. All of this was translated at the level of daily practices into numerous forms of resistance, notably in the factory: for example, the "dawdling about," denounced elsewhere by Taylor, which justified attempts at reorganization. This sentiment of

---

[87] F. Furet and J. Ozouf, *Lire et éccire: L'alphabétisation des Français de Calvin à Jules Ferry* (Paris: Ed. de Minuit, 1977).

identity expressed and reinforced itself in speech, symbols, and action. More than any other, the strike confirmed itself as the major form of working-class action; there were always over one thousand strikes per year after 1906, as opposed to a hundred or so around 1880. Decisions with respect to them were usually taken at the level of the basic work community. An instrument for exercising pressure, the strike was then also, to a greater extent than in our own time of industrial and union concentration, a means of expression in which the working class and the people within which it encased, meet again in the street they have reclaimed. Through the strike, the workers tested their strength, held themselves up as models for their brothers, and wrote their names in the common history. To go on strike was such a positive act, from the vantage point of working-class morality, that those who stayed out of it were called, by a significant twist of language, "idle." And why should it then be surprising that the revolutionary project and its scenario were embodied in the general strike? The producers' decision to withdraw, to cross their arms, will cause the world to collapse and a new society to arise. The general strike, in those days, was not a "myth" but a literal belief.

The celebration of the First of May, purposely instituted to unify the working class across national boundaries around a quasi-religious rite— all doing the same thing at the same time—has had a much broader drawing power than that of any organization.[88]

It is, of course, very difficult to measure the real extent of this consciousness of a shared identity, particularly at the individual level. Several factors contributed to foster its widespread acceptance: first, on the part of syndicalism, a strong sense of stagecraft, combining traditional symbols (religious, for example) with new ones; second, the fears voiced by the dominant classes, truly obsessed by the working-class "peril"; and finally, the works of historians themselves, fascinated by the process of crystallization. Perhaps we are dealing with a myth; but it is a strong myth, to which public opinion truly subscribed.

Minority Syndicalism. The influence of minority syndicalism exceeded its enrollments. The contrast between the widespread endorsement of syndicalist beliefs and the movement's organizational weakness is very striking. Approximately 10 percent of wage earners in 1913 were union members with, however, enormous sectoral differences: thus, miners of the north were highly unionized, as were printers. The CGT, founded in 1895 and reorganized in 1902, then numbered 100,000 members and at

---

[88] M. Perrot, "The First of May 1890 in France: The Birth of a Working-Class Ritual," in *The Power of the Past: Essays in Honor of Eric Hobsbawm*, ed. P. Thane, G. Crossick, and R. Floud (London: Thomson Press, 1984).

its prewar high point around 1910-1911, 350,000, or about 3 percent of the population eligible for union membership. This is very little in comparison with England or Germany.

French syndicalism was not only minoritarian but internally divided. Although the CGT as a whole has usually been identified with revolutionary syndicalism, this is an error; in reality, perhaps as much as half of its membership subscribed to a reformist orientation. As Jacques Julliard points out, if instead of the electoral system in use within the CGT they had adopted proportional representation, as demanded by the "reformist" leaders of the printers' and railroadmen's unions, the revolutionaries would have been reduced to a minority as early as 1904.[89] Recent works have shown that certain regions, such as Brittany, resisted revolutionary syndicalism.[90]

Nevertheless, this minority was very active in its ideological expression—direct action—and in concrete struggles, so that its influence vastly exceeded its size. More generally, as far as France is concerned, the number of formal dues-paying members cannot be used as the sole indicator of a movement's size. Most historians agree that one can consider this direct-action syndicalism "representative," as can be seen most clearly in the course of certain strikes and on the occasion of May First celebrations.

Committed to a revolutionary project, syndicalism advocated the complete overturn of social relationships and refused to accept reformism as a final solution, while being very realistic and pragmatic in daily demands. It aimed at "the total emancipation" of workers through "the disappearance of the wage system and of employers," an objective that concurrently entailed the "expropriation of capitalism" and the abolition of hierarchical relationships. The future society would be without classes, that is, without private ownership of the means of production and of exchange, but also without state authority. The legacy of Marx (in reality poorly known in France) here merges with that of Bakunin and Proudhon and to an even greater extent with the rich experience and tradition of the workers themselves.

Viewed as inevitable—there arose, at certain moments, a real revolutionary messianism—the revolution would be made by the working class, the only class that is genuinely subversive and bearer of a future. It carries on the daily struggle on the very grounds where production is going on, in the workshops and factories against the employers, and in the neighborhoods against the landlords. Everywhere the individual must

[89] Rebérioux, ed., *Jaurès*, p. 111.
[90] Claude Geslin, "Le syndicalisme ouvrier en Bretagne avant 1914" (state doctorate thesis, Paris X-Nanterre, 1982).

defend his right to freedom, to responsibility. The great revolutionary instrument is the general strike, which will make it impossible for capitalism to survive. The general strike will be turned into an insurrection by the resistance of the owners; but the violence of the confrontation, the duration of the battle—perhaps as short as a single "Great Evening"— will be limited by the solidarity of the soldiers, sons of the people, who will "raise their weapons upside down": hence the crucial importance of antimilitarist propaganda, which proliferated between 1900 and 1905.

The society of the future will be founded on the labor of all; organized according to the principle of self-management, it will rely on workers' associations to manage the factories, to regulate the pace of production, and on labor exchanges (local organizations) to regulate exchange, with barter replacing monetary exchanges whenever possible, as financial transactions are considered pernicious.

To the narrowly political vision of authority concentrated in the constitutional organs of government, the CGT opposed another and much broader one, centered on factories and working-class neighborhoods. A conflict with socialism, embodied since 1905 in the reunified SFIO (French Section of the Workers' International), was inevitable.

Syndicalism and Socialism. From the 1880s to the beginning of the twentieth century, French socialism had grown like a tree of Jesse, by the splitting of various sects and parties.[91] The unification of 1905 occurred on the basis of the propositions set forth by the Guesdists, the Marxist branch. But in reality, it was Jaurès who increasingly dominated the evolution of French socialism from 1905 to 1914. The movement was growing rapidly: 90,000 members in 1914; 1,400,000 votes and 103 seats in the April-May elections of 1914, which established the SFIO as the second largest French party, behind the Radicals.

Gaining considerable strength in rural areas, the Socialist party assuredly did not mobilize the entire working class, the more so in that it is necessary to take into account a substantial number of unregistered voters. Moreover, certain working-class communities, despite their willingness to engage in very difficult strikes, sometimes voted on the right: for example, the wool shearers of Mazamet.[92] The issue of electoral participation was a major source of confrontation between syndicalism and

[91] The basic facts are found in M. Rebérioux, "Le socialisme français," vol. 2 of *L'histoire générale du socialisme* (Paris: Presses Universitaires de France, 1974); see also the same author's *La République radicale? 1898-1914*, vol. 11 of *Nouvelle histoire de la France contemporaine* (Paris: Seuil, 1975), and *Jaurès*.

[92] Rémy Cazals, *Avec les ouvriers de Mazamet dans la grève et l'action quotidienne, 1904-1914* (Paris: Maspéro, 1978).

socialism. According to the former, the individual nature of the vote was contrary to the notion of "collective will," as expressed in meetings; and universal suffrage wrongly placed the active and the passive on the same footing. The anarcho-syndicalists struck hard at the *Votards* (ballot-box lovers), who entrust their fate to politicians, bourgeois intellectuals; they advocated massive abstention. However, it is difficult to establish to what extent they were persuasive. The urban populations remained strongly attached to the Republic and to universal suffrage; regional studies (around Lyon and in Brittany) have established a growing political integration on the eve of 1914, and an increasing level of working-class voting. Other points of friction between syndicalism and socialism included the question of arbitration, which the former believed sapped the class struggle; the role of the state; the place of the working class; and the value of patriotic sentiment.

However, their relations, which were very tense at the beginning of the century, evolved toward a mutual recognition, and a rapprochement clearly took place. This is largely attributable to the personality of Jaurès. He was concerned with achieving social unity, after having achieved the unity of socialism, and with integrating the working class into the democratic political game in order to transform democracy itself and bring about a socialist Republic. After 1905, especially, Jaurès acknowledged the representative character of the CGT and the socialist nature of the struggle waged by the syndicates, fundamentally anticapitalist organizations, well suited for mobilizing the world of work. He gradually made room for the general strike as a potential instrument of action, side by side with universal suffrage. Above all, he recognized the independence of unions affirmed in the Charter of Amiens (1906): "Syndicalism can be powerful and a friend of socialism only if it possesses the pride of autonomy," he wrote in 1912.[93]

The CGT was undergoing an evolution of its own. There were several reasons for this: the hardening of the Radical regime's stance toward the labor movement, of which Jaurès emerged as the most eloquent defender; the rise of international tension, which revealed to syndicalist leaders the fragility of proletarian internationalism and fostered a rally of the French left; the failure of the attempted general strike of May 1, 1906; the increasing percentage of strike failures, indicative of the growing resistance of employers, also manifested by tough lockouts.

---

[93] *1906: Le Congrès de la Charte d'Amiens*, full proceedings, published by the C.G.T.'s Institut d'Histoire Sociale, in *Les Congrès de la C.G.T.* (Paris, 1983). The famous document known as the "Charte d'Amiens," often referred to by the French labor movement, established the complete autonomy of political and union functions and proclaimed the absolute necessity of union independence.

To these classic reasons, I would add innovative thinking among CGT leaders between 1910 and 1914, notably around Alphonse Merrheim and the magazine *La Vie Ouvrière*. This stream of thought insists on the importance of economic problems, the complexity of capitalist society, and the necessity of studying these questions in order to develop a more appropriate form of action.[94]

All these reasons account for the rapprochement between the CGT and Jaurès. In 1913-1914, facing the likelihood of war, the French labor movement acknowledged Jaurès as one of its leaders, and regarded the SFIO no longer as an adversary but as a potential ally. This perhaps marked the beginning of a broad-gauged transformation of syndicates and the acknowledgment of a new system of industrial relations. Tragically interrupted by the war and the Russian Revolution, this evolution is perhaps resuming its course in France today.

[94] Dominique Baillaud, "La C.G.T. et les problèmes économiques (1905-1914)," unpublished study summarized by myself in *Histoire économique et sociale de la France*, ed. Labrousse and Braudel, vol. 4, pt. 1, pp. 530ff.

4 The Distinctiveness of Working-Class Cultures in France, 1848-1900

• *Alain Cottereau*

I. *From Employers' Dissatisfactions to the Illusion of Worker Acculturation*

Throughout the nineteenth century, the French working class had the reputation of being particularly rebellious toward industrial discipline. Compared with its counterparts in Britain, the United States, and Germany, it was characterized in the eyes of contemporary observers by an obstinate resistance to the order of the factory system, the rhythms of industrial activity, and the morality of productive labor. But an examination of the conditions under which these judgments were produced casts doubt on their validity. It reveals that the flood of moralistic, philanthropic, and public health literature on which they are founded stems from a common origin of employer discourse. The same perceptual mechanism of worker behavior turns up repeatedly: employers, never satisfied—by definition—with the extent to which workers accepted their exploitation, communicated to the great nineteenth-century surveys a whole range of judgments concerning the gap between actual and ideal behavior, as they dreamed of it: hence the record of lack of discipline, laziness, absenteeism, neglect of savings, inability to plan for the future, and the like.

On this foundation was erected a very general conceptual system, shared from the very onset of industrialization by all the dominant social strata, employers, notables, officials, Catholic clergy, and social workers. The various behaviors of workers were perceived, in opposition to employer norms, as the result of dispositions particular to certain groups, trades, or regions. These dispositions were dressed up in a multiplicity of conceptual guises: trade or regional temperaments, mentalities, customs, and work habits; or finally various moral qualities, such as docility or lack of it, love of work or its rejection.

THIS ESSAY was translated from the French by Aristide R. Zolberg.

These intellectual constructs stem from a logical process similar to that which led to viewing as "routine" all peasant practices that did not conform to the dreams of agronomists and modernizing rural notables. In both cases, the demands of social change—industrial capitalism in the one, agrarian capitalism in the other—are taken as unquestioned givens; in the face of these demands, worker and peasant practices are considered merely in terms of their degree of adaptation or resistance to change. In this manner, there emerged an implicit problematic to the formation of the French working class that might be dubbed "culturalist." As used here, the term refers to (1) a problematic of social change imposed from the outside, to which dominated classes can respond only by adapting or resisting; and (2) a problematic that entails the internalization of external demands, that is, acculturation, the incorporation of new habits and new values.

A variety of social scientific currents have contributed to reinstate this culturalist approach. In the field of French working-class history, the rare studies concerned with the life of workers more often than not merely take up the vision of philanthropic surveys, without subjecting them to critical evaluation. Particularly illustrative of this tendency is the work of G. Duveau, which is still used as a standard reference.[1] More surprisingly, the same employer perspective has recently been reinvigorated in France on the basis of the work of Michel Foucault. New compilations of the philanthropic literature have simply transcribed bourgeois obsession with the development of an industrial morality into Foucault's language: what would be called in the United States "industrial acculturation" is termed in France "disciplinarization," "deployment of technologies of authority," and the like.[2]

To the extent that they uncritically adopt the perspectives of industrialists, philanthropists, and government officials without taking into consideration those of the workers, and to the extent that they fail to deal with the actual industrial practices of both, such problematics obscure the most important questions raised by the formation of industrial working classes.

However, the rejection of culturalist illusions also leads to a critique of certain self-proclaimed Marxist approaches, and more particularly the

[1] G. Duveau, *La vie ouvrière en France sous le Second Empire* (Paris: Gallimard, 1946).
[2] The consequences of Foucault's philosophical position for social history have been demonstrated by Danielle Rancière in "Le philanthrope et sa famille," *Les révoltes logiques* 8/9 (1979), pp. 99-116. Within Foucault's framework, historical research becomes a sort of paranoid analysis, as any social control is interpreted as a coherent consequence of magical intentions of "le pouvoir."

use of the notion of "class consciousness." It is not merely a matter of rejecting the teleological vision of a progressive growth of consciousness; it is the very notion of "class consciousness" that becomes a problem, once it is used as an operational concept to characterize degrees or levels of worker consciousness in historical processes. There is here a sort of symmetry with the culturalism discussed earlier: social change is conceived as resulting from the initiative of capital alone, in the face of which the working class has no choice but to submit or to rebel. Moreover, this approach also entails a questionable problematic of internalization; but this internalization is now located between two poles—either internalization of the interests of capital, or of the higher interest of the working class, which one would pretend to be determinable, at least from the transcendent point of view of a historian.

Against these approaches, the reconstitution of worker practices and points of view can shed light on a crucial dimension of working-class formation: how the practices of workers proceed from logics and strategies adapted to the situations that they confront and how these practices sometimes bring about a reversal of such situations. Once the blinders imposed by "acculturation" or industrial "disciplinarization" are eliminated, the subject of "working-class formation" itself comes to be replaced by a multitude of uncertainties and questions. For example, instead of a so-called process of disciplinarization within the factory, one is led to detect an abundance of dialectics and of sequences between, on one side, exploitative mechanisms, and on the other, dodges devised by workers against them. In this light, it can be seen that every one of the multiple paths leading toward "modern" industrial forms entails a response to some concomitant form of worker resistance, with each of the latter itself constituting an adaptation to some older technique of exploitation. But, reciprocally, the workers can sometimes pull ahead of the game and temporarily defeat established techniques of exploitation.

In the same manner, it no longer makes sense to focus the analysis on the greater or lesser degree of "class consciousness." Instead, one is faced with questions concerning different logics and practices, both individual and collective and more or less mutually contradictory. Instead of an idealist problematic of "degrees of consciousness," it becomes possible to develop an understanding of oppositions and divisions among workers, a concrete analysis of the conditions under which particular groups of workers establish their social identities, and of fixations and displacements among these identities.

The formulation of such questions does not pretend to map a new approach.[3] However, it will be noted that in the literature on French working-class formation, the questions set forth here are rarely faced all at once. Conceptual revisions have seldom gone beyond the stage of essays based on secondary or even more remote evidence. In contrast with this, French social history has not been very receptive to philosophical and anthropological questions concerning the production of "meaning." Hence, this presentation of the French case will be limited to a sketch of various aspects of the overall question and to a formulation of questions appropriate for a comparative approach. The essay relies on a limited number of published works, as well as on the firsthand research I have conducted on the cultures of French workers during the past decade, most of it still unpublished.[4]

II. *Workers' Experience of the Industrial Revolution: The Productivist Race*

To understand how workers experienced the industrial revolution, it has turned out to be particularly useful to reconstitute in detail practices and points of view of workers, and to compare them with the better-

---

[3] The debate between E. P. Thompson and the English Althusserians has revealed some of the stakes involved in the analysis of "working-class cultures." See, among others, R. Samuel, ed., *People's History and Socialist Theory* (London: Routledge and Kegan Paul, 1981), the last section, "Culturalism: Debates around 'the Poverty of Theory.'"

[4] For a critical review of the state of French historiography on working-class formation, see A. Lincoln, "Through the Undergrowth: Capitalist Development and Social Formation in 19th century France," in Samuel, ed., *People's History*, pp. 255-67. Outstanding examples of conjunctions between contemporary philosophical critiques and firsthand historical research are provided by the journal *Les révoltes logiques*, 1976-1982. To be noted as well is the fundamental work by Jacques Rancière, *La nuit des prolétaires* (Paris: Fayard, 1981), which thoroughly alters our understanding of French utopians by initiating us to their very modes of thought. My own previously published work on the subject, which includes further discussion of problems of interpretation, includes the following: "Pouvoir et dérision du pouvoir dans le Paris de l'avant—et l'après Commune, in *Prendre la ville, esquisse d'une histoire de l'Urbanisme d'Etat* (Paris: Ed. Anthropos, 1977); "Déjà au XIXe siècle, ouvriers et luttes urbaines," *Autrement* (June 1976):207-217; "Méconnue, la vie des enfants d'ouvriers au XIXe siècle," *Autrement* (August 1977); "La tuberculose à Paris, 1882-1914: Maladie urbaine ou maladie de l'usure du travail? Critique d'une épidémiologie officielle," *Sociologie du travail* (June 1978); "Les jeunes contre le boulot: Une histoire vieille comme le capitalisme industriel," *Autrement*, no. 21 (October 1979); "Vie quotidienne et résistance ouvrière à Paris en 1870," introduction to the reprint of Denis Poulot, *Question sociale: Le sublime* (Paris: Maspéro, 1980); "Usure au travail, destins masculins et destins féminins dans les cultures ouvrières en France au XIXe siècle," *Le mouvement social*, no. 124 (July-Sept. 1983):71-112; "La prévoyance, des uns, imprévoyance des autres: Questions sur les cultures ouvrières, face aux principes de l'assurance mutuelle, au XIXe siècle," *Prévenir* 9 (May 1984):57-68; "Les règlements d'atelier au cours de la révolution industrielle en France," introduction to Anne Biroleau, "Les règlements d'atelier, 1798-1936," Bibliothèque Nationale, Paris, 1984.

known practices and views of their employers. This perspective leads to a reconsideration of accepted historical wisdom concerning the industrial revolution, and calls into question the three classical oppositions that are generally considered self-evident: between work at home and in the factory; between craft and industry; and between manual and mechanized labor. Generally speaking, the experiences of workers cut across these oppositions and hence challenge their analytic relevance. For many French workers, change occurred in the form of the industrialization of "collective works," a process that can be analyzed by examining the case of weaving.

The *fabrique collective* ("collective works") was a familiar category of nineteenth-century France, largely forgotten by historians. The term did not refer to a physical establishment (e.g., a workshop or factory) but rather to a system of production, encountered as early as the seventeenth century, within which specialized enterprises of all sizes (from the very large establishment to the cottage) contributed to the elaboration of an article of trade. Within such works, relationships between enterprises could range from cooperation between capitalists to wage earning in the form of piecework. In its most usual sense, a "collective works" was thus a whole consisting of parts located in close proximity to one another and linked by the fate of their merchandise on the market. For example, one can speak of the "Lyon silk works," the "Sedan woolers fabrique," or the "furniture fabrique of the Faubourg Saint-Antoine" (in Paris). The term "collective" appears at first rather odd, because the enterprises under consideration are not concentrated but rather dispersed and are linked by a division of technical operations. At the level of social relationships, the contours of the "fabrique collective" are somewhat blurred and must be more precisely delineated for each case.

In nineteenth-century France, the system of "fabrique collective" pertained to most branches of industry, with the exception of mining, as well as parts of steel, metallurgy, and wool and cotton spinning. Everywhere else, the "collective works" was the usual framework within which the industrial revolution took place. This included, among others, weaving, hosiery, lacemaking, ready-to-wear clothing, most of mechanical engineering, furniture making, building, the bulk of the food industry, and so forth—in short, over nine-tenths of nineteenth-century French industrial activity.

The Case of Handweaving. Contrary to the impression of "decline" suggested by French economic historians, handweaving in fact underwent considerable expansion until 1874-1875, and one can infer from various statistical series that only from the mid-1890s on did more weavers work at mechanical than at hand looms.[5] Even in the cotton sector, symbol of the most rapid progress of mechanization, power weaving of a given type of cloth might coexist with the production of new types of cloth manufactured by handlooms.[6]

This suggests a most elementary comparative question: what is the significance, for working-class formation, of the expansion and then the vitality of handweaving in France throughout the second half of the nineteenth century? One cannot be satisfied with an explanation in terms of technological or developmental "backwardness," as if there were merely a time lag between France and Britain, when it is most evident that we are in fact faced with a difference of processes. Let us remember that in Britain, handweaving collapsed to the benefit of the mechanical sector within a very short time span, 1830-1840, especially in cotton weaving, and that this process gave rise to national crises, vast political economy debates, and profoundly shaped the formation of the English labor move-

[5] These statements are based on two series of sources gathered by the Ministry of Commerce, the Commission on Customs, and annual economic statistics. These series are not very consistent and can be used only to establish an order of magnitude. This was cross-checked with totals obtained by estimating, for each fiber and period, the relationship between the number of looms and the number of workers, on the basis of extrapolations from local monographs. In his thesis on *Les paysans de la Normandie orientale* (Paris: A. Colin, 1909), J. Sion analyzes the decline of handweaving during the second half of the nineteenth century, and his work remains the standard reference to this day. Yet by way of periodization, he merely identifies the moment when cotton weaving is "terminal," in the sense in which a patient is declared "terminal" by medical authorities. He locates this moment in 1839. For the subsequent period, during the last two-thirds of the century, he speaks of the "resistance" or "stubbornness" of the peasants. However, by the same token, he seems to see nothing of the economic transformations of handweaving, ignoring, particularly, the redivision of labor between factories and handlooms. The approach of the classic work of Claude Fohlen, *L'industrie textile au temps du Second Empire* (Paris: Plon, 1956), is hardly different, symbolized as it is by vitalist metaphors of the same genre. Textile centers that have lasted to this very day are studied under the title of "residual industries." These analyses as a whole stage a Manichaean struggle between the industries of the past and the industries of the future. In his overall periodization, he labels as irreversible the regression of handweaving in the cyclical crisis of 1867, without examining what happened to them after the Second Empire.

[6] For example, in Roubaix in 1884-1886, the number of handloom workers was equal to those in the mechanized sector. In Thizy, a cotton-weaving town where a rapid wave of mechanization occurred in 1876-1877, handweavers remained the majority as late as the mid-1890s. Local monographs with confirming information include: E. Juillard, *La vie rurale dans la plaine de Basse Alsace* (Paris: Société d'edition Les belles-lettres, 1953); Gabriel Désert, *Les Paysans du Calvados, 1815-1895* (Lille: Université de Lille 3, Service des thèses, 1975); M. Marcheteau, "L'industrie textile à Laval," *Bulletin du cercle d'études géographiques du Bas-Maine*, nos. 4, 5, and 6 (1952). The assertion concerning the rate of mechanization of cotton weaving in France is even more applicable to wool and silk, where mechanization always came later and was more spread out in time. New silk handweaveries were still being established in the Dauphiné in the 1890s, and employment in mechanical weaving of silk exceeded handweaving only around 1906-1910. See Yves Lequin, *Les ouvriers de la région lyonnaise, 1848-1914* (Lyon: Presses de l'Université de Lyon, 1977), 1:84-85.

ment. Although this raises numerous prior questions concerning the French economy, technological transfers, and the like, we cannot deal with these here and will turn immediately to the implications of this process for the specific experiences of French weavers.[7]

In contrast with the emphasis on "survival" found in the literature, the weavers' vision of their work evokes a universe of permanent change. The very rare individual testimonies suggest this by descriptions of injustices perpetrated by employers. Among other things, they enumerate the constant flow of initiatives by supervisors to accelerate the rhythm of work. These pressures began very early and might operate openly by means of a specification of ever more restrictive schedules and deadlines.[8] Most of the time, however, they come into play implicitly by the mechanism of subcontracting—probably as important in the industrialization of France as J. H. Clapham has shown it to be for Britain—and the regulation of wage levels.[9] This is extremely well documented by the weavers' perennial concern with the issue of piece prices (tarifs).[10] The general innovation, which from the perspective of workers fundamentally altered the meaning of the old collective works, was the near-permanent revision of the rates: at the beginning, seasonally, from two to four times a year; and then with each new order, each time a piece of cloth was turned in. In the eighteenth century it had already appeared scandalous from the workers' point of view that "work no longer has a price." Now, however,

---

[7] The basic reference for comparisons between the French and British economies in the nineteenth century remains, on the French side, the series of studies published by the *Cahiers de l'ISEA*, 1961 to 1965, whose main contribution was to cast doubt on the superiority of British "development" by demonstrating the similarity of per capita income in the two countries. The problem was taken up again more recently by Patrick O'Brien and Caglar Keyder in *Economic Growth in Britain and France, 1780-1914: Two Paths to the Twentieth Century* (London: Allen and Unwin, 1978). Using the same data base, they criticize the historiography of French retardation and elaborate the hypothesis of two different paths of development. Another interpretation of this was set forth by M. Lévy-Leboyer, "Les processus d'industrialisation: Le cas de l'Angleterre et de la France," *Revue historique* (Apr.-June 1968):281-99.

[8] Among recently reprinted testimonies, see: C. Noiret, *Mémoires d'un ouvrier rouennais* (1836; Paris: Editions d'Histoire Sociale, 1979); and Norbert Truquin, *Mémoires et aventures d'un prolétaire à travers la Révolution* (Paris: Maspéro, 1977), pp. 130-86.

[9] J. H. Clapham, *An Economic History of Modern Britain: The Early Railway Age, 1820-1850* (Cambridge: Cambridge University Press, 1926). An important exception for the French case is: B. Mottez, *Systèmes de salaires et politiques patronales* (Paris: CNRS, 1966). Additional information can be found in Rémi Gossez, *Les ouvriers de Paris, Livre 1, L'organisation, 1848-1851*, vol. 24 of Bibliothèque de la Révolution de 1848 (Paris: Société d'histoire de la Révolution de 1848, 1967).

[10] Although references to the issue of rates can be found in all the well-known archival sources (Interior, Agriculture, Commerce, Justice) as well as in parliamentary and governmental inquiries, the adoption of a narrowly economic perspective has caused them to be neglected because they did not lend themselves to the construction of time series. However, the decoding of strategies and social relationships renders them highly interesting.

all written or tacit piece-price agreements, which regulated interactions within the old collective works like a series of cease-fires, were eliminated.

Another fundamental facet of the same phenomenon was the constant decline of piece rates. Historians are quite familiar with this; but they have hardly taken into consideration its challenging implications for the classical view of industrialization, namely that it points to the considerable and generalized increase of the individual physical productivity of French handweavers throughout the nineteenth century.[11]

This highlights a crucial feature of the formation of the French working class in comparison with the classic English case. Analyses of the rapid collapse of English handweaving are concerned with explaining the occurrence of a catastrophic process—"catastrophic" in the precise sense in which a process has no other outcome than its destruction. They bring into consideration the following more or less concurrent sequence: (1) the lasting invasion of the labor market by a surplus of weavers in the course of conjunctural crises; (2) within this context of surplus manpower, a lowering of wages by internal competition; (3) the progressive abandonment of the handweaving market by traditional male weavers, to the benefit of women and Irish immigrants; (4) the failure of all attempts to fix rates in the face of declining wages. In most cases, it is only when an advanced degree of "sweating" is reached that there is a massive disappearance of handlooms, while within the same employment pools, competing mechanical looms easily pick up the manpower that has been cast adrift. "Easily" means here at low wages and within the framework of a factory discipline whose imposition is facilitated by the fact that the "factory system" appears on the scene as an economic savior.[12] It should be noted that in contrast with the French case, one does not observe in

---

[11] There are other possible ways of measuring individual physical productivity, in particular by reconstructing over the long term quantities of raw materials or of finished product by occupation or per capita. For example, here are the results of some rough calculations regarding the dispersed ribbon manufacture (ribbon "collective works") of Saint-Etienne, for which a great deal of economic data, deriving from employer sources, is available. The data deal with the average per capita consumption of silk and cotton by the workers performing the weaving and its ancillary tasks (i.e., the preparation and loading of the looms but not the dyeing and finishing) and have been calculated for boom years, supposing full employment of the workers and looms. The consumption of raw materials per weaver in the dispersed manufacture of Saint-Etienne in 1839 (ribbons only) was 6.8 kg of silk; in 1855 (ribbons and velvet), 26 kg (21.4 kg of silk and 4.6 kg of cotton); and in 1895 (ribbons and velvet), 59 kg (32 kg of silk and 27 kg of cotton). If the products remained homogeneous, this would imply that real productivity per weaver increased by a factor of 8.7 in fifty-six years. Since products actually evolved, the increase in individual productivity was probably a little less.

[12] I. Pinchbeck, *Women Workers and the Industrial Revolution, 1750-1850* (London: Virago, 1981), pp. 157-82; M. Berg, *The Machinery Question and the Making of Political Economy, 1815-1848* (Cambridge: Cambridge University Press, 1980), pp. 226-52; D. Bythell, *The Handloom Weavers* (Cambridge: Cambridge University Press, 1969).

England a renewal of handlooms on the basis of growing productivity, except in isolated cases. This absence may be to a certain extent an artifact attributable to historiographic blinders; but the victory of the "factory system" is so rapid and general that we must conclude that the labor productivity of factories was much more evident in Great Britain than in France.

From the vantage point of productivity, the relationships between work in the factory and at home would thus appear to have been reversed on the two sides of the Channel. Echoing this are the views of weavers concerning work discipline. In France, until the 1890s, weavers might feel themselves much more free in factories than when they worked at home. Concomitantly, employers justified "putting-out" not only by the fact that it entailed a lesser amount of fixed capital, but also because it facilitated the imposition of rhythms, rates, and labor discipline on dispersed weavers. In contrast, in the course of the struggles and debates on mechanization of weaving in England, the domestic system came to be associated very early with the "love of freedom," whereas the factory meant the "mechanization of men."[13]

Such reversals constitute a paradox as long as one insists on attributing a single meaning to the opposition of factory work to domestic work; to resolve it, it is necessary to revise the link between productivity and mechanization taken for granted in the classical view of industrialization. The spectacular achievements brought about by the mechanization of cotton spinning have too often been erected into generalizable prototypes of the processes of industrial mechanization; yet cotton spinning is merely one type of technological change and is perhaps even a thoroughly exceptional one. Indeed, it is this very exceptionalism that led to its becoming the star case of classical political economy, and of its Marxist critique. But weaving represents another type altogether, and perhaps a much more usual one. Throughout the nineteenth century, the "technical" effect of weaving operations, whether steam or manual, remained absolutely inseparable from the intensification of work and hence from the array of nonmechanical devices to control its rhythm. M. Berg has brought out this relativity of procedures with respect to English weaving factories:

It was quite clear to many that the productivity of the power loom was not its greatest asset. Consistent production time, and control and supervision over manufacturing processes in the factory were rather its most powerful attrac-

---

[13] See Berg, *The Machinery Question*, pp. 244-45. This same classical alternative between the craftsman's freedom and the mechanization of men within the factory system is used as the analytic framework for U.S. workers by R. Rogers, *The Work Ethic in Industrial America, 1850-1920* (Chicago: University of Chicago Press, 1978), pp. 65-94.

tions to the manufacturer. Working-class discipline also had something to do with the differing labour conditions between the two techniques. The Bolton Committee was aware of this: "The chief advantage of powerlooms is the facility of executing a quantity of work under more immediate control and management, and the prevention of embezzlement, and not in the reduced cost of production."[14]

To the contrary, the prevailing stereotype concerning the "traditionalism" of the handlooms has hidden from view a multiplication of transformations of the organization of work and of the techniques of handweaving, less spectacular than the Jacquard or the flying shuttle, but nevertheless highly effective in bringing about an acceleration of the individual work rhythm for all kinds of cloth.[15] There was also a steady increase in the control supervisors exercised over the organization of work. Testimony from workers enables us to trace this growing control on many different levels: conception of the drawings, invention of new weaves, treatment of the thread, disposition of the workplace, and many others. There are also a number of hagiographical museum-minded monographs that insist on the former feats of skill carried off by the "traditional weavers." But a major change in work ethics and aesthetics remains to be analyzed: a slippage of the criteria of skill away from an ability to conceive products and production processes toward the contest for speed and reliable repetitive gestures set up by the employers' "design."

These hidden dimensions of control over work procedures are summarized in the particularly fortunate formula of a Rouen handweaver: *"Today's workers are not workers, but machines, totally deprived of intelligence*, and this because the masters corner all the industry's profits, so that the interest of workers is limited to the greater or lesser ease they experience in securing work, and also because *daily misery and worry fetter their genius."*[16]

[14] Berg, *The Machinery Question*, pp. 241-42.

[15] It would be very interesting to examine the manner in which the analysis of the mechanization of cotton spinning was transferred uncritically to the analysis of the mechanization of weaving. Yet throughout the nineteenth century, the multiplier effect of mechanical looms fell far short of the claims set forth by cultists of Progress. Most historians of technology have fallen into the trap set by promoters, accepting as a norm productivity levels achieved under ideal conditions. For example, David S. Landes has written that by the mid-1820s, "one boy on two mechanical looms could do up to fifteen times as much as the cottage artisan," a technical advantage raised further to the level of 20:1 by 1833 (*The Unbound Prometheus* [Cambridge: Cambridge University Press, 1969], p. 86). Were this true, the history of weaving in nineteenth-century France would make no sense whatsoever.

[16] Noiret, *Mémoires*, p. 64 (emphasis added). With respect to the downgrading of intelligence and the illegitimacy of capitalist organization of work, Noiret's book should be

Whereas the classical view posits the "mechanization of men" as a consequence of the mechanization of tools, Noiret posits the mechanization of men as a process prior to the mechanization of tools. He locates, in his way, the de-skilling process of handweaving. The formulation "workers deprived of intelligence," coupled with the image of the "fettered genius" presupposes, as if it were self-evident, that work brings about a demobilization of intelligence. Yet that does not mean intelligence is thereby destroyed; rather, it is made to suffer in the face of the violence of the market and of the organization of work. Thousands of protests and conflicts involving weavers brought before tribunals, hundreds of answers to parliamentary inquiries from 1848 to 1886, could thus be decoded as indicators of the forced demobilization of know-how, and as worker-initiated challenges to the legitimacy of the organization of work.

That industrialization, in France, largely involved the industrialization of domestic work, demonstrates the irrelevance of the classic opposition between "domestic work" and "factory work"; much in the same vein, an elucidation of the system of industrial subordination demonstrates the irrelevance of the craft/industry polarity. Beneath the apparent stability of the "craftsman" label, there took place a complete transformation of the organization of work—its rhythms, techniques, and stimuli—and of accompanying modes of conflict between employers and workers. The example of weaving, simultaneously rural and urban, can be extended to the whole range of French collective works.[17] The "mechanization of men" Noiret speaks of occurred among all of them, regardless of the degree of mechanization of tools. Here, the most significant phenomenon is not the degree of subordination to automatic machines, but the fact that the employers systematically begin to intervene in the organization of work, breaking the direct link between workers' conception and execution of tasks.

In this manner, the criteria of industrialization, elaborated in a way that transcends the English model, lead to the delineation of a more general theory of the social relationships that constitute "industrialization"—and other equivalent terms such as "takeoff," "growth," and industrial "development." We must limit ourselves here to merely suggesting the possibility of such a theory, by an outline of a few characteristic traits. Globally, industrialization can be characterized as the

---

read in conjunction with his two long letters, written five years later, published by Jacques Rancière in *La parole ouvrière* (Paris: UGE, 1976), pp. 105-141.

[17] For examples of industrialization of collective works under the cover of so-called craft shops, see Lequin, *Les ouvriers*, 1:52-76; and Cottereau, "Les jeunes contre le boulot," as well as "Vie quotidienne," pp. 63-81.

permanent exercise of productivist pressure over labor and capital:

(a) Productivist pressure is brought to bear on the organization of work itself, on its rhythms and procedures. In this, it can be distinguished from the old autonomies of work, with their customs and relatively stable crafts. The old modes of subordination to capital occurred more indirectly, through transactions and commercial policing.[18]

(b) This results in permanent pressure to reorganize labor and to lower qualifications. The centers of capitalist control—international trade, department stores, brokers, industrialists—redistribute work, constantly rearrange operations, entrusting the largest share of the process to a labor force that is unskilled, that is, without acknowledged skills: day laborers, women, youths, elderly, and so forth.

(c) Capitalist control extends over work procedures: it is interposed between the wage earner's thought and gestures. The transformation of tools into machines is one of the possible strategies to achieve this objective, but not its necessary condition.[19]

(d) Productivist pressure is limited only by the resistance of workers. Herein lies, in my view, the most universal foundation of working-class cultures. On this basis it might be possible to reconstruct a general reevaluation of all the formative experiences of capital/labor

---

[18] In the language of French Marxist debates of the past decade concerning the "transition" to capitalism, it is a matter of analyzing the processes of the "real" subordination of wage labor to capital, against its "formal" subordination. Unfortunately, the debate is itself sometimes very formal. Most of the time, it relies on the most classical model of industrialization, labeling "formal appropriation" anything that does not fit within it. But the interesting problem is to establish how "real" appropriation can occur under the appearance of a maintenance of traditions. One should also avoid imagining that the older collective works allowed workers greater autonomy in the organization of production. What was new was not the advent of capitalist control, but rather a change in the mode of capitalist control. For an analysis of the changing modalities of control of older French collective works, see in particular J. C. Perrot, *Genèse d'une ville moderne: Caen au 18ème siècle* (Paris: Mouton, 1975).

[19] These four points are an extension of the problematic developed by Harry Braverman, *Labor and Monopoly Capital* (New York: Monthly Review Press, 1974); and by M. Freyssenet, *Le processus de déqualification-surqualification de la force du travail* (Paris: Centre de Sociologie Urbaine, 1974), as well as the same author's *La division capitaliste du travail* (Paris: Savelli, 1977). Using the example of weaving, we have tried to suggest that it would be fruitful to move even farther from technological evolutionism. In that spirit, see in particular R. Samuel, "The Workshop of the World," *History Workshop*, 3 (1977). Everything he writes on the importance of technologies that fall outside of the classical model for nineteenth-century Britain is even more applicable to the French case. Much of what he says on the subject is still applicable to contemporary industrial countries. For example, a recent survey by the French Ministry of Labor shows that even today, only a very small minority of workers are subjected to mechanical contraints on their work rhythm; only 8 percent work on the assembly line. See: "Enquête sur les conditions du travail, Octobre 1978," *Bulletin mensuel des statistiques du travail* 71 (1979). We are far from the stereotype of mechanized work and from the realization of Andrew Ure's utopia of the subordination of industrial work to great automata.

relationships. This new focus on domination might also be stated in terms reflecting the familiar experiences of all generations of wage earners, whether among early or late industrializers, when first entering into the domain of industrialized work: they must of necessity set a limit to the rhythm of work demanded of them, whatever the level of the limit might be, lest they succumb beneath the burden of their task.[20]

III. *Workers' Cultures against the Functioning of a Labor Force*

With respect to the contributions of various patterns of industrialization to the formation of workers' cultures, the French case can be viewed as a hinge between the group of early industrializers—among them Britain, the United States, Germany, and France itself—and Latin Europe—Italy, Spain, and Portugal. Industrialization through dispersed collective works is commonly encountered in Latin Europe, but it is rarer

---

[20] This broad reconceptualization of "industrialization" recaptures forgotten dimensions outlined by nineteenth-century theorists, and in particular by Frédéric LePlay and his school. The concept of "collective works" was elaborated by LePlay himself in *Les ouvriers européens*, 2d ed., 6 vols. (Tours: Mame, 1877-79); and later in *Les ouvriers des deux mondes*, five series, 12 vols. (Paris, 1857-1913: Société Internationale, then Firmin Didot, then Société d'économie sociale). Subtle analyses of industrialization and of exploitation in dispersed urban collective works are to be found in the studies of LePlay's disciple Pierre Du Maroussem, among them *La question ouvrière*, 4 vols. (Paris: A. Rousseau, 1891-94); and in the official publications of the Ministère du Commerce, Office du travail, *La petite industrie: Salaire et durée du travail*, 2 vols. (Paris: Imprimerie Nationale, 1893-1896). This conceptualization is also consistent with many of Marx's observations, later repressed by economistic Marxist traditions, as in the following unambiguous passage that extends the concept of industrialization beyond the mere mechanization of tools and the concentration of workers in factories: "Along with the development of the factory system and of the revolution in agriculture that accompanies it, production in all the other branches of industry not only extends, but alters its character. The principle, carried out in the factory system, of analysing the process of production into its constituent phases, and of solving the problems thus proposed by the application of mechanics, of chemistry, and of the whole range of the natural sciences, becomes the determining principle everywhere. . . . Independently of this, a radical change takes place in the composition of the collective labourer. . . . This is the case not only with all production on a large scale, whether employing machinery or not, but also with the so-called domestic industry, whether carried on in the houses of the workpeople or in small workshops. This modern so-called domestic industry has nothing, except the name, in common with the old-fashioned domestic industry, the existence of which pre-supposes independent urban handicrafts, independent peasant farming, and above all, a dwelling-house for the labourer and his family. That old-fashioned industry has now been converted into an outside department of the factory, the manufactory, or the warehouse. Besides the factory operatives, the manufacturing workmen and the handicraftsmen, whom it concentrates in large masses at one spot, and directly commands, capital also sets in motion, by means of invisible threads, another army: that of the workers in the domestic industries, who dwell in the large towns and are also scattered over the face of the country" (Karl Marx, *Capital* [London: L. Wishart, 1974], 1:434).

in Germany, and even more so—but not altogether absent—in Great Britain and North America. In keeping with this, one would expect to encounter in France more Latin forms of conflict. However, the French case is closer to Great Britain, the United States, and Germany with respect to the articulation between the political sphere and other dimensions of workers' cultures. Therein lies the distinctiveness of the cultures of French workers in the second half of the nineteenth century.

The Common Experience of Dispossession and the Variety of Resistance Practices: The Example of Shoemakers. The analysis developed by E. P. Thompson concerning the entry of "artisans" into the sphere of industrial capitalism might, as a first approximation, account at the same time for common features and for differences among the two sets of countries indicated above. In all cases, the reaction of "artisans" in the face of industrialization is founded on the same fundamental logic: illegitimacy of the new economic order; enhancement of independence and freedom; claims in the name of the rights of man against the liberal-utilitarian order; universalization of public references in the name of a working class. Within this, variations could be explained in terms of two dimensions. First, that of time: what took place over about forty years in England stretched over nearly a century in France, and was similarly spread out in the other Latin countries. Second, to the extent dispersed collective works were relatively more important in the Latin group, the dialectic of dispossession of so-called craft work went on for a longer period as well.

Paralleling Thompson's analysis, and against the illusion that the consciousness of workers was formed by the factory experience, Jacques Rancière set forth the following general formula for the formation of the French working class:

The idea of the proletarian revolution is inexorably contemporaneous with the discourse of this workers' vanguard (i.e., the "utopian" artisans of the first half of the nineteenth century), who think and act not in order to prepare a future where the proletarians would inherit the legacy of a great capitalist industry formed by the dispossession of their labor and their intelligence, *but rather to arrest the mechanism of this dispossession.* This does not represent an attachment to the past—in what sense are the large collective workshops in which tailors seek to manufacture ready-made clothing less modern than the domestic work that is being organized by capitalists?—but rather the sentiment of a present that is the threshold of two equally likely futures: that of capitalist organization that, in each craft, announces, by the reorganization of the work process, an exacerbation of competition among workers, or the reinforcement of shop discipline, the instoration of a new slavery; or that of the "free and voluntary" association of workers. It is on the basis of an awareness of this choice that the idea of workers' emancipation is formed, an idea to which the theory of proletarian revolution comes to be grafted later on. The starting point is not the consciousness of proletarians formed in the "school of the factory" but rather that the consciousness of those determined to reject this school altogether.[21]

In recent years, a number of works inspired by Thompson have drawn attention to the importance of the conflict between capitalists and "craftsmen" in Latin countries, and a focus on this has in turn revealed the multiplicity of attempts by workers to arrest the process of dispossession. But a consideration of these various experiences casts some doubt on what Thompson held to be a certainty: the correspondence between varieties of work experience on the one hand, and workers' cultures and the relationship to the political sphere on the other.

Let us take the example of shoemakers, comparing analyses drawn from the United States and Great Britain with the French situation in the second half of the nineteenth century. Some features of "collective works" emerged in all three cases, but machines and factories entered into play very differently. Amazing similarities can be traced between forms of work and of culture among shoe industry workers in Paris and London.[22] Among other things, one finds the same types of division of labor and the same types of antagonisms among workers. Contemporary inquiries relate these work situations to the shoemakers' alleged "character," "temperament," or "mentality": in Paris as in London, they were reputedly very concerned over their independence and inclined to engage in meditation, which was predicated on the availability of long stretches of work suitable for solitary thought, without requiring the mobilization of their attention to the activities of their fellow workers.

Given these similarities, how can one explain the divergences between Paris and London shoemakers, which became quickly manifest from the 1884 economic crisis on? Whereas of all the London trades threatened

---

[21] J. Rancière, *La parole ouvrière*, pp. 22-23. Emphasis in original.

[22] This is based on an unpublished comparative work on Paris and London trades in the second half of the nineteenth century. For London shoemakers, I have used classic printed sources, among them: Henry Mayhew, in *The Unknown Mayhew*, ed. E. P. Thompson and Eileen Yeo (London: Pelican, 1973); C. Booth, *Life and Labour of the People in London*, esp. 1st series (London: Macmillan, 1892-1903), 4:69-137; French and English reports by workers' delegations to various world's fairs, 1862-1889; A. Fox, *History of the National Union of Boot and Shoe Operatives, 1874-1857* (Oxford: Oxford University Press, 1958); E. J. Hobsbawm, *Labouring Men* (London: Weidenfeld and Nicolson, 1964). For Paris, I have used mostly unpublished archives from various ministries, the Prefecture of Police, as well as workers' and employers' newspapers. Among printed sources, see: Ministère du Travail, Office du travail, *Enquête sur le travail à domicile dans l'industrie de la chaussure* (Paris: Imprimerie Nationale, 1914).

by the institution of a sweatshop system, shoemakers put up the most successful resistance, in Paris the resistance of shoemakers collapsed altogether, and a certain kind of sweatshop system was more successfully established in the shoe industry than in other Parisian apparel trades. In London, the employers' strategy quickly came to be opposed by effective counterpressures directed against the system of production itself. The employers had imposed a partial mechanization of the lasting and finishing processes, in order to develop a type of sweating called the "team system," involving the employment of unskilled personnel—children, women, elderly—as adjuncts to the skilled workers who subcontracted shoe parts at home. Workers in London—and in other centers such as Leicester and Bristol—reacted by completely overturning the erstwhile production ideal: in 1887-1892, unions and strikes secured considerable support by advocating a shift to the factory system, as opposed to domestic subcontracting, in order to be in a better position to impose workers' control over wages, qualifications, and rhythms and procedures of production. The compromises that came to be established after a period of very strong control by workers (1890-1895) maintained the development of the factory system as a consequence of the convergence of employers' and workers' strategies. The employers regained the initiative as far as mechanization and organization of work were concerned, but worker pressure led to collective negotiation and to local wage scales that put dispersed production systems at a disadvantage.

In Paris, the ideals of quality, made-to-measure, handsewn shoes and of autonomous mobility outside the factory were to be maintained until the 1920s. The relationship between Paris and the provinces was very different from its counterpart in Britain, even if some decentralization began to occur in both cases. In France, there was a moderate growth of the factory system in the provinces, whereas the capital acquired a system very close to the sweatshop, and yet distinct from the English type. The Paris system remained skill intensive and recruited craftsmen expelled by provincial mechanization. The team system did make its appearance in Paris in the course of the 1884 crisis, but remained less widespread than in London.[23] The difference between the systems of pro-

[23] I have taken the concept "skilled intensive" from a working paper by C. Sabel and J. Zeitlin, "Historical Alternatives to Mass Production" (October 1981), which the authors kindly made available. The use they make of it in their comparative analysis of forms of production in Great Britain and France is very persuasive and enlightening. A new version of this paper, "Historical Alternatives to Mass Production: Politics, Markets, and Technology in Nineteenth-Century Industrialization," was published in *Past and Present*, no. 108 (August 1985):133-76. It provides new views on many of the questions raised here, but the present chapter, completed some time ago, was not able to discuss

Table 4.1. Boot and Shoe Operatives by Sex and Type of Employment

	France		England and Wales	
	Number	%	Number	%
Working on own account				
men	94,831	54.0	38,190	17.0
women	6,147	3.5	1,300	0.6
total	100,978	57.5	39,490	17.6
Employed in workshops or factories				
men	59,492	34	138,185	63
women	15,728	9	41,644	19
total	75,220	43	179,829	82
Total work force				
men	154,323	88	176,375	80
women	21,875	12	42,944	20
total	176,198	100	219,319	100

SOURCES: *Census of England and Wales, 1891. Age, Conditions as to Marriage, Occupations . . .* , vol. 3 (London: HMSO, 1893), table 5; *Statistique générale de la France. Résultats statistiques du recensement général . . . 1901,* vol. 4, 2d section (Paris: Imprimerie Nationale, 1905), table 7.

duction of the two countries thereby became so marked that it was discernible in official census statistics (see table 4.1).

The contrast between Paris and London is no less sharp when one considers mechanisms of resistance to employer pressure. In Paris, the trade unionism of shoemakers was extremely weak and functioned only in spurts, on the occasion of strike movements that were hardly "organized" but that revolutionary leaders attempted to channel. In London, within the shoemakers' organization, roles were reversed; leaders were relatively moderate and leaned toward compromise solutions, whereas more radical delegates influenced decisions during periods of improving strategic posture. But the most remarkable contrast yet is to be found in the patterning of daily conflict. In London, shop practices usually relied on usages, scales, and local regulations supported by unions; in Paris, daily resistance usually arose without the benefit of a normative framework formulated by a workers' organization.

Should we attempt to establish a one-to-one correspondence between particular experiences of work and particular forms of working-class cul-

them. It seems to me that many of our propositions are convergent. When our perspectives differ, they are very compatible and complementary. In particular, the dimension of "flexibility" of production, developed in their article and omitted here, might complete and reinforce my analysis.

ture, we would find that the evidence mustered for each case separately would be invalidated by the juxtaposition of the several cases. For example, it might be argued that in the case of London, the craftsmen's shared experience of dispossession facilitated the organization of an effective reaction against sweating and disqualification of the shoemaking trade, on the grounds that this previous experience provided sufficiently strong cohesion to enable workers to overcome their internal divisions, fostered a common front against the team system, and contributed to a compromise outcome—a negotiated factory system. But in Paris, the same common experience of dispossession and of de-qualification would explain just as self-evidently how workers reacted on behalf of the preservation of work autonomy, how the spirit of independence fostered a certain suspicion toward trade union discipline, and how shoemakers responded to the most varied ideologies, as these expressed a radical demand for social relationships founded on something other than competition among workers and capitalist accumulation among businessmen.

An examination of small-manufacturing towns devoted to shoemaking further suggests that common work experiences do not necessarily result in the same culture and political orientation. Let us take the cases of Lynn, in the United States, as studied by Alan Dawley, and of Fougères, in France.[24] Describing the transition from a dispersed industrial system to a factory system, Dawley suggests that the "mentality" of Lynn shoemakers was fashioned in the course of the first phase:

Their lives were intersected by contrary historical crosscurrents: small-scale household production and large-scale mass production, the personal ties of small-town life and the gnawing impersonality of the city. Despite the impact of industrial capitalism, preindustrial influences were still strong. Thus the consciousness of the artisans was shot through with contradictions; they proclaimed they were freemen who knew no master, but worried they were slaves to their employers. They spoke for a community of harmonious citizens, but organized themselves to strike. They were the lords of creation, but also the wretched of the earth.[25]

The transition toward the factory was accelerated by the economic crisis of 1857 and the great strike of 1861. In contrast with Britain, the factory system was founded on defeats in strikes. Then, however, workers quickly built up considerable strength. Dawley attributes their coherence

---

[24] Alan Dawley, *Class and Community: The Industrial Revolution in Lynn* (Cambridge: Harvard University Press, 1976). For Fougères, in addition to archival sources, I rely on the series of articles by Claude Geslin, "Le combat des chaussonniers de Fougères, 1887-1907," in *Le Pays de Fougères*, nos. 1-5 (Fougères, 1975).

[25] Dawley, *Class and Community*, p. 63.

and capacity for protest and organization to the old common experience of the craft:

Factory workers in the shoe industry were able to organize because most of them had been shoemakers in prefactory days. This gave shoeworkers a common identity through a continuity of shared ideas and experiences. They remembered the self-reliance of the artisan and recalled the time when the tasks of shoemaking intimately intermingled with the tasks of family and community life: when the journeyman was husband to the binder, father to the young helper, neighbor to the shoemaker family next door; a time when the binder was at once shoemaker and homemaker, arranging time for each task according to the needs of the day; a time when the journeyman was both shoemaker and householder, whose daily activity followed the intertwining rhythms of both roles.[26]

The small town of Fougères in Brittany also contained until the 1870s a majority of "craftsmen," working in scattered shops, at home, regrouped into a local community and inserted into mass production. However, the very same factors that would seem to account for the cultural and organizational strength of the craftsmen of Lynn appear to account in Fougères for their weakness. At the organizational level, most visible of all, one observes the absence of any lasting labor organization until 1887. The few small strikes noted before this date ended in defeats. At the cultural level, official observers and labor spokesmen concur in their reports of a barely constituted milieu, without coherence, marked by competition among individuals and categories. Neither the defensive outlook of craftsmen nor that of factory workers had penetrated Fougères. In case of unemployment, the population could live from agricultural wage labor, whereas in prosperous times, they could hope to become agricultural owner-operators, small businessmen, craftsmen, or small independent producers of shoes. The rapid development of factories in the early 1870s apparently did not modify this picture until the end of the 1880s. One could provide for Fougères an explanation that is the exact opposite of the one Dawley gives for Lynn: "In Fougères, factory workers in the shoe industry were *unable* to organize because most of them had been shoemakers in prefactory days." Indeed, as was commonly said by militants disappointed in their potential troops, preindustrial habits can involve individualism, rivalries, and a desire to get by on one's own.

We thus become aware of the indeterminacy of the notion of "shared experience" or of "common identity." The "personal ties" of the small town do not necessarily lead to the beautiful—overly beautiful?—spec-

[26] Dawley, *Class and Community*, p. 176.

tacle of solidarity and harmonious citizenship suggested by Dawley in the case of Lynn. As for Fougères, a more subtle inquiry that does not stop at "nonorganization" suggests patterns of activity among workers opposite to those reported in Lynn, and more or less opposed to one another. One finds, on the one hand, rules of urban mono-industrial clientelism; and on the other, rules of collective defense by means of individual mobility, common to French collective works more generally, and carried over into Fougères factories.

The urban clientelism of Fougères, which is found in other French mono-industrial small towns as well, is very different from the paternalism associated with the locally dominant large establishment. Its distinctive feature is a sort of tacit compromise between employer and worker controls. Employers secure from stable workers a certain degree of allegiance, whereby they are willing to ignore frontiers between place of work, family life, and urban life; the counterpart of this is that the authority of employers is contained within strict limits. Symmetrically, the spheres of worker autonomy ignore the frontier between private life, public life, and life in the factory. This is manifested among other things, from 1870 to 1896, by the workers' refusal of employer control over the organization of work procedures; conflicts over the authority of foremen or work procedures often resulted in at least partial worker victories.

Although collective defense by means of individual mobility may appear to constitute an antagonistic reaction to clientelism, in practice the two patterns could coexist either by segmenting a given workplace between stable and unstable workers, or by alternating practices from factory to factory. The guiding principle of this type of collective defense was simple: leave the factory as soon as an employer tries to impose wages, work procedures, or disciplinary rules that are too strict in the eyes of workers, yet do not resort to real strikes or "damnations." It should be noted that such practices, in appearance individualistic, are part of a collective game and require the collusion of the entire worker community. Mobility took place at the same time between factories, between factories and domestic work, between industrial sectors, and between industrial and agricultural work, within the same region or in different regions.

Industrial Discipline and Control of Work by Workers. Urban clientelism and collective defense by mobility provide two examples of collective practices that were very current in the second half of the nineteenth century. In a sense, we find ourselves here at the level of what David Montgomery called "group ethical codes" that were internal to certain trades, to be distinguished from two more formally organized levels: the level of "union work rules," also internal to trades, and the level of "mutual supports" between different trades.[27]

The examples chosen so far have suggested the importance in France of informal conflicts, hardly visible if one adopts the usual state-centered vantage point. These conflicts cast doubt on the historiographic traditions according to which strikes and formal organization are the most reliable indicators of "worker militancy" or class consciousness. In the case of Fougères, the absence of unions and the near-absence of strikes before 1887 suggest "apathy," although in reality other systems of defense and control were operating. In fact, this example can probably be generalized to all of France, which appeared "silent" from the vantage point of political listening posts and the repressive judicial apparatus.

The mechanisms by which French labor exercised such implicit power have hardly been studied per se, but it is possible to trace their manifestations in numerous local histories and monographs. A very suggestive example concerning the rural textile and hosiery industry in Picardy is mentioned by P. Pinchemel.[28] In the course of the locally prosperous period of 1870-1882, workers were able to raise their wages while reducing work time to only four days a week. This suggests that rural workers were able to impose among themselves and on employers a control of weekly rhythms that according to historiographic tradition was reserved to the most skilled and most traditional trades of large cities. It is possible to identify beyond formal organizations a universe of worker controls made up of unstable practices, the objects of constant pressures and counterpressures, that concerned scales, wage systems, hiring and firing, allocation of space, and so forth.[29] A few monographs regarding particular trades at the national level also provide descriptions of such informal practices; but in those cases, they are founded on exceptionally strong formal organizations, as with printers and hatmakers, among whom worker controls are closest to the trade controls recorded in the British and U.S. historical literature.[30]

[27] David Montgomery, *Workers' Control in America* (Cambridge: Cambridge University Press, 1979), pp. 11-27.

[28] P. Pinchemel, *Structures sociales et dépopulation rurale dans les campagnes picardes de 1836 à 1936* (Paris: A. Colin, 1957), p. 114.

[29] Poulot, *Le Sublime*, and A. Cottereau, "Vie Quotidienne." Practices similar to the ones denounced by Poulot can be spotted in all large cities by reading between the lines of employer complaints. These practices often preceded organized forms or survived their disappearance. This is where worker controls are closest to the trade controls identified by David Montgomery for the United States and abundantly documented in the tradition of social history for Great Britain.

[30] J. Vial, *La coutume chapelière: Histoire du mouvement ouvrier dans la chapellerie* (Paris: Domat-Montchrestien, 1941); P. Chauvet, *Les ouvriers du livre en France de 1789 à la constitution de la Fédération du Livre* (Paris: M. Rivière, 1956).

In the absence of published materials, I suggest the following working hypothesis on the basis of my own research:[31] In France, throughout the nineteenth century, wherever industrial productivist pressures came to be systematized, there arose forms of collective control that were independent of any institutionalized organization—that is, outside mutual aid societies, unions, and strike committees. This is the key to the distinctive character of French working-class formation in comparison with Britain, the United States, and Germany. The originality does not lie in the existence of informal controls, since current research is tending to discover such controls in all countries; rather, it consists of the particularly acute disjunction between informal controls and institutionalized organizations.

Every workers' community reputed to be unorganized and apathetic that I have studied has revealed the existence of collective control practices. An example is the Mayenne cotton cloth works, a "fabrique collective," simultaneously rural and urban, reputed to be among the most conservative and apathetic of nineteenth-century France.[32] Yet it is possible, on the basis of the archives of local magistrates, to reconstruct permanent pressures on local practices concerning hiring, payment, mobility, and contract enforcement. Furthermore, employers complained that in the years 1860-1882, they were unable to impose the production of certain novelties, because workers accepted only products that enabled them to maintain freedom of work rhythms and to maintain a multiplicity of annual activities and resources, tied to agricultural cycles. One can guess at sharp divisions between the minority of households no longer making a living from anything but cloth, disadvantaged by these rules, and the majority of households, playing on the diversification of resources. Of course, the establishment of these rules was part of a compromise outcome; if employers failed to impose the production of certain novelties, they made up for it by paying much lower wages than in the neighboring Laval works, thus using the diversification of worker resources to force them to transfer some income from agriculture and thereby letting the agricultural sector bear part of their manpower costs.

The Thiers cutlery works provides a similar example of worker controls that remain invisible in terms of the usual indicators. The abundant local literature has insisted on the permanence of "craft" traditions because of

[31] These statements are based on my current research, generally based on local archives, on the daily conflicts, collective practices, and local practices among French working-class cultures at the time of the industrial revolution.

[32] For published manuscript sources, see J. Omnes, "Les débuts du syndicalisme ouvrier en Mayenne (1890-1901)" in the journal of a very lively society for local history, L'oribus, No. 1 (December 1980):B1-B31.

the persistence of dispersed manufacturing in the town and its environs. For 130 years, from 1852 to 1982, the authors of local monographs dramatized the timing of their observations, believing themselves to be on the eve of an inevitable transition to the factory system, as had occurred in the two other competing world centers, Sheffield and Solingen. Each time, the authors attributed the apparent apathy of local workers, paralleling the alleged traditionalism of employers, to an individual craft "mentality." Yet it is the case that in keeping with the gradual industrialization of the cutlery works, which would bear reexamination, worker counterdisciplines arose against employer controls, against piecework wages, against pressures to foster competition among workers. In their correspondence, employers complained about the strict rules imposed by workers against the productivist race, sanctioned by anonymous sabotage, which could not be repressed in an authoritarian manner.[33]

The existence of informal worker controls among urban and rural collective works invites us to reexamine worker-imposed discipline in large-scale establishments, mines and factories. The various forms of worker discipline did not evolve independently from one another. It is possible to find among French factories types of controls similar to those found among collective works. Earlier attention was drawn to the case of weaving factories: in France, they operated in general more slowly than their English counterparts, because of the control workers exercised over rhythms. Since factories were components of large production systems, pressure to speed up rhythms within the factory was constrained by the norms established among dispersed workshops.

French historiographic tradition has often presented large factories as places of total bondage, under the conjoined impact of misery, machines, and paternalist policy. But such images rest on very questionable interpretations. They rely mostly on the literature generated by philanthropic employers who played up the factories they considered best managed, those that succeeded in imposing their order via draconian shop regulations and in stabilizing their personnel by means of company-run institutions of social assistance. Among the star factories were the Mulhouse mills and a handful of mills in the north; a few large metallurgical factories (among them Le Creusot and Imphy); and a few large mining companies (Compagnie d'Anzin, the Douchy mines). A roster of top management honors, which one can easily retranslate into a roster of

---

[33] The vast literature on the cutlery industry in Thiers uses as its principal source the encyclopedic study by Camille Pagé, *La coutellerie depuis les origines jusqu'à nos jours*, 6 vols. (Châtellerault: H. Rivière, 1896-1904).

maximum bondage, was established by E. Cheysson in his report to the Social Economy Section of the 1889 world's fair.

Unfortunately, too often historians have unduly generalized on the basis of such documents, presenting as "employer ideologies" or as "employer policies" results that were exceptional and the opposite of the most common employer habits. For example, if one were to examine the correspondence of employers with ministries and parliamentary representatives, one would become aware that most employers in the largest factory and mine sectors were opposed to recommendations advocating employer paternalism, which they considered unrealistically utopian and attributable to a handful of particularly privileged employers who were in a position to dominate local manpower markets. Their arguments always came down to this: if they attempted to apply the paternalistic models of Mulhouse, Le Creusot, or Anzin, they would no longer be able to recruit anyone because workers would surely reject such humiliating conditions. Coming back to the well-worn formula of nineteenth-century French employers, whose full implications have not yet been fully appreciated, they insisted that they "preferred to keep their freedom" rather than attempt to link the fate of the workers to that of their factories.

One is thus forced to admit the reality of informal worker controls from this negative reading—a consideration of the constraints that imposed limits on employer practices. These limits are at the source of all the charges of "lack of discipline" with which official discourse on the French working class is replete. But when instead of stopping at this "lack of discipline" one reconstructs positively the collective practices that are at their source, the landscape of social relationships takes on a new meaning. At the most general level, there emerges a fundamental illegitimacy of social relationships, manifested indirectly through the always unstable and circumstantial character of compromises established between employers and local worker groups. These are similar to the collective practices analyzed by Montgomery and Thompson.

Those contemporary academic investigators most concerned to understand social relationships, and who did not distort their descriptions in order to legitimize the status quo at that level, made no mistake about this. Adolphe Blanqui concluded his 1848 inquiry by insisting on the rooting of the social movement in "ordinary" relationships. In his view, something irreversible had occurred. The return to political calm after the revolution should not hide the new antagonism on which social relationships were now founded:

The troubles that sometimes make so many good people lose their bearings stem from the abuses of which they have had grounds to complain, without being able to quite explain them. The extreme severity of manufacturing regulations, the abuse of fines for slight rule-breaking, the excitement produced by so many unexpected and sudden events, the sufferings that resulted from them, the disloyal preachings that soured them, everything has contributed to aggravate the moral malaise of the working classes; and this great pressure has hidden from sight the special causes whose impact is greatest in ordinary times. Today, one can no longer hope that we shall so soon navigate in calm waters, with a good breeze and under mild latitudes. All social relationships, even the ones that undergo least change at the sound of revolution, will have to cope with gale winds, and it will be necessary for us to act together in order to make the house livable for tenants who have become more demanding.[34]

In 1873-1874, a retrospective balance sheet of employer-worker relationships established by the "Parliamentary Commission on Working Conditions in France" noted, according to questionnaires answered by industrialists and various collectivities throughout France, that employer-worker antagonisms had steadily progressed over the past thirty years. In its summary report, the subcommittee that dealt with relationships within the firm deplored the fact that this state of fundamental disagreement extended to all of industry and all regions, well beyond the realm of open struggles and the influence of working-class organizations. As they expressed it in their conclusion, "the spirit of antagonism seems in some sense to have become a way of life."[35]

Manpower Recruitment and Worker Defense Systems. How is the disjunction between informal controls and institutionalized organizations found in France to be explained? One likely explanatory factor has already surfaced in the various examples cited: the ability of workers to acquire some control over the work process presupposed a relative shortage of manpower. In the weaving industry, sweating in France was never as catastrophic as in Britain because the dumping of alternative manpower on the market—substitution of women for men, of immigrants for locals—was not possible. This relative shortage is intimately linked to the relations between rural labor and urban wage earning, between family structure and occupational mobility.

The elucidation of these questions is rendered difficult by the compartmentalization between historical demography and social history, between history of the industrial world and rural history. The major exception to this is the study of Yves Lequin on the recruitment and

[34] Adolphe Blanqui, *Des classes ouvrières en France pendant l'année 1848* (Paris: Pagnerre, 1849), pp. 221-22.
[35] Assemblée Nationale, Commission d'enquête sur les conditions de travail en France, *Rapport présenté au nom de la 2ème sous-commission par M. L. Favre* (A.N., Archives parlementaires, C. 3025), p. 4. The official report is more stereotyped and distorts the answers given to questionnaires and the subcommittee syntheses.

mobility of workers in the Lyon region from 1852 to 1914.[36] His extensive intergenerational research should put an end to a persistent myth, already undermined by more limited findings: French industrial workers in the second half of the nineteenth century did not constitute an uprooted mass. With respect to geographical areas of recruitment, Lequin refines the gross understanding that might be drawn from official census statistics and a handful of local demographic studies, that is, in comparison with other western countries, immigration contributed in a very limited way to the growth of cities and industrial zones, a growth whose rate was itself more moderate than most. Most internal migration within France came from neighboring areas. Lequin shows that the only exceptions to this in the Lyon region pertained to more distant areas with traditional links to the receiver and hence confirm that, at this level, there never was any "uprooting." More generally, French censuses, which distinguished early on among native-borns between those originating in the department and others, suggest that the incidence of internal migration was lower in France than in other industrializing countries.

Lequin's most original contribution pertains to intergenerational mobility. Against the notion that the worker population was formed by agricultural recruitment, he shows the proportion of industrial workers whose fathers were agriculturalists to have been very low and to have declined further in the course of the second half of the nineteenth century. This finding completely invalidates numerous economic and demographic interpretations that assumed, on the basis of censuses and economic history, that the French agricultural crisis of the last quarter of the century precipitated an agricultural exodus toward industry. Another remarkable conclusion is the very large share of what Lequin calls "occupational heredity." In the middle of the nineteenth century, between 54 and 65 percent of urban workers at the time of their marriage belonged to the same occupation as their fathers; at the beginning of the twentieth, the proportion still ranged between 43 and 53 percent.

With respect to more general demographic processes, there are unfortunately very few class-specific studies of natality, fertility, and family structure.[37] It appears that from the very beginning of the century, workers nearly everywhere engaged in Malthusian practices, much as the

[36] Lequin, *Les ouvriers*, vol. 1, *La formation de la classe ouvrière régionale*. A partial summary of Lequin's findings concerning geographical and intergenerational mobility can be found in "La formation du prolétariat industriel dans la région lyonnaise au 19ème siècle: Approches méthodologiques et premiers résultats," *Le mouvement social* 97 (Oct.-Dec. 1976).

[37] The major statistical source remains: Statistique générale de la France, *Statistique des familles en 1906* (Paris: Imprimerie Nationale, 1911). The work of J. L. Flandrin,

rural population was doing. Temporary increases in fertility occurred, but overall, compared with other western countries, the French working-class family was distinctive in its small number of children. Here again, the only regional exceptions are found in the north and the northeast, and the only atypical industrial sector in the country as a whole is mining, within which families are always larger. L. Tilly and J. Scott have sketched the "household wage-earning economy" of these two important exceptions;[38] but one should not generalize about France as a whole on the basis of these cases.

The lower general fertility of France, and in particular of worker households, constitutes a factor of crucial importance that gives an original stamp to all aspects of working-class culture and to social relationships. One way of expressing the quantitative difference with other western countries is to compare age pyramids—for the total population, for the gainfully employed, and by occupation. An illustration is a comparison of female populations in France and Britain (see figure 4.1). The proportion under twenty-five percent among active women was 30 percent in France, against 54 percent in England and Wales. Similar differences would be found between France, on the one hand, and the United States and Germany, on the other. All by itself, such a situation would already provide a good indicator that the issue of industrial recruitment and concomitantly of worker control posed itself differently in France.

Another peculiarity, which opens up a number of questions concerning the sexual division of labor in France, emerges from the comparative

---

Familles, parenté, maison, sexualité dans l'ancienne société (Paris: Hachette, 1976) contains relevant comparative observations, even though his major concern is with peasant families under the Ancien Régime. The study of P. Guillaume, *La population de Bordeaux au 19ème siècle* (Paris: A. Colin, 1972), provides a historical demographic overview applied to social-class differences. Concerning the geographical mobility of workers in the course of their lives, the classic foundation is the large work by A. Châtelain, *Les migrants temporaires en France de 1800 à 1914*, 2 vols. (Lille: Université de Lille 3, 1976). With respect to rural depopulation, one could cite many geographical studies. In the matter of intergenerational mobility, few works were available before Lequin's thesis; some elements can be found in P. Guillaume. William Sewell, Jr., in "La classe ouvrière de Marseille sous la Seconde République: Structure sociale et comportement politique," *Le mouvement social* 76 (July-Sept. 1971):27-65, has published data on geographical recruitment by occupation in Marseille and proposed a framework of analysis for occupational recruitments in terms of whether the trades were open or closed to persons from outside the city. The research of L. Tilly and J. Scott on household economies are examined in the text below. There is a great deal of firsthand research currently under way. All these studies, based on civil registry records or individual census returns, reveal the fanciful character of older demographic interpretations based on official censuses alone and on bourgeois "common sense," such as the interpretations of L. Chevalier.

[38] L. A. Tilly and J. W. Scott, *Women, Work, Family* (New York: Holt, Rinehart and Winston, 1978).

Figure 4.1. Age Pyramids of Economically Active Women and the Total
Female Population in France (1901) and in England and Wales (1893)

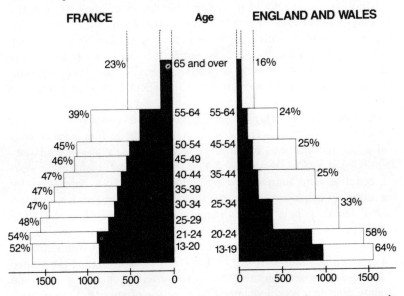

SOURCES: For France, *Statistique générale de la France. Résultats statistiques du recensement général . . . 1901*, vol. 4 (Paris: Imprimerie Nationale, 1905); for Great Britain, *Census of England and Wales, 1891. Age, Conditions as to Marriage, Occupations . . .*, vol. 3 (London: HMSO, 1893).
NOTE: Each bar represents total female population (in thousands) for age group indicated; dark portion represents number economically active. Percentage is rate of activity for each age group.

analysis of rates of economic activity of married women among early industrializers (see table 4.2): 40 percent active among married women in France, as against less than 10 percent in the United Kingdom, Germany, and the United States! To consider all the questions suggested by this dramatic variation would require a vast research program, all the more so because it does not seem to have aroused much attention among French labor historians.[39]

[39] The variation itself has occasionally been noted in demographic works, and is particularly emphasized by J. Daric, *L'activité professionnelle des femmes en France: Etude statistique, évolution, comparaisons internationales*, INED, cahier 5 (Paris: Presses Universitaires de France, 1947). Tilly and Scott are aware of the variation but underestimate its significance by attributing the French situation mainly to certain demographic factors, namely lower marriage age and lower general fertility. In reality, a careful comparative examination of age pyramids by occupational sectors would show that statistical

Table 4.2. Economically Active Women by Marital Status (percent active of total population within each marital status category)

Country and Year	Unmarried	Married	Widows
France, 1901	58.3	40.0	37.6
United Kingdom, 1911	69.3	9.6	29.4
Germany, 1895	52.3	9.1	40.5
United States, 1900	43.5	5.6	32.5

SOURCE: T. Deldycke, H. Gelders, and J. M. Limbor, "La population active et sa structure," *Statistiques internationales retrospectives,* vol. 1 (Brussels: Université Libre de Bruxelles, 1969).

These overall differences must be related to the singularity of nineteenth-century France in its relationship between agricultural and industrial development. Once more, it is necessary to begin by pointing to the absence of research on agricultural wage earners and therefore of analysis concerning the links between agricultural and industrial work.[40] However, with respect to agricultural development, research oriented' toward the rural economy has provided us with explanatory models of the growth of small-scale agricultural enterprise that overcome the conventional problematic of French "backwardness" in relation to agricultural capitalism of the English type.[41] They demonstrate how a capitalist dynamic could subject rural parcelization to productivist pressure, taking advantage of familial labor without resorting to concentration, large-scale enterprise, or the expansion of agricultural wage earning. The difference in patterns of development resulted in impressive divergences in the numbers of agricultural wage earners in France and Britain.[42] Capi-

differences stem from fundamental differences in the structures of female employment and that these differences pertain to all sectors of economic activity.

[40] An important but relatively isolated exception is the historical panorama of social relationships in French agrarian capitalism by G. Postel-Vinay, *La rente foncière dans le capitalisme agricole* (Paris: Maspéro, 1974). On the relative importance of rural wage labor, see Gabriel Désert, *Les paysans du Calvados, 1815-1895* (thesis, Université de Lille 3, 1975), in which the author speaks of "rural deproletarianization" throughout the nineteenth century. But the most important evidence is to be found in pre-1914 law theses.

[41] See the theoretical synthesis by J. Servolin, "L'absorption de l'agriculture dans le mode de production capitaliste," *L'univers politique des paysans dans la France contemporaine,* ed. Y. Tavernier, M. Gervais, and C. Servolin (Paris: A. Colin, 1972). This work initiated an important intellectual trend that subsequently influenced rural economics and "sociology of development" more generally. See, for example, A. Mollard, *Paysans exploités: Essai sur la question paysanne* (Grenoble: Presses de l'Université de Grenoble, 1977).

[42] For a synthesis of historical statistics, see J. C. Toutain, *La population française de 1700 à 1959* (Cahiers de l'ISEA. AF 3, January 1963).

talist farming in England—not including Scotland—was reflected in a ratio of 83 percent wage earners against 17 percent farmers or independent producers. In France wage earners constituted merely 45-50 percent of the agricultural active population in the first half of the nineteenth century, and their relative share subsequently decreased steadily until they constituted only 39 percent of the total in 1911. Nonetheless, in a country where agriculture still accounted for 42 percent of all active at the beginning of the twentieth century, the importance of small family farms should not blind us to the substantial contribution of rural wage earners to the formation of industrial manpower. In 1851, the mass of rural wage earners was one-third larger than the industrial; sixty years later, the industrial mass was one-third larger than the rural. On the other hand, it should be noted as well that the number of rural actives who were not wage earners was approximately equal to the number of industrial workers.

Considered in purely economic terms as a "labor market," France was characterized from 1852 on by a permanent relative shortage of rural and industrial wage labor. From this date on, the lack of agricultural wage workers is a subject of perennial distress and the object of a multitude of reports and inquiries by local societies and advisory boards. One of the most striking features of the situation is the permanent competition between agricultural and industrial employers. The complaints of the latter enable us to identify the exercise by workers of a variety of defensive strategies, and the constant two-way flow between agricultural and industrial work. The "temporary migrations" of agricultural wage earners, enumerated in detail in the agricultural survey of 1852 and analyzed by A. Châtelain, seem to extend throughout the second half of the nineteenth century, though changing character.[43] Contrary to what occurred earlier, one never again finds masses of day laborers driven out by unemployment in the course of economic crises. Hence, on the recruitment side, industrialists could rarely rely on "reserve armies." Most of the time, they had to divert workers by offering them higher wages, which helps to explain why in France the implantation of factories and mines tended on the whole to be viewed initially by local wage earners and businessmen as a blessing, before giving way to phases of disenchantment.

This context invites us to raise a series of questions concerning the links between the formation of French working-class cultures and the evolution of rural cultures. One of the most original characteristics of French

---

[43] Statistique générale de la France, *Enquête agricole de 1852* (Paris, 1852); Ministère de l'Agriculture, du Commerce et des Travaux Publics, *Enquête économique de 1866*, 28 vols. (Paris, 1867-72); A. Châtelain, *Les migrants temporaires.*

working cultures can be located in the fields of family lifestyles and the social division of labor.

With respect to the sexual division of labor and household economies, France distinguishes itself by the parallel importance of the work of married women in both the agricultural and industrial sectors. Martine Ségalen has shown effectively how ideologies pertaining to the sexual division of roles in peasant families could hide actual practices. In reality, peasant women devoted a considerable share of their time to working in the fields and their activities extended widely beyond the so-called feminine tasks to which they were confined by contemporary ideologies.[44]

These remarks could be extended to agricultural wage work. In France, an exceptionally high proportion of married women and aged widows remained within the agricultural wage-work sector throughout the nineteenth century, whereas female wage work in agriculture disappears from English agrarian capitalism as early as the first half of the nineteenth century, in accordance with an English process revealed by I. Pinchbeck.[45] One encounters the same originality among female day laborers in industry and commerce, together with a high degree of mobility with respect to employment in all three of these sectors at all stages of life.[46]

Tilly and Scott have undertaken a comparative analysis of various models of "household economy" and proposed global interpretations that can serve as a basis for further analyses.[47] However, their models are not sufficiently precise to highlight the originality of the French case. They analyze the passage to industrial wage work as a slower transition than elsewhere, between "household production" and the "family wage economy." But these two categories remain too general and vague. J. Servolin has already reminded us that, in relation to the peasant family economy, the industrial wage-work environment transformed the small peasant into a sort of self-employed person, who paid himself a salary shaped by the level of ongoing industrial wages.

But the most original feature of the French transformation, it seems

---

[44] Martine Ségalen, *Mari et femme dans la société paysanne* (Paris: Flammarion, 1980). Her historical monograph, *Nuptialité et alliance: Le choix du conjoint dans une commune de l'Eure* (Paris: Maisonneuve et Larose, 1972), provides an exemplary study of what an historical anthropology of the transition from agricultural labor to rural industries might be, far removed from the folklorist commonplaces and the stereotypes of the *mentalité* approach.

[45] Pinchbeck, *Women Workers*, pp. 85-110.

[46] These phenomena of recruitment and mobility have not, to my knowledge, been brought out for France, and I can support these contentions only by referring to the census sources, the great governmental surveys of the nineteenth century, as well as to my own ongoing research based on archives and civil registry records.

[47] Tilly and Scott, *Women, Work, Family*.

to me, is the development of a household economy founded on multiple sources of income. In France, worker households living on industrial wages alone constituted a small minority. In addition to one or more industrial wages, there were agricultural incomes (revenue from the sale of owner-produced crops, gathering, agricultural wages, rent revenue);[48] wages as employees or as domestics; revenue from small businesses or gardening; and income from exchanges among relatives and friends outside of commercial circuits. Moreover, the rural sector contributed to the distinctive patterning of productivist pressure in France. "Pressure" is to be understood here literally: in England, the New Poor Law of 1834 was designed to cut off the possibility of "escaping" from the productivist race. But it was impossible to institutionalize such mechanisms in France, notwithstanding "philanthropic" protests against what was considered the overindulgence of Catholic charity. As it was, the agricultural sector and its rural environment functioned as a permanent refuge from industrial productivist pressures. It constituted, so to speak, the French proletarian's unemployment compensation, his hospital, and his poorhouse.[49] The possibility of escape worked in both directions: in the zones of agrarian capitalism (in the north and the Parisian basin), large farmers were increasingly complaining of the lack of discipline among agricultural day laborers, who resorted to techniques of resistance developed in the industrial sector, displaying a spirit of "insolence" moralists believed to be characteristic of skilled workers in large cities.

IV. *Working-Class Cultures and the Political Sphere*

We have seen that the configuration of the labor market enabled French workers to defend themselves effectively without relying on legally recognized formal organizations. However, it would be one-sided to limit ourselves to this explanation. We have tried to compensate up to this point for narrowly organizational and political analyses that consider the working class merely as a source of political intervention. But this is not to say that politics does not matter; rather, the adoption of a vantage point external to the political sphere should enable us to identify more

[48] In *La rente foncière*, Postel-Vinay insists on the importance of rent income for agricultural as well as other wage earners until the end of the nineteenth century. According to Ministry of Agriculture surveys, the proportion of agricultural day laborers who owned some landed property was 56.6 percent in 1862 and still 48.7 percent in 1892.
[49] A. Cottereau, "La tuberculose," and "Usure au travail, destins masculins et destins féminins dans les cultures ouvrières françaises au 19ème siècle," *Le mouvement social* (July-Sept., 1983).

precisely the role of the state and other political structures in the process of working-class formation.[50]

The Disjunction between the Labor Movement and Labor Organizations. Considered from the vantage point of the political sphere, the most evident characteristic of the French labor movement in the second half of the nineteenth century is the great weakness of labor organizations in comparison with Germany, Great Britain, or the United States. Whether one speaks of mutual aid societies, unions, or labor parties, the so-called "organized" segment of the working class was always relatively smaller than in the other three countries.[51]

This numerical weakness is linked to a weak institutionalization. When one observes the daily life of French unions in the latter third of the nineteenth century, one wonders how appropriate it is to think of French syndicates as "unions" in the British or German sense. In France, belonging to a syndicate did not quite mean belonging to an "organization"; most often, it meant accepting a certain solidarity for the purpose of carrying out some action against employers and officials—an operation that might use the strike as its principal weapon, but also petitions, delegations, dem-

---

[50] The term "public sphere" is used here in the sense in which Habermas defined his concept of *Offentlichkeit* in *Strukturwandel der Offentlichkeit* (Neuwied am Rhein and Berlin: Herman Luchterhand Verlag, 1965). Habermas signaled in his preface that he left aside, in his study, the "plebeian public sphere" as it manifested itself in the Robespierrism of the French Revolution and later in the European labor movement, especially in its anarchist traditions.

[51] Mutual aid societies, whose development was encouraged by the Second Empire, reached a total membership of about 800,000 in 1870, of whom workers accounted for a large share. Later, while enrollments increased, the worker share declined, and probably reached a plateau of slightly under 400,000. There is no thorough recent study of mutual aid societies; for a short synthesis, see Thierry Laurent, *La mutualité française et le monde du travail* (Paris: Coopérative d'information et d'édition mutualiste, 1973). However, there is a large pre-1914 bibliography. Older classic studies include: G. Hubbard, *De l'organisation des sociétés de prévoyance* (Paris: Guillaumin, 1852); E. Laurent, *Le paupérisme et les associations de prévoyance*, 2d ed. (Paris: Guillaumin, 1865); A. Weber, *A travers la mutualité* (Paris: Rivière, 1908). Official counts of union membership were as follows: 1890–139,692; 1891–205,152; 1892–288,770; 1893–402,125; 1894–408,025; 1895–419,172; 1896–422,777; 1897–431,794; 1898–419,761; 1899–492,647; 1900–588,832; 1901–614,204. The oldest figures are the most underestimated. The rate of unionization in relation to the wage-earning population counted in the census was as follows: 1891, 2.07 percent; 1896, 4.57; 1901, 6.31; 1911, 8.38. There was no genuine "mass" labor party in the modern sense of the term before the development of the SFIO (French Section of the Workers' International), constituted by the unification of various small political sects between 1896 and 1914. Before 1896, the largest party, the Parti Ouvrier Français (so-called Guesdists) reached a maximum of 16,000 members. The total membership of "workers' parties" probably fluctuated between 1879 and 1896 from a few thousand to a maximum of 30,000 members.

onstrations, and the like. Once the action was completed, regardless of
its outcome, there was no reason to continue belonging to the syndicate,
unless one faced the prospect of a follow-up action in the case of victory,
or of revenge in the case of defeat. Although officially recorded enrollment figures overestimate membership and the regularity of their adherence, they do point toward very wide and rapid fluctuations; within a few
months or a few years, enrollments could rise from a few dozen to several
hundred, and go down again just as suddenly.

Contrary to German and British unions, French syndicates did not
take over existing institutional traditions. They became legally tolerated
only in 1864, except for a brief period during the 1848 revolution; in
contrast with Great Britain and Germany, where the legalization of
unions preceded democratization and contributed to bringing it about, in
France it occurred sixteen years after the institutionalization of universal
suffrage. Early French syndicates should rather be considered as the
heirs of certain clandestine practices of collective struggle, particularly
of secret strike committees that were perennially established throughout
France among all sectors and forms of production from the 1800s to the
1880s, for the duration of a given action. As against this, the spirit of the
compagnonnage tradition was not really taken up by syndicalism. Its
most formal aspect, which reflected a desire to institute particularist
trade corporations, was firmly rejected in the name of democratic citizenship. All moralizing aspects of compagnonnage, its loyalism toward
well-wrought work and faithfully executed contracts, were rejected on
behalf of the benefit of informal collective practices. The only features of
this tradition taken up by syndicalism were certain clandestine techniques, which were by no means limited to compagnonnage alone.

A particularly revealing indicator of the specificity of French syndicalism during this period is the conception of organizational finance and
the meaning of dues. The pattern of financial development of French syndicates is the reverse of British, German, or U.S. unions. Among the latter countries, union funds grew steadily in importance; they were more
and more institutionalized and sometimes acquired quasi-official authority for the purpose of carrying out welfare functions. To the contrary, in
France, the Ancien Régime tradition of "common purses," revived
among some trades in the first half of the century, was subsequently rapidly rejected. The level of dues, set fairly high in the statutes of early
syndicates, later continuously declined, and members paid very irregu-
larly. Here also, it was particular work actions—whether strikes, aid to
fellow workers, national or even international class solidarity—that stimulated the largest contributions. But never again did the mass of French
workers consider it legitimate to contribute regularly to the financing

of a worker insurance institution: social assistance must be paid by the
state and by the social classes that had illegitimately enriched themselves.[52]

The organizational weakness of the French labor movement has long
been attributed to the conjunction of a romantic revolutionary faith and
of an apocalyptic mythology disconnected from concrete realities.[53] But
this tenacious stereotype underestimates the workers' historical experiences and the situational logic that led various groups of workers to adopt
this or that mode of action. It was always by way of sudden actions and
outbursts, unexpected by political observers, that the French labor movement achieved its most "concrete" economic and political successes.

There is a striking parallel between the informal, small-scale collective
practices, and the eruptions of the labor movement into the national political arena. At work in both cases was a deep suspicion toward delegation
of authority. This suspicion affected secretaries of mutual aid societies or
of unions just as much as parliamentary or municipal representatives.
The original conception of "unity" within the labor movement reveals, in
the same manner, a certain continuity between collective practices in the
workplace and actions in the political arena. In contrast with what
occurred in Britain, Germany, and the United States, all attempts to
unite on the basis of a federation of trades or of national political parties
failed between 1872 and 1896. It was only when unity came to be
founded on resistance practices, without seeking to achieve unity of decision making or of political doctrine, that the scattering of small unions
agreed to cooperate at the regional and national level. This accounts for
the success of the labor exchanges in the late 1880s and their rapid
regrouping into the Federation of Labor Exchanges from 1892 on.

The initiative for the development of labor exchanges was taken by
reformist municipal councils, concerned with regularizing the function-

[52] Of the immense literature on syndicalism, strikes, and the labor movement, I have
relied on two fundamental works. First, Michelle Perrot, *Les ouvriers en grève, 1871-1890*
(Paris: Mouton, 1974); this work marked a turning point in French historiography, taking
the study of the labor movement beyond the purely organizational level and situating it
in the multidimensional universe of worker practices. The second fundamental work is
Lequin, *Les ouvriers*.

[53] This stereotype was perpetuated by retrospective interpretations from a variety of
political points of view. The political-academic cadres of the early Third Republic (Joseph
Barberet, Emile Levasseur, official publications of the Office du Travail) produced a heroic history of the progress of "associationism," centering on the image of courageous and
realistic pioneers who struggled against the supposedly unrealistic mentality of workers,
impatient to achieve immediate results and subject to the demagogic appeal of romantics
who aspired to great revolutionary upheavals. For a very long time, the historiographic
tradition of the French Communist party adopted the same premise in order to demonstrate that the French working class could achieve nothing solid before 1918 for lack of
a vanguard party and of a unified leadership.

ing of labor markets by entrusting to labor unions the means of gathering job offers under conditions considered equitable by both sides. Materially, the creation of a labor exchange entailed the provision of a hall for the unions of a given town or small region, together with limited municipal subsidies toward paperwork, the whole process being entrusted to the collective management of the unions concerned. The principal leader of the Federation of Labor Exchanges, F. Pelloutier, had in mind the development of a revolutionary practice on the basis of an extension of these institutions and the broadening of their scope to include, in addition to job placement, the establishment of unemployment funds, travel aid, mutual aid funds, educational institutions, labor museums, "propaganda" services, and cooperatives.[54]

However, the success of the labor exchanges did not at all follow the path envisaged at the start. Their main dynamic rested on the local cooperation of small unions, through the mutual reinforcement of their ability to launch strikes and related actions, and their capacity to impose the legitimacy of labor actions at the level of a town or a small region. This unanticipated dynamic came to be called "direct-action syndicalism"; but to understand it properly, one must relate it to informal collective practices. When this is done, the labor exchange movement emerges as the broadening, on a territorial basis, of the collective practices of the trades. The labor exchanges mobilized within a given residential community the militants who had already become the agents of collective practices in their respective trades, thus reinforcing their power. They fostered a transposition of the cohesion achieved at the level of the work environment into a class cohesion at the level of the local community, relying on the high degree of interoccupational mobility and thereby rendering the resistance mechanisms established within the trades accessible to unskilled workers.

This touches on a key point of the articulation between the political culture of workers and other dimensions of their collective practices. Even before the institutionalization of "direct-action syndicalism," there was at work in the culture of workers what might be called a "pragmatic of direct action," whose tenets can be expressed as follows: avoid separating action on behalf of specific demands from the development of parallel worker power; reject the compartmentalization between the public

---

[54] F. Pelloutier, *Histoire des bourses du travail: Origines, institutions, avenir*, with a preface by Georges Sorel (repr., Paris: Gordon and Breach, 1971). Sorel's preface is perhaps still the best theoretical study of the original characteristics of the French labor movement of that period. See, as well, Jacques Julliard, *Fernand Pelloutier et les origines du syndicalisme d'action directe* (Paris: Seuil, 1971); and H. Dubief, *Le Syndicalisme révolutionnaire* (Paris: A. Colin, 1969).

sphere (the state, elected representatives, public opinion) and the economic or "private" sphere proposed by parliamentary democracy; emphasize at all levels of the movement the illegitimacy of established social relationships and propose a different legitimacy, to be acknowledged by other social classes.

Frenchmen, Citizens, and Workers. It will not do to conceptualize the direct-action outlook in terms of "class autonomy." In general, the political practices of workers are systems of communication, power, and legitimacy, in constant interaction with all the other social forces and symbolic systems of the society at large. In the case under consideration, direct action implies a certain way of utilizing the democratic regime and confronting forces hostile to "worker emancipation." The very ambiguity of the labor exchanges on the local political scene illustrates this insertion of worker practices into the larger society: on the one hand, the labor exchanges rejected hierarchical leadership models in the name of an anti-bourgeois conception of democracy; but on the other, they accepted aid from often very bourgeois reformist municipalities, and allowed themselves to become dependent on subsidies to secure offices and in many cases paid secretaries, something unheard of for unions at the time.

The broadest features of the French working class's ambivalence toward the larger society emerged in the course of the democratic experience of the Second Republic, when a lasting rift was established between the political sphere and the labor movement.[55] Most important, the experience of the Second Republic revealed the possibility of reactionary democracy and the isolation of workers in the national community. What struck those concerned most was of course the slight weight of industrial workers in relation to the electorate in general and to the peasant world in particular.

The special place of Catholicism in France should be related to the singular configuration of the peasantry within the sphere of social relationships. Throughout the nineteenth century, French Catholicism remained linked to the peasant world. The ecclesiastical hierarchy's preferred form of social control was the direct ascendancy of notables over peasant families, and a concomitant system of clientelism.[56] These forms

[55] Maurice Agulhon, *1848 ou l'apprentissage de la république, 1848-1852* (Paris: Seuil, 1973); ibid., *Une ville ouvrière au temps du socialisme utopique: Toulon de 1815 à 1851* (Paris: Mouton, 1970); ibid., *La république au village* (Paris: Plon, 1970). See also: P. Vigier, *La seconde république* (Paris: Presses Universitaires de France, 1963); Gossez, *Les ouvriers de Paris*: Livre I.

[56] Michel Denis, *Les royalistes de la Mayenne et le monde moderne (XIXe-XXe siècle)* (Paris: C. Klincksiek, 1977). He criticizes, at the end of his work, the historiography

of social control worked very well in numerous rural regions. But they constituted the most repulsive forms that can be imagined in relation to working-class cultures.

These Catholic clientelisms may explain why, unlike Germany, France did not experience great Catholic organizations, parties, and labor unions, aspiring to regroup the working class.[57] In contrast with German social Catholicism, French clericalism emphasized two objectives until the beginning of the twentieth century: First, to demand the support of the central state apparatus to influence consciences. In this regard, there was a sort of gradual "right Jacobinism" of the French clergy, until church and state were separated in 1904-1905. Second, to maximize the clientelist influence of charity by denying workers any autonomous service or representative institutions.

The failure of a series of attempts to organize worker-controlled social welfare institutions in large industrial cities provides indirect evidence of the strength of these tendencies. As soon as experiments of this sort gained some support among workers, they were repressed by the French ecclesiastical apparatus: they were perceived as dangerously democratic, and appeared in the eyes of the hierarchy as insane or demagogic adventures.[58]

However, in 1849, there also emerged a strand of "rural socialism."[59] Although repressed in 1851, it reemerged triumphantly with the creation

---

based on the traditionalism-modernization couplet, after having shown that the political and social conservatism of the Mayenne region was no more archaic or less modern than other local political orientations. It was the local power system that operated a selection among mechanisms for controlling economic and social relationships.

[57] Attempts at Catholic labor unions did occur, following two distinct paths: on the one hand, in the white-collar sector, and on the other a "yellow" (company) unionism, promoted by employers against "red" syndicalism. Their membership remained limited to a few thousands in the years 1880-1890 and grew to several tens of thousands on the eve of World War I. See M. Gros, *Etudes du mouvement syndical ouvrier en France: Syndicats jaunes ou indépendants* (thèse de droit, Dijon, Paris, 1904).

[58] See in particular: J. B. Duroselle, *Les débuts du catholicisme social en France, 1822-1870* (Paris: Presses Universitaires de France, 1951). See also Y. M. Hilaire, *Une chrétienté an XIXème siècle? La vie religieuse des populations du diocèse d'Arras (1840-1914)* (Lille: Presses de l'Université de Lille, 1977); M. Ozouf, *L'école, l'église et la république, 1871-1914* (Paris: A. Colin, 1963); F. Bedarida and J. Maitron, eds., "Christianisme et monde ouvrier," *Les cahiers du mouvement social*, no. 1 (1970).

[59] Numerous studies have had to react against the simplification and retrospective idealization of village democracy and of the egalitarian spirit of communities in small-property regions. See the works of Vigier cited in note 55, as well as his *Essai sur la répartition de la propriété foncière dans la région alpine: Son évolution des origines du cadastre à la fin du Second Empire* (Paris: Presses Universitaires de France, 1963). Among numerous holistic regional monographs, the classic work remains G. Dupeux, *Aspects de l'histoire sociale et politique du Loir-et-Cher, 1848-1914* (Paris: Mouton, 1962).

of the Third Republic. The "Social and Democratic Republicans" of 1849-1850, nicknamed for short "Democ-socs," "Socialists," or "Reds," were more commonly called "Radicals" at the end of the Second Empire, and later "Radical-Socialists." On the surface, rural and urban radical strands shared many common traits; their discourse was very similar, and they were considered as one in Parliament as well as by the political press. However, from the very beginning, they were separated by a number of "misunderstandings." Within the most narrowly construed Marxist tradition, these have been reduced to the differences between petty-bourgeois socialism and that of workers. Recent research has not denied the validity of such a distinction but has challenged its reductionist implications.

To properly appreciate the originality of Radicalism and of the French petty bourgeois, one might locate the French case within the framework developed by S. Volkov for Germany and Britain.[60] Volkov stresses how, in the Germany of 1848, there was simultaneously a struggle for civil, political, and social rights. In contrast in England, the middle and lower-middle classes moved toward radicalism very early, distinguishing their interests from those of the great liberal capitalists on the basis of the achievements of liberalism itself. These conditions for the genesis of radicalism on the foundation of prior liberal achievements recur in the French and U.S. cases. But the distinctiveness of France can be outlined by noting two features: first, that civil and political right fluctuated in keeping with revolutionary and counterrevolutionary rhythms; and second, that social rights (legality of associations, the right to work protection and to welfare) came much later in France than in Britain, Germany, and the United States.

During the Second Empire and the beginning of the Third Republic, the radical currents of the political scene took on a mainly urban character; their ideologies came to be colored by a profound contempt and bitterness toward the world of the peasant. In the working-class environment, this negative stance was fueled by the two-way mobility between industrial and agricultural wage work: the two were in constant communication, but this communication was a source of antagonisms—between, on one side, the mobile worker, free of any bonds, who circulated between the agricultural and industrial sectors; and on the other, the world of peasant, servants, and masters, the bondage of rural domes-

---

[60] S. Volkov, *The Rise of Popular Antimodernism in Germany: The Urban Master-Artisans, 1873-1896* (Princeton: Princeton University Press, 1978). See also the chapters on Germany in this volume.

tics, a world that extended to urban domestics of rural origin, to servant girls, drivers, some day-laborers, and some commercial employees.[61]

In terms of classes, the basis of urban radicalism extends beyond petty-bourgeois and worker strata to include the whole set of urban cadre whose position was not founded on economic property, such as the liberal professions, teachers, and government employees. Yet more broadly, radicalism could be found among industrialists with a liberal and progressive ideology, who preferred the opposition to a potential alliance of state bureaucracy, Catholic hierarchy, agrarian notables, and commercial capitalism.[62] The cultural and ideological tone of French radicalism stressed "modernism" and faith in "progress." At the same time, until the end of the century, it maintained a populist appearance, showing little respect for middle-class styles and proprieties, which gives it a very different coloring from that of English and American radicalisms.[63]

---

[61] The union movement among agricultural wage workers was weaker in France than in all other large western countries, and industrial-type strikes in that milieu rarer. See A. Souchon, *La crise de la main-d'oeuvre agricole en France* (Paris: A. Rousseau, 1914); and P. Barral, ed., "Aspects régionaux de l'agrarisme français avant 1930" (special issue no. 67 of *Le mouvement social*).

[62] R. Aminzade, who has analyzed the class base of radical republicans for Toulouse, concludes: "During the 1870s bourgeois Republican party leaders elaborated a political ideology that provided the basis for a recasting of the class alliance that had previously underpinned republican politics. The new republican alliance proved successful primarily because workers were excluded from it, in sharp contrast to the central role they had played in the political class alliance forged by the Republican party prior to the revolutionary communes. A political class alliance of industrial capitalists, petty bourgeois and small-holding peasants emerged to confront both the revolutionary aspirations of socialist workers and the anti-republicanism of aristocrats and of the financial fraction of the bourgeoisie. This alliance of small-scale urban and rural producers with the industrial bourgeoisie was forged around a socially conservative republican ideology that appealed to political equality, property (of all sorts), and entrepreneurial freedom—all of which appeared to promise opportunity to energetic capitalists and security to small producers" (*Class, Politics, and Early Industrial Capitalism: A Study of Mid-Nineteenth-Century Toulouse, France* [Albany: State University of New York Press, 1981], pp. 286-87). See also Y. Guin, *Le mouvement ouvrier nantais, essai sur le syndicalisme d'action directe à Nantes et à Saint-Nazaire* (Paris: Maspéro, 1976); P. Pierrard, *La vie ouvrière à Lille sous le Second Empire* (Paris: Bloud et Gay, 1965). Concerning the "petty bourgeois," one can compare the antimodernist evolution of German small masters and the "progressivism" of French small masters, tied to differences in their economic and political integration. See in particular two special issues, "L'atelier et la boutique," *Le mouvement social*, no. 108 (July-Oct. 1979) and "Petite entreprise et politique," *Le mouvement social*, no. 114 (Jan.-March 1981).

[63] French radicalism, like the American radicalism studied by David Montgomery in *Beyond Equality: Labor and the Radical Republicans, 1862-1872* (New York: Alfred A. Knopf, 1967), advocated the broadening of individual rights beyond individualism and sought to broaden the collective practices of the trades by establishing them on institutional ground, with a strong ideology of the progress of law. However, its moral style was very different; far from sharing in the quest for honorability and for moral recognition by other social classes, the style of the French radicals was very populist and perhaps even

Within this radical political camp, working-class support was genuine and massive but never unconditional. On the contrary, a refined analysis of the vast number of written observations concerning "public spirit," recorded most minutely by officials of the Second Empire and the Third Republic, would show that workers said different things, held different discourses, depending upon the situation. If the issue was one of promoting civil liberties in the face of arbitrary action by authorities, police, and judges, then the language and style of workers emphasized their universalist identity as "citizens," utilizing the Jacobin symbolic material of the French Revolution—beginning with the greeting "Citizen" and its concomitant familiar form of address—to signify an inter-class alliance against conservative and bureaucratic forces.[64] It is also likely that a precise analysis of the circumstances in which workers identified themselves strongly as "Frenchmen" and "patriots" would show that this occurred mainly in opposition to the progressive disarmament of the people and of the popular militias.[65] Here again, it is evident that the persistence of revolutionary symbols should not be interpreted as mere attachment to "traditional myth" or as the reenactment of a historical tragedy as farce.

These identities as citizens and as Frenchmen could coexist among workers alongside class identities. However, workers appear to have never bought the notion of limiting themselves solely to civil and political rights, as the Radical alliance wished them to do. It is at the level of these

---

"demagogic" in the eyes of the most "honorable" social classes. More fundamentally, the difference is attributable to the fact that in France, radicalism was effective in the sphere of public opinion rather than in the realm of associations. A parallel might be drawn as well with G. Stedman-Jones's study of the evolution of English working-class cultures, in relation to the evolution of other social strata ("Working-class Culture and Working-class Politics in London, 1870-1900: Notes on the Remaking of a Working Class," *Journal of Social History* [Summer 1974]:460-508). The major difference among working-class cultures can be ascribed, of course, to the greater weight of "defensive" institutions in Great Britain, which imply a de facto recognition of capitalism as a limiting condition. Another difference, emphasized by Stedman-Jones, is the gradual distancing of petty-bourgeois strata from workers and their adoption of the lifestyles of the "middle classes" in 1870-1900. A similar process took place in France as well, but not until 1900-1930.

[64] Regarding republican symbolic material, see Maurice Agulhon, *Marianne au combat* (Paris: Flammarion, 1979). It is not without interest to note that the downright "petty-bourgeois" radical program of Gambetta in 1869, founded on a demand for direct democracy against authoritarian bureaucracy, bears a greater similarity to the practical part of the orthodox Marxist Erfurt program of 1891 than to the Gotha program considered overly "petty bourgeois" by Marx's friends. All the considerations developed up to now obviously entail consequences for the analysis of the revolutionary periods of 1848 and the Commune of 1871, which there is no room to draw out here. See, e.g., Cottereau, "Vie quotidienne." It is not a question simply of the effects of everyday practices upon the revolutionary phases, but also of the effects of the revolutionary phases upon everyday practices.

[65] Louis Girard, *La garde nationale, 1814-1871* (Paris: Plon, 1964).

complex strategies that the pragmatics of direct action take on their full meaning: they got around the constraints of action in the political arena in order to establish the de facto power of workers at the level of the relations of production, bypassing the quest for its public legitimation. The experiences of workers led them to think that in France, the chances of legal reformism were very weak; in contrast with Germany and Britain, there were no great landed aristocrats who might ally themselves to reformist forces in opposition to the power of industrial capitalists.

But it is the absence of a genuine "labor aristocracy" that is the most telling hallmark of the conjunction between the offensive on behalf of freedoms in the political arena and the exercise of direct action—without publicity—to achieve worker power in the sphere of relations of production. Although some doubt has been cast on the appropriateness of the concept of "labor aristocracy" even for the British case, it is nevertheless true that there is a significant difference in this respect between French and British workers, which pertains to the effects of the political sphere on hierarchical divisions among them. In Britain, social reforms were possible to the extent that they relied on segments of the working class already organized in mutual aid societies and unions. In France, attempts to similar effect were rare and uniformly failed. Internal hierarchies did come into play, and direct-action tactics relied on the strata whose skills made resistance most effective; but this form of action implied extending mobilization to include less skilled workers every time success was achieved, so that the "associationist" perspective held out by Napoleon III to the mutual aid societies and later by the Radical Republicans toward the unions always failed in the attempt to separate out a leadership stratum from the mass of workers, and to secure their collaboration.

The anti-intellectualism of the French labor movement is congruent with this configuration. It is attributable, in the first instance, to the lack of economic and sociological relevance of the French academic milieu; but D. Lindenberg has also shown how anti-intellectualism originated in the workers' negative experiences of theorists who offered themselves as leaders, in the name of a self-proclaimed double vocation as leaders of political parties and as intellectuals.[66] Most theorists never overcame the perspectives of the public sphere and thus provoked, by reaction, a desire on the part of workers to engage in a sort of direct action with respect to intellectual reflection.[67]

[66] D. Lindenberg, *Le marxisme introuvable* (Paris: Calmann-Lévy, 1975). Lindenberg shows in addition how the French Communist party, which long aspired to the honor of a great national ancestor who was a Marxist, manufactured the legend of a Guesdist party recognized by Marx as the authentic vanguard of French proletarians.

[67] An example of direct-action practices in the intellectual sphere is provided by the public meetings movement in Paris, 1868-1870. The importance of this movement can be

If by playing such a complex game in relation to the political sphere French working-class cultures avoided the formation of a politically relevant "labor aristocracy," they did little or nothing to overcome the antagonism between men and women within the working class. Here is, undoubtedly, the major failure of the labor movement, more marked in France than in Anglo-Saxon countries. At the level of feminist and union organization, the difference is striking and has long been emphasized. Female participation in union organizations was very low and came very late;[68] and most feminist organizations had a bourgeois orientation and were concerned with matrimonial rights within the civil code, an issue that had little relevance to the family problems of workers. The exclusion of female workers from citizenship was particularly acute in France, and all the more paradoxical in that it occurred in a country where male universal suffrage was secured very quickly and where a much larger proportion of married women were wage earners than elsewhere. Female union members themselves often appeared to "internalize" this noncitizenship, or at least found it impossible to challenge it under existing circumstances. In the final analysis, this paradox underlines the strength of national culture with respect to male domination and citizenship, so that the only remarkable thing about the political culture of workers in this respect is its conformity with the nation at large.[69]

But this female noncitizenship could, at the same time, be turned offensively against established social relationships; something that was marginal to politics could be transformed into something that went

rediscovered thanks to the book by A. Dalotel, A. Faure, and J. C. Freiermuth, *Aux origines de la Commune: Les réunions publiques à Paris, 1868-1870* (Paris: Maspéro, 1980). Similar efforts, which Pelloutier sought unsuccessfully to systematize, were launched later among some of the labor exchanges. At the level of individual works, the labor movement inspired two distinct lines of theoretical development: the first, linked with direct-action syndicalism, produced the writings of Georges Sorel; the other, linked to the democratic socialist—and later radical—ideologies, focused politically on the "progress of law" and found its principal theorist in Jaurès. See H. Goldberg, *Jaurès* (Paris: Fayard, 1971); and M. Reybérioux, *Jaurès et la classe ouvrière* (Paris: Maspéro, 1978).

[68] A very detailed fundamental work has been published by M. Guilbert, *Les femmes et l'organisation syndicale avant 1914* (Paris: CNRS, 1966).

[69] An exceptional example of conjunction between a feminist movement and a movement of female workers is analyzed by Guilbert, *Les Femmes*, pp. 420-30. But this is more reminiscent of French situations in 1960-1970 than in the nineteenth century. Michelle Perrot has published a synthesis of various practices of resistance to relations of domination among women of the popular classes, in "La femme populaire rebelle," *L'histoire sans qualité* (Paris: Galilée, 1979), pp. 125-157. See also the other essays in that book, as well as the new journal *Pénélope, pour l'histoire des femmes* (Paris: Publications du groupe d'études féministes de l'Université de Paris 7 et du Centre de recherches historiques de l'EHESS). A theoretical synthesis of relationships between sexual oppositions and class oppositions is provided by D. Kergoat in "Ouvrier = ouvrière?" *Critiques de l'économie politique*, nouvelle série, no. 5 (Paris: Maspéro, 1978).

beyond politics. There is a great deal of current research that attempts to bring to the fore these dimensions in the everyday practices of female workers. Perhaps zones of female power and changes of social relationships were able to establish themselves outside the usual channels of public legitimacy. Many of the practices of women workers infringed upon the separation between the private and the public sphere, between work and nonwork, between the political and the nonpolitical. The task is thus to detect worker practices whose effects were erased by the usual historical memories.

Part Two

The United States

5 Becoming American: The Working Classes in the United States before the Civil War • *Amy Bridges*

The three decades preceding the Civil War were an important time in the creation of the American working classes. The first generation of a modern proletariat appeared at the workplace; the last property restrictions on the suffrage were abolished; and massive immigration lent the working classes the ethnic diversity that has characterized them to the present day. In the same decades the social and economic expectations of working people, their understanding of themselves and their social betters, and their political demands were substantially altered.

These transformations are better understood today than a decade ago as a result of the growth of social historical research in the United States. In particular, social historians have explored and charted the values, habits, and feelings of American artisans in the Jacksonian era. The same studies that provide us with a richer picture of the early working classes than ever before available also effectively discredit older theories of working-class development in the United States. The work of John R. Commons and his colleagues dominated research in labor history and inquiries about working-class formation in the United States until very recently. Insisting that by the Civil War workers had retreated from politics to "trade unionism pure and simple," Commons and his colleagues painted a portrait of an adamantly nonpolitical working class resolutely focused on earnings. Political activity only engaged workers when, as in the great nineteenth-century depressions, trade union activity lapsed.[1] From this vantage point the most interesting questions seemed to be not who workers in the United States were but who, somehow intransigently, they had failed to become. Various parts of this portrait have been redrawn by the last generation of social historical research. Where Louis Hartz saw "incipient entrepreneurs,"[2] Paul Faler found that Horatio

MY THANKS to the editors of this volume, colleagues in the state and capitalism seminar at the Center for European Studies at Harvard University, and Joshua Brown for most helpful comments.

[1] John R. Commons et al., *History of Labour in the United States*, 4 vols. (New York: Macmillan Co., 1926).

[2] Louis Hartz, *The Liberal Tradition in America* (New York: Harcourt, Brace & World, 1955), p. 122.

Alger was "an outcast in the minds" of American workers.[3] In place of
"trade unionism pure and simple," a number of studies have shown that
political activity was most sustained where the union movement was
strongest.[4] If still haunted by the failings of the American working
classes, social historians have succeeded in changing their focus from the
absence of a particular consciousness to the reality of working-class values and political culture. And although social historians have tended to
be suspicious of party politics—inclined to regard political action as
either ritual or social control—they have nevertheless begun to grapple
with the meanings of the long political history of the American working
classes.

The present moment, then, is an opportune one for providing some
summary arguments and offering hypotheses about the making of the
first generations of the working classes in the United States. The changes
in the working classes in the antebellum era might be summarized by
saying that by 1860 the working classes were more distinctively "American" than they had been in 1780, 1800, or even 1830. On the eve of
industrialization in the United States, in 1830, the American working
classes evidenced striking dispositional and ideological similarities to
their English cousins. Workers in the United States shared with the
English working classes a world view that has been variously termed
"artisan republicanism," "Painite," and "Jacobin."[5] English and American workers understood the advent of the industrial system in similar
terms. Workingmen's advocates in both places saw the ascendancy of
trade and industrialism as corrosive of social morals. Robert Owen and
Clinton Roosevelt alike denounced the selfishness encouraged by the new
order:

[Merchants are] trained to buy cheap and sell dear. This occupation deterio-
rates, and often destroys, the finest and best faculties of our natures. . . . I am
thoroughly convinced that there can be no superior character formed under this
thoroughly selfish system. Truth, honesty, virtue, will be mere names. . . . Under
this system . . . all are trained . . . to oppose and often to destroy one another.

[3] Alan Dawley, *Class and Community: The Industrial Revolution in Lynn* (Cambridge: Harvard University Press, 1976), p. 219.

[4] See, e.g., David Montgomery, "The Working Classes of the Preindustrial American
City, 1780-1830," *Labor History*, no. 9 (1968):3-22 and Dawley, *Class and Community*,
pp. 196-97.

[5] On "artisan republicanism," see Robert Sean Wilentz, "Ritual, Republicanism, and
the Artisans of Jacksonian New York," paper presented at the annual meeting of the
Organization of American Historians, New York, April 1978; on "Painite," see E. P.
Thompson, *The Making of the English Working Class* (Harmondsworth, England: Penguin Books, 1970), chap. 16; on "Jacobin," see Eric Hobsbawm, *The Age of Revolution,
1789-1848* (New York: New American Library, 1962), p. 249.

... It is a low, vulgar, ignorant and inferior mode of conducting the affairs of society[6]

wrote one; the other explained,

The dealer has the habit of operating alone against his fellows, selfishly, and his motto is "laissez-nous faire". ... The teaching that no other feeling is to be consulted, or can be, in our intercourse in society, tends to contract our sympathies, and man being the creature of habit and education, he will soon become entirely what he is taught to be and has the habit of being.[7]

Cobbett and the National Trades Union alike anticipated the advance "to the state in which there are but two classes of men," "masters and slaves"; the "present system of manufacturing" was declared in both places "a system of mental and physical slavery," an "unnatural" system.[8] Workingmen in England and the United States agreed that labor produced all wealth, and that government conspired with the wealthy to rob them of it—through the "taxing and funding system" in England and through banks in the United States.[9] Workingmen in England and the United States saw machinery, "the peoples' legitimate servants ... become their rivals and masters."[10] Finally, in both England and the United States the advantages of capital over labor were seen as largely political advantages. John Knight in England and the *Workingman's Advocate* in the United States opposed the "monopoly of wealth" on elective office. As one lamented,

candidates for public offices, especially for our representatives in the ... legislature ... have been taken entirely from the class of citizens denominated, or supposed to be rich, or property holders, thereby leaving our own most numerous body without a voice in making those laws which we are compelled to obey.[11]

[6] Robert Owen quoted in Raymond Williams, *Culture and Society, 1780-1950* (1958; pbk., New York: Harper & Row, 1966), p. 28.

[7] Clinton Roosevelt, *The Mode of Protecting Domestic Industries* (1831; repr., New York: Benjamin H. Tyrrel, 1889), pp. 10-11.

[8] Compare Seth Luther at the 1835 National Trades' Union Meeting ("the present system of manufacturing is a system of mental and physical slavery") with Cobbett, arguing that although once there were rich and poor, "now ... it is an affair of *masters* and *slaves*." Luther is quoted in John R. Commons et al., eds., *A Documentary History of American Industrial Society* (Cleveland: Arthur H. Clark Co., 1910), 6:245, and Cobbett in Williams, *Culture and Society*, pp. 14-15 (emphasis in original).

[9] For the United States see the Locofoco statement in Fitzwilliam Byrdsall, *The History of the Loco-Foco or Equal Rights Party* (1842; repr., New York: Burt Franklin, 1967), p. 73, or Isaac Smith's statement quoted in ibid., p. 75; for similar views from Cobbett, see Williams, *Culture and Society*, p. 13.

[10] *Working Man's Advocate*, Feb. 2, 1830, quoted in Seymour Savetsky, "The New York Workingmen's Party" (master's thesis, Columbia University, 1948).

[11] *New York Sentinel and Workingman's Advocate*, Jan. 16, 1830, quoted in Commons, *History of Labor in the United States*, 1:233.

His cousin meanwhile protested:

The making and administering of laws is exclusively enjoyed by men of property, and, therefore, in the promotion of their own interests they are continually
diminishing the rights of all the labouring classes. No plan hitherto laid for the
benefit of the labourers has been successful; and so far as the legislative power
remains exclusively in the hands of men of property, no such plan will ever be
effectual.[12]

It was not only these most articulate spokesmen who had sentiments in
common. Paul Gilje has written of "Anglo-American" mob traditions;
Eric Foner and others have pointed to an American "moral economy,"
and Sean Wilentz has documented the continuing ties that bound
together an "Anglo-American world of labor."[13]

Although these themes, traditions, and dispositions were shared across
the emerging modern working classes, the setting in which American
workers encountered industrial transformation was a radically distinctive
one. Two elements of this setting were particularly important in shaping
the character of the working classes. First, the wage labor force in the
United States was largely urban, and as it was created, the agricultural
labor force continued to expand. In the nineteenth century both agricultural and nonagricultural labor forces grew. Indeed, the labor force in
mining, construction, and manufactures did not exceed the agricultural
labor force until 1920. Although there was rural-urban migration in the
United States as elsewhere, those numbers were overwhelmed by immigration from overseas and constant movement westward. Even counting
quite small towns (population 2,500) as "urban," the population of the
United States in 1850 was 85 percent rural.[14] The political construction
of this geography intensified the isolation of labor. State legislatures, like
the U.S. House of Representatives, are elected from single-member districts. Largely urban, workers were not only a numerical minority in
every state but Rhode Island, but also suffered from district lines that
favored the representation of rural areas. The national situation was
worse, since in the Senate states are represented, rather than population.

[12] John Knight quoted in John Foster, *Class Struggle and the Industrial Revolution:
Early Industrial Capitalism in Three English Towns* (New York: St. Martin's Press,
1974), p. 148.
[13] Paul Gilje, "The Baltimore Riots of 1812 and the Breakdown of the Anglo-American
Mob Tradition," *Journal of Social History* 13, no. 4 (Summer 1980):547-64; Eric Foner,
Tom Paine and Revolutionary America (New York: Oxford University Press, 1976), ch.
5; Wilentz, "Ritual, Republicanism."
[14] U.S. Dept. of Commerce, Bureau of the Census, *Historical Statistics of the United
States, Colonial Times to 1970, Part I* (Washington, D.C.: Government Printing Office,
1975), pp. 138, 12.

Between 1800 and 1850 the number of states nearly doubled (from seventeen to thirty-three), as territories gained sufficient population to secure admission to the Union. These new admissions, nearly all from the great plains of the Midwest, had little industrial development. This is the mirror image of the frontier thesis: wage labor was largely confined to the cities and nationally to minority status.

Second, the very first generation of the industrial labor force in the United States, as well as the great majority of their artisan forebears, were entitled to vote. The franchise changed the arena in which the newly created working classes struggled to achieve their goals. In that arena sheer numbers, the search for allies, geographical dispersion or concentration, and the rules of the electoral game all affected the political capacity of the working classes. If elsewhere the Painite ideology of republicanism and rights cherished by artisans provided powerful programmatic insights that fostered artisan–wage labor alliances, in the American setting it was of little programmatic help. As Alan Dawley has written, the People's Charter of American artisans "was already written into the Federal Constitution."[15] Enfranchisement also meant that the debates of the working classes about society and their vision of it, about the meaning of the industrial system, and about the sources of social honor were conducted in dialogue with—if not under constant barrage of arguments from—other classes and, of course, politicians.

If American workers began that dialogue in 1830 as "industrious mechanics," by 1860 they had become Republicans and Democrats. The habits of unionism were widespread. Workers' analyses of their misfortunes were centered less on politics and more on the "industrial system." They no longer believed that the election of workingmen or governmental "even-handedness" would ensure prosperity, but they did insist that government insure them against the worst perils of the accumulation process.

In this essay I relate these transformations of the working classes to the distinctive setting in which they worked, argued, and promoted their own political visions. In structuralist language, the argument is that the distinctive character of the American working classes at mid-century is a product of the differential timing of the development of economic, ideological, and political structures.[16] A set of values and sentiments, largely shared with their western European counterparts, and placed in a radically different political and economic setting, produced transformations

[15] Dawley, *Class and Community*, p. 71.

[16] For suggestions on such an implicitly comparative structural framework, see Nicos Poulantzas, *Political Power and Social Classes* (London: New Left Books, 1973), pp. 147-57.

in the culture and dispositions of the working classes that marked them as distinctively American by 1860. The same argument can be couched in the less deterministic language of Sidney Mintz. If, as he has suggested, culture is a set of "resources," and society is an "arena," then the development of the working classes in the United States is best understood by paying close attention to the arena.[17] Social arenas, after all, are not large empty spaces, but highly structured settings in which institutional arrangements and the general configuration of social forces contribute to how social conflicts are resolved and how political cultures and subcultures evolve in response to a changing world.

The dynamics of these relations between culture and setting are discernible in the 1830s. The first section of this essay describes the labor movement of that decade, charting its values, its political efforts, and its successes and failures. The subsequent section examines changes in the structure of the work force in the antebellum years. A third section traces changes in sentiment and disposition among the working classes as artisans gave way to wage workers. The final section explores the political action those values provoked in the last decade before the Civil War. For both the 1830s and the 1850s a contradictory reality emerges: that the franchise politically empowered workers, even as the logic and practice of politics constrained that power and made Democrats and Republicans of workers.

I. *Tradition and Action: The 1830s*

The antebellum years embrace two quite distinct periods of activisim among working people. The 1830s saw the rise and collapse of Workingmen's parties and the first modern labor movement. The 1840s was largely a period of quiescence, as the depression of the late 1830s destroyed most labor organizations. Nevertheless, in quite a few states a continued and sometimes bitter campaign for laws limiting the workday provided continuity from the 1830s to the renewed activism of the 1850s. In the 1850s the labor movement flowered again, though by then the working classes were quite different than they had been a generation before: much more heavily proletarian and largely composed of immigrants. It is useful to look briefly at the first period of labor activism, describing the cultural resources with which the working classes entered the industrial age. Their successes and failures highlight the contours of the arena in which the modern working classes would do battle.

---

[17] Quoted in Herbert Gutman, *Work, Culture, and Society in Industrializing America* (New York: Vintage Books, 1977), p. 16.

A variety of organizations claimed to speak for labor. The Working-men's parties were an insurgent political force in nearly every state between 1827 and 1831. The General Trades' Unions in New York and elsewhere, the New England Workmen's Association, and the National Trades' Union were organizations of unions. The member unions were rarely common laborers but rather were unions of journeymen artisans, though some member "unions" were crafts organizations that included masters. The Workingmen's parties, the General Trades' Unions of New York and counterpart organizations in Philadelphia, Newark, and Baltimore, the New England Workingmen's Association, and the National Trades' Union voiced a common republicanism and a common set of political demands.[18] The Workingmen's parties were the last in a tradition in which "mechanics" opposed the domination of government by wealth.[19] Though the last of such efforts, the parties were also somewhat different. The eighteenth-century mechanics' factions were local political protests; in the Jacksonian era there were counterparts in nearly every state. In addition, there was in the later parties an effort to keep out any "boss who employed a large number of hands," indicating emerging tensions undermining craft solidarity among masters and journeymen.[20] The trades' unions more emphatically insisted on the rights and virtues of journeymen, though the metropolitan area Trades' Unions included crafts organizations (and excluded the unskilled).

This organizational life reveals the artisans of the Jacksonian era as the proud bearers of the ideology of Paine and the American Revolution. Their political economy identified them as the creators of social wealth and as liberty's best defenders.[21] If their world view was "Painite" or "Jacobin," it was so not only in meaning but also in language. Their rhet-

[18] Historians of the Workingmen's parties will object strongly to this statement. The history of these parties is complicated not only because they varied from state to state, but also because they were subjected to opportunistic (and destructive) intrusion from supporters of Jackson and Clay and because there were among the Workingmen a variety of radical spokesmen. By contrast, the union movement was more autonomous of the parties. Nevertheless, for my purposes here it is appropriate to emphasize common themes of the Workingmen's parties and the labor movement that distinguish them from the major parties and from working-class views a generation hence.

[19] The interventions of mechanics in politics had a history predating the Revolution, in which from time to time mechanics ran tickets for assembly or city office (even under restricted franchise artisans formed a majority of the electorate). The later years of the Sons of Liberty, once merchants and lawyers had been pressed out of positions of leadership, were equally mechanics' interventions and, after the Revolution as before, mechanics' slates were occasionally launched to demonstrate disaffection and to increase the representation of craftsmen in government.

[20] Commons, *History of Labour*, 1:234.

[21] Montgomery, "Working Classes," p. 13. Philip S. Foner, *History of the Labor Movement in the United States* (New York: International Publishers, 1975), 1:196.

oric opposed the freeman to the slave and aristocracy to republicanism; it denounced demagogues and championed the industrious and virtuous artisan and farmer; it demanded even-handed regulation of the pursuit of wealth by the state; and it based its claims squarely on equality and natural right. These emphases gave eighteenth-century republicanism its power and nineteenth-century journeymen principles justifying their interests and a radical political critique of their opponents. "Our republicanism," New York City's General Trades' Union declared, is "founded in the laws of nature, of equality, and of reciprocity."[22]

Working people needed to organize because "while those who subsist by labour, who are in fact the producers of the wealth of the country, are becoming poorer, the non-producers . . . are . . . growing richer."[23] Government, abandoning its "true object," "the health and happiness of its citizens," was assisting the few and forsaking the many. "The poor," asserted the Association of Working People of New Castle County, Delaware, "have no laws; the laws are made by the rich and of course for the rich."[24] The same dominance meant that artisans failed to receive the social respect due to them. Thus working people needed a party to regain "a proper standing in the community, and representation in the councils of state."[25] Republican language also justified organizations of unions. When employing curriers in New York City refused to hire union members, the General Trades' Union praised the journeymen curriers for having "properly resisted this attempted tyrannical coalition like freemen"; the Lowell mill girls invoked "the spirit of our patriotic ancestors," and employing tailors in Baltimore were likened in "greed and avarice" to those who wrote the Stamp Act.[26]

The fate of republican government was also linked to the perpetuation of the industrious, virtuous, independent character of its citizens. The advancing industrial and "speculating" system not only left men with little time for self-education but also was more insidiously corrosive of character. Since "no individual foresight can prevent failure in business," speculation led "to intemperance and despair" among those who failed.[27] Similarly, speculation created "a distaste for the steady pursuit of those modes of business by which wealth is gradually acquired," awakening

[22] *The Union* (New York), Apr. 28, 1836, p. 2.

[23] Commons, *History of Labour*, 1:292.

[24] P. Foner, *History of the Labor Movement*, 1:121.

[25] *Working Man's Advocate*, May 8, 1830, quoted in Savetsky, "The New York Workingmen's Party," p. 79.

[26] On curriers: *The Union*, Apr. 23, 1836, p. 2; on Lowell: quoted in P. Foner, *History of the Labor Movement*, 1:109; on Baltimore: *ibid.*, 1:113.

[27] Roosevelt, *The Mode of Protecting Domestic Industries*, p. 34.

instead "a desire for enterprises which hold out the dazzling prospect of sudden riches."[28] Since, far more than any other form of government, republican government rested squarely on the moral fiber of the citizens, it was incumbent on journeymen to "arouse our fellow citizens to the peril of these departures from the purity and simplicity of our republican system."[29] In both their political activity and their organization for economic self-defense, then, workers were finishing "the glorious work of the [American] revolution."[30]

This world view was quite different from those put forward by the major political parties. From the first election of Andrew Jackson to the presidency, in 1828, until well into the 1850s, the two major national parties were the Democratic Republicans (usually called simply "Democrats," the party of Jackson), and the Whigs. These two parties are generally referred to as the "second American party system." Like the Workingmen, Whigs argued that the state should guide interdependent interests to a prosperous common good, but Whigs also endorsed the "credit system" and an "American system" of which many workers were profoundly suspicious. Democrats took up a militant workerism and an insistence on equality, but they too failed to protect the "industrious mechanics." Neither party, moreover, welcomed the political assertiveness of common men. Thus like the Workingmen's parties, the Trades' Unions were critical of both Whigs and Democrats. The most articulate spokesmen for working people were likely to find themselves stranded between the parties and, although both parties succeeded in gaining votes from the working classes, neither party succeeded in winning the allegiance of the labor movement. The Jacksonian working classes maintained their own distinctive political culture.

The few years of political independence in the Workingmen's parties reveal much about the situation of the Jacksonian working classes and, by implication, their descendants. The Workingmen's parties defined the producing classes broadly, including anyone who "followed any *useful* occupation, mental or physical, for a livelihood,"[31] and their demands represented broadly felt needs. The demands of the labor movement too attracted others as well as journeymen. Both the parties and the trades' unions demanded an abolition of prison labor, expanded public educa-

---

[28] G. H. Evans in the *Working Man's Advocate*, quoted in Walter Hugins, *Jacksonian Democracy and the Working Class* (Stanford: Stanford University Press, 1960), p. 179.

[29] Commons, *Documentary History*, 1:293.

[30] P. Foner, *History of the Labor Movement*, 1:127.

[31] Susan E. Hirsch, *Roots of the American Working Class: The Industrialization of Crafts in Newark 1800-1860* (Philadelphia: University of Pennsylvania Press, 1978), pp. 113-14.

tion, laws limiting the working day to ten hours, and reform of state militia systems. The parties also demanded a variety of democratizing reforms. In New Jersey the party demanded ballot rather than voice voting, judicial reform, and reapportionment, as well as reforms affecting the economic life of artisans.[32] In New York, the party opposed voter registration and demanded compensation for city council members, jurors, and witnesses, direct election of the mayor, a single-member district system, and simplification of laws. In addition, the party there and elsewhere demanded an abolition of imprisonment for debt and the enactment of lien laws (giving construction workers title to property they constructed if contractors failed to pay wages). The unions, of course, also demanded the right to unionize.

Since the party's agenda addressed the needs of many small producers, in most rural places farmers were organized into the parties, and branches of the Workingmen bore names like the "Committee of Farmers, Mechanics, and other Working Men." In the city, democratizing demands drew the support of small-property owners and other reforms—of the laws and education, for example—were supported by additional groups for their own reasons. These bases of support were important, for most of the agenda of the labor movement required action by state governments. The coalitions supporting particular demands had everything to do with the successes and failures of the labor movement.

A look at the response to labor's demands in New York shows that demands directed at state government were most likely to be won when small tradesmen and farmers shared journeymen's interests. A lien law was passed in 1832 (and subsequently more stringent lien laws were passed in 1844, 1851, 1855, and 1861). Imprisonment for debt, an important issue to farmers and small tradesmen as well as journeymen, was abolished in 1831. The militia system, too, though it was not abolished, was not rigorously enforced, and in 1846 was essentially discontinued under the new state constitution. Similarly, democratizing reforms for the city were also largely achieved. The mayor became an elected official in 1834, simplification of the laws was proceeding under additional impetus, voter registration (which Workingmen regarded as a measure that would decrease the participation of the working classes) was not seriously attempted until the mid-1840s, and although the Common School system was not extended to New York City until 1842, a real estate tax for the purpose of funding public schools was levied by the state assembly in 1829 and the rate raised in 1831.

[32] G. H. Evans quoted in P. Foner, *History of the Labor Movement*, 1:136; see also Dawley, *Class and Community*, p. 64.

Those issues directly affecting mechanics and wage laborers received less attention. Compensation for the common council, jurors, and witnesses in New York City was not achieved, nor was legislation for the ten-hour workday or the abolition of prison labor. Ten hours was established as the length of the regular workday in New York and elsewhere by economic action. Indeed, although the attempt of employers to lengthen the working day was the immediate provocation for the formation of the Workingmen's parties, the issue was settled in New York City before the first election in which the party ran candidates. Similarly, in Philadelphia the ten-hour working day was won from private and public employers by a citywide strike. By the Civil War labor in New York was agitating for an eight-hour day despite the fact that legislation limiting the workday had never been passed.[33]

New York was hardly unusual. Generally, by the middle of the 1840s, states had abolished imprisonment for debt, made their militia systems less oppressive, expanded their public school systems, and enacted lien laws. The issues affecting wage laborers and artisans more directly—prison labor, contract labor on public works, and length of workday—were not resolved so successfully.[34] The political effectiveness of wage laborers on the issues more peculiarly their own, and especially on the one of greatest importance—ten-hours legislation—was largely determined by their numerical strength in the electorate and their concentration in urban locations. Urban location mattered because the malapportionment of districts for the election of state legislators discriminated in favor of rural interests. Thus the political capacity of wage workers was largely a product of their numbers and their geographical dispersion. If states are compared, using the census of 1840, for the size and dispersion of those engaged in "manufactures and trades," the fate of ten-hours legislation is largely explained.

Throughout New England, with its large and widely distributed factory population, the struggle for ten-hours legislation was sustained and bitter. Rhode Island was the only state in which those engaged in "manufactures and trades" outnumbered the farming population. New Hampshire, Maine, New Jersey and Connecticut passed ten-hours legislation, as had Rhode Island. In these states the single largest concentration of those engaged in manufactures and trades accounted for less than 10 percent of the manufacturing population. In Massachusetts, the state

[33] See P. Foner, *History of the Labor Movement*, for general account of ten hours conflicts, and Commons, *History of Labor*, vol. 1, ch. 4.

[34] For general summaries, see P. Foner, *History of the Labor Movement*, and Commons, *History of Labor*, 1:326-34.

that, after Rhode Island, had the highest proportion of its gainfully employed engaged in manufactures, the struggle for ten-hours legislation was intense. Many of those factory workers were women and so without the vote; waging the ten-hours struggle convinced the New England Workingmen's Association that female suffrage should be endorsed. That many of the women were from rural families also enhanced farmer-worker alliances. In Pennsylvania, to Philadelphia's many artisans and workers were added the large concentration in the Allegheny area (Pittsburgh), enhancing their political strength. Finally, in New York, which did not pass ten-hours legislation, fully 25 percent of all those engaged in "manufactures and trades" lived in New York City, and their political power in state politics was slim indeed.

If the logic and dynamics of this situation were obvious enough, the implications were profound. Labor's experience in the Jacksonian era foreshadows much that happened a generation later. Workingmen's most effective spokesmen were stranded between the parties. The labor movement was successful when the issues it raised concerned artisans as they concerned farmers and small tradesmen, and much less so when issues concerned wage laborers alone. At the same time, minority status in the population and concentration in the cities meant that the working classes needed the parties to achieve their goals in the nation's state capitals. Parties, after all, organize coalitions of constituents into effective political majorities. The more proletarianized and foreign-born the working classes became, the more their political strength was confined to the cities and the more they needed the parties to be effective politically in state politics (though that effectiveness was, of course, compromised by coalition). Here is the importance of the mirror image of the frontier thesis: the same frontier that welcomed the pioneer and the farmer made of the working classes an urban minority. Their greatest political strength, of course, was in the cities, and there the parties were bent, in ways we will see, to their will.

II. The "Industrial System"

Well into the nineteenth century the American city was a city of artisans and merchants. By the election of Andrew Jackson in 1828 there were strong disorganizing pressures on the crafts. Some factories had even made their appearance. Yet it was probably the case that half of the working classes were still engaged in traditionally organized trades. By 1860 the cities of the United States were cities of workers, employers, and financiers. The overwhelming majority of the working classes were wage workers, many in reorganized crafts, with more among the thousands of laborers, domestics, and longshoremen. Those crafts retaining traditional production patterns accounted for perhaps one in five in the working classes. This is the dramatic change in social structure that is summarized in the term "industrialization." The single word embraces thousands of fits, starts, and experiments, hundreds of complex paths from the craft to waged work. Industrialization had many starting points—the investment needs of Boston merchants, the foundries of Pittsburgh, the mills of Lowell, and the shipbuilding of New York. Across that diversity, however, industrialization meant the erosion and eventual disappearance of production by artisan and craftsmen and the creation in their place of "putting out" systems, wage labor, manufacture, and modern industry.

The most important symbol of these transformations was of course the factory. The mills and shoe producers of New England, the producer industries in Pittsburgh, Philadelphia, and the suburbs of Baltimore offered machine, order, and smokestack to those who aspired to surpassing England's greatness. If the experience of the mill girls was wholly new, producer industries and shoe manufactures drew more closely on the crafts. In the foundries and iron and steel mills many places remained for craftsmen and skilled workers. For these compensation was high and so was status.[35] In shoemaking and printing, however, innovation and an increased division of labor destroyed the craft and facilitated the introduction of unskilled labor. James Harper and his brothers, the successful publishers, were well-known examples of industrious "small masters made good" whose marketing skill, innovative production techniques, and impressive managerial skills put them at the forefront of their business. A contemporary children's book, *The Harper Establishment, or How the Story Books are Made*, describes an elaborate and precise division of labor among dozens of men, women, boys, and girls. The compositor, the author tells us, "has every inducement to learn to work fast, for he is paid, not by the time, but by the quantity of work which he accomplishes," more precisely, "the amount of *corrected* work that they do." Girls rubbing type were "so dextrous and quick, indeed, that you will have to look very closely to follow." Men and boys smoothing paper also worked "with a dexterity and rapidity that is surprising." The foreman, meanwhile could "survey his whole dominion, and observe the action of all the presses and machinery" from the vantage point of an elevated desk.[36] Apprenticeship, of course, had disappeared entirely. By

---

[35] Michael Holt, *Forging a Majority: The Formation of the Republican Party in Pittsburgh, 1848-1860* (New Haven: Yale University Press, 1969), ch. 3.

[36] Jacob Abbott, *The Harper Establishment or How the Story Books are Made* (New York, 1855; repr., Hamden, Conn.: Shoe String Press, 1956), passim.

1850 a committee of the printers' union was complaining of irregular pay and the invasion of women, boys, and girls, as well as inexperienced men whose presence undermined the wage scale.[37]

James Harper and his brothers represented the most successful of small masters who became industrialists. There were many aspiring master craftsmen in the 1830s, but few of these ended up presiding over neatly organized factory establishments, and few workers were employed in factory environments. Rather, industrializing transformations reorganized crafts work in smaller shops, homes, and garrets. Although rapid from a historical point of view, these transformations involved complex and gradual changes in the organization of work. In clothing manufacture, for example, the transition from craft production to manufacture took this more common nonfactory path. Perhaps into the 1830s, clothing was only produced by master tailors, working with journeymen and apprentices, in small shops. Clothing was almost always made for the "custom" trade, that is, for individual customers (people who could not afford custom-made clothing bought second-hand clothing). A small amount of ready-made clothing, mostly for servants' uniforms, was produced in the off-season. Slaves also wore ready-made work clothes, and the increase in demand for these meant that by 1840 establishments with no relation to the custom trade began to appear. This market and the appearance of other markets put pressure (via merchants) on the traditional relations of manufacture, and although custom and ready-made production were still associated, three kinds of production were found. The first, traditional relation was called the "inside shop." In the second, journeymen and their families worked at home for a master tailor functioning more or less as a contractor. In the third form, contractors contracted out-work to be done at home, and perhaps ran workshops. Contractors, not themselves master tailors, used less-skilled labor for mass production.

By mid-century, a fourth form, the wholesale manufacturer, prevailed. For the manufacturer, tailors might work at home, in a room rented in cooperation with others, or in the shop of a small contractor (the latter two termed "outside shops"). Wholesale manufacturers also increased the participation of women in the trade. These were divided into two groups: older, more skilled women, with home responsibilities, might buy or rent a sewing machine and work at home. Younger, less-skilled women worked in supervised workshops. Workers were often required to furnish machines, fuel for irons, needles, thread, trimmings, or buttons for their

---

[37] The report appears in Geo. A. Stevens, *New York Typographical Union No. 6* (Albany: J. B. Lyon Co., 1913), pp. 209ff.

work. The manufacturer increased the division of labor, separating out from the abilities of master tailor the occupations of cutter, baster, operative, finisher, and presser. In some branches the tailor was eliminated completely. By mid-century, the great mass of workers in clothing manufacture were unskilled or semiskilled. In off-season periods they were simply out of work, unlike the journeymen working with the master tailor. Nor could they aspire either to learn the craft of tailoring or to develop their own clientele. Rather, whether working at home or in the shop, they were wage laborers dependent on securing employment from a manufacturer or contractor. Because the crafts basis of manufacture had been destroyed, new workers might easily be brought into the labor force.[38]

More generally, a master craftsman with expanding trade was likely to find himself more and more occupied with his suppliers and buyers, and with finances, credit, and bookkeeping. The ambitious master was more contractor than industrial captain. At the same time he was reorganizing production if not engaged in it himself. Apprenticeship was rapidly becoming illusory, a euphemism for child labor. Journeymen too were restricted in their field of operation, performing an ever narrower range of tasks as part of a broadening division of labor. Work was increasingly subdivided, the piece wage used as both carrot and stick in efforts to increase productivity. Some of this reorganization took place in workshops, but more often employer and employee were not at the same site—as the size of a master's payroll was increasing, a greater proportion of workers were employed outside his immediate supervision. Employees commonly rented workspace in lofts or shacks, or worked at home. These "outworkers" accounted for the majority of employees in the industrializing crafts; their situation signified the replacement of the artisan by the wage laborer.[39]

The same period was also one of mass immigration, and as industrialization and growth reshaped the social structure new and old citizens found different kinds of places within it. Thus industrialization was accompanied by a dramatic cultural division of labor. The distribution of workers, by nativity, may be examined across class structure in Boston in 1850 and New York City in 1855. (See table 5.1) In each city, wage workers II represented about 35 percent of the work force, but less than 20 percent of either German- or U.S.-born workers and more than 50

---

[38] Jesse E. Pope, *The Clothing Industry in New York* (Columbia: University of Missouri Press, 1905), esp. pp. 11-39.

[39] Sean Wilentz, *Chants Democratic: New York City and the Rise of the American Working Class, 1790-1850* (New York: Oxford University Press, 1984), offers a description of the contractor and the ambitious master in ch. 3.

Table 5.1. Two Examples of the Cultural Division of Labor at Mid-Century

Class Structure	U.S.-Born	Irish-Born	German-Born	Whole Work Force[g]
Boston, 1850				
Owners[a]	8.3	0.6	2.8	5.2
Small Proprietors[b]	15.2	4.0	9.9	10.5
Professionals[c]	7.1	0.8	7.7	4.8
Artisans[d]	19.2	5.3	21.9	13.9
Wage workers I[e]	36.4	19.7	40.5	30.1
Wage workers II[f]	13.8	69.6	17.2	35.5
Totals	100.0	100.0	100.0	100.0
	(20,734)	(14,096)	(886)	(39,344)
New York City, 1855				
Owners	9.9	0.4	1.5	3.4
Small Proprietors	18.4	4.3	13.9	10.5
Professionals	10.8	1.2	2.3	6.4
Artisans	13.0	8.9	18.7	12.2
Wage workers I	36.9	26.2	45.5	28.3
Wage workers II	11.0	59.0	18.1	39.2
Totals	100.0	100.0	100.0	100.0
	(50,075)	(84,700)	(43,027)	(191,059)

SOURCES: Boston data computed from Oscar Handlin, *Boston's Immigrants, 1790–1880* (New York: Atheneum, 1968), table 13, pp. 250–51. New York City data computed from Robert Ernst, *Immigrant Life in New York City, 1825–1863* (New York: Columbia University Press, 1949), app. 1.

[a] Includes bankers, merchants, large manufacturers.

[b] Grocers, clothiers, boardinghouse keepers and other storekeepers.

[c] Attorneys and counselors, physicians, higher governmental employees, etc.

[d] Cabinetmakers, gunsmiths, musical and other instrument makers, some in construction, shipbuilding, and similar trades.

[e] Proletarianized crafts: Textile workers, hatters, clerks, bakers, printers, glassworkers, etc.

[f] Occupations that were always wage labor: domestics, cartmen, coachmen, common laborers, watchmen, etc.

[g] Whole work force includes others born outside the U.S., Ireland, or Germany.

percent of Irish workers. In neither city did many Irish secure occupations of artisan status, though in New York 13 percent of those born in America and nearly 19 percent of the Germans worked in artisan trades; in Boston about 20 percent of each of these groups were artisans.

Across America's cities the social structure was reorganized by industrialization and immigration. Not only in factory towns like Lynn and Lowell, Massachusetts, but also in the nation's metropolises, getting, spending, and producing were reordered in the antebellum years. In New York City by 1855 wage workers accounted for 82 percent of the working population, and 70 percent of the manufacturing labor force worked for employers with twenty-five or more hands.[40] In Baltimore manufacturers and corporate directors rose to prominence, challenging the city's merchant elite. More than New York, in Baltimore manufactures were conducted in factories, but even in the handicraft trades an increased division of labor and the labor of women and children displaced the artisan. Independent, small-shop craftsmen were decimated: fewer than one in ten of the shops in 1850 remained in business in 1860.[41] In Philadelphia industrialization took many forms. Alongside the artisans' or neighborhood shops the new forms—out-work, the sweatshop, large-scale manufactures, and factories—employed the preponderance of productive workers by 1850.[42] Philadelphia exhibited an elaborate cultural division of labor by the same date. Nearly half of the Irish immigrants there were employed as day laborers, at carting, or in handloom-weaving. Nearly 12 percent of the Germans worked as day laborers; two-thirds worked in skilled trades. Even fewer native-born whites were engaged in unskilled labor and the industrialized crafts. They were concentrated instead in "the prestigious building trades and printing and disproportionately represented in commerce and the professions."[43]

In Newark, New Jersey, an increased division of labor and the invention of productive machinery "rendered craftsmen's skills obsolete."[44] At the time of Andrew Jackson's election as President, the city's major productive pursuits—hatting, leathermaking, trunk making, jewelry making, saddlemaking, shoemaking—were all, save shoemaking, performed in traditional ways. By the election of Lincoln all had been industrialized to some extent.[45] Here too the foreign-born were concentrated in the most industrialized, least skilled, and least secure employments.[46] In Boston industrial expansion was fueled by massive immigration, with the number employed in major industries doubling between 1845 and 1855 and again between 1855 and 1865. In the sewing trades, sugar refining, and furniture-making industries, cheap labor facilitated a more elaborate

[40] For class structure, see table 5.1. On firm size, see Carl N. Degler, "Labor in the Economy and Politics of New York City, 1850-1860: A Study in the Impact of Early Industrialism" (Ph.D. diss., Columbia University, 1952), p. 9.

[41] Gary Lawson Browne, *Baltimore in the Nation, 1789-1861* (Chapel Hill: University of North Carolina Press, 1980), pp. 178-84.

[42] Bruce Laurie, *Working People of Philadelphia 1800-1850* (Philadelphia: Temple University Press, 1980), pp. 15-27.

[43] Bruce Laurie, Theodore Hershberg, and George Alter, "Immigrants and Industry: The Philadelphia Experience, 1850-1880," *Journal of Social History* 9, no. 2 (1975), pp. 219-67, quotation at 234.

[44] Hirsch, *Roots of the American Working Class*, p. 37.

[45] Ibid., p. 35.

[46] Ibid., p. 48.

division of labor and mechanical invention changed the practice of the craft. In the 1850s new rolling mills, forges, ironworks, and rail factories were also established in the city. With more women employed in the needle trades alone than in the entire male work force, Boston was the site of the archetypal Irish neeedlewoman. Since very nearly half of the Irish-born men worked as day laborers, they took their place here as elsewhere near the bottom of the cultural division of labor.[47] Pittsburgh's iron, glass, and cotton industries all expanded in the antebellum era, the first most spectacularly; Pittsburgh was the site of considerable industrial combat. Ironworkers struck repeatedly in the 1840s, as did women in the cotton mills. While "capitalistic aristocrats lolled on sofas and lounges in their princely mansions," their workers were "ground into poverty."[48]

There were artisans who escaped, at least for this generation, these disorganizing changes. In New York's shipbuilding industries craft solidarity, a strong apprentice system, and artisan militance in favor of a limited workday survived until the Civil War. In the building trades, too, craft organizations persisted even as unions were being organized among some journeymen. Mechanics Mutual Protection, a secret organization primarily of building trades artisans, was organized in 1841. Its leaders made much of their Christian principles, argued that the interests of masters and journeymen were the same, and declared strikes both unnecessary and pernicious. Some jewelers, coopers, pipemakers, and cabinetmakers also maintained craft or "protective" organizations.[49]

These men were the exceptions, for by the middle of the 1850s most urban employees were artisans no longer. Most of those engaged in trades producing consumer goods were simply wage workers. Outworkers in a number of trades tried to organize cooperative workshops and stores but these quickly succumbed to competition. More frequently and more successfully men and women organized unions. Most journeymen's associations founded in the 1830s did not survive the depression of 1837 and the hard years of the decade that followed. There were exceptions—the New England mill towns were sites of vigorous wage and ten-hours agitation. In Pittsburgh men and women organized in the iron industries,

[47] Oscar Handlin, *Boston's Immigrants 1790-1880* (New York: Atheneum, 1968), pp. 74-80, 250-51 (app., table 12).

[48] Holt, *Forging a Majority*, pp. 29-30.

[49] On Mechanics Mutual Protection, see Commons, *Documentary History*, 8:243-63, and Helen Zahler, *Eastern Workingmen and National Land Policy 1829-1862* (New York: Columbia University Press, 1941), p. 71. On shipbuilding trades, see Robert G. Albion and Jennie B. Pope, *The Rise of the New York Port, 1815-1860* (1939; repr., Charles Scribner and Sons, 1970). On Protective Unions, see Stevens, *New York Typographical Union No. 6*, pp. 4-7.

and militantly—at times violently—defended their wage demands and insisted on a ten-hour day.

As prosperity returned, organization flowered. In 1850 there was a sudden upsurge in union formation. In New York, hat finishers, whitework weavers, turners, upholsterers, button and fringe makers, quarrymen, marble cutters, stonecutters, boot and shoe workers, saddle and harness makers, boilermakers, iron moulders, journeymen silversmiths, type founders, and tailors organized or reorganized to raise wages or better working conditions. Straw and pamilla sewers organized a union in the same year. Journeymen house carpenters and journeymen painters, who had been organized in the 1830s, formed new organizations after 1850 and laborers in the building trades organized as well.[50] In Boston, tailors, granite cutters, and others organized at about the same time.[51] In Newark, shoemakers, curriers, carpenters, masons, and tailors organized as the economy revived.[52] In Milwaukee, too, the closing years of the 1840s saw a flowering of worker organization, and tailors, shoemakers, cabinetmakers, printers, and cigarmakers all formed unions by 1860.[53] In Pittsburgh in 1850 fourteen organized trades joined forces in the United Trades and Labor Organizations of Allegheny County.[54]

This burgeoning organizational life was accompanied by a protest against the degradation from independence to "wage slavery." One union broadside, for example, declared that "competition is an evil only because labor is a marketable commodity, or because labor is dependent upon capital in the hands of other persons than laborers. . . . Equally possessed of the means of earning a livelihood, they would be content to do so."[55] Strikes would "prevent the growth of an unwholesome aristocracy, whose only aim is to acquire wealth by robbery of the toiling masses" and enable labor to "take that position which God intended men should fill— truly independent of his fellow, and above the position of mere 'wageslaves.' "[56]

Even more numerous than the first group of wage workers was a second: those laborers, retail clerks, drivers, porters, and domestics whose work had never held the status of the crafts. These formed 49 percent of the working classes in New York in 1855 and 45 percent of the working

[50] Stevens, *New York Typographical Union No. 6.*
[51] Handlin, *Boston's Immigrants*, pp. 159-60, 217.
[52] Hirsch, *Roots of the American Working Class*, p. 116.
[53] Kathleen Conzen, *Immigrant Milwaukee 1836-1860: Accommodation and Community in a Frontier City* (Cambridge: Harvard University Press, 1976), p. 113.
[54] Holt, *Forging a Majority*, p. 89.
[55] Degler, "Labor," p. 263.
[56] Ibid., p. 262.

classes in Boston in 1850. There were many women in this class, for it
included domestic servants, housekeepers, and laundresses. It was also
the most heavily foreign born of the classes. Perhaps because they had
so many sisters, brothers, husbands, and cousins among the labor movement's wage workers I, the upsurge of unionism in 1850 embraced wage
workers II as well. In New York City that year not only those in needle
and building trades but also omnibus drivers, public porters, and coachmen formed unions. Between 1849 and 1852 boot and shoe clerks, dry
goods clerks, grocers' clerks, actors, and barbers also formed employees'
organizations.[57] In 1843 common laborers had organized the Laborers'
Union Association. Chartered as a benevolent society by the legislature
in 1845, the laborers went on strike in 1846 and again in 1850. Masons'
laborers also organized a union.[58] In 1846 unskilled Irishmen in Boston
organized the Boston Laborers Association, which included dock and
warehouse workers. Waiters in Boston also organized.[59] In New York
the Irish Societies Convention served as an umbrella for all organized
Irish workers and as a voice advocating labor's interests; elsewhere
too there were federated labor organizations for the Irish and the
Germans.[60]

   The resurgent organizational life of the 1850s suggests that the cultural division of labor in the American work force had both divisive and
binding effects. On one hand, cultural difference increased the social distance between artisans, largely born in the United States, and wage
workers, who were predominantly immigrants. Many of the organizations that supported nativist parties (which were anti-immigrant and,
usually, anti-Catholic) emphasized their artisan membership as well as
their Protestantism. Both the Order of United American Mechanics and
Mechanics Mutual Protection, for example, were involved with nativist
parties. More generally, the organizational life that bound master and
journeyman together in the crafts—and bound them against encroaching
industrialism facilitated by immigration—excluded those who accepted
a future of wage labor.

   On the other hand, the cultural division of labor may well have
strengthened ties between those wage workers whose occupations were
proletarianized crafts—like shoemakers or tailors—and those whose
work had no crafts antecedents, like common laborers, retail clerks, bus
drivers, and the like. Rather than rejecting the latter "dishonorable
trades," wage workers I who embraced a unionist strategy of self-defense

[57] Stevens, *New York Typographical Union No. 6.*
[58] Ibid., pp. 7-10.
[59] Handlin, *Boston's Immigrants*, p. 160.
[60] Degler, "Labor," p. 148.

saw common ties with wage workers II. And for those common laborers, retail clerks, drivers, dockworkers, and grooms who organized, it may well have been the example set by the Irish and German cousins, brothers, and sisters in the labor movement that encouraged their own efforts. These ties contrast sharply with the organizational life of the first labor movement: in the 1830s citywide trades congresses, as well as the labor movement more broadly, had rejected laborers and unskilled workers. Workers of the 1850s inherited a republican self-respect and workplace militance from artisans, but the new class identity and the organizational life of the 1850s could embrace all those who experienced labor as "a marketable commodity."

III. Sentiment and Disposition

In the generation from 1830 to 1850 massive immigration and profound reorganizations of labor made the working classes suddenly diverse. If in the 1830s the organizations of the working classes offered a coherent political economy of their own, by the 1850s the sentiments of the working classes were more varied and diffuse. The organizations of the 1830s for the most part represented artisans, if emphatically journeyman artisans. By the 1850s there were more spokesmen of the unskilled parts of the working classes, and more who identified themselves simply as wage laborers. In addition, the ideology of 1830s radicals and artisans itself underwent certain transformations. Across the working classes, the sentiments and dispositions of the final antebellum decade evidenced both a persistence of themes from a generation before and amendments reconciling strongly held values with new realities.

Republicanism not only informed the early labor movement in the antebellum years but also provided key values for the labor movement of the 1850s in politics, in popular organizations like the volunteer fire companies, and in the struggle against the cultural offensives of Protestant evangelicalism and the temperance movement. Republican rhetoric was also prominent in the statements of the new unions of the 1850s. Omnibus drivers organizing in 1851 argued, much as unionists had in the 1830s, that they regarded the "equality of rights and opportunities as the only basis upon which Society can rest and be productive of happiness, virtue, and freedom." Bakers claimed they needed organization to decrease the hours of work lest they be too weary after their "week's unnatural toil" to "study Nature and Nature's God." Strikes and increased wages were necessary to workers "to prevent the growth of an unwholesome aristocracy" and to guarantee the "independence" of workingmen. Education and fair remuneration were necessary because they "confer an honor on the workingman ... which gives him a nobility of soul, and an erect and manly republican independence."[61] Firemen campaigned continuously for an increased democratization of procedures within the volunteer fire department—like the election of fire chiefs and station leaders—and fought to maintain the autonomy of fire companies from city government and the political parties. Fire company names exhibited the importance of republican thought and memorialized the heroes of republicanism; these included Lafayette, Franklin, and Washington.[62]

The language of republicanism and civil liberties was also at the heart of resistance to evangelical Protestanism, anti-Catholic organization, and the temperance movement. Temperance legislation was denounced as a "sumptuary law" and as such the "bane of all republics." The "right to drink" was a civil liberty especially precious to the poor man and the immigrant; what recommended democracy over monarchy if not that the "rights of the poor man, as well as the rich, are respected?" Nativists were denounced as "traitors to the Constitution," the repeal of temperance legislation celebrated as "a triumph of social, political, and religious rights."[63] If these cultural issues were particularly important to Irish Catholics, the language of liberty and republicanism was one they surely shared with other workers. It was the Irish, after all, who invented the slogan "no taxation without representation." The language of republicanism pervaded the activities of the working classes in the antebellum period.

Republicanism's deep meaning and special appeal had everything to do with the important role of common men as the republic's citizens. For the artisan, the "nobility of soul, and ... manly *republican* independence" were one with craft pride, skill, and independence. The world view that ascribed to the artisan the role of producing all values and safeguarding political liberty made him militant in defense of his craft and his rights. If the artisan's autonomy was significantly eroded in the generation from 1830 to 1850, the militance was passed on intact. Alan Dawley, for example, has written that "the militancy of the factory worker is hard to imagine without the legacy of artisan protest against the encroachments of capital into the sphere of production."[64] Militance

[61] Commons, *Documentary History*, 8:256.
[62] Bruce Laurie, "Fire Companies and Gangs in Southwark: the 1840s," in *The Peoples of Philadelphia, A History of Ethnic Groups and Lower Class Life, 1790-1940*, ed. Allen F. Davis and Mark H. Haller (Philadelphia: Temple University Press, 1973); George W. Sheldon, *The Story of the Volunteer Fire Department of the City of New York* (New York: Harper and Bros., 1882).
[63] By New York's Democratic party, *New York Times*, November 11, 1854.
[64] Dawley, *Class and Community*, p. 228.

and self-assertion were not only for use in defense of wages and work prerogatives. Among casual laborers and putting-out home workers as well and in the fire departments in Philadelphia, Bruce Laurie found "an indefatigably autonomous culture" that insisted, among other things, on "an abiding hatred of upper-class reformers."[65]

The critique of industrialism as immoral and promoting selfish values also persisted well into the 1840s and 1850s. Indeed, hardly an organization that claimed to speak for the working classes before the Civil War failed to defend a society remembered, if rather romantically, as characterized by mutuality, reciprocity, and familial relations between high and low. Those labor organizations that united master and journeyman made special claim to preserving these values that were, to their regret, passing away. Mechanics Mutual Protection spokesmen argued that neither the strike nor violence but mechanics' solidarity and a feeling of Christian brotherhood would promote the goals of higher pay, an end to prison labor, and the institution of a ten-hour workday. Hostility between classes was in this view not inevitable, but followed from a "spirit of competition" that could be rooted out by an emphasis on Christian brotherhood.[66] Others preached a more militant Christianity, as the Pawtucket evangelist who wrote a pamphlet on the Biblical text, "Do not rich men oppress you? Lo to ye rich men, weep and howl for the miseries that shall come upon you."[67]

More militant unions insisted that "the system of competition" was "subversive of morality, religion, and virtue." Organization was necessary, they argued, because the industrial system "causes those to be oppressors who wish to be just."[68] The temperance movement, too, saw increasing social disharmony and argued that temperance was "the most effectual means of closing this fatal chasm in our social system of knitting up those social sympathies again."[69] For others, the "fatal chasm" was clearly tied to the creation of a new social order. One speaker at a Boston mechanics' meeting explained the change in the following way: "The division of society in the producing and the non-producing classes, and the fact of the unequal distribution of value between the two, introduces us at once to another distinction—that of capital and labor. ... Labor now becomes a commodity, wealth capital, and *the natural order of*

[65] Laurie, *Working People*, pp. 54, 66.

[66] Commons, *Documentary History*, 8:246-56.

[67] Quoted in Gary Kulik, "Pawtucket Village and the Strike of 1824: The Origins of Class Conflict in Rhode Island," *Radical History Review*, no. 17 (Spring 1978): 5-38, quotation at p. 17.

[68] Degler, "Labor," p. 266; Stevens, *New York Typographical Union No. 6*, pp. 23-24.

[69] Bruce Laurie, "Nothing on Compulsion: Life Styles of Philadelphia Artisans, 1820-1850," *Labor History*, no. 15 (1974):337-66, quotation at p. 350.

things is entirely reversed. Antagonism and opposition of interest is introduced in the community; capital and labor stand opposed."[70] In this new
social order, the virtuous, industrious, independent mechanic was
replaced by "labor," the "hard working masses," and "laboring classes,"
who conceded that "it is useless for us to disguise from ourselves the fact
that, under the present arrangement of things, there exists a perpetual
antagonism between labor and capital."[71] It was this system that undermined the virtue and vigor of the laboring classes. In response to the
moral stewards who preached salvation and temperance for self-improvement, more than one labor spokesman argued that drink was not the root
of degradation and crime, but degradation the root of crime and drink.
New York Democrat Mike Walsh expressed the view succinctly: "The
great and fruitful source of crime and misery on earth is the *inequality
of society*, the abject dependence of honest, willing industry upon idle and
dishonest capitalists."[72]

The working classes supported what may be called moral-economic
concepts of justice, as opposed to the emerging contractual notions of
justice subscribed to by their social betters.[73] E. P. Thompson explains
the moral economy in this way:

[Popular] grievances operated within a popular consensus as to what were legitimate and what were illegitimate practices in marketing, milling, baking, etc.
This in its turn was grounded upon a consistent traditional view of social norms
and obligations, of the proper economic functions of several parties within the
community, which, taken together, can be said to constitute the moral economy
of the poor. An outrage to these moral assumptions, quite as much as actual
deprivation, was the usual occasion for direct action.[74]

The food riot is the classic expression of the moral economy, both because
it expresses outrage at the immoral hoarding of food and because it pun-

---

[70] Dawley, *Class and Community*, pp. 63-64, emphasis added.
[71] Quoted in Degler, "Labor," p. 258.
[72] *Sketches of the Speeches and Writings of Michael Walsh: Including His Poems and
Correspondence Compiled by a Committee of the Spartan Association* (New York:
Thomas McSpeden, 1843).
[73] On changing values in the middle and business classes, see, e.g., Morton J. Horwitz,
The Transformation of American Law, 1780-1860 (Cambridge: Harvard University
Press, 1977) and Clifford S. Griffen, *Their Brothers' Keepers: Moral Stewardship in the
United States, 1800-1865* (New Brunswick: Rutgers University Press, 1960).
[74] E. P. Thompson, "The Moral Economy of the English Crowd in the Eighteenth Century," *Past and Present*, no. 50 (1971):76-136. The "moral economy" is often offered as
a "precapitalist" social phenomenon. Nevertheless, certain kinds of crowd behavior and
values associated with Thompson's moral economy persist well past the period he writes
about. As these values and behaviors persist and change only gradually with the coming
of industrialism, it seems unfortunate to set up a categorization that does not recognize
them as "moral economic" when continuity and persistence are clear.

ishes those who fail to perform the social obligations of the rich to the poor. There were food riots in the United States in the depression of 1837. Yet as Thompson explains of eighteenth-century England, it was the government that was expected to enforce these obligations by, for example, regulating markets. Here I want to distinguish between desires for social familism, on one hand, and on the other an insistence on governmental adherence to what Thompson calls "the paternalist tradition of the authorities." After 1850 some workers gave up on the possibility of social familism; others insisted it could be preserved. Militant and non-militant workers alike, however, were not ready to let government off the mutualist hook. This change in target invoked a change of rhetoric from obligation to rights.

Here, as in the towns Thompson discusses, city government had a long history of involvement in the market and the protection of the consumer. Eighteenth-century city government in the United States regulated and owned markets, ensuring that consumers were brought face to face with farmers and eliminating the middleman. Wholesalers were forbidden to enter the market before late in the day; various monopoly practices were illegal. The city council set prices on provisions and the assize on bread and also at times curtailed the export of commodities for local consumption.[75] By the nineteenth century most of the functions had eroded considerably, but the erosion was contentious. Although there were elite pressures for government to withdraw from this activity, there were intense popular pressures that it not do so. There were, for example, repeated popular calls for the revival of the assize on bread up to the Civil War. In the West the difference between popular and elite notions of "right" or "justice" was clearly brought out in the question of the bonds counties and states had issued to promote railroad development.[76] In the depression of the 1850s it was very popular for state and county governments to renounce these bonds because in such times the taxes required to make payment on the bonds were oppressive. From the popular and "moral-economic" point of view it was also "just" that bankers not require payment when that payment would be oppressive. From the bankers' point of view, right and justice of course lay in fulfillment of contractual obligation. On the eastern seaboard in the 1850s the depres-

---

[75] On eighteenth-century New York, see my *A City in the Republic: Antebellum New York and the Origins of Machine Politics* (New York: Cambridge University Press, 1984), ch. 4; on Philadelphia, see Sam Bass Warner, Jr., *The Private City: Philadelphia in Three Periods of its Growth* (Philadelphia: University of Pennsylvania Press, 1968), pt. I; on Baltimore, see Browne, *Baltimore in the Nation*, pt. 1.

[76] On the bonds issue, Holt, *Forging a Majority*, ch. 6 and Griffen, *Their Brothers' Keepers*, pp. 94-95.

sion brought with it demands for "work or bread" from city government, demands that joined notions of popular "rights" with governmental obligations. There were simultaneous demands for restoration of the assize on bread and the curtailment of exports. If their social betters viewed these as "foreign" and even "communistic" doctrines threatening the stability of the republic (and they did), from the workers' point of view they were simply the obvious course for a government committed to the common good, in which the poor stood on an equal footing with the rich. In this way popular republicanism and a persistent morality were adapted to industrial society.

In the last antebellum decade the working classes were more ideologically diverse and ethnically pluralist than in the Jacksonian era. They were also substantially more proletarian than the working classes of the age of Jackson. Proletarianization was accompanied by a new sense of class, announced by labor spokesmen at the workplace, in the neighborhood and in politics, and institutionalized in unions. Although this new sense of class was not shared by all of the working classes, nevertheless common themes existed across working-class diversity. In general, the working classes no longer saw the domination of government by wealth, or government policy overall, as the source of economic distress. Rather, they recognized an autonomous economy "making oppressors of those who wish to be just." Although their understanding of society changed, certain values and a distinctive sense of justice continued. The working classes resisted the harsh morality of laissez faire, supply and demand, and contract obligation that was rapidly winning the favor of their social betters. In their stead there persisted an assertion that the weak not be left as the prey of the strong and the poor not be abandoned to the heartless forces of the market.

IV. *Politics*

Labor's political efforts in the 1840s were dominated by the struggle for ten-hours legislation on one hand and by a variety of radicals like land reformers and cooperationists on the other. The resurgence of unionism in the 1850s also meant a quickened pace of political demands. These were for the most part familiar: better public education, a ten-hour work day, abolition of contract labor on public works, lien laws, homestead legislation, and democratizing reforms (e.g., election of judges). Overwhelmingly urban, the working classes needed to work through the major parties to achieve their goals, since these goals usually required action by state or national government. There labor necessarily worked through partisan coalitions. In contrast, local political life was strongly marked by working-class citizens. In the 1830s local political debate had simply echoed the national arguments of Whig and Democratic parties; in the 1850s local politics had more rhythm and rhetoric of its own, and this was largely (though not exclusively) due to the presence and the pressures of the working classes.

The recognition that the "industrial system" was not government's creation did not mean a withdrawal from political activity. If anything those who were most insistent on the antagonism of labor and capital, those who were in the most militant unions, and those radicals who claimed their program was in labor's interest were also those who most loudly championed political activity. Some of this activity was in loose working relationships between radicals and labor spokesman. The Industrial Congresses formed in 1849-1850 represented both land reform and labor sentiment. The congresses insisted that "political action on measures designed to elevate the condition of the industrial classes is the surest, speediest, and most effective plan for effecting the exodus of the producing classes from the oppressions and grievances under which they are suffering."[77] From the federal government the Industrial Congresses demanded land limitation and plans foreshadowing the Homestead Act. From the states, woman suffrage, ten hours legislation, and an end to prison labor; in the state and city, public construction undertaken by government itself and a minimum wage on public works. The political method for achieving these goals was to ask candidates whether or not they approved the congress platform and to endorse candidates who responded positively. The congress suffered from antagonism between radicals and those who favored "unionism pure and simple" and, more seriously, from interference by the political parties; as a result the congresses had folded by the middle of the 1850s.

The congresses had, nevertheless, served an important function. Where labor made demands on local government in the 1850s its platform was much like that presented by the congress: abolition of the contract system on public works, public employment without partisan preference, and a minimum wage on public works. Those demands were loudly voiced in the depression of the mid-1850s. There were "bread or work" demonstrations in Newark, Philadelphia, Providence, and New York. Interestingly, none of these was accompanied by food riots, though the looting of food stores was sometimes suggested. The charity of the wealthy, although recognized, was declared both inadequate and degrading. In these demonstrations the obligations of the rich to the poor were no

[77] Accounts of the Industrial Congresses may be found in Commons, *Documentary History*, 8:285-309 and Commons, *History of Labor*, 1:547-63.

longer at issue; rather, the demand was that government alleviate the suffering of its working-class citizens. Radical William West, for example, who was prominent in the demonstrations of the unemployed in New York, argued that it was obvious that "private capital is insufficient to satisfy the demands of labor. Unless you, therefore, substitute the public for private capital, in the employment of these thousands of idle workmen, it must be apparent that the men cannot live except upon charity."[78]

To the argument that workers should be patient and wait for the workings of the market to end the depression, the *Irish News* replied, "When famine stares fifty thousand workmen in the face—when their wives and little ones cry to them for bread, it is no time to be laying down stale maxims of economy, quoting Adam Smith or any other politico-economical old fogy."[79] In Philadelphia it was German workmen who first formed an association to fight for relief. They rapidly allied with the American-born in a Central Workingmen's Committee, which demanded that Philadelphia's Common Council float a bond of $50 million for public works. In Newark, too, a joint committee petitioned the mayor and city council for relief.[80]

These demonstrations and demands, the new sense of class identity, and the bond issue in the West provided opportunities for politicians taking a militant workerist stance to build followings. Their popularity was based on a rhetoric of class hostility abusing speculators, exploiters, and the like, and championing the working man as the "bone and sinew of the republic." Democrat Leckey Harper expressed solidarity with Pittsburgh's striking workers when he denounced "the unholy and unjust attempts of the capitalists to crush and destroy the souls and bodies of men, women, and children."[81] New York Democrat Walsh took the occasion of a party nominating meeting to insist that

the best protectors of the laboring classes are the laborers themselves, and to Whig capitalists who volunteer on our behalf we reply. . . . [We] grew by your neglect . . . the instincts of wealth are the same everywhere . . . the affection of capitalists for the labouring classes is not more [hypocritical] in Great Britain than in the United States . . . in monopolizing the earning of labour in the former, they march . . . boldly to their object, while here they work to obtain it by tricks in Tariff, Currency, and Debt.[82]

[78] Degler, "Labor," p. 166.
[79] *Irish News*, Nov. 14, 1857, p. 2.
[80] P. Foner, *History of the Labor Movement*, pp. 237-40; Hirsch, *Roots of the American Working Class*, p. 129.
[81] Holt, *Forging a Majority*, p. 69.
[82] *New York Herald*, Oct. 19, 1842, p. 2.

Walsh was an outspoken critic of party and government policy, a militant labor advocate whose popularity—and hard-fisted followers—made it impossible for the party to deny him a place on either the podium or the ticket. In Trenton a Workingman's Union was organized by union members to question candidates for political office on a long list of state and national demands. In some places such efforts were ignored, but there not a candidate for office failed to endorse the general agenda of labor demands.[83] During the great shoemakers' strike in New England, congressional candidates in Lynn contributed to the strike fund. In the same city a Workingmen's party was organized to put in the mayor's office a man who would keep the police out of labor disputes and—himself a worker—demonstrate that the working classes were capable of self-government. Successful then and again later in the century, supporters of the Workingmen's party could support the Republicans in national elections but balked at supporting for local government those who claimed that "in our free states property is constantly changing hands."[84]

In New York, the great depression of the mid-1850s provided an excellent opportunity for an insightful Democrat to become the most powerful politician in the city. When unemployed workers demanded "work and bread" from city hall, Mayor Fernando Wood responded by echoing their own reasoning. In good times, he argued, workers "labor for a mere subsistence, while other classes accumulate wealth"; in bad times workers suffer while others have the resources to sustain themselves. Public action was necessary lest it be said here as in Europe that "those who produce everything get nothing, and those who produce nothing get everything."[85]

Workers won real concessions as well as rhetorical support from city government: expanded public employment in the depression (one thousand jobs per day on Central Park in New York City in the late 1850s), expanded health care provided by city government, unionization of public works and a minimum wage there, noninterference of police with labor disputes and the earliest of housing codes. Militance might also mean the cultural defense of the working classes. In this way, the militant stance mobilized an ethnically diverse political majority, and often a Democratic one. In New York it is clear that militant class rhetoric on the part of the Democratic party was used to recruit immigrant voters without alienating native-born voters. The Irish Societies Convention was consistent in supporting the demands of the Industrial Congresses, and oppo-

[83] P. Foner, *History of the Labor Movement*, pp. 240-45.
[84] Dawley, *Class and Community*, chs. 4, 8.
[85] See Bridges, *A City in the Republic*, ch. 6.

sition by Irish Catholics in particular to the cultural offensives of the evangelical movement fit in well with this militant style of local politics.

Not all workers agreed with the printers that "there exists a perpetual antagonism between labor and capital." Those who continued to be organized along the lines of the craft—the least proletarianized trades—insisted on the importance of craft solidarity. Mechanics Mutual Protection, the secret organization of building-trades artisans, serves as an example. Workers in these trades and in others still organized as crafts continued to emphasize the "independence" of the artisan as opposed to the "wage-slave," and Mechanics Mutual Protection continued to put forward a version of the labor theory of value, insisting that the "happiness of our whole people depends upon the remuneration which our Mechanics receive for their labor and skill and our freedom reposes on this anchor."[86]

In addition, there were everywhere workers who refused to identify with the "hard-working masses." Unable to distinguish themselves from the mass of "wage slaves" by their "independence," these workers attempted to do so by their sobriety, industry, and thrift.[87] These workers and those in the crafts experienced status anxiety on one hand and material anxiety on the other, and evidenced fears of a future of degrading "wage-slavery." Although those in more proletarianized trades had, generally speaking, embraced unionism as a class strategy for ameliorating their position within the industrial system, unionism was not a possible strategy for the craftsmen and militant unionism was an unacceptable strategy for others. Both groups of workers saw a threat in continued immigration, which facilitated industrialization by increasing the supply of labor, and both groups had ties to nativist politics. Indeed, the threatened but as yet unproletarianized crafts—also, not coincidentally, the occupations most clearly dominated by the American-born—were at the heart of that movement, in organizations like the Order of United American Mechanics, and temperance activity was also strongly associated with nativism.

It was possible, then, to mobilize these workers into cross-class political coalitions emphasizing shared interests. In contrast to the militant workerist style of politics in the cities just described, this sort of mobilization may be described as "mutualist." Here the unity of master and journeymen was updated to include employer and wage worker. Whiggish,

[86] Commons, *Documentary History*, 8:256.

[87] Paul Faler, "Cultural Aspects of the Industrial Revolution in Lynn, Mass.: Shoemakers and Industrial Morality, 1826-1860," *Labor History* 15 (Summer 1974):367-94. Joseph R. Gusfield, *Symbolic Crusade: Status Politics and the American Temperance Movement* (Urbana: University of Illinois Press, 1963), ch. 2.

Republican, and nativist, mutualist politics insisted on the primacy of the American interests and the subordination of class divisions. Two things particularly favored such mobilization. The first might be called "ostentatious paternalism," employer reinforcement of social familism and elite acceptance of moral-economic precepts. Wealthy Democrats in New York who wished to rout the "demogogues" from the party, for example, recognized that "action on the part of the moneyed classes, in such a manner as should prove to the working men that the sympathy of those who held the purse strings in their hands was not wanting to them" was required (they did not succeed).[88] In Providence the lavish display of charitable efforts on the part of wealthy men in the depression of the 1850s was accompanied by reminders that those who provoked class hostility in the United States were out of place. The *Providence Daily Journal*, denouncing "bread or work" agitation in New York City, described the errors of class warfare, arguing that it was not difficult to convince the hungry that the government and the rich were responsible for the lack of work and the high price of food, but that those leading them astray should be prevented from insisting on conflict "between the different classes whom the laws of nature and a just political economy have made mutually dependent."[89]

The second facilitator of mutualist politics was the tariff. The tariff was the policy cement of the view that labor and capital shared the same interest, and mutualist settlements, which were largely Republican, trumpeted the tariff as the best protection of American labor from English competition. The national platform of that party was largely devoted to other matters in the elections from 1856 to 1860, but local and working-class Republican partisanship was hardly based on a desire to destroy the "peculiar institution." In some places the possibility of the Homestead Act, quiet concessions to nativism, and more generally the tariff were the basis of working-class attraction to the party. Pittsburgh and Newark provide examples of the transition from Whiggery to Republicanism by such accommodations to the changing working classes. In Newark the tariff was "sacred," and Whigs and later Republicans never abandoned the rhetoric of the mechanic as "the very blood and muscle of society."[90] In Pittsburgh the tariff, Homestead Act, and "free labor," carefully wedded to racist and anti-Catholic sentiment, provided enough promise to win the city for the Republicans.

Although militance and mutualism were the dominant alternatives,

[88] *New York Herald*, Oct. 1, 1859, p. 4.
[89] *Providence Daily Journal*, Jan. 12, 1854.
[90] Hirsch, *Roots of the American Working Class*, p. 123 and ch. 6, passim.

there were other political styles as well (though without the power of a national presence they were inevitably minor themes). There were more than a few nativist politicians who, like the militants, based their appeal on a strong sense of class, a tough public image, and close association with rough supporters. Joel Barlow Sutherland in Philadelphia and Joel Barker in Pittsburgh serve as examples. Baltimore's Know-Nothing party became a political force when striking factory workers abandoned the Democrats en masse for supporting their employers; Know Nothing administrations in Massachusetts enacted a long list of labor reforms.

Nowhere did urban politicians succeed without softening the hard line of the dominant parties. The common theme of these concessions was to ameliorate the harshness of the "industrial system." In the cities I have called "mutualist," these concessions took the form of continued employer paternalism. Elsewhere, successful urban politicians supported one or another form of primitive, *sub rosa*, or informal welfarism. In New York and Philadelphia Democrats supported public works in times of distress. In Baltimore urban reformers did the same; in Boston it was a nativist boss who offered relief and public health reforms.

Beyond concessions enhancing social welfare local politics exhibited important commonalities from place to place. First, if from a national point of view the working classes were divided between the parties, in many local settings there was very little political competition after 1860. Instead large majorities were opposed by the intermittent campaigns of minority parties (usually municipal reformers). From this local perspective it would be a mistake to view the working classes as utterly divided against themselves, for one party (if not everywhere the same party) claimed the loyalty of most voters.

Second, the various styles of local politics incorporated a strong sense of class and a vision of the relation between classes. For many voters that sense was reinforced by ethnic solidarities or cultural interests, as when the New York Irish voted Democratic both because the Democracy was the "true home of the working classes" and because it protected their "right" to drink. As one might suspect where ethnicity and class were themselves so closely related, "class" and "ethnicity" were not always loyalties in competition with one another. Rather, they were often, especially in political life, reinforcing loyalties.

Third, local political life was considerably more than the simple expression of popular political culture (or, for that matter, minority efforts at social control). A variety of ties to state and national politics continued to play a role. Party leaders needed the contributions of wealthy men to keep the coffers full; party funding was to a considerable extent organized through national networks; party leaders desired access to patronage controlled by state and national governments that was only available if their own party was in power. To say this is simply to recall the many ways in which republicanism falls short of democracy. These general constraints on the many placed limits on the political capacity of the working classes in particular ways. The fact that much of the workers' agenda continued to be directed at higher governments meant that the working classes—largely urban—had the strongest incentives to join the major parties to achieve their political aims. If the artisans of the Jacksonian era had "natural allies" in other small-property owners everywhere, the wage workers of mid-century had no such good fortune; what alliances they were able to make were achieved through the party system. This, however, bound their political fate with the dynamics of party life. Local politicians made concessions to wage workers in the style and substance of local political life, but wage workers were subject to the discipline of party.

Fourth, antebellum cities shared a future of machine politics. Indeed, central elements of machine politics were already in place in the cities described. This was so because the institutions of machine politics coordinated an accommodation between the working classes and their social betters. The machine enabled politicians to behave in "mutualist" ways, perpetuating the "paternalist tradition of the authorities," sometimes accompanied by militant rhetoric, while simultaneously allowing government to withdraw formally from market relations. The "private" (and not incidentally coercive) welfare provided by machine politicians was acceptable to local elites; institutionalization of the New Deal–style demands of the working classes was not.

Finally, political leaders everywhere were tireless in their efforts to promote particular visions of society in order to create reliable majorities. Although local political life bore the imprint of the working classes and other social groups, it also reflected the successes of political leaders at creating partisan solidarities. It was these partisan solidarities that made the working classes of the United States "American" by the eve of the Civil War. Partisanship embraced ethnicity, class identity, and a vision of the relations between classes. This is not to say that the working classes were unreflective party loyalists. There was skepticism and insurgency in the antebellum period and well beyond. It suggests nevertheless that the result of the particular patterns of American political development—of the encounter between Painite artisan ideology and the setting of the United States—was that party incorporated and transcended class and status.

V. *Summary*

The first generation of an industrial working class appeared in the United States in the second quarter of the nineteenth century. The artisans of the Jacksonian era subscribed to views that have elsewhere been described as "artisan republicanism," "Painite," and "Jacobin." They saw the emerging industrial system as an immoral and unnatural one, fostering pernicious values and undermining the character of the citizenry. They blamed its advance on the control of government by wealth, and they resisted it by exhortation, organization, and political action.

By the Civil War the working classes were more proletarian and more ethnically diverse than in the age of Jackson. They no longer resisted the "industrial system" as much as they sought ways to make it more bearable. They located the sources of their distress less in government policy than in the workings of the economy. Many had forsaken hopes of mutualistic relationships with their social betters. If artisans saw themselves as industrious, independent mechanics, the newer working classes had a more modern self-consciousness as "laboring classes" and "hard-working masses." They were also Republicans and Democrats.

For all of these changes, certain important values and perceptions persisted. Republicanism informed working-class activity of many sorts. Everywhere working people continued to speak of themselves as the "bone and sinew" of the republic and the producers of all wealth, while their political culture centered on equality and rights. A persistently distinctive morality and sense of justice, moreover, distinguished their political life and demands from that of their social betters.

I have suggested here that these transformations came about as workers with certain cultural resources encountered industrialization in the United States. Although it has often been asked "what elements of American *culture* account for the consciousness of the working classes," I have instead emphasized what American artisans culturally *shared* with nineteenth-century artisans elsewhere. From this standpoint the logical question is "what elements of the American *setting* meant that a working class that, in 1830, evidenced striking dispositional and ideological similarities to its European counterparts developed in a quite distinctive way?" I have argued that two aspects of the American arena were particularly important: widespread suffrage and the urban locale of industrialization in a growing agricultural country.

The suffrage had radically disarming effects on artisans' ideology. Even though the Painite ideology that American, French, and British workers shared armed them for political battle, it was an inadequate political resource in the presence of the franchise. If artisans everywhere bequeathed to their proletarian successors militance, pride, and a firm belief in their entitlement to rights and political equality, Painite ideology had a strategic imperative elsewhere that was quickly made irrelevant in the young United States. That obvious programmatic imperative was to win the right to vote. That done, what program followed? In the United States the franchise deprived artisans of the cultural resources enabling them elsewhere to provide political leadership and forge a working class from the working classes.

Second, the logic of voting hinges on numbers and, in a country based on geographical representation, on location. As the working classes became increasingly proletarian they became increasingly confined to the cities. The American working class of the antebellum period was, from a national point of view, a very small group. When women, blacks, and youths who could not vote are subtracted, it becomes politically an even smaller group, an urban group in a rapidly expanding agrarian country. Once the working classes had lost those petty bourgeois characteristics of the artisan that enabled the Workingmen's parties to form alliances of mechanics, other small-property owners, and rural groups, the possibilities for a national or, in most places, even a state-level political presence for the working class were for all practical purposes nonexistent.

To the extent that the working classes could and did have a distinctive political impact it was in local politics. To the extent that the working classes desired influence at the state or national level they were dependent on the major parties, and through them joined cross-class alliances. Joining the political parties, however, meant among other things that the culture of the working classes, particularly in periods when labor organizations could not be maintained, was shaped, in ways that are sometimes hard to identify, by party rhetoric. Participation also meant that workers became Republicans and Democrats.

What was most distinctively American about the working classes in the United States in 1860 is that they *were* Republicans and Democrats. This is not to say that they were unreflectively or unreservedly so—insurgencies, rebellions, and later, withdrawal from politics abound. It is to say that partisan identity was "larger" than ethnic or class identity, and not simply reflective of either of them (or of anything else). That a man was Irish, a laborer, and sending his children to Catholic schools might all contribute to his vote; a man who was a master carpenter, Protestant, and hoping to move west might similarly cast a vote for a party that made him promises in all three respects. That partisan identity was "larger" than other identities makes intuitive sense when one thinks that a citizen need not choose to be ethnic *or* a member of a particular class *or* of a certain faith; one can be all of these things at once. By contrast a voter may choose only one party.

In emphasizing the importance of the suffrage some disclaimers should be made. I am not saying here, as Reinhard Bendix did, that workers in the United States were less angry about industrialization than voters elsewhere because they had the vote as "compensation."[91] Nor am I saying, with Alan Dawley and Paul Faler, that the vote offered a "ritual" of democracy that made politics a safety value for working-class discontent.[92] I am arguing that when workers had political goals (e.g., laws limiting the workday or the abolition of contract labor), were entitled to vote, and were an urban minority, they were inevitably drawn into electoral politics and party politics—and those practices just as inevitably shaped their consciousness and their culture. Workers became Republicans and Democrats not as the result of "symbolic" or "ritualistic" activities but in the service of quite objective working-class goals.

The idea that men of the working classes thought of themselves as Republicans and Democrats will encounter resistance. Among social historians two predispositions stand as barriers. One, the legacy of Commons, is that working people only engaged in politics when their "unionism pure and simple" was inadequate to their needs. Little in the antebellum history of the working classes supports this view. Second, contemporary social historians for the most part have assumed that the major political parties were institutions of the middle and upper classes and, insofar as workers were concerned, were at best agencies of social control and at worst alien excrescences on the consciousness of the lower orders.

Political scientists will also find the importance of partisanship counterintuitive. The behavioral approach to politics, focusing as it does on party choice, presupposes that partisanship is the result of other, more salient identities, and so in itself is superficial. Typically the analytic goal of students of politics is to say "Religion [or nation of origin, or class] mattered to this group of voters, and so they voted for this party." The contemporary political scene reinforces disciplinary predisposition: party

[91] Reinhard Bendix, *Nation Building and Citizenship* (New York: John Wiley & Sons, 1964), esp. pp. 61-74.

[92] Alan Dawley and Paul Faler, "Working Class Culture and Politics in the Industrial Revolution: Sources of Loyalism and Rebellion," *Journal of Social History* 9, no. 4 (1976):466-80, esp. pp. 474-75. The authors write that "for the first generations of industrial workers, politics was a continual re-enactment of a ritual embodying the social relations of an earlier era of unity."

competition, increasing independence (that is, lack of party identification), "cross-cutting cleavages," and low turnout all suggest that half of
the electorate is indifferent to party politics and most of the other half
might easily vote for either party.

Like students of politics, students of working-class formation have
searched for those sentiments and predispositions that caused workers to
choose particular political paths. Within this framework one is likely to
claim that because ethnicity mattered, or because the liberal tradition
mattered, or because "community" mattered, class did not matter, and
so workers in the United States did not form a labor party. Within this
framework it is not possible to answer the question, "what group identity
summarized the experience of the working classes?" by saying "party."
I am reminded of the day my sister Nancy, then a toddler, was being
taught the difference between boys and girls. After the critical evidence
was described, she was asked, was brother Bill a boy or a girl? Amy?
mom? dad? Having answered all these correctly, she was asked, "and
yourself, Nancy?" There was a pause, and then the answer, "I'm a
Unitarian."

Despite our predispositions there are good historical reasons to believe
that "Republican" or "Democrat" served as answers to the question of
public identity, and did so because partisanship embraced ethnic, class,
and religious experience as well as political reality and so was not simply
reflective of any one of them. These historial reasons are found in characteristics of nineteenth-century society and politics. First, the social
structure was not one of "cross-cutting cleavages" but rather, for most
people, one of mutually reinforcing positions. The cultural division of
labor meant that class, religion, and ethnicity most often reinforced one
another. In this setting the self-images and visions of society that parties
offered served to summarize much of individual experience. For that reason we have lengthy accounts of Jacksonian, Whig, and Republican persuasions, and these demonstrate that parties represented not simply interest but also morality, disposition, and ethic. Second, in many localities in
the 1850s, party competition was quite lopsided, pitting not one choice
against another but the many against the few. Third, to be an "independent" voter in the nineteenth century was unthinkable, considered as
absurd as the idea of a third sex. For all of these reasons, partisanship
served as a viable and meaningful public identity. As Robert Marcus has
written, in the nineteenth century "party politics was available as a labeling device defining who one was and offering a shorthand account of one's
general attitudes and objects of hero worship. . . . They placed people in

a context."[93] In our own time we recognize that partisanship may provide identity and organize solidarities when we say "he is a lunch-pail Democrat," "she is an old-line Republican," "he is a party regular," or even, "she is in the party."[94]

This argument may be more than a little contentious and certainly it is hardly proven here. The argument does, however, suggest some research directions that will clarify the "making" of American workers. The outpouring of scholarship on Jacksonian artisans has left those interested in working-class formation anxious for the answers to related questions. For example, I have argued that in general the setting of widespread suffrage meant that artisans lacked the cultural resources (or a program) for providing leadership to the working classes. It has often been suggested, moreover, that for cultural reasons they were not inclined to do so and sought, if anything, to distance themselves from immigrant wage workers. In some places, like Lynn and Pawtucket, artisans indeed "led," instructed, and surely supported the emerging proletariat. In New York and Philadelphia artisan radicals provided leadership to the working classes at crucial moments. In the same two cities, however, wage workers and artisans seem to have ended up in different parties. We need to know much more about the kinds of coalitions made among different sectors of the working classes and also about the role of other classes and politicians in these coalitions.

Asking these questions will raise more fundamental ones. Much of the research on Jacksonian artisans (and earlier ones) was undertaken to learn with what cultural resources the working classes encountered industrialization. In this essay I have followed suit. Yet in the most literal ways the American working classes did not have artisan origins, and surely not origins in Jacksonian workers. Of the wage workers of mid-

[93] Robert D. Marcus, *Grand Old Party, Political Structure in the Gilded Age, 1880-1896* (New York: Oxford University Press, 1971), p. 261.

[94] There are also good theoretical reasons to argue that partisanship was a viable public identity. Two brief suggestions may be offered here. First, it might be said, following Althusser, that sentiment follows practice, rather than the other way around. Althusser paraphrases Pascal: "Pascal says, more or less: 'Kneel down, move your lips in prayer, and you will believe.' He thus said scandalously of other things. . . ." (Louis Althusser, *Lenin and Philosophy and Other Essays* [New York: Monthly Review Press, 1971], p. 168.) Without embracing Althusser's determinism (believing that people make history, if not under conditions of their own choosing) I have tried here to recognize the ways in which practice, and unchosen conditions, influenced sentiment and disposition. A second argument follows from Hartz's *Liberal Tradition*: in a political culture so centered on individualism, and a society so taken with its "republican experiment," what would be more likely than that collective indentity be based not on ascription or achievement but on citizenship?

century, a great majority were not American-born and a good number were not artisans before they emigrated. Whatever their initial cultural resources (about which we know precious little), they became the great majority of the American working classes. Social historians have yet to focus attention on the tailors, carpenters, cabinetmakers, and shoemakers who were not born in the United States, much less on the common laborers, dockworkers, cartmen, drivers, domestics and needlewomen of all national origins who formed an even larger portion of the working classes at mid-century. Much—indeed nearly everything—remains to be written about their organizations (particularly their unions), their values, and their politics. Too little is known of the sometimes ephemeral but constantly appearing and reappearing organizations of laborers, dockworkers, and others who learned economic self-defense just as artisans were excluding masters from unions and themselves organizing modern labor organizations.

Since the publication of *Origin of the Species* our natural tendency is to think that the anatomy of the ape holds the key to human anatomy. Marx argued that the relationship is really the other way around: since apes evolved into humans, it is the anatomy of the latter that reveals what is significant about apes.[95] We are very much in need of a portrait. of American workers at mid-century, especially those whose work had no crafts antecedent. In New York City and perhaps elsewhere, aging former Workingmen's party and General Trades' Union leaders reappeared in the 1850s to give their blessing to a renascent labor movement. That younger movement, and the working class it represented, was more female and more foreign-born than the labor movement of the 1830s, and it was overwhelmingly proletarian. These men and women, in unions and clubs, churches, factories, and on docks, in party insurgencies and party loyalty, were the working class that was formed in the United States. Their portrait, comparably subtle and rich as the one so lately produced for the Jacksonian artisan, will both be a key to artisan culture (as the human to the ape) and enable us to make more sense of working-class formation in the United States.

Important elements of any account of working-class formation in the United States will be found in the antebellum years. Yet in 1860 the

---

[95] The complete thought is as follows: "Human anatomy contains a key to the anatomy of the ape. The intimations of higher development among the subordinate animal species, however, can be understood only after the higher development is already known. The bourgeois economy thus supplies the key to the ancient, etc." Karl Marx, "Grundrisse," *Foundations of Political Economy (rough draft)* (Harmondsworth, England: Penguin Books, 1973), p. 105.

American working class was not "made" ideologically, culturally, or economically. The cataclysm of the Civil War lay just ahead. The institutionalization of machine politics was a long and arduous process. Industrialization had just begun. The crises of Homestead and Lawrence were far in the future; the workers who would be there were not yet born, nor were their parents, for the most part, yet on American soil. In many ways the working classes had barely begun to become American.

6 Trade Unions and Political Machines: The Organization and Disorganization of the American Working Class in the Late Nineteenth Century • *Martin Shefter*

The decades following the outbreak of the Civil War witnessed the consolidation of the major organizations through which workers were to make demands upon, and reach accommodations with, other elements of American society during much of the twentieth century: trade unions and political machines. It was during this period that many of the practices and institutions of contemporary "labor relations" emerged: carefully planned and highly organized strikes, collective bargaining between employers and representatives of their employees, the oldest surviving national labor unions, and the American Federation of Labor. At the same time the Republicans and Democrats became entrenched as the nation's major parties, and their local organizations carved out a similar position for themselves in cities throughout the country. By the end of the nineteenth century the dominant segment of the nation's trade union movement and the local machines affiliated with the nation's major parties had institutionalized a series of distinctions between the claims workers made upon their employers and the state, the modes of collective action through which they asserted those claims, and the composition of the groups with which workers allied in pursuing their goals in the economic and political arenas.

Trade unions were organized at workplaces—factories, mines, construction sites, railroad yards—and the targets of their organization were employers. The constituency of the trade union movement at the end of the nineteenth century was composed largely of skilled wage laborers. Excluded, on the one hand, were employers and members of the middle class and, on the other hand, most unskilled workers, all Orientals and most blacks, and, at various times and places, members of one or another of the nation's newer immigrant groups. The major demands made upon employers concerned the terms and conditions under which union mem-

I WOULD like to thank the editors and other contributors to this volume for their valuable comments on an earlier version of this essay.

bers labored. Both the rhetoric and the behavior of trade unions were quite militant: they insisted that a fundamental conflict of interest existed between employers and employees, and the characteristic collective activity in which they engaged was the strike. In the main, however, American trade unionists at the end of the nineteenth century were not revolutionaries: they called strikes to extract concessions from employers, not to topple the state; they were prepared to concede control over the nation's political institutions to the Democratic and Republican parties; and they were prepared to negotiate national trade agreements that bound workers at the plant level not to strike. In other words, by the 1890s a majority of trade unionists in the United States rejected anarchism, socialism, and syndicalism.

Political machines differed from trade unions in each of these dimensions. The constituency of political machines tended to be defined along ethnic lines and to cut across lines of social class—unskilled workers, unionized skilled workers, and middle-class elements of various ethnic groups were united with segments of the local business community. The sites of their grass-roots organizations were the neighborhoods in which workers lived; the major demands they organized into politics concerned the allocation of public jobs among the city's various ethnic groups and of public facilities among its various neighborhoods; and the machine secured these benefits for its constituents by organizing them for combat in the electoral arena. And though there were substantial variations among American cities in the relationship between local machines and trade unions, in at least the nation's largest cities differences between the two institutions enabled them to establish a *modus vivendi* with one another.

Although many of the organizations and practices of twentieth-century American labor relations and politics became institutionalized in the postbellum decades, the trade union and the political machine were by no means the only types of organizations to which workers belonged in these years. Similarly, demands for higher wages and for political patronage were not the only claims workers made upon other segments of American society, nor were voting their approval or disapproval of trade agreements negotiated by national union leaders and marching to the polls to cast their ballots for the Democratic or Republican ticket the only forms of collective action in which workers engaged. The late nineteenth century was a period in which major changes occurred in the structure of the American economy, cities, and political system that profoundly altered the conditions workers faced on their jobs, in their communities, and in the political realm. In responding to those changes that affected them adversely, workers exhibited dispositions to engage in numerous modes of collective action and to establish many types of organizations that to a greater or lesser degree challenged the ethos of acquisitive individualism that was preached by the upper and middle classes and the patterns of behavior that factory managers and public officials allied with those classes were seeking to impose upon workers.

These differences between the interests, values, and behavioral dispositions of workers and employers sparked conflicts during the post–Civil War years that at times approached full-scale class warfare. The labor union and the political machine institutionalized an accommodation between these warring forces. By no means did the emergence of these organizations put an end to such conflicts. Nonetheless, this essay argues, the institutionalization of the trade union and the political machine established the characteristic manner in which class conflicts in the United States could be channelled and thereby contained.

This argument is elaborated below. The first section analyzes the character of and major changes in the realms of production, community life, and politics in the United States between 1861 and 1894, and describes the ways in which these were experienced by members of the working class. (In the terminology of the introduction to this volume, it discusses the first and second levels of class.) The second discusses the numerous ways in which workers responded to these changes—the variety of claims they asserted, modes of collective action in which they engaged, and types of organizations they created or joined; the third analyzes the conditions that influenced the disposition of workers to respond in these different ways. (Together these sections provide an analysis of the third level of class.) The fourth section seeks to explain how one set of these organizations, the trade union and the political machine, came to be institutionalized (the fourth level of class). The concluding section briefly analyzes the implications of this process of class formation for the character of the working class in the United States and discusses some of the challenges that confronted trade unions and political machines in the twentieth century, thereby shaping the subsequent evolution of the American working class.

I. *The Organization of Production, Community Life, and Politics, 1861-1894*

The period between the Civil War and the depression of 1894 was one of enormous growth and change in the American economy. In 1860 the manufacturing sector in the United States was by no means insignificant—it generated 12 percent of the nation's private production income and America ranked fourth among the world's industrial powers—but it was dwarfed by the agricultural sector, which produced 31 percent of the nation's income. (The balance was generated by commerce, transportation, and services.) By the eve of the 1894 depression the nation's industrial production, railroad mileage, and gross national product had more than tripled; manufacturing generated more income than agriculture; and the United States had become the world's leading industrial power.[1] The American economy did not, however, grow at a uniform rate over these thirty-five years. The nation suffered a major depression in 1873-1878 and a somewhat less severe one in 1882-1885.[2] In the timing and rapidity of its industrialization and the severity of the depressions that punctuated it, American economic development during the late nineteenth century resembled that of Germany.

The United States occupied a distinctive niche in the world economy of this period. Relative to other industrializing nations, natural resources—agricultural land, coal, iron ore, and timber—were abundant in America and labor was scarce, which had important consequences for the nation's pattern of economic development.

Once the extension of the railway network and the invention of the steamship made it possible to ship bulk commodities cheaply from the Midwest and Great Plains to the cities of the United States and Europe, American farmers could compete on favorable terms with grain and meat producers anywhere. Except where tariff barriers stood in their way, American farmers fed industrial workers throughout the western world.[3] As farmers specialized in cash crops, they began to purchase goods they formerly had produced themselves, and this created an enormous internal market for the products of American industry.

At the same time, food exports from the Midwest and Great Plains contributed to the decimation of agriculture in the American Northeast and throughout much of Europe. Many displaced American farmers and European peasants (as well as many European industrial workers and miners) migrated to American cities, because the scarcity of labor there made industrial wages relatively high. From the 1860s through the mid-1890s, immigration to the United States averaged more than 300,000 persons a year. (An indication of the extent to which there was an integrated international labor market in the late nineteenth century is the

[1] Gilbert Fite and Jim Reece, *An Economic History of the United States* (Boston: Houghton Mifflin, 1973), ch. 16.

[2] Edward Kirkland, *Industry Comes of Age: Business, Labor, and Public Policy 1860-1897* (New York: Holt, Rinehart and Winston, 1961), ch. 1.

[3] Peter Gourevitch, "International Trade, Domestic Coalitions, and Liberty: Comparative Responses to the Crisis of 1873-1896," *Journal of Interdisciplinary History* 8 (1977):281-313.

fluctuation of emigration from Europe to America with the demand for labor in the United States: emigration rose to 400,000 a year during the peaks of the American business cycle and fell to half that number at the troughs of American depressions.) The immigrants who came to the United States during the three decades following the Civil War played a crucial role in the industrialization of America. England, Wales, and to a lesser extent Germany supplied many of the skilled workers in the American textile, mining, and metal industries; Ireland, Scandanavia, and China supplied many of the laborers who constructed the railroads and worked as common laborers in manufacturing and mining.

Another aspect of the organization of production in this period also had important consequences for the working class. Even in the most advanced sectors of the economy—the iron and steel industries, the railroads, coal mining, and textiles—skilled workers "exercised broad discretion in the direction of their own work and that of their helpers," as David Montgomery has noted. He cites the example of iron rollers in a mill in Ohio in the mid-1870s, whose workers

negotiated a single tonnage rate with the company for specific rolling jobs the company undertook. The workers then decided collectively, among themselves, what portion of that rate would go to each of them . . . ; how work should be allocated among them; how many rounds of the rolls should be undertaken per day; . . . and how members should be hired and progress through the various ranks of the gang. To put it another way, all the boss did was buy the equipment and raw materials and sell the finished product.[4]

The knowledge of productive techniques monopolized by skilled workers in the late nineteenth century and the key role they played in the organization of production gave them leverage to extract high wages from employers, to enforce work rules, and to establish output quotas that restricted managerial discretion and further increased unit labor costs.

The high wage bill they faced by virtue of both the relative scarcity of labor in the United States and the crucial role of skilled workers provided factory owners with an incentive to reorganize production in ways that reduced their dependence upon this costly input. The creation of a national railway network and thereby a national market in manufactured goods turned this incentive into an imperative. With the destruction of local monopolies, any firm that failed to reduce labor costs could be undersold by firms in other cities.[5] By mechanizing production and/or

---

[4] David Montgomery, *Workers' Control in America* (Cambridge: Cambridge University Press, 1979), pp. 11f.

[5] See, e.g., Alexander Saxton, *The Indispensable Enemy: Labor and the Anti-Chinese Movement in California* (Berkeley: University of California Press, 1971), pp. 68-78.

increasing the division of labor, employers sought to increase the output per worker or, better still, substitute lower-wage unskilled labor for higher-wage skilled labor. (A case in point is the McCormick Harvesting Machine Company, which, in the wake of a successful strike by skilled iron molders in 1885, installed pneumatic molding machines, fired all its unionized molders, and replaced them with unskilled—and less well paid—machine-tenders.)[6]

To be sure, Taylorism still lay in the future. The effort by employers to restructure the jobs performed by their workers was not as methodical in the decades immediately following the Civil War as it was to become in the first two decades of the twentieth century. Moreover, the introduction of new technologies created entirely new skilled trades, such as steamfitters and structural iron workers in the construction industry. Consequently the number of skilled workers actually increased from roughly 1 million to 2 million between 1870 and 1890, and the proportion of the urban working class belonging to this aristocracy of labor remained more or less constant during this period, fluctuating between 17 percent and 20 percent.[7] Nonetheless the possibility that employers would introduce machinery or otherwise reorganize production to reduce the autonomy, dilute the skills, and lower the wages of their employees was a major fear of workers and a central theme in conflicts between labor and capital in the late nineteenth century.[8]

Efforts by employers to increase output per worker and to reduce labor costs by purchasing new machinery, introducing prefabricated parts, tightening supervision of their employees, and changing methods of compensation (for example, paying piecework rates rather than hourly wages or subcontracting out jobs to work crews through competitive bidding) had profound implications for workers. These were particularly great for first-generation factory workers, whether they had previously been farmers, rural outworkers, or artisans in Europe or America. The factory system demanded a new sense of time and, indeed, a new way of life among workers—one that stressed sobriety, industry, and frugality.[9] The owner of a factory whose very functioning (or, at least, whose profitability)

[6] Robert Ozanne, "Union-Management Relations: McCormick Harvesting Machine Company, 1862-1886," *Labor History* 4 (1963):149.

[7] Andrew Dawson, "The Paradox of Dynamic Technological Change and the Labor Aristocracy in the United States, 1880-1914," *Labor History* 20 (1979):330-31.

[8] Irwin Yellowitz, *Industrialization and the American Labor Movement* (Port Washington, N.Y.: Kennikat Press, 1977).

[9] Herbert Gutman, *Work, Culture, and Society in Industrializing America* (New York: Alfred A. Knopf, 1976), ch. 1; and Alan Dawley and Paul Faler, "Working Class Culture and Politics in the Industrial Revolution: Sources of Loyalism and Rebellion," *Journal of Social History* 9 (1975):466-80.

depended upon the close integration of specialized tasks performed by different workers would not tolerate half his employees staying home Monday mornings to sleep off hangovers from weekend drinking bouts. The conflicts between workers and employers in the late nineteenth century, however, were not simply the expression of the disjunction between the world views of "traditional" workers and the demands of a "modern" economy. Workers who were born and brought up in the economic and moral worlds of industrial capitalism experienced the efforts of employers to extract more output from them as attacks upon their independence.[10]

The Painite vocabulary of antebellum artisans remained available later to both first- and second-generation industrial workers for expressing their opposition to such attacks. Among the key words in this vocabulary were "slavery" and "manliness." Irwin Yellowitz reports that Toledo cigar workers striking against the introduction of the cigar mold in 1871 conceded that such opposition had failed in Europe, but European workers were "only 'a grade above the slave' whereas American workers would assert their rights." Similarly, coopers objecting to the introduction of machinery into their trade in the 1870s argued that "employers were attracted to machinery because it allowed them 'to make money and enslave coopers' by superceding the skilled worker."[11] The term "wage slavery" was also widely used in the years following the Civil War by all segments of the American labor reform movement. One major argument made for the movement's central demand during this period—the eight-hour day—was that if workers were to be subject to the control of their employers while on the job, the length of the working day should be limited so that those subject to the "wages system" at least would have an equal number of waking hours in which they were their own masters, and which they could devote to self-improvement and the exercise of the rights that were theirs as citizens of a republic.[12]

In the vocabulary of American workers of the time "slavery" or "slavishness" was contrasted with "manliness." As David Montgomery notes:

Few words enjoyed more popularity in the nineteenth century than this honorific, with all its connotations of dignity, respectability, defiant egalitarianism, and patriarchial male supremacy. The worker who merited it refused to cower before the foreman's glares—in fact, often would not work at all when a boss was watching. When confronted with indignities, he was expected to respond like the machinist in Lowell, who found [restrictive] regulations posted in his

[10] David Montgomery, "Gutman's Nineteenth-Century America," *Labor History*, no. 19 (1978):416-29.

[11] Yellowitz, *Industrialization*, pp. 65, 72.

[12] David Montgomery, *Beyond Equality: Labor and the Radical Republicans, 1862-1872* (New York: Alfred A. Knopf, 1967), p. 238.

shop in 1867. . . . "Not having been brought up under such a system of slavery, . . . I took my things and went out, followed in a few hours by the rest of the men."[13]

This code also demanded manliness in dealing with one's fellow workers. It enjoined them to observe informal restrictions on output in order not to deprive other workers of jobs; even when piece-rate systems promised higher earnings to those who produced more, workers were expected to observe these restrictions as an act of "unselfish brotherhood." In a similar fashion they were enjoined to resist the lure of the profits to be made by becoming subcontractors and exploiting their fellow workers. In these respects, an important segment of the working class rejected the acquisitive individualism of middle-class society.

The late nineteenth century also witnessed major changes in the character of the communities in which American workers lived. The first industrial revolution occurred initially in the towns and small cities of New England's river valleys. Textile mills in the 1830s and 1840s relied on water power to drive their machinery, barges to transport their raw materials and finished products, and the daughters and sons of American farmers as a source of labor. Consequently they were located in places such as Lowell and Lawrence, Massachusetts; Manchester, New Hampshire; and Pawtucket, Rhode Island. Even in the 1860s, when the adoption of steam power and the construction of an extensive railroad network made it possible for factories to locate elsewhere, manufacturing employment grew somewhat more rapidly in small cities than in the nation's great metropolises. After 1870, however, manufacturing began to concentrate more heavily in big cities. Over the next three decades smaller industrial cities scarcely stagnated—manufacturing employment in the cities ranked 21st through 50th in population grew by 158 percent between 1870 and 1900—but industrial growth was even more rapid in the largest cities in the United States. During these thirty years manufacturing employment in New York, Philadelphia, and Chicago increased by 245 percent.[14]

Major changes occurred in the distribution of people not only among cities, but also within them. The days were long past when persons unrelated by ties of blood or matrimony (other than servants) lived in the household of their employers. In addition, the invention of the trolley enabled members of the middle class to move from the sooty and con-

---

[13] Montgomery, *Workers Control*, pp. 13f.

[14] David Gordon, "Capitalist Development and the History of American Cities," in *Marxism and the Metropolis*, ed. William Tabb and Larry Sawers (New York: Oxford University Press, 1978), p. 39.

gested neighborhoods downtown and into "streetcar suburbs" miles from the heart of town.[15] Through this process, the population of inner-city neighborhoods became more uniformly working class in composition. It was not until the twentieth century, however, that zoning codes were enacted that sought to separate residential and industrial districts. Before this workers lived in the shadows of the factories, mills, and foundries that employed them, and sweatshops were established in the tenement houses in which poor workers resided.

Ethnicity was as important as social class in shaping the residential patterns of American cities in the late nineteenth century. Because immigrants found housing through relatives or fellow townsmen from the old country or through boarding-house runners (who specialized in recruiting immigrants from a single country), foreign-born workers generally lived in neighborhoods inhabited by other members of their ethnic group. The Boston Tenement House Survey of 1892, conducted by the Massachusetts Bureau of Labor Statistics, gathered very complete data on the birthplaces of tenement dwellers. In 1892 there were 204 electoral precincts in Boston, with an average tenement population of 1,518. Of Boston's 7,905 Russian-born tenement dwellers (the vast majority of whom were Jewish and who comprised Boston's largest foreign-language ethnic group) only 14 percent lived in the 188 precincts inhabited by fewer than 100 other Russian-born Jews (see table 6.1). Almost double this proportion—25 percent—lived in the eight precincts in which there was a significant presence of between 100 and 400 Jews, and fully 61 percent lived in the eight precincts inhabited by more than 400 Jews. Similarly, 82 percent of Boston's Italian tenement residents lived in only ten of the city's 204 precincts, and of these well over half lived in the three most heavily Italian precincts in the city. The Irish, who were Boston's largest immigrant group and whose countrymen had lived in large numbers in Boston for a half-century by 1892, were more evenly dispersed through the city than either the Russian-born Jews or the Italians, but there also was some unevenness in their distribution among the city's precincts. At one extreme, sixty-one precincts (30 percent of the city's 204) had very small Irish tenement populations; at the other, 38 precincts had more than 400 Irish tenement residents, and 43 percent of Boston's Irish population lived in such heavily Irish neighborhoods. It should be noted, moreover, that these figures refer only to the foreign-born. These data do not classify second-generation immigrants, including young children living with their families, in the same category as their parents, and there-

[15] Sam Bass Warner, *Street Car Suburbs: The Process of Growth in Boston 1870-1900* (Cambridge: Harvard University Press, 1962).

Table 6.1. Residential Concentration among Russian-, Italian-, and Irish-born Tenement Dwellers in Boston, 1892

Country of Birth	Number of Group in Precinct	Number of Precincts	Number of Persons	Percent of Group's Population
Russia	0–99	188	1,126	14.2
	100–399	8	1,953	24.7
	400+	8	4,826	61.1
Italy	0–99	194	1,065	17.8
	100–399	7	1,771	29.6
	400+	3	3,148	52.6
Ireland	0–99	61	3,427	7.2
	100–399	105	23,509	49.6
	400+	38	20,478	43.2

SOURCE: Compiled from Massachusetts Bureau of Statistics of Labor, *Twenty-Third Annual Report* (Boston: Wright & Potter Printing Co., 1893), pp. 170–87.

fore understate the extent to which the members of Boston's major ethnic groups tended to live in clusters.

The neighborhoods inhabited by the great majority of workers in large American cities of the late nineteenth century differed dramatically from the middle-class sections of these cities. In particular, most working-class neighborhoods were characterized by very high population densities, extraordinary rates of population turnover, an absence of many of the public facilities that now are taken for granted—and as a result of all of these, a great deal of congestion, dirt, and disease. These differences between working- and middle-class neighborhoods were chiefly a consequence, in turn, of the distribution of income between and within the social classes and the character and modes of financing of public services in the nineteenth-century city. There were, however, important variations within the working class, and therefore all working-class neighborhoods were not identical.

Approximately 40 percent of the American working class in the late 1880s lived in poverty, earning less than the $500 a year that was minimally necessary for a family of five to afford an adequate diet.[16] One out of every four members of this group was at best a marginal member of the labor force and survived by scavenging, begging, and stealing. The

[16] The estimates of the income of various strata of the working class in this and the following two paragraphs are drawn from David Montgomery, "Labor in the Industrial Era," in *The U.S. Department of Labor Bicentennial History of the American Worker*, ed. Richard B. Morris (Washington, D.C.: Government Printing Office, 1976), pp. 117-18.

remaining three-fourths were unskilled laborers whose wives and children had to work if their family was to get by. Because the amount they could afford to spend for shelter was sharply limited, they lived in extremely crowded conditions: families in one or two rooms in cheap tenements; single men, as Jacob Riis's photographs indicate, in flophouses or even coal cellers.[17] Moreover, because "public improvements" such as street paving, street lighting, and the installation of sewer and water lines characteristically were financed through assessments on local property owners and the owners of tenements had no incentive to incur these costs, these basic public services often were not provided to neighborhoods inhabited by the poor.[18] (Jane Addams reported that she and some fellow residents of Hull House once decided to see how far down through the compacted garbage on a local street it was necessary to dig to reach the pavement below: the answer was a foot and a half.)[19] The combination of inadequate nutrition, congestion, and poor sanitation led to extremely high morbidity and mortality rates among both adults and children in poor neighborhoods. For example, in 1890 the mortality rate in one of Boston's poorest wards, the thirteenth, was 3,365.36 per 100,000—more than twice the rate of 1,578.95 in the predominantly middle-class eleventh ward; and the mortality rate in the thirteenth ward from childhood diseases (diptheria, croup, whooping cough, and measles) was 312.85—more than five times the eleventh ward's rate of 55.40.[20] People living in such conditions had few reasons to be attached to their city, and this helps explain why Stephen Thernstrom found that more than 44 percent of the unskilled workers living in Boston in 1880 had moved from the city by 1890.[21]

A slightly larger segment of the working class—45 percent in the late 1880s—lived in better circumstances. Skilled workers earning from $500 to $800 per year did not go hungry as long as they remained employed, could rent an apartment with a separate bedroom for the parents and another for the children, and could afford the dues for a fraternal organization and trolley fare for an occasional outing. Even so residential den-

[17] Jacob Riis, *How the Other Half Lives: Studies Among the Tenements of New York* (New York: Dover, 1971).

[18] Victor Rosewater, *Special Assessments* (New York: Columbia College, 1893).

[19] Jane Addams, *Twenty Years at Hull-House* (New York: Macmillan, 1938), p. 286.

[20] U. S. Department of Interior, Census Office, *Report on Vital and Social Statistics in the United States at the Eleventh Census, 1890. Part II. Vital Statistics of Cities of 100,000 Population and Upward* (Washington, D.C.: Government Printing Office, 1896), p. 392.

[21] Stephen Thernstrom, *The Other Bostonians: Poverty and Progress in the American Metropolis, 1880-1970* (Cambridge: Harvard University Press, 1973), p. 40.

sities were high by present-day standards (the boarder was a common figure in working-class households), public services were limited (landlords here too had a limited incentive to pay local assessments for public improvements), and mobility rates were high (37 percent of the skilled workers in Thernstrom's sample moved from Boston between 1880 and 1890). None of these conditions was as extreme as in neighborhoods inhabited by common laborers, however, and if the skilled worker's wife through constant cleaning managed to rid their apartment of the dirt from the streets below and the soot from the factory chimneys above, if the family was able to survive periods of unemployment, and if its members joined with their friends and neighbors to avoid being demoralized by the bleakness of their surroundings, they could lead lives that accorded with the ideals of cleanliness, thrift, temperance (if not total abstinence), and also mutuality.[22]

The top 15 percent of the working class, composed of the most highly skilled workers—such as glass blowers, pattern makers, and railroad engineers—lived in neighborhoods similar to those inhabited by the lower middle class. Indeed, as members of the middle class moved to newly built streetcar suburbs, this upper stratum of the working class purchased their homes. The residential densities in their neighborhoods were relatively low; as homeowners they had an incentive to pay for public improvements; and they had a stronger reason than their fellow workers to remain in their neighborhood and city. Thus, in conjunction with shopkeepers, clerks, and lawyers newly risen from the working class, they often were in a position to be major contenders for the political leadership of their city.[23]

One final point about the relationship between social class and residential communities in post–Civil War America should be made. The distance between working- and middle-class neighborhoods was socially as well as physically greater in large cities than in small ones. The gang was a prominent institution in the working-class neighborhoods of large cities; its members regarded themselves as manly and looked with some scorn upon middle- and upper-class "long hairs"; and they gave a hard time to any such intruders into their neighborhood, as well as to intruders from other working-class neighborhoods. Members of the middle class relied upon professional police forces to keep undesirables out of their neighborhoods, and their sense of distance from the working class was

[22] Susan J. Kleinberg, "Technology and Women's Work: The Lives of Working Class Women in Pittsburgh, 1870-1900," *Labor History* 17 (1976):58-72.

[23] Estelle Feinstein, *Stamford in the Gilded Age* (Stamford, Conn.: Stamford Historical Society, 1973).

expressed in the use of such terms as "the dangerous classes" to refer to the poor.[24] In small cities the social distance between such neighborhoods was not so great. Herbert Gutman argues that the residents of small cities were more likely than their counterparts in the nation's greatest metropolises to regard themselves as members of a common community and that the middle class was more inclined to consider factory owners, rather than workers, as the disruptive force there.[25] This had important consequences when conflicts between labor and capital erupted in such settings.

Three characteristics of the nineteenth-century American political system had important consequences for the formation of the nation's working class. The first was the early advent of universal suffrage (or, more precisely, white manhood suffrage) and the concomitant mobilization of the working class into politics by parties whose leaders already occupied positions of power in the American regime. The second was the peculiar character of the "output" institutions of American government. In contrast to the major regimes of continental Europe, America was not governed by a centralized administrative apparatus. Rather, power was divided among genuinely independent local, provincial, and national governments and, within each of these governments in turn, authority was shared by legislative, executive, and judicial officials. During the Federalist and Jeffersonian eras various arrangements to cope with this fragmentation and give the government some administrative capacity had been tried, but it was only in the 1830s that the one that was to prevail through the remainder of the nineteenth century emerged—a "state of courts and parties," as Stephen Skowronek has termed it.[26] Laws were administered chiefly through the courts, and political parties played the major role in staffing and achieving a measure of coordination among the nation's political institutions. The third aspect of American politics that had important implications for the working class was the pattern of cleavages and alignments among the political elites of the day. The major event of the 1860s was of course the Civil War, and the major source of contention in politics after Appomattox was what to do with the institutions that had been created and the policies that had been enacted during

---

[24] Charles Loring Brace, *The Dangerous Classes of New York* (New York: Wynkoop and Hallenbeck, 1880).

[25] Herbert Gutman, "The Workers Search for Power: Labor in the Gilded Age," in *The Gilded Age: A Reappraisal,* ed. H. Wayne Morgan (Syracuse: Syracuse University Press, 1963).

[26] Stephen Skowronek, *Building a New American State: The Expansion of National Administrative Capacities, 1877-1920* (Cambridge: Cambridge University Press, 1982), ch. 2.

the war. This touched upon questions of concern to various contenders for the leadership of American workers.

The advent of suffrage was experienced most directly by the working class. There was an extraordinarily high level of popular involvement in party politics during the late nineteenth century.[27] Turnout rates in elections averaged 85 percent or more of the eligible electorate, and because aliens who merely declared their intention of becoming citizens were permitted to vote in a number of states and machine politicians were more than willing to help aliens obtain naturalization papers in many of the remaining ones, even recent immigrants were part of that eligible electorate. Moreover, elections for city, county, state, and national offices characteristically were not conducted simultaneously, and therefore electioneering occurred throughout the year: as one contemporary politician observed, "We work through one campaign, take a bath, and start in on the next."[28] These campaigns were a major form of popular entertainment, involving torch-light parades, brawls, and the marching of voters to the polls. This does not, however, mean that politics had no other significance to members of the working class. Voters were prepared to listen to two-hour orations extolling the virtues of American democracy at Fourth of July celebrations and to equally long speeches during election campaigns expounding party principles.[29] The mobilization of the working class into politics through the nation's political institutions, rather than in opposition to them, made its members intensely loyal to the American regime.[30]

The peculiar structure of the American state—its relatively limited domain and its fragmentation—also had implications for working-class daily life. As indicated above, in working-class neighborhoods officials performing public services—or, more precisely, services that now are regarded as public—were more notable for their absence than for their presence, and many public works were constructed only in neighborhoods whose residents could afford to finance them. What little relief was available to the poor at times of distress was provided by private charitable organizations. Moreover, the repeal during the Jacksonian era of licensing requirements to enter many trades, the abolition of imprisonment for

---

[27] Walter Dean Burnham, "The Changing Shape of the American Political Universe," *American Political Science Review* 59 (1965):7-28.

[28] Morton Keller, *Affairs of State: Public Life in Late Nineteenth Century America* (Cambridge: The Belknap Press of Harvard University Press, 1977), p. 241.

[29] Walter Dean Burnham, "Theory and Voting Research: Some Reflections on Converse's Change in the American Electorate," *American Political Science Review* 68 (1974):1002-1023.

[30] Dawley and Faler, "Working Class Culture," pp. 474-75.

debt, and the absence of a system of internal passports left most American workers free to move among jobs as they chose. In a similar fashion, the absence of any laws regulating private associations left workers free to form mutual aid societies and trade unions. Where workers faced restrictions in these areas they were less likely to be imposed by the state than by employers' associations (which maintained blacklists of union members), private security forces (such as the Pinkerton Detective Agency), and that extreme manifestation of the rights of private property, the company town.

The fragmentation of public authority in the United States and the dominance by political parties over public agencies and employees at all levels of the federal system were also experienced quite directly by the working class. The substantial decentralization of government in nineteenth-century America meant that the public officials and employees with whom workers and their families were most frequently in contact—policemen, magistrates, teachers, inspectors—were more likely to be employees of the municipal than of the national government, and they were relatively accessible to the people upon whose lives they impinged. In small cities and towns it often was possible for members of the working class in coalition with groups immediately above them in the social structure to boot out mayors or police chiefs who directed their subordinates to behave in undesirable ways, and such coalitions also found it possible to block the proposals of the city's business elite.[31] In large cities, in which the municipal government was not as immediately accessible, the party organizations that slated and deslated elected officials and hired and fired public employees found it in their interest to direct their functionaries to behave in ways that would serve the party's electoral interests. One need not accept the romanticized picture of the generous ward politician and the friendly neighborhood cop—ignoring the fact that parties had an incentive to respond to pressures from above as well as those from below, and overlooking the coercive aspects of the relationship between machine politicians and citizens—to recognize that at least public officials and employees could be "reached" by the working class. A member of the family could be sprung from jail or gotten a job on a public works crew by speaking to the ward leader. Workers in the United States, in contrast to their German counterparts—to cite the other extreme—did not find themselves subjugated by an official, and officious, class. This in conjunction with the relatively narrow domain of government in the United States during the late nineteenth century meant that on the whole what-

[31] Gutman, *Work, Culture, and Society*, ch. 5.

ever oppression or exploitation American workers experienced was not oppression by the State.

There were some exceptions to this rule, all of which were to have important implications for patterns of working-class activity and organization. The first of these was that pietistic forces did attempt to use public authority to alter the way of life of the immigrant working classes, most importantly by regulating the sale and consumption of liquor.[32] The targets of this Protestant crusade regarded this as an assault upon their personal liberty. Secondly, although private security forces played a more important role than the U.S. Army in breaking strikes, state militias and municipal police forces, under conditions to be described, were used quite regularly to protect strikebreakers during labor disputes.

Finally, there was the Civil War. In 1861-1865 a state was constructed that dwarfed anything with which Americans were familiar. President Lincoln was commander in chief of an army in which more than 2,000,000 men served, and that, along with its Confederate counterpart, killed 600,000 of the nation's citizens. This army eventually relied upon conscription to fill its ranks, an exercise of state power that ignited the New York Draft Riot of 1863, the bloodiest riot in American history. In large sections of the country martial law was declared, the right of *habeas corpus* suspended, politicians and editors suspected of being disloyal to the Union cause summarily arrested, and military force used to break strikes in plants producing war matériel. The imperatives of financing the war led to the enactment of a system of national taxation and to the creation of a national debt and a national currency. The burdens of the former and the inflation generated by the latter ate into the real income of the working class. And the Thirteenth Amendment, enacted at the end of the war, released a major fraction of the nation's laborers from bondage, converting them from subjects of their masters into citizens of the United States.[33]

The war was a central event in the lives of most Americans, workers and nonworkers alike. But not everyone—not even all northern whites—experienced it in the same way. If some regarded the measures that were adopted to prosecute the war as oppressive, others experienced them as liberating—providing them with the opportunity to fight on behalf of the noble causes of national unity and free labor, in opposition to a society based upon slave labor. The divisions generated by the war, it should be noted, cut across class lines. Workers and their employers could agree,

---

[32] Richard Jensen, *The Winning of the Midwest: Social and Political Conflict, 1886-96* (Chicago: University of Chicago Press, 1971), ch. 3.

[33] Keller, *Affairs of State*, ch. 1; Montgomery, *Beyond Equality*, chap. 3.

and millions did, that the taxes and tariffs enacted during the war were onerous, that the efforts by Republicans to extend the rights of blacks threatened the hegemony of the white race, and that the powers exercised by the army during and after the war were tyrannical. It was equally possible for millions of other workers and their employers to endorse whatever measures were necessary to ensure that the rebellion was crushed and to guarantee that the principles for which the war was fought would not be lost after it ended.

This brings us to the final major aspect of American politics in the late nineteenth century that had important implications for the working class—the pattern of cleavages and alignments among major political forces. During Reconstruction, issues related to the war continued to dominate political discourse and determine political alignments—in particular, the terms upon which the southern states and their black population should be integrated into the Union and the extent to which the institutions constructed, and the policies enacted during the war should be maintained. The cleavages generated by these issues, like those evoked by the war itself, cut across class lines.

The changes in the American economy described above contributed to the emergence of another issue in the 1860s and subsequent decades: What position should the increasingly numerous class of wage laborers occupy in the nation's economic and political life? The very depth of the cleavages generated by the issues of the Civil War and Reconstruction created opportunities for working-class spokesmen to insist forcefully and effectively that the injustices associated with the system of wage slavery cried out for redress as much as did those associated with the system of chattel slavery. The effort to cope with these demands ultimately led political and economic elites to regroup in a new alignment—with major implications for the nation's working class.[34]

II. *The Working-Class Response: Patterns of Behavior*

Workers responded in a wide variety of ways to the changes they experienced in their daily lives during the 1860s, 1870s, and 1880s. They exhibited dispositions to engage in many different forms of collective action and to create or join many different types of groups and organizations in an effort to cope. These collectivities, groups, and organizations asserted a broad spectrum of claims against the state, employers, and

---

[34] C. Vann Woodward, *Reunion and Reaction: The Compromise of 1877 and the End of Reconstruction* (Boston: Little, Brown, 1951).

members of the working class itself, for during this period the position
workers were to occupy in industrial America was very much an open
question. Institutions and values that are widely accepted in the United
States today—the wage-labor system, the concept of managerial prerogatives, the division of labor between union leaders and party politicians,
the ethos of acquisitive individualism in the realms of both production
and consumption—were matters of sharp contention a century ago.

The most characteristic form of collective action by workers in the late
nineteenth century was the strike. Strikes were certainly not unknown
prior to the Civil War, but in the late 1860s important changes began to
occur in the way they were initiated, conducted, and concluded. Previously strikes had taken one of two forms. The first, characteristic of
strikes by unskilled laborers, was the unplanned walkout. Generally not
in a position to organize unions, these workers walked off their jobs more
or less spontaneously and staged marches calling upon other workers to
join their walkout. This pattern was exemplified in a strike by miners at
the Cooper and Hewitt ironworks in 1867:

Led by a local political aspirant, they closed eighteen mines within two days by
marching in body from pit to pit, stopping teamsters from hauling ore, and,
when the owners tried shipping ore by canal boat, filling in large sections of the
canals. When state militia arrived to escort the boatmen, the strike was broken.
It is noteworthy that even amidst this undisciplined action there was no violence.
. . . The miners sought to raise their wages from $1.65 to $2.00 a day, but, said
proprieter Abram Hewitt: "They struck first without making any demand."[35]

Strikes by skilled workers, able to organize trade unions, followed a
somewhat different pattern. Representatives of unions and employers did
not engage in collective bargaining in the present-day sense. Rather, to
increase the wages of its members, a trade union would enact a "rule"
declaring that after a designated date its members no longer would work
for less than a stipulated rate. The union would "banner" any "rat shop"
that refused to pay the new rate as a way of warning its members against
working in the shop and encouraging consumers to boycott its products.
"Rats" who violated the rule and worked for less than the new rate would
be expelled from the union. A union would regard a strike as successful
once all of its members were employed at the new rate, even if there were
some shops in the city that employed nonmembers at a lower wage.

As Montgomery notes, "Union methods based on the unilateral adoption of rules to control the sale of their labor were peculiarly appropriate

---

[35] Montgomery, *Beyond Equality*, p. 144; see also Henry Leonard, "Ethnic Cleavage
and Industrial Conflict in Late 19th Century America: The Cleveland Rolling Mill Company Strikes of 1882 and 1885," *Labor History* 20 (1979):524-48, quotation at p. 536.

for the workingmen who had progressed but partway down the path from journeyman artisan to factory wage-laborer."[36] On the one hand, the rise of the factory system made collective action by workers against their employers considerably more feasible than it had been when workers lived in their employer's household. On the other hand, these methods—which are closer to those of present-day trade associations than labor unions—did not limit the independence of individual workingmen to any great degree. It is true that union members bound themselves to observe the rules enacted by a majority of their fellow tradesmen, but this involved no delegation of authority to, or submission to the leadership of, union officials.

These methods, however, had their limitations—in particular, they were extremely rigid. They gave employers no alternative but to capitulate to the union and pay the wages it decreed or to defy the union and insist on the old rate. Conflicts between employers and employees over rates of pay are inherent in the wage-labor relationship, and the potential for conflict was heightened still more by the different views nineteenth-century craftsmen and employers characteristically had of their rights and obligations in this relationship. Consequently employers always had an incentive (which, to be sure, might be outweighed by countervailing considerations in any given case) to pursue the latter course of action if it appeared that they could hold out longer than their striking employees or could find a sufficient number of craftsmen who were prepared to work at less than the union scale.

Beyond this, the changes in the American economy described above gave some employers in the post–Civil War years additional incentives to resist the demands of their workers. The expansion of the nation's railway network made it impossible for manufacturers to pay wages higher than those paid in the lowest-wage city in their market area. At the same time, the easier it became for workers to move among cities, the less likely it was that the great majority of craftsmen seeking employment in any given trade in a given city would belong to the local trade union and regard themselves as bound by its rules. In some cases mechanization also made it easier than it previously had been to replace striking craftsmen because reduced skills were required to do their jobs.[37]

To overcome the limitations inherent in their older practices and to cope with these changing conditions, unions embarked upon new modes

---

[36] Montgomery, *Beyond Equality*, p. 143.

[37] See Alan Dawley, *Class and Community: The Industrial Revolution in Lynn* (Cambridge: Harvard University Press, 1976), pp. 143-48, 175-84; John R. Commons, "American Shoemakers, 1648-1895," in his *Labor and Administration* (New York: Macmillan, 1913), pp. 219-66.

of collective action and adopted new forms of organization. Unable to promulgate and enforce wage rates unilaterally, unions undertook to negotiate wage scales with employers before staging walkouts, and even if no agreement could be reached and a strike was called, they sought to negotiate the terms of a settlement. This procedure—then termed "treating with employers" and striking only as a "dernier resort"—was more likely to yield a mutually acceptable conclusion. Moreover, when unions did strike, they took care to accumulate strike funds beforehand; they called walkouts during those seasons of the year or phases of the business cycle when employers were least willing to see their factories shut down and/or could most afford to accede to the unions' demands; and they sought to ensure that all firms operating within a market area were shut down simultaneously. In the language of the day such careful planning was termed "acting conservatively."[38]

These changes presupposed and further encouraged the strengthening and extension of union organization. Collective bargaining could only take place if workers were prepared to delegate to union leaders the authority to speak for them. Workers in established trades were not all willing to renounce their traditional independence, and strikes were defeated because of the resulting divisions in their ranks. This lesson was not lost upon workers at the time, however, and the 1860s and early 1870s witnessed the emergence of the nation's first professional union leaders, who perfected the organization of their unions and imposed a substantial measure of discipline upon their members. One aspect of this strengthening and extension of union organizations was the formation of national trade unions, which sponsored the creation of new union locals, raised and distributed strike funds, and sought to control the supply of labor and to establish uniform wages for their trade throughout the nation. Another was the emergence of municipal trade assemblies, which, among other things, raised strike funds and organized boycotts of shops that employed nonunion labor.[39]

There were, however, four interrelated differences between the strikes of this period and those of today. First, in the absence of the Wagner Act's provisions defining the legal obligations of workers and employers in the process of collective bargaining and guaranteeing the stability of labor unions, and in the absence of multimillion-dollar strike funds (let alone unemployment compensation for striking workers), strikes required a very strong sense of solidarity among the workers participating in them.

[38] David Montgomery, "Strikes in Nineteenth Century America," *Social Science History* 4 (1980):81-104, quotation at p. 89.
[39] Lloyd Ullman, *The Rise of the National Trade Union* (Cambridge: Harvard University Press, 1955); Montgomery, *Beyond Equality*, pp. 151-76.

Second, workers who did not belong to unions often were caught up in strike movements, and strikes mobilized their participants outside their places of work. Third, strikes at times were used as a political weapon, and their target could be the state as much as the employers of the participants in the strike. Fourth, both in the content of their demands and the rhetoric with which these were justified, strikes were used to pursue a broader ranger of goals than is the case today.

The workers who participated in strikes during the post–Civil War years commonly had to be prepared to make substantial sacrifices and take great risks. It was not until the 1880s that unions began to amass permanent strike funds, and therefore workers had to go without any assured income during strikes; they also faced the possibility of not being rehired—and often of being blacklisted—after a strike was terminated. In addition, the benefits strikers sought most notably, higher wages— were "collective goods" that would accrue to workers who did not make these sacrifices as much as to those who did, and unions as yet did not possess the legal authority to levy sanctions against such "free riders."[40] Nonetheless, strikes did occur, and workers at times stayed off their jobs for weeks or months. That they were prepared to do so reflects the strong solidarities linking workers to one another on the job. This is the significance of the ethical code of the craftsman described above and of the rejection of "hoggish" behavior and the praise of "unselfish brotherhood" that was at the heart of that code: many nineteenth-century American workers did not conform to the model of *homo economicus* that generates the free-rider problem in neoclassical economic theory. Or at least, in contrast to their employers, they did not hold up that model as an ideal. As a banner carried by members of the Detroit coopers' union in an 1880 parade asserted:

> Each for himself is the bosses' plea
> Union for all will make you free.[41]

[40] To be sure, strikers in the late nineteenth century could and often did rely upon extralegal sanctions to deal with free riders—that is, they used threats of ostracism and violence to intimidate strikebreakers. Union leaders, however, recognized that the use of violence was a very risky strategy for workers, because it enabled employers to call upon local authorities to intervene on their behalf to protect law and order. Thus, for example, the leaders of the Amalgamated Iron and Steel Workers during their strike against the Cleveland Rolling Mill Company in 1882 appointed marshals to patrol the streets near the mills to prevent such violence and urged their members to use only "honorable means" against strikebreakers and to "respectfully talk to them and convert them" (Leonard, "Ethnic Cleavage," p. 529).

[41] Quoted in David Montgomery, "To Study the People: The American Working Class," *Labor History* 21 (1980):485-512, at p. 502; Dawson, "Paradox of Dynamic Change," pp. 345-48; James Q. Wilson, *Political Organizations* (New York: Basic Books, 1973), p. 123.

This points to the second distinctive characteristic of strikes in the late nineteenth century: they often drew upon the strong communal and ethnic solidarities in working-class neighborhoods, and wives and/or neighbors of the striking workers often became involved. An episode during a strike by Slavic miners in Wilkes-Barre, Pennsylvania, is indicative of this pattern:

As soon as the [strikebreakers] appeared at the mine head and prepared to leave, violence broke out. "The strikers assailed their enemies with clubs, stones, and pistols, and beat some of them in a terrible manner." The assault was definitely a group affair, as women also participated. Their nationality was obvious from a banner held aloft proclaiming in Polish, "Kill the men who have taken the bread out of our mouths."[42]

A common feature of large strikes during this period was a march by crowds from factory to factory in working-class neighborhoods, calling upon all employees to walk off their jobs. The railway strike of 1877, the largest of the nineteenth century, precipitated sympathetic walkouts by coal miners and factory workers in dozens of cities and full-scale general strikes in Toledo and St. Louis. The marches and open-air meetings that occurred in the course of these strikes invited the participation of all segments of the population in working-class neighborhoods: unionized workers, nonunionized workers, unemployed men, women, and children.[43] A number of strikes during this period were also associated with riots—most notably, the 1863 draft riot in New York, an 1867 strike on behalf of the eight-hour day in Chicago, and the 1877 railroad strike in Pittsburgh and Baltimore. The participants in these riots extended far beyond the striking workers and the crowd actions of these episodes were not centered on the workplaces of the rioters.[44]

Another important feature of many strikes during the 1860s and 1870s was their political or quasi-political character. During these years workers struck to "enforce" state laws defining the length of a legal day's work and the procedures to be used in weighing the coal produced by miners who were paid on a per-ton basis—laws that state governments were unable to implement in the face of resistance by employers. These statutes had been enacted initially as a result of electioneering and lobbying

---

[42] Victor Greene, *The Slavic Community on Strike: Immigrant Labor in Pennsylvania Anthracite* (Notre Dame: University of Notre Dame Press, 1968), p. 99.

[43] David T. Burbank, *Reign of the Rabble: The St. Louis General Strike of 1877* (New York: Augustus M. Kelley, 1966), passim.

[44] Adrian Cook, *The Armies of the Streets: The New York City Draft Riots of 1863* (Lexington: University Press of Kentucky, 1974), p. 56; Montgomery, *Beyond Equality*, pp. 309-310; David Bruce, *1877: Year of Violence* (Indianapolis: Bobbs-Merrill, 1959), chs. 6, 8.

efforts by labor reformers, and inasmuch as strikes were the only means to secure the implementation of these laws, they were yet another weapon in the political arsenal of labor.[45] And in some instances the strike was used as a weapon to secure the enactment of legislation. The public meeting that authorized the 1877 general strike in St. Louis resolved

that, as the condition of an immense number of people now forced in idleness, and the great suffering for the necessaries of life caused by the monopoly in the hands of capitalists, appeals strongly to all industrial classes for prompt action, therefore, to avoid bloodshed or violence, we recommend a general strike of all branches of industry for eight hours as a day's work, and we call on the legislature for the immediate enactment of an eight hour law, and the enforcement of a severe penalty for its violation, and that the employment of all children under fourteen years of age be prohibited.[46]

More generally, as Montgomery notes of the 1877 strikes, "everywhere the first target of the crowd's fury was the interlocking directorate of railroad executives, military officers, and political officials, which constituted the apex of the country's new power structure."[47] The destination of the largest mass march during the St. Louis general strike was the Four Courts building—the symbol of the Law in that city and, significantly, the major strongpoint being garrisoned by the militia that the city's political and business elite established in response to the strike.[48] In San Francisco Denis Kearney, the leader of the Workingmen's party that was created in the aftermath of the 1877 upheaval, led marches of his supporters not only to the Central Pacific Railroad and other major employers, demanding that Chinese workers be fired and white men hired in their stead, but also invaded ward meetings of the major parties. Alexander Saxton observes,

Kearney's style was that of a declaration of war against the two-party establishment. Not only must the Chinese go. The boodlers, and monopolists and corruptionists of both parties must go with them. To this end Californians would organize a new party of their own. "We propose to elect none but competent workingmen and their friends to any office whatever. The rich have ruled us until they have ruined us. We will take our own affairs into our own hands. The republic must and shall be preserved, and only workingmen will do it."[49]

Related to these political characteristics, the goals workers pursued through strikes extended well beyond wages to the central question of the

[45] Montgomery, *Beyond Equality*, ch. 8.
[46] Burbank, *Reign of the Rabble*, frontispiece.
[47] Montgomery, "Strikes," p. 95.
[48] Burbank, *Reign of the Rabble*, p. 103.
[49] Saxton, *Indispensable Enemy*, p. 118.

day: Who was to control and benefit from the new economic and political order being constructed in the United States? This was most clear in those strikes that escalated into violent attacks upon the powers that be, but it was true as well of more peaceful strikes on behalf of the central goal of the labor movement during the post–Civil War decades—the eight-hour day. Its proponents argued that the hours of labor should be limited so that workers would have the time not only for relaxation but also for self-improvement and for fulfilling their obligations as citizens of a democracy. At stake in strikes over the eight-hour day was whether workers and their children would, like Chinese coolies or Russian serfs, spend virtually all their waking hours and working lives toiling so that a privileged class could live in luxury or whether they would be free men, the equal of all others in the American republic. Labor reformers commonly spoke of the "emancipation of the working class" as the goal of their movement, and this term—as well as "wage slavery," also often used in the late nineteenth century—had both political and economic connotations.[50]

Although the strike was the most dramatic form of collective action of the period, it was not the only form. Groups of workers also formed producer cooperatives. For example, to release its members from the grip of the "wages system," the iron molders' union established twelve cooperative foundries in the 1860s, and the coopers' union established seven cooperative barrel factories during that decade. There was another spurt in the formation of producer cooperatives in the early 1880s, with the Cooperative Board of the Knights of Labor serving as the major source of financial assistance and advice.[51]

Workers also engaged in collective actions and constructed cooperative institutions within the realm of consumption—boycotts, union labels, and consumer cooperatives. "Non-intercourse" proclamations had been issued against offending merchants by the Sons of Liberty during the Revolutionary period, by abolitionist societies during the antebellum era, and by municipal trades assemblies as early as 1863, but the term "boycott" itself is of Irish origin, and Michael Gordon argues that it became a major weapon in the hands of workers in the United States through the adaptation of this Irish institution to conditions in large American cities.[52] As practiced by the Land League in Ireland, the boycott involved

[50] Montgomery, "Strikes," p. 96.
[51] Joseph Rayback, *A History of American Labor* (New York: Free Press, 1966), pp. 114, 160.
[52] Michael Gordon, "The Labor Boycott in New York City, 1880-1886," *Labor History* 16 (1975):184-229.

total social ostracism of landlords, their agents, and others who refused
to acknowledge peasant claims. During strikes in the United States Irish
immigrants did ostracize—or, as it was termed, "leave severely alone"—
fellow workers who acted as scabs, but this scarcely served as a meaningful sanction against employers who lived in another part of town, with
whom workers had no social relations to sever. They could, however,
injure an employer by refusing to buy his products and by urging other
workers to do the same. To succeed such a tactic presupposed the existence of a fairly high degree of class consciousness among workers in
their capacity as consumers.

The converse of the consumer boycott was the union label, a device for
encouraging consumers to purchase products manufactured by union
labor. (Probably the earliest manifestation of this device, however, was
the "white label," developed in the 1860s in California to distinguish
cigars manufactured by shops that hired white men exclusively and
would not employ Chinese.)[53] Another institution involving joint efforts
among workers in the realm of consumption was the consumer cooperative. During the 1860s municipal labor federations established thirty-
seven cooperative stores in cities from Maine to California. In the 1870s
the Sovereigns of Industry, a nationwide cooperative society, had ninety-
six local branches that sponsored such stores. And in the 1880s the Cooperative Board of the Knights of Labor carried on this tradition.[54]

Workers also banded together for the purposes of fellowship in good
times and mutual assistance in times of need. For the most part they
joined with other residents of their neighborhood or members of their
ethnic group—in neighborhood saloons and in fraternal organizations
and mutual aid societies that defined their membership along ethnic or
religious lines. But some of these groupings and organizations were created by workers at (or in association with) their places of work. A number of restaurants in the factory district of Lynn, Massachusetts, for
example, catered to an exclusively—and self-consciously—working-class
clientele: so many unemployed shoe workers spent their days at Hunt's
Cafe that it came to be known as "Crispin's Congress," and Mackenzie's
Lunch found it useful to advertise itself as a "strictly union house."[55]
Some fraternal organizations restricted their membership to persons
belonging to the working (or producing) classes—the Supreme Mechanical Order of the Sun was the largest of these in the 1860s—and others

[53] Saxton, *Indispensable Enemy*, p. 74.
[54] Rayback, *History*, p. 112; Montgomery, "Labor in the Industrial Era," pp. 121f.
[55] John Cumbler, "Labor, Capital, and Community: The Struggle for Power," *Labor History* 15 (1974):395-415, quotations at p. 401.

were organized along craft lines. A number of craft-based fraternal societies functioned as trade unions, as the names of some of the major labor unions of the 1860s and 1870s indicates: the Knights of St. Crispin, the Brotherhood of the Footboard, and the Sons of Vulcan. The secrecy, the ritual, and the fraternal spirit of such organizations served a number of purposes for labor unions. Secrecy as a way of dealing with blacklists; elaborate rituals, oaths, and titles enabled organizations, which did not enjoy the protection or control the sanctions that the Wagner Act later granted unions, to distribute "solidary inducements" to their members; and, most important of all, the fraternalism that characterized such organizations was quite similar to the spirit of mutual assistance among brother workers that labor unions drew upon and sought to strengthen among their members.[56]

Another way in which workers sought to improve the conditions under which they lived and labored was through participation in labor reform associations. These associations were roughly comparable to the abolitionist societies of the 1840s and 1850s and the civil rights groups of the 1940s and 1950s. They sought through education, agitation, and lobbying to secure the enactment of legislation beneficial to workers. Their membership was open to anyone who shared their principles, workers and nonworkers alike. The most prominent of these organizations were the Eight Hour Leagues, which sought to get state legislatures to enact statutes declaring eight hours to be a "legal day's work."[57]

Labor parties were another component of the labor reform movement during the quarter century following the outbreak of the Civil War. In 1869 the Independent party, organized by the Knights of St. Crispin, elected two dozen state legislators from industrial towns in Massachusetts; in 1878 the Greenback-Labor party elected a number of mayors in industrial and mining towns in Pennsylvania and New York; and in 1886 labor tickets won municipal elections in dozens of communities throughout the country. Labor reformers also organized a succession of national labor or farmer-labor parties during the 1860s, 1870s, and 1880s; none of these, however, managed to win a substantial number of working-class votes.[58]

Many of these disparate goals, modes of collective action, and organizational forms characterized the largest labor reform organization of the

---

[56] See, e.g., P. M. Arthur, "The Rise of Railroad Organization," in *The Labor Movement: The Problem of Today*, ed. George McNeill, quoted in Philip Taft, *Organized Labor in American History* (New York: Harper & Row, 1964), p. 58.

[57] Montgomery, *Beyond Equality*, pp. 135-39.

[58] Rayback, *History*, pp. 125-26, 136-39, 169-73.

late nineteenth century, the Knights of Labor. The organization, whose full name was the Noble and Holy Order of the Knights of Labor, was founded as a fraternal society among Philadelphia garment workers in 1869, and especially during the first decade of its life it shrouded its affairs in secrecy (members were forbidden to mention the organization's name to outsiders, let alone the names of fellow members), and practiced an elaborate ritual of oaths, passwords, and ceremonies.[59] Members of the Knights—sometimes with the sanction of the organization, and sometimes without—also participated in strikes, and the organization's leaders engaged in collective bargaining with employers.[60] In connection with these activities the Knights sponsored boycotts and attached an identifying label to goods manufactured by firms that negotiated contracts with the organization.[61] The Cooperative Board of the Knights, as mentioned above, helped set up both producer and consumer cooperatives. The Knights also participated actively in electoral politics. Terrence Powderly, the organization's Grand Master Workman, was elected mayor of Scranton, Pennsylvania, in 1878 and district assemblies of the Knights played a major role in the surge of labor activity in the elections of 1886.[62]

A noteworthy feature of most of the organizations established by workers was their extremely amorphous structure. The Knights provide a striking example of this. After the order shed its secrecy in 1879, it was very easy to join it and consequently its total membership fluctuated wildly. The most dramatic fluctuation occurred during the second half of the 1880s: between July 1885 and July 1886 the Knights' membership increased from 104,000 to 703,000; it then reversed direction and declined to its original level by the end of the decade.

Not only was movement into and out of labor organizations easy and frequent, so too were the boundaries between them highly permeable. Many skilled workers belonged to both a trades union and the Knights; Samuel Gompers himself was such a "two card" man. Similarly, many socialists played an active role in the Knights and in the trade unions of the day. As Alexander Saxton says of the San Francisco labor movement of the early 1880s, "Everything in the house of labor in those days was interpermeable; ideas overlapped; and personnel swapped places. Haskill

[59] See, e.g., John R. Commons et al., eds., *A Documentary History of American Industrial Society* (Cleveland: Arthur H. Clark Co., 1910-1911), 10:19-32.
[60] See, e.g., Katherine Harvey, "The Knights of Labor in the Maryland Coal Fields, 1878-1882," *Labor History* 10 (1969):555-83; James M. Morris, "The Cincinnati Shoemakers' Lockout of 1888," *Labor History* 13 (1972):505-519.
[61] M. Gordon, "Labor Boycott," pp. 211-18.
[62] Leon Fink, *Workingmen's Democracy: The Knights of Labor and American Politics* (Urbana: University of Illinois Press, 1983).

[a Socialist], editing what had become the official organ of the Trades Assembly, devoted his columns to the service of the Knights with impartial enthusiasm."[63]

It was possible for trade unionists, Knights, socialists, and other labor reformers to work together because to a considerable degree they shared a common vocabulary and set of objections to the dominant institutions and values of the late-nineteenth-century American economic order. There were differences among them, but the similarities were sufficiently great to make it possible to speak of the existence of a single, albeit amorphous, labor reform movement in the United States during the twenty-five years after the outbreak of the Civil War.[64]

The focus of traditional American labor historiography upon the conflict between bread-and-butter trade unionists (who supposedly shared the materialistic values of American society and simply wanted to secure higher wages for the members of their trade) and impractical reformers (who either wanted to return to a simpler age or who preached doctrines alien to American workers) obscures the rather substantial areas of agreement among trade unionists, Knights, and socialists and the very profound objections they all raised to some of the central practices and values of industrial capitalism.[65] Trade unionists, as much as Knights and socialists, spoke of "the abolition of the wages system" and "the emancipation of the working class" as their ultimate goal.[66] And all segments of the labor movement regarded themselves as engaged in a struggle with "capital" or "wealth" over the very shape of American society. The preamble to the constitution adopted by the Knights of Labor in 1878 declared that, as summarized by Joseph Rayback:

"Wealth" . . . had become so aggressive that "unless checked" it would lead to the "pauperization and hopeless degradation of the toiling masses." If the toilers, therefore, wanted to enjoy the "blessings of life" they had to organize

---

[63] Saxton, *Indispensable Enemy*, p. 165. See also Richard Oestreicher, "Socialism and the Knights of Labor in Detroit, 1877-1886," *Labor History* 22 (1981):5-30.

[64] I used the term "labor reform movement," which I borrow from David Montgomery, rather than "working-class movement," because the latter term would prejudge the central question this essay addresses—how America's distinctive working class (in the full sense of class levels three and four) came to be formed. The character and boundaries of the American working class were very much a matter of contention in the period 1861-1886, and by no means can all the dispositions toward collective action exhibited by American workers or all the organizations they formed be classified as part of a common working-class movement.

[65] Cf., Gerald Grob, *Workers and Utopia* (Evanston: Northwestern University Press, 1961).

[66] Stuart Kaufman, *Samuel Gompers and the Origins of the American Federation of Labor, 1848-1896* (Westport, Conn.: Greenwood Press, 1973), pp. 168, 199.

"every department of productive industry." . . . The ultimate aim of the order would be the establishment of "cooperative institutions productive and distributive."[67]

The preamble of the constitution adopted by the American Federation of Labor (AFL) in 1886 asserted, in a rather similar vein, that a

struggle is going on in all the civilized world between oppressors and oppressed of all countries, between capitalist and laborer which grows in intensity from year to year. . . . It therefore behooves the Representatives of the Trades and Labor Unions of America . . . to adopt such measures and disseminate such principles among the mechanics and laborers of our country as will permanently unite them.[68]

It is in this context that the rather substantial role socialists played in the American labor movement of the post–Civil War decades can be understood. For reasons to be discussed, socialism was not a significant force in American electoral politics during this period. Socialist doctrines concerning the inevitability of conflict between capital and labor, however, resonated with experiences that many workers had had on their jobs, and when such conflicts were especially intense other elements of the labor reform movement were prepared to associate themselves with socialists. In particular, in 1869, when the campaign for an eight-hour day was sweeping the nation, the National Labor Union announced its intention of affiliating with the International Workingmen's Association (IWA)—the First International.[69] The IWA's successor, the Working-men's Party of the United States, played an important role in the leadership of the 1877 strike movement in a number of cities, most notably in St. Louis, where a majority of the members of the executive committee that ran the general strike were members of the party.[70] Socialists also gained a major voice in the Knights of Labor and the AFL during the crisis of the 1890s.

In addition, the commitment of Marxian socialists (as opposed to Lassalleans) to the organization of labor unions meant that men who were, or once had been, socialists played a major role in the American trade union movement. In New York City, for example, members of the "Stanton Street group"—a circle of IWA members and their associates, the most prominent of whom were Adolph Strasser, Samuel Gompers, and Peter Maguire—led the drives to organize the city's cigarmakers and

[67] Rayback, *History*, p. 145.
[68] Quoted in Taft, *Organized Labor*, p. 115.
[69] Montgomery, *Beyond Equality*, pp. 327-28.
[70] Philip Foner, *The Great Labor Uprising of 1877* (New York: Monad Press, 1977), ch. 9.

carpenters in the 1870s.[71] In San Francisco a similar grouping, which Saxton terms "the socialist academy," played a major role in organizing the Coast Seamen's Union and the city's Trades Assembly in the 1880s.[72] The important role socialists played in the organization of unions laid the groundwork for socialists and nonsocialists in the American labor movement to influence one another.

One final characteristic of the collective endeavors in which workers engaged and the organizations they formed during the post–Civil War years is worth emphasizing again at this point—the often close articulation between the claims that workers made upon their employers and the state, and the activities and organizations through which they asserted these claims. Workers sought both to pressure employers directly and to obtain the support of state governments for their efforts to secure the eight-hour day, to increase mine safety, and to secure relief from the competition of "coolie labor." They pursued these goals by staging strikes, threatening to switch their votes between the major parties, entering labor tickets in elections, and lobbying. It was not uncommon during this period for labor organizations (the Knights were the most important example) to engage in several of these activities; thus workers often made claims upon both their employers and the state through one and the same organization. It is true that most trade unions, for reasons to be discussed below, scrupulously avoided official involvement in electoral politics; it remains the case, however, that the leaders of these "pure and simple" unions played a major role in founding labor reform organizations that were heavily involved in political action.

What all of this means is that the wide array of groups and organizations established by workers in the decades following the Civil War were more the vehicles through which a social movement—the labor movement—operated than a set of interest groups occupying an established and limited niche in the American economic and political order. Their goals were broad—involving nothing less than transforming the position workers occupied in American society—and quite threatening to the nation's upper class and its political leadership. Moreover, these groups and organizations were not highly "institutionalized"; they were not characterized by a high degree of organizational "autonomy," "coherence," and "adaptability," to use Samuel P. Huntington's terminology.[73] This is especially clear in the case of the period's largest labor reform organization, the Knights of Labor. Far from enjoying a substan-

[71] Kaufman, *Samuel Gompers*, p. 58.

[72] Saxton, *Indispensable Enemy*, ch. 8.

[73] Samuel P. Huntington, *Political Order in Changing Societies* (New Haven: Yale University Press, 1968), pp. 12-24.

tial measure of autonomy from its social base, the Knights quite accurately reflected the temper of the working class: its membership shot up in the mid-1880s as the number of persons caught up in the spirit of the labor movement increased—the hope that workers could improve their lives through their collective efforts. These new members, sharing the militant mood of the day—that workers should "give no quarter" in the fight for their rights—drew the Knights into the great strike wave of 1886.[74] Correlatively, the leaders of the Knights were able to exercise little control over their members; in particular, they were not in a position to decree when strikes would be called and terminated and, as we shall see, they were unable to shed old goals and methods and to adopt new ones for the sake of preserving their organization.

Although it makes sense to speak of a single, albeit amorphous, labor reform movement in the United States during this period, this is not to say that all elements of that movement had identical goals or that there was unanimity among them on questions of strategy and tactics, any more than speaking of a civil rights movement in the 1960s implies that all blacks who participated in the quest for "freedom now" or "black liberation" had a common understanding of the meaning of those slogans or agreed on the best means to achieve those ends. One of the most important divergences among participants in the labor reform movement concerned their view of the scope of the movement's constituency—their understanding of the boundaries of the working class. In their words and deeds labor reformers revealed a wide range of views on the boundaries of the collectivity whose interests they sought to advance.

The most comprehensive of these understandings regarded "labor" as including all members of the "producing classes"—common laborers, skilled workers, farmers, members of the middle class, and even manufacturers. This view was especially prevalent during the early part of the period. In the 1860s and early 1870s the term "working classes" always was used in the plural; "labor" was used to refer both to workers and manufacturers; and its antonym, "capital," referred exclusively to financiers and *rentiers*. Those sharing this comprehensive understanding believed that there were no inherent conflicts of interest between employers and employees, and that the labor reform movement need not be one of wage laborers alone.[75] During the 1860s and early 1870s members of the middle class played an important role in the Eight Hour Leagues, in

---

[74] Rayback, *History*, p. 165.

[75] Samuel Walker, "Varieties of Workingclass Experience: The Workingmen of Scranton, Pennsylvania, 1855-1885," in *American Workingclass Culture: Explorations in American Labor and Social History,* ed. Milton Cantor (Westport, Conn.: Greenwood Press, 1979), p. 366.

many sections of the International Workingmen's Association, and in the National Labor Union and the National Labor Reform Party.[76] Under the constitution adopted by the Knights of Labor in 1878, membership in the order was open to any person "working for wages, or who at any time worked for wages," with the exception of bankers, lawyers, doctors, and liquor dealers—whose very businesses and professions involved the exploitation of productive labor. Significantly, employers were not excluded from the order.[77]

Although the national leaders of the Knights argued that the interests of employers and employees were fundamentally similar and were therefore reluctant to endorse strikes, the members of numerous local assemblies of the order indicated that they had a less inclusive understanding of the boundaries of the working class by walking off their jobs to put pressure on and extract concessions from their employers.[78] Trade unionists, who in word and deed excluded employers from the working class—who used the term "working class" in the singular and did not hesitate to use the strike as a weapon—established the Federation of Organized Trades and Labor Unions (FOTLU) in 1881, the first national labor reform organization composed of wage laborers alone, and the precursor of the American Federation of Labor.[79]

Participants in the labor reform movement—and American workers generally—also displayed a variety of dispositions toward those who differed from them in race and sex. Whites, blacks, and Orientals often competed for the same jobs, as did men and women; moreover, employers at times used blacks, Orientals, and women as strikebreakers. Labor reformers responded in two different ways to this situation. On the one hand, many local and national crafts unions excluded the members of racial minorities and women from their ranks and sought to drive them from their trades.[80] And all national labor organizations, from the NLU through the AFL, sought to ban all immigration to the United States from China. In California the Workingmen's party, the Knights, and San Francisco's Federated Trades Council went even further and sought to expel the Chinese. During the 1880s in several small cities and mining camps in the Far West white workers (and small businessmen) took the law into their own hands and drove the Chinese out of their communities by force.[81]

[76] Montgomery, *Beyond Equality*, chap. 10.
[77] Fink, " 'Irrespective of Party,' " p. 329.
[78] See, e.g., Harvey, "Knights of Labor"; Morris, "Cincinnati Shoemakers' Lockout."
[79] Kaufman, *Samuel Gompers*, ch. 6.
[80] Gutman, *Work, Culture, and Society*, p. 193.
[81] Saxton, *Indispensable Enemy*, ch. 10.

On the other hand, white and black workers and also male and female workers at times united across these lines in strikes, election campaigns, and in labor reform organizations. Black sewer workers in Louisville, Kentucky, and black stevedores in Cairo, Illinois, took part in the strike movement that swept the country in the summer of 1877.[82] In the municipal elections in Richmond, Virginia, in 1886 the Knights of Labor and black Republicans endorsed a common slate of candidates, and together they won control of the city council.[83] The NLU and the Knights encouraged the organization of blacks, albeit often in segregated locals; in 1886 the Knights had 60,000 black members.[84] Among labor unions, the United Mine Workers was especially active in recruiting blacks and a black organizer, Richard Davis, served on that union's national executive board in the 1890s.[85] As for women, the NLU seated delegates from Working Women's Protective Unions at its national conventions and advocated equal pay for equal work; many local and district assemblies of the Knights in the shoe and garment industries admitted women to their ranks; and strikes in these industries often mobilized both male and female workers.[86]

Immigrants comprised a much larger proportion of the industrial work force than blacks or women in the late nineteenth century, and thus the relationship between ethnicity and class—the tendency of workers to divide along ethnic lines or to unite across them—is a matter of great importance that will be discussed further below. Suffice it to say here that this relationship was also a multifaceted one. Many strikes were lost because employers brought in gangs of immigrants to serve as strike-breakers.[87] For this reason all national labor organizations in the post–Civil War years sought to ban the importation of immigrant contract labor, and the passage of the Foran Act in 1885, which outlawed this practice, was generally regarded as one of labor's major legislative victories in the nineteenth century.[88] On the local level many trade unions dominated by native-born workers or the members of older immigrant groups refused to admit newer immigrants to their ranks. In Scranton, Welsh miners who dominated the Workingman's Benevolent Association took such a stance toward Irish and Germans; in Milwaukee the Irish

[82] Rayback, *History*, p. 136.

[83] Fink, " 'Irrespective of Party,' " p. 333.

[84] Montgomery, "Labor in the Industrial Era," p. 128; Kenneth Kann, "The Knights of Labor and the Southern Black Worker," *Labor History* 18 (1977):49-70.

[85] Gutman, *Work, Culture, and Society*, ch. 3.

[86] See, e.g., Mary Blewitt, "The Union of Sex and Craft in the Haverhill Shoe Strike of 1895," *Labor History* 20 (1979):352-75.

[87] Charlotte Erickson, *American Industry and the European Immigrant, 1860-1885* (Cambridge: Harvard University Press, 1957), ch. 6.

[88] Ibid., ch. 9.

and Germans who dominated that city's labor unions refused to recruit into their ranks members of that city's large Polish community.[89]

Nativism, however, was not a major theme in the labor reform movement during the postbellum years. Immigrants from England, Wales, and Germany played a major role in organizing trade unions (and also consumer cooperatives) during this period. A major reason that the Knights of Labor shed its secrecy in 1878 was to enable Catholic immigrants to join the order without violating the Church's ban on membership in secret societies. And many trade unionists recognized that the only way they could effectively counter the tactic of using immigrants as strikebreakers was to recruit the latter into their ranks.[90]

III. The Working-Class Response: Sources of Variation and Change

As amorphous in structure as the labor reform movement of the late nineteenth century was and as disparate the views of its members, by no means did most American workers respond to the changes they were experiencing by participating in that movement. Only a minority of the nation's wage earners ever took part in a strike, belonged to a trade union or other labor reform organization, or voted for a labor ticket. Moreover, significant changes occurred during the period in the relative importance and character of both the various modes of collective action in which workers engaged and the organizations to which they belonged. These variations across groups of workers and through time were a function of the structure of and changes in the patterns of economic, community, and political life within which workers were situated.

Variations and Changes. Although it is impossible to obtain data on the numbers involved, it is probably true that more workers sought to overcome the difficulties they faced through individual endeavors than by joining in a collective effort to improve their lives. As mentioned above, rates of population mobility were extraordinarily high, especially among persons at the bottom of the class structure; those unable to find work in one city would move on to another. The most extreme manifestation of this phenomenon was tramping: thousands of men rode the rails from city to city to eke out an existence. Occasionally these transient laborers would join together under the leadership of a tribune who gave voice to their common grievances: Denis Kearney in the late 1870s and Jacob

[89] Walker, "Varieties," pp. 368-69; Gerd Korman, *Industrialization, Immigrants, and Americanizers: The View from Milwaukee* (Madison: State Historical Society of Wisconsin, 1967), pp. 51-53.

[90] See, e.g., Greene, *Slavic Community*, ch. 5.

Coxey in 1894 drew many followers from this source.[91] More commonly, however, they suffered their fates in solitude.

Moreover, though many workers rejected the acquisitive and individualistic values preached by the Henry Ward Beechers and Horatio Algers of the time, many others did not. The ubiquity of small shops in working-class neighborhoods gives testimony to the determination of many workers to scrimp and save so that they and their children could move out of the factories. And the proliferation of subcontracting practices in American industry—the most notorious being the sweatshop system in the garment trades—indicates that there were large numbers of workers who could not resist the temptation of becoming small entrepreneurs and profiting from the exploitation of other workers. The ideal of self-improvement that animated the labor movement was separated by only a narrow line from the impulse to move up the class scale through one's individual efforts. Mutualistic and individualistic manifestations of this ethos could coexist in the late nineteenth century because America in the Gilded Age was a land in which workers both suffered massive exploitation and had genuine opportunities (or at least their children did) to move out of the working class or up within it.[92]

When workers did join with others in an effort to improve their lives, ethnicity was at least as likely as social class *per se* to be the basis of association. It will not do, however, to speak of ethnicity and class as competing principles of identification and organization—the prevailing fashion in the historiography of the period—as many examples cited below will indicate. Nonetheless it was not uncommon for ethnic subcommunities to unite behind those of its members who broke strikes called by workers belonging to other ethnic groups. For example, during a coal strike in Scranton in 1871, Irish and German mine laborers broke ranks with striking Welsh miners, hoping to take their jobs and provoking violent clashes between the ethnic subcommunities.[93] It is also true that ethnicity and religion were the most common bases of association for mutual aid and fraternal societies that provided members with such benefits as burial insurance, mutual support in abstaining from alcohol, or good fellowship to accompany their liquor.

Also, though labor tickets were entered in hundreds of local and state elections in the postbellum period and the effort to create a national farmer-labor party was a persistent theme, the victories labor reformers

[91] Saxton, *Indispensable Enemy*, pp. 143-47; Donald L. McMurry, *Coxey's Army: A Study of the Industrial Army Movement of 1894* (Seattle: University of Washington Press, 1968).
[92] Gutman, *Work, Culture, and Society*, chaps. 2, 4.
[93] Walker, "Varieties," p. 369.

won in the electoral arena were at best evanescent and the great majority of American workers cast their ballots for the Democratic and Republican parties. Indeed, the institutions with which the largest number of American workers almost certainly identified were these national parties, the common activity in which they most frequently engaged was voting the Democratic or Republican ticket on election day, and the organizations to which the largest number of them belonged were the local machines affiliated with the major parties. The two major parties and their local machines could not be indifferent to the concerns of their working-class constituents, but the cleavage between them cut across class lines—however broadly or narrowly the boundaries of the nation's social classes might be defined—and this meant that all the hoopla of nineteenth-century electioneering divided the working class and stressed the ties that workers had with their fellow partisans from other social classes.

Not only did substantial differences exist at any given time in the disposition of various segments of the working class to participate in the labor reform movement, significant changes occurred during the late nineteenth century in the activities and organizations comprising that movement. In particular, major changes occurred both in the frequency and the character of strikes during the three decades following the Civil War. The number of workers involved in strikes increased over time, but there were substantial fluctuations within this trend. Equally important, changes occurred in the role unions played in strikes: the proportion of strikes that were called by unions (as opposed to unorganized, spontaneous walkouts) rose during 1869-1874, fell during the remainder of the 1870s, and then resumed climbing from just under 50 percent in 1881 to over 70 percent in the early 1890s. With increasing organization came changes in the goals of strikers. The proportion of strikes in which wages were the central issue fell from 75 percent in the early 1880s to 50 percent in the early 1890s, and the number dealing with organizational issues—such as strikes to secure union recognition or to defend union members against retaliation—rose steadily. In addition, between 1885 and 1894 the number of sympathy strikes increased dramatically. In one respect, however, both the focus and setting of strikes became narrower during the second half of our period. During the decade and a half following 1877, strikes were not used as a political weapon to the extent they had been during the previous fifteen years and, correspondingly, they were more likely to occur exclusively at workplaces than to take the form of community uprisings.[94]

[94] Montgomery, "Strikes," pp. 89-100.

These variations in participation in the labor reform movement and changes through time in its activities and organizations were a function of the character of and changes in broader economic, community, and political relationships. Workers, after all, did not exist *in vacuo*; as the relationship between any segment of the working class and other social forces varied—and as the relationship among these other groups changed—so too did the behavior of the workers in question.

Relations of Production. The modes of collective action in which different workers engaged and the types of organizations they formed were shaped first by the web of economic relations in which they were enmeshed— their relationship with competitors for their jobs, with other workers on their jobs, and with their employers. The image of a web is particularly appropriate because changes in any one of these relationships could alter the others, and changes in economic relations in which workers were not directly involved, such as the relationship between their employer and his competitors, could alter those that did touch them directly. A number of such changes occurred during the last decades of the nineteenth century.

The relationship between workers and potential competitors for their jobs is the focus of the central law of neoclassical labor economics: the more completely a group of workers can restrict entry into a labor market, the more readily they can form a trade union and compel their employer to bargain with them.[95] The ability to restrict entry into a labor market is, in turn, heavily influenced by the skill required to do the job in question. The oldest and most stable labor unions in the nineteenth century were those organized by highly skilled workers—among them typographers, iron molders, machinists, locomotive engineers, carpenters, and bricklayers—because employers faced with a walkout by such craftsmen could not readily replace the strikers and therefore had an incentive to come to terms with the unions these workers formed. By contrast, unskilled workers who walked off their jobs could easily be replaced, and employers had little reason to enter into stable bargaining relationships with labor unions unskilled workers might seek to form.

The relationship of skilled workers to their fellow workers on the job was at least equally important, however, in explaining why they were able to organize unions and conduct strikes successfully. As indicated above, skilled workers played a crucial role in the organization of production in the nineteenth-century factory. They often knew better than their employer himself how the production end of his business was conducted, and they exercised more control over the day-to-day operations of his

[95] Ullman, *Rise of the National Trade Union*, ch. 2.

plant than he did. To the extent that this was true, these workers were indispensable and had considerable bargaining leverage.[96] Moreover, the relationship of skilled workers to each other on the job had an ethical dimension that was fundamentally collectivist (as opposed to individualist) in orientation, and the unions these workers organized drew upon these solidarities.[97]

The business cycle also influenced the ability of workers to control labor markets. Strikes could be more successfully conducted and unions more readily organized during periods of prosperity, when the labor market was tight, than during depressions, when firms could easily replace striking workers with the unemployed, including unemployed union men who were driven by necessity to work for less than the union scale. Thus the first great wave of union organization in the late nineteenth century occurred during the flush years of the late 1860s and early 1870s; union membership declined precipitously during the depression of 1873-1878; and the Knights of Labor grew in membership during the relatively prosperous 1880s. With some important qualifications to be noted, the number of workers involved in strikes also rose and fell with the business cycle.

The relationship between fluctuations in the business cycle and rates of strike activity and union formation was not perfect, however. As mentioned earlier, there was a secular increase both in the number of workers involved in strikes and in the extent to which strikes were carefully planned and organized. This rising baseline is to be explained in the first place by a number of changes in the structure of the American economy that affected the relationship of business firms to one another, of employers to employees, and ultimately of workers to each other.

Prior to the depression of 1873 most manufacturing firms in the United States were quite small—in 1869 the average factory had only eight employees—and the great majority of such establishments were family firms or partnerships whose owners played an active role in their management.[98] In these circumstances it was possible for employers to maintain something of a personal relationship with their employees, and the concept of the "producing classes" made sense phenomenologically. Samuel Walker says of the workingmen of Scranton during this period:

Many Scranton workingmen ... had worked side by side with the George Scrantons and Thomas Dicksons [the city's two leading industrialists] in the

[96] Benson Soffer, "A Theory of Trade Union Development: The Role of the 'Autonomous' Workman," *Labor History* 1 (1960):141-63.

[97] Dawson, "Paradox of Dynamic Change," pp. 344-48.

[98] Montgomery, *Beyond Equality*, pp. 3-15.

1850s and 1860s. George Scranton, for example, wielded hammer and chisel in his initial attempts to manufacture iron. One workingman recalled the time when "Thomas Dickson . . . appeared in blue denim trousers and blouse on him. He took the hammer from one man and took his place for about fifteen minutes, then stepped over to the other side and spelled another man for fifteen minutes."[99]

Conflicts between employers and employees existed, to be sure, and workers staged strikes to increase the wages they earned and reduce the hours they labored, but union leaders continued to insist that the interests of the two sides were fundamentally in harmony, and they sought to resolve such disputes by dealing personally with their employers.

Economic developments during the late nineteenth century disrupted such relationships. As noted, the extension of the railroads made it difficult for any employer to treat his employees more decently than his least scrupulous competitors in other cities. Beyond this, the absorption of small firms by stronger ones during the depressions and recessions of the period, the spread of the corporate form of business organization, and the emergence of a class of professional managers destroyed the organizational base upon which personal relations between employers and employees had been grounded. Workers for a time resisted the reduction of all relations to the cash nexus. Walker reports that as late as 1877, well after corporations based in New York City had taken control of Scranton's major industries, delegations of workers sought to settle disputes by traveling to New York to talk personally to the president of the corporation that employed them.[100] Such appeals, of course, fell on deaf ears, and workers in time learned how to organize themselves more effectively to advance their interests in this new economic environment.

Class divisions became more pronounced and strikes became more frequent and more highly organized not simply because manufacturers, driven by the lure of profits and the lash of competition, sought to squeeze more output from their men, but also because workers themselves, in striving to advance their collective interests, took steps that sharpened the line between employers and employees. Work-rules unions enacted that established output quotas and prohibited participation in various subcontracting schemes served the collective interests of the union's members by imposing restraints on the efforts of individual wage laborers to get ahead at the expense of their brothers. These work rules were essentially a codification of the informal norms, described above, that had emerged in the course of earlier struggles between craftsmen and their employers.

[99] Walker, "Varieties," p. 364.
[100] Ibid., p. 366.

Unions codified these norms and established formal procedures to enforce them—shop committees to monitor compliance, strikes called against employers who violated the union's rules, and eventually sympathy strikes against employers who violated the work rules of other unions— to better ensure that employers would adhere to the union's standards. These developments in union practice heightened class divisions.[101]

Factory owners, on their part, undertook to reorganize the process of production in their plants—adopting new and improved technologies and new techniques of supervision, reward, and punishment—in order to overcome the limitations that their employees sought to impose upon them. The employers' associations they established and the mergers into which they entered were influenced by this same consideration.[102] This in turn shaped the tone and tenor of relations between employers and employees. There was, then, a dialectical interaction between changes in the organization of production and changes in the character and extent of class conflicts, class consciousness, and working-class organization.

Finally, from time to time during the late nineteenth century there were bursts of strike activity above and beyond what can be explained by this rising trend and fluctuations of the business cycle. In the summer of 1877, during the American economy's worst depression up to that time, the nation was convulsed by a strike wave larger than any it had previously experienced. In 1886 the number of workers involved in strikes shot up to 407,000 from an average of 124,000 in the years between 1881 and 1885. Finally, in 1894, at the trough of the worst depression of the nineteenth century, the number of strikers shot up to its highest level in that century—505,000, a figure roughly double that of the preceding and following years.

The strikes of 1877 and 1886, and to a lesser extent those of 1894, spread in a contagious fashion and involved workers who had not previously participated in the labor reform movement. Each of these strike waves was precipitated by a walkout of railway men. The central role that railroads played in the American economic order of the nineteenth century was well understood at the time, and the spectacle of workers rising up against the nation's key economic institution inspired others to do the same. As each strike wave gathered momentum it appeared that

[101] Montgomery, *Workers' Control*, ch. 1.

[102] The classic example was the effort of Franklin B. Gowen to unite the railroads that owned the coal fields of eastern Pennsylvania against the anthracite miners' union, the Workingmen's Benevolent Association. See, e.g., Marvin W. Schlegel, *Ruler of the Reading: The Life of Franklin B. Gowen* (Harrisburg: Archives Publishing Company of Pennsylvania, 1947).

the entire structure of authority, both industrial and political, to which workers were subjected was crumbling. If the sense that workers could indeed change the conditions under which they labored led increasing numbers to join these strike movements, it provoked fear and outrage among the upper and middle classes and led them to stage counterattacks.[103]

The years following the Great Uprising of 1886 witnessed an especially sustained antilabor crusade. The Knights were its first target. As Rayback notes:

Leaders of the campaign against them were the employers from whom the order had secured concessions. . . . [They] began to organize into associations which openly and deliberately moved to destroy the order by systematic violation of trade agreements, refusal to arbitrate industrial disputes, and resort to lockouts, black listing, and yellow-dog contracts. Such activity led to some fearsome conflicts. Nearly 100,000 Knights were involved in strikes and lockouts in the latter months of the year 1886.[104]

In addition, business firms that competed with the cooperative enterprises sponsored by the Knights induced other firms to refuse to sell equipment and supplies to them, and within two year's time all of these enterprises were destroyed.

During these years many employers also undertook to destroy the trade unions that organized their workers. Their employees responded by striking and by calling upon their brother workers to stage sympathy strikes. These confrontations led to some of the largest and most bitter strikes of the nineteenth century—the strikes at Homestead, Coeur d'Alene, and on the New Orleans docks in 1892, and the Pullman and bituminous coal strikes in 1894. As will be discussed, employers were able to get the militia, the army, and the courts to intervene on their behalf in many of these conflicts.

This counteroffensive by business and the state threatened the very survival of the labor movement. It also fostered deep divisions within the movement over the question of how, in this increasingly hostile environment, workers could best improve the conditions under which they labored.

Community Life. The size and structure of the communities in which workers lived also shaped the modes of collective action in which they

---

[103] Montgomery, "Strikes," pp. 94-98; for a discussion of such "moments of madness" in France, see Aristide Zolberg, "Moments of Madness," *Politics and Society* 2 (1972):183-207.

[104] Rayback, *History*, p. 174.

engaged. In small cities and mining towns where a majority of wage earners might work in a single industry or even for a single firm, ties of community and class often reinforced one another: a wage cut or lockout in
the town's key industry was an attack upon all or most workers in the
town. At the same time, the division between the working and middle
classes characteristically was not as pronounced in small cities as in large
ones. The neighborhoods in which workers lived were, quite literally, less
distant from those inhabited by the middle class, and there were greater
opportunities for interaction between individuals across class lines. This
made it less likely that the members of the working and the middle
classes in small cities would come to view the world in entirely different
ways.

These aspects of community life had a number of important consequences. The doctrines of labor reform organizations, such as the Knights
of Labor, that sought to unite all "producers"—laborers, skilled workers,
shopkeepers, and farmers—in the battle against "monopoly" found their
readiest audience in smaller cities, and the mixed assemblies of the
Knights—whose membership was not confined to a single craft—was a
widely adopted form of organization in these locales. Strikes in smaller
cities commonly were community affairs, with the workers involved
receiving the support of their fellow townsmen. As one coal miner said
of a strike in St. Clair County, Illinois, in 1868, "We had support from
the shopkeepers, farmers, and everyone else to stand out against our
oppressors."[105] Just as trade unions and unorganized strike movements
were able to draw upon the strong solidarities linking workers to one
another on the job to sustain themselves in the absence of the sanctions provided by the Wagner Act, so too were they able to draw
upon the solidarities linking workers to their neighbors. For example,
the coal miners who staged a strike in Tioga County, Pennsylvania, in
1874 were able to hold out for three months until the company capitu-
lated, even though they had no strike fund to draw upon, because
local shopkeepers and householders provided them with food and
shelter.[106]

These same community solidarities also often ensured that workers did
not have to fear that the local government would intervene on behalf of
their employers during strikes. During a strike by coal miners in Braidwood, Illinois—a town of 6,000—in 1874, the mine operators hired Pinkerton agents and sought to have them deputized by the sheriff so that

[105] Montgomery, *Beyond Equality*, p. 145.
[106] Gutman, *Work, Culture, and Society*, p. 341.

they could arrest striking workers for trespassing on company property. The sheriff, however, refused to do so. Instead he and the mayor appointed as special deputies a dozen members of a committee the strikers had established to prevent violence and property destruction.[107] Labor reformers also enjoyed greater success in small cities than in large ones when they entered the electoral arena. Three years after the miners' strike in Braidwood, for example, the president of the miners' union was elected mayor. More generally, the candidates nominated by the Greenback-Labor party in the mid- and late-1870s won hundreds of councilmanic, state legislative, and congressional elections in small cities, but very few in the nation's great metropolises.

What was true of small towns as a whole was usually true of the ethnic subcommunities within them. The great majority of both Irish-Americans and immigrants from southern and eastern Europe in these towns tended to be laborers and workers, and hence the small number of middle-class members of these groups could scarcely escape identification with the class position of their countrymen: to be a Polish or Hungarian shopkeeper in the mining towns of northeastern Pennsylvania was to belong to an ethnic group whose members were overwhelmingly proletarian. This meant that strikes by such mine workers were actions of the entire ethnic subcommunity. In his account of a strike by East European miners in the Pennsylvania anthracite fields in 1888, appropriately titled "A Slavic Community Strikes," Victor Greene reports that a rally to support the strikers called by a Ukrainian priest was addressed by the editors of the local Lithuanian and Ukrainian newspapers, a Slovak merchant, and a Polish shoemaker.[108] And ethnically based organizations in these communities were more likely to be dominated by working-class militants than by members of the group's middle class. For example, following the destruction of the anthracite miners' union in the "Long Strike" of 1874, the Molly Maguires, a secret society within the Ancient Order of Hibernians, emerged as the vehicle for the miners' struggle against their bosses. At this point homicide—both extralegal and legal—became the chief means through which class conflict was conducted in the coal fields: the Mollys murdered mine superintendents, and the mine operators secured the conviction and execution of twenty alleged members of the order by hiring a Pinkerton agent to infiltrate it, collect evidence, and testify against its members.[109] In the early 1880s, branches of the Land

[107] Gutman, "The Workers' Search for Power," p. 40.

[108] Greene, *Slavic Community*, ch. 5.

[109] Wayne G. Broehl, *The Molly Maguires* (Cambridge: Harvard University Press, 1964).

League—at the time the most prominent Irish nationalist organization—
in the mining towns of Pennsylvania and the Far West and in the small
manufacturing cities of the Northeast and Midwest were dominated by
leaders who asserted that the struggle of American workers against their
employers was the same as the struggle of Irish tenant farmers against
their landlords. Significantly, many of these league branches were organized at workplaces and even included members of ethnic groups other
than the Irish.[110]

In the nation's major metropolises there was more residential and
social segregation of the working and middle classes. Especially in large
commercial and financial centers, with their armies of clerks, the middle
class was numerous enough for its members to establish a full set of institutions enabling them to shop, pray, play, and educate their children
without coming into contact with members of the working class. Correspondingly, shopkeepers, preachers, teachers, and newspaper editors
could cater exclusively to a middle-class clientele. Beyond this, different
segments of the working class—defined along lines of income and/or ethnicity—generally lived in different neighborhoods. Even in the middle-
sized city of Scranton, the predominantly Welsh miners, who were the
aristocracy of the local working class, lived apart from the Irish and German mine laborers and workers in other trades.[111] These aspects of community life in large cities affected patterns of working-class behavior and
organization.

The residents of large cities were less available than their small-town
counterparts for mobilization by organizations that sought to unite all
producers. If the geographic center of gravity of the mixed assembly of
the Knights was small-town America, the center of gravity of the trades
assemblies of the Knights and of craft unions was in the nation's larger
cities. Moreover, though workers in large cities often united across craft
and ethnic lines when conflicts between capital and labor were most
intense, when such episodes passed, these cleavages reemerged to divide
the working class. During the 1877 general strike in St. Louis, for example, the employed and unemployed and the German- and non-German-
speaking members of the city's working class displayed a remarkable
degree of unity and discipline. Yet in the elections after the strike, the
Workingmen's party, whose members occupied a majority of seats on the
executive committee that ran the strike, was able to elect candidates only

---

[110] Eric Foner, "Class, Ethnicity, and Radicalism in the Gilded Age: The Land League
and Irish America," *Marxist Perspectives* 2 (1978):6-55.
[111] Walker, "Varieties," p. 368.

in the city's German neighborhoods.[112] When Terrence Powderly was elected mayor of Scranton on the Greenback-Labor ticket immediately following the 1877 strike, which had involved workers in the city's iron mills and coal mines as well as railroads, he won the votes of the traditionally Republican Welsh as well as the traditionally Democratic Irish. Within a year's time, however, the city's Welsh voters had returned to the GOP, and Powderly only won reelection because he received the Democratic as well as the GLP nomination. He won a third term running on the Democratic ticket alone.[113]

In large and medium-sized cities labor reformers not only faced difficulties overcoming ethnic and craft divisions within the working class but also had to contend with sharp cleavages between the working and middle classes. In particular, members of the middle class in large cities were more likely to sympathize with employers than with employees in labor disputes. This freed municipal governments in large cities to intervene against workers in strikes and at labor demonstrations. In Chicago Mayor John Rice mobilized the police and a local militia company to break a strike by unions seeking to enforce the eight-hour day in 1868; the New York City police broke up an entirely peaceful meeting in Tompkins Square in 1874 at which speakers called upon the city to put the unemployed to work on public construction projects; and the "pick handle brigade," upon which the city government of San Francisco relied to restore order during the July 1877 riots against the Chinese and the business firms that employed them, was drawn primarily from the city's middle class.[114]

In large cities the middle-class elements of local ethnic groups were also more likely to assume the leadership of their subcommunity. A major reason they were in a position to do so was that in large cities this segment tended to be both numerically and proportionately larger than in smaller factory and mining towns. The Irish Land League of the 1880s again serves as a case in point. In Boston and New York City, in particular, the league was controlled by members of each city's large Irish mid-

[112] Burbank, *Reign of the Rabble*, p. 189.

[113] Walker, "Varieties," pp. 372-73.

[114] Montgomery, *Beyond Equality*, p. 310; Herbert Gutman, "The Tompkins Square 'Riot' in New York City on January 13, 1874: A Re-examination of Its Causes and Its Aftermath," *Labor History* 6 (1965):44-70; Saxton, *Indispensable Enemy*, pp. 114-16. It is revealing that the railroad strike of 1877 involved uprisings of entire communities—including members of the middle class—in many small cities, whereas it precipitated sharp class divisions in larger cities. Contrast Rayback, *History*, p. 136 and Burbank, *Reign of the Rabble*, passim.

dle class, who craved respectability in the eyes of their city's Protestant upper class.[115]

Employers reacted in a variety of ways to these differences. One response, especially prevalent in industries like mining with no locational flexibility, was to establish company towns that were structured to deprive workers of an autonomous community life. Another was to call upon higher authorities for assistance when local officials refused to intervene on their behalf in labor disputes. Firms that had some locational flexibility reacted to the hostile climate of smaller cities by moving to or initially setting up shop in the nation's great metropolises. This helps explain why manufacturing employment in America's largest cities grew more rapidly in the 1870s, 1880s, and 1890s than in smaller cities— reversing the pattern that had characterized the 1860s.[116]

Politics. The distinctive character of the American political regime and changes in the structure of national politics during the postbellum years also influenced the successes and failures of the various organizations workers joined and the various modes of collective action in which they engaged. This in turn helped determine which of these organizations and patterns of behavior would survive into the twentieth century.

The strong attachments members of the working class developed to the two major parties by virtue of having been mobilized into politics through the nation's political institutions had particularly important consequences for American labor unions. The constitutions and by-laws of unions in the late nineteenth century invariably prohibited them from taking stands on political issues or endorsing candidates for public office, because this would alienate rank-and-file members who had other commitments and might well lead these members to quit the union. The secretary of the Bricklayers International Union expressed this in 1872: "We have excellent trades' unionists, who are warm democrats and zealous republicans ... and who are ready to point with suspicion to every movement on our part towards the formation of political organizations. ... The only way we can be successful with our local and national trades unions is by excluding politics from them."[117]

At the same time, union leaders recognized that government actions and policies had important implications for the well-being of both members of their organizations and the working class at large, and they

[115] E. Foner, "Class, Ethnicity, and Radicalism," p. 22.
[116] D. Gordon, "Capitalist Development," p. 39.
[117] Quoted in Montgomery, *Beyond Equality*, p. 195.

wanted to be able to influence those policies. In an effort to accomplish this without risking splitting their unions, many of them sought to establish the various local and national labor parties mentioned above—parties that were organizationally distinct from unions. The labor leaders who founded these parties were hedging their bets. They hoped that the members of their unions—and of the "producing classes" in general—would cast their ballots for labor's candidates. But if their members' attachment to the Democratic and Republican parties was so strong that they would not vote for a labor ticket, the absence of any official union involvement in these third-party campaigns would ensure that "warm democrats" and "zealous republicans" would have no reason to walk out of the union. It turned out that trade unions leaders were wise to take these precautions. The labor reform parties of the period either were totally insignificant electorally (e.g., the National Labor Union and National Labor Reform party) or at most succeeded in winning isolated elections and were unable to repeat their victories (e.g., the Greenback-Labor party).

These labor parties were the victims of a dilemma that ultimately sprang from the openness of the American political system to the participation of working-class voters. On the one hand, that openness compelled unions to detach themselves from partisan activity. On the other, the absence of organizational ties between the labor parties and trade unions of the postbellum decades often enabled middle-class reformers to dominate the parties because they alone could afford to devote their time to party business between annual conventions. Consequently the ideologies and programs of post–Civil War labor parties spoke as much to the concerns of middle-class activists within the labor reform community as to those of working-class trade unionists.[118] The National Labor Union, for example, eventually devoted more attention to the greenback issue than to the eight-hour day. This detached trade union leaders who participated in politics through third parties from rank-and-file union members—who at the same time, however, were becoming increasingly willing to follow these leaders when they called strikes, negotiated contracts, and so forth. Thus the openness of the American political system fostered a division between the organizations through which workers pursued their interests at their workplace, on the one hand, and in the realm of politics, on the other.

This is the converse of the British experience. In an effort to win the elective franchise during the nineteenth century, the leaders of England's skilled workers entered into a political coalition with the class beneath

[118] Ibid., pp. 421f.

them in the social structure rather than with the one immediately above. During this common struggle to gain the right to vote, artisans transmitted their ideology to laborers, and skilled and unskilled workers came to regard themselves as belonging to a single class, with interests in both the political and economic realms that were distinct from those of other social classes.[119]

The political behavior of the postbellum labor movement was also shaped by the fragmented structure of the American regime. This is indicated by the way labor reformers worked to achieve one of their major goals of the late nineteenth century—the eight-hour day. In the late 1860s and early 1870s the National Labor Union and its state and local affiliates sought to get Congress and the state legislatures to declare eight hours to be a "legal day's work." At the outset, however, they conceded that it was entirely beyond the authority of the national government to regulate the hours of workers in the private sector: all they asked of Washington was that it serve as an exemplary employer by limiting the hours of the workers on its own payroll. The statutes they proposed at the state level did apply in the private sector, but they included no governmental mechanism to compel employers to comply with the law. Labor reformers never proposed—indeed, they never conceived of—the creation of public bureaucracies to serve this function. They simply sought to get the state legislature to declare that the community at large regarded eight hours as an appropriate working day. The actual task of "enforcing" the law, however, would remain in the hands of trade unions, and the means they would use to secure compliance was their usual one— the strike. Nonetheless, labor reformers anticipated that their victories in the political arena would strengthen their hand by bringing the force of public opinion to bear against recalcitrant employers.[120]

As it turned out, labor's legislative victories did not have these effects. Few employers were moved to reduce the hours of their employees simply because the legislature passed what amounted to a nonbinding resolution commending such a course of action. And when unions struck to enforce the eight-hour law, the only ones that succeeded were those that were in a position to secure this concession regardless of the state legislature's action. One result of this experience in the 1860s and early 1870s was that when the Federation of Organized Trades and Labor Unions decided to embark upon a new eight-hour campaign in 1886, it eschewed legislative action entirely and sought to accomplish its goal entirely through economic action.

[119] See the essay by Amy Bridges, above.
[120] Montgomery, *Beyond Equality*, ch. 8.

Although government institutions in the United States were highly fragmented, the American regime had the capacity to defend the prerogatives of employers against the efforts of workers to circumscribe them. This was accomplished through two mechanisms, each described by Toqueville in the 1830s and much in evidence later: the extraordinary authority of the American judiciary and the remarkable capacity of Americans—in this case members of the upper and middle classes—to organize private associations to advance their interests.

During the late nineteenth century the federal courts developed several doctrines that hindered (though they did not entirely block) the efforts of labor reformers to improve the lot of the working class through both political and economic action. One of these, developing from Justice Stephen J. Field's dissenting opinion in the Slaughterhouse cases of 1873, recognized corporations as persons subject to the protection of the due process clause of the Fourteenth Amendment and interpreted that protection as rendering unconstitutional any legislation that limited the right of its owners and managers to do what they pleased with their property. Once this doctrine of "substantive due process" was accepted by a majority of Field's brethren, the Supreme Court began striking down state laws regulating railroad rates, safety conditions in mines and factories, and the like. A parallel development involved judicial interpretations of the constitutional prohibition against laws impairing contracts: the courts cited the contract clause to invalidate legislation regulating the relations between employers and employees. In 1876 the federal eight-hour law became one of the first casualties of this interpretation. And beginning in the 1890s the federal courts refashioned the doctrine of relief in equity so as to enable employers to secure injunctions against strikes.[121]

Members of the American upper and middle classes also displayed a notable ability to organize in their own defense against threats from below. Where regular army troops or militia companies were not available in adequate numbers, local businessmen organized Committees of Public Safety, Citizens Volunteer Companies, or Citizens Alliances to fill in the gap. This occurred during the Draft Riots in New York City in 1863, the anti-Chinese riots in San Francisco in July 1877, and during the Great Railway Strike in Indiana and Missouri in the summer of 1877.[122]

It must be noted that the structure of the American state, the influ-

---

[121] Arnold Paul, *Conservative Crisis and the Rule of Law* (Ithaca: Cornell University Press, 1960); Rayback, *History*, pp. 205-207.
[122] Cook, *Armies of the Streets*, p. 108; Saxton, *Indispensable Enemy*, pp. 115-16; Skowronek, *Building a New American State*, ch. 4.

ences to which it was subject, and the uses to which it was put did not remain completely constant during the late nineteenth century; changes occurred as the composition of the nation's governing coalition shifted. Shifting patterns of cleavage and alignment within the nation's political system, in turn, shaped the incentives workers had to channel their energies through the regime's dominant institutions and the availability of allies and prospects for success if they engaged in collective actions outside those institutions.

Broadly speaking, the late nineteenth century witnessed an increasing tendency on the part of the nation's economic and political elites to close ranks in an effort (that largely succeeded) to stave off challenges from below to their prerogatives. This occurred in two phases. The first was the period of Civil War and Radical Reconstruction, whose peak years were 1861-1868 but which did not fully end until the compromise of 1876-1877; this was a period of intense and violent conflict among elites both across and within the nation's major regions. The second was the classic phase of American competitive party politics, which began in 1868, reached its peak in 1876-1886, and collapsed in 1894; during this period the major parties displayed an extraordinary capacity to channel and contain political conflicts, although some conflicts still erupted outside the nation's dominant institutions and ultimately contributed to another realignment in 1896. As this periodization indicates, the boundaries between these phases were not sharply defined; during each one there were subordinate (or contradictory) tendencies that eventually undermined the dominant pattern of elite cleavages and coalitions and set the stage for the succeeding one.

The central events of the 1860s and early 1870s were the Civil War and Reconstruction, and both involved the use of force to settle conflicts between the dominant political groupings in the North and South: the armies of the Union and Confederate governments together killed 600,000 persons, and the U.S. Army occupied the defeated Southern states for periods extending from three to twelve years after the war ended. In addition, bitter intrasectional conflicts erupted during the war over the policies the administrations in Washington and Richmond pursued to fight and finance the war, as well as over the terms upon which peace should be sought. And after Appomattox such conflicts raged over the conditions that should be established for admitting the southern states back into the Union, the rights that should be extended to blacks, and the extent to which the policies Washington had enacted during the war—especially protective tariffs and the greenback currency—should be maintained or repealed.

There were two different lessons that the lower classes—both urban and rural—drew from these conflicts. On the one hand, the war strengthened the attachment of the working class to the American regime. It united wage workers and employers in defense of a nation that was the world's only democracy and in opposition to a society based upon the principle of slave labor. Although American labor conflicts were more violent than those of any other industrialized nation, the number of workers killed by the Confederate Army exceeded by a factor of more than one hundred the number killed in conflicts with their employers. The loyalties to the regime forged during this titanic conflict were strong and enduring.[123]

To be sure, the measures the Lincoln administration adopted to prosecute the war were extremely controversial, and the effort of the Radical Republicans to preserve many of the wartime institutions and policies during Reconstruction defined the central political issues and divisions of the immediate postwar years. However, the divisions aroused by the issues of Reconstruction, like those generated by the war itself, cut across class lines. And inasmuch as these issues were the central source of contention between Democratic and Republican parties in the 1860s, the very intensity of the passions they aroused cemented the loyalty of most American workers to the major parties.

On the other hand, Barrington Moore to the contrary notwithstanding, cleavages among the nation's political and economic elites enabled and even encouraged radical currents to bubble up from below.[124] The violent language Democratic politicians used to denounce the Conscription Act of 1863 both legitimated the indignation the poor felt against a statute that permitted members of the middle and upper classes to purchase an exemption from the draft and almost certainly contributed to the numerous episodes obstructing its implementation by force.[125] The principles the Radical Republicans used to justify confiscating the property of southern slaveholders and depriving them of political power could be extended to justify placing restrictions on the privileges and powers of northern industrialists. Such a conclusion was drawn by the Boston Labor Reform Association, which in 1865 resolved: "So too must our dinner tables be reconstructed . . . [and] our dress, manners, education, morals, dwellings, and the whole Social System."[126] To bring about this reconstruction, workers

---

[123] Dawley and Faler, "Working Class Culture," pp. 475-76.
[124] Cf. Barrington Moore, *Social Origins of Dictatorship and Democracy* (Boston: Beacon Press, 1966), ch. 3.
[125] Cook, *Armies of the Streets*, p. 52.
[126] Montgomery, *Beyond Equality*, p. ix.

were prepared to use the strike as a political weapon in the manner already described. In addition, the assault that Democrats launched against the legitimacy of every policy the Republicans had enacted since coming to power in 1861 implied that the entire corpus of public policy was open to question. Such questioning could come from more than one direction; in particular, the rural districts in the Midwest where Democrats were strongest during the war and the early years of Reconstruction became centers of Greenbackism in the late 1860s and the 1870s, and Democratic elites in the South also faced challenges from agrarian radicals.

The eruption of class conflicts in the cities and of agrarian radicalism in the countryside raised the possibility that disaffected workers and farmers might join in an attack upon industrialists, bankers, and railroad barons, and throw out the Republican and Democratic politicians allied with these interests. The effort in the 1870s to deal with this threat led to a reorganization of coalitional patterns at the peak of the American political system.

The lead in fashioning the political settlement that contained the turbulence of the Civil War and Reconstruction eras was taken by a group of professional politicians who moved into a dominant position in the Republican and Democratic parties in the 1870s.[127] These politicians searched for compromises on the issues that had so deeply divided the nation during the previous decade. It is crucial to note, however, that the stands taken by the major parties on the central issues of the 1870s and 1880s were not identical; there were areas of disagreement as well as agreement between them, which had important consequences for the political behavior of the working class.

With regard to the "southern question," the Republican party by 1877 abandoned the effort to use the U.S. Army to protect the rights of blacks in the south and to sustain state governments that depended upon black votes. Nonetheless, Republican candidates in the North regularly denounced "southern outrages" and "waved the bloody shirt" in their campaigns; and as late as 1890 the GOP threatened to reintroduce a federal presence in the South to protect the rights of blacks.[128] The Democrats, in the so-called "New Departure," accepted the legitimacy of the three Reconstruction amendments to the U.S. Constitution and, after gaining control of southern state governments, permitted blacks to vote, hold public offices, serve on juries, and patronize many of the same public

[127] Keller, *Affairs of State*, p. 561.
[128] J. Morgan Kousser, *The Shaping of Southern Politics* (New Haven: Yale University Press, 1974), ch. 1.

accommodations as whites.[129] However, lynching and kindred acts of terror against blacks were not suppressed, northern and southern Democrats in Congress insisted that the doctrine of states rights precluded the federal government from acting to protect the rights of blacks, and they backed this up by drastically reducing the size of the army and outlawing its use as a posse comitatus to enforce the law.[130]

On the currency and tariff issues, Republican and Democratic leaders sought to hammer out compromise positions that could keep their respective parties from fracturing along regional lines, though here too differences between the parties remained. Generally, Republican congressional leaders and presidential candidates were more flexible on the currency issue than their Democratic counterparts, whose defense of sound money tended to be more doctrinaire. The GOP was identified with high tariffs, as the party with the closest ties to manufactures; the Democrats were most closely aligned with commercial interests that were advocates of free trade.[131]

The Republican and Democratic parties after Reconstruction also differed in their stands on sumptuary legislation. The GOP was open to influence by prohibitionists, sabbatarians, and nativists. The Democratic party stood squarely for "personal liberty" on these issues.[132]

Finally, and of special relevance here, professional politicians in both parties were prepared to make concessions to labor reformers. In the 1870s six states established bureaus of labor statistics, and Congress created such an agency on the national level in 1884.[133] Between 1883 and 1886 Democratic legislatures in four industrial states and Republican legislatures in two others enacted statutes limiting the use of convict labor.[134] And, as mentioned above, in 1885 Congress passed the Foran Act, prohibiting the importation of immigrant contract labor. Most significantly, the state and federal governments tacitly acknowledged the legitimacy of the institutions and procedures that were emerging for resolving industrial disputes. Strikes, boycotts, and trade unions were not for the most part outlawed, enjoined, and suppressed by legislators, judges, and executive officials.

---

[129] C. Vann Woodward, *The Strange Career of Jim Crow* (New York: Oxford University Press, 1974), chs. 1-2.

[130] Skowronek, *Building a New American State*, ch. 4.

[131] Robert Sharkey, *Money, Class, and Party: An Economic Study of Civil War and Reconstruction* (Baltimore: Johns Hopkins University Press, 1959).

[132] See, e.g., Samuel McSeveney, *The Politics of Depression* (New York: Oxford University Press, 1972), ch. 1.

[133] Burbank, *Reign of the Rabble*, p. 191.

[134] Rayback, *History*, p. 163.

Public officials were only prepared to tolerate strikes, however, if they were confined to workplaces and did not turn into community uprisings or attacks upon the regime. This limitation was enforced chiefly by the National Guard. In the wake of the 1877 railroad strike, which did turn into an uprising against the new order by the working class in some cities (and by the entire community in a number of others), every state in the nation reorganized and strengthened its militia.[135] Especially in the industrial states of the northeast, armories were constructed in major cities to provide facilities for training National Guard units and storing weapons, and garrisons from which the guard could be deployed to put down civil disorders in general and disruptive strikes in particular.

The political settlement that ended Reconstruction had several significant effects on the working class. First, the great majority of workers and working class leaders acquiesced to the limitations it imposed on the modes of political action in which they could engage. After the suppression of the 1877 railroad strike and the local upheavals connected with it, there was talk within the Socialist Labor party—whose members had played a prominent part in some of these disruptions—of forming military clubs and of using strikes as a political weapon, but the closing of ranks by the nation's political and economic elite and the formation of military clubs—otherwise known as the National Guard—by the upper and middle class made it so unlikely that such a strategy could succeed that few workers were prepared to associate themselves with such a great gamble. Moreover, the possibility of using the ballot to influence the conduct of public officials encouraged the great majority of American workers to channel their political energies through the nation's institutions, rather than seeking to overturn them. Under these conditions anarchists who called upon workers to rise up and smash the state were unable to acquire a substantial following.[136]

Second, the issues Democratic and Republican politicians organized politics around in the 1870s and 1880s were deeply meaningful to most workers. Democratic denunciations of "black Republicanism" and the waving of the bloody shirt by GOP politicians drew upon the loyalties and hatreds that Americans, workers and nonworkers alike, had developed during the Civil War and its immediate aftermath. Moreover, the argument by party politicians that employees shared the interests of their employers on the tariff issue was substantiallly correct. Politicians drove this point home further by arguing that their party's stance on these

---

[135] Skowronek, *Building a New American State*, ch. 4.
[136] Burbank, *Reign of the Rabble*, pp. 190-191; Montgomery, "Strikes," pp. 96-100.

questions was of a piece with its position on sumptuary legislation. Democrats argued that the Republican impulse to tax (via the tariff) every article the workingman consumed and to elevate blacks to a position of equality with whites was related to its desire to tell him what he could or could not do on his Sundays and that the Democratic party's devotion to Jeffersonian principles and personal liberty provided him with his best defense against this meddling fanaticism. Republicans argued that the Democrats' indifference to the plight of the American workingman facing unemployment as a result of the importation of goods produced by cheap foreign labor was akin to its indifference to the plight of blacks and the morals of American citizens.

Nonetheless there were challenges to the hegemony of Republican and Democratic party politicians during the 1870s and 1880s by spokesmen for political forces who regarded the compromises struck by these politicians as bad bargains. One such challenge came from an influential group of intellectuals and professionals who had close ties to the northeastern financial and commercial elite and who opposed the concessions that professional politicians made to workers, farmers, and manufacturers in seeking to win electoral majorities.[137] Small farmers who were exploited through the credit system—exploitation compounded by the relentless deflation of the period, which kept them in bondage to their creditors—also periodically rose up against the major parties.[138]

In addition, labor reformers were not satisfied with the concessions the major parties made in their efforts to secure working-class votes. Greenbackism, with its promise of expanding the money supply sufficiently for industry to prosper so that workers and employers need no longer be at each other's throats, exerted a persistent appeal to that segment of the labor reform movement devoted to the producer ethic.[139] The legislative program adopted by FOTLU at its founding in 1881 provides a typical statement of the other policies labor reformers wished to see enacted. In addition to eight-hour laws, bureaus of labor statistics, prohibitions on convict labor and immigrant contract labor, and Chinese exclusion, FOTLU called for factory safety legislation, increasing the liability of employers for industrial accidents, prohibitions on child labor, and compulsory education.[140] Rank-and-file workers were willing to abandon the major parties and vote for labor tickets when public officials intervened

[137] Skowronek, *Building a New American State*, ch. 3.
[138] Lawrence Goodwyn, *Democratic Promise: The Populist Moment in America* (New York: Oxford University Press, 1976).
[139] Montgomery, *Beyond Equality*, chap. 11.
[140] Rayback, *History*, pp. 157-58.

in industrial disputes on behalf of employers. Such episodes led workers to respond to leaders who argued that if Democratic and Republican officials were using their authority to protect capital at the expense of labor, workers had no choice but to form a party of their own and elect officials sympathetic to their cause.

The intensification of industrial strife and agrarian unrest in the years following 1886 shook the foundations of the political settlement worked out in the 1870s. As the number of workers involved in strikes increased, as employers launched their counterattack upon the Knights and the trade union movement, and as the Farmers Alliance gathered support, Democratic and Republican leaders struggled to keep their political coalitions from fragmenting. In their efforts to maintain the support of workers, legislators in the industrial states enacted many of the measures labor reformers had been advocating for the previous twenty years; major party politicians in the agrarian South and West made concessions on some of the less threatening measures in the program of the Farmers Alliance; and Republicans and Democrats beat the drum on so-called ethnocultural issues—especially liquor legislation—ever more loudly. On the other hand, executives, legislators, and judges rose to the defense of public order and the rights of property. President Benjamin Harrison dispatched the army to break the strike of silver miners at Coeur d'Alene in 1892; President Grover Cleveland used federal troops to break the Pullman strike in 1894; and the National Guard was mobilized by governors with increasing frequency during the period—most notably in the Homestead strike of 1892. And, as Rayback notes, after the Haymarket affair drove the upper and middle classes to new heights of hysteria over the menace of anarchy in the United States, "state legislatures rushed laws curbing the freedom of action of labor organizations onto the statute books. The courts began to convict union members of conspiracy, intimidation, and rioting in wholesale lots."[141] This counteroffensive presented the labor movement with the pressing question of how best to respond.

IV. *Trade Unions and Political Machines: The Institutional Legacy of the Late Nineteenth Century*

Confronted with this trend toward an increasingly hostile environment, labor reformers could respond in a number of ways. They could organize as many workers as possible into labor unions and pursue a strategy of escalation on the economic front. Alternatively (or at the same time),

---

[141] Ibid., p. 168.

they could escalate the conflict on the political front by attempting to take control of the state through electoral or other means. Finally, labor reformers could retreat to their strongest redoubt and seek an accommodation with the forces arrayed against them—thus attempting to protect the gains of at least a segment of the working class by narrowing the constituency of labor unions and seeking to placate politicians and public officials by agreeing to stay out of the political arena.

There were advocates of each of these courses of action within the labor reform movement, and the 1890s witnessed sharp conflicts among them over which of these paths to take. It would be a mistake, however, to regard these conflicts as disputes between completely distinct types of labor leaders—backward-looking idealists in the Knights, ideologies out of touch with American realities in the socialist movement, and hardheaded realists in the AFL. Substantial commonalities in the outlook of these segments of the labor movement remained into the 1890s.[142] Moreover, though the choices national labor leaders made were crucial in determining the direction the American labor movement took, these issues were not decided simply through debates and votes at national conventions of the Knights, the Socialist Labor party, and the AFL. There was constant interaction among the views of labor activists, the outcomes of conflicts in the economic and political arenas, and the modes of organization the labor movement adopted. Ultimately a majority of the nation's trade union leaders opted for the last of the above-mentioned courses of action. The unions they led emerged as the dominant force in the American labor movement because (1) efforts to pursue the other strategies met with defeat, (2) "pure and simple" trade unionism proved to be capable of meeting the imperatives of organizational maintenance, and (3) this mode of working-class organization was a mutually acceptable arrangement to important segments of America's political leadership, economic elite, and the working class itself. The organizational manifestations of this accommodation among these social forces were the trade unions and political machines that became institutionalized in the 1880s and 1890s.

The Defeated Alternatives. Organizing unskilled as well as skilled workers into unions and escalating the conflict with capital on the industrial front enjoyed widespread support among labor reformers. Indeed, all segments of the labor movement expressed their dedication to this approach in one form or another. Although Terrence Powderly and his associates

---

[142] Dawson, "Paradox of Dynamic Change," pp. 345-46.

in the national leadership of the Knights did not believe it was possible
to achieve the emancipation of the working classes through strikes
alone—"Strike at the boss and hit yourself," he had warned Maryland
coal miners who walked off their jobs in 1882—local assemblies
that counted unskilled as well as skilled workers among their members
staged numerous strikes throughout the order's history, especially in
response to the counterattack employers launched against them in the
late 1880s.[143]

The late 1880s and early 1890s also witnessed an upsurge of strikes by
trade unions affiliated with the AFL, and these trade unionists also spoke
of the necessity of organizing the unskilled as well as the skilled. The
constitution of the AFL provided for the organization of unskilled workers into "labor" unions (as distinguished from "trade" unions), and in
the early 1890s the two most important industrial unions of the nineteenth century—the United Mine Workers and the American Railway
Union—were organized.

Finally, the dominant faction within the American socialist movement
in the 1890s also advocated pursuing a strategy of mobilization on the
economic front. A number of national unions and municipal labor federations were controlled by socialists during this decade—among them
the Bakers and Confectioners, the Boot and Shoe Workers, the United
Brewery Workers, and the New York and Brooklyn Central Labor Federations—and the leaders of these unions sought to win industrial conflicts by bringing all workers in their industry into their union, drawing
upon the energy and solidarity that unskilled workers had displayed during the 1886 strike wave, and, as Martin Dodd says of the Shoe Workers,
stressing "class consciousness and locally controlled and financed strikes
as organizing tools."[144]

These efforts to pursue a strategy of mobilization in the economic
arena encountered serious difficulties. Businessmen fought back
furiously: they organized employers' associations, drove unions to strike,
and then called upon the government to defend their right to hire strikebreakers. In these confrontations workers found it increasingly difficult
to win the support of the middle-class residents of their communities.
This was a consequence partly of the anti-union hysteria following the
Haymarket affair and partly of changes in the economy. The merger
movement of the 1890s and the emergence of multiplant firms made it
easier for employers plausibly to threaten to close down any plant whose

[143] Harvey, "Knights of Labor," p. 570.
[144] Martin H. Dodd, "Marlboro, Massachusetts and the Shoeworkers' Strike of 1898-
1899," *Labor History* 20 (1979):376-97.

workers were too obstreperous. This could decimate the economy of the community in question, and such threats therefore frequently led retail merchants and other members of the local middle class to identify their interests with the town's or city's factory owners, rather than its industrial workers.[145]

The Knights as a national organization had no effective answer to these problems. The order never had offered striking local assemblies much financial support and in 1888 it decided to devote even more of its resources to an educational campaign on behalf of its political program. The insistence of the order's national leadership that the interests of employers and employees were fundamentally harmonious—Powderly, for example, insisted that businessmen could be persuaded that it was in their interest to grant workers an eight-hour day—simply did not accord with the experiences of the bulk of their members. This led the great majority of members to abandon the Knights in the late 1880s and early 1890s, and many of the skilled workers among them joined trade unions that accepted class conflict as a fact of life.[146]

The trade unions belonging to the AFL may have accepted the inevitability of class conflict, but the great majority of them sought to cope with the hostile climate they faced at the end of the nineteenth century by reaching a tacit accommodation with employers to be discussed further below. Among its terms was the abandonment by the AFL of its professed intention of organizing unskilled workers and the imposition by national union leaders of very severe restraints on the right of union locals to call strikes.

Such an accommodation, of course, could only be reached if both employers and union leaders were prepared—even if reluctantly—to make a deal. Where employers could count on the local, state, or national government to back them, however intransigent they might be in dealing with their employees, unions found it almost impossible to survive. And though there were some exceptions, unions controlled by socialists or other radicals who proclaimed the impossibility of achieving a satisfactory resolution of class conflicts as long as the capitalist system remained intact generally found that the only alternative to adopting the technique of organizational consolidation advocated by the leadership of the AFL was defeat and destruction.[147]

---

[145] Ibid., p. 391; David Brody, *Steelworkers in America: The Non-Union Era* (New York: Harper & Row, 1969), pp. 112-24.

[146] See, e.g., Morris, "Cincinnati Shoemakers' Lockout," p. 505.

[147] John Laslett, "Reflections on the Failure of Socialism in the American Federation of Labor," *Mississippi Valley Historical Review* 50 (1964):634-51.

An equally widespread impulse among labor reformers was to respond to the increasingly hostile environment that confronted them in the years after 1886 by entering the electoral arena at the local, state, and national levels. The prospects for the success of such a strategy seemed especially good because the hegemony of the nation's political elite was then being challenged by millions of farmers in the South and West—first through the Farmers Alliance and then through the Populist party. It thus appeared that the coalition of dissatisfied workers and farmers that the Greenback-Labor party had sought with only limited success to mobilize in the 1870s might sweep the field in the 1890s.

The Knights threw themselves into this endeavor. The order played a leading role in the selection of and campaigning for labor tickets in local and state elections in 1886 and 1887.[148] And in 1888 the national convention of the Knights, at Terrence Powderly's urging, decided to concentrate the resources of the order on promoting a national political program of currency reform, government control of railroads and telegraphs, and government taxation and management of the land. Powderly himself thought that through education and agitation all producers—including employers—could be convinced that their interests would be served by such a program, and that the major parties thus would be compelled to adopt it by 1892. To rally agrarian support, he led a delegation of Knights to the 1889 national convention of the Southern Farmers Alliance. The Knights endorsed the alliance's program, merged its Washington lobby with the one run by the alliance, and agreed to endorse only those candidates who would support the alliance program. In the early 1890s, especially in the South and the West, local assemblies of the Knights cooperated with the electoral activities of the alliance and its political arm, the Populist party.[149]

Many trade unionists also responded to the events of the late 1880s and the 1890s by entering the electoral arena. Municipal labor federations participated along with Knights, socialists, and single-taxers in selecting and campaigning for labor slates in the local elections of 1886. And many local trade unions, chiefly in the South and the West, campaigned for Populist candidates in elections in the 1890s. In 1892 socialists within the AFL introduced a resolution at the federation's national convention that cited the recent defeats of labor—a reference, in particular, to the use of troops to break the strikes at Homestead and Coeur d'Alene—as indicating the "impotency" of pure and simple trade unionism to "cope with the great power of concentrated wealth" and that would commit the AFL to lead an independent political movement. This

---

[148] Fink, *Workingmens' Democracy*.
[149] Kaufman, *Samuel Gompers*, pp. 185-86.

resolution was defeated, though the convention did endorse some planks in the Populist platform, including one calling for government ownership of the telephone and telegraph systems. Heartened by this, the socialists submitted a political program to the 1893 AFL national convention advocating, among other things, "the collective ownership by the people of all means of production and distribution." This time the convention voted to submit the program to its constituent unions for their consideration. After the great majority endorsed the socialist program and it was presented to the AFL's 1894 national convention for a substantive vote, it only was defeated as a result of parliamentary sleight-of-hand of Gompers and other leaders of the federation.[150] The delegates who supported the program retaliated by defeating Gompers' bid for reelection to the presidency of the AFL (1894 was the only year from the federation's founding in 1886 until Gompers' death in 1924 that he did not serve as president) and part of the compromise that secured his return to the presidency in 1895 involved the AFL's adopting the socialists' political program as its "legislative platform."

The various efforts by labor reformers in the 1890s to secure fundamental changes in government policy through electoral activity ultimately were defeated. Powderly's expectation that the major parties could be compelled through such pressure to adopt the program of the Knights and the Farmers Alliance in the 1892 election proved, of course, to be unfounded. Cleveland and Harrison, the Democratic and Republic presidential candidates that year, were scarcely the men to lead a crusade that Powderly envisaged to "control the dollar, curb the power of money, and kill the trusts."[151] In 1893 he was deposed as Grand Master Workman by a coalition of socialists and agrarian radicals within the Knights who sought, in effect, to merge the organization with the Populist party.

The strategy of working through a third party, the Populists, was also defeated, however. The sources of this defeat were somewhat different in the states of the South and the West, on the one hand, where alliances between workers and poor farmers were most easily established, and the states of the Northeast, where such alliances never emerged. In the South the leaders of the Democratic party, who were closely tied to that region's agrarian, commercial, and financial elites, managed to overcome the threat of Populism by relying upon a combination of race baiting, force, and fraud and by exploiting the political incapacity of the poor farmers who provided the Populists with much of their leadership.[152] The Demo-

[150] Rayback, *History*, p. 198.
[151] Kaufman, *Samuel Gompers*, p. 181.
[152] C. Vann Woodward, *Origins of the New South, 1877-1913* (Baton Rouge: Louisiana State University Press, 1951), chs. 9-10.

crats then attracted many of that party's supporters into its ranks by
adopting the free-silver doctrine—the plank in the Populist platform that
least threatened the interests of regional elites. In the West the lure of
controlling the nomination of a major party also eventually led the Populists to fuse with—and disappear into—the Democratic party. In 1896
a coalition of southern and western silverites secured the Democratic
presidential nomination for William Jennings Bryan.

In the nation's industrial heartland—the belt of states running from
Illinois to New England—where the great majority of workers lived in
large cities and had no contact with farmers, it was considerably more
difficult to forge the sort of alliance that the Populists and the national
leadership of the Knights of Labor sought to establish. The greatest
impediment the proponents of such an alliance faced was convincing
workers, who were subject to exploitation through the wage-labor system,
to identify their interests with farmers, who were subject to a different
mode of exploitation, the credit system.[153] (An excellent example of the
difficulty of doing so is provided by Samuel Gompers himself, who considered the small farmers who formed the mass base of the Populist party
to be exploiters, rather than victims of exploitation, because many
of them employed wage laborers.) For this reason eastern workers
were not attracted to the vision of a cooperative commonwealth of all
producers that the Populists put forward. Beyond this, the local
machines of the Democratic and Republican parties tended to be stronger
in the Northeast than elsewhere, and the Populists found it
difficult to shatter the ties linking workers to these machines. The
Populists also had difficulty countering the not implausible argument
of Republican and Democratic politicians that protective tariffs and/or
sound money, by making it profitable for businessmen to invest their
capital, would contribute to the prosperity of employers and workers
alike.

The nomination of Bryan by the Democrats did little to change this
situation. It drove most members of the northeastern upper and middle
classes into the Republican party and also drove many workers in this
region into the GOP: the doctrine of free silver did not speak to their
interests; the evangelical Protestant tone of Bryan's campaign was
threatening to the heavily Catholic urban working class; and the Republicans, in contrast, successfully presented themselves as the party of
industrial prosperity and ethnocultural tolerance. All of this contributed

---

[153] Lawrence Goodwyn, "The Cooperative Commonwealth and Other Abstractions: In
Search of a Democratic Premise," *Marxist Perspectives* (Summer 1980):8-42.

to a landslide victory for the Republicans and the passing of America's "populist moment."[154]

The economic and ethnocultural cleavages that divided poor farmers in the South and West from workers in the East were not inherently unbridgeable: after all, in the 1930s Franklin D. Roosevelt managed to forge together a coalition that included these groups. Labor unions were to play a major role in the New Deal coalition. At the end of the nineteenth century, however, a number of organizational, economic, and political considerations encouraged the top leaders of America's trade union movement to pursue a different course of action.

"Pure and Simple" Trade Unionism. Despite their flirtation with alternative responses to the crisis confronting the labor movement, a majority of the nation's trade unionists followed a more accommodating strategy, and their unions came to overshadow the organizations that pursued less conciliatory policies. Unions affiliated with the AFL in the main chose this course of action because their leaders concluded from the experiences of the late nineteenth century that "pure and simple" craft unionism was the only viable form of working-class organization in the United States as the twentieth century began: the only form that at once could meet the imperatives of internal organizational maintenance; carve out a niche for itself in the age of corporate capitalism; and accommodate itself to the harsh political climate confronting labor at the time.

The experience of the post–Civil War decades clearly indicated the great difficulties trade unions confronted to sustain themselves in the face of periodic business depressions, bitter employer resistance, and hostile public authorities. To cope with these problems, Gompers and his associates—first in his home union, the Cigar Makers International Union, then in the FOTLU, and finally in the AFL—argued that unions had to "perfect" their organization and establish themselves on a "permanent" basis by providing their members with unemployment benefits, burial insurance, sick pay, and strike benefits. This would give workers an incentive to remain in their union despite the inevitable setbacks to be expected during depressions, strikes, eras of political reaction, and periods of personal distress. A second element of organizational perfection was the centralization of authority in the hands of national union officials. Local unions engaged in strikes or experiencing unusually high levels of unemployment could only afford to provide their members with benefits if they could draw on the resources of union locals in other cities whose members

[154] Jensen, *Winning of the Midwest,* ch. 10; Goodwyn, *Democratic Promise,* ch. 9.

were still working. This, in turn, entailed transferring to the national level the authority "to decide whether a strike is practicable," so that impetuous members of one local would not be in a position to squander the funds collected by their more prudent brothers in other cities.[155]

This mode of organization was far easier to establish with unions that represented skilled rather than unskilled workers. Unions could only provide their members with meaningful benefits and pay the salaries of full-time officers if they levied higher dues than unskilled workers could readily afford. In addition, it was more difficult for union leaders to assert control over unskilled workers, who tended to move from job to job, than over skilled workers, who were more likely to establish enduring ties to the other members of their local and to its leaders. These problems were demonstrated in the enormous difficulty Terrence Powderly had influencing the behavior of the hundreds of thousands of workers who flooded into the Knights in the mid-1880s, called strikes he deemed inadvisable, and then left the organization in droves when these were defeated.

The case of the Boot and Shoe Workers union illustrates quite clearly why a majority of the nation's trade unions came to adopt the organizational forms advocated by the AFL. The union was founded by socialists, who sought to organize skilled and unskilled workers alike. Its dues were low; it provided little in the way of financial benefits to its members; and its national leaders did not seek to restrain local strikes. In the 1890s the union lost a number of strikes because manufacturers organized themselves more effectively than ever before to rid themselves of the " 'annoying' intercession of labor agents" and because, for the reasons mentioned above, striking workers no longer could count upon the support of the local middle class in their battles with their employers. As a result of this experience the shoemakers, like workers in many other industries, "learned to mistrust their communities and came to rely instead on . . . craft solidarity." In 1899 the Boot and Shoeworkers Union adopted a new constitution that sharply increased dues, established strike and sick-benefit funds, and placed authority over the dispersal of these funds in the hands of the union's national leadership. Arguing for the new constitution, the union's national secretary drew the following lesson from recent experience: "Numerous examples can be cited where organizations with high dues and benefits have even passed through defeat and still maintained their organization and quickly rallied, ready once more to face the enemy, but all cheap unions go down alike regardless of what their theory or philosophy."[156]

---

[155] Kaufman, *Samuel Gompers*, pp. 93-95, 98-99, 117-18.
[156] Dodd, "Marlboro, Massachusetts," pp. 377, 395.

One other aspect of trade union organization is worth noting here. It was a concern for organizational stability in particular that led to the founding of the AFL. In 1886, after the Knights and New York's cigar manufacturers reached an agreement that froze out the New York local of the Cigar Makers International Union, the FOTLU demanded that the Knights disband its trades assemblies in crafts already organized by a union, refuse to enroll anyone who had been expelled from a union or worked for less than the union scale, and not place its own label on any product for which there was a union label. When the Knights refused to accede to these demands, the trade unions organized themselves into the American Federation of Labor and declared war on the order. The founders of the AFL were prepared to wage war over these issues because where they were unable to establish themselves as the exclusive bargaining agent for the members of a trade it was difficult for them to exert discipline over their members and win conflicts with employers. It is significant that it was a concern for mundane questions of organization, exclusive jurisdiction, and discipline, rather than loftier ideological disputes, that led to the formation of the AFL, that ultimately enabled trade unions to survive the crisis of the 1890s better than any other component of the nineteenth-century labor reform movement, and that made it possible for a federation of trade unions, which enrolled only a small fraction of the American working class, to claim to be *the* representative of labor in the United States.

The second lesson that most trade unionists drew from the events of 1886-1894 was that the great industrial combines that were being organized during this period were powerful adversaries indeed. The two largest sympathy strikes of the day—the Homestead and Pullman strikes—were unequivocal victories for, respectively, the Carnegie Steel Corporation and the railroads belonging to the Chicago General Managers' Association. More generally, the counterattack upon labor launched by the upper and middle classes in the 1890s threatened the existence of all trade unions. This threat took its most serious form in the open shop movement of the following decade.

To deal with this threat, a majority of the nation's trade unionists sought to demonstrate to employers that the labor movement was reasonable and responsible. The AFL and many of the national trade unions affiliated with it renounced sympathy strikes, indicated their willingness to cooperate with the efforts of employers to increase labor productivity, insisted that they regarded contracts negotiated through collective bargaining to be binding upon workers as much as on employers and therefore undertook to restrain "wildcat strikes" by union locals or dissident workers, and provided manufacturers who signed such contracts with union labels that helped them sell their products in the working-class market. In addition, the AFL never carried out its professed intention of organizing unskilled workers. The trade unionists who made these concessions hoped that employers in return would accept the unionization of at least the skilled workers in their plants and make wage concessions to them, however they might treat unskilled workers.

A third conclusion drawn by a majority of trade unionists from the events of the late nineteenth century was that workers had to rely chiefly upon economic rather than political action to achieve their goals. In so doing they abandoned the strategy of constructing a political alliance among all "producers," which had been pursued by the two largest labor organizations of 1861-1886, the NLU and the Knights.

The leadership of the AFL renounced this strategy for a combination of reasons. First, they feared that such a course of action, like any other foray into the electoral arena, might divide their unions. Second, even the most impressive efforts at forging such a coalition—including those of 1886-1887 and those associated with the Populist party in the early and mid-1890s—ultimately had failed. The labor campaign of 1886-1887 had demonstrated once again that workers would rise up in anger against the Democrats and Republicans when public officials elected by the major parties blatantly used their authority to help capital in its conflicts with labor, but this outburst like earlier ones, subsided after the major parties made some concessions; workers then returned to their former political homes. The labor campaigns of 1886-1887 and the Populist campaigns of the early 1890s also demonstrated that a majority of middle-class voters could be whipped into hysteria, and their loyalties to the major parties reinforced, by the charge that these efforts represented nothing less than an attempt to foment class warfare in the United States and involved an assault on the institution of private property.

Even those members of the middle class who did not swallow this line were regarded by the AFL leadership as more of a burden than a benefit to the labor movement, because they had their own political agenda that was based upon the false premise that employers and employees had harmonious interests and that diverted workers from militantly pursuing their interests where they did conflict with their employers. As Stuart Kaufman notes, Gompers insisted that "the emancipation of the working class had to be achieved by the workers themselves. This at base was the issue between the Federation and the Knights of Labor. From the beginning the greatest danger to the AFL appeared to Gompers to be 'the unnecessary desire of persons thrusting their individual opinions upon organized workers.' "[157]

[157] Kaufman, *Samuel Gompers*, p. 175.

Gompers also rejected the counsel of socialists, who shared his understanding of the boundaries of the working class but who argued that the only way to secure its emancipation was for the labor movement to enter the political arena with a program calling for the collective ownership of the means of production. In addition to fearing the divisive effects this might have upon the labor movement, Gompers read the evidence of the times as indicating that when the government involved itself in issues of concern to the working class it was less likely to serve the interests of workers than those of capital. He said in a speech in 1891: "Against us we find arrayed a host guarded by special privilege, buttressed by legalized trusts, fed by streams of legalized monopolists, picketed by gangs of legalized Pinkertons, and having in reserve thousands of embryo employers who, under the name militia, are organized, uniformed, and armed for the sole purpose of holding the discontented in subservient bondage to iniquitous conditions."[158] In his autobiography Gompers asserted that the Tompkins Square "riot" of 1874—in which the New York City police brutally attacked a peaceful protest meeting called by the IWA— convinced him that it was self-defeating for labor to identify itself with radical groups and causes because this simply provided its enemies with ammunition to discredit the labor movement and to justify the use of force against it. The Haymarket episode reinforced this conclusion.

The eight-hour day was the central demand of the American labor movement during the half-century following the Civil War. The changes in the way labor reformers pursued this goal provide a telling indication of the transformations that occurred during the late part of the century in the labor movement's orientation to politics, in the modes of collective action and organization through which workers sought to accomplish their goals, and in the vocabulary working-class leaders employed to justify their claims. The first nationwide campaign for the eight-hour day was initiated by the National Labor Union in the late 1860s, and the various labor reform organizations affiliated with the NLU directed this demand to both the state and employers: they sought to get state legislatures to declare eight hours to be a "legal day's work," and after succeeding they staged strikes to "enforce" these laws. Moreover, as Jama Lazerow argues, "in the 1860s, the most significant aspect of the eight-hour demand had been its class nature. By establishing a specific part of the day which could not be purchased by an employer, working people challenged the prevalent concept of private property and struck a blow for freedom from wage slavery."[159] It is important to note that the con-

---

[158] Ibid., p. 201.
[159] Jama Lazerow, " 'The Workingman's Hour': The 1886 Labor Uprising in Boston," *Labor History* 21 (1980):200-220, quotation at p. 212.

cept of wage slavery had political as well as economic connotations. In arguing for the eight-hour day labor reformers claimed that it would give workers the time to devote themselves both to self-improvement and to exercising the rights and obligations of republican citizenship.

As discussed above, the eight-hour campaign of the late 1860s and early 1870s bore little fruit, and labor reformers initiated new campaigns in 1886 and 1890. Rhetorically there were some similarities between the earlier campaign and these later ones. In Boston, for example, George McNeill—who had participated in the eight-hour movement of the 1860s, was a prominent figure in the Knights, and was a major leader of the 1886 campaign—linked it to the other major struggles for liberty in American history, the Revolution and the Civil War. Speaking at a meeting of the Knights on the anniversary of the Battle of Lexington, he said: "I am glad to welcome you here tonight on this 19th day of April, a day ever dear to the heart of every American . . . and as this is the anniversary of the day when the Christian soil of virgin villages was stained with the blood of our fathers, and as they died to put down that chattel system of slavery, so we stand here remembering that blood shed and that sacrifice."[160] He concluded that "the success or failure of the republican experiment rests with us," implying that if the status quo persisted, the United States would not warrant being called a republic.

Trade unionists used some of the same republican vocabulary. In striking to secure the eight-hour day from the Master Builders Association in 1886, the Carpenters Union denounced their target for the "unrepublican" character of its name: the name "master," they asserted, was "foreign and offensive to our sense of citizenship, as well as offensive to the fundamental principles on which the republic is based." And Frank Foster, a leader of the AFL in Boston, argued in 1890 that "the man whose hours of toil are fixed for him by another is not free."[161]

Nonetheless, there were some important differences between the eight-hour movements of 1886 and 1890 and those of the late 1860s and early 1870s. The later demand for an eight-hour day was directed exclusively against employers, and the strike was labor's weapon of first rather than last resort to secure this goal. By 1890 the campaign for an eight-hour day no longer had the character of a mass movement: not only did the AFL eschew appeals to the state legislature or to the public at large through mass demonstrations, it also drew back from its initial plans for calling a general strike to secure shorter hours for the members of all unionized trades. Rather, it decided that only one union, the Carpenters,

---

[160] Quoted in ibid., p. 209.
[161] Ibid., pp. 209, 213.

which had a great deal of bargaining leverage, would strike, and that the members of other unions would continue working and would provide the Carpenters with financial support during their strike. The major arguments used by trade unionists in 1886 and 1890 on behalf of the eight-hour day were economic, not political, and they implicitly accepted the existence and persistence of the wage-labor system. Boston's Central Labor Union argued in 1886 that by reducing the hours of labor, unemployment would drop and therefore wages would rise: "Overwork and machinery combine to increase the army of the unemployed. Every unemployed man is an obstacle to our common advancement. An army of unemployed men is an army of obstacles. To remove them they must be employed by reducing the hours of labor. Let us act!"[162] And a statement issued by Boston's carpenters during their strike in 1890 implied that they fully accepted that labor was a commodity, to be bought and sold like any other: they demanded "the right to name both the price and length of our day's labor, the same as any other merchant selling his commodity."[163] The culmination of this trend can be seen in a statement issued by striking workers at the Bethlehem Steel Corporation in 1910, whose arguments on behalf of shortening their working day referred exclusively to the private sphere of life: "The overtime feature of employment having been a detriment to our health, our homes, and our families, we ask for its abolition. If it must be a feature of future employment, we ask for an additional compensation in the form of time and 1-half time for overtime, so that we may procure additional nutriment to give strength to our bodies to perform the task."[164]

Although by the end of the nineteenth century the dominant wing of the trade union movement in the United States abandoned efforts to change the character of the American regime fundamentally, this is not to say that its members no longer sought to influence particular public policies. The AFL, state and local labor federations, and individual trade unions lobbied to secure the enactment of laws limiting the working hours of women and children, requiring safety inspections of factories and mines, and providing for the arbitration of industrial disputes; Gompers admonished workers when voting to reward the friends of labor within the Democratic and Republican parties who supported such legislation and to punish their enemies who refused to do so. Of equal significance, local craft unions, especially in the building trades, established ties with the locally dominant political party in an effort to get municipal govern-

[162] Ibid., pp. 212-13.
[163] Ibid., p. 213.
[164] Robert Hessen, "The Bethlehem Steel Strike of 1910," *Labor History* 15 (1974):3-18, p. 8.

ments to enact and enforce regulations, such as building codes, that provided additional jobs for their members. In some ways most interestingly of all (because it revealed how the boundaries of the American working class ultimately came to be defined), the AFL campaigned to restrict immigration from China, Japan, and eventually southern and eastern Europe. The precedent for this campaign was the anti-Chinese movement in California of the 1860s and 1870s. The initial social base of anti-coolie sentiment was among unskilled workers facing competition from Chinese laborers who could be hired at very low wages. Skilled workers did not face such competition, but their unions rallied to the anti-coolie cause as a way of mobilizing support among unskilled workers for legislation that was of benefit to skilled workers. Democratic and Republican politicians joined the crusade, because proposing restrictions on Chinese immigration was an easy way of winning votes among skilled and unskilled workers alike. As Saxton argues, this same calculation—and the same arguments that had been used in California against the Chinese—led the AFL beginning in 1897 to call for limitations on immigration from Latin and Slavic Europeans well as from the Orient and to acquiesce in efforts to drive blacks from the skilled trades, along with efforts to reverse almost every other gain blacks had made since the Civil War.[165] Thus racism was one of the terms in the accommodation organized labor sought to establish with the powers that be in twentieth-century America.

In sum, the doctrine of "pure and simple" trade unionism advocated by and institutionalized in the AFL asserted that workers—or at least a subset of them—could organize to advance their common interests in the economic arena largely apart from what they or the nation's governing elite did in the political realm. Indeed, it presupposed a distinction between the economic and political realm that was foreign to the thought of those labor reformers who earlier had spoken of "wage slavery" or America's "republican experiment." By enjoining workers to reward labor's friends and punish its enemies within the Democratic and Republican parties—and to restrict their political efforts to the act of voting— the dominant wing of the trade union movement largely renounced efforts to influence the fundamental character of the American regime and the composition of the nation's governing class. They hoped that in return the public officials elected by the Democratic and Republican parties would not interfere with the operation of trade unions within the domain to which they were prepared to confine themselves.

[165] Saxton, *Indispensable Enemy*, pp. 270-78.

Political Machines. The political and class conflicts of the late nineteenth century also led to the institutionalization of the American party system in its classic form. On the national level the Republicans and Democrats became entrenched as the nation's major parties and professional politicians securely established their leadership over them. On the local level, these politicians increasingly perfected the organizations through which they mobilized the mass electorate—that is, they constructed political machines. At least in the nation's major cities, these machines consolidated their position as the most important vehicle through which the working class participated in politics.

The machine politicians who moved to the fore of American urban politics late in the century established their political hegemony by arranging an accommodation among the major political forces in the city. The precise terms varied from city to city, as did the process through which the locally dominant machine became institutionalized. It is not feasible to describe these variations here; the account below will focus upon a single city, New York. Nonetheless, the events that led to the institutionalization of New York's Tammany machine were basically similar to those that occurred in other large American cities.[166]

Machine politicians in New York, as in other cities, appealed in a number of ways to the working-class voters who provided them with the bulk of their popular support. First, they picked up and enacted many of the legislative proposals advanced by labor reformers. For example, the New York state legislature, with the support of the Tammany delegation, created a board of mediation and arbitration, prohibited employers from coercing union members, and established a ten-hour day for women and children.[167] Second, the machine created an elaborate unofficial welfare system. During the severe winter of 1870-1871, for example, Tammany's Boss Tweed spent $50,000 of his "own" money (whose ultimate source, of course, was the city treasury) to buy coal for the poor in his ward. Machine politicians also relied upon ethnic appeals to win the support of working-class voters: they provided public subsidies and grants of public authority to charitable institutions run by members of the city's major ethnic groups;[168] they nominated and appointed a substantial number of immigrants—especially the Irish—to public offices; and they defended

---

[166] See, e.g., Geoffrey Blodgett, *The Gentle Reformers: Massachusetts Democrats in the Cleveland Era* (Cambridge: Harvard University Press, 1966), ch. 6; William A. Bullough, *The Blind Boss and His City: Christopher Augustine Buckley and Nineteenth Century San Francisco* (Berkeley: University of California Press, 1979), ch. 4.

[167] Rayback, *History*, p. 170.

[168] John W. Pratt, "Boss Tweed's Public Welfare Program," *New York Historical Society Quarterly* 45 (1961):396-411; Erickson, *American Industry*, p. 95.

the political rights of immigrants. In the "naturalization frauds" of 1868, for example, the machine's functionaries brought hundreds of immigrants at a time before Tammany judges, who turned them en bloc into citizens, voters, and, not least, Tammany Democrats. Over the next twenty-five years, Tammany defended these voters against efforts by the Republicans to disfranchise them.[169] Moreover, in 1870 Boss Tweed secured the enactment of a new city charter abolishing a number of state-appointed metropolitan commissions that controlled policing, fire fighting, public health, and parks in the city; in their stead the new charter created municipal departments whose commissioners were appointed by the mayor. There were a number of impulses behind the creation and abolition of the metropolitan commissions, but the one of greatest relevance here is that Tweed's charter placed control over these important public functions in the hands of officials who ultimately were responsible to the city's heavily immigrant electorate.

It is important to note that the methods the machine used to appeal to foreign-stock voters buttressed the political position of middle-class elements of the city's ethnic groups relative to less respectable or more radical contenders for the leadership of the group in question. The charitable institutions that benefited from this public support were run by the wealthier members of the city's immigrant subcommunities and the recipients of the most lucrative forms of patronage the machine distributed were not members of the working class, but rather contractors, lawyers, and the owners of firms that sold supplies to the municipal government. It was these same elements of the city's ethnic subcommunities that rose to positions of leadership in the machine. Seymour Mandelbaum has written of Tammany's first Irish leader, John Kelly, who came to power in 1872, "In Kelly, the Irish middle class asserted its claim to a place on the dais."[170]

At the same time, the machine politicians who rose to prominence in the 1870s enjoyed the support of and provided substantial benefits to important segments of the upper class. Considering again the case of New York, John Kelly's candidacy for the leadership of Tammany Hall was backed by, among others, August Belmont, the representative of the House of Rothschild in the United States and the chairman of the Dem-

---

[169] John I. Davenport, *The Election and Naturalization Frauds in New York City, 1860-1870* (New York: n.p., 1894); Richard Franklin Bensel, *Sectionalism and American Political Development 1880-1980* (Madison, Wis.: University of Wisconsin Press, 1984), p. 83.

[170] Seymour Mandelbaum, *Boss Tweed's New York* (New York: John Wiley & Sons, 1965), p. 93.

ocratic national committee, Samuel Tilden, one of New York's leading corporation lawyers and the Democratic party's presidential candidate in 1876, and Abram Hewitt, an iron manufacturer and the national Democratic party's leading spokesman for free trade. The Tammany-backed administrations that controlled city hall in the 1870s pursued extremely tight-fisted financial policies; in particular, they cut the wages of city laborers during that decade's depression. On the affirmative side, the machine sent congressmen to Washington and backed presidential candidates who were staunch advocates of the monetary and tariff policies that were favored by the Democratic party's allies within the business community.[171]

As Amy Bridges argues, the political parties of the antebellum era also had constructed cross-class coalitions, and the package of policies upon which such coalitions were based was roughly similar to those pursued by Kelly's machine. There was, however, an important difference between Kelly's Tammany Hall and the Tammany of earlier party leaders in New York up to and including Boss Tweed. In the 1850s and 1860s the Democratic machine was quite fragmented and amorphous: Democratic machine politicians were for the most part independent political entrepreneurs and the institutions through which they mobilized votes in working-class neighborhoods—volunteer fire companies, gangs, militia companies—were not fully subject to party control.[172] Indeed, one reason that the Tweed ring engaged in massive corruption was that bribery was the only reliable way in which Tweed could influence the behavior of other politicians.[173] In contrast, Kelly undertook to centralize and strengthen the Tammany organization. Under his leadership, Tammany's Committee on Organization purged members of the party's district committees deemed to be disloyal to the organization; it distributed patronage through these reorganized district committees rather than granting it to individual ward politicians; and it regularly gave instructions to legislators elected with Tammany's support. Finally, under Kelly and his successor Richard Croker, Tammany extended throughout the city a mode of organization—the district club—that was found to be a more successful means of ensuring voter loyalty to the machine than working through autonomous neighborhood institutions. In short, under

[171] Ibid., pp. 92, 126; David Hammack, *Power and Society: Greater New York at the Turn of the Century* (New York: Russell Sage Foundation, 1982), ch. 5; Martin Shefter, *Political Crisis/Fiscal Crisis: The Collapse and Revival of New York City* (New York: Basic Books, 1985), pp. 16-21.

[172] Amy Bridges, *A City in the Republic: Antebellum New York and the Origins of Machine Politics* (New York: Cambridge University Press, 1984), chs. 4, 7-8.

[173] Mandelbaum, *Boss Tweed's New York*, ch. 7.

Kelly and Croker, the Tammany machine became increasingly institutionalized.[174]

The institutionalization of the machine was a response to two developments—the mobilization of a mass electorate and the emergence of an increasingly well organized labor movement—that gathered force in the years following the Civil War and that culminated in crises to which party leaders were compelled to respond. The spiral of competitive mobilization that was initiated in the Jacksonian era and reached a crescendo in the naturalization frauds of 1868 presented party leaders with the problem of controlling the thousands of ward politicians who linked these voters to the machine. When Tweed's response to this—widespread and costly corruption—became public knowledge in 1871, it threatened to discredit the Democratic party in New York City and to destroy Tammany Hall. Kelly and the Tilden-Hewitt forces had a stake in preserving the organization that provided them with a political base, and hence they sponsored the centralizing reforms mentioned above, which enabled them to purge politicians implicated in the Tweed scandals and to control local politicians without relying upon Tweed's methods.

The second development that contributed to the institutionalization of the machine was the emergence of an increasingly well organized labor movement. This development, however, did not confront Tammany with a major crisis until a decade and a half after the fall of Tweed. In the late 1860s and early 1870s New York's Workingmen's Union and its German-language counterpart, the Arbeiter-Union, were the strongest municipal trades assemblies in the United States, but nonetheless when they staged a foray into electoral politics in 1869 they were unable to prevent their movement from being captured by regular party politicians. And the depression of the 1870s greatly weakened the city's trade union movement.

In 1882 a new municipal federation of trade unions, the Central Labor Union (CLU), was organized in New York. Leaders of the radical wing of the Irish nationalist organization, the Land League—most prominently, Patrick Ford and Robert Blissert—played a major role in the founding of the CLU. Indeed, the new labor federation grew out of a meeting of 12,000 union members who, like Ford and Blissert, believed that major economic reforms were called for in the United States as well as in Ireland. In 1886 the CLU and the Knights of Labor formed the United Labor Party (ULP) and nominated Henry George for mayor; Ford and many veterans of the Land League's radical wing actively par-

---

[174] Martin Shefter, "The Emergence of the Political Machine: An Alternative View," in *Theoretical Perspectives in Urban Politics*, ed. Willis Hawley and Michael Lipsky (Englewood Cliffs, N.J.: Prentice-Hall, 1976).

ticipated in the ULP campaign. George went on to win a substantial portion of the working-class and Irish vote in New York.[175] As Eric Foner notes, the struggle for the leadership of Irish-Americans—a struggle that in New York City culminated in the George campaign—reflected

> the existence of two overlapping but distinct centers of power, or poles of leadership, within the Irish-American community. Those who opposed Ford reflected the views of a nexus composed of the Catholic Church, the Democratic party, and the Irish-American middle class. The social dominance of this triple alliance was challenged in the 1880s by the organized social radicalism articulated and institutionalized in the Land League's radical branches and the Knights of Labor. Here were the only organized alternatives to the Tammany-oriented saloon and local clubhouse, as a focus for working class social life in the Irish-American community. . . . [They] embodied a social ethic that challenged the individualism of the middle class and the cautious social reformism of the Democratic party and Catholic Church.[176]

The ULP's mayoral campaign had some enduring consequences for New York politics. Tammany responded to the labor party's challenge to its political hegemony within New York's Irish-American community—and other ethnic subcommunities as well—by extending a network of district clubs throughout the city. This institutionalization of the party's base strengthened the bonds linking both working- and middle-class foreign-stock voters to the machine, making it that much more difficult for any subsequent competitor for the leadership of these groups to succeed. Moreover, Gompers, who had supported George's mayoral candidacy, concluded from the ULP's defeat that it was pointless for labor to devote its energies to political campaigns. Gompers and the AFL unions that followed his leadership were willing to acquiesce to the Democratic and Republican parties' dominance of both national and local politics. In return they sought above all to ensure that public officials elected by these parties would not intervene in labor disputes. Eventually such a *modus vivendi* between political machines and trade unions was established.

V. *The American Working Class on the Eve of the Twentieth Century*

In sum, the craft unions and political machines that became solidly established at the end of the nineteenth century were the organizational manifestations of an accommodation between one segment of America's

---

[175] Martin Shefter, "The Electoral Foundations of the Political Machine: New York City, 1884-1897," in *The History of American Electoral Behavior*, ed. Joel Silbey et al. (Princeton: Princeton University Press, 1978).

[176] E. Foner, "Class, Ethnicity, and Radicalism," p. 54.

wage-labor force and other social forces in the United States. The organizations that embodied this accommodation institutionalized only a limited subset of the numerous dispositions American workers had exhibited in the decades immediately following the Civil War. In so doing they largely defined—and delimited—the shape and character that the American working class (in the full sense of the fourth level of class) was to assume for the next several decades.

Three terms of the accommodation embodied in the craft union and the political machine are particularly noteworthy. First, this accommodation institutionalized a distinction between the organizations through which workers asserted claims upon their employers and upon the state: the former was the province of trade unions, the latter the province of party machines. As indicated above, the labor reform organizations of the post–Civil War years and the strike movements of that period had not always drawn this sharp distinction.

Second, the settlement embodied in the craft union and the political machine institutionalized a multifaceted definition of the collectivities to which workers belonged. In the economic realm the AFL unions officially defined their constituency—"labor" or the "working class"—to include only wage earners, thereby excluding the employers, farmers, shopkeepers, and clerks who formerly had been defined as belonging to the producing or working classes. (In practice, the definition of organized labor's constituency was even narrower, excluding unskilled laborers and frequently the members of racial and ethnic minorities as well.) Along with this narrower understanding of the boundaries of the working class went a militance in fighting for its distinctive interests that was considerably greater than that of those nineteenth-century labor reformers who regarded the interests of workers and employers as harmonious and who endorsed strikes only with the utmost reluctance. The machines that dominated the political arena in America's industrial cities at the end of the nineteenth century emphasized a different set of cleavages. On the whole, they organized cleavages of ethnicity and community into politics, uniting under a common banner skilled workers who belonged to trade unions, unskilled laborers for whom unions refused to accept responsibility, and members of the middle and upper classes. And these machines displayed a militance in their campaigns (as Richard Jensen has noted, both the rhetoric and practice of party warfare in the late nineteenth century was drawn from the military)[177] that was akin to that of contemporary trade unions, though the groups and issues on behalf of which they fought were rather different.

[177] Jensen, *Winning of the Midwest*, ch. 6.

Finally, the accommodations that were embodied in craft unions and political machines institutionalized at least a partial distinction between the claims workers asserted against their employers and those they asserted against the state. The former centered on wages, hours, and, for a time at least, control over the workplace. The latter centered on issues of ethnicity and community—which ethnic groups would be rewarded with jobs on the public payroll and which neighborhoods would benefit from the construction of public works. However, an important qualification to this last point must be noted. Although machine politicians generally sought to emphasize issues that would keep their party from fracturing along class lines, they were prepared to enact measures that had initially been proposed by trade unionists when electoral conditions required them to do so, even if these measures were opposed by some of the business interests with which their party was allied. The willingness of machine politicians to accept conflict—including class conflict—as a fact of life enabled them to stay in tune with the sentiments of their constituents at times of industrial strife and to triumph over that segment of the labor reform movement whose quest for ways to restore harmony between employers and employees—such as currency reform or the single tax—made it lose touch with workers for whom such conflicts were part of their daily lives.[178]

It is important, however, not to overestimate the extent to which the accommodation institutionalized in the craft union and the political machine was accepted by employers, political elites, leaders and would-be leaders of the working class, and workers themselves. This accommodation embodied a number of tensions and was subject to persistent challenges from above, from below, and from without. Employers chafed under the restrictions that unions placed upon their ability to control and deploy their labor force, and many sought to overcome these restrictions by adopting the changes in the organization of production advocated by Frederick W. Taylor and taught in the nation's new schools of engineering and business admininstration, and/or by joining the open-shop drive of the National Association of Manufacturers. And within the political arena, Progressive reformers argued that the class compromise institutionalized in the machine was a bad deal: businessmen and members of the middle class should not have to bear the financial and moral costs of machine government in order to avoid the dangers of working-class and agrarian radicalism. To eliminate this necessity the Progressives advocated changes in election laws, municipal charters, and procedures for recruiting public employees that, when enacted, contributed to a weak-

[178] Montgomery, *Beyond Equality*, p. 447.

ening of political machines, a reduction in voter turnout, and the election of candidates committed to conducting public affairs according to business principles.[179]

The hegemony of machine politicians and "pure and simple" trade unionists also was challenged by other competitors for the leadership of the working class, who at times managed to win a substantial following. During the first two decades of the twentieth century the Socialist party elected thousands of its candidates to local offices in cities and towns across the country, and socialists continued to be a substantial force within the AFL: socialists of various persuasions controlled a number of the national unions affiliated with the AFL, as well as many union locals; at the 1902 AFL national convention the Socialist platform was defeated by the remarkably close vote of 4,171 to 4,897; and at the 1912 AFL convention the Socialist candidate secured one-third of the votes in a bid to unseat Gompers from the federation's presidency.[180]

During this same period there was a considerable amount of strike activity in the United States that was conducted outside the confines of the AFL or without the sanction of its national leadership. Among the miners, lumbermen, migratory farm workers, and casual laborers in the West, strikes were led by the Western Federation of Miners (WFM) and the International Workers of the World (IWW)—organizations that were bitterly opposed to the AFL. During the second decade of the twentieth century there was an enormous surge in wildcat strikes by skilled craftsmen resisting the introduction by their employers of scientific management techniques—especially incentive-pay schemes. And simultaneously there was a wave of strikes by unskilled workers, the majority of whom were immigrants from southern and eastern Europe seeking wage increases that would maintain their standard of living in the face of inflation.[181]

There were three noteworthy characteristics of these strikers and their strikes. First, they involved workers who either were excluded from the set of accommodations embodied in the craft union and the machine or who explicitly rejected those accommodations. The AFL and, for the most part, the major party organizations did not undertake to organize the highly transient unskilled workers in the extractive industries of the West or the factory operatives—who, in the main, were new immigrants

---

[179] Walter Dean Burnham, *Critical Elections and the Mainsprings of American Politics* (New York: W. W. Norton, 1970), ch. 4.

[180] Rayback, *History*, pp. 232, 240.

[181] Montgomery, *Workers' Control*, pp. 100-104; Graham Adams, *Age of Industrial Violence, 1910-1915* (New York: Columbia University Press, 1966), chs. 4-8.

from eastern and southern Europe—in the nation's industrial heartland; this left these workers available for mobilization by other leaders. And the skilled craftsmen who struck on behalf of "workers' control" (a term that came into common use after World War I) did not believe that the AFL leadership's willingness to concede managerial control over the workplace in exchange for binding trade agreements was a bargain that served their interests. Second, the modes of collective action in which these workers engaged, the forms of organization they adopted, and the ideology their leadership espoused differed sustantially from those advocated by the dominant faction in the AFL. These workers relied on direct action (spontaneous walkouts, massive rallies); they established ad hoc workers' councils to coordinate strikes whose jurisdiction crossed craft lines; they sought to decentralize authority to shop committees; and their leaders were revolutionaries.[182] All of this contrasted with the AFL's advocacy of carefully accumulating strike and benefit funds; the negotiation of national contracts that would commit union locals not to strike; and the centralization of authority in the hands of national craft union leaders, who were prepared to make their peace with the nation's captains of industry and political leaders. Third, and finally, the great majority of these strikes failed: they had to contend with the concerted opposition of Citizens' Alliances, local police forces, the judiciary, and not infrequently, the military; and striking workers generally could be replaced with new recruits from the reserve army of the unemployed. In the final analysis, the AFL's assessment of the political and economic constraints within which the American labor movement was compelled to operate during the early decades of the twentieth century was, in fact, a rather accurate one.[183]

These challenges to the set of institutions and accommodations that linked the American working class to the nation's economic and political order reached a new crescendo during the Great Depression of the 1930s, and was expressed by changes in the behavior of workers (and also farmers and businessmen) in factories, on the streets, and in voting booths. In the heat of this crisis a number of new institutions were forged—among them industrial unions, welfare bureaucracies, and the New Deal wing of the Democratic party. The craft unions and political machines that had been organized in the late nineteenth century found it necessary to adjust to these changes in the dispositions of their members and constit-

---

[182] Montgomery, *Workers' Control*, chaps. 4-5.

[183] For a comparative assessment of these constraints see James Holt, "Trade Unionism in the British and U.S. Steel Industries, 1888-1912: A Comparative Study," *Labor History* 18 (1977):5-35.

uents, and to reach a *modus vivendi* with these new institutions. Some were incapable of making these adjustments and collapsed; others were more adaptable and survived. The precise nature of these adaptations and their implications for the character of the contemporary American working class is, however, another story.[184]

[184] See, e.g., Montgomery, *Workers' Control*, ch. 7; Frances Fox Piven and Richard Cloward, *Poor People's Movements: Why They Succeed, How They Fail* (New York: Vintage Books, 1979), ch. 3.

Part Three

Germany

7 Problems of Working-Class Formation in Germany: The Early Years, 1800-1875 • Jürgen Kocka

In West Germany in recent decades, labor and working-class history has become a quickly growing and diversifying field. The earlier stress on the history of labor organizations, programs, and politics has been supplemented and partly replaced by research on the history of protests and strikes, industrial relations and the workplace, social mobility, migration and fluctuations, housing and food, and the families and life cycles of workers. Most recently the experiences, perceptions, and "cultures" of the working class have become topics of research. Much progress has been made, but the concept of "class" has not been a major conceptual tool for West German historians. Most studies have been highly specialized and have not seen the need for such a comprehensive concept. In addition, the terms *Klasse* and *Arbeiterklasse* carry with them strong Marxist connotations. To many non-Marxist historians, they may seem to overstress the homogeneity and common characteristics of different categories of workers and to exaggerate the basic conflict between them and the rest of society.[1]

AN EXTENDED version of this essay has been published in German: *Lohnarbeit und Klassenbildung: Arbeiter und Arbeiterbewegung in Deutschland 1800-1875* (Berlin/Bonn: Verlag J.H.W. Dietz Nachf., 1983).

[1] Bibliographies on German workers and labor history include: H.-J. Steinberg, *Die deutsche sozialistische Arbeiterbewegung bis 1914: Eine bibliographische Einführung* (Frankfurt and New York, 1979); D. Dowe, *Bibliographie zur Geschichte der deutschen Arbeiterbewegung, sozialistischen und kommunistischen Bewegung von den Anfängen bis 1863*, 3d ed. (Bonn, 1981); K. Tenfelde and G. A. Ritter, eds., *Bibliographie zur Geschichte der deutschen Arbeiterschaft und Arbeiterbewegung 1830-1914* (Bonn, 1981). A good sample of recent research and an informative introduction may be found in: D. Langewiesche and K. Schönhoven, eds. *Arbeiter in Deutschland: Studien zur Lebensweise der Arbeiterschaft im Zeitalter der Industrialisierung* (Paderborn, 1981). See also W. Conze and U. Engelhardt, eds., *Arbeiterexistenz im 19. Jahrhundert: Lebensstandard und Lebensgestaltung deutscher Arbeiter und Handwerker* (Stuttgart, 1981). Most recently emphasis has shifted to the study of workers' everyday life, experiences, and perceptions, usually on a microhistorical level. Cf., e.g., Heiko Haumann, ed., *Arbeiteralltag in Stadt und Land: Neue Wege der Geschichtsschreibung* (Berlin, 1982). A critical assessment of this recent trend ("Alltagsgeschichte") is Jürgen Kocka, "Klassen oder Kultur? Durchbrüche und Sackgassen in der Arbeitergeschichte," *Merkur* 36 (1982):955-65. See also Klaus Tenfelde, "Schwierigkeiten mit dem Alltag," *Geschichte*

With some justification, this avoidance of "class" has been criticized, particularly by Marxist writers. They have argued that in discarding the concept historians risk losing sight of those elements that are common to all workers and of the relationship between workers and nonworkers in a given society. It has also been noted that the present stage of highly specialized research badly needs synthesis and that the concept of "class" could perhaps aid in this endeavor.[2]

A Marxist-Leninist concept of the term "working class" has been held by most East German historians working in the field. Recent research in particular has made good use of it. By relating their findings to an overall notion of "class evolution," these historians have avoided the dangers of producing unconnected, fragmented research and of overstressing the undeniable differences between various groups of workers. They have been sensitive to tensions and conflicts between workers and other social groups and to the dynamic relations between the workers and society at large.[3]

On the other hand this type of class analysis has tempted historians to overgeneralize. When specific conditions regarding one group of workers are uncovered, it is easily assumed or implied (but neither questioned nor demonstrated) that these conditions were characteristic of the working class in general. Similarly, the political maneuvers of certain labor organizations (usually Marxist groups of a specific type) are quickly taken as

und Gesellschaft 10 (1984), with numerous references. The stress on differences within the working class is very clear in two influential articles: W. Fischer, "Innerbetrieblicher und sozialer Status der frühen Fabrikarbeiterschaft," in his Wirtschaft und Gesellschaft im Zeitalter der Industrialisierung (Göttingen, 1972), 258-84; and W. Köllmann, "Politische und soziale Entwicklung der deutschen Arbeiterschaft 1850-1914," Vierteljahrschrift für Sozial- und Wirtschaftgeschichte (1963):480-504.

[2] Such criticism appears in: H. Zwahr, Zur Konstituierung des Proletariats als Klasse: Strukturuntersuchung über das Leipziger Proletariat während der industriellen Revolution (Berlin, 1978), pp. 18-23; G. Hardach, "Klassen und Schichten in Deutschland 1848-1970," Geschichte und Gesellschaft 3 (1977):503-524.

[3] On the state of research, see Historische Forschungen in der DDR 1970-1980: Analysen und Berichte, Zum XV. Internationalen Historiker Kongress in Bukarest 1980 (Berlin, 1980); a corresponding volume on the occasion of the International Congress of Historians in Moscow appeared in Berlin in 1970 (same title). A good bibliographical essay about research on the nineteenth century is H. Handke, "Forschungen zur Geschichte der Sozialstruktur in der DDR 1970-1980," Jahrbuch für Wirtschaftsgeschichte, no. 2 (1981):339-51. See particularly Zwahr, Zur Konstituierung; see also H. Zwahr, "Zur Genesis der deutschen Arbeiterklasse," Zur Entstehung des Proletariats (Magdeburg, 1980), 25-49; and the influential article by E. Engelberg, "Quellen und Methoden zur Erforschung der Herausbildung und Strukturwandlung des deutschen Industrie-Proletariats im letzten Drittel des 19. Jahrhunderts," Die Volksmassen: Gestalter der Geschichte (Berlin, 1962), pp. 231-36. A good selection of influential articles by East German historians is: H. Zwahr, ed., Die Konstituierung der deutschen Arbeiterklasse von den dreissiger bis zu den siebziger Jahren des 19. Jahrhunderts (Berlin, 1981).

an expression of the interests of *the* working class. Differences and tensions between different working-class groups are frequently underestimated. In addition, this type of class analysis often has a teleological bent. Consequently, the emergence of the working class as a social and political unit with a common radical consciousness seems to be the "normal" development to such an extent that it does not require empirical explanation. Instead, it is deviations from this course that need to be explained. Marxist consciousness (of a specific type) is regarded as a yardstick by which to measure the process of working-class formation. From this point of view, the weakness or absence of a revolutionary Marxist consciousness among workers can only be regarded as a sign of the immaturity of the class, an example of "false consciousness," or the result of manipulation. Those who do not share the underlying political creed usually find such grading unconvincing.[4]

It should be possible to utilize the power of class analysis while avoiding its trappings.[5] It is useful to distinguish four analytical dimensions:

(1) Fundamental and interrelated processes of change—the rise of capitalism, the intensification of state building, population growth, and perhaps other factors—contributed to the erosion of older patterns of social inequality and to the formation of classes. The emergence of labor markets and the restructuring of the productive system are arenas of change most important for the formation of the working class.

(2) To the extent that these processes became effective, an increasing proportion of work was turned into work for wages (*Lohnarbeit*). An increasing number of those who worked with their hands (and some

[4] Weaknesses of this type are very apparent in Institut für Marxismus-Leninismus beim Zentralkomitee der SED, ed., *Geschichte der deutschen Arbeiterbewegung*, 8 vols. (Berlin, 1966-69). Within a similar ideological framework, though with very helpful materials, is D. Fricke, *Die deutsche Arbeiterbewegung 1869-1914: Ein Handbuch über ihre Organisation und Tätigkeit im Klassenkampf* (Berlin, 1976). See also Jürgen Kuczynski, *Die Geschichte der Lage der Arbeiter unter dem Kapitalismus*, 38 vols. (Berlin, 1961-72). Nor is Zwahr's work free of such limitations.

[5] For the methodological implications, cf. Max Weber, *Gesammelte Aufsätze zur Wissenschaftslehre*, 3d ed. (Tübingen, 1968), p. 191; Jürgen Kocka, *Sozialgeschichte* (Göttingen, 1977), pp. 86-88. Also see Jürgen Kocka, "The Study of Social Mobility and the Formation of the Working Class In the 19th Century," *Le mouvement social*, no. 111 (April-June 1980):104-107, 115-17; Jürgen Kocka, *Klassengesellschaft im Krieg; Deutsche Sozialgeschichte 1914-1918*, 2d ed. (Göttingen, 1978), pp. 1-6. As an easy introduction to Marx's theory of wage work (*Lohnarbeit*), cf. K. Marx, "Lohnarbeit und Kapital" (1848, rev. by F. Engels in 1891) in K. Marx and F. Engels, *Werke* (Berlin, 1973), 6:397-423; and Engels' introduction of 1891, ibid., pp. 593-99 (on the difference between *Arbeit* and *Arbeitskraft*); see also of course, K. Marx, *Das Kapital*, vol. 1 (Marx and Engels, *Werke*, vol. 23), esp. pp. 181-91 (on the difference between "Klasse an sich" and "Klasse für sich").

of those who did nonmanual work) became lifetime "wage workers."[6] The opportunities or risks for such workers are determined by markets and market changes. They do not possess the tools they use, the raw materials they process, or the products they produce. Their work is determined by those who possess all this in the form of capital and who, on this basis, employ and direct them (often through managers, supervisors, or other types of middlemen). The relation between wage workers and employers is based on a contract of exchange (work for wages), terminable by both sides, and not by extraeconomic compulsion or tradition. Those workers who share these characteristics share a common class position in contrast to the class position of capitalist owners and employers. Class on this level is a multitude of persons (and families) who, due to this joint socioeconomic position, share structural presuppositions of common interests, in contrast to the related and potentially conflicting interests of at least one other class. Working class on this level is not more than a potentiality—a category, not a group.

(3)   Under certain conditions those who share this common socioeconomic position may become aware and conscious of what they share. They may, on this basis, develop a common social identity: some degree of internal cohesion and mutual communication, common experiences and dispositions, common fears and aspirations, manifest interests and loyalties, something like a common consciousness as a class—distinguished from the members of other classes. Considered in this way, "working class" ceases to be a mere category and develops the characteristics of a group. The contrast between workers and capitalists/employers becomes an overt tension that is felt and experienced by those concerned. Whether class in this sense came into existence or not, to what extent, and in which way depends on many economic, social, political, and cultural factors that have varied a great deal and that need to be studied empirically. Whether, to what extent, and in what way a working class in this sense emerged should be studied with respect to the places of work and residence, the social origins and careers, the marriage patterns and family structure, the cultures and life styles, etc., of the group involved.

---

    [6] In German: *Lohnarbeiter*. In contrast to the common use of the term in English, "wage worker" as used in this article includes highly skilled artisans and craftsmen in employed positions, as well as unskilled workers, but it excludes self-employed persons. If I speak of "worker" (Arbeiter) on the following pages, I mean wage worker (Lohnarbeiter) in this sense.

(4) In addition, under certain conditions those who share a common class position and become a social class (as outlined in the paragraph above) may, on the same basis, act collectively and perhaps organize, in conflict with other classes and perhaps the state. Again, whether and to what extent this occurs depends on many factors and is, consequently, an empirical question. The same holds true with respect to the organizational form, the ideological content, the rhetoric, and the degree of radicalism that characterize processes of class formation on this level. Labor protests and associations, clubs and societies, unions, parties and politics need to be studied from this point of view.

This concept of four levels does not imply unilinear causality. It is compatible with the conviction that there has been some historical variability in the interrelations between the four levels. In general it assumes that processes of working-class formation have occurred in different forms and with different contents due to the impact of conditions that are not defined by it. The concept is not teleological. Rather, it is based on the assumption that processes of class formation are never complete and can be reversed. It permits the identification of tendencies and counter-tendencies. In this understanding, classes are always in the process of becoming or disappearing, of evolution or devolution.

On the basis of this concept one can distinguish periods with more or less "class." One can distinguish periods of accelerated and retarded class formation and devolution. But within this framework it would be difficult to state that the process of working-class formation was finished at a certain point of time (e.g., by the 1830s in England, and by the 1860s in Leipzig).[7] It is equally difficult to determine when processes of class formation begin.

I. *The Lower Classes in 1800*

At the beginning of the nineteenth century "Germany" was made up of roughly 1,800 more or less autonomous political units. About 23 million people lived on the territory that after 1870-1871 was to become the German Reich.[8] The population was largely rural. There were only two

---

[7] Without much justification, these two dates are given by Zwahr, *Zur Konstituierung*, and E. P. Thompson, *The Making of the English Working Class* (London, 1963). For my reservations about Thompson's class concept, see "The Study of Social Mobility," pp. 98, 115.

[8] In contrast to the "Holy Roman Empire" (which was dissolved in 1806) and the loose "German Federation" (1815-1866), the German Reich of 1871 excluded Austria (i.e., Austria-Hungary), but included the eastern parts of Prussia.

large cities with more than 100,000 inhabitants: Berlin (172,000) and Hamburg (130,000). Only 7 to 8 percent of the population lived in cities with 10,000 or more inhabitants; the respective figures for England and the Netherlands at the time were 21 and 30 percent. About 73 percent of the Prussian population lived in hamlets and villages and about 27 percent in towns and cities, according to a legal definition that included even places with fewer than 1,000 inhabitants in the category of "town/ city."[9]

It is safe to say that more than half of the total population in 1800 belonged to the lower classes, the laboring and nonlaboring poor.[10] In the countryside, the peasants and farmers who had enough land to sustain themselves (usually after transfering 20 to 40 percent of their production to the lord and/or to state authorities) were nearly everywhere in the minority, accounting for one-third to one-half of the rural population (including a small number of free peasants and 1 to 2 percent noble owners of large estates). About one-third to one-half of the population were small holders who had only a little piece of land that was not enough to sustain them. They did subsidiary work for the peasants and for the lords to whom they belonged and sometimes worked on other holdings; had temporary engagements like road or canal construction; did handicraft work for local demand;[11] and were engaged in spinning, weaving, and other types of cottage industry for the export trade. Often they did several things at the same time. Depending on the size and quality of the land they had, these additional occupations ranged from being minor supplementary employment to providing the major income of the family. And finally there were those who had no land at all, who formed roughly 25 percent of the total rural population. They lived in rented cottages and rooms, usually had an inferior legal status, and did similar work as the small-holding families. Many of them did casual work of all sorts.

---

[9] Cf. A. F. Weber, *The Growth of Cities in the 19th Century: A Study in Statistics* (1899; repr. Ithaca, N.Y., 1967), pp. 15f (for definition), 82, 144. Most of Weber's figures refer to 1816 and to Prussia, but there was not much change between 1800 and 1816, and after 1815 Prussia was, in this respect, rather representative for Germany.

[10] In the West German literature, "Unterschicht" is the most common category used for this conglomerate of different groups; also used are "Vierter Stand" and "unterbäuerliche und unterbürgerliche Schichten." East German historians often speak of "Landarme" and "Stadtarme."

[11] A minority of these rural craftsmen were relatively well-off, with standing similar to full peasants, particularly millers and blacksmiths. But the great majority of them belonged to the rural lower classes in terms of life style, earnings, status, and social relations. Altogether, the rural craftsmen amounted to more than 10 percent of the rural households, in some regions up to 30-40 percent. But it is hard to isolate them both from agricultural workers, due to the frequency of multiple and part-time jobs, and from the export-oriented cottage workers. Cf. H. Schultz, "Landhandwerk und ländliche Sozialstruktur um 1800," *Jahrbuch für Wirtschaftsgeschichte*, no. 2 (1981):11-49.

Others were often on the move, alternating between town and countryside. Some were permanent tramps. This extremely mobile layer—casual workers, paupers, beggars and thieves, sometimes traveling in bands—may have included 5 percent of the whole population as the century began. In economically advanced rural regions, especially in the west in Saxony and Silesia, many landless persons (and families) were absorbed into cottage work for export, particularly spinning and weaving. Regional differences were great, of course. The ratio between peasants (*Vollbauern*) and smallholders/landless persons was 1:0.5 in some strictly agricultural precincts of the east but perhaps 1:15 in the district of Tecklenburg/Westphalia, a stronghold of proto-industrialization.

There were great variations between towns and cities, as well. These included, for example, a small Brandenburg town full of peasants and smallholders, the medium-sized capital of a small princely state like Weimar with about 7,000 people, and the huge industrial port city of Hamburg with more than 100,000 inhabitants and a proud tradition of self-government. If nevertheless a very crude overview of the urban population is sought, one can distinguish a small upper stratum of about 3 to 5 percent, the composition of which varied with the character of the place (including high civil servants; men of the court; the higher clergy; landowners and *rentiers*; rich wholesale merchants, shippers, and other successful businessmen; members of the town government; professors, doctors, lawyers, and other men of education). A broad middle stratum of perhaps 35 to 45 percent included most master artisans, merchants, shippers, retailers, innkeepers, also in many cases owners of neighboring farmland, nonacademic civil servants, teachers, community employees, better-off clerks and commercial employees, and so forth. These people were not wealthy but relatively secure; they had a family and a moderate but stable life style. They either had some property and were self-employed or were in salaried public or semipublic service; they were not engaged in manual or wage labor. There were of course many borderline cases, for example, the self-employed craftsmen who worked without any help. For a master artisan to be such an *Alleinmeister* was not infrequent, particularly weavers, spinners, shoemakers, tailors, and clothmakers—perhaps 15 percent of the urban "labor force" altogether. They had small and not completely regular earnings and often became dependent on merchants and larger shops.

With some qualifications, the remaining 50 to 60 percent can be labelled the "lower classes" and divided in four segments of roughly the same size: (a) most journeymen and apprentices working with master-artisans; (b) domestic servants working for upper-class and middle-class households; (c) a mixture of transport workers and day laborers, casual out-workers, and most of those who had found employment in manufactories; and finally (d) those who were unable or unwilling to work, recipients of charity or poor relief; the inmates of poorhouses and workhouses; trampers of different kinds, beggars, and petty criminals: their numbers increased in times of recession. These four categories all worked with their hands, in very dependent positions, or not at all. Most of them were unmarried. They had no property, no means of production, and no house of their own. Their earnings were irregular and small, near or below the poverty line. Most of them were inhabitants of the town, but not citizens (*Bürger*) in legal terms; they had inferior legal status in contrast to nearly all members of the middle and upper strata.[12]

Still, this is a heterogeneous category with many ambiguous cases, particularly among the journeymen. On the one hand they shared the lower-class attributes specified in the last paragraph. A traveling journeyman, not finding work, could easily become a tramp. On the other hand journeymen, in contrast to other lower-class groups, did highly qualified work. Although recent migrants from the rural areas clearly dominated among the urban poor, day laborers, and domestic servants, this was much less true among the journeymen. Many of them came from urban-industrial backgrounds and a strong minority were sons of masters themselves. Statistically there were two masters for every journeyman/ apprentice in 1800, although in single cities the journeymen outnumbered the masters. Many journeymen, except in the building and textile trades, had a good chance of later becoming masters and there were many married journeymen, particularly in the building trades, textiles, and printing. Some of them acquired houses of their own and citizen status. In values, respectability, social expectations, and work experiences, most journeymen felt close to their masters (in whose house they usually lived); they looked down on day laborers and domestic servants. In contrast to all other low-class groups they were able to organize themselves, although their brotherhoods had been severely weakened by 1800. Thus there are good reasons to treat the journeymen as a group per se, between the middle and lower classes.[13]

[12] Sources and literature quoted in Kocka, *Lohnarbeit*, pp. 36, 39-40. A starting point is D. Saalfeld, "Die ständische Gliederung der Gesellschaft Deutschlands im Zeitalter des Absolutismus," *Vierteljahrschrift für Sozial- und Wirtschaftsgeschichte*, 67 (1980):457-83.

[13] A good case study on journeymen in Bremen is K. Schwarz, *Die Lage der Handwerksgesellen in Bremen während des 18. Jahrhunderts* (Bremen, 1975); further evidence is in: Jürgen Kocka, "Craft Traditions and the Labour Movement in Nineteenth-Century Germany," in *The power of the Past: Essays for Eric Hobsbawm*, ed. Pat Thane et al. (Cambridge, 1984), pp. 95-118.

The rural and urban lower classes and certain borderline categories—like small masters and better-off journeymen—were the social reservoir out of which the emerging working class would later on be recruited. But at the beginning of the nineteenth century a working class did not yet exist. Most of the persons and families who belonged to the lower classes were not really wage workers as defined above. Most had income from different sources, wages playing only a partial, often only subsidiary, role. For many smallholders and self-employed artisans, wage work was a temporary and irregular experience. Most cottage workers and a minority of self-employed craftsmen had become very dependent on merchants and other employers but still usually owned their tools and the rooms in which they worked, mostly together with their families. Some even employed helpers themselves. The domestic servants, many agricultural workers, and most unmarried journeymen were integrated into their employers' households; the bulk of their income came in kind (lodging and food) and was for the most part independent from market changes.

Although the legal freedom of both the employer and the employee is an essential aspect of wage work proper, the observable elements of wage work, at the beginning of the century, were still deeply embedded in various feudal and corporate ties, household structures, government regulations, rules of custom, and other nonmarket relations. In such a situation it cannot be expected that large numbers would identify themselves as wage earners and develop common experiences and loyalties on this basis. Lower-class loyalties were often tied to family and household, village, and parish, in the case of the journeymen to the specific craft, and often to the king or the prince. Besides these highly fragmented, mostly "vertical" loyalties there probably was a vague, non-class-specific feeling, based on experience, that one belonged to the little people, the small folk, the laboring poor.[14] The dominant pattern of eighteenth-century collective protest supports this view. In the countryside, riots rarely mobilized the rural laboring poor against the peasants—more often the two groups (frequently together with smallholders and laborers of different kinds) were mobilized against the demands of the lord and the territorial state. The urban and urban-rural crowds who took part in food riots and other collective protests (against rising taxes, "unjust" prices, enforcement of new property rights, authorities capitalists—or Jews) were of a heterogeneous composition, including master artisans, small merchants, and

<hr>

[14] There are many examples with respect to the Bavarian lower classes in W. K. Blessing, *Staat und Kirche in der Gesellschaft: Institutionelle Autorität und mentaler Wandel in Bayern während des 19. Jahrhunderts* (Göttingen, 1982).

peasants together with journeymen, day laborers, and the urban poor. Even the frequent strikes, boycotts, and riots of journeymen hardly reflected an emerging class identity. Journeymen kept clearly apart from unskilled workers and the lower class in general; their actions were strictly fragmented along trade lines; and in every sixth case they were supported by their masters—more frequently than they were joined by journeymen of other trades. Corporate solidarity was still more effective than solidarity along class lines.[15]

II. *Forces of Change*

By 1800 fundamental changes were on the way and their momentum accelerated in the following decades. For the sake of analysis one can distinguish between state building, population growth, and the rise of capitalism. These processes were interrelated, but none of them can be deduced from any of the others.

Particularly in the large German states of the eighteenth and early nineteenth century, the absolutist monarchs and their well-established bureaucracies contributed to the erosion of corporate and feudal structures. The aim was "internal state building": insurance of state power against outside competitors and autonomous groups within; modernization of internal resources to increase the country's standing in a highly competitive system of international relations; centralization and bureaucratic control of different spheres of life for the sake of order and efficiency. The ideas of the Enlightenment had gained influence in the higher levels of the civil service and inspired some of the government-sponsored reforms. Recent research has correctly stressed the limits of the absolutist state's impact on social relations. On the other hand, the economic and social policies of the state were not without consequence. For example, the governments did strengthen their control of the handicraft guilds and of the "moral economy" for which they stood. Their

---

[15] On rural riots: P. Bierbrauer, "Bäuerliche Revolten in Alten Reich: Ein Forschungsbericht," in *Aufruhr und Empörung? Studien zum bäuerlichen Widerstand im Alten Reich*, ed. P. Blickle et al. (Munich, 1980), pp. 1-80; W. Schulze, ed., *Aufstände, Revolten, Prozesse: Beiträge zu bäuerlichen Widerstandsbewegungen im frühneuzeitlichen Europa* (Stuttgart, 1983). On the 1780s to the 1840s: C. Dipper, *Die Bauernbefreiung in Deutschland 1790-1850* (Stuttgart, 1980), pp. 143-53. On crowd riots: Charles Tilly, Louise Tilly, and Richard Tilly, *The Rebellious Century, 1830-1930* (Cambridge, Mass., 1975), pp. 192, 232f, passim; A. Herzig, "Vom sozialen Protest zur Arbeiterbewegung: Das Beispiel des märkisch-westfälischen Industriegebietes (1780-1865)," in *Sozialer Protest*, ed. H. Volkmann and J. Bergmann (Opladen, 1984), pp. 253-80. On journeymen: A. Griessinger, *Das symbolische Kapital der Ehre: Streikbewegung und kollektives Bewusstsein deutscher Handwerksgesellen im 18. Jahrhundert* (Berlin, 1981).

autonomy was slightly curbed, some of their customs were regulated, and the founding of enterprises unrestricted by guild rules was facilitated. The authorities proved even more energetic and successful when they encroached upon the financial bases, traditional rites, and power to strike of the journeymen brotherhoods (semi-autonomous bodies within the guilds). The governments of the larger states also facilitated the gradual intrusion of capitalist principles into the feudal structure of large-scale agriculture by freeing the peasants, smallholders, and laborers on the government-owned estates and by other measures as well.[16]

These "reforms from above" increased in the first two decades of the nineteenth century under the challenge and influence of first the French Revolution and then the Napoleonic wars. The legal foundations of a capitalist agriculture were laid. The lords lost most (not all) of their privileges, but gained economically, due to generous indemnities; the feudal ties and obligations of the peasants were removed, but they had to compensate the lords in land, services, or money. Many smallholders and servants became agricultural workers and the commons were dissolved, the land becoming private property that could be bought and sold in the market. The reforms slowed after 1820, but were largely perfected in 1848-1849.

The powers of the guilds were further weakened, particularly in Prussia where "freedom of trade" (*Gewerbefreiheit*) became the official policy. But in most other states (except on the left bank of the Rhine, where French laws continued to be effective) some guild restrictions were maintained until the 1860 and even in Prussia they were partially restored in 1845 and 1849.[17]

[16] The classic studies on this topic are by Otto Hintze. The most important of his essays are available in English: F. Gilbert, ed., *The Historical Essays of Otto Hintze* (New York, 1975). Cf. G. Oestreich, "Strukturprobleme des europäischen Absolutismus," *Vierteljahrschrift für Sozial- und Wirtschaftsgeschichte* 55 (1968): 329-47; R. Vierhaus, *Deutschland im Zeitalter des Absolutismus (1648-1763)* (Göttingen, 1978); H. Rosenberg, *Bureaucracy, Aristocracy, and Autocracy: The Prussian Experience, 1660-1815* (Cambridge, Mass., 1958); G. Schmoller, "Das Brandenburgisch-Preussische Innungswesen von 1604-1806," *Forschungen zur Brandenburgischen und Preussischen Geschichte* 1 (1888):57-109, 325-83. W. Fischer, *Handwerksrecht und Handwerkswirtschaft um 1800* (Berlin, 1955).

[17] Two readers with good introductions: B. Vogel, ed, *Preussische Reformen 1807-1820* (Königstein, 1980); H. Berding and H.-P. Ullmann, eds., *Deutschland zwischen Revolution und Restauration* (Königstein, 1981), on Germany outside Prussia. See also Dipper, *Bauernbefreiung*; R. Koselleck, *Preussen zwischen Reform und Revolution: Allgemeines Landrecht, Verwaltung und soziale Bewegung von 1791-1848*, 2d ed. (Stuttgart, 1975); F.-W. Henning, "Die Einführung der Gewerbefreiheit und ihre Auswirkungen auf das Handwerk in Deutschland," in *Handwerksgeschichte in neuer Sicht*, ed. W.Abel et al. (Göttingen, 1970), pp. 147-77; J. Jeschke, *Gewerberecht und Handwerkswirtschaft des Königreichs Hannover im Übergang 1815-1866* (Göttingen, 1977).

The governments had the support of the masters when they dissolved many journeymen brotherhoods in the years after 1800 as part of an anti-corporate, modernizing reform policy. After the turn of the century journeymen's strikes and boycotts, so frequent throughout the eighteenth century, became rare and usually unsuccessful. To the extent that brotherhoods reemerged or continued, their functions were severely limited (usually to insurance against sickness, burial funds, and care for journeymen passing through the area). The local masters' guilds and the town authorities were in charge of observing the associations as well as the traveling journeymen in general.[18] It is true that the reality of control varied from state to state, from community to community, and from decade to decade. Below the surface some journeymen brotherhoods, customs, and rites did survive; the efficiency of the bureaucracy had its limits. But this was a period of authoritarian rule in most of Germany. In the Vormärz, the period between 1815 (which marked the defeat of Napoleon, the Congress of Vienna, and the foundation of the Deutsche Bund, a loose federation of about forty relatively independent political units, dominated by the kingdom of Prussia and the Hapsburg monarchy) and the outbreak of the revolution in March 1848, most states had a monarchical or monarchical-bureaucratic government. If they had courts or representative bodies, they were not indepenent or strong. There were of course remarkable differences: compare for example, the states of southern Germany (Baden, Württemberg, and Bavaria), which had relatively liberal constitutions but remained rather slow in terms of economic policy and development; Prussia, which had an authoritarian political structure (no written constitution, no representative body on the supraregional level, an effective bureaucracy, and a strong standing army) and promoted a liberal economic policy and economic growth; and Saxony, economically most advanced, constitutionally conservative, but with some reforms after 1830. But in general the period after 1819, again after the French revolution of 1830, and even more so in the "hungry '40s" was characterized by the repression of political opposition, the prosecution of radical ideas and activities, censorship, suppression of strikes and boycotts, and government supervision of associations, clubs, and meetings. Although economic integration advanced (the German Customs Union was formed under Prussian leadership in 1834 and expanded in the years following), national unification did not, despite liberal and democratic demands. Strong pressures for building a German nation-

[18] Cf. Schwarz, *Die Lage der Handwerksgesellen*; Griessinger, *Das Symbolische Kapital*; K. Bücher, "Frankfurter Buchbinder-Ordnungen vom XVI. bis zum XIX. Jahrhundert," *Archiv für Frankfurter Geschichte und Kunst*, 3d ser., 1 (1888):243ff.

state, a liberal constitution, and democratic reforms built up under the surface of the authoritarian state (*Obrigkeitsstaat*); they burst into the open during the short months of the revolution in 1848-1849. Then the freedom of association and the right to strike were again effectively denied, censorship and government control restored, and liberal and democratic reforms refused in the period of "reaction," 1849-1859.

It was only in the more liberal 1860s that journeymen and workers were able to form associations and unions more freely and acquired the right to strike. In the same decade national unification was finally achieved, not by the power of liberals and democrats, but by the Prussian monarchy under Bismarck's leadership. Austria was defeated in 1866 and the loose Deutsche Bund was replaced by the North German Federation in 1867 and, after the victory over France, by the German Reich under Prussian hegemony in 1871. The constitution (1867 and 1871) contained some liberal elements and granted male suffrage. But it restored decisive government prerogatives and prevented the parliament from becoming the center of power. Although most of the liberals made their peace with this modified authoritarian structure, the growing social-democratic labor organizations moved into opposition. New forms of state repression reached a climax with the Anti-Socialist Law of 1878.[19]

Government policies contributed to the process of decorporation (which was pushed forward by other forces as well), the rise of capitalism, and the emergence of wage work, particularly in the late eighteenth and early nineteenth centuries. In the following decades, too, government policies tended to weaken traditional corporate identities, for example, among journeymen. The continuity between the eighteenth-century brotherhoods and the unions that emerged in the 1860s was severely weakened. Government supervision and repression did not focus on specific occupations but on journeymen and workers in general. Probably this helped them to identify as workers instead of as members of particular crafts or special skill groups.

[19] A detailed constitutional history is provided by E. R. Huber, *Deutsche Verfassungsgeschichte*, vol. 1 (1789-1930), vol. 2 (1830-1850), and vol. 3 (Bismarck und das Reich) (Stuttgart, 1967, 1968, 1963). For a short overview, see F. Hartung, *Deutsche Verfassungsgeschichte*, 8th ed. (Stuttgart, 1950), chs. 12-15. See also T. S. Hamerow, *The Social Foundations of German Unification, 1858-1871* (Princeton, 1972); W. Ritscher, *Koalitionen und Koalitionsrecht in Deutschland bis zur Reichsgewerbeordnung* (Stuttgart, 1917); A. Kraus, "Die rechtliche Lage der Unterschichten im Übergang von der Agrarzur Industriegesellschaft," in *Vom Elend der Handarbeit*, ed. H. Mommsen and W. Schulze (Stuttgart, 1981), pp. 243-58. G. A. Ritter, *Staat, Arbeiterschaft und Arbeiterbewegung in Deutschland: Vom Vormärz bis zum Ende der Weimarer Republik* (Berlin, 1980), esp. pp. 33ff (see pp. 26-33 with respect to other important aspects—role of the schools, the churches, and the military—not discussed in this essay).

Turning to the second major force of change, population growth throughout the eighteenth century was remarkable; it accelerated around 1750 and again in the 1770s and 1780s. From 1740-1750 to 1800, the German population grew 40 to 50 percent, well beyond the European average of about 30 percent. The annual growth rate of the German population averaged 0.84 in 1800-1850 and 0.95 in 1850-1900, which was more than in France (0.47 and 0.25), but less than in Great Britain (1.30 and 1.14). The growth rate peaked around 1820, reaching 1.4 to 1.5, a figure that was only surpassed in the 1890s and 1910s. In the territory covered by the German Reich (of 1871), the population was about 17 million in 1750, 23 million in 1800, 43 million in 1875, and 67 million in 1913.[20]

Declining death rates were more important than rising birth rates throughout the period. Improvement in medical services probably played a limited role (for example, increasing numbers of doctors and facilities per person, hygienic training, inocculations). Quarantine measures and other bureaucratic provisions may have contributed to the disappearance of the plague after 1750 and to the reduction of other epidemics as well. In some periods and regions, increases of food supply due to intensified agricultural production and improved circulation may have helped reduce the number of deaths. But other factors were involved as well. Regional variations were pronounced, and the situation is far from completely understood.

In the late eighteenth century and in the first decades of the nineteenth, marriage and birth rates were particularly high in agrarian regions of the east with large estates producing grain for the market and in the proto-industrial regions with a concentration of cottage industries. In both cases having a family became somewhat independent from having a "position" (*Stelle*). Production was partially integrated in emerging capitalist markets, but not yet separated from household and family. In comparison, marriage and birth rates were lower in rural areas with less market-oriented, medium-sized peasant property and the right to entail (*Anerbenrecht*) as well as in towns and cities, at least until the 1860s.[21]

---

[20] Cf. E. A. Wrigley, *Population and History* (New York, 1969), p. 185; for time series for 1815-1875 in all German states (excluding Austria): W. Köllmann, ed., *Quellen zur Bevölkerungs-, Sozial- und Wirtschaftsstatistik Deutschlands 1815-1875* I (Boppard, 1980); summaries in: W. Fischer et al., *Sozialgeschichtliches Arbeitsbuch I-Materialien zur Statistik des Deutschen Bundes 1815-1870* (Munich, 1982), pp. 15-43; W. G. Hoffmann et al., *Das Wachstum der deutschen Wirtschaft seit der Mitte des 19. Jahrhunderts* (Berlin, 1965), pp. 172-74.

[21] Cf. W. Köllmann, "Bevölkerungsgeschichte 1800-1970," in *Handbuch der deutschen Wirtschafts- und Sozialgeschichte*, ed. H. Aubin and W. Zorn (Stuttgart, 1976), 2:9-50; W. Köllmann, *Bevölkerung in der industriellen Revolution* (Göttingen, 1974), pp. 61-98;

As a consequence (or a part) of this pattern of fast population growth, the stratum below the traditional corporate structure, the lower classes, expanded both before 1800 and even more so in the decades that followed. The population grew faster than the number of positions and earnings offered by the economy. Unemployment or rather underemployment became a mass phenomenon; misery and hardship increased. In rural areas those with a highly fragmented ownership structure suffered most. In some proto-industrial areas (e.g., Silesia, Minden-Ravensberg), unemployment, poverty, and hunger reached catastrophic dimensions in the 1840s and 1850s when the consequences of overpopulation and crop failures were aggravated by international market fluctuations and the impact of factory-produced goods (particularly textiles) from abroad, against which cottage spinners and handloom weavers could not really compete. In cities like Hamburg, Cologne, Barmen, and Elberfeld, 10 to 20 percent of the population received regular public poor relief. In the years of particularly severe crises (1816-1818, 1830-1831, 1845-1848, 1857) it was estimated by local authorities that about half of the population could not live without some support from public funds or private charity. Westphalian industrial towns in the 1840s and 1850s spent more than half of the local taxes for poor relief. In 1857, 22 percent of those living in Berlin were transients without permanent residence. A deep feeling of crisis became widespread and found expression in the public debate on "pauperism" and its causes.[22]

W. R. Lee, "Germany," in *European Democracy and Economic Growth*, ed. W. R. Lee (London, 1979), pp. 144-95; H. Harnisch, "Bevölkerung und Wirtschaft: Über die Zusammenhänge zwischen sozialökonomischer Struktur und demographischer Entwicklung im Spätfeudalismus," *Jahrbuch für Wirtschaftsgeschichte*, no. 2 (1975):57-87; H. Harnisch, "Bevölkerungsgeschichtliche Probleme der industriellen Revolution in Deutschland," in *Studien zur Geschichte der Produktivkräfte Deutschlands zur Zeit der industriellen Revolution*, ed. K. Lärmer (Berlin, 1979), pp. 283, 286, 289; A. Fircks, *Rückblick auf die Bewegung der Bevölkerung im preussischen Staate während des Zeitraums vom Jahre 1816 bis zum Jahre 1874* (= *Preussische Statistik* 48a) (Berlin, 1879), pp. 22-25, 137-39; *Stand und Bewegung der Bevölkerung des Deutschen Reichs und fremder Staaten in den Jahren 1841-1886* (*Statistik des Deutschen Reichs*, N.F. 44) (Berlin, 1892).

[22] Cf. B. Weisbrod, "Wohltätigkeit und 'symbolische Gewalt' in der Frühindustrialisierung: Städtische Armut und Armenpolitik im Wuppertal," in *Vom Elend der Handarbeit*, ed. Mommsen and Schulze, p. 341; A. Kraus, *Die Unterschichten Hamburgs in der ersten Hälfte des 19, Jahrhunderts* (Stuttgart, 1965), pp. 43, 49; J. Schwarz, *Das Armenwesen der Stadt Köln vom Ende des 18. Jahrhunderts bis 1918* (Cologne, n.d.), p. 64; C. Sachsse and F. Tennstedt, *Geschichte der Armenfürsorge in Deutschland: Vom Spätmittelalter bis zum Ersten Weltkrieg* (Stuttgart, 1980), p. 214; H. Schwabe, *Die Berliner Volkszählung vom 3, December 1867* (Berlin, 1869), quoted in *Jahrbücher für Nationalökonomie und Statistik* 13 (1869):151; see examples of widespread poverty in Jürgen Kuczynski, *Darstellung der Lage der Arbeiter in Deutschland von 1789-1849* (Berlin, 1961) and *Darstellung der Lage der Arbeiter in Deutschland*

The processes contributed to what has been called "negative proletarianization."[23] People were "set free," detached from old corporate structures and made available for new structuring forces. An increasing number of them had to move. In general the towns and cities grew faster than the population, particularly after 1850, mostly due to short-distance migrations until the 1870s and later both short- and long-distance migration. Urbanization was slow in the Vormärz, stepped up after 1850, and again after 1870 (see table 7.1). But the towns and cities could not fully absorb the rural "overpopulation" before industrialization took hold in the 1850s. This is made very clear by the emigration figures. The average number of emigrants per year was about 2,000 in the 1820s, 15,000 in the 1830s, 42,000 in the 1840s, and 110,000 in the 1850s. In 1854 nearly 0.7 percent of the German population left the country; this was the peak. Then the numbers slowly decreased: 87,000 per year in the 1860s, 63,000 per year in the 1870s, 60,000 per year in the 1890s, and 28,000 per year in the 1900s, with an interruption in the 1880s (a peak of 136,000 due to a severe depression). More than 90 percent went to the United States.[24] After the mid-1850s, large-scale migrations from the countryside to the towns and cities gradually replaced emigration. This was due to the effects of capitalist industrialization, which created new jobs and earnings in and around the emerging factory system.

The third force of change, capitalism, had of course contributed to the destruction of the old order and to the slow formation of a working class long before industrialization proper (characterized by the extended use of machines and new types of energy in an increasingly centralized system of production) began. These major capitalist criteria—profit-oriented decisions within relatively autonomous business units, production of commodities for sale on the market, private ownership and accumulation of capital, contractual wage work—had already intruded into large-scale agriculture in the eighteenth century and particularly after the legislative reforms of 1800-1820, as indicated above.[25] Capitalist prin-

---

von 1849-1870 (Berlin, 1962); the contemporary debate on "pauperism" is documented in Die Eigentumslosen, ed. C. Jantke and D. Hilger (Munich, 1965).

[23] Cf. G. Lenhardt and C. Offe, "Staatstheorie und Sozialpolitik," Kölner Zeitschrift für Soziologie und Sozialpsychologie, special issue 19 (1977): 102, 104.

[24] Fisher et al., Sozialgeschichtliches Arbeitsbuch, p. 38f (on the basis of F. Burgdörfer's figures); G. Hohorst et al., Sozialgeschichtliches Arbeitsbuch II: Materialien zur Statistik des Kaiserreichs 1870-1914, 2d ed. (Munich, 1978), pp. 38-39; M. Walker, Germany and the Emigration 1816-1885 (Cambridge, Mass., 1964); P. Marschalck, Deutsche Überseewanderung im 19. Jahrhundert (Stuttgart, 1973).

[25] Even the legally privileged Prussian estates (Rittergüter) became commodities on the real estate market. More than two-thirds of them were sold, sometimes by auction, between the 1820s and the 1870s. Although in 1800 nearly all of the East German Rit-

Table 7.1. Distribution of the German Population by Size of Community (in percent)

Population	1830	1871	1910
More than 100,000	1.3	4.8	21.3
50,000–100,000	1.5	4.1	5.4
10,000–50,000	4.9	8.5	14.4
Less than 10,000	92.3	82.5	58.8

SOURCES: H. P. Thummler, "Zur regionalen Bevölkerungsentwicklung in Deutschland 1816–1871," *Jahrbuch für Wirtschaftsgeschichte* (1977), 1:55–72, p. 65; Statistisches Bundesamt, ed., *Bevölkerung und Wirtschaft 1872–1972* (Wiesbaden, 1972), p. 94. The figures for 1830 refer to the German Bund, the others to the German Reich.
NOTE: Not all columns add up to 100% due to rounding off.

ciples had guided the economic behavior of merchants, particularly wholesale merchants for centuries. Some of them had penetrated and reorganized large parts of the productive system, sometimes by founding and directing manufactories, that is, centralized business, usually urban, with perhaps ten to fifty employees according to different patterns of specialization, but without machines. It is estimated that about 1,000 of them existed in 1800, producing textiles, weapons, porcelain and ceramics, glass, tobacco, carpets, carriages, paper, leather goods, and so forth. Their numbers slowly increased.[26] Much more important, both quantitatively and in regard to the dynamic of change, was the "putting-out" system and similar forms of decentralized production, in which cottage workers and dependent craftsmen produced with their hands in traditional patterns—in their homes and usually together with their families—but for a merchant or putter-out, who would sell their products on the market according to capitalist principles and influence their work in many ways. It has been estimated that of the 2.2 million individuals primarily engaged in industry around 1800, nearly one million or 44 percent worked in the putting-out system (mostly textiles), 51 percent in the tra-

---

tergüter belonged to noble families, about 64 percent had middle-class owners by 1880. F.-W. Henning, *Landwirtschaft und ländliche Gesellschaft in Deutschland II (1750-1796)* (Paderborn, 1978), p. 60.

[26] S. Pollard, *Peaceful Conquest: The Industrialization of Europe 1760-1970* (Oxford, 1981), pp. 78-83. Number of manufactories is according to Wolfgang Zorn in *Handbuch*, ed. Aubin and Zorn, 1:550. Less than 10 percent of the manufactories were owned and run by government authorities although there was often some government support involved. Cf. H. Krüger, *Geschichte der Manufakturen und der Manufakturarbeiter in Preussen: Die mittleren Provinzen in der zweiten Hälfte des 18. Jahrhunderts* (Berlin, 1958); R. Forberger, *Die Manufaktur in Sachsen vom Ende des 16. bis zum Anfang des 19. Jahrhunderts* (Berlin, 1958); Jürgen Kocka, "Entrepreneurs and Managers in German Industrialization," *Cambridge Economic History of Europe* (Cambridge, 1978), 7:501-508.

ditional handicrafts (as masters, journeymen, and apprentices), and only 5 percent in centralized enterprises (manufactories, mines, early factories, and the like).[27] Even in the handicraft sector some capitalist principles—production for extended markets, competition, elements of wage work—gradually made themselves felt when population pressures mounted, the integration of markets proceeded, and guild rules crumbled, both before and increasingly after 1800.[28]

But the decisive breakthrough of capitalism occurred in the form of industrial capitalism, that is, in the first phase of industrialization proper, the "industrial revolution" from the 1830s and 1840s to the mid-1870s.[29] This was the period when market integration proceeded quickly, on the political level (the German Customs Union in 1834, the North German Federation in 1866-1867, and the German Reich of 1870-1871 without internal tariff lines, with a unified economic policy, uniform currency, etc.) and in terms of traffic and transportation, due to the multiplication of roads and quick construction of railroads (the first one in 1835).[30]

In the 1860s the remaining guild restrictions were finally abandoned. Economic change accelerated. Although the absolute number of persons working primarily in agriculture continued to grow and was much higher in any case than in England, the distribution percentage changed at the cost of the primary sector.[31] This redistribution sped up after the 1840s.

It has been estimated that total national income per person slowly climbed from about 250 Mark in 1800 to about 265 Mark in 1850, but it jumped to 427 Mark in 1875 and 593 Mark in 1900 (expressed in 1913 values).[32] The factory population tripled between 1850 and 1873, while the number of cottage workers in the putting-out system began to decline quickly. Centralization of production proceeded rapidly; the handicraft

---

[27] F.-W. Henning, *Die Industrialisierung in Deutschland 1800-1914* (Paderborn, 1973), p. 130. These are very rough estimates because in reality distinctions were not clearly drawn.

[28] Cf. Pollard, *Peaceful Conquest*, pp. 59-63.

[29] For a short periodization of German industrialization cf. R. H. Tilly, "Capital Formation in Germany in the 19th Century," *Cambridge Economic History of Europe* (Cambridge, 1978), 7:383-87. Also see K. Borchardt's contribution on Germany, 1700-1914, in *The Fontana Economic History of Europe*, ed. C. M. Cipolla (London, 1973), vol. 4, pt. 1, pp. 76-160. A similar periodization by a Marxist author is H. Mottek, "Zum Verlauf und zu einigen Hauptproblemen der industriellen Revolution in Deutschland," *Studien zur Geschichte der industriellen Revolution in Deutschland* (Berlin, 1960), pp. 11-63; see a different approach in Pollard, *Peaceful Conquest*.

[30] The German railroads extended 6 km in 1835, 579 km in 1840, 7,123 km in 1850 and 24,769 km in 1870. Cf. Fischer et al., *Sozialgeschichtliches Arbeitsbuch I*, p. 90. The great importance of the railways as a "leading sector" is demonstrated in R. Fremdling, *Eisenbahnen und deutsches Wirtschaftswachstum 1840-1879* (Dortmund, 1975).

[31] Henning, *Industrialisierung*, p. 20.

[32] Ibid., p. 25.

sector, though stagnating in terms of percentage of workers employed, did not shrink but grew in absolute numbers (see table 7.2). The number of journeymen expanded faster than the number of masters, but factory and mine workers had by far the fastest growth (table 7.3).

Of the 5.44 million persons active in German industry (factories, crafts, mining, building) in 1875, only 70,000 (1.3 percent) were owners and directors of shops and factories with more than five persons; 85,000 (1.5 percent) were listed as technical, commercial, and supervisory personnel, who worked only in units of more than five; 2.2 million (40 percent) were self-employed persons who worked by themselves, with (parts of) their families, or in units with up to five employees (small masters, cottage workers, domestic workers within and outside the putting-out system); the largest category—3.1 million (57 percent)—consisted of skilled and unskilled wage workers in craft shops, factories, mines, etc., including journeymen, apprentices, day laborers and others. Of them, 1.1 million (20 percent), mostly journeymen, worked in craft shops and the like with not more than five persons; 2 million (37 percent) worked in units with more than five employees, most of them in factories.[33]

Of those 2 million industrial workers about 400,000 worked in mining and metal production; 380,000 in textiles; 310,000 in the production of machinery, tools, and metal goods in general; 240,000 in the food indus-

Table 7.2. Gainfully Employed Workers in German Secondary Sector by Type of Enterprise, 1800–1913

Year	Putting-Out System		Factories, Mining, Manufactories		Handicrafts		Totals for Secondary Sector	
	1 (millions)	2 (%)	1 (millions)	2 (%)	1 (millions)	2 (%)	1 (millions)	2 (%)
1800	0.96	9.0	0.12	1.5	1.12	10.5	2.2	21.0
1835	1.40	10.0	0.35	2.0	1.50	11.0	3.2	23.0
1850	1.50	10.0	0.60	4.0	1.70	12.0	3.8	26.0
1873	1.10	6.0	1.80	10.0	2.50	14.0	5.4	30.0
1900	0.50	2.0	5.70	22.0	3.30	13.0	9.5	37.0
1913	0.50	2.0	7.20	23.0	4.00	13.0	11.7	38.0

SOURCE: F. W. Henning, *Die Industrialisierung in Deutschland 1800–1914* (Paderborn, 1973), p. 130. These are very rough estimates because in reality distinctions were not clearly drawn.
NOTE: Column 1 indicates millions of gainfully employed workers (*Erwerbstätige*); column 2 represents their percentage of total Erwerbstätige.

[33] Calculated on the basis of Dr. Engel, *Die deutsche Industrie 1875 und 1861* (Berlin, 1881), pp. 240-41.

Table 7.3. Increases in Selected Job Categories in Prussia, 1816–1861 (in thousands)

	1816	1861	Difference (in %)
Master Artisans	259	535	+107
Journeymen	146	559	+283
Servants	1,082	1,470	+ 36
Day Laborers and Hands	880	2,229	+153
Factory Workers	44	414	+848
Mine Workers	15	117	+680
Total Population	10,349	18,491	+ 79

SOURCE: G. Schmoller, *Zur Geschichte der deutschen Kleingewerbe im 19. Jahrhundert* (Halle, 1870; repr. Hildesheim, 1975), pp. 65, 71; *Jahrbuch des Preuszsichen Staates* (1867), 2:23lff. The figures for factory workers, servants (*Gesinde*), and day laborers and hands in particular are probably very inaccurate, due to problems of delineation and changes in statistical categorization. The Prussian figures were roughly representative for all Germany. In 1875 Prussia included 60 percent of the population and 57 percent of the nonagrarian economic units (*Betriebe*) of the German Reich.

tries; 160,000 in construction; and 160,000 in works producing and processing stone, sand, clay, glass, cement, etc. The rest were distributed among nine smaller industries.

It is doubtful whether many of the units with six to ten persons qualified as "factories" if by that we mean centralized institutions of production with at least some machinery and, more important, a clear separation between the roles of owners/employers and wage workers. But the great majority of these 2 million people worked in larger units, most of which were certainly factories. Take the Prussian industry, which employed roughly 60 percent of all German industrial workers. There were 15,191 units with 6-10 persons; 17,972 with 11-50; 4,232 units with 51-200; 894 with 201-1,000; and 87 with more than 1,000 (71 of which were in mining). Roughly 1.3 million workers were employed in these units. Only 9 percent of them worked in units with 6-10 persons, and 29 percent in units with 11-50. The majority was employed in medium-sized and large establishments: 27 percent in units with 51-200; 25 percent in units with 201-1,000; and 9 percent in units with more than 1,000.[34]

Regional and local variations were great. In Prussia as a whole in 1861, factory workers amounted to 5-6 percent of all gainfully employed workers (*Erwerbstätige*). But while in the rural district of Gumbinnen (East Prussia) this figure was only 2 percent, it amounted to 9 percent in

[34] *Statistik des Deutschen Reichs* 35, pt. 1 (= Die Ergebnisse der Gewerbezählung vom 1. Dezember 1875 im Deutschen Reich) (Berlin, 1879), p. 582; *Preussische Statistik* 40, pt. 1 (= Die definitiven Ergebnisse der Gewerbezählung vom 1. Dezember 1875 im Preussischen Staate) (Berlin, 1878), p. 15.

the old industrial district of Düsseldorf, 11 percent in the city of Berlin, and 32 percent in the newly industrializing city of Essen (Ruhr). The industrial revolution occurred only in some German regions, usually those with an old industrial/commercial tradition.[35]

But by and large one can say that when the "Great Depression" began in the mid-1870s, the German economy had gone through its first phase of industrialization; It had experienced a "big spurt," to use Gerschenkron's phrase. After a relatively late start (relative to western Europe, particularly England) Germany had proceeded quickly. Although France had been ahead with respect to most conventional measures of economic development in 1830, Germany had caught up by the mid-1870s.[36]

III. *The Emergence of Wage Work and Its Meaning for Workers*

The fundamental changes sketched above contributed to the emergence of wage work in some sectors of the traditional lower classes. But the impact was different depending on the specific lower-class group.

Servants, Agricultural Workers, and Others. In Prussia in the 1860s, Servants (*Gesinde*) still accounted for about 14 percent of all gainfully employed workers as counted by the statisticians. Only a minority of them, less than 20 percent, were primarily domestic servants, most of them girls and young women in towns and cities. The majority, more than 80 percent (half male, half female), did primarily agricultural work on farms and estates. Although enjoying personal freedom and working on a contractual basis in principle, they continued to have special legal status and remained part of their employers' households. Their work was not clearly defined or measured. Large parts of their wages continued to be paid in kind. In many personal respects as well, they remained subject to the authority of their masters. Typically such a worker was single and would be a servant only for a limited number of years before getting married and taking another job as a day laborer, smallholder, cottage

---

[35] But there were rapidly industrializing regions (like the Ruhr territory after 1850) that had been largely agricultural before. And some of the old rural centers of industry (like the Siegerland) became primarily agricultural again. Percentage figures have been estimated on the basis of various data in *Jahrbuch des Preussischen Staates* 2 (1867).

[36] This can be shown with respect to the sectorial distribution of the labor force, the production of coal and pig iron, consumption of raw cotton, railroad lines opened and urbanization. See the relevant figures in B. R. Mitchell, *European Historical Statistics 1750-1970* (London, 1975), pp. 53-54, 61, 184-86, 215-17, 251-53, 315-17. Compared with other countries the speed of German industrialization appears to be not particularly high. Cf. H. Kaelble, "Der Mythos von der rapiden Industrialisierung in Deutschland," *Geschichte und Gesellschaft* 9 (1983):106-123 (based mainly on Bairoch's figures).

worker, or industrial worker in a neighboring town. Work and living situations varied. Records exist of servants' grievances, petitions, and protests, particularly in 1848-1849, in the early 1870s, and again toward the end of the century. But for the most part their situation, did not teach them solidarity with each other. The right of association was explicitly denied to them until 1918. As servants they did not take part in the activities of the early labor movement. But many of them became industrial workers and, perhaps even more important, wives of industrial workers, transporting their specific experiences into the new working-class milieu.[37]

Agricultural workers, a highly heterogeneous category, accounted for roughly 15 percent of all gainfully employed workers in Prussia in the 1860s (the smallholders, not included, made up another 12 percent). Though personally free, most of them continued to be bound to the land and their employers by semifeudal ties, particularly on the large estates east of the river Elbe. They lived on the estates and had the right to cultivate a small piece of land (part of the estate) by themselves, with the employers' tools and horses. They received a small proportion of the grain they helped to thresh, and other goods as well, in addition to a small amount of cash. In the West and the South it was different; there the division between lower-class agricultural groups was more fluid. A great deal of cohesion existed within the villages due to old traditions of mutual help and family relations among peasants, smallholders, and agricultural workers.

This remained the basic pattern until the 1870s (and later), but changes were visible. When the "separations" (a type of enclosures) proceeded, primarily between 1820 and 1850, many landless workers lost the right to participate in the use of the commons, a right that had distinguished them from "pure" wage workers. With increasing market integration, agricultural employers preferred "free" agricultural labor to semifeudal relations. The number of "free" agricultural laborers grew;

---

[37] The best study of domestic servants is in R. Engelsing, *Zur Sozialgeschichte deutscher Mittel- und Unterschichten*, 2d ed. (Göttingen, 1978), pp. 180-283; R. Engelsing, "Der Arbeitsmarkt der Dienstboten im 17., 18. und 19. Jahrhundert," *Wirtschaftspolitik und Arbeitsmarkt*, ed. H. Kellenbenz (Vienna, 1974):159-237; a good introduction into the problems of nondomestic servants in Prussian agriculture is K. Tenfelde, "Ländliches Gesinde in Preussen: Gesinderecht und Gesindestatistik 1810-1861," *Archiv für Sozialgeschichte* 19 (1979):169-229 (with many references to the older literature). Also see K.-S. Kramer, "Gutsherrschaft und Volksleben," *Rheinisch-Westfälische Zeitschrift für Volkskunde* 22 (1976):14-33, 27-28; K.-S. Kramer, "Einiges über die Lage des Gesindes in einem ostelbischen Gutsbezirk," *Zeitschrift für Volkskunde* 70 (1974):20-38; T. Vormbaum, *Politik und Gesinderecht im 19. Jahrhundert (vornehmlich in Preussen 1810-1918)* (Berlin, 1980).

the cash proportion of agricultural income slowly increased. New tensions appeared in the countryside between landless laborers and those who owned land, superimposed upon the older tensions between the small folk and the lord.

But pure wage work continued to be a minority phenomenon in the countryside into the 1870s. The mechanisms of integration were powerful on the estates and in the villages, and there is evidence of group-specific identities, morals, and loyalties among agricultural workers on the estates. But communication between different groups of workers and between different locations was difficult and rare. Class consciousness was slow to develop here. After 1850, an increasing proportion of those who were dissatisfied and sufficiently motivated to take action preferred to move to the towns and cities. Protests of agricultural workers and smallholders were rare after 1848. Like the servants, agricultural workers were legally forbidden to strike or to form unions, in Prussia and other German states, until 1918. When the Social Democrats started to work for support in the countryside in the early 1870s, they had very little success.[38]

There were other categories of workers that should be included in a more thorough investigation: nonagricultural day laborers, casual workers, road and railroad construction workers, transport workers, and unskilled manual workers of different kinds. For most of them wage work continued to be a temporary experience; they were highly mobile, moving back and forth between town and countryside, between the work force and the unemployed poor; they belonged to the lowest layer of the emerging working class if not to the strata below, the subproletariat, about

---

[38] Cf. G. F. Knapp, *Die Bauernbefreiung und der Ursprung der Landarbeiter in den älteren Theilen Preussens*, 2d ed. (Munich, 1927), 2:333-40: this contains good descriptions of the situation of agricultural workers on large estates in 1842 and 1843; Th. Frh. v.d. Goltz, *Die ländliche Arbeiterfrage und der preussische Staat* (Jena, 1893), pp. 92-155; J. Mooser, "Gleichheit und Ungleichheit in der ländlichen Gemeinde: Sozialstruktur und Kommunalverfassung im östlichen Westfalen vom späten 18. bis in die Mitte des 19. Jahrhunderts," *Archiv für Sozialgeschichte* 19 (1979):231-62; H.-G. Husung, "Zur ländlichen Sozialschichtung im norddeutschen Vormärz," in *Vom Elend der Handarbeit*, ed. Mommsen and Schulze, pp. 259-73. See the interesting remarks on differences among Germany, England, and France in Harnisch, "Bevölkerungsgeschichtliche Probleme," pp. 301-302. See also H. Bleiber, "Bauern und Landarbeiter in der bürgerlich-demokratischen Revolution von 1848/49 in Deutschland," *Zeitschrift für Geschichtswissenschaft* 17 (1969):289:309; H. Hübner and K. Kathe, eds., *Lage und Kampf der Landarbeiter im Ostelbischen Preussen: (Vom Anfang des 19. Jahrhunderts bis zur November-Revolution 1918/19)*, 2 vols. (Berlin, 1977); F. Schaaf, *Der Kampf der deutschen Arbeiterbewegung um die Landarbeiter und werktätigen Bauern 1848-1890* (Berlin, 1962); F. Wunderlich, *Farm Labor in Germany 1810-1945: Its Historical Development within the Framework of Agricultural and Social Policy* (Princeton, 1961); A. Eggebrecht et al., *Geschichte der Arbeit* (Cologne, 1980), pp. 292-94.

which we know little.[39] Particular attention should be paid to the miners. In Germany they were well paid and highly thought of workers with great cohesion and a strong, state-protected corporate tradition. This was progressively challenged in the 1850s to the 1870s by capitalist principles that increasingly structured the growing mining industries.[40] In this essay they are left aside, concentrating instead on three broad categories of workers, each of which comprised roughly 7 percent of all gainfully employed workers in the 1860s: workers in domestic industries, journeymen, and factory workers.

Workers in Domestic Industries. The master artisan sold his product directly to the consumer or to the local merchant without being dependent on him; the domestic worker (*Heimarbeiter*), although formally self-employed and usually owning his tools, depended on a putting-out merchant who provided the raw materials and intermediate products at various stages, monopolized "his" workers, and bought their product for a predetermined price (wage). He often controlled and changed the process of work in indirect ways and sometimes even owned the tools. But dependence on the merchant could take many forms and in reality the distinction between master artisan and domestic worker was a fluid one.[41]

The majority of domestic workers belonged to the textile sector, lived in the countryside, and were largely recruited from agricultural workers' and smallholders' families. The overall changes of the nineteenth century affected them in two ways. First, specialization increased in that an expanding proportion of spinners, weavers, nail makers, and the like performed their tasks for the most part as a full-time job, whereas in the

[39] Research on these categories has been minimal, except on railroad construction workers: K. Obermann, "Zur Rolle der Eisenbahnbauarbeiter im Prozess der Formierung der Arbeiterklasse in Deutschland," *Jahrbuch für Wirtschaftsgeschichte*, no. 3 (1970):129-140; W. Wortmann, *Eisenbahnbauarbeiter im Vormärz: Sozialgeschichtliche Untersuchung der Bauarbeiter der Köln-Mindener Eisenbahn in Minden-Ravensberg 1844-1847* (Cologne, 1972); E. Wolfgramm et al., *"Die sozio-ökonomischen Kämpfe der Eisenbahnbauarbeiter in Sachsen 1844-1848," Aus der Frühgeschichte der deutschen Arbeiterbewegung* (Berlin, 1964), pp. 65-101. On the construction of a port: A. Kraus, "Arbeiteralltag auf einer Grossbaustelle des 19. Jahrhunderts," *Hamburger Jahrbuch für Wirtschafts- und Gesellschaftspolitik* 24 (1979):109-120. On poverty: Sachsse and Tennstedt, *Geschichte der Armenfürsorge in Deutschland*, pp. 179ff; W. Fischer, *Armut in der Geschichte* (Göttingen, 1982), pp. 56-90; a case study: B. Balkenhol, *Armut und Arbeitslosigkeit in der Industrialisierung: Dargestellt am Beispiel Düsseldorf 1850-1900* (Düsseldorf, 1976).

[40] Cf. K. Tenfelde, *Sozialgeschichte der Bergarbeiterschaft an der Ruhr im 19. Jahrhundert* (Bonn, 1977); L. Schofer, *The Formation of a Modern Labor Force: Upper Silesia, 1865-1914* (Berkeley, 1975).

[41] Very helpful for conceptual clarification: Karl Heinrich Kaufhold, *Das Gewerbe in Preussen um 1800* (Göttingen, 1978), pp. 224-42.

early years these jobs had largely been done on a part-time basis.[42] This means that cottage workers became a more clearly defined category, more distinguished from agricultural workers and smallholders, and more dependent on their industrial work, the merchants, and the markets. Second, due to rising population pressures and to the superior competition of the factory system (particularly in spinning, later on weaving, first from English and Belgian imports, later from German factories as well), most rural domestic industries experienced a structural crisis that reached a climax in the 1840s and 1850s. Declining prices and expanding volumes of yarn and linen were characteristic. Cottage workers as a group were trapped with no way out except emigration and, after the 1850s, migration to the towns and the factories. Their numbers quickly declined after 1850. Some of their most numerous subgroups virtually disappeared within a few decades (spinners); others continued to exist in precarious situations and even expanded (e.g., toymakers), until the twentieth century.[43]

A minority of domestic workers had a different collective history. They had been fully developed self-employed masters in highly qualified and often guild-regulated trades (metal trades, qualified weavers, dyers, later on tailors and shoemakers, etc., usually in towns and surroundings, mostly in regions with an old industrial tradition) before being integrated into growing supralocal markets and becoming dependent on merchants, putters-out, and later of factories as well. These were often very gradual processes of transformation, extending over generations and moving through several stations, defined by different degrees of dependence on the merchant or putter-out as in the textile trades of Glauchau and Meerane, Saxony.

Most domestic workers of this second type suffered from pressures and

[42] On nonspecialization in a West German textile region, see T. C. Banfield, *Industry of the Rhine*, Series 2: Manufactures (1848; repr. New York, 1969), I:51-52, 56, 70-73 II:7; F. Le Play, *Les ouvriers, européens* (Tours, 1877), 3:162.

[43] See table 7.2 above. J. Mooser. *Ländliche Klassengesellschaft 1770-1848. Bauern, Unterschichten und ländliche Industrie im östlichen Westfalen* (Göttingen, 1984), with a good survey of the literature; B. Schöne, *Kultur und Lebensweise Lausitzer Bandweber (1750-1850)* (Berlin, 1977); G. Adelmann, "Strukturelle Krisen im ländlichen Textilgewerbe Nordwest-Deutschlands zu Beginn der Industrialisierung," in *Wirtschaftspolitik und Arbeitsmarkt*, ed. Kellenbenz, pp. 110-28; G. Adelmann, "Die ländlichen Textilgewerbe des Rheinlandes vor der Industrialisierung," *Rheinische Vierteljahresblätter* 43 (1979):260-88. An impressive description of textile cottage workers' misery: "Bericht über den Notstand in der Senne zwischen Bielefeld und Paderborn (1853)," *64. Jahresbericht des Historischen Vereins für die Grafschaft Ravensberg 1964/65* (Bielefeld, 1966), pp. 1-108. On the recent debate about proto-industrialization: Pollard, *Peaceful Conquests*, pp. 62-78. For the later period: G. Schnapper-Arndt, *Fünf Dorfgemeinden auf dem hohen Taunus: Eine sozialstatistische Untersuchung über Kleinbauernthum, Hausindustrie und Volksleben* (Leipzig, 1883).

challenges similar to those of workers from agricultural origins: market-conditioned insecurity, waves of poverty and underemployment, pressures from overpopulation, decline due to the competition of the rising factory system, low wages, and increasing control by the putting-out merchant. In addition, domestic workers with a background in autonomous crafts, in contrast to those growing out of the agricultural lower classes, usually experienced what happened as a process of degradation, loss of control, and violation of traditional codes of conduct that had formerly provided pride in their work and meaning to their life.[44]

There was at least one other type of domestic worker: relatively unskilled and poorly paid persons who did highly specialized work within new and expanding urban systems of decentralized production. For example, consider the sewing girls employed and directed by a subcontractor who in turn worked for a ready-made clothier's shop or a large store. Forerunners of such businesses existed in Berlin in the 1820s and 1830s, but the breakthrough of this type of production came only with the sewing machine and with quickly developing urban markets in the 1860s and 1870s, particularly in Berlin and in other urban centers. Similar developments can be traced in the production of shoes, other leather goods, caps, gloves, umbrellas, and similar products. But these developments were more typical for the cities of the late nineteenth century than for the industrial revolution proper. As was true everywhere, a large proportion of women and children workers, long hours, low pay, unhealthy working conditions at home or in little shops, harsh exploitation by competitive agents and selling organizations were characteristics for the sweatshop system in imperial Germany.[45]

In contrast to servants and most agricultural workers, domestic industrial workers experienced the powerful impact of capitalist markets directly. They also experienced the conflict of distribution between wage

[44] The best materials in A. Thun, *Die Industrie am Niederrhein und ihre Arbeiter* (Leipzig, 1879), vols. 1 and 2; R. Boch, "Was macht aus Arbeit industrielle Lohn-'Arbeit'? Arbeitsbedingungen und -fertigkeiten im Prozess der Kapitalisierung: Die Solinger Schneidewarenfabrikation 1850-1920," *Sozialwissenschaftliche Informationen* 9 (Stuttgart, April 1980):61-66; R. Boch, *Handwerker-Sozialistengegen Fabrikgesellschaft: Lokale Fachvereine, Massengewerkschaft und industrielle Rationalisierung in Solingen 1870 bis 1914* (Göttingen, 1985); Le Play, *Les ouvriers européens*, 3:156-81 (life and work of a Solingen armorer).

[45] Cf. O. Baader, *Ein steiniger Weg: Lebenserinnerungen einer Sozialistin*, 3d ed. (Berlin, 1979), pp. 19ff (experiences of a sewing girl in the early 1870s); K. Hausen, "Technischer Fortschritt und Frauenarbeit im 19. Jahrhundert: Zur Sozialgeschichte der Nähmaschine," *Geschichte und Gesellschaft* 4 (1978):152-53. Further examples are in J. Ehmer, *Familienstruktur und Arbeitsorganisation im frühindustriellen Wien* (Munich, 1980). There are types of domestic industrial work that do not easily fit into the threefold typology proposed (e.g., cigar production).

labor and capital (in bargaining processes; on every payday; and in periods of depression, when the merchant "delegated" the market risks to them by withdrawing and withholding orders). Other elements of their situation, however, impeded the development of a general wage workers' identity or even class consciousness. In contrast to journeymen and factory workers, they did not experience the conflict between capital and labor in the form of a direct conflict of authority: they worked by themselves without direct control by any employer. Most of them were part of closely knit families serving as units of production, consumption, and re–creation as well. Loyalty to the family was a very concrete experience to them; in comparison, loyalty to their class was abstract and removed, difficult to experience. It seems that the family tended to absorb anger, disappointment, frustration, and aggression, diverting these feelings from being channeled into collective actions. The family served as a device of protection, emotionally and materially, within limits, and contributed to the individualization of the experiences of hardship and deprivation. Most domestic workers had their own tools, and a large minority of them were employers themselves. This explains why they rarely identified as wage workers but rather tended to see themselves as self-employed masters.[46]

In the 1820s, 1830s, and 1840s domestic workers (mostly urban) participated in riots directed against early factories, machines, and the houses of capitalists and civil servants, although crowd actions of a Luddist type were apparently less frequent in Germany than in England or France. Although they were partly products of desperation, without much effect and usually put down by military action in short order, at least some of them were guided by anticapitalist and anticompetitive norms that derived from the corporate handicraft tradition and its ideal of protected guilds, mutual self-help, just prices, and honorable sustenance (*ehrbare Nahrung*).[47] When in 1848-1849 grievances and claims

---

[46] Cf. W. H. Schröder, *Arbeitergeschichte und Arbeiterbewegung: Industriearbeit und Organisationsverhalten im 19. und frühen 20. Jahrhundert* (Frankfurt, 1978), pp. 101-109; J. Mooser, "Bäuerliche Gesellschaft im Zeitalter der Revolution 1789-1848: Zur Sozialgeschichte des politischen Verhaltens ländlicher Unterschichten im östlichen Westfalen" (diss., University of Bielefeld, 1978), pp. 105ff, 567f (on the role of the family and the rural environment); also Shöne, *Kultur*, pp. 63ff, 70; Thun, *Industrie*, 1:45f; Adelmann, "Die ländlichen Textilgewerbe," pp. 178f; W. Mager, "Haushalt und Familie in proto-industrieller Gesellschaft: Spenge (Ravensberg) während der ersten Hälfte des 19. Jahrhunderts," in *Familie zwischen Tradition und Moderne*, ed. N. Bulst et al. (Göttingen, 1981), pp. 141-81. Life in a domestic workers' family in the second third of the nineteenth century is documented in the autobiography *Die kleine, mühselige Welt des jungen Hermann Enters: Erinnerungen eines Amerika-Auswanderers an das frühindustrielle Wuppertal*, 2d ed. (Wuppertal, 1971).

[47] Many examples from the Rhineland are reported in Thun, *Industrie*, 1:31ff, 2:62ff,

could be openly formulated, the Krefeld silk weavers, for example, successfully fought to be recognized as master artisans (*Handwerksmeister*)
and to be protected by guild rules; they also demanded regular income
on the basis of collective bargaining with the merchants and contracts to
be enforced by the local authorities. In Bielefeld, spinners and weavers
demanded monopoly rights, support for spinning schools, credit institutions, and government action in order to guarantee their self-employed
status.[48]

But this desire for craft autonomy and self-employment was not
always incompatible with support for the early labor movement. In some
of the protests of 1848-1849 and again in the 1860s it was clear that
domestic workers supported plans for cooperatives (*Assoziationen*). On
the other hand, the idea of cooperative societies with productive functions
was an important element of the emerging socialist vision, from the 1840s
to the 1870s, and supported by early labor leaders like Stephan Born and
August Bebel. Consider the Solingen cutlers of the early nineteenth century. Small masters (sometimes with journeymen and apprentices) were
confronted by putting-out merchants who defined their place in the
divided and complex process of knife production, provided the semifin-
ished materials, took back the products after the cutlers had worked on
them, and handed them on to the next stage of production. The cutlers
(who worked in small shops, not at home) did everything they could to
remain as autonomous as possible. They rented steam energy once it had
become indispensable in the second third of the nineteenth century. They
tried to continue with guildlike free associations, which they increasingly
legitimized in socialist terms; the Prussian administration stopped these
initiatives in the 1840s. But in the early 1870s the cutlers founded a local
trade union that organized 90 percent of them. They succeeded in getting
a piece-rate contract with the merchants in 1872 that was modelled after
a similar statute of 1789 between the guild and the merchants. In 1877
they struck. Later on this "union" applied guildlike practices: only one
apprentice and one journeyman per master were admitted. At the same

---

89f, 102f, 196; D. Dowe, *Aktion und Organisation: Arbeiterbewegung, sozialistische und
kommunistische Bewegung in der preussischen Rheinprovinz 1820-1852* (Hannover,
1970), pp. 25-32, on protests of a Luddist type; less important is M. Henkel and R. Taub-
ert, *Maschinenstürmer* (Frankfurt, 1979), on riots in Eupen in 1821 and in Solingen in
1826 and 1848. On the famous riots of the Silesian weavers: L. Kronenberg and R. Schlos-
ser, eds., *Weber-Revolte 1844: Der Schlesische Weberaufstand im Spiegel der zeitgenöss-
ischen Publizistik und Literatur* (Cologne, 1979). Also Zwahr, "Zur Genesis," pp. 25-
49, esp. 41f; H.-J. Rupieper, "Die Sozialstruktur der Trägerschichten der Revolution von
1848/49 am Beispiel Sachsen," in *Probleme der Modernisierung in Deutschland*, ed.
H. Kaelble et al. (Opladen, 1978), pp. 80-109, esp. 96-101.

[48] Cf. Thun, *Industrie*, 1:114f, 142, 2:31ff.

time they identified as "workers" (*Arbeiter*) vis-à-vis the merchant-entre-
preneurs who tried to centralize production.[49]

The Solingen cutlers may have been an exception. Unions did not easily organize domestic workers as far as we know. They were clearly
underrepresented among the participants of the many strikes of the
1870s. But they seem to have participated in general (not trade-specific)
workers' clubs, and many of them seem to have supported the socialist
parties in the 1860s and 1870s. The strongholds of the early labor movement were usually located in areas with old industrial traditions (e.g.,
Glauchau, Meerane and Crimmitschau in Saxony; Solingen, Wuppertal,
Elberfeld-Barmen in Prussia; Apolda in Thuringia; Nuremberg in
Bavaria). Domestic workers, particularly those of the second type, may
have contributed more to the early labor movement than has been previously thought.[50]

Journeymen. In contrast, journeymen (*Handwerksgesellen*)—artisans
working for small employers (*Meister*) in unmechanized or scarcely
mechanized units below factory size—are known to have contributed a
great deal to the rising labor movement from the 1830s to the 1870s. It
is difficult to generalize about them. Journeymen in rapidly declining
crafts (weavers, glove makers, button makers, wig makers) had different
problems from those in expanding trades (most building trades, printing,
butchers, bakers, etc.). In Nuremberg at the middle of the century, the
annual income of journeymen was about 450 Mark for furriers and 401
Mark for bookbinders, but only 267 Mark for weavers, 264 Mark for
filers, and 199 Mark for box makers. Unit size made a difference: in Berlin, the ratio in 1867 between masters and journeymen/apprentices varied from 1:13 (masons) and 1:10 (printers, carpenters) to 1:4 (cabinetmakers) to 1:1 (shoemakers, glove makers) and less. States in which
guild rules existed until the 1860s, though in a weakened form (as in
South Germany, Hannover, Saxony), differed from those with relatively
liberal laws (like Prussia), but everywhere enough of the old corporate
law was preserved to make the distinction between *Handwerk* and *Industrie* (handicraft and factories) a self-evident one that has continued to
structure law, public statistics, social language, politics, and the historiography of the working class in Germany down to the present (in contrast with England and the United States).[51]

[49] Ibid., 1:152ff, Boch, "Was macht aus Arbeit industrielle Lohn-'Arbeit'?"

[50] Cf. Zwahr, "Zur Genesis," pp. 31-33; Schöne, *Kultur*, p. 74; Thun, *Industrie*,
1:196ff, 2:156f.

[51] Journeymen earnings in Nuremberg: R. Gömmel, *Wachstum und Konjunktur der
Nürnberger Wirtschaft (1815-1914)* (Stuttgart, 1978), pp. 111f; Berlin figures in

If one summarizes in spite of so many differences, certain changes that made the journeymen increasingly similar to the ideal-type of wage worker as defined above cannot be overlooked. In the case of the journeymen the emergence of wage work was much more pronounced and definite than in the case of domestic workers, agricultural workers, and the servants. It was a very gradual and diverse process, protracted over decades and not without temporary setbacks, but all over Germany by the late 1860s free labor contracts had become the rule and remnants of corporate laws had been largely destroyed with respect to the relationship between masters and journeymen. Traditional nonmarket practices of placing new journeymen with masters or sending them on the road again if there were no openings broke down, particularly in the reforms around 1810, in the crisis years of the 1830s and 1840s when there was high unemployment, and finally in the industrialization boom of the late 1860s and early 1870s. Local authorities had tried to continue to determine wage rates in a few trades (masons, carpenters, pavers) in some regions, but increasingly these attempts for "just" regulation were overwhelmed by market pressures and given up in the 1860s, at the latest (as in most Prussian coal mines in which state control was replaced by a free market system, 1851-1865). Fluctuations of wages increased as did differentials between journeymen incomes and masters' incomes, at least in the cases that have been studied. One of the most important steps in changing the journeyman-master relationship into a wage worker–employer relationship occurred when the journeyman moved out of the master's house. This meant a decisive reduction of social control; changing issues of conflict (from battles over the quality of food and the right to have a house key to conflicts over wages and working time, to put it crudely); increasing probability that journeymen would develop a self-understanding, a "culture" and aims apart from and in contrast to the masters; and that the cash proportion of the wages jumped from about 40-50 percent (room and board may be estimated to have made up half of the wages) to 100 percent. In Frankfurt nearly all journeymen (except those in the building and printing trades) lived with their masters in 1832; in 1850 at least three of four Nuremberg journeymen "lived in." In both cases these proportions quickly declined, though exact figures are lacking. In Berlin in 1867 the proportion of those "living in" had reduced to 29 percent, and 30 percent lived in apartments of their own, 17 percent with family and

---

H. Schwabe, *Resultate der Berliner Volkszählung vom 3. December 1867* (Berlin, 1869), p. 94 (excluding tailors). The guild system was weakened early in Berlin, but largely maintained in Hannover; cf. J. Bergmann, *Das Berliner Handwerk in den Frühphasen der Industrialisierung* (Berlin, 1973); Jeschke, *Gewerberecht* (on Hannover).

relatives, 6 percent in rented rooms and 18 percent as *Schlafgänger* (having no room but paying for using a bed, usually in the household of another lower-class person). It should be remembered that Berlin was more advanced in the process of dissolving the living-in system than most other places,[52] but the figures are indicative of what took place elsewhere.

Journeymen status also became somewhat less transitory. Even so, in 1847 only a small minority of Hannover journeymen (those in the building trades) had been married (partly due to legal restraints); in contrast, nine of ten masters were married. In the following decades the proportion of married journeymen rose in most trades (see table 7.4).[53]

This must have meant decreasing mobility for an increasing proportion of journeymen who had been extremely mobile in preceding decades. The chances of leaving the journeyman status and becoming a self-employed master may have increased temporarily whenever a step of legal liberalization occurred. But over the decades it slightly decreased. An indirect measure is the rising average size of the craft shops (factories excluded): 1.6 persons per shop in 1816 and still in 1834; 1.7 in 1837 and 1840; 1.8 from 1843 to 1855; 1.9 in 1858; 2.0 in 1861; and 2.8 in 1895.[54]

[52] In addition to the two major studies on Berlin and Hannover by Bergmann and Jeschke (see notes 51 and 17 above), see scattered materials in G. Schmoller, *Zur Geschichte der deutschen Kleingewerbe im 19. Jahrhundert* (1870; repr. Hildesheim, 1975); P. Kampffmeyer, "Vom Frankfurter Zunftgesellen zum klassenbewussten Arbeiter" (=Generalkommission der Gewerkschaften Deutschlands/Arbeiter-Sekretariat [Frankfurt]), *Jahresbericht* I [1899], App. (Frankfurt, 1900). Nuremberg and Berlin figures from Gömmel, *Wachstum*, pp. 101-103; Schwabe, *Resultate*, p. 98. On the role of the Herberge: J. Ehmer, "Rote Fahnen—blauer Montag," in *Wahrnehmungsformen und Protestverhalten: Studien zur Lage der Unterschichten im 18. und 19. Jahrhundert*, ed. D. Puls (Frankfurt, 1979), pp. 143-74, esp. 158; Jeschke, *Gewerberecht*, pp. 254ff. See also the recent volume *Handwerker in der Industrialisierung: Lage, Kultur und Politik vom späten 18. bis ins frühe 20. Jahrhundert*, ed. U. Engelhardt (Stuttgart, 1984), which contains many important pieces of fresh and ongoing research on masters and journeymen.

[53] In Berlin, 51 percent of the shoemakers, 38 percent of the butchers, 51 percent of the masons, 46 percent of the carpenters, 39 percent of the printers, and 47 percent of the cabinetmakers were married in 1867; the figures are for male journeymen (Schwabe, *Resultate der Berliner Volkszählung*, p. 94). Wages rarely rose when a journeyman married. Cf. W. Köllman. *Sozialgeschichte der Stadt Barmen im 19. Jahrhundert* (Tübingen, 1960), p. 139. Legal restraints on marriage of workers and journeymen were abandoned in Prussia, but effective in most other states to a different degree until the 1860s. Cf. H. Eckert, *Liberal- oder Sozialdemokratie: Frühgeschichte der Nürnberger Arbeiterbewegung* (Stuttgart, 1968), pp. 30ff; and, most comprehensive, K. J. Matz, *Pauperismus und Bevölkerung: Die gesetzlichen Ehebeschränkungen in den süddeutschen Staaten während des 19. Jahrhunderts* (Stuttgart, 1980).

[54] In 1858 the average size was 1.9 in the metal, 1.6 in the textile, 1.7 in the wood, 1.7 in the food, and 7.9 in the building trades. See Fischer et al., *Sozialgeschichtliches Arbeitsbuch I*, p. 69. Many trades had a dualistic structure: many one-man units (usually 30-50 percent of the total) and a few large ones (with more than five). There are no good mobility studies on the career opportunities of journeymen. In addition, it should not be

Table 7.4. Percentage of Married Persons among Leipzig Journeymen and Workers

	1849	1875
Tailors (male)	10	12
Shoemakers (male)	8	13
Butchers (male)	2	4
Locksmiths (male)	23	33
Cigar Makers (male)	31	69
Factory Workers (male, unskilled)	38	88
Masons (male)	74	51
Cigar Makers (female)	9	11
Factory Workers (female)	0	1
Maids	0	0.2

Source: H. Zwahr, *Zur Konstituierung des Proletariats als Klasse: Strukturunter-suchung über das Leipziger Proletariat während der industriellen Revolution* (Berlin, 1978), pp. 126f.

It is difficult to generalize about how journeymen experienced those changes. Certainly, many of them experienced the rise of the market principle, the capitalist transformation of the journeyman-master relations, the increasing division of labor, the rise of the factory, and the destruction of corporate laws and customs as a challenge, degradation, and threat to their claims and expectations, which were still oriented toward a precapitalist "moral economy." Market-determined wages and prices contradicted their nonacquisitive and noncompetitive assumptions about "just" wages and prices. When their employers, under the pressure of competition, adopted new production and sales techniques, when the division of labor advanced and small machines were adopted, when they suddenly had to work closely with unskilled helpers, when costs became more important than quality and time-consciousness grew at the expense of traditional customs, when masters and local authorities stepped up their century-old attacks on Saint Monday, and particularly when they had to change over to work in the newly built factories, journeymen often experienced this as a violation of their pride and standards—not just as unpleasant, but as morally wrong. Under new conditions old customs changed their meaning or were misunderstood. For instance, to ask for a "gift" (*Geschenk, Zeichen*) had for centuries been normal and respectable for the traveling journeyman. But the same behavior could now easily be regarded as beggaring and prosecuted as such when the young small-

overlooked that the change from a position of journeyman to master was not always a gain in terms of income, security, or opportunity. Cf. Jeschke, *Gewerberecht*, pp. 456-58, with respect to small masters whose standard of living was similar to that of poor journeymen.

town journeyman came to a large city where guild rules and customs were largely forgotten. His reaction would be disappointment and anger. Other examples could be given to illustrate the basic conflict between traditional cultures and capitalist modernization.

But on the one hand one should not overdo this argument. In the decades of extreme poverty, unemployment, hunger, and misery (particularly the 1830s to 1850s), many journeymen (especially those with a family) were probably more concerned with how to survive than with worries about the widespread violation of old cultures and life styles.[55] On the other hand, with respect to Germany, the argument needs to be supplemented and modified in two different ways.

First, the destruction of the old order was not just a loss and a threat but also an opportunity and improvement for many journeymen. Close analysis shows that the nonmarket rules of corporate origins according to which journeymen were still often placed and hired in the first part of the nineteenth century favored the interests of the masters to the disadvantage of journeymen. The same was frequently true for the rules of dismissal. Guild rules as far as they continued to exist made it difficult for journeymen to rise into masters' positions (except for the masters' sons)—even more difficult than it would have been anyway, due to economic and demographic reasons. Due to the corporate tradition the masters had legal privileges (full representation in the guilds or guildlike institutions, more rights in the community, a specific authority on the journeymen) by which they distinguished themselves from journeymen and apprentices until the 1860s. In other words, the line of distinction between master and journeyman was particularly pronounced in Germany due to the survival of corporate traditions. Increasingly, journeymen seem to have experienced the living-in system primarily as a device of control and deprivation. They opposed it and were glad to move out of the master's house as soon as they could afford it.

Other examples could be added, but the message should be clear. Elements of the old corporate order survived much longer in Germany than in France and Britain, into the midst of the industrial revolution. But

[55] This is the dominant feeling one gets from reading workers' autobiographies. Cf. W. Emmerich, ed., *Proletarische Lebensläufe* 1 (Reinbek, 1974), vol. 1. The history of strikes and particularly of strike aims would seem to support this view, although it may be conceded that the declared goals of strikes were not always identical with the more complex motives and grievances of the strikers: 76 percent of journeymen and factory worker strikes of the 1870s were concerned with improving or defending wages; 27 percent with questions of working hours; only 9 percent with other working conditions, including problems of job control and supervision; in 7 percent of the cases union rights were at stake, and in 4 percent of the cases questions of piece rates were central. For sources see note 80 below.

they remained in an unbalanced way. The master guilds survived much better than the journeymen brotherhoods, which had been deeply weakened by government policy. From the perspective of the journeymen, the restrictive elements of the old order lasted more successfully than its protective aspects did. Under changing conditions these restrictive elements became more manifest. Corporate institutions and rules, as far as they endured, became part of a social system in which elements of class played a growing role; but their functions changed. They increasingly served class-specific purposes to the advantage of the masters-employers and to the disadvantage of the journeymen-workers. Corporate remnants served to sharpen class distinctions and tensions.

Consequently, journeymen suffered from both the gradual destruction and the protracted resistance of the old order. Understandably, although they were no admirers of the emerging system of capitalism, they were no staunch defenders of the old order as it existed, either.[56]

In addition to the destruction of the old order and its protracted resistance there was a second source of journeymen's anger, distress, and frustration: the state. State and local authorities made a strong and independent contribution to the taming of traditional journeymen's customs and the destruction of the bases of journeymen's autonomies. From the late eighteenth century to the 1860s, they probably contributed more than the employers to suppressing Saint Monday, to forbidding large demonstrative funerals, feasts, and parades, to regulating journeymen's insurance schemes, to destroying or weakening their brotherhoods, and to disciplining them at work and in general. State control and supervision were of course often not very effective, and they were more intensive in Prussia than south of the Main River, Saxony being somewhere in between. But generally speaking, the state was present in the everyday life and experiences of German journeymen to an extent that would have surprised their counterparts in England and the United States, perhaps also in France.

The letters, diaries, and autobiographies of traveling journeymen express many complaints about police arbitrariness and chicanery. They make clear how burdensome it was to live under the elaborate system of passports, obligatory travel records, work licenses, and prohibitions. Traveling journeymen had to register with the local authorities and hand in their documents on arrival; they would get them back on departure

---

[56] On surviving guild regulations and traditions biased in favor of the masters: Jeschke, *Gewerberecht*, pp. 85f, 94, 133ff; Kampffmeyer, "Vom Frankfurter Zunftgesellen," pp. 83-100; H. Laufenberg, *Geschichte der Arbeiterbewegung in Hamburg-Altona und Umgebung* (Hamburg, 1911), 1:75.

only if they had behaved well. There were many frontiers in Germany and thus many occasions for checking, searching, and examining those who passed. It was an atmosphere of permanent suspicion and surveillance, particularly after the French revolution of 1830, again in the 1840s when public fear of social unrest grew, and again in the reaction period of the 1850s. When journeymen tried to settle down, they often had to fight for many years to overcome legal obstacles and bureaucratic suspicion. And they could experience a particularly harsh form of state authority if they joined a secret brotherhood, a political club, or an initiative for improving their wages and working conditions. Although government actions of this kind were by and large functional for the rise of capitalism and the interests of the employers, it would be wrong to understand these government actions as simply a result, byproduct, or instrument of the rise of capitalism. They had dynamics of their own in the German tradition of bureaucratic absolutism and "reform from above," a tradition that had never been weakened by a successful revolution from below.[57]

Similar to, but later than, domestic industrial workers, journeymen experienced the powerful impact of capitalist markets and the conflict between labor and capital. In contrast to domestic workers they experienced this conflict in both forms: as a conflict of distribution and as a very direct conflict of authority (aggravated by corporate remnants). In contrast to domestic workers they gradually ceased to be fully integrated (with their work) into a family or a household. This made it easier for them to define themselves on the basis of occupation or class and to act collectively. But many of them still owned their tools; a sizable minority would eventually work on their own and even employ workers themselves—situational elements that help to explain why many of them continued to identify themselves as members of a specific trade rather than as journeymen or even as workers in general.

Unlike most domestic workers or unskilled laborers, journeymen had special resources that made it easier for them to respond collectively to common challenges and to strive for common improvements. It is true

---

[57] There are many examples in H. Bopp, *Die Entwicklung des deutschen Handwerksgesellentums im 19. Jahrhundert* (Paderborn, 1932); E. Kloth, *Geschichte des Deutschen Buchbinderverbandes und seiner Vorläufer* (Berlin, 1910), 1:42-45; G. Beier, *Schwarze Kunst und Klassenkampf: Geschichte der Industriegewerkschaft Druck und Papier und ihrer Vorläufer seit dem Beginn der modernen Arbeiterbewegung* (Frankfurt, 1966), 1:164-65; M. Quarck, "Von der Zunft zur Arbeiterbewegung," *Kölner sozialpolitische Vierteljahresschrift* 3 (1923):82-91; E. F. Vogel, *Das Zunft- und Innungswesen beym deutschen Handwerksstande aus dem Gesichtspuncte seiner zeitgemässen Erneuerung* (Leipzig, 1848), pp. 40-45.

that their (trade-specific) brotherhoods had been partially destroyed and weakened around 1800 and again in the 1840s. But some of them continued to exist underground (particularly the masons). Others restricted themselves to insurance and social purposes, at least on the surface, and thus were tolerated by the local authorities. Journeymen of the same trade stayed in supralocal contact with one another: most journeymen still took a few years, after finishing their apprenticeship, to travel through Germany and other parts of Europe. The local brotherhoods had intensive correspondence with one another; the knowledge of trade-specific symbols and rites was handed down from generation to generation; similar qualifications and work experiences meant an additional bond. These bases of trade-specific loyalties could be mobilized under new conditions.[58]

It is not surprising that journeymen were the main supporters of the early labor movement. However, not all of them supported it to an equal extent. On the one hand, bakers, butchers, barbers, and similar crafts were underrepresented. Their work and lives had changed very little and most of them continued to be integrated into their masters' households. On the other hand, crafts that were rapidly fragmented, reduced, degraded, or destroyed by industrialization (spinners, most categories of weavers, certain leather and wooden trades) did not play a large role, either. Artisans of this type were probably too poor and too powerless and quickly lost the resources (stable common experiences, pride, communication, financial support from colleagues) that would have facilitated both protest and organization.

Rather, it is the printers and cigar makers, tailors and shoemakers, joiners, carpenters, and masons who are most frequently mentioned in the sources on early friendly societies (*Kassen*), clubs, protests, strikes, unions, and parties. These were large categories, mostly urban crafts that had great continuity, stability, and cohesion, usually guild traditions (except the cigar makers, who are a special case), and relatively good bargaining powers. These were also categories that had come into close contact with the technical-commercial changes and resultant challenges mentioned above. They usually worked in relatively large, market-oriented units (building, printing, cigar makers), or they worked in trades

---

[58] This is clearly shown by the early history of many craft unions, e.g., in the case of the printers and typesetters. Cf. W. Krahl, *Der Verband der Deutschen Buchdrucker*, vol. 1 (Berlin, 1916), esp. pp. 61ff, 81ff; Beier, *Schwarze Kunst und Klassenkampf*, pp. 173ff, passim. This connection is very clear in the case of Hamburg, where journeymen brotherhoods survived for a long time and unions rose early. CF. H. Bürger, *Die Hamburger Gewerkschaften und deren Kämpfe von 1865-1890* (Hamburg, 1899), esp. pp. 16f, 23, 30, passim.

that were increasingly challenged by merchant capitalists and competing factories (tailors, shoemakers). Some of them probably had had the experience of working in a factory for a time before returning to a craft shop. Artisans of this type usually lived outside the households of their employers. They were far advanced in the process of transformation from traditional journeyman to qualified wage worker, but they still retained much of what held the trade together traditionally and used this as a basis of protest and organization. In other respects these trades differed strongly, as did their actions and ideologies.[59]

It is also not surprising that the journeymen's actions and organizations were usually trade-specific. Whether we examine their demands, friendly societies, boycotts, and strikes in the Vormärz, their prolific actions and movements in the revolution of 1848-1849 and the early unions (printers and cigar makers in 1848-1849, and a large number of unions founded in the second part of the 1860s), or the wave of massive strikes in the late 1860s and early 1870s, we usually find that the basis was a single trade (or a small group of closely related trades, like masons and carpenters). Actions and organizations frequently stretched over different localities and reached regional and even national extension, but they usually did not unite journeymen of many different trades.

This was the traditional pattern, well known in the eighteenth century, when conflicts over customs and privileges of brotherhoods, questions of honor and dignity, work relations, wages, and lodging were usually carried out within the boundaries of the craft. But the situation had changed, as sketched above. Given the structural disparity between masters and journeymen; given the fundamental changes that tended to turn the master-journeyman relationship into one of employer and employee without providing for new and adequate mechanisms of conflict solution on either side; and given the involvement of the state that tended to define as political what, under other conditions, would not have been political at all (e.g., strikes), even rather specific demands of the journeymen easily acquired a very principled character transcending the boundaries of the craft. When carpenters claimed the use of the wood cuttings left over on the construction site where they had worked in the name of the "old

[59] Cf. H. Berndt, "Die auf Grund des Sozialistengesetzes zwischen 1881 und 1890 Ausgewiesenen aus Leipzig und Umgegend: Eine Studie zur sozialen Struktur der deutschen Arbeiterklasse und Arbeiterbewegung" (Phil. diss., Humboldt-Universität Berlin, 1972), pp. 399-419; Zwahr, "Zur Genesis," pp. 42f; R. Stadelmann and W. Fischer, Die Bildungswelt des deutschen Handwerks um 1800 (Berlin, 1955), p. 189; J. Bergmann in Die frühsozialistischen Bünde in der Geschichte der deutschen Arbeiterbewegung (Berlin, 1975), p. 147; Zwahr, Zur Konstituierung, p. 322; H.-G. Husung, Kollektiver Protest und politische Krisen in Norddeutschland zwischen Restauration und Revolution 1848 (Göttingen, 1983).

rights," they raised the issue of private property. When printers fought the installation of a mechanical press, they fought against a small indicator of a fundamental change that they could not halt by one specific victory. When masons united for boycott and strike in the 1840s or 1850s, they implicitly raised a constitutional problem. Some of them may have vaguely understood this when they saw how serious—how "systemic"—their actions were taken to be by the public authorities who quickly intervened, often with military means. In the period of transition, every specific conflict tended to become a conflict about the rules of the game.[60]

In other words, many journeymen faced problems that were difficult to understand except in a broader context. At this point religious, ideological, and theoretical explanations could enter and fulfill certain needs, especially for relatively educated journeymen.[61] These were problems not specific to single trades and usually not shared by their masters and employers. It was a constellation in which class-specific, intercraft organizations with comprehensive programs could be appealing.

Factory Workers. In a much more direct way, class-specific (instead of craft-specific) experiences occurred in the factories. This is one of the reasons why factory workers, more than any other category of workers, have received attention by contemporary observers, theoreticians like Marx, and labor historians.[62] What was so different for them?

Dependence on the market and the division of labor were not unique to factory work, although the division of labor (which tended to destroy the traditional profile of the crafts concerned) could proceed faster and further in centralized rather than decentralized systems of production. If we look at the workers, machines were not the central innovation and

---

[60] Cf. E. Todt and H. Radandt, *Zur Frühgeschichte der deutschen Gewerkschaftsbewegung 1800-1849* (Berlin, 1950); E. Todt, *Die gewerkschaftliche Betätigung in Deutschland von 1850-1859* (Berlin, 1950).

[61] On the education of masters and journeymen, cf. Stadelmann and Fischer, *Bildungswelt.*

[62] Even before 1848, public opinion tended to interpret the workers' problems as problems of factory workers. Cf. H. J. Teuteberg, *Geschichte der industriellen Mitbestimmung in Deutschland* (Tübingen, 1961), pp. 1ff; in the second third of the nineteenth century the imagination of novelists was stimulated by factory workers, not by journeymen or out-workers. Cf. O. Scholz, *Arbeiterselbstbild und Arbeiterfremdbild zur Zeit der industriellen Revolution. Ein Beitrag zur Sozialgeschichte des Arbeiters in der deutschen Erzähl- und Memoirenliteratur um die Mitte des 19. Jahrhunderts* (Berlin, 1980). Factory workers are thought to play a central role in the formation of the working class in F. Engels, "Die Lage der arbeitenden Klasse in England" (1845), and K. Marx and F. Engels, "Manifest der Kommunistischen Partei," in Marx and Engels, *Werke,* 2:225ff and 4:459ff.

basic difference, either. Certainly for the public at large the machines symbolized what was new, bad, or promising in the factory; they mobilized hopes and fears. Certainly, the application of machines (steam engines and machine tools) was decisive in economic historical terms and the most important reason for the centralization of production in factories. It is also true that many factory workers had something to do with machines. Machines often threatened and destroyed traditional forms of qualified work and were usually resented by the artisans directly concerned. But many factory workers (in fact most of them, in the 1860s and 1870s) had little to do with machines, since the installation of machines proceeded unevenly and slowly. The application of new mechanical and chemical processes frequently did bring particular hardship to the workers: noise, dust, heat, more accidents, and increasing intensity of work. However, monotonous, strictly determined, hard, and "alienated" work existed outside the machine departments as well.

Still, more than any other industrial institution, factory work promoted and symbolized the breakup of the old order because of the combination and cumulative effect of three factors: (1) Nowhere else did workers of different crafts as well as unskilled laborers work so closely together under the same roof, at the same time, and under the same system of authority. (2) In the factories (in contrast to all decentralized systems) the conflict between labor and capital was both a conflict of distribution and of authority. Moreover, it was easier to experience as such because (in contrast to the small craft shop where masters and journeymen, in spite of their basic distinctions and tensions, usually shared the same type of manual work) in the factories, mines, and the like the role of the owners, employers, and managers[63] on the one hand and the role of the workers on the other were clearly differentiated and the gap between them was thus more evident. (3) In contrast to most traditional work situations, factory work was clearly separated from the workers' home and household.[64]

The fact that different crafts and occupations worked within the same factories did not mean that the differences between them were extinguished. Nor did it mean that there was automatic communication or solidarity between them. Frequently, different categories worked side by side, in different rooms, without too much interconnection. Recent

[63] These three concepts refer to different roles at the top of an enterprise. But in the period of the industrial revolution they were usually fulfilled by the same person (or the same group of persons) who owned and directed the factory. Cf. Kocka, "Entrepreneurs," pp. 493f.

[64] This situation was, of course, not completely new. It had existed for a minority of workers for a long time (e.g., in the manufactories and mines).

research has correctly stressed the differences—among factory workers
of different skills, crafts, occupations, and functions, between the (usually
skilled) minority of workers who remained over the years and the quickly
fluctuating majority, between male and female workers, different age
groups, and different origins. We know that hierarchies based on income
and status and also in terms of power (elements of the subcontracting
system, frequent in early textile factories) existed among workers. The
situation and experiences, the rewards and risks of workers differed
within the same factory and differed even more if factories of different
size, branch, and region are compared. The factory workers were never
a homogeneous mass, and the differences between them apparently did
not decrease in the course of the nineteenth century.[65] But as a rule factory workers, in spite of these differences, shared two important experiences.

First, it was not the rule that whole families went to work in the same
factory. In fact, though most wives of workers contributed something to
the family income (as servants, washing women, part-time domestic
workers, petty traders, etc.), they usually did not do factory work.[66]
After the middle of the century child labor was quickly reduced in the
factories (though not in domestic industries), even in textiles, where
it had been widespread in the decades before.[67] To the extent that
married women and children worked in factories, they usually did not
work where their husbands and parents did—some exceptions notwithstanding.[68]

It was rare that workers spent the nights in the factories.[69] Even when

[65] Cf. Fischer, *Wirtschaft und Gesellschaft*, pp. 258-84; K. Ditt, "Technologischer
Wandel und Strukturveränderung der Fabrikarbeiterschaft in Bielefeld 1860-1914," in
Arbeiter im Industrialisierungsprozess, ed. W. Conze and U. Engelhardt (Stuttgart,
1979), pp. 237-61; R. Vetterli, *Industriearbeit, Arbeiterbewusstsein und gewerkschaftliche Organisation: Dargestellt am Beispiel der Georg-Fischer AG (1890-1930)* (Göttingen, 1978).

[66] Cf. G. Mayer, "Statistik der in bayerischen Fabriken und grösseren Gewerbebetrieben zum Besten der Arbeiter getroffenen Einrichtungen," *Zeitschrift des Königlich Bayerischen Statistischen Bureau* 7 (1875):38-157, esp. p. 137; a survey of 72,097 workers
(50,960 male; 21,137 female) in 692 Bavarian factories in the early 1870s showed that
25 percent of the female and 49 percent of the male workers were married.

[67] In the 1850s and 1860s about 10 percent of those employed in the Bielefeld textile
works were children, fourteen years old and younger. After that the proportion quickly
decreased. Cf. K. Ditt, *Industrialisierung, Arbeiterschaft und Arbeiterbewegung in
Bielefeld 1850-1914* (Dortmund, 1982), p. 107.

[68] Textile workers employed their children in early textile works, see M. Hilbert, "Kinderarbeit im Industriebezirk Glauchau," *Sächsische Heimatblätter* 9 (1963):18. But in
the early Bielefeld textile industry the employment of whole families was the exception,
see Ditt, *Industrialisierung*, pp. 107f.

[69] Again, there are exceptions in the early periods; see Thun, *Industrie*, 1:63.

they lived near their workplace, for example in factory-owned housing available only to a minority of them,[70] household and workplace were separated. Often, there was a long distance between factory and home. Factory work happened outside the context of family and household. It had to be done in rooms and furnishings that were neither owned nor shaped by the workers. It was more clearly abstracted from other dimensions of life than cottage work or work in a small master's craft shop, usually situated directly beside the living quarters. In the centralized factory or mine more than in other settings, work became a dimension by itself. The difference between work and nonwork became more systematic and pronounced. It became easier to experience work as such as well as its capitalist context, and to recognize its mechanisms, rules, and "logic." It became more likely that work relations included other dimensions of social relations, loyalties and antagonisms that would affect life outside the workplace as well.[71]

There was, certainly, a liberating element in this separation of family and household from the workplace. The private sphere was freed of the constraints inherent to hard, market-oriented work under conditions of scarcity and rules set by others. But this did not mean much when the average workday, for instance in the textile factories, lasted twelve to fourteen hours (not including breaks) and the way to and from work could easily take another two hours or more.[72] Rather it worked the other way: the separation between household and workplace probably made work less pleasant and more coercive for those who experienced the change. The large majority of domestic workers feared and avoided factory work because it was outside the family and the house, although it paid better. It was rare at the time, though it happened, for a journeyman or a maid to prefer factory work because it would free them from the hard personal discipline and restriction of their previous workplace in the

[70] An example (St. Blasien, 1809-1848) is described by Fischer, *Wirtschaft und Gesellschaft*, pp. 408-427. Of all Prussian enterprises with more than thirty employees, 1,655 offered houses, apartments, and/or dormitories to their workers in 1875. Cf. *Die Einrichtungen für die Wohlfahrt der Arbeiter der grösseren gewerblichen Anlagen im preussischen Staate* (Berlin, 1876), 1:11-32, 76-163.

[71] Cf. H. Steffens, "Arbeitstag, Arbeitszumutungen und Widerstand: Bergmännische Arbeitserfahrungen an der Saar in der zweiten Hälfte des 19. Jahrhunderts," *Archiv für Sozialgeschichte* 21 (1981):1-54, esp. p. 1 and the references in notes 2 and 3.

[72] Average daily and weekly work hours 1800-1914: K. Ditt, "Arbeitsverhältnisse und Betriebsverfassung in der deutschen Textilindustrie des 19. Jahrhunderts unter besonderer Berücksichtigung der Bielefelder Leinenindustrie," *Archiv für Sozialgeschichte* 21 (1981): 63 (in the German textile industries); Gömmel, *Wachstum*, pp. 188-95 (Nuremberg); C.-L. Holtfrerich, *Quantitative Wirtschaftsgeschichte des Ruhrkohlebergbaus im 19. Jahrhundert* (Dortmund, 1973), pp. 62ff (mining). On the whole, average work time slowly decreased after 1850-1860.

house.[73] The separation of the traditional unity of household and work-place was, by and large, experienced as a calamity. Work changed its character in this separation. As an illustration, child labor had been common and noncontroversial in domestic industrial and agricultural work; it turned into a scandal when it became work outside the household and family—factory work.[74]

Second, work in the factories was characterized by particular forms of discipline. It has been convincingly argued by recent research that factory discipline was rather imperfect in the early decades. Many loopholes existed. Coffee was boiled and distributed during working hours, and sometimes hard liquor, too. In contrast to what the shop rules said, time discipline was not always strict. Saint Monday did not disappear with the factory. Well-qualified artisans, in particular, still enjoyed great autonomy, and they were skillful and inventive in defending their small niches of customary self-determination and uncontrolled communication.[75]

Still, in contrast to most traditional forms of work, factory workers were confronted with unusually harsh measures of discipline and control. They were required to adjust to new rhythms of work and time, contrary to what they were used to. In smaller factories the authority relationship between employer and workers had a strongly personal and often patri-archical flavor, similar to the situation in the craft shops. In larger fac-

[73] See as one of many similar statements the testimony of a sewing woman who changed from domestic work to the factory in the early 1860s: Baader, *Ein steiniger Weg*, pp. 15-19. Also see J. Loreck, *Wie man früher Sozialdemokrat wurde: Das Kommunikations-verhalten in der deutschen Arbeiterbewegung und die Konzeption der sozialistischen Par-teipublizistik durch August Bebel* (Bonn–Bad Godesberg, 1977), p. 142, a working-class father advises his son to become a shoemaker because this trade would not compel him to work in a factory or to do out-work (in the 1880s). But see Bürger, *Die Hamburger Gewerkschatten*, pp. 3, 14; in the 1850s, journeymen-workers preferred factory work over work in a small shop because it offered more freedom.

[74] With references to the older literature, see W. Feldenkirchen, "Kinderarbeit im 19. Jahrhundert: Ihre wirtschaftlichen und sozialen Auswirkungen," *Zeitschrift für Unter-nehmensgeschichte* 26 (1981):1-41. The fact that in many factories, persons of both sexes worked side by side or together was regarded as a moral danger and a basis of vice. Cf. Adolf Schmidt, *Die Zukunft der arbeitenden Klassen* (Berlin, 1845), p. 25.

[75] Cf. P. Caspard, "Die Fabrik auf dem Dorf" in *Wahrnehmungsformen*, ed. Puls, pp. 105-142 (on an example in the French part of Switzerland); A. Lüdtke, "Arbeitsbeginn, Arbeitspausen, Arbeitsende: Skizzen zu Bedürfnisbefriedigung und Industriearbeit im 19. und frühen 20. Jahrhundert," in *Sozialgeschichte der Freizeit. Untersuchungen zum Wandel der Alltagskultur in Deutschland*, ed. G. Huck (Wuppertal, 1980), pp. 95-122; L. Machtan, "Zum Innenleben deutscher Fabriken im 19. Jahrhundert: Die formelle und die informelle Verfassung von Industriebetrieben, anhand von Beispielen aus dem Bereich der Textil- und Maschinenbauproduktion (1869-1891)," *Archiv für Sozialgeschichte* 21 (1981):179-236, esp. 207ff. Machtan, not fully convincingly, interprets these imperfec-tions of factory discipline as signs of workers' "resistance."

tories, of which there were many, authority relations became more impersonal and formalized.

The larger the factories, the more likely it was that written shop rules (*Fabrikordnungen*) existed. These said a great deal about the duties of workers and the penalties in case of violation, but little about their rights. Shop rules became more and more similar in the course of the 1860s and 1870s. They stressed the necessity of order and cleanliness, inside and outside the factory. They demanded obedience and respect to the foremen and other members of management. They often forbade talking during work and trespassing into other rooms. Workers were forbidden to do "unproductive" things or anything except what they were ordered to do. They could not use the tools for personal purposes. The rules provided for harsh penalties in case of damages and petty thievery; sometimes personal searches were provided for, against the protests of the workers. The factory rules appear to have been strongly influenced by bureaucratic and military models.[76]

In the context of this essay it is particularly important that these rules and controls were related to the workers as workers, not as members of a specific craft. The same was also true of most welfare plans, which were introduced in many of the larger factories in the 1860s and 1870s (health and accident insurance, pension plans, housing, and health care, particularly).[77] The personnel management of nineteenth-century factories clearly distinguished all manual workers of different skills and crafts (*Arbeiter*) from all supervisory, technical, and commercial employees (*Beamte, Angestellte*). A clear demarcation between "blue collar" and "white collar" workers developed earlier in Germany than in England and the United States, both within the factories and in the society at large, partly due to the impact of bureaucratic models that played an important role in Germany but not in the Anglo-American world. The more pronounced the "collar line," the less pronounced were skill and

---

[76] Comprehensive analysis of work rules are offered by Ditt, "Arbeitsverhältnisse" and Machtan, "Innenleben." On bureaucratic and military traditions, cf. Jürgen Kocka, *Unternehmensverwaltung und Angestelltenschaft am Beispiel Siemens 1847-1914* (Stuttgart, 1969), pp. 86-92, 115f, passim; C. Helfer, "Über militärische Einflüsse auf die industrielle Entwicklung Deutschlands," *Schmollers Jahrbuch* 83 (1963):597-609.

[77] The most comprehensive surveys of industrial welfare schemes are *Die Einrichtungen für die Wohlfahrt* and *Ergebnisse einer Erhebung über die im Bayerischen Fabriken und grösseren Gewerbebetrieben zum Besten der Arbeiter getroffenen Einrichtungen* (Munich, 1874). On the pattern and purposes of these "welfare institutions," cf. Jürgen Kocka, "Management und Angestellte im Unternehmen der Industriellen Revolution," in *Gesellschaft in der industriellen Revolution*, ed. R. Braun et al. (Cologne, 1973), 162-204, esp. 172-74; also H. Pohl, ed., *Betriebliche Sozialpolitik deutscher Unternehmen seit dem 19. Jahrhundert* (Wiesbaden, 1978) and the critical review of I. Costas in *Archiv für Sozialgeschichte* 21 (1981):756-59, esp. p. 757.

craft distinctions within the blue-collar work force in terms of managerial controls and rewards, obligations and rights, status, and perhaps expectations. The social distance between salaried employees and wage workers was very pronounced. This probably made it easier for workers of different skills and occupations to identify themselves as Arbeiter (in contrast to Angestellte—to stress what they had in common in contrast to "those above."[78]

Even if many of the early shop rules were not fully enforced, their mere existence and rigor indicated an atmosphere of high tension, possible conflict, and demand for control. We know from other sources that newcomers experienced the work discipline of the factory as a shock. Workers deeply felt and often resented managerial control and authority, which, in larger units, appeared to them concentrated in the powerful foremen and symbolized by the office. It was probably the highly skilled factory worker—usually a former journeyman, domestic worker, or little master—who resented the close controls and tight regulations the most because they contradicted his sense of autonomy. It is not surprising that questions of discipline and work rules, penalties and control, dismissals and misuse of authority played a larger role in the strikes of factory workers than in the strikes of journeymen in the 1870s (although in both types of strikes the issues of wages and length of workday were paramount).[79]

Factory workers resembled the ideal-type of the wage worker more than any other category of workers. Eventually, at the end of the nineteenth and in the twentieth century, (skilled) factory workers would be the mainstay of the labor movement. But in the period investigated here they were not. We do not hear much of factory workers' strikes in the Vormärz. In the revolution of 1848-1849 they were certainly much more reluctant to join the protesting masses than were the journeymen and the small masters; they played a rather conservative role. They were underrepresented in the clubs, unions, and working-class parties of the 1860s and 1870s. And in the strikes of the 1870s, even if we adopt a very broad concept of "factory worker," they were responsible only for about 36 per-

[78] Cf. Jürgen Kocka, "Capitalism and Bureaucracy in German Industrialization before 1914," *Economic History Review*, 2d ser., vol. 33, no. 3 (August 1981):461-68 (on the relative sharpness of the "collar line" in Germany, in comparative perspective).

[79] On migration, fluctuation, and the experience of factory discipline, see the contributions in *Arbeiter im Industrialisierungsprozess*, ed. Conze and Engelhardt, pp. 94-119, 228-363, 494-512. Much can be found in early autobiographies of workers. Cf. K. Fischer, *Denkwürdigkeiten und Erinnerungen eines Arbeiters*, 2 vols. (Leipzig, 1903-1904); Machtan, "Innenleben." A preliminary analysis of about 740 strikes in the 1870s shows that 15 percent of factory workers' strikes but only 8 percent of journeymen's strikes were concerned with questions of discipline and authority, work rules, and the like (for sources of this data, see note 80).

cent of the strikes (journeymen: 41 percent; cigar makers: 7 percent; domestic workers, mixed groups, unknown cases: 16 percent), despite the fact that in the industrial sector at large they already outnumbered the journeymen.[80] Why was this?

In the first half of the century their numbers were small. In 1848-1849, conservative options by lower-class groups were not completely unusual and were sometimes a way for them to express their rejection of liberal middle-class values. Through the entire period most factory workers had a better and more regular income (and more security) than most domestic workers and journeymen. Factory workers were also often faced with strong managerial controls; factory-owned housing and factory-based insurance plans increased the risks of striking for them. The proportion of married persons was larger among factory workers than among journeymen, and consequently factory workers were less mobile: this reduced their power and readiness to strike in a period when unions hardly existed. And when they struck their chance of succeeding was remarkably lower than in strikes of journeymen.[81]

Finally and perhaps most important, although journeymen could use their specific craft tradition and the resulting cohesion as a resource for collective action, the workers of a factory did not have such common traditions. They usually belonged to different crafts and many of them had no craft at all. They needed new bases of solidarity, which took time to develop. It is true that most skilled factory workers of the time were recruited from the crafts—from the groups of journeymen, masters, and qualified domestic workers. These did play a role in the emerging labor movement together with the journeymen; the distinction between jour-

[80] This is based on a rather exhaustive tabulation of 1,150 strikes in the German Reich, 1871-1878, collected by Dr. Lothar Machtan (Bremen, 1870-1875) and Dr. Dietrich Milles (Konstanz, 1876-1878) in a semistandardized form. I am grateful to both authors for having made available their data to me before publication. Cf. D. Milles, "Tabellarische Übersicht der Streiks und Aussperrungen im Deutschen Reich von Januar 1876 bis Dezember 1882" (ms., Konstanz, 1980); L. Machtan, *Streiks und Aussperrungen im deutschen Kaiserreich 1871-1875: Eine sozialgeschichtliche Dokumentation* (Berlin, forthcoming); L. Machtan, *Streiks im frühen deutschen Kaiserreich* (Frankfurt, 1983). On the basis of the very imperfect figures of Todt and Radandt, *Zur Frühgeschichte* (at present, the best we have for up to the 1850s), E. Dittrich has summarized the evidence for the Vormärz: Of thirty-five categorized strikes, 26 occurred in Handwerk and 7 in mining and manufacturing. Cf. E. Dittrich, *Arbeiterbewegung und Arbeiterbildung im 19. Jahrhundert* (Bensheim, 1980), pp. 116, 118; p. 125 on the strikes of 1848.

[81] In the 1870s, 43 percent of journeymen strikes and 23 percent of factory worker strikes were fully successful in terms of the aims of the strikers. By the same standard, 23 percent of the journeymen strikes and 52 percent of the factory worker strikes were outright failures. More than 40 percent of the journeymen strikes, but only 30 percent of the factory worker strikes had support from some sort of organization, especially (local) unions. See note 80 for sources.

neymen and skilled factory workers was fluid in any case, because both groups had been apprenticed in the same way and many moved back and forth between craft shop and factory.[82] Most of the unskilled, however, came from agricultural backgrounds, cottage workers' families, and the urban poor. They had great endurance, small expectations, and no tradition of collective action to build on. For them the factory was unpleasant in many ways but certainly not an experience of degradation or loss of autonomy. Compared to where they had been previously, the factory often meant progress for them. Many maintained close affiliations with their rural background, moving back during part of the year or expecting to return after some years of factory work. Unskilled workers were also easy to replace; their bargaining power was thus extremely weak. For all these reasons, it was difficult to draw them into sustained common action and organization. Although artisans dominated in the machine-producing factories and metalworks in general, they were outnumbered by unskilled or semiskilled persons from the countryside in other branches—in most textile factories (where the majority of workers were women) in the foundry works, in stone, clay, and cement production, and the like.[83]

IV. *The Limited Emergence of a Class*

In the preceding sections some of the deep differences between various groups of workers have been discussed. Work situations and work experiences varied greatly. Workers differed by occupation and skill, by social and regional origin, by sex, age, and family status, by income and life style, and by group-specific traditions and attitudes. Different categories of workers expressed different grievances and hopes and followed different patterns of protest and organization. One could easily continue depicting how lacking in homogeneity the emerging working class was by comparing men and women, Catholics and Protestants, and regional and local specificities. In view of these tremendous distinctions among different workers, is it at all meaningful to speak of an emerging working class in these decades?

It is true that in the course of the first two-thirds of the nineteenth century, wage work emerged as the dominant form of manual work as

[82] Cf. G. Adelmann, "Die berufliche Aus- und Weiterbildung in der deutschen Wirtschaft 1871-1918," in *Berufliche Aus- und Weiterbildung in der deutschen Wirtschaft seit dem 19. Jahrhundert*, ed. H. Pohl (Wiesbaden, 1979), pp. 9-52.

[83] Cf. Fischer, *Wirtschaft und Gesellschaft*, pp. 262ff; K. Ditt, "Technologischer Wandel" (a comparison of textiles and metalwork); also the good introduction in *Arbeiter in Deutschland*, ed. Langewiesche and Schönhoven, pp. 9-20.

far as it was done in dependence on others. Consequently an increasing number of workers shared the basic and most "objective" criterion defining class position. The emergence of wage work accelerated in the periods of legal reform around 1810 and in the 1860s. It proceeded in a more gradual way with the advancing integration of the markets, and sped up with the breakthrough of the factory system from the 1840s to the 1870s. But on the one hand wage work remained frequently embedded in different types of non-wage-work relations, as in the case of servants, many agricultural workers, most domestic industrial workers, and a minority of journeymen. And on the other hand, wage work may have been a rather abstract shared characteristic, not very important for the experiences, self-identification, consciousness, aims, collective actions, and organizations of workers if compared with those characteristics in which they differed. Even if one concedes that there emerged, to a certain extent, a working class in the sense of a multitude of persons sharing a common ("objective") class position, did there also emerge a working class in the sense of a social class with shared identities and perhaps even with the propensity for collective action and organization? This occurred to a certain extent, but within narrow limits. It is difficult, if not impossible, to know what large groups of workers really felt and thought. But there are indirect indicators, one of which is the language of class.

Language. In the early years of the nineteenth century, the concept of "Arbeiter" (worker) was not very prominent in the social and political language, in contrast to general categories like *Volk* (people) and in contrast to occupational corporate categories (like masons or *Handwerker*).[84] Arbeiter was used as a residual category for those doing unskilled manual work without having a qualified occupation ("hands"), and sometimes for both skilled and unskilled workers in the post-corporate systems of production, the putting-out system and the early factories (*Fabrikarbeiter*). Yet the concept was also used as a very broad descriptive category, usually in phrases like "arbeitende Klassen" or "handarbeitende Klassen," including journeymen and masters, domestic and factory workers, servants, agricultural workers, and sometimes even peasants. These meanings continued to exist through the nineteenth century in addition to other nuances not mentioned here. Semantic changes are rarely clear-

---

[84] Cf. W. Conze, "Arbeiter," in *Geschichtliche Grundbegriffe: Historisches Lexikon zur politischsozialen Sprache in Deutschland* (Stuttgart, 1972), 1:216-42, which contains much evidence for this section. See further evidence in Kocka, *Lohnarbeit*, pp. 130-36; W. Conze, "Vom 'Pöbel' zum 'Proletariat': Sozialgeschichtliche Voraussetzungen für den Sozialismus in Deutschland" (1954), repr. in H.-W. Wehler, ed., *Moderne deutsche Sozialgeschichte*, 5th ed. (1976; repr. Königstein, 1981), pp. 111-36, esp. 113ff.

cut. But from the 1830s onward the concept underwent two significant changes.

In some senses the concept became more comprehensive: it tended to include journeymen and workers of all different trades and skills (but rarely servants) and cut across traditional lines of occupational and corporate distinctions. In other ways it became more exclusive: it tended to exclude those who employed others and, somewhat later and not without ambiguity, all those who were self-employed masters and peasants. This process occurred in the context of politics. The redefined concept was used both from the outside as a tool of categorization by the middle class and as a means of self-identification by different workers.

In the 1830s and particularly in the 1840s, with their crowds, riots, and strikes, the "soziale Frage" (social question) was hotly debated by an alarmed public, and it was increasingly identified with the "Arbeiterfrage," the workers' question. Middle-class writers with very different political positions identified the workers, the "workers' estate" (*Arbeiterstand*), or the "working class" (*Arbeiterklasse*) as a threat or a challenge to the system and in this context they were of course not as interested in occupational distinctions as in the potential or actual fronts of conflict. The socialist and particularly the Marxist class theory was just one variation of a generally dichotomous view of society that was widespread in the 1840s. In the same period (1840s and 1850s) and in the same context the concept of "Arbeiterbewegung" (labor movement) emerged, first usually expressed in the plural (Arbeiterbewegungen, or labor movements).

About the same time—perhaps a bit later—the term Arbeiter slowly began to be used by journeymen and different types of workers as a means of self-categorization. In using the word they tried to stress what they had in common across occupational and corporate distinctions, in contrast to others—employers, capitalists, and bureaucrats. This occurred first in the radical, socialist, and communist clubs formed by wandering German journeymen and political émigrés, workers, and intellectuals in Zurich, Bern, Paris, Brussels, and London, in the 1830s and 1840s.

In 1848-1849, Arbeiter served as an emphatic tool of self-identification for politically active journeymen and other workers. Journeymen book printers formed one of the two first nationwide unions—on a craft basis, of course. But while still doubtful to what extent they should accept close cooperation with the employers, they called themselves "the most intelligent part of the working class," which was thought to be oppressed by capitalists and which was supposed to become the core and the strength of human society. When journeymen from different trades walked out of the master-dominated Handwerk convention of Frankfurt in 1848, they started to convene by themselves and adopted the name Allgemeiner Deutscher Arbeiterkongress (General German Workers' Congress). Later they joined the Berlin-centered Arbeiterverbrüderung, a partly radical, partly socialist, largely social-democratic organization recruiting workers of different trades and skills and representing their interests in conflict and cooperation with "Arbeitgebern oder Meistern" (employers or masters). "When the journeymen call themselves workers, they misunderstand their rights and degrade themselves," said the representative of a Berlin masters' guild in 1848. But for those journeymen and workers who called themselves Arbeiter, the concept had lost its traditional degrading connotation. Rather it had gained an emphatic anticorporatist and antiparticularistic connotation that expressed generalized claims for equality and emancipation and adapted these middle-class ideas to working-class needs.

In contrast to the word "proletarian," which most workers did not like to use for self-identification, the concepts Arbeiter and Arbeiterklasse, were clearly established by the 1860s and 1870s as positive terms in the rhetoric of the emerging labor movement. It is true that there remained some uncertainty whether these terms could include the self-employed small masters, but the tendency was to exclude them. Although the term Arbeiter narrowed down to Lohnarbeiter (wage worker), the term Handwerker also became more exclusive though in the opposite direction: increasingly, it was reserved for the self-employed Handwerksmeister, whether they employed others or not. It is interesting that the corresponding English concepts changed the other way: "artisan" and "craftsman" increasingly meant skilled workers who earned their wages by working for others.

Key concepts of the social and political language reflect perceptions of reality and the underlying experiences dominant among those who use them, often in group- or class-specific ways. From the 1830s to the 1870s was the crucial period in which a redefinition of the terms Arbeiter and Handwerker took place, reflecting a growing awareness of class, though in slightly different ways among different groups and with different values attached to what they called Arbeiter.

Protest, Mobility, Marriage. There are many other indirect ways to investigate whether, to what extent, and in which ways class formation proceeded. In the study of social protest, for example, it has been shown that among cases of violent protest those having something to do with labor relations became more frequent while food riots and some other non-work-related protests became less frequent, particularly after 1850.

More specifically, non-work-related protests were replaced in part by early industrial protests (machine breaking, protests against merchant-capitalists, and reactions to extreme scarcity and exploitation, particularly in the 1840s) and later on by boycotts and strikes for better pay and improved working conditions and against employers' control and other work-related grievances. It has also been shown that the aggregate number of violent collective protests reached high points around 1830 and in the 1840s (particularly 1848). After this they remained at a moderate level for the rest of the century in absolute numbers and clearly declined per capita. At the same time the number of strikes, mostly nonviolent, increased, reaching early peaks in the revolution of 1848, in the depression of 1857, and, after legalization, in 1869-1873.[85]

Both the changing pattern of violent protests and the gradual and limited replacement of violent protests by mostly nonviolent strikes implied that the protesting groups gradually became more class-specific in composition. Although lower-class and poor people were of course heavily overrepresented in food riots and the like, the social composition of crowds did not follow class lines. The protesting groups in Luddist and similar early industrial protests were somewhat more specific and more defined by their position in the system of production. But frequently masters and journeymen were on the same side (against factories, merchants, stores, etc.), whole families often participated, persons from other lower-class groups frequently joined, and the protest forms resembled those of more traditional crowd actions. In contrast, participants in strikes, which became so frequent in the 1860s and 1870s, were more homogeneous in terms of class position. They were workers of different kinds and directed actions against members of another class, usually capitalist employers.[86]

A comparison of journeymen strikes of the late eighteenth century and strikes by journeymen and factory workers in the 1870s points in the same direction. On the one hand, cooperation of journeymen/workers

[85] Cf. R. Tilly, "Popular Disorders in Nineteenth-Century Germany: A Preliminary Survey," *Journal of Social History* 4 (1970):1-41; Tilly et al., *The Rebellious Century*, pp. 191-238 (on Germany, by R. Tilly); R. Tilly, *Kapital, Staat und sozialer Protest in der deutschen Industrialisierung* (Göttingen, 1980), pp. 143-96.

[86] Needless to say, this was only the general trend; there were many exceptions and much coexistence and overlapping of different types of protest throughout the century. On the history of strikes: H. Volkmann, "Modernisierung des Arbeitskampfs? Zum Formwandel von Streik und Aussperrung in Deutschland 1864-1975," in *Probleme der Modernisierung*, ed. Kaelble et al., pp. 110-70; K. Tenfelde and H. Volkmann, eds., *Streik. Zur Geschichte des Arbeitskampfes in Deutschland während der Industrialisierung* (Munich, 1981). In general, see D. Geary, *European Labour Protest 1848-1939* (London, 1981).

across skill and trade lines slightly increased. Only in 2 percent of the cases had journeymen of different crafts struck together in the eighteenth century; by the 1870s, however, this had risen to 10 percent (20 percent of the factory workers' and 6 percent of the journeymen's strikes). In the eighteenth century support for strikers from other crafts is documented in 13 percent of the cases; in the 1870s, every third strike was supported by one or several labor organizations, most of which were affiliated or had some connection with either the Allgemeiner Deutscher Arbeiterverein (ADAV), the Sozial demokratische Arbeiterpartei (SDAP), or the First International—labor organizations with an intercraft basis (discussed below). On the other hand, although at least 16 percent of the eighteenth-century journeymen strikes had been supported by self-employed masters and their organizations, support for strikers by employers had dramatically declined by the 1870s to less than 1 percent. This is understandable, since the strikes of the 1870s concentrated much more exclusively than those of the eighteenth century on issues that were obviously disputed by those who employed and those who were employed—conflicts of distribution (wages, hours) and, less important, conflicts of authority. In contrast, issues of honor, life style, and guild privileges, with respect to which journeymen and masters could share some interests and opinions, had lost their previous predominance.

Although the strikes in the 1870s still displayed a very high (though declining) degree of fragmentation along craft lines, they were clearly structured by the distinction between employers and workers, unlike before 1800. Particularly in this respect, the changing pattern of strikes indicated the advancing formation of class.[87]

Slowly advancing class formation is indicated by recent studies on social mobility and marriage patterns as well. It has been shown that in Leipzig and several Westphalian localities the interconnections among different groups of workers (skilled, unskilled, industrial, domestic, agricultural), measured by intergenerational social mobility, increased over time while the distinction between workers and non-workers continued to be a major barrier for intergenerational mobility. It has also been shown that cases of intermarriage between different working-class groups became more frequent and that marriages across the class line did not. Of course, these were only small trends; fragmentation by industry, trade, or skill was still very visible within the emerging working class and there continued to be occupational exchange and intermarriage between

---

[87] For a more detailed comparison see Kocka, "Craft Traditions."

workers' and nonworkers' families. But mobility and marriage patterns were increasingly structured along class lines.[88]

What did this mean for the spread of common experiences and perhaps common attitudes within the emerging working class, and for its separation from other social groups and classes? Do we find decreasing fragmentation between different types of workers and deepening divisions along class lines if we study housing patterns, health records and life expectancy, cultures and life style, the structure of the educational system, leisure, or the composition of voluntary associations? In the present state of research it is difficult to answer these questions.

Organizations and Politics: The Early Years and the Rise of the Unions. More is known, however, about labor organizations and politics. And indeed, the slow and limited formation of a working class is indicated by the history of the early labor movement, as well. During the Vormärz one can distinguish three types of organizations that were roots of the German labor movement.

First, there were hundreds of usually craft-specific (sometimes factory-based) local friendly societies with varying names (such as Unterstützungskassen, Unterstützungsvereine, Bruderschaften, Buchdruckerverein "Typographia"). Among them we find the surviving but weakened journeymen brotherhoods. Their main tasks, because of which they were tolerated and even encouraged by the local authorities and the laws (in Prussia of 1845, 1849, 1854), were health and accident insurance, financial help in the case of death, support for wandering journeymen (particularly the Viaticum).[89] The more the old corporate institutions were eroded, the greater need there was for alternative mechanisms to take care of those protective tasks that state authorities were too weak to assume. Frequently these friendly societies were closely supervised by

---

[88] I have summarized the evidence in: "The Study of Social Mobility," Jürgen Kocka, "Family and Class Formation: Intergenerational Mobility and Marriage Patterns in Nineteenth-Century Westphalian Towns," *Journal of Social History* 12 (1983):412-33. On the role of the family and of shared experiences in this process of limited class formation see Kocka, *Lohnarbeit*, pp. 137-53 (with additional references). A very well integrated collection of interesting essays on Hamburg workers is A. Herzig et al., eds., *Arbeiter in Hamburg* (Hamburg, 1983).

[89] Payments to departing journeymen were a disguised form of unemployment benefits, which could be used for controlling the labor market of the specific craft, particularly when organized on a supralocal level. This was attempted by some crafts (e.g., printers) in 1848-1849, and discussed even earlier. Journeymen and masters/employers often disagreed about which side should control and administer the viaticum. Cf. F. Zahn, "Die Organisation der Prinzipale und Gehülfen im deutschen Buchdruckgewerbe," in *Arbeitseinstellungen und Fortbildung des Arbeitsvertrags*, ed. L. Brentano (Leipzig, 1890), pp. 337, 341, 344-45, 364-65, 369-71, 394-97.

masters, employers, and/or local authorities, but usually the journeymen and workers sought as much self-control as possible. The question of who should control and administer the insurance schemes was highly controversial and a subject of ongoing conflict. Printers and cigar makers played a leading role. In addition to being institutions of insurance and mutual self-help, these friendly societies usually functioned as social clubs and educative institutions whose programs and discussions might deal with general social and political questions as well, sometimes with a radical or socialist flavor, particularly in the 1840s. Some of them resembled local unions by representing their members' economic and social interests to employers and authorities. But the repressive administrative practices, reenforced by an all-German decree in 1834, set very clear limits to these activities.[90]

Before the revolution of 1848-1849 thousands of journeymen and workers were involved in a second type of organization, general artisans' clubs (*Handwerkervereine*) and workers' education societies (*Arbeiterbildungsvereine*). These were neither craft-specific nor reserved for workers, but usually open to other citizens as well, particularly to masters, intellectuals, professionals, and reform-minded citizens in general. Education was their main purpose, particularly general education (*Bildung*). They were influenced by the numerous liberal and democratic middle-class reading societies, which had grown out of the eighteenth-century Enlightenment tradition. They were fully in tune with the contemporary stress on voluntary associations that were thought to take the place of the corporate organizations slowly fading away. They also expressed the liberal belief in education as the main instrument of self-help and social progress. For the most part they were founded by middle-class reformers from the 1820s onward. Very few of them were creations of workers themselves, like the radical Mannheim club, which was dissolved by the

---

[90] Cf. Beier, *Schwarze Kunst*, pp. 199-200, 296 (on printers' clubs in different cities, esp. Leipzig, in the 1840s); Todt and Radandt, *Zur Frühgeschichte*; Kloth, *Geschichte des Deutschen Buchbinderverbandes*, 1:87f, 115f, 133ff (on friendly societies of book binders); D. Dowe, "Legale Interessenvertretung und Streik: Der Arbeitskampf in den Tuchfabriken des Kreises Lennep (Bergisches Land) 1850" in *Streik*, ed. Tenfelde and Volkmann, p. 40f; Geary, *European Labour Protest*, pp. 42f; G. Plumpe, "Die Württembergische Eisenindustrie im 19. Jahrhundert" (diss., Marburg, 1979), pp. 71f (on friendly societies in ironworks from the 1820s on); B. Miller, *Die deutsche Arbeiterbewegung* (Leipzig, 1863), pp. 16-20; Krahl, *Der Verband*, 1:162f, 172ff, 255f, 259f, 293f, 329, 381f (on printers); Teuteberg, *Mitbestimmung*, pp. 115-200; W. Reininghaus, "Die Gesellenladen und Unterstützungskassen der Fabrikarbeiter bis 1870 in der Grafschaft Detmold," *Der Märker* 29 (1980):46-55; on friendly societies and health insurance, U. Frevert, *Krankheit als politisches Problem 1770-1880: Soziale Unterschichten in Preussen zwischen medizinischer Polizei und staatlicher Sozialversicherung* (Göttingen, 1984), ch. 4.

authorities in 1847. In addition to emphasizing education, they fulfilled important social functions and sometimes adopted insurance schemes. Among these clubs and societies there was great variation, from antisocialist bulwarks controlled by the middle class to radical and socialist strongholds that served as "schools for revolutionaries" (Stephan Born), like the clubs in Berlin and Hamburg. Intellectuals from the Hegelian left, democratic leaders like Gustav von Struve and Friedrich Hecker in Mannheim, and socialists of different types (e.g., in Cologne) used some of these clubs as long as they were not forbidden, as platforms. In the 1840s a radicalization of these clubs took place, frequently against the will of their sponsors. Stephan Born, Wilhelm Liebknecht, and later on August Bebel and other labor leaders were exposed to early politicizing influences in such associations.[91]

Under the more liberal laws of France, Switzerland, England, and Belgium, a third kind of association, of wandering German journeymen, workers, and intellectual émigrés, emerged in the 1830s and 1840s. These were neither craft-specific nor strictly working class, but socialist and communist in different ways. Karl Marx and Friedrich Engels were leading members of the Communist League, based in Paris, Zurich, and London. It developed in 1847 out of a previous organization, the Bund der Gerechten, founded in 1836, whose precursors reached back at least to 1832. These clubs were small, with a few hundred members altogether at any point in the 1840s. They were influenced by the political debates in the more advanced western European countries. They exerted ideological influence on artisans' and workers' clubs within Germany, secretly first and without disguise in 1848-1849.[92]

[91] Cf. K. Tenfelde, "Lesegesellschaften und Arbeiterbildungsvereine," in *Lesegesellschaften und bürgerliche Emanzipation: Ein europäischer Vergleich*, ed. O. Dann (Munich, 1981):253-74; K. Birker, *Die deutschen Arbeiterbildungsvereine 1840-1870* (Berlin, 1973); H.-J. Ruckhäberle, "Bildung und Organisation: Zur Kultur der Handwerker und Arbeiter 1830-1914," *Internationales Archiv für Sozialgeschichte der deutschen Literatur* 3 (1978):191-207; Todt and Radandt, *Zur Frühgeschichte*, pp. 81ff; on middle-class reformers: J. Reulecke, *Der Centralverein für das Wohl der arbeitenden Klassen in Preussen in der Frühindustrialisierung* (Wuppertal, 1883).

[92] W. Schieder, *Anfänge der deutschen Arbeiterbewegung: Die Auslandsvereine im Jahrzehnt nach der Juli Revolution von 1830* (Stuttgart, 1963); E. Schraepler, *Handwerkerbünde und Arbeitervereine 1830-1853: Die politische Tätigkeit deutscher Sozialisten von Wilhelm Weitling bis Karl Marx* (Berlin, 1972); W. Kowalski, *Vorgeschichte und Entstehung des Bundes der Gerechten* (Berlin, 1962); B. Andreas, *Die Gründungsdokumente des Bundes der Kommunisten* (Hamburg, 1969); W. Blumenberg, "Zur Geschichte des Bundes der Kommunisten," *International Review of Social History* 9 (1964):81-122; *Der Bund der Kommunisten: Dokumente und Materialien I (1836-1849)* (Berlin, 1970); O. Büsch and H. Herzfeld, eds., *Die frühsozialistischen Bünde in der Geschichte der deutschen Arbeiterbewegung: Vom "Bund der Gerechten" zum "Bund der Kommunisten" 1836-1846* (Berlin, 1975); W. Schieder, "Bund der Kommunisten," in

The distinctions among these three types of organizations (particularly between the first two) were imprecise in reality. There were many contacts between them. Young, highly mobile journeymen-workers predominated among the membership of all three.

Of course, only a small minority of journeymen was at all politically conscious and active. And only a minority of this minority found socialist and communist ideas attractive. They were appealing because they seemed to confirm some of their basic precapitalistic ideals (mutuality instead of competitive individualism, just distribution of common goods instead of market mechanisms, protection instead of risks, moral economy instead of a sharp disjunction between morals and economic behavior) and to combine them with revolutionary ideals of equality and emancipation, and claims for citizenship and human rights. Socialism rejected much of the new and emerging capitalist order without leading back to the old one with all its repressive restraints and unpleasant inequalities. It was this mixture of backward-looking and forward-looking elements that made different variants of socialism attractive to the journeymen, who suffered both from the pressures of the emerging new capitalist system and from the resistant remnants of the old corporate one.[93] In some ways, religious ideas could serve similar functions, as in Wilhelm Weitling's religious socialism around 1840 and in the Catholic Kolping societies from 1845 on.[94]

But the majority of the politically active journeymen as well as most of the workers' clubs and artisans' associations were part of the left-liberal, democratic, or radical movements of the 1830s and 1840s, and most of them, at the same time, would have welcomed the restoration of some elements of the old corporate order at the cost of the emerging capitalist system. A clear separation between radical-democratic and socialist politics did not occur before 1848. Nor was there as yet a clear organizational separation along class lines.[95]

Sowjetsystem und demokratische Gesellschaft, ed. C. D. Kernig (Freiburg, 1966), 1:900-909; D. Dowe, "Der Bund der Kommunisten in der Rheinprovinz nach der Revolution von 1848/49," *Rheinische Vierteljahrsblätter* 34 (1970):267-97.

[93] On this affinity between precapitalist values under challenge and early Marxism see Kocka, "Craft Traditions." Also see E. Nolte, *Marxismus und Industrielle Revolution* (Stuttgart, 1983).

[94] As to the Kolping-Vereine: J. Kracht, "Adolph Kolping und die Gründung der ersten Gesellenvereine in Westfalen," in *Studia Westfalica: Beiträge zur Kirchengeschichte und religiösen Volkskunde Westfalens*, ed. M. Bierbaum (Münster, 1973), pp. 195-213. On Weitling see Dowe, *Biblographie*, pp. 213-14.

[95] Cf. W. Koeppen, *Die Anfänge der Arbeiter- und Gesellenbewegung in Franken (1830-1852)* (Erlangen, 1935), pp. 18-38; Ehmer, "Rote Fahnen," pp. 169ff (on Vienna); H. Bock, "Bürgerlicher Liberalismus und revolutionäre Demokratie: Zur Dialektik der sozialen und nationalen Frage in den deutschen Klassenkämpfen 1831-1834," *Jahrbuch*

Such separation proceeded in 1848-1849. The revolution was a decisive step toward an independent labor movement. When government repression was suddenly removed and when, in broad segments of society the general climate abruptly changed from restrained anger and apathy to enthusiastic hopes and far-reaching expectations, there surfaced demands and protests, loyalties, alliances, and lines of division that had been hidden or mere potentials previously. It is true that the mass movements of the revolution, from the victorious street fights in March 1848 to the desperate civil war trying in vain to defend the national assembly and constitution against the forces of reaction in the spring of 1849, were not class-specific. Journeymen and workers of different kinds fought on the barricades and in the popular battalions together with self-employed artisans, students, and members of other social groups, while peasants, small landholders, and agricultural laborers rioted in the countryside (only in the first months of the revolution). But three developments indicated that the process of class formation had advanced.

First, numerous strikes, particularly in the large cities, brought to the surface and reenforced the tension between the interests of journeymen and workers on one side and masters and employers on the other. Unions, usually craft-specific, emerged, partly anew, partly from earlier friendly societies. Communication beyond the local level quickly intensified; regional conventions were held and federations formed. Two crafts founded nationwide unions: the book printers and the cigar makers. Other trades would have followed soon. Corporate traditions did continue to play an important role: the printers in particular were not quite certain what direction to take, toward a union of journeymen or a democratized guild, organizing journeymen and masters on the basis of parity. Nor was the divide between journeymen and masters already completed in the other trades. But strikes and unionization tended to sharpen the class line within each trade, despite the fact that opposition to machines, the free enterprise system, and noncorporate practices in general could still unite masters and journeymen in many cases.[96]

---

für Geschichte 13 (1975):109-151; O. Büsch and W. Grab, eds., *Die demokratische Bewegung in Mitteleuropa im ausgehenden 18. und frühen 19. Jahrhundert* (Berlin, 1981); D. Fricke, *Deutsche Demokraten 1830-1945: Die nicht-proletarischen demokratischen Kräfte in der deutschen Geschichte* (Cologne, 1981); H. J. Rupieper, "Die Sozialstruktur demokratischer Vereine im Königreich Sachsen 1848-55," *Jahrbuch des Instituts für Deutsche Geschichte* 7 (1978):460ff.

[96] Cf. Beier, *Schwarze Kunst*, on the printers; on the cigar makers: W. Frisch, *Die Organisationsbestrebungen der Arbeiter in der deutschen Tabakindustrie* (Leipzig, 1905); Schröder, *Arbeitergeschichte*, pp. 237-253; Todt and Radandt, *Zur Frühge-*

Second, in July 1848 a general convention of masters and journeymen from different crafts met in Frankfurt in order to oppose the free enterprise system and to propose the outlines of a semicorporate economic order. But the convention quickly split along class lines. The journeymen, who were in the minority, walked out because they felt discriminated against—not given equal rights in the debates and not treated as equal partners—by the masters. Legally and in terms of their self-understanding the masters were different from and superior to the journeymen, due to the unbalanced corporate tradition that had survived in Germany. The tensions resulting from this tradition contributed more to this early split along class lines than anything else. The masters continued the convention and sent to the National Assembly an anticapitalist resolution that advocated the resurrection of a modified corporate order under government protection. The journeymen started a convention on their own, which they called the General Workers' Congress. Their debates reflected a mixture of radical political demands, corporate sympathies, socialist perspectives, and cooperative plans. Later they joined the Allgemeine Arbeiterverbrüderung.[97]

The Allgemeine Arbeiterverbrüderung (General Workers' Brotherhood), the third evidence of advancing working-class formation, was founded in Berlin in August 1848 and consequently was run from Leipzig. It was a flexible federation of different workers' and artisans' clubs, unions, and ad hoc initiatives. Although it did not strictly exclude the small masters, its quick rise reflected and reenforced the growing awareness of workers from different trades and skills that they had enough in common in order to form a comprehensive organization apart from the bourgeoisie and other non-working-class groups. The federation did not break all ties to the democratic and left-liberal groups, but it did develop

schichte; Eduard Bernstein, *Die Geschichte der Berliner Arbeiter-Bewegung: Ein Kapitel zur Geschichte der deutschen Sozialdemokratie*, 3 vols. (Berlin, 1907-1910), 109ff; Dowe, *Aktion*, pp. 130ff; E. Dittrich, *Arbeiterbewegung und Arbeiterbildung im 19. Jahrhundert* (Bensheim, 1980), pp. 126ff.

[97] D. Dowe and T. Offermann, eds., *Deutsche Handwerker- und Arbeiterkongresse 1848-1852: Protokolle und Materialien* (Berlin/Bonn, 1983). Cf. P. H. Noyes, *Organization and Revolution: Working-Class Associations in the German Revolutions of 1848-1849* (Princeton, 1966), pp. 163ff; Barrington Moore, Jr., *Injustice: The Social Bases of Obedience and Revolt* (London, 1978), pp. 144ff; W. E. Biermann, *Karl Georg Winkelblech (Karl Marlo): Sein Leben und sein Werk*, 2 vols. (Leipzig, 1909); T. S. Hamerow, *Restoration, Revolution, Reaction: Economics and Politics in Germany, 1815-1871* (Princeton, 1958), pp. 145-46. C. Lipp, "Württembergische Handwerker und Handwerkervereine im Vormärz und der Revolution 1848/49," *Handwerker*, ed. U. Engelhardt, pp. 347-80; M. Simon, *Handwerk in Krise und Umbruch: Wirtschaftliche Forderungen und sozialpolitische Vorstellungen der Handwerksmeister im Revolutionsjahr 1848/49* (Cologne, 1983).

a political identity of its own. This combined self-help in the tradition of the friendly societies and an emphasis on education with the aim of both fundamental social and economic reform from a socialist cooperative perspective and the struggle for democratic or left-liberal constitutional change, if necessary by revolutionary means. Adhering to these goals, the Arbeiterverbrüderung saw itself increasingly deprived of its middle-class allies who were less interested in or hostile to far-reaching anticapitalist social reforms and tended to be more modest in the constitutional debate (with the exception of some radical democrats). The Arbeiterverbrüderung also worked with unions and supported strikes. It absorbed ideological influences from different sides, Marxist and other communist inputs among them. Led by the typesetter Stephan Born, a pragmatic socialist, it became the first workers' mass movement in Germany, with about 170 locals and nearly 15,000 members in 1849 and about 18,000 members in 1850.[98]

The rise of an independent workers' movement on the left was one of several factors explaining the defeat of the revolution. Confronted with this challenge from below, large segments of the middle class found it necessary to scale down their opposition to the authoritarian bureaucracy and its semifeudal basis.[99] The defeat of the revolution and the triumph of reaction sharply interrupted the rise of the not yet consolidated labor movement. The Arbeiterverbrüderung was suppressed and dissolved, as were all other political workers' organizations (including the Communist League) and most of the unions. The right to form a coalition for the purpose of collectively improving one's working conditions was again effectively denied. The more radical labor leaders, like democrats, socialists, and communists in general, were persecuted. Many of them went

[98] Max Quarck, *Die erste deutsche Arbeiterbewegung: Geschichte der Arbeiterverbrüderung 1848/49* (Leipzig, 1924); F. Balser, *Sozial-Demokratie 1848/49 bis 1863: Die erste Arbeiterorganisation "Allgemeine deutsche Arbeiterverbrüderung" nach der Revolution* (Stuttgart, 1962), pp. 73-75: membership figures; Noyes, *Organization and Revolution*, pp. 212-30, 290-314; H. Schlechte, *Die Allgemeine Deutsche Arbeiterverbrüderung 1848-1850: Dokumente des Zentralkomitees für die deutschen Arbeiter in Leipzig* (Weimar, 1979). A good short characterization is W. Schieder, "Die Rolle der deutschen Arbeiter in der Revolution von 1848/49," *Archiv für Frankfurts Geschichte und Kunst*, issue 54 (Frankfurt, 1974):43-56, esp. pp. 50-53; on "Arbeiterverbrüderung," "Bund der Kommunisten," and other workers' associations in the Rhineland 1848-1849, see Dowe, *Aktion*, pp. 133-234.

[99] Cf. R. Stadelmann, *Soziale und politische Geschichte der Revolution von 1848*, 3d ed. (Munich, 1973); W. Schmidt, "Zur historischen Stellung der deutschen Revolution von 1848/49," in *Die grosspreussisch-militaristische Reichsgründung 1871*, ed. H. Bartel and E. Engelberg (Berlin, 1971), 1:1-23; M. Stürmer, "1848 in der deutschen Geschichte," in *Sozialgeschichte heute. Festschrift für Hans Rosenberg zum 70. Geburtstag*, ed. H. -U. Wehler (Göttingen, 1974), pp. 228-42.

abroad. In general, workers' organizations had a choice of being forbidden, dissolving themselves, or devoluting into forms tolerated by the restrictive laws and the authorities: nonpolitical, workers' education associations influenced by the middle class, artisan clubs, reading societies, social clubs, and most important, friendly societies. Such organizations continued to exist as long as they stayed clear from politics and from union activities. The friendly societies (Hilfskassen) were even strongly encouraged by law (in Prussia in 1849 and 1854); they could be made obligatory on the community level; they were restricted as to their functions; increasingly they were organized on an intercraft basis; and usually they existed under employers' influence. Nevertheless they served as means through which workers of different kind communicated and had experiences in collective "self-help" and self-administration. And within these workers' associations and friendly societies survived some of the ideas, activists, and circles that had been officially eliminated.[100]

The war between Austria and Italy and the fundamental competition between Prussia and Austria influenced the softening of government repression in 1859, when the political climate became more liberal. The liberals and the democrats again organized (the Nationalverein, or National Association, in 1859; the Fortschrittspartei, or Progressive party, in Prussia 1861) in favor of national unification and constitutional reform, though in a moderate, postrevolutionary mood. The decade between the early 1860s and the early 1870s was a period of decisive constitutional struggles, particularly in Prussia, ending with Bismarck's constitution of the German Reich, which granted male suffrage and a few concessions to the liberals but prevented parliamentarization and preserved important prerogatives of the crown, the bureaucracy, the military, and other traditional ruling elites, in violation of the principles for which liberals and democrats had fought. It was also the decade in which the German nation-state was formed, with the help of three wars, by excluding Austria and under the hegemony of Prussia—under conservative and military auspices, "from above," not as a consequence of a liberal and democratic initiative "from below" as attempted in 1848.[101] In addition, it was a period of accelerated industrialization and the decade in which the breakthrough of the German labor movement occurred on two fronts: as a movement of unions (and strikes), and as a movement of workers' (education) associations changing into working-class parties.

---

[100] The best work on the period after the revolution is T. Offermann, *Arbeiterbewegung und liberales Bürgertum in Deutschland 1850-1863* (Bonn, 1979).

[101] Cf. H.-U. Wehler, *Das Deutsche Kaiserreich 1871-1918*, 3d ed. (Göttingen, 1977); Gordon A. Craig, *Germany 1866-1945* (Oxford, 1978), ch. 1.

The connections between these two movements had never been completely absent but they became close and decisive from the late 1860s on.

Ulrich Engelhardt's painstaking research has convincingly shown how, in the 1860s, a trade union movement developed that was not primarily a creation of the emerging working-class parties but grew "from below." When all kinds of associations and clubs had a chance to flourish after 1859, and when the right to form a coalition for collectively improving one's working conditions was conceded step by step between 1861 (Saxony) and 1869 (Norddeutscher Bund), the dynamics of unionization picked up again. As before, the previously existing organizations facilitated the emergence of unions, particularly the friendly societies and other workers' clubs that had experimented with cooperative schemes and other devices of self-help in previous years. The experience of conflict between labor and capital played an important role. Strikes became less illegal and more numerous in the 1860s. Increasingly, union-type organizations developed out of strikes, and once they existed and survived, they tried to support (and, increasingly in the 1870s, to regulate and restrict) strike activities. Between 1800 and the 1860s the history of strikes and the history of working-class organizations had largely developed apart, mostly due to the illegal character of the strikes; now they became intertwined.[102]

But even apart from the strikes, to many workers self-organization and collective self-help appeared to be a quasi-natural way of protection against the insecurities of the market economy and the superiority of the employers. Unions provided for health, accident, and other types of insurance, and frequently for legal aid. They experimented with cooperative enterprises; some tried, usually in vain, to set up union-influenced labor exchanges. Many workers saw the unions as indispensable tools for getting at least a modest share of the increasing returns of the economic progress that they were helping to generate. Collective bargaining with the employers and, if necessary, organized pressure (e.g., strikes) on them were important union functions in this period of fast industrialization, growing wealth, belief in progress, and rising expectations.[103] In addition, organizations like unions served social and cultural needs, offer-

---

[102] This point is made by Dittrich, *Arbeiterbewegung und Arbeiterbildung*, pp. 129f, 196. The most comprehensive study on the early unions: U. Engelhardt, *"Nur vereinigt sind wir stark": Die Anfänge der deutschen Gewerkschaftbewegung 1862/63 bis 1869/70*, 2 vols. (Stuttgart, 1977); on the following decades: W. Albrecht, *Fachverein—Berufsgewerkschaft—Zentralverband: Organisationsprobleme der deutschen Gewerkschaften 1870-1890* (Berlin/Bonn, 1982).

[103] This is stressed by the good short synthesis: U. Engelhardt, "Gewerkschaftliches Organisationsverhalten in der ersten Industrialisierungsphase," in *Arbeiter*, ed. Conze and Engelhardt, pp. 372-402.

ing experiences of community and recognition that workers were usually denied in the associations and social networks dominated by the middle class. The drive for unionization was supported by the two socialist labor parties and the left wing of the liberals from 1868 on.[104]

But the obstacles were great. For workers money and time were extremely short, and both were needed for union membership. Apathy was widespread; networks of stable communication and mutual trust that facilitate organization were largely restricted to skilled workers with artisan backgrounds. Employers' resistance was stiff, and usually the public authorities were hostile to autonomous workers' organizations as well. The early organizations were extremely weak. What benefits could they really promise? Still another factor impeded unionization. Old craft-specific traditions of self-organization had been severely weakened and partially interrupted by state repression and also by the recent speed of industrialization. The German unions could not simply grow out of the old Handwerk organizations, the guilds (which had become master guilds and later employers' associations), or the journeymen brotherhoods.

The unions grew, nevertheless. Beginning at the local level, usually in the big cities, they soon federated at a regional, and some of them at a national level. Regional and national organizations then reached back to the local level and organized membership drives. In nationwide organizations, the cigar makers and the book printers–typesetters were first again, in 1865-1866. Other crafts followed. The pattern of organization was highly unstable, decentralized, and fragmented.

From 1868 on, the political parties played both a stimulating and disintegrating role. Within the same trade unions of three different political directions frequently existed, often attacking each other: those connected with the Allgemeiner Deutscher Arbeiterverein (ADAV), the party created by Ferdinand Lassalle in 1863; those supported by the German section of the First International and the related Sozialdemokratische Arbeiterpartei (SDAP), growing out of a federation of workers' (education) associations and finally established under the leadership of Bebel and Liebknecht in 1869; and the liberal unions (Gewerkvereine), promoted by left-liberals like Max Hirsch from 1868 on. There were also Catholic associations, founded in the 1860s and 1870s, particularly in the mining industries of the Ruhr and in Silesia. Some nationwide unions like the printers-typesetters and many local organizations did not subscribe

---

[104] For the period after 1869: Albrecht, *Fachverein*; A. Bringmann, *Geschichte der deutschen Zimmerer-Bewegung*, vol. 1, 2d ed. (1909; repr. Berlin, 1980); Hermann Müller, *Die Organisationen der Lithographen, Steindrucker und verwandten Berufe*, vol. 1 (1917; repr. Berlin, 1978); W. Ettelt and H.-D. Krause, *Der Kampf um eine marxistische Gewerkschaftspolitik 1868-1878* (Berlin, 1975).

to any of these parties and tried to stay out of party politics. In many other cases the political affiliation remained formal and superficial. But frequently, particularly in the case of the weaker unions, support from the party was important and political divisions were real.[105]

It is thought that there were 60,000 to 80,000 unionized workers, mostly journeymen and skilled factory workers, in 1869-1870, perhaps 40 percent liberal, another 40 percent with socialist affiliations (about equally divided between ADAV and SDAP), and the rest independent or Catholic.[106] Further union growth in the years that followed was largely prevented by the Franco-German war of 1870-1871; increasing disappointment with the liberal unions, whose politics of mediation and rational conflict solution was increasingly discredited by the employers' hard stand; the erratic politics of ADAV with regard to union autonomy; ongoing struggles among the parties; and finally the depression of 1873. After the unification of the two socialist parties in 1875, unions of the same craft (or branch) merged as well (some of them even earlier). In 1877 a survey was taken. About 50,000 workers belonged to unions with socialist affiliations or sympathies. The cigar makers (tobacco workers) were first (8,100 members), and the book printers–typesetters second (5,500). There were 5,100 joiners (*Tischler*) and 3,100 cabinetmakers (*Zimmerer*). A metalworkers' union had 4,000 members; the shoemakers' union reported 3,600; the shipbuilders (*Schiffszimmerer*) 3,000; the tailors 2,800; and the masons 2,500. The others were smaller. In addition to these, the liberal unions still had about 20,000 to 25,000 members, particularly mechanics, other skilled metalworkers, joiners, and carpenters. In addition, there were about 10,000 members, particularly miners, in Catholic associations with unionlike characteristics.[107]

Even apart from its political segmentation, the union movement of the

---

[105] The strong printers' union stayed relatively "neutral"; cf. Beier, *Schwarze Kunst*. In contrast, the masons and the cigar makers had unions with strong party affiliation (ADAV); cf. F. Paeplow, *Die Organisation der Maurer Deutschlands von 1869-1899* (Hamburg, 1900); F. Klüss, *Die älteste deutsche Gewerkschaft: Die Organisation der Tabak- und Zigarrenarbeiter bis zum Erlass des Sozialistengesetzes* (Karlsruhe, 1905).

[106] Cf. Engelhardt, "Gewerkschaftliches Organisationsverhalten," pp. 390-91.

[107] August Geib's statistics were first printed in the labor periodical "Pionier," Jan. 26, 1878, and reprinted several times: *Correspondenzblatt der Generalkommission der Gewerkschaften Deutschlands* 3, no. 30 (Dec. 18, 1893), pp. 1, 5f; Müller, *Lithographen*, between 468 and 469. Recent researchers tend to think that Geib's figures are on the low side (by roughly 10 percent). Cf. G. A. Ritter and K. Tenfelde, "Die Mitglieder der Freien Gewerkschaften 1877/78 bis 1895 (1900)," in *Vom Sozialistengesetz zur Mitbestimmung*, ed. H. O. Vetter (Cologne, 1975), pp. 61-120 (table between pp. 120 and 121). Figures for the liberal unions: W. Kulemann, *Die Berufsvereine* I/2 (Jena, 1908), pp. 29-31. On the Catholics: Tenfelde and Ritter, *Bibliographie*, p. 112, n. 353.

1860s and 1870s differed from a class movement in several respects. First, it comprised only 2-3 percent of all industrial workers (in factories, craft shops, construction, and mining), 4 percent if we exclude those in the smallest craft shops (with five persons or fewer). Unionization proceeded very unevenly. Although the cigar makers and book printers–typesetters organized more than 20 percent of their branches, the proportion of organized textile workers was negligible, well under 1 percent.[108] Second, even the socialist unions usually did not exclude self-employed masters working on their own. Sometimes they even admitted small employers. By including cooperative enterprises (*Produktivgenossenschaften*) as one of their aims until the early 1870s, the unions may have appealed to hard-pressed small masters as well as to the Handwerk-oriented aspirations of skilled workers with artisan backgrounds. The liberal unions were of course even less hostile to the employers. The class line was not yet sharply drawn.[109] Third, the movement was clearly divided by craft. The strongest unions (e.g., the printers-typesetters), particularly, were highly skeptical of any proposal for close cooperation between different trade unions.[110]

On the other hand, the number of employers organized in the unions was extremely small: 1.5 percent in the union of book printers and typesetters in 1869 and probably fewer in the other unions, with a tendency to decline. Most of the unions' aims and services did not appeal to self-employed persons, especially after the early 1870s, when the socialist unions gradually ceased to advocate cooperative enterprises. When strikes occurred, divergent interests became most manifest, particularly regarding wages, hours, and control at the workplace. The more the unions used socialist rhetoric, the more they tended to offend the self-employed masters, not to mention the employers. The masters, in any case, increasingly had organizations of their own.[111]

---

[108] On total figures of industrial workers see above and *Statistik des Deutschen Reichs* 34 (Berlin, 1879), pt. 2, pp. 552ff: 42,000-43,000 printers, typesetters, and the like (some of whom were women and helpers, i.e. not eligible); 100,000 tobacco workers (however, again, women and unskilled helpers not recruitable); 380,000 in textiles (but excluding cottage workers and semidependent artisans; if these categories were included textile workers would add up to more than one million). The union for textile workers (Gewerkschaft der Manufaktur- und Handarbeiter beiderlei Geschlechts) had only 1,250 members in 1877, but had been stronger in previous years.

[109] Cf. Engelhardt, *"Nur vereinigt sind wir stark,"* 2:781f, 795f, 800; on the liberal unions: K. Goldschmidt, *Die deutschen Gewerkvereine* (Berlin, 1907); W. Gleichauf, *Geschichte des Verbandes der deutschen Gewerkvereine (Hirsch-Duncker)* (Berlin, 1907).

[110] Cf. Beier, *Schwarze Kunst*, p. 404 (on 1868).

[111] This process of separation between masters and journeymen-workers is shown, with respect to Berlin and Würzburg tailors in the 1870s, by W. Renzsch, *Handwerker und*

Supporting the argument, it should also be noted that the fragmentation of the union movement along craft and trade lines was not absolute. Compared with the English trade unions, the German organizations may have been more comprehensive. For example, the association of book printers and typesetters organized different specializations within one union that in England were organized by fourteen specialized unions. There are other examples of this kind. Early on, some German craft unions were "compound craft unions" with strong elements of "amalgamated craft unions."[112] One also may stress that there were very early attempts to form rudimentary industrial unions, at least on the local level (e.g., metalworkers' unions and wood workers' unions). Although most unions concentrated on skilled workers, there were early attempts to organize the unskilled as well (1869).[113] The party-initiated attempts to unite the different unions into a comprehensive federation (particularly in 1868) did not get very far, but one cannot dismiss altogether the constant emphasis, from both the party leaders and the party press, on interunion cooperation and general workers' class solidarity. Most unions had no newspapers of their own, but used the pages of the *Socialdemokrat* and the *Neue Socialdemokrat* (ADAV), and the *Volksstaat* (SDAP) for communicating with their locals and their members. And though early attempts to form a union of unions (in 1872 and 1874) failed, there was another attempt to form a cartel of unions in 1878, which had to be interrupted because of renewed government suppression.[114]

The rhetoric of the unions was craft-specific only to some extent. Their agitation came out in favor of the rights of the workers and the mission of the working class in general. In practice, of course, they worked first for the interests of their specific memberships. But in comparison with the English trade unions, the German organization had less inclination or less leverage to stress craft exclusivity. For instance, among German unions guild-type labor-market controls (e.g., union-controlled apprenticeship rules, the rejection of nonapprenticed colleagues, control of access to and dismissal from the shop floor, closed shop, and union shop)—mechanisms that not only reduce the power of management but implicitly discriminate against other workers as well—did not play a

---

Lohnarbeiter in der frühen Arbeiterbewegung: Zur sozialen Basis von Gewerkschaften und Sozialdemokratie im Reichsgründungsjahrzehnt (Göttingen, 1980), pp. 85-97, 98-104 passim.

[112] I follow Beier, *Schwarze Kunst*, pp. 34-35.

[113] Cf. Bürger, *Die Hamburger Gewerkschaften*, pp. 79, 111f; Engelhardt, "*Nur vereinigt sind wir stark*," 2:775ff, 802ff: Julius Motteler's "Internationale Gewerksgenossenschaft der Manufaktur-, Fabrik- und Handarbeiter (beiderlei Geschlechts)."

[114] Cf. Müller, *Lithographen*, pp. 120-131, 255-75, 289-302, 347-58, 397ff.

large role either in practice or in union goals. Neither did the fight against dilution or the defense of traditional, dignified work rules against innovation have much prominence. German unions felt and indeed were more clearly distinguished from the old corporate guilds than their English counterparts.[115] The reasons have been mentioned above: the unbalanced survival of corporate tradition (including the suppression of brotherhoods) and probably also the impact of late, high-speed industrialization. Although the Handwerk tradition continued to affect the masters and small employers for an extremely long time (a distinction between Handwerk and Industrie is still customary in Germany today), the Handwerk tradition was perhaps less formative for the emerging German working class than for the English. Consequently, certain internal divisions of the emerging working class along craft lines and the distinction between skilled and unskilled were somewhat less influential in the German case than in the English. This may be one of several factors that explains the subsequent greater appeal of Marxist ideals and ideologies to German than to English workers.

Party and Class. The very early rise of a strong independent labor party distinguishes Germany from the West European pattern. Nevertheless, the following evidence points in a direction similar to others'. The emerging party, whose name included the word Arbeiter, addressed itself to workers in general, not to workers of a specific craft or sector (including the unskilled and agricultural workers). It tried to base its appeal on class interpretations of social reality and made extensive use of socialist and communist class rhetoric although its programs and campaigns contained other elements as well. The party did not exclude nonworkers from membership. Indeed, intellectuals have always played a large role in German Social Democracy; other social groups were represented as well, including small masters and even businessmen.[116] But a large majority of the total membership (in 1874, 34,000-39,000) were certainly workers in the sense of this essay. And it is likely that at this early point in time (in contrast to later) the large majority of socialist votes came from members of the (non-Catholic) working class, particularly in the large cities and

---

[115] Cf. L. Brentano, *Die Arbeitergilden der Gegenwart I: Zur Geschichte der englischen Gewerkvereine* (Leipzig, 1871). The type of organizations Brentano described with much sympathy could hardly be found on the contemporary German scene.

[116] Among 158 politically active persons expelled under the Anti-Socialist Law in Leipzig, 1881-1890, there were 92 workers (including journeymen), 23 persons who were either master artisans or journeymen, 12 master journeymen, 4 innkeepers, 4 petty traders, 5 booksellers, 4 publishers, 6 journalists, 3 clerks, 2 students, and 1 doctor. Cf. Berndt, "Die auf Grund des Sozialistengesetzes," pp. 579-83.

in some regions with domestic industries. (In the Reichstag elections of 1871 and 1874, the two socialist parties received 124,655 and 351,952 votes, i.e., 1.6 and 4.1 percent of the total vote. But in Berlin they received 21.6 and 27.7 percent and in Hamburg 24.1 and 40.9 percent of the total).[117] Although there remained some connections and partial congruences between the rising Social Democratic party and the democratic or left-liberal forces throughout the *Kaiserreich*, and although support for the SPD came from only a (growing) minority of the working class, a split along class lines structured the party system in Germany much earlier than in England and France, not to mention the United States.

The German labor party developed out of the workers' (education) associations, which had also organized workers of different crafts. When the liberals became active again around 1860, their left wing tried to cooperate with the workers' (education) associations, as did many democrats. They hoped to enlist the political support of the workers in the fight for unification and constitutional reform. They actively offered them a reform program that stressed general and trade-oriented education, cooperative schemes, and saving institutions. It was not until 1865 that a majority in the liberal camp supported the demand for general (male) suffrage and the right of coalition: those liberals interested in a (liberal) union movement remained a minority. Instead, liberals and democrats encouraged the founding of new workers' associations and their coordination on the national level, hoping to lead the movement in the right direction.

But by 1863 some of these associations had already turned against them, under the leadership of the Leipzig Arbeiterverein, which invited the philosopher, journalist and political agitator, Ferdinand Lassalle— Hegelian, radical democrat, socialist, and critic of liberalism—to help launch a nationwide congress and organization of workers' associations.

---

[117] Figures from D. Fricke, *Die deutsche Arbeiterbewegung 1869-1914* (Berlin, 1976), pp. 34, 526; G. A. Ritter and M. Niehuss, *Wahlgeschichtliches Arbeitsbuch: Materialien zur Statistik des Kaiserreichs 1871-1918* (Munich, 1980), pp. 67-97, 99. The Social Democratic vote (as percent of the total vote) was, in predominantly Protestant voting districts, 5.7 in 1871 and 14.4 in 1874; in predominantly Catholic voting districts, 1.8 in 1871 and 3.8 in 1874. The voting districts of Wuppertal-Elberfeld and Solingen (ADAV) and Glauchau-Meerane and Zwickau-Crimmitschau (SDAP) were socialist voting strongholds from the late 1860s onward, and all of them had a large proportion of domestic industrial workers (textiles and, in Solingen, metalwork). On handweavers voting socialist in the 1860s, cf. F. Engels to E. Bernstein, Nov. 30, 1881, in: Marx and Engels, *Werke* 35:237f. However, this was not true for spinners and weavers everywhere. In Bielefeld, e.g., they were deeply religious (Protestant with a strong evangelical bent), and showed their distrust in capitalism and liberalism by voting conservative (Ditt, *Industrialisierung*, p. 147ff).

They succeeded in building up ADAV (Allgemeiner Deutscher Arbeiterverein), a centralized mass movement or unstable party that advocated socialist revolution, democratic suffrage, and production on a state-supported, state-financed cooperative basis. Lassalle and his successors were extremely hostile to liberalism as well as to the German bourgeoisie, but ready to consider temporary cooperation with Bismarck and the conservatives. ADAV found more support among weavers and other cottage workers in semirural areas, cigar makers, masons, and carpenters—most of whom had never been politically involved before—than among highly skilled urban workers. The Berlin mechanics, for example, still remained faithful to the liberal cause in the 1870s. Theoretically at least, ADAV rejected friendly societies, unions, and strikes as useless deviations from the course toward revolution and dangerous to the organization's strength until 1868, when its leadership reversed itself and supported unions in order to benefit from them.[118]

The majority of workers' (education) associations—"education" was increasingly dropped from the name—closely cooperated with the left-liberals and the democrats. They formed a loose nationwide federation (Verband Deutscher Arbeitervereine or VDAV) that met once a year. In 1865 it included about 100 associations with more than 20,000 members, mostly south of the Main River and in Saxony (Lassalle's ADAV had its strongholds in Prussia). From 1863 to 1868 a complicated process of reshuffling and faction building took place in this organization, reflecting important changes that occurred at its base. Many local associations extended their functions beyond education and insurance plans; they supported strikes, dealt with cooperative projects, and demanded better pay and improved work conditions. They became increasingly political, concerned with suffrage questions, association laws, and the problem of parliamentarization, and increasingly dissatisfied with the liberals, who could not approve of these changes and who tended to arrange themselves with the status quo, particularly after Bismarck's victory over Austria in 1866. At the Nuremberg convention of 1868, the majority of the federation, led by Bebel, expressed its solidarity with the First International and its principles inspired by Karl Marx. The liberal minority (about one-third) left the organization. In 1868, August Bebel and the radical, Marx-influenced journalist Wilhelm Liebknecht founded the Sozialdemokratische Arbeiterpartei (SDAP), which emerged out of a previous party of Saxon democrats and absorbed the federation in addition to

---

[118] A good recent treatment of ADAV: A. Herzig, *Der Allgemeine Deutsche Arbeiter-Verein in der deutschen Sozialdemokratie: Dargestellt an der Biographie des Funktionärs Carl Wilhelm Tölcke (1817-1893)* (Berlin, 1979).

some socialists who had left the ADAV. The new party had a democratic and socialist program, stressed cooperation with the unions, agreed with the necessity of worker-controlled insurance plans, and half-heartedly supported cooperative plans. In contrast to ADAV, it did not break all ties with the democratic and left-liberal groups but kept a strict distance from the conservatives. Also unlike ADAV, SDAP was strongly opposed to a Prussian leadership in the emerging Reich.[119]

Despite sharp competition and bitter fights between the two parties, they moved closer to each other within the next few years. The Bismarckian solution of the German question created a *fait accompli* and removed one of the major points of disagreement between them; this Prussian-led system was heavily criticized by both of them. Because they protested continuing the war with France after the first battles had been won, declared sympathy with the Paris Commune, and remained skeptical toward the wave of nationalism in the wake of the war, both parties faced widespread hostility, discrimination, and persecution. When the creation of the Reich was celebrated by Bismarck, the princes, and many dignitaries in the palace of Versailles, some leaders of the workers' parties were jailed.

The public was alarmed by the successes of the socialist parties at the polls and the waves of strikes; state repression increased. In 1875 the two parties united and formed the Sozialistische Arbeiterpartei Deutschlands (SAP), renamed Sozialdemokratische Partei Deutschlands (SPD) in 1890 and still existing today.[120]

It is not easy to explain why an independent, strong, and successful labor party was established in Germany so early, in the breakthrough phase of industrialization. The increasing tensions between capital and labor, dramatized by the waves of strikes and other disputes, had to strain a liberal-radical alliance comprising workers and businessmen.

---

[119] On the VDAV: S. Na'aman, "Arbeitervereine, Arbeitertage und Arbeiterverband—drei Etappen auf dem Weg zur Arbeiterpartei," in *Berichte über die Verhandlungen der Vereinstage deutscher Arbeitervereine 1863-1869*, ed. D. Dowe (Berlin, 1980), pp. 9-51; E. Eyck, *Der Vereinstag Deutscher Arbeitervereine 1863-1868* (Berlin, 1904); Dittrich, *Arbeiterbewegung und Arbeiterbildung*, pp. 211-83. On SDAP: F. Mehring, *Geschichte der deutschen Sozialdemokratie* II ([1st ed. 1898, 2d ed. 1904] Berlin, 1960), pp. 159-370; G. Mayer, *Friedrich Engels: Eine Biographie* (1934; repr. Cologne, 1975), 2:148-295; Fricke, *Die deutsche Arbeiterbewegung*, pp. 5-59; for additional (more specialized) titles cf. Tenfelde and Ritter, eds., *Bibliographie*, pp. 440-48.

[120] Cf. G. Eckert, "Die Konsolidierung der sozialdemokratischen Arbeiterbewegung zwischen Reichsgründung und Sozialistengesetz," in *Sozialdemokratie zwischen Klassenbewegung und Volkspartei*, ed. H. Mommsen (Frankfurt, 1974), pp. 35-51; S. Miller, *Das Problem der Freiheit im Sozialismus: Freiheit, Staat und Revolution in der Programmatik der Sozialdemokratie von Lassalle bis zum Revisionismusstaat* (Berlin, 1974), esp. pp. 68-79 (good on the program and ideology of the SPD).

One can observe that the strikes of 1865 heightened the tension within the VDAV, and that the Waldenburg miners' strike of 1869 tested and discredited the liberal unions' movement.[121] It is also to be expected that workers like the hand weavers, for example, who were threatened by rapid industrialization, had little enthusiasm for any program that defended such changes as signs of progress, which to some extent liberalism did. Thus anti-liberal politics—of the Catholic church, ADAV, or sometimes even of the conservatives—[122] could gain support from depressed groups of workers who were not strong enough for unionization. It is also not surprising that the liberals were confronted with the rising expectations and claims of skilled industrial workers, who had reached new forms of self-consciousness, experienced the changeability of social relations, and challenged traditional patterns of inequality. Their desire for suffrage was an example, as was their increasing resentment of the paternalistic attitudes that even well-meaning liberal spokesmen displayed toward workers.[123]

The English liberals were faced with similar challenges, but they succeeded in integrating workers' associations, unions, and their own interests until the end of the century.[124] The German liberals most likely had a more difficult task. Given the German tradition of bureaucratic reform from above, the liberals had always been relatively weak and certainly

[121] The strains within the liberal-radical alliance can best be studied by looking at the VDAV 1863-1869. Cf. the titles in note 119 above and Birker, *Die deutschen Arbeiterbildungsvereine*, pp. 56-83; G. Mayer, "Die Trennung der proletarischen von der bürgerlichen Demokratie in Deutschland 1830-1870" (1912), in G. Mayer, *Radikalismus, Sozialismus und bürgerliche Demokratie* (Frankfurt, 1969), pp. 108-178; on the Waldenburg strike of 1869: U. Engelhardt, "Zur Verhaltensanalyse eines sozialen Konflikts," in *Soziale Innovation und sozialer Konflikt*, ed. O. Neuloh (Göttingen, 1977), pp. 69-94.

[122] On the role of Catholicism for Bavarian workers: W. K. Blessing, *Staat und Kirche in der Gesellschaft: Institutionelle Autorität und mentaler Wandel in Bayern während des 19. Jahrhunderts* (Göttingen, 1982); an interesting case study: H. Lepper, "Kaplan Franz Eduard Cronenberg und die christlich-soziale Bewegung in Aachen 1868-1878," *Zeitschrift des Aachener Geschichtsvereins* 79 (1968):57-148; on the role of evangelical protestantism for the Westphalian lower classes: J. Mooser, "Religion und sozialer Protest: Erweckungsbewegung und ländliche Unterschichten im Vormärz am Beispiel Minden-Ravensberg," in *Sozialer Protest*, ed. Volkmann and Bergmann, pp. 304-324; on the conservative orientation of Bielefeld workers in the second third of the nineteenth century cf. Ditt, *Industrialisierung*, pp. 147ff. On the ADAV see above note 118 and S. Na'aman and H.-P. Harstick, *Die Konstituierung der deutschen Arbeiterbewegung 1862/63: Darstellung und Dokumentation* (Assen/Holland, 1975); S. Na'aman, *Lassalle* (Hannover, 1970), pp. 527ff.

[123] Cf. Birker, *Die deutschen Arbeiterbildungsvereine*, p. 54.

[124] On the British-German comparison, cf. J. Breuilly, "Liberalismus oder Sozialdemokratie? Ein Vergleich der britischen und deutschen politischen Arbeiterbewegung zwischen 1850 und 1875," in *Europäische Arbeiterbewegungen im 19. Jahrhundert: Deutschland, Österreich, England und Frankreich im Vergleich*, ed. Jürgen Kocka (Göttingen, 1983), pp. 129-68.

were after their defeat of 1848-1849. This became apparent in the Prussian constitutional conflict of the 1860s, when they could not effectively challenge the uncompromising stubbornness of the government. In addition, most of them retreated from a vigorous advocacy of the liberal position after Bismarck's victories on the battlefield, which also helped to turn off labor leaders—some of them early, like Lassalle, and some later, like Bebel.[125]

The liberals faced particular difficulties because of the timing of German modernization. The problems of nation building, conflict over political participation and the constitutional order, and the "social question" brought about by capitalist industrialization (the conflict of capital and labor, the challenge of a rising working class) may confront a nation at different points in its history, perhaps one after the other, as was the case in most of Europe and North America.[126] In contrast, Germany faced these three issues or crises within the same quarter of a century, particularly in 1848 and in the 1860s. The result was a superimposition of problems that easily overwhelmed the actors, in this case the liberals in particular. They would have had more resources and more means for bridging the gap with labor had they been the ruling party in an established parliamentary system like the English. In addition, the early and sudden introduction of the suffrage in 1867 did not make their task easier. The electoral law (modified proportional representation) facilitated the rise of independent parties—in contrast to England. And perhaps the liberals' quest for constitutional reforms would have been bolder than it was in the 1860s if they had not been faced by an already powerful "second front," the challenge of labor resulting from advancing industrialization. The memory of 1848-1849 played a role on both sides: as a liberal failure in the minds of some radical labor leaders and probably many workers and as a dangerous mass movement slipping out of control in the memories of many liberals. The conflict between labor and society at large might have been less fundamental if the emergence of the working class had occurred within a well-established and self-assured, consolidated nation-state.[127]

[125] Of course, both had other motives as well. Cf. H. Mommsen, "Lassalle," *Sowjetsystem und demokratische Gesellschaft* (Freiburg, 1969), 3:1339f; H. Hirsch, *August Bebel: Pionier unserer Zeit* (Cologne, 1973).

[126] Cf. A. Marschall, *Citizenship and Social Class* (Cambridge, 1950).

[127] Since the formation of working-class parties, which displayed some internationalist inclinations, coincided with the wave of nationalist mobilization and the formation of the national state, these new working-class organizations were defined and rejected as antinational outsiders. The complicated relationship between the national movements and the rising labor movement is skillfully discussed in W. Conze and D. Groh, *Die Arbeiterbewegung in der nationalen Bewegung: Die deutsche Sozialdemokratie vor, während und*

Finally, it seems that those liberals who tried to keep labor under liberal influence underestimated the degree to which the society was already structured in class terms. Consider Hermann Schulze-Delitzsch, the liberal most admired by workers in the 1860s. His proposals of cooperative associations did not clearly distinguish between wage workers and self-employed masters. Indeed, he still used the term Arbeiter in its older, non-class-specific meaning. He had to learn that proposals that appealed to self-employed individuals frequently did not appeal to wage workers and that class-related rhetoric as used by his socialist competitors struck a chord in the souls of the workers and apparently fit into their experience and expectations. Or consider the liberal unions. Although they displayed remarkable strength in the late 1860s, it was clear in the mid-1870s that they had no chance in the long run. Their leaders propagated a program of rational conflict solution and reasonable intermediation that was increasingly weakened and contradicted by the heat of the controversies and the bitterness of the struggle between workers and employers. They were laughed at by many workers and let down by their more business-oriented colleagues in the party. They tried to follow the English example and praised the English trade union system (of the 1860s and 1870s). But in Germany they were too late, and perhaps also too early.[128]

DID A working class exist in Germany in the 1870s? On the basis of the definitions used in this essay, such a question can only be answered ambivalently: in some respects yes, in others no. This would be the answer with regard to any later period in German social history, as well. What can be said with more certainty is that in 1800-1875 the process of class formation clearly progressed. There was much more of a working class in 1875 than in 1800. The trend was clear and it was to continue at least until World War I.[129] But as of 1875, its results remained very limited.

In the first three quarters of the nineteenth century, wage work

---

nach der Reichsgründung (Stuttgart, 1966). The most important recent piece on why a separate working-class party was founded so early in Germany is W. Schieder, "Das Scheitern des bürgerlichen Radikalismus und die sozialistische Parteibildung in Deutschland," in *Sozialdemokratie*, ed. Mosen, pp. 17-34; see also Mayer, "Trennung" and Kocka, ed., *Europäische Arbeiterbewegungen.*

[128] Cf. Bernstein, *Berliner Arbeiter-Bewegung*, pp. 237-41, for interesting comments on why the liberal proposals to create unions and mechanisms of reconciliation on the British model did not work in Germany.

[129] On the long-term trends in class formation, see Jürgen Kocka, "Stand—Klasse—Organisation: Strukturen sozialer Ungleichheit in Deutschland vom späten 18. bis zum frühen 20. Jahrhundert im Aufriss," in *Klassen in der europäischen Sozialgeschichte*, ed. H.-U. Wehler (Göttingen, 1979), pp. 137-65.

emerged as the dominant form of manual work that was done in dependence on others. But the work of large sectors of the lower classes was
either not yet transformed in this way or only to a limited extent (Gesinde, agricultural workers). Even when wage work became the dominant
mode it continued to be mixed with non-wage-work elements (especially
in the domestic industries, less so with the journeymen and hardly at all
with the factory workers).

Interests, experiences, opportunities, and risks greatly varied among
those who, more or less, became wage workers. But as the discussion of
social language, protest, mobility, and marriage patterns intended to
show, something like a common identity developed that included wage
workers in spite of those differences and increasingly excluded those who
were not workers. The limits of these tendencies, however, were even
clearer and more pronounced than in the case of the emergence of wage
work. We have also examined the beginnings of organizations and politics structured along class lines. On this third level class formation was
particularly slow, limited, and only in its initial stage by 1875.

Class was initially defined here on different levels. It is not surprising
to find that many more people belonged to the emerging working class
on the most basic level (defined as those who do work for wages) than to
the working class defined as a social class (social cohesion, self-identification); again, only a fraction of those who belonged to the working class
on this intermediate level was part of the working class on the third
level—participating in class-specific collective actions and organizations.
There are many factors explaining why some wage workers developed
class-identification to this extent, and why a minority, in addition, participated in class action and organization, while many others, certainly
the majority, did not develop in this way. These factors cannot be easily
summarized. In conclusion I want to stress only two, suggested by comparisons among servants, agricultural workers, domestic workers, journeymen, and factory workers.

The more clearly a category of workers was transformed into wage
workers (but see again the broad definition of wage worker above), the
more likely it was that it also became part of the emerging working class
in terms of social cohesion and action/organization. Yet wage workers
were more likely to develop class cohesion and class identities and even
to participate in class-specific collective action if and to the extent that
they stood in particular, usually corporate, traditions that were challenged but not yet destroyed by the rise of industrial capitalism. As the
example of some categories of journeymen in contrast to others and in
contrast to most factory workers seems to show, the experience of wage
work (including market dependency and subordination to an employer)

was indispensable but usually not sufficient for producing class consciousness and readiness for class-based action in that early period. The conflict between traditional ways of life, cultures, and expectations on one side and the new imperatives and restraints, as defined by capitalist industrialization and the state, on the other side frequently played a supplementary, enforcing role, and this explains the different degrees and forms of a group's participation in class formation. The emerging conflict between labor and capital was central. But with it a conflict between tradition and modernization was intertwined that of course varied over time and space.

Again and again the important role of tradition for the process of working-class formation has been discussed. On the one hand, the long but unbalanced survival of the corporate order appeared decisive. On the other hand, the early rise of strong state bureaucracies played an important role. And third, the belated formation of the nation-state and the weakness of liberalism were also very influential. In the comparative consideration of working-class formation, these must be seen as the major elements of the German experience.

8 Economic Crisis, State Policy, and Working-Class Formation in Germany, 1870-1900 • *Mary Nolan*

Although Britain experienced the first industrial revolution and France developed the first significant socialist associations, Germany produced the largest and best-organized workers' movement in the late nineteenth century. By the mid-1890s, German social democracy had successfully built a mass party and a centralized trade union movement in spite of—or, it could be argued, because of—its espousal of deterministic Marxism, its practice of ambivalent parliamentarism and its isolation from the state and much of society. Drawing on and transforming older forms of economic and political organization and protest, the German Social Democratic party (SPD) and the socialist trade unions recruited primarily journeymen and skilled factory workers for whom the movement was a vehicle not only for demanding political reform and defending material interests but also for adapting to a new urban industrial environment and creating working-class communities and culture within it.

If social democracy became the movement of those who saw themselves as members of the working class, it simultaneously reflected and reenforced divisions among workers and between them and other classes. Miners, peasant workers, the permanently unskilled, and women remained indifferent to the appeals of social democracy and master artisans and peasants were hostile to it. In addition, the rise of social democracy, with its demands for political democracy, extensive social reform, and ultimately working-class emancipation through socialism, could not thwart the expansion of a more conservative, corporatist Catholic workers' movement, loyal to the Catholic Center party. In the late nineteenth century, social democracy in Germany laid the basis for becoming both the model of success for socialist workers elsewhere and the embodiment of the limits of social democracy as a social movement, a political practice, and an ideology of revolutionary transformation.

The character of the late-nineteenth-century German working class and the Social Democratic movement that issued from it was both a product of and a complex response to the tumultuous transformations of the Great Depression era. The first phase of the German industrial revolution and working-class formation was brought to an abrupt end by the economic crisis of 1873, which ushered in two decades of restructuring and reorientation in the economy, in politics, and in the working class.[1] Between the 1840s and the early 1870s Germany had experienced late but rapid industrialization while simultaneously achieving national unification and solving, albeit on controversial terms, the long-disputed constitutional question. During that period both a working class and an embryonic, independent workers' movement, under socialist but not Marxist auspices, had emerged.

Significant as these changes were, however, they had not definitively established either the structure of the economy or the social and political basis of the new German state. The composition of the working class, its relationship to other classes, its forms of struggle and accommodation, and the importance and meaning of the socialist movement still remained open questions. From the 1870s to the 1890s the tentative solutions given to these problems in the previous decades were reviewed and found wanting, and new ones were tried.

The period of the Great Depression marked a transition from the institutions, practices, and values that had evolved since the 1840s to those that developed fully after the mid-1890s. The earlier period was characterized by the first industrial revolution, elite politics, the dominance of constitutional and national issues in political debate, and the flourishing, although not the triumph, of economic and political liberalism. The later period witnessed the second industrial revolution and more organized forms of capitalism, extensive state intervention and the primacy of economic issues in political organization and discussion, a new mass politics, and the prevalence of generally conservative forms of "collective protectionism."[2] Between 1873 and 1896 these new trends emerged, although few came to full fruition and all coexisted with older institutions and practices.

For workers this was also a period of transition. Industrial capitalism, economic crisis, and massive migration transformed the recruitment of wage labor, the skill and occupational structure of the labor force, the labor process, and community forms. External class boundaries became more clearly delineated and internal ones diminished but by no means

[1] The classic work on this period is Hans Rosenberg, *Grosse Depression und Bismarck Zeit* (Berlin: Walter de Gruyter, 1967). See also, Hans-Ulrich Wehler, *Das deutsche Kaiserreich, 1871-1918* (Göttingen: Vandenhoeck and Ruprecht, 1973). For a critique of Wehler and Rosenberg, see David Blackbourn and Geoff Eley, *The Peculiarities of German History* (Oxford: Oxford University Press, 1984).

[2] For an overview of the earlier period, see Jürgen Kocka's essay in this volume. For the later period, see Richard Evans, ed., *Society and Politics in Wilhelmine Germany* (London: Croom Helm, 1978) and Heinrich A. Winkler, ed., *Organisierter Kapitalismus* (Göttingen: Vandenhoeck and Ruprecht, 1974).

disappeared. Economic struggles and organizational forms reflected a learning of the rules of the capitalist game and the linking of local interests with wider class ones, but the process proved slow. Backward- and forward-looking goals, spontaneity and planning, and old and new tactics continued to coexist throughout the period. Working-class politics, both in the dominant Social Democratic form and in the less pervasive Catholic one, underwent unprecedented expansion and fundamentally altered their social base, organizational structure, ideology, and strategy. The transformation of working-class politics, like that of economic struggles, promoted class formation, radicalization, and isolation from the state. It redrew internal class divisions and solidified the external boundaries that material conditions had created.

Three principal forces shaped the particular composition, organization, politics, and consciousness of the German working class in the late nineteenth century: economic crisis, religion, and state policy. Economic crisis had profound structural and political effects on a society that had just experienced simultaneously three processes that were temporally separate in other countries—rapid industrialization, national unification, and constitutional disputes. The Great Depression prolonged the disruptive impact of these processes as well as the controversies surrounding them and significantly altered the character of the wage labor force that was created by and confronted with them. Religion, specifically Catholicism, proved a particularly central and divisive force for workers and for German society as a whole, not only because the Protestant-ruled country had a large, geographically concentrated Catholic minority[3] but also, and above all, because Catholicism became politicized, organized, and popular. Finally, institutionalized, legalized repression, only marginally moderated by paternalistic state social welfare, was implemented by an authoritarian state that rested on a conservative alliance of aristocrats and industrialists. The interaction of state policy and structure played a decisive role in shaping working-class actions, organizations, and ideologies by delineating, subordinating, isolating, and radicalizing workers.

This essay will explore from four perspectives how these forces shaped the German working class. Section one analyzes the restructuring of economic and political life in the wake of the Great Depression and sketches the contours of state policy toward workers and their movements. Section two moves from the structures and relations of society as a whole to those

[3] In 1871 Germany had 25,581,685 Protestants and 14,869,292 Catholics. The latter were concentrated in south Germany, the Rhineland, and the Polish-speaking areas east of the Elbe. Gerd Hohorst, Jürgen Kocka, and Gerhard A. Ritter, *Sozialgeschichtliches Arbeitsbuch* (Munich: Beck, 1975).

of work, the occupational order, and community. Capitalist expansion, the labor process, migration, urbanization, and living standards will be examined in order to explain the material basis on which internal and external class boundaries developed. Section three explores dispositions and attitudes, focusing on the sense different workers made of economic and political change, the identities they developed, and the strategies they pursued outside the arena of workplace struggles and politics. Section four examines the demands, actions, and organizations of the working class in the economic and political spheres and explores how they were shaped by the developments analyzed in sections one and two and articulated or not articulated by the groups discussed in section three.

I. Economic Crisis, Politics, and the State

The Great Depression of 1873-1896 brought in its wake a restructuring of Germany's economy, a transformation of its political parties, and a refounding of the Reich. This reorientation of state and society set the framework within which the working class and workers' movements developed. Of equal importance, the working class and workers' movements were central elements of that new framework. They were both the objects of repressive and paternalistic state policies and the "enemy within" against whom the tenuous Bismarckian synthesis united.

The Great Depression involved the entire industrial capitalist world, but its impact on Germany was particularly pronounced, testifying both to Germany's new integration into the world economy and to the instabilities and vulnerabilities generated by rapid industrialization. For Germany this prolonged crisis entailed three periods of intense economic downturn—1873-1879, 1882-1884, and 1891-1893—interspersed with tentative and short-lived upswings. It abruptly ended two decades of rapid growth and prosperity, shattered the brash optimism of new industrialists and the quieter confidence of Junker agriculture, and intensified the insecurities of the traditional petty bourgeoisie and peasantry.[4]

In Germany this crisis displayed peculiar characteristics that shaped both its impact and the responses to it. During the depression, production and investment slowed but did not decline precipitously. Whereas economic growth averaged 4.5 percent per year in the decades preceding and following the depression, it slowed to 3 percent during it. Whereas 2.9

---

[4] For discussions of the impact of the Great Depression see Paul Massing, *Rehearsal for Destruction* (New York: Harper, 1949); Fritz Stern, *The Failure of Illiberalism* (Chicago: University of Chicago, 1976); Hans-Ulrich Wehler, *Bismarck und der Imperialismus* (Munich: Deutscher Taschenbuch Verlag, 1976).

billion marks went into joint stock companies between 1871 and 1873 alone, precisely the same amount was invested in the entire period 1874-1895. Deflation was acute, with wholesale prices falling by one-third between 1874 and 1879 and staying at roughly that level until the mid-1890s.[5] Although wages dropped as well, the collapse was not as dramatic or rapid. Deflation, in addition to limited domestic markets and highly competitive, increasingly restricted foreign ones, led industrialists to complain about overcapacity and overproduction and financiers to lament the lack of profitable investment opportunities.[6]

Complaints and crisis notwithstanding, per capita industrial production did increase and industrialization proceeded, even if at a slower pace. Coal production, for example, expanded from 34 million tons in 1870 to 89 million tons in 1890 while steel production grew from 0.2 million tons to 2.2 million tons in the same period.[7] Although the Ruhr and the cities of south Germany were to experience their most dramatic economic transformation after 1896, the former was first developed on a large scale in this period and the latter underwent slow but steady industrialization. Producer goods grew faster than consumer ones and the new industries of the second industrial revolution made their appearance. This enhanced existing differentials and laid the basis for the undisputed primacy of heavy industry after the 1890s.[8]

For both agriculture and *Handwerk* (artisanal or craft work) the depression marked a structural as well as a cyclical crisis. Due to the importation of cheap American agricultural goods into Europe, Germany became a high-cost agrarian area, and its large-scale grain sector, dominated by the Junker aristocracy, either had to reorganize or be preserved artificially by state intervention. For master artisans and journeymen the period required adjustment to the previous rapid industrialization and the ongoing slower changes—adjustment that could entail clinging to a precarious independence or abandoning it for the factory, adopting more capitalist forms or shifting into retail and repair, or moving to rural areas or employing women to cut costs.[9]

Although the depression weakened agriculture and the artisanal sector

[5] Rosenberg, *Grosse Depression*, pp. 40-43.

[6] Wehler, *Bismarck*, pp. 65-66, 139-55.

[7] Jürgen Kuczynski, *Geschichte der Lage der Arbeiter unter dem Kapitalismus*, Bd. 3, *Darstellung der Lage der Arbeiter in Deutschland von 1871 bis 1900* (Berlin: Akademie Verlag, 1962), p. 122.

[8] Rosenberg, *Grosse Depression*, pp. 40-41.

[9] On agriculture, see Alexander Gerschenkron, *Bread and Democracy in Germany* (Berkeley: University of California, 1943). On *Handwerk* see, Wilhelm Heinz Schröder, *Arbeitergeschichte und Arbeiterbewegung* (Frankfurt: Campus, 1978), pp. 78-87.

it by no means eliminated them. Although Germany emerged from the period with a different and much larger industrial sector, uneven development remained pronounced. In addition to the widespread coexistence of Handwerk and advanced industry, north Germany continued to be considerably more industrialized than the south and areas east of the Elbe River were overwhelmingly devoted to large-scale market agriculture with patriarchal social relations.[10] This contradictory pattern of combined and uneven development, which had characterized the first phase of German industrialization, was perpetuated less by the depression itself than by the economic and political responses to it.

Among industrialists, agrarians, and master artisans the Great Depression generated profound pessimism and a rejection not only of free trade but also of all aspects of laissez-faire economics. There were strong demands for state aid and intervention in the economy, most particularly for tariffs to protect agriculture and industry and, as the slogan went, to "defend national work." These tariffs, which were introduced in 1879, raised in the 1880s, and retained until 1918, represented discriminatory class legislation at its most blatant, for they benefited heavy industry and preserved inefficient Junker agriculture while hurting the consumer-goods sector and raising the cost of living. A form of indirect taxation, tariffs bore most heavily on those least able to pay, the rapidly expanding wage labor force.[11]

Nor were tariffs the only response. For key economic groups, organization on an unprecedented scale became the favorite means of promoting particular policies and augmenting a strategy of "collective protectionism."[12] Industry became more concentrated and vertically integrated, with heavy and new industries leading the way. Cartels multiplied in this period, although they were only gradually transformed from unstable expedients into permanent institutions. Industrialists organized a variety of sectoral, regional, and national economic interest groups that lobbied both the government and political parties vigorously.[13] Following suit, Junker agriculture rallied its forces into powerful associations. Even master artisans tried to build a national Handwerk movement and pressure for the reinstitution of restrictive guild legislation.[14]

[10] Tom Kemp, *Industrialization in Nineteenth Century Europe* (London: Longman, 1969), pp. 81-118.

[11] Rosenberg, *Grosse Depression*, pp. 62-81, 169-91.

[12] Ibid., pp. 78-79.

[13] Kuczynski, *Geschichte*, Bd. 3, pp. 54-55, 130. Heinz Josef Varain, *Interessenverbände in Deutschland* (Cologne: Kiepenheuer and Witsch, 1973).

[14] Hermann Aubin and Wolfgang Zorn, eds., *Handbuch der deutschen Wirtschafts- und Sozialgeschichte* (Stuttgart: Klett, 1976), 2:657.

The depression and the protectionist response to it were central to the transformation of politics, to the discrediting and discarding of liberalism not only as an economic policy but also as a political ideology and movement. Political liberalism was attacked from without by agrarians, artisans, workers, and Catholics of all classes and abandoned from within by most of its previous industrial and professional middle-class supporters. The crucial date in this process was 1879. The tariff legislation created a profoundly conservative political alliance between Junker agriculture and heavy industry, an alliance that accepted the Bismarckian state and provided it with the firm social base it had lacked. This "refounding of the Reich" stabilized the Bismarckian system but also precluded reform and working-class political integration, as an examination of political parties and the state shows.[15]

In response to economic crisis and as part of the ruling classes' strategy of collective protectionism, political parties became narrowly class-based economic interest groups, giving priority to economic and social rather than political or constitutional questions. Even the multiclass Catholic Center party gave primacy to religion and in practice, if not in ideology, favored agrarians and master artisans over workers and capitalists. Parties operated in a parliament in which there was no ministerial responsibility and only limited parliamentary control of budgets, the military, and foreign policy. Instead of challenging this authoritarian, pseudoparliamentary system, the National Liberals, Conservatives, and Catholics adapted to it, extracting important economic and social concessions in return for accepting their political impotence.[16] The power of the Bismarckian state, industrialist and agrarian preoccupation with economic issues, the prevalence of extraparliamentary economic interest groups, and a pervasive fear of the working class and social democracy all promoted this form of party development, which in turn facilitated and perpetuated the refounding of the Reich on a conservative basis.

If parties became narrower in the interests that they articulated and served, they nonetheless expanded their social base. Elite parties gave way to mass politics as German society was gradually reorganized into highly structured, strongly ideological, and mutually exclusive political milieus.[17] In response to the Kulturkampf, Bismarck's attack on the Catholic church in the 1870s, political Catholicism began to organize its

---

[15] See Helmut Böhme, *Deutschlands Weg zur Grossmacht* (Cologne: Kiepenheuer and Witsch, 1966) and Eckhart Kehr, *Primat der Innenpolitik* (Berlin: Walter de Gruyter, 1965).

[16] See Rosenberg, *Grosse Depression*, pp. 118-68; also Wehler, *Kaiserreich*.

[17] M. Rainer Lepsius, "Parteiensystem und Sozialstruktur: zum Problem der Demokratisierung der deutschen Gesellschaft," in *Die deutschen Parteien vor 1918*, ed. Gerhard A. Ritter (Cologne: Kiepenheuer and Witsch, 1973), pp. 56-80.

lower-class supporters into a variety of associations that could be mobilized to support the Center party at the polls. The Junker-based Conservative party made tentative overtures to the peasantry in the 1880s and recruited them into the Agrarian League in the 1890s. Only the National Liberals, who organized primarily among the industrial and financial bourgeoisie, remained an elite party of the old type.[18] On the one hand, this general politicization encouraged worker organization and activism. On the other, the major parties were hostile to working-class interests and effectively mobilized potential class allies of a workers' movement. If workers were to act, they had to do so alone or in conjunction with the Center party.

The authoritarian state institutions established in 1871 encouraged and reenforced the animosity of the dominant classes toward the working class and workers' movements. The German state, like the process of unification it crowned, was the product of a conservative revolution from above, not a popular uprising from below. The impotent parliament threatened neither the autonomy of the right-wing military and bureaucracy nor the power of the prime minister. Universal male suffrage for the Reichstag, conferred by Bismarck in an effort to win the loyalty of the lower classes, promoted mass politics without empowering the masses. Moreover, on the regional and local level everywhere except in southern Germany, inequitable systems of class suffrage ensured the primacy of the bourgeoisie and Junker aristocracy.[19]

If the authoritarian state structure made democratic reform and working-class integration unlikely, the state policies adopted during the depression made them impossible. The refounding of the Reich was a complex process, affecting all classes. The state sought to bolster its legitimacy and benefit its supporters by means not only of tariffs but also of colonial policy, social imperialism, and the purge of liberals from the bureaucracy. The state also intervened actively in an effort to shape working-class formation and defuse activism.[20] Only if the latter strategy complemented the former could the authoritarian state and conservative social order be permanently stabilized.

Although the government had devoted relatively little attention to

[18] On National Liberalism, see James Sheehan, *German Liberalism in the Nineteenth Century* (Chicago: University of Chicago, 1978). On Conservatism, see Gerschenkron, *Bread and Democracy*, and on political Catholicism, see Ronald Ross, *Beleaguered Tower* (Notre Dame: University of Notre Dame, 1976).

[19] Under this income-based suffrage in Prussia, for example, roughly the wealthiest 5 percent elected one-third of the deputies, the next 10 percent elected one-third, and the remaining 85 percent elected one-third.

[20] See Kehr, *Primat der Innenpolitik*, pp. 64-85 and Rosenberg, *Grosse Depression*, pp. 192-255.

workers prior to 1873, it made them a prime object of policy thereafter. Repression, aimed at containing both workplace unrest and the political potential of social democracy, was the dominant strategy adopted. Beginning in the mid-1870s the police and judiciary intensified their harassment of the still insignificant socialist unions and political organizations. Persecution of the fledgling workers' movement culminated in the passage of the Anti-Socialist laws in 1878. This legislation, initiated by Bismarck and widely supported by other parties, simultaneously singled out social democracy as the "enemy within" and, in conjunction with the tariff bill, rallied Liberal industrialists and Conservative agrarians behind the Bismarckian state. Under the terms of the Anti-Socialist laws, the Social Democrats could legally run for political office, but all Social Democratic political organizations, publications, and activities were declared illegal and in practice the ban applied to Social Democratic cultural associations and trade unions as well. The laws, whose application was accompanied by vituperative antisocialist and anti–working class rhetoric from the state and other parties, proved ineffective in curbing the workers' movement. In 1890 parliament, which recognized the failure of the Anti-Socialist laws but was unwilling to strengthen them, re-legalized the Social Democratic party.[21] But twelve years of institutionalized repression were to shape the ideology, strategy, and organization of the working class profoundly.

A subordinate and equally ineffective theme of government policy was paternalistic social welfare. In the 1880s Bismarck pushed through health, accident, and old-age insurance programs that were administered by the three contributing groups—the state, employers, and workers. The threefold aim was to secure the state and social order by eliminating need in its most acute forms, to deradicalize workers by making them state pensioners, and to build corporatist institutions that might ultimately replace political forms of representation.[22] The "social question," the question of the relationship of the working class to state and society, was to be given a social welfare rather than a political answer.

State policy was thus an ambitious attempt to preclude working-class political independence while integrating workers into a hierarchical

---

[21] See Richard Höhn, *Die vaterlandslosen Gesellen* (Cologne: Westdeutscher Verlag, 1964) and Vernon Lidtke *The Outlawed Party* (Princeton: Princeton University Press, 1966).

[22] Karl Erich Born, *Staat und Sozialpolitik seit Bismarck's Sturz* (Wiesbaden: Franz Steiner, 1957), pp. 23-27; Albin Gladen, *Geschichte der Sozialpolitik in Deutschland* (Wiesbaden: Franz Steiner, 1974), pp. 56-57, 66; Volker Hentschel, "Das System der sozialen Sicherung in historischer Sicht, 1880 bis 1975," *Archiv für Sozialgeschichte* 18 (1978):311.

social order. Although Bismarck's legislation gave Germany the most progressive social welfare system in Europe, social insurance did not bring social reform or achieve Bismarck's political goals. Eligibility was limited; benefits were meager and often uncollectable. The state endorsed repression and refused to pass much-needed and strongly demanded protective legislation.[23] In both its repressive and paternalistic forms, state policy promoted not only working-class political opposition but the very process of working-class formation. State policy treated workers as workers, rather than as members of particular crafts or of an amorphously defined fourth estate. It placed workers at the center of political debate and made them more aware of their interests and needs without convincing them of the state's ability to serve them.

Economic crisis, ruling-class response, and state policy were to define, unify, marginalize, and radicalize the emerging working class and the workers' movement. Before turning to that process, however, the effects of the depression on the material conditions of wage labor must be examined. Only then can we study the process by which class boundaries were drawn and understand the response of those who formed the working class to the massive transformations on all levels of German economic, social, and political life.

II. The Restructuring of Wage Labor

The Great Depression had pervasive but contradictory effects on the structure and condition of wage labor. The work force expanded and its recruitment altered. The labor process as well as occupational and skill hierarchies were transformed. Urbanization escalated and new forms of working-class communities emerged. Real wages rose but unemployment, migration, and emigration also increased. Both the individual processes of change and their collective impact on different sectors of the wage labor force need to be explored in depth, for these changes played a formative role in eroding old solidarities and encouraging new ones, in strengthening workers' capacity for organization and action, and simultaneously drawing the internal and external limits of class identification.

Due to economic crisis and high rates of emigration, the overall composition of the German labor force underwent slow and steady restructuring rather than dramatic change. Although there was no massive exodus from the countryside, there was a continuous flow from farm to mine, factory, and shop, because the severe agrarian crisis compounded the

[23] Hentschel, "System der sozialen Sicherung," pp. 314, 329-31; Wehler, *Bismarck*, pp. 459-63.

Table 8.1. Employment in Major Sectors of Manufacturing

Sector	1875		1895	
	Labor Force	%	Labor Force	%
Mining	286,000	5.3	432,000	5.4
Basic Metal	150,000	2.8	225,000	2.8
Metalworking	601,000	11.0	964,000	12.1
Chemicals	65,000	1.2	138,000	1.7
Textiles	926,000	17.0	992,000	12.5
Construction	530,000	9.7	1,025,000	12.9
Wood	522,000	9.6	679,000	8.5
Printing	46,000	0.8	116,000	1.5
Clothing, shoes	1,078,000	19.8	1,392,000	17.5
Food	676,000	12.4	1,029,000	12.9

SOURCE: Gerhard A. Ritter, *Arbeiterbewegung, Parteien und Parlamentarismus* (Göttingen: Vandenhoeck and Ruprecht, 1976), p. 63.
NOTE: Percentage is of those employed in mining, industry, and Handwerk only.

preexisting problems of rural overpopulation and landlessness. In 1875, 49.5 percent of the economically active worked in agriculture; by 1895 only 41.8 percent did. During the same period, those in mining and manufacturing (a category that includes factory and artisanal production as well as construction) grew from almost 5.5 million to nearly 8 million, or from 29.1 percent to 34 percent of the economically active. An increasing proportion of this group were dependent workers. In 1875, 41.7 percent of those in manufacturing and mining were independent producers and 56.7 percent were wage laborers; in 1895 the figures were 24.9 percent and 71.9 percent, respectively.[24]

Although all sectors of manufacturing grew absolutely and all but textiles grew as a percentage of total employment, the rates in different sectors varied considerably (see table 8.1), demonstrating the transitional character of the era. The occupations characteristic of the first industrial revolution, such as textiles, clothing, and wood working, declined relatively, and decline was frequently accompanied by a feminization of the labor force. Yet the newer occupations, indicative of the second industrial revolution, did not gain the predominance they were to enjoy after the turn of the century. As a result of the extensive development of mines in the Ruhr and the replacement of state supervision by fully capitalist forms of ownership and production, the absolute number of miners

[24] Aubin and Zorn, *Handbuch*, p. 614. Hohorst et al., *Sozialgeschichtliches Arbeitsbuch*, p. 69. Gerhard A. Ritter, *Arbeiterbewegung, Parteien und Parlamentarismus* (Göttingen: Vandenhoeck and Ruprecht, 1976), p. 63. The percentage of white-collar workers increased from 1.6 to 3.2.

increased substantially, but their representation in the labor force remained stagnant.[25] The metal sector underwent a similar development. Only metalworking, in which Handwerk persisted along with factories, experienced a relative as well as an absolute increase. New industries, such as chemicals, employed only a minuscule portion of the labor force.

Reflecting Germany's uneven development, the artisanal sector continued to be a major locus of employment, even though its relative significance diminished. Prior to the Great Depression nearly one-half of the economically active in the secondary sector worked in Handwerk, and afterwards more than one-third still did. As the *Alleinmeister* (a craftsman working alone) diminished and the ratio of journeymen to masters steadily increased, especially in urban areas, an increasing proportion of those in Handwerk were wage laborers.[26] For a significant segment of German workers, Handwerk was thus a part, if not the totality, of their work experience.

Although Handwerk as a general category persisted, different sectors of it suffered varied fates. The most marked growth occurred in construction, reflecting Germany's rapid urbanization and continued industrialization. Wood, clothing, and food workers, all of whom had figured prominently in the early manufacturing labor force, increased slightly in absolute terms but declined somewhat in relation to other groups. In shoes and clothing this surprising decline despite population growth and urbanization resulted from a partial shift to factory production. For many artisans survival meant increased specialization or a shift to repair and retail trade. Other threatened sectors moved from guildlike production to "putting out," but home work did not prove as adaptive as Handwerk in general and diminished both absolutely and relatively in this period.[27]

In terms of both numbers and position, women were marginal to this expanding and changing labor force. In 1875 women comprised 9.2 percent of those in industry and Handwerk; in 1895, 11.8 percent. Women were overwhelmingly concentrated in textiles, food, and clothing, especially in the precarious and declining parts of those sectors, where wages were notoriously low and hours long. Against 992,000 women workers in manufacturing in 1895, there were 201,000 doing home work, a form of

[25] Klaus Tenfelde, *Sozialgeschichte der Bergarbeiterschaft an der Ruhr im 19. Jahrhundert* (Bonn: Verlag neue Gesellschaft, 1977), pp. 164-70.

[26] Schröder, *Arbeitergeschichte*, pp. 84-85; Wolfram Fischer, *Wirtschaft und Gesellschaft im Zeitalter der Industrialisierung* (Göttingen: Vandenhoeck and Ruprecht, 1972), p. 329.

[27] Those employed in home work decreased from 476,075 in 1882 to 457,748 in 1895. Schröder, *Arbeitergeschichte*, p. 103.

production whose feminization reflected and reenforced its deterioration. Even more striking, by 1895 there were 1,339,000 female domestics, most of whom lived with their employers and all of whom were subject to the particularly repressive constraints of the servants' law (*Gesindeordnung*), which required unqualified obedience to one's employer, forbade organization, and excluded domestics as well as farm servants from protective legislation and social insurance programs.[28]

If the structure of the work force changed, so too did the nature of the work being performed. Industrialists' desire to cut costs and increase productivity in order to expand operations and maintain profits in a time of crisis led to significant changes in the labor process. Concentration and intensification were the general strategies pursued. Factory expansion and integration meant that the percentage of employees in firms with a labor force of fifty-one or more (that is, in what were then labelled large firms) increased from 22.8 percent to 33.5 percent between 1882 and 1895. Productivity per worker rose 54 percent in the two decades after 1875, while hours generally fell slightly.[29]

Mechanization, dequalification, and new forms of supervision and wage payment were capital's preferred means to attain its ends, especially in larger factories. Recent research suggests the extent and variety of attacks on more traditional labor processes. In Bochum's large-scale basic metal industry, mechanization was increased, the work pace was intensified, piece rates were lowered, and two twelve-hour shifts per day were introduced in iron and steel. In a Bielefeld sewing machine factory, productivity per worker nearly doubled between 1868 and 1889 due to mechanization, the simplification of tasks, and the introduction of piece rates. The factory, which had initially been like a large Handwerk shop, came to resemble a textile mill. From the late 1870s on, machine makers in a Württemberg machine factory saw their skill and prestige eroded. As management became bureaucratized and rationalized, it increased its control over individual workshops. Apprenticeship was restructured so that youths were given narrow training for specific factory jobs rather than wide-ranging artisan expertise. Piece rates were steadily lowered to the point where the wages and lifetime earning prospects of skilled workers were scarcely better than those of the semiskilled and unskilled. If such an extreme narrowing of wage differentials was exceptional, the

---

[28] Kuczynski, *Geschichte*, Bd. 18, *Studien zur Geschichte der Lage der Arbeiterin in Deutschland von 1700 bis zur Gegenwart* (Berlin: Akademie, 1963), pp. 105-106, 110-12, 127, 143; Rolf Engelsing, *Zur Sozialgeschichte der deutschen Mittel- und Unterschichten* (Göttingen: Vandenhoeck and Ruprecht, 1973), pp. 235-36, 255.

[29] Hohorst et al., *Sozialgeschichtliches Arbeitsbuch*, p. 75. Rosenberg, *Grosse Depression*, p. 49.

general pressure on the earnings of the skilled was not. At Siemens, the major producer of electrical equipment, more flexible forms of supervision, resembling those of journeymen by masters, were replaced by increasingly strict and detailed factory ordinances and sharper surveillance for laxity, theft, and the like. At least formally, although not always in practice, foremen gained complete control over the labor process, workers' access to materials, and their relationship with other workers. Not all capitalist initiatives were, to be sure, immediately successful. In a Berlin machine factory, internal subcontracting was eliminated and piece rates were introduced but worker opposition led to the reinstitution of hourly wages in the early 1890s. After the turn of the century, however, the premium bonus system was imposed to increase productivity and intensify work.[30]

The same general processes were operative in mining. In the 1870s, Ruhr mine owners responded to the crisis by cutting wages and firing workers; in the 1880s, by rationalizing and intensifying work. Although mechanization was not introduced, the average size of mines grew from 234 workers in 1870 to 722 in 1890. As a result, the division of labor increased, miners were more isolated from one another, and supervision became more formal. Owners sought to increase productivity and lower labor costs by eliminating the traditional eight-hour day, violating work rules, imposing arbitrary fines, and manipulating company housing and welfare programs to ensure acquiescence to these harsher conditions.[31]

The situation in the artisanal sector was more varied. Construction, for example, remained immune from mechanization and concentration, allowing workers to retain their skills and control of the labor process. Woodworking shops remained small, but some mechanization and specialization occurred. Less fortunate branches of Handwerk were fundamentally transformed as employers sought to cope with the depression and compete with factories by cutting labor costs. In cigar making, for example, the position of the skilled male was destroyed by ruralization,

---

[30] David Crew, *Town in the Ruhr* (New York: Columbia University Press, 1979), pp. 39-41; Helwig Schomerus, "Soziale Differenzierungen und Nivellierung der Fabrikarbeiterschaft Esslingens, 1846-1914," in *Forschungen zur Lage der Arbeiter im Industrialisierungsprozess*, ed. Hans Pohl (Stuttgart: Klett, 1978), pp. 21-47; Karl Ditt, "Technologischer Wandel und Strukturveränderung der Fabrikarbeiterschaft in Bielefeld, 1860-1914," in *Arbeiter im Industrialisierungsprozess*, ed. Werner Conze and Ulrich Engelhardt (Stuttgart: Klett, 1979), pp. 243-47; Jürgen Kocka, *Unternehemensverwaltung und Angestelltenschaft am Beispiel Siemens, 1847-1914* (Stuttgart: Klett, 1969), pp. 212-15; Heinrich Reichelt, "Die Arbeitsverhältnisse in einem Berlin Grossbetrieb der Maschinenindustrie" (Ph.D. diss., Berlin, 1900), pp. 12-13.

[31] Tenfelde, *Sozialgeschichte*, pp. 203-207, 220-23, 277-78; Klaus Tenfelde, "Die bergmännische Arbeitsplatz während der Hochindustrialisierung," in *Arbeiter*, ed. Conze and Engelhardt, p. 297.

feminization, and simplification of tasks as a once-thriving artisan trade moved not into the factory but into the home. Similarly, shoemaking was transformed from Handwerk to home work, but it then shifted to factory production, with its labor force becoming increasingly female.[32]

Both skill hierarchies and the meaning of skill were modified by these changes. The numerical preponderence of the skilled in manufacturing persisted. Indeed, in 1895 there were roughly three skilled and semi-skilled workers for every two unskilled. But such global statistics mask the disproportionately rapid rise in the unskilled as well as the emergence of that amorphous category, the semiskilled, who were recruited from the dequalified skilled workers, from independent artisans, and from formerly unskilled manual laborers who became machine operatives.[33] Although some highly trained workers retained or even upgraded their skills, others saw their autonomy and expertise limited by transformations in the industrial labor process. Those limits were evident in wages, hours, and forms of supervision. Language also reflected the growing similarities in the condition of all wage labor. In government statistics and social insurance programs, skilled and unskilled alike were treated as part of the universal category "workers" (Arbeiter). At Siemens "the use of the collective designation 'worker' for all non-clerical and non-managerial employees became ever more widespread" from the 1870s on.[34] Although in some sectors of Handwerk skill was simply destroyed, in others it was not skill per se but rather the link between skill and independence that was eliminated. Rather than an age-specific and temporary status, the position of journeyman increasingly became a lifelong situation of dependence. Those in declining trades, like shoemaking, where capital requirements were low and tools simple, might make the "flight into independence" but they seldom succeeded in escaping wage labor in the shop or factory permanently.[35]

These changes in occupational structure, work, and skill both promoted and hindered class formation. To begin with, the processes themselves were contradictory. Concentration, for example, brought large numbers of workers together in a common situation but also intensified supervision and worker isolation. Second, although capitalist responses to the crisis engendered disaffection, the crisis itself fostered demobilization.

[32] See Schröder, Arbeitergeschichte, pp. 101-185.
[33] Ibid., pp. 68-69. The unskilled formed 34.7 percent of workers in manufacturing in 1895 and 41.6 percent in 1907 (ibid.). See also Ditt, "Technologischer," p. 247 and Kocka, Unternehemensverwaltung, p. 208.
[34] Kocka, Unternehemensverwaltung, p. 208. For a discussion of the changing meaning of Arbeiter see Geschichtliche Grundbegriffe (Stuttgart: Klett, 1972), 1:216-42.
[35] Schröder, Arbeitergeschichte, p. 87.

Dequalification angered the skilled, for instance, but unemployment and state repression lessened their prospects of effectively combatting it. Third, and perhaps most important, those experiencing these changes came from very different backgrounds and had very different expectations of and experiences with new forms of wage labor. To understand worker response, the patterns of recruitment into the labor force and the types of involvement with industrial and artisanal work must be reconstructed. Mobility is the key to understanding these issues.

Germany in the Great Depression was a nation on the move. The striking magnitude of geographic mobility was a reflection of and response to three factors. First, unlike France, whose population hardly grew in this period, Germany suffered from continuous demographic pressure, its population increasing 27 percent from 1873 to 1896.[36] Second, this population expansion, coupled with the crisis in agriculture, forced many to leave the land temporarily or permanently. Third, the crisis-ridden expansion of manufacturing and mining meant that although a demand for labor existed, it was neither steady nor as great as the potential supply. These processes interacted to create high rates of emigration, internal migration, and job fluctuation.

Emigration was one possible response to pervasive crisis. To be sure, it was hardly a viable option in the 1870s due to the severity of the depression in the United States; the number leaving Germany declined from over 110,000 a year in 1873 to under 23,000 at the low point of 1877. Crisis abroad compounded that at home. Between 1880 and 1893, however, 1.8 million Germans emigrated, primarily to the United States. The exodus was fed above all by the unskilled in agriculture and manufacturing, 39 percent of whom came from east of the Elbe.[37] On the one hand emigration slowed working-class formation by providing an alternative to organization and protest, even to wage labor. On the other hand, it facilitated it by limiting the deterioration of workers' position and the influx of agrarian laborers into industry.

For most landless agrarian laborers, small peasants, artisans, and workers, internal migration rather than emigration was the response chosen. Germany's mass migration was composed of those moving from the country to the city and from one urban area to another as well as those returning to the land from a town. It included those who relocated one

---

[36] Rosenberg, *Grosse Depression*, p. 40.

[37] Ibid., p. 40; Hohorst et al., *Sozialgeschichtliches Arbeitsbuch*, p. 38; Klaus Bade, "Massenwanderung und Arbeitsmarkt im deutschen Nordosten von 1800 bis zum ersten Weltkrieg," *Archiv für Sozialgeschichte* 20 (1980):270, 281; Heinzpeter Thummler, "Zum Problem der Auswanderung aus dem deutschen Reich zwischen 1871 und 1900," *Jahrbuch für Wirtschaftsgeschichte* (1973), pp. 75, 90.

time as well as the many who migrated seasonally or moved frequently. Although it is impossible to estimate the total volume of migration, a sense of its magnitude can be sketched. From the 1880s on, the volume of people migrating in and out of cities of over 100,000 was the equivalent of one-fourth to one-third of those cities' populations. Between 1880 and 1890 the ratio of in- and out-migrants to population growth in the industrial cities of Essen and Chemnitz was 10–11:1.[38] Of greater importance, distinct patterns of migration that greatly affected working-class formation can be distinguished.

Skilled and unskilled workers moved literally in different worlds.[39] Skilled workers from small and medium-sized towns formed the vast majority of long-distance (more than 50 kilometers) migrants. Possessing skill, bargaining power, pride, and often urban experience and a little money, they sought out larger urban centers or moved between cities but seldom returned to their original home. Young factory workers or journeymen in Handwerk continued the artisan tradition of the wandering years, and those in their twenties or older moved either in search of work or as a form of protest.

The unskilled moved more frequently but rarely traveled over 50 kilometers, usually seeking out small towns and frequently returning to the countryside from which they had come. From the 1850s to the 1870s, landless agrarian laborers or their children as well as members of peasant families and some rural Handwerker sought unskilled jobs on a seasonal or one-time basis, their movements being dictated by the rhythms of agriculture and the economic situation on the land. The Great Depression disturbed this pattern, for it made rural conditions more precarious and industrial jobs less available. The unskilled traveled farther for temporary jobs and an increasing number of rural children, unlike their parents, remained permanently in the manufacturing sector. Mining provided the most dramatic instance of this. Through the 1870s, Ruhr mines employed skilled miners from elsewhere or peasant miners from the region; thereafter they recruited from the proletarianized rural laborers

[38] Dieter Langewiesche, "Wanderungsbewegungen in der Hochindustrialisierungsperiode," *Vierteljahresschrift für Sozial- und Wirtschaftsgeschichte* 64, no. 1 (1977): 6-7, 13.

[39] Tenfelde, *Sozialgeschichte*, pp. 230-31; Bade, "Massenwanderung," p. 277; Peter Borscheid, "Schranken sozialer Mobilität und Binnenwanderung im 19. Jahrhundert," in *Arbeiter*, ed. Conze and Engelhardt, pp. 38-49; Wolfgang von Hippel, "Regionale und soziale Herkunft der Bevolkerung einer Industriestadt: Untersuchung zu Ludwigshaven," in ibid., pp. 57-59, 100-108; Gunther Schulz, "Integrationsprobleme der Arbeiter in Metall, Papier und Chemie in der Rheinprovinz, 1850-1914," in *Forschungen zur Lage*, ed. Pohl, pp. 779.

east of the Elbe, for whom the transition to mining on the other side of Germany was as traumatic as emigration.[40] Significant segments of the labor force were thus drawn from the impoverished rural underclass, which lacked job skills or urban experience, money, or property. They had few prospects for job security, advancement, and integration into industrial work and urban life. Indeed, they had little desire for them.

For a given factory, shop, or mine, these patterns of migration meant extraordinarily high job turnover. Between 1870 and 1890 fluctuation rates for the unskilled were between 70 and 80 percent and for the industrial labor force as a whole between 40 and 50 percent. Although mines and factories made little effort to retain the unskilled, who often left within a few months, they did build a small stable core of skilled workers, who were tied to the firm by high wages, company housing, and welfare programs.[41]

Migration, emigration, and job fluctuation, which had begun well before the Great Depression, continued to erode corporatist traditions in Germany and to transform the "social question" from one of rural overpopulation and proletarianization in a *Ständestaat* (society of estates) to one of workers in a capitalist industrial society. They brought ever larger circles into contact with new forms of wage labor. But these processes also served as a safety valve and alternative to protest. They created new divisions among workers and enormous obstacles to organization. They promoted urbanization in ways that both created new forms of community and reenforced the divisions generated by patterns of mobility.

Although Handwerk remained a rural and small-town phenomenon as well as an urban one, industry was increasingly concentrated in cities and mining villages became populous towns. Between 1871 and 1890 the percentage of the population residing in towns of over 20,000 increased from 12.5 to 21.9 percent. The number of cities with populations over 100,000 rose from 12 to 17. The Rhineland, Saxony, and north Germany experienced the most pronounced urbanization. In many big cities and medium-sized industrial towns, large proletarian neighborhoods and increased residential segregation by class developed. Even in a relatively small Württemberg town, exclusively working-class apartment buildings and streets appeared, testifying to the increased contact among workers

---

[40] Silesian mines drew their labor force from dwarf farms and landless laborers in the region. Lawrence Schofer, *The Formation of a Modern Labor Force in Upper Silesia, 1865-1914* (Berkeley: University of California, 1975), pp. 50-55.

[41] Crew, *Town*, pp. 148ff; Schofer, *Formation*, pp. 100-101, 122; Schulz, "Intergrationsprobleme," pp. 78-79.

in various trades and the decreased association of skilled metalworkers with the middle and lower-middle classes.[42]

With increased urban density and speculative building, the percentage of workers owning their own homes, always a minority in any case, decreased. Generally a young single worker would either live at home or room with his or her employer or another working-class family. After marriage a small apartment would be rented from a speculator. Once children arrived and budgetary pressures mounted, a still smaller dwelling would be sought or roomers taken in. This "half-open" family structure of kin and roomers, which was especially prevalent in the Ruhr and big cities, provided workers with solidarity and support on a subpolitical level.[43]

If certain aspects of urbanization subjected workers to a collective fate, others intensified differences in experiences. Except in Ruhr mining communities, for example, the mass of highly mobile unskilled lived apart from both the stable element and the migratory skilled.[44] Housing forms laid the basis for different types of communities. In cities like Berlin, workers crowded together in high-density, unsanitary apartment houses, aptly called "rental barracks." In the Rhineland and south Germany they lived in low-density dwellings. Both types of housing brought together workers from different trades, even if not from all skill levels. In the Ruhr, small apartments or vast new "company colonies" with little apartments and garden plots predominated. Although housing structures there were better than in places like Berlin and Düsseldorf, housing shortages and overcrowding were acute. Moreover, miners were often dependent on the company and were always isolated from other workers. Older industrial towns, such as Barmen, Remscheid, or Berlin, and newer ones, such as Düsseldorf, were multiclass, well-established urban centers in which a physical and social infrastructure of roads, schools, hospitals, churches, and pubs had been developed before the 1870s and was expanded, albeit inadequately, thereafter. There was an urban working-class culture built on a social base of craftsmen, small tradesmen, and second- or third-generation factory workers. This greatly facilitated political, economic, and educational organizing among workers. In the completely new and overwhelmingly proletarian Ruhr towns, however, there was neither an

[42] Hohorst et al., *Sozialgeschichtliches Arbeitsbuch*, pp. 35, 43; Schomerus, "Soziale Differenzierungen," pp. 78-81.

[43] Lutz Niethammer, "Wie wohnten Arbeiter im Kaiserreich," *Archiv für Sozialgeschichte* 16 (1976):78-81. Franz Brüggemeier and Lutz Niethammer, "Schlafgänger, Schnapskasinos und schwerindustrielle Kolonie," in *Fabrik, Familie, Feierabend*, ed. Jürgen Reulecke and Wolfhard Weber (Wuppertal: Peter Hammer, 1978), pp. 150-54.

[44] Borscheid, "Schranken," p. 42.

urban infrastructure nor a working-class culture. This both made organization more difficult and shaped consciousness and activism in different
directions.[45]

The Great Depression altered the standard of living of workers just as
it changed other aspects of their situation. The conventional wisdom
about this period—that the standard of living rose because money wages
fell more slowly than prices—is accurate on the most general level but in
need of substantial qualification. Taking 1895 as the base year, workers'
average yearly real income did rise from 70 in 1871 to 100 in 1895.[46] But
this significant improvement came only after the early 1880s. The first
decade of the crisis was disastrous on all counts. After 1873, average real
weekly wages rose briefly and then dropped precipitously, where they
remained until the mid-1880s. Simultaneously unemployment rose
sharply, further lowering earnings and increasing insecurity. The meager
statistics available only hint at the magnitude of the problem. Between
1873 and 1879 employment in mining dropped from 289,000 to 275,000.
Two major companies, the Dortmunder Union and the Bochemer Verein,
cut their labor force in half, while Krupp dropped wages 50 percent. In
1883, a year when over 173,000 Germans emigrated, between 200,000
and 400,000 roamed the country in search of work.[47]

From the mid-1880s on, improvement affected all workers, but the
skilled, who earned 30 to 50 percent more than unskilled men and 50 to
65 percent more than women, were the principal beneficiaries. A skilled
male might cover over 90 percent of his family's needs with his wage
alone, but an unskilled worker could only cover 75 percent, making the
contribution of his wife and/or children absolutely essential for survival.
The skilled paid roughly 50 percent of their income for food and another
20 to 25 percent for rent; figures for the unskilled were even higher.[48] For
most male workers remaining in manufacturing full time, earnings rose
from their first employment in adolescence through their thirties and
then declined. This meant that young workers could save a bit before
marriage and with luck maintain their standard of living through their
early forties. Thereafter, however, lower wages, unstable employment,

[45] Niethammer, "Wie wohnten Arbeiter," pp. 101-107; Franz Brüggemeier, "Ruhr
Miners and Their Historians," in *People's History and Socialist Theory*, ed. Raphael
Samuel (London: Routledge and Kegan Paul, 1981), p. 330.

[46] Hohorst et al., *Sozialgeschichtliches Arbeitsbuch*, p. 107.

[47] Ibid., p. 38; Rosenberg, *Grosse Depression*, pp. 46-47; Wehler, *Bismarck*, p. 79;
Ritter, *Arbeiterbewegung, Parteien*, p. 65.

[48] Hans-Dieter Gimbel, "Sozialistengesetz und 'grosse Depression' " in *Geschichte der
deutschen Gewerkschaftsbewegung*, ed. Frank Deppe et al. (Cologne: Pahl-Rugenstein,
1977), p. 47; Aubin and Zorn, *Handbuch*, p. 621; Niethammer, "Wie wohnten Arbeiter,"
p. 48.

and illness eroded previous gains. For the unskilled, the transient, the temporary, and women, improvement in mid-life was less likely but decline in later years even more certain.[49]

Workers' perceptions of their standard of living are even more difficult to ascertain than statistical averages. There are, however, good reasons to doubt that a pervasive sense of improvement existed. The first decade of the depression was undoubtedly traumatic due to both the severity of the crisis and the sharp contrast with the prosperity of previous years. Throughout the period, unemployment, migration, job fluctuation, and changes in the labor process lessened gains and dulled the perception of what gains did occur. For skilled workers, increased wages could not be translated into upward mobility because the barrier between manual and nonmanual labor was insurmountable. Nor could it mean adequate housing, schools, and communities. For miners, better wages were counterbalanced by a loss of their privileges and position as the best-paid workers in Germany. For unskilled migrants, improving wages offered scant compensation for the erosion of their traditional values and way of life.[50] And the economic factors limiting perception of improvement were compounded by repressive state policies.

This complex restructuring of the labor force, the labor process, work, community, mobility, and living standards created the conditions not of their own choosing under which wage laborers developed their identities. In the face of these pervasive and disruptive changes, which brought few benefits, wage laborers increasingly felt that they shared a collective fate. Different groups, however, defined that fate in quite different ways.

III. *Class Consciousness, Craft Particularism, and Precapitalist Identities*

Although cyclical crisis and structural change led to the erosion of older solidarities and dispositions among wage laborers, they by no means molded workers into a homogeneous group with a shared identity. Although external class boundaries were delineated more sharply, they were also drawn more narrowly. In the period from the 1870s to the 1890s, there emerged three main groups within the wage-labor population: first, those who identified themselves primarily as working class, had a permanent commitment to wage labor and urban life, and associated with one another at work, in the community, and through marriage; sec-

---

[49] Helwig Schomerus, "Lebenszyklus und Lebenshaltung in Arbeiterhaushaltungen des 19 Jahrhunderts," in *Arbeiter*, ed. Conze and Engelhardt, pp. 196-99.

[50] Crew, *Town*, pp. 80ff; Tenfelde, "Die bergmännische Arbeitsplatz," pp. 317-20.

ond, those whose self-conception, community, and culture were built predominantly around their trade; and third, those whose self-definition did not center around industrial work and urban life, whose commitments and associations lay elsewhere. The remaining links were severed between those with class and craft consciousness on the one hand and master artisans, new white-collar employees, small farmers, and rural laborers on the other, while wage laborers without such consciousness remained embedded in the preindustrial, patriarchal order.

Those who considered themselves workers, and members of the working class, as opposed to the workers' estate, were a varied and expanding lot. Many artisans, such as wood workers and shoe and cigar makers, and those factory workers who were born proletarians, such as textile workers and printers, had developed a working-class identity that transcended craft particularism before the 1870s. New groups of dependent artisans, especially in construction, and growing numbers of skilled factory workers, above all in the metal industries, did so thereafter.[51] This heterogeneous group embraced the designation "Arbeiter," which was a "fighting concept" with clear political connotations and not simply a social category.[52] These workers shared a collective fate on and off the job. It was not the fact of a collective fate, however, but its character and the way it interacted with the background, outlook, and expectations of these workers that promoted class solidarity.

Nearly all skilled workers, regardless of where they ultimately worked, received their training in Handwerk. This initiation into artisan work gave them not only skill but a shared definition of work based on the abilities and control that characterized artisanal work. They absorbed the pride and culture of the artisan as well as his determination to defend his position and prerogatives, but they were not imbued with narrow craft exclusiveness, for the corporate tradition was extremely weak due to rapid industrialization and state policy. This shared experience of apprenticeship as well as the growing necessity for many artisans to seek skilled or semiskilled factory jobs helped to diminish significantly the previously existing divisions and hostilities between journeymen and skilled factory workers.[53]

In terms of work, earnings, and expectations, skilled factory workers and journeymen in Handwerk remained privileged and distinct from the unskilled throughout the Great Depression. Yet, as seen earlier, skills

---

[51] Ritter, *Arbeiterbewegung, Parteien*, pp. 55-95.

[52] *Geschichtliche Grundbegriffe*, 4:228-33.

[53] Schulz, "Integrationsprobleme," p. 75; Schröder, *Arbeitergeschichte*, pp. 22-23; see also the essay by Kocka in this volume.

were steadily being eroded, employment was insecure, wage gains were hardly dramatic, and upward mobility, whether through self-employment or within the factory, was rare. The resulting sense of a shared fate and of collective proletarianization was enhanced by the pattern of migration common to the skilled, who moved frequently over long distances and within regional or national labor markets. This pattern taught some skilled workers that their situation was determined by systemic economic and political factors, not by local or personal ones. It made many others receptive to such structural arguments once social democracy offered them. Mobility also enabled workers to spread that awareness more widely.

The skilled shared both a commitment to urban life and similar urban life experiences. These workers had broken their ties with the land and saw the capitalist industrial system as a way of life to which they must adjust rather than simply a temporary place in which to work. Although they experienced a division between work and home/community, both were located in the same urban world, one increasingly structured by class relations. They lived in working-class housing, migrated among working-class neighborhoods, married other workers, participated actively in the emerging working-class culture, and socialized their children as well as their young, single lodgers into this world. Community and culture reenforced class identity particularly strongly in older industrial cities such as Leipzig, Elberfeld-Barmen, and Berlin, but created either weaker or different and conflicting solidarities in new economic centers, such as those in the Ruhr or in Catholic cities, such as Düsseldorf.[54]

Finally, those who considered themselves working class were overwhelmingly Protestant, for Catholic workers remained loyal to their religion and its political movement until after the turn of the century. The Protestant Church failed to develop a rich sociocultural milieu into which workers could be organized and with which they could identify. There were some evangelical workers' associations, but these emphasized religion and patriotism and were the only link between workers and religion. The Catholic Church, in contrast, constructed a multifaceted institutional network. Catholic Workers' Associations, which pursued secular as well as religious goals and recreational and cultural as well as economic activities, were supplemented by political associations, parish societies, and welfare organizations. Of equal importance, political Catholi-

---

[54] Niethammer, "Wie wohnten Arbeiter," pp. 100ff. See also Hartmut Zwar, *Zur Konstituierung des Proletariats als Klasse* (Berlin: Akademie, 1978) and Mary Nolan, *Social Democracy and Society* (New York: Cambridge University Press, 1981).

cism offered workers a comprehensive ideology that mixed religion, politics, and economics, that was critical of the Bismarckian state (if only because it persecuted Catholics) and that criticized capitalism (albeit from a corporatist perspective). Even if political Catholicism did not grant Catholic workers equality or promise extensive economic and political reform, it did provide them with political representation, social services, and a modest defense of their material interests. It offered workers a secure but subordinate place in the Catholic culture and community. Protestant workers needed a new vocabulary and alternative community to a much greater extent than Catholic workers did.[55]

Miners shared many aspects of the objective situation of journeymen, construction workers, and skilled factory workers. They were permanent wage laborers, whose skills, control, and earnings were under steady attack and who increasingly lived in isolated, concentrated working-class neighborhoods. Yet, for both ideological and social reasons, miners did not move from an occupational to a class identity in this period.

Corporate ideology, which was a reflection of reality until the 1850s and a strong residual force thereafter, made it difficult for miners to recognize the full implications of their changed situation. Older miners sought to restore the status that their trade had enjoyed before government regulation of mining and the corporate privileges of miners associated with it ceased. They handed down precapitalist assumptions and solidarities as well as beliefs about miners' special relationship with the state. To the extent that new miners, who came directly from agriculture, transcended their rural ties—and they did so much more in the Ruhr than in Silesia—they were either influenced by older ideologies or identified only with their new work. And the nature of mine work strongly reenforced the primacy of occupational identification. Miners worked in groups, whose members had little direct supervision but were heavily dependent on one another for wages and safety. The hierarchy of skills was rudimentary and most could expect to move through it, from hauler to apprentice hewer to hewer.[56]

Community and culture further encouraged craft identification. Miners lived in new towns that were overwhelmingly proletarian if not exclusively populated by miners. In company housing or rented apartments, mining families lived with other mining families and took in fellow miners, often members of the husband's work group, as lodgers. These towns

[55] Vernon Lidtke, "Social Class and Secularization in Imperial Germany: The Working Classes," in *Year Book* 25, Leo Baeck Institute (1980), pp. 31-33, 36; Nolan, *Social Democracy*, pp. 42-47.

[56] Tenfelde, *Sozialgeschichte*, pp. 340-42; Tenfelde, "Die bergmännische Arbeitsplatz," pp. 301-303; Schofer, *Formation*, pp. 50-55, 120-22.

lacked an urban infrastructure and traditional working-class culture that might have integrated miners into a larger community. Thus, miners' cultural and recreational life centered on work; their associational forms were built on the traditional miners' organizations, the *Knappenvereine*, which were a sort of friendly society. Finally, religion reenforced miners' isolation from the working class, for most miners were Catholic and the Church was active among them, especially in the Ruhr.[57]

Miners, especially younger ones who were second-generation workers in the capitalist mines, did become increasingly militant and organized in the 1880s, but it was still more in defense of craft than of class, of their position as *Bergmänner* and not as *Bergarbeiter*.[58] State policy no longer supported the corporate identity that it had helped create, but miners were slow to realize this.

What of those wage laborers who identified neither with class nor with craft? Peasant workers and the permanently unskilled who were recruited from them did share a collective fate. They suffered inadequate wages, low status, job insecurity, and work intensification. They moved frequently but within a small radius and returned often to the land. Work and home were not only separate but in different social worlds, and peasant workers were residentially and culturally marginal to the urban life and the skilled working class in the towns where they sought employment. These common experiences, however, produced divided identities. Industrial work was a way to maintain agrarian life; it was to the latter that peasant workers were committed, and with others from the rural world that they married and socialized. Even those forced to work in industry all their lives often clung to the illusion of returning or commuted from the countryside daily or weekly. Those without such ties or illusions, whose number increased during the Great Depression, nonetheless lacked the material and cultural prerequisites to identify with the journeymen and skilled factory workers who formed the working class.[59]

Employed girls and women are more difficult to categorize.[60] Domestic servants, the largest occupational group, can be safely excluded from the working class. They were predominantly rural in origin, lived with middle- and upper-class families rather than in proletarian neighborhoods, often returned to the countryside to marry, and were relegated to a sep-

[57] Brüggemeier, "Ruhr Miners," pp. 330-31; Klaus Tenfelde, "Bergmännisches Vereinswesen im Ruhrgebiet während der Industrialisierung," in *Fabrik, Familie, Feierabend*, ed. Reulecke and Weber, pp. 315-44.

[58] Tenfelde argues that class consciousness did supplant craft consciousness (*Sozialgeschichte*, pp. 511-96).

[59] Schröder, *Arbeitergeschichte*, pp. 41-49.

[60] Virtually no work has been done on female workers. For a good collection of documents, see *Frauenarbeit und Beruf*, ed. Gisela Brinker-Gabler (Frankfurt: Fischer, 1979).

arate legal status by the Gesindeordnung. Women in the increasingly feminized home-work sector also occupied a marginal position, but for different reasons. Unskilled home work, which was often located in rural areas, isolated laborers from one another and encouraged identity with the family as the key unit of production and survival rather than with craft or class. Women in industry and Handwerk were in a more ambiguous position. For most, wage labor was either restricted to the phase of their life between school and marriage or was resorted to sporadically in times of family crisis, such as a husband's illness, unemployment, or death. Their identity was not with their job, which was unskilled, or with wage labor, which was particularly exploitative for women, as much as it was with the family and the family wage economy.

Whether this identification could broaden into class consciousness depended on the complex interaction of family of birth, work, and family of marriage. The daughters or wives of peasant workers probably shared their families' identification with the land. Those of unskilled but permanent wage laborers would of necessity work themselves, but like their husbands or fathers—and like working single women and widows—they would be excluded from the economic, cultural, and political world of the skilled. Wives and daughters of the Protestant skilled, regardless of whether they relied solely on the man's wage or took in boarders, home-work, and laundry, were likely to identify with the working class. But they were relegated to a subordinate status in a working class that defined itself by skill, maleness, and the public culture built around those attributes. Catholic women tended to remain closely tied to the Catholic milieu, whatever their own work situation or that of their husbands and fathers.

Those who formed the working class remained separate not only from many wage laborers but also, and even more so, from other social groups. Prior to the 1870s master artisans, the self-employed, and journeymen had not always been distinct and hostile groups. In trades where capital requirements were low and the product could be made by one person, many crossed and recrossed the line between wage labor and independence. Conflicts between journeymen and employers, which first emerged in serious form during the revolution of 1848, coexisted with a residual corporatist defense of the interests of the trade in particular and Handwerk in general. In response to continued industrialization and the depression, however, master artisans sought to increase their power and protect their privileges by organizing along corporatist lines and securing legislation to strengthen guilds. Their dual aim was to bolster Handwerk vis-à-vis capitalist industry and to keep journeymen out of the workers' movement. As master artisans engaged in a conservative collective protectionism similar to that of Junker landlords and industrialists, the economic conflicts with journeymen multiplied and areas of common interest shrank. As journeymen developed a consciousness of being working class, master artisans developed one as *Mittelstand* (middle estate), a designation from an older corporatist vocabulary, whose essence was independence and distance from the working class.[61]

The boundaries between the working class and those in agriculture, whether peasants or laborers, remained sharp during this period, even though unskilled workers and miners were often of rural origin. Both economic development and state policy fostered the preservation of remnants of the patriarchal order in the countryside. After the 1870s, as before, rural workers lived not only in a separate economic and cultural world, characterized by dependence and deference, but also in a separate legal one, embodied in the Gesindeordnung. Their closest social and kin relationships were with one another or with those wage laborers most marginal to the working class. Although economic conditions in the countryside deteriorated, temporary or permanent migration and emigration offered an alternative to organization and protest.

The political changes of the depression eliminated the admittedly meager possibilities that the barrier between rural and urban workers would be lessened. Junker agriculture sought to mobilize the countryside behind an ideology of conservative agrarianism, protectionism, anti-Semitism, and antisocialism. Political Catholicism offered a program mixing religion, tariffs, and the defense of rural life. And while Conservatives and Catholics were successfully organizing, the Social Democrats alternated between ignoring the rural sector and complacently predicting its demise.[62]

Based on their different backgrounds and experiences, German wage laborers thus developed different identities that divided them from one another and from other social groups. Of equal importance, their ideological and organizational responses to their different collective fates also diverged markedly.

IV. *Protest and Politics*

The era of the Great Depression saw a fundamental transformation of worker politics in the economic arena and in society at large. In the wake of economic crisis, repressive state policies, and the restructuring of the

---

[61] Alfred Förster, *Die Gewerkschaftspolitik der deutschen Sozialdemokratie während des Sozialistengesetzes* (Berlin: Tribune, 1971), pp. 191-99. *Geschichtliche Grundbegriffe*, 4:81-84.

[62] Bade, "Massenwanderung," pp. 302-303.

labor force, the embryonic Social Democratic organization of the 1870s became a mass movement by the 1890s. To those workers who had developed a class identity, the Social Democratic movement offered a persuasive analysis of their situation, an effective vehicle for protest, and a cohesive community in industrial urban society. But social democracy was to be profoundly shaped—indeed limited—ideologically and organizationally by the very conditions that promoted it. Its deterministic Marxism, ambivalent parliamentarism, and organizational centralization were reflections of and responses to industrial capitalist development and authoritarian politics—replies, at once effective and problematic, to the contradictory position of the working class in Imperial German society. Social democracy both united workers and deepened divisions among them. If the Social Democrats became the spokesmen for those considering themselves working class, the movement failed to broaden its appeal to those with craft consciousness and with precapitalist identities. If social democracy provided a new vocabulary, institutions, and goals for Protestant workers, it could not curb the growth of a Catholic workers' movement, which was itself transformed by the conditions of the era and by competition from social democracy.

The changing character of worker politics and protest emerges clearly if we isolate three areas—strikes, trade unions, and political parties—and trace their complex interconnections. Only then can the unique outcome of class formation in Germany be understood: the emergence of a mass, Marxist, Social Democratic movement and a minority corporatist Catholic one, both of which resulted from but could not transcend the economic, social, and political marginalization of the working class.

From the 1870s to the 1890s, economic struggles were transformed as workers learned to understand capitalism and to fight it from within rather than to attack it with precapitalist values and strategies. Workplace protest became increasingly rationalized, disciplined, centralized, and coordinated with both economic cycles and trade union strength. But the process was slow and uneven. Until the 1890s, unions were neither a prerequisite for nor a necessary result of workplace militancy. Old strike demands and tactics coexisted with new ones, and job changes, absenteeism, slowdowns, and alcohol provided many with alternative forms of protest to strikes and organization.

Strike statistics nonetheless reveal workers' growing perception of conflicts between capital and labor. In the 1870s, acute economic crisis and then the Anti-Socialist laws virtually eliminated protest. The number of strikes per year fell from 225 in 1873 to 3 by 1878, a level at which it remained through the early 1880s. Between 1883 and 1888, however, there were 508 strikes and in 1888-1889 alone there were 670, including a massive walkout by over 90,000 Ruhr miners. Thereafter strikes declined sharply as the depression deepened once again.[63] Although strikes were heavily concentrated among skilled factory and construction workers and journeymen, protest also occurred among Ruhr miners and occasionally among women textile workers and the unskilled. This spread of strikes beyond those who initially were in or came to be in the working class reflected the pervasiveness of structural change, intensification, and dequalification as well as the limited effectiveness of individual, informal protest.

Certain large and significant groups, however, remained uninvolved in strikes. In the Saar mining area, for example, the state's role in the mines and the authoritarian paternalism of capitalists in the firm and community bolstered miners' corporatist identity and quelled protest.[64] Peasant workers, who knew their sojourn in the factory or shop would be brief, preferred regular pay to risky and potentially costly protest. The unskilled had no bargaining power and received little aid from the skilled until the 1890s. Most women workers, trapped in home work, the sweatshop, or domestic service and often burdened by housework and child care, were understandably quiescent. Political Catholicism actively condemned strikes until the mid-1890s, when it reluctantly conceded their legitimacy in an effort to retain the loyalty of Catholic workers.

The demands of strikers, which included backward- and forward-looking elements, reflected the growing realization that craft exclusiveness and residual corporatism were unsuitable to new conditions. Workers' demands centered on increased wages and shorter hours. The form of payment was seldom attacked, for although trade union leaders insisted that "piecework is murder," skilled workers objected more to the unilateral lowering of rates than to piecework itself. Workers' demands sometimes represented the defense of tradition, as with the Ruhr miners, who had once had a state-guaranteed eight-hour day and privileged pay, and at other times the logic of subsistence. Increasingly, however, these demands were justified in terms of the right to a normal workday and the need to compensate for increased intensity and to combat the manipulation of piece rates.[65] As late as the early 1880s, protesting journeymen accompanied their demands with appeals for cooperation between masters and men in the creation of a harmonious workplace. By the decade's

---

[63] Wehler, *Bismarck*, p. 80. Klaus Schönhoven, *Expansion und Konzentration: Studien zur Entwicklung der Freien Gewerkschaften im Wilhelmischen Deutschland* (Stuttgart: Klett, 1980), p. 97.

[64] Tenfelde, *Sozialgeschichte*, p. 533.

[65] Ibid., pp. 595-96; Dieter Groh, "Vorläufige Überlegungen zur Formierung der deutschen Arbeiterklasse" (University of Konstanz, 1979), pp. 16, 20-21.

end, however, the conflict between capital and labor, even in Handwerk, was unequivocally acknowledged.[66]

Tactics, like demands, were a mixture of the old, the new, and the old used in new ways. Although journeymen's strikes in the eighteenth century had been rationally timed, thoroughly organized, and strategically sophisticated, in the early nineteenth century journeymen's organizations had declined and with them the earlier effective strike tradition. By the 1860s and 1870s, strikes were largely local and spontaneous affairs, undertaken by one occupation with relatively little regard to the state of the economy and the size of strike funds. Gradually they became more carefully planned and executed by local organizations, which increasingly preceded and promoted protest. With growing frequency strikers appealed to workers in other occupations and locales—a clear indication of diminishing craft exclusiveness and developing links between local issues and wider class concerns. Throughout the period, Ruhr miners resorted to their time-honored tactic of petitioning government officials for the redress of grievances and the restoration of privileges. Other workers, however, used such petitions both to promote union organization and to demand more general rights, as in the ten-hour workday petition movement of 1882. In addition, they looked not only to the state but also to public opinion for support. Even the Ruhr miners, who painfully discovered that capital was intransigent and the state hardly neutral, learned the necessity of supplementing traditional petitions with strikes and ultimately with ongoing union organizations.[67]

The increasing frequency of strikes and their changing goals and forms resulted in part from structural changes in the economy, labor force, migration, and urbanization and in part from the learning process undergone by many workers, whatever their political proclivities. By the 1880s, a third factor was dwarfing these two—direct Social Democratic intervention in the organization and execution of strikes. The importance and nature of Social Democratic involvement in strike behavior was confirmed in the early 1890s, when advocates of centralized trade unions triumphed over proponents of local autonomy and imposed their vision of the rational, disciplined, and centrally directed strike.[68] Trade union development explains this outcome.

The Great Depression was an era of spectacular if erratic growth and

[66] Förster, *Gewerkschaftspolitik*, pp. 130-39, 198-99.

[67] Ibid., pp. 108-110; Groh, "Vorläufige Überlegungen," pp. 18-19; Tenfelde, *Sozialgeschichte*, pp. 508-573; Andreas Griessinger, *Das symbolische Kapital des Ehre* (Frankfurt: Ullstein Materialien, 1981).

[68] See Gerhard A. Ritter, *Die Arbeiterbewegung im Wilhelmischen Reich* (Berlin: Colloquium Verlag, 1959).

fundamental transformation for the German trade union movement. If workplace militancy provides an index of growing class conflict and consciousness, trade union development demonstrates the institutionalization of both, and in new ways. As the union movement—or movements, for Social Democrats, Catholics, and liberals each had one—grew, they changed their social base, leaders, organizational forms, and relationships to political parties. The relative power of these highly ideological union movements shifted as well. Indeed, union organization, along with electoral activity, was the principal means by which the Social Democrats gained predominant influence in the working class. The Social Democratic unions, which were commonly referred to as the "free" trade unions, in turn illustrate the strengths and limits of that power.

Although trade unions had a checkered history during this period of economic crisis and political repression and membership statistics were not systematically collected until the early 1890s, the broad contours of unionization can nonetheless be reconstructed. In the 1870s the depression, the police, and judicial harassment created major obstacles to union organizing. So too did divisions within social democracy between the Lassalleans, who adhered to the iron law of wages and thus considered unions to be useless for improving the workers' material situation, and the Eisenachers, who gave primacy to politics but viewed unions as economically beneficial and organizationally advantageous. By 1877-1878, roughly 52,000–56,000 workers, or only slightly more than in 1869-1870, were in socialist unions, and another 16,000 had joined the Hirsch-Duncker movement, whose liberal outlook led it to emphasize cooperatives and self-help and to eschew strikes and collective bargaining. The proclamation of the Anti-Socialist laws initially decimated the free trade unions, for the government, recognizing the close links between the political and economic wings of the Social Democratic movement, outlawed fifty national associations and many local ones.[69]

Although repression disrupted union growth and caused organizations to appear and disappear rapidly in the early 1880s, it failed to stop the momentum of social democracy on the economic front just as it failed on the electoral one. Social Democratic unions grew steadily from the mid-1880s on, winning over 100,000 members by 1888 and nearly 300,000 by 1890, when the movement was again made legal. The liberal union movement, by contrast, had just over 63,000 members. Although political Catholicism had many Catholic Workers' Associations, devoted to "the strengthening of faith" and "the promotion of the virtues of one's estate (*Standestugenden*)," it did not establish Christian trade unions until

---

[69] Ritter, *Arbeiterbewegung, Parteien*, pp. 59, table following p. 96.

1894. By the mid-1890s the free trade unions, to which just under 4 percent of blue-collar workers belonged, were not yet the mass movement they were to become after 1900. Yet socialist dominance was established. The inadequacy of the liberal unions' solution to the problems of the German working class was evident in their failure to grow substantially despite the repression of the Social Democrats and the inactivity of the Catholics. And the Catholic union movement never recovered from its late start, the religious limits of its appeal, and the necessity of acting like and cooperating with the free unions in order to win demands.[70]

As the free union movement grew its social base altered. In the 1860s and 1870s workers in tobacco, printing, and trades with a Handwerk tradition dominated the movement; in the 1880s tobacco, construction, and carpenters' unions led the way. By the 1890s the five largest unions were, in order, those of the metalworkers, woodworkers, printers, textile workers, and masons.

The union movement reflected both changes in the structure of the economy and the limits of working-class identification. Organization was strongest in artisan shops and small and medium-sized factories in the finished-goods sector, but even there it was only skilled and dequalified semiskilled male workers who joined. Peasant workers, who had little enough reason to join given their expectations of returning to the land, and the permanently unskilled were ignored and disparaged by the organized. As a result the fragile factory workers' union attracted only 1 percent of its potential constituency. Although unions formed among Ruhr miners in the wake of the 1889 strike, they lost 90 percent of their members by 1895 due to economic crisis, religious differences, and the persistence of traditional views. And even this transitory success was absent in the Saar and Silesia. The free trade unions had little success in either the large and low-skilled factories of the heavy industrial sector or in home work with its dispersed and diverse labor force. Workers employed by the state railroads might join liberal or later Catholic unions but never socialist ones; those in the tertiary sector remained unorganized. A scant 2 percent of free trade union members were female, for unions were strongest where women's wage labor was weakest. Equally important, the antifeminist tradition of skilled male workers and the Social Democrats' ambivalence about women's right to work encouraged unions to ignore or even to exclude women.[71] After 1895 the free trade

[70] Ibid., table following p. 96; Groh, "Vorläufige Überlegungen," p. 27; Tenfelde, *Sozialgeschichte*, pp. 368-69.

[71] Ritter, *Arbeiterbewegung, Parteien*, table following p. 96; Schönhoven, *Expansion*, pp. 28-30, 43; Werner Thönnessen, *Frauenemanzipation* (Frankfurt: Europäischer Verlagsanstalt, 1969).

unions recruited in depth from the occupational base established during the Great Depression, but they were never able to transcend it.

The free trade unions became a movement not only of the skilled and the male but also of the relatively young and the distinctly urban. From the mid-1880s on, leaders and probably most members as well were recruited from a younger generation of born proletarians who were less influenced by residual corporatist attitudes than older workers, who had been exposed to the guilds.[72] These younger workers, who joined in their twenties and thirties when the wandering years of their adolescence were over, enjoyed brief decades of peak earnings but were also burdened by family responsibilities, economic crisis, and political repression. They were mobile and hence knowledgeable about conditions in many areas, but nonetheless anchored in an urban, industrial world. Although in 1895 half the labor force in industry and Handwerk lived in towns of fewer than 5,000 people, only 6.8 percent of trade unionists did. Conversely, over 45 percent of trade unionists were in cities of over 100,000 while only about 20 percent of workers were.[73] Urbanization, skilled migration patterns, growing working-class residential segregation, and the resulting flourishing of working-class culture proved conducive to unionization.

In response to economic transformation, state policy, capitalist organization, and a new membership, the free trade unions gradually altered their structure. The loosely interconnected, relatively autonomous local craft unions of the 1860s and 1870s were revived in the mid-1880s but criticized and partially rejected by Social Democrats in the early 1890s. The establishment of industrial unions in metal, wood, and textiles on the one hand and of the trade union general commission under Karl Legien on the other marked the triumph of centralization, bureaucraticization, and the principle of industrial unionism.[74] Within and among unions, patient organization, coordination from above, and cautious planning would be the hallmarks of Social Democratic leadership. Thus, even before the vast free trade union expansion of the late 1890s, the movement's institutional parameters had been set, its localist and syndicalist elements defeated, and its craft character weakened.

The relationship between the free trade unions and the SPD, however, was not definitively established in these years. Prior to 1878 party leaders and theorists regarded the unions as useful defenders of working-class material interests and as recruiting schools for the party—important

---

[72] Ritter, *Arbeiterbewegung, Parteien*, p. 66; Schönhoven, *Expansion*, p. 93.
[73] Deppe, *Geschichte der deutschen Gewerkschaftsbewegung*, p. 54; Ritter, *Arbeiterbewegung, Parteien*, p. 93.
[74] Schönhoven, *Expansion*, p. 107.

tasks to be sure but subordinate to those of the political wing of the move-ment. With the outlawing of the SPD the ties between the party and the unions were greatly strengthened, for unions became the major organi-zations in and through which Social Democrats agitated, educated, and organized. The return to legality divided what repression had united and raised once again the troubling questions of the appropriate relationship between the party and the unions, between economic and political strug-gles. Although both wings of the movement agreed to return to the status quo of pre-1878, verbal proclamations could not contain the growing size, autonomy, or reformism of the union movement after 1895. Nor could pledges of solidarity solve the vexing problem of how to coordinate eco-nomic and political action for an effective assault on the structures of Imperial German society. The tense and unsettled relationship of the SPD and free trade unions in the early 1890s was symptomatic of the movement's deeper difficulty in developing an analysis and strategy that coordinated economics and politics.[75] That difficulty cannot be under-stood without an investigation of the party itself.

Despite—or perhaps more accurately, because of—repression and eco-nomic crisis, social democracy became the political ideology and organ-ization of many of the skilled factory workers, construction workers, and journeymen who formed the working class. In 1871, the Social Demo-crats won 124,000 votes and two Reichstag seats; in 1877, 493,000 votes and twelve seats. Thereafter, repression and persistent economic crisis eroded socialist support and seemingly confirmed the shrewdness of Bis-marck's strategy. By the mid-1880s, however, the Social Democratic electorate began to expand once again and in 1890, a few months before the Anti-Socialist laws were lifted, the party polled nearly 1.5 million votes, more than any other single party, and won thirty-five seats.[76] The basis for a mass Social Democratic movement was securely laid. But in responding to economic crisis and political change, the Social Democratic movement and its supporters transformed their political demands, their practice, and their ideology. The party that was relegalized in 1890 was very different from the one that had been outlawed in 1878.

Prior to the 1870s, the Social Democrats had focused their demands on political reforms—on the attainment of a "free people's state." This democratic republic would, it was assumed, be achieved by political means and in conjunction with national unification. It would provide the

[75] See Hans Manfred Bock, *Geschichte des "Linken Radikalismus" in Deutschland* (Frankfurt: Suhrkamp, 1976).

[76] Koppel Pinson, *Modern Germany* (New York: Macmillan, 1954), pp. 572-73. Party membership statistics do not exist for this period.

basis on which social reform and ultimately socialism would be achieved. The Prussian solution to the German question—a revolution from above that established a unified but authoritarian state—destroyed Social Democratic efforts to link political democracy, nationalism, and socialism. Thereafter the Social Democrats relegated the free people's state to the category of distant end goals rather than immediate political tasks. Simultaneously, the leadership adopted an internationalist perspective and reinterpreted socialism as a product of economic development rather than political action. They turned their attention away from political issues.[77] The Social Democrats did campaign vigorously for an end to the Anti-Socialist laws, demand improvements in the right to organize, and bitterly criticize the class character of the state. Yet they made few demands for reforming political structures and devoted most of their energies to social and economic policy.

From the late 1870s on, the Social Democrats insisted that the state pass extensive protective legislation to regulate hours, working conditions, and the like. With equal vigor they demanded a social insurance system that would cover all wage laborers, pay adequate benefits, be totally funded by employers and the state, and grant workers a major administrative role. Unable to achieve this, they publicly repudiated both the form and underlying motive of Bismarckian social policy. And, given the peculiarities of the Anti-Socialist laws, they had ample opportunity to do so in parliament, in election campaigns, and in the many open meetings that Bismarck held to popularize his insurance scheme.[78]

This shift from politics to social policy both resulted from and reenforced working-class disillusionment with the structures and policies of the state, as they had developed first after unification and even more after the refounding of the Reich in 1879. It paralleled the evolution of other political parties, who were becoming narrowly class-based economic interest groups, engaging in collective protectionism. Social Democratic demands thus recognized the limits of politics in Imperial Germany. They also responded to the agenda that Bismarck set. By focusing their agitation around social insurance and protective legislation, the Social Democrats coopted for their own ends the key weapon in Bismarck's campaign to pacify the working class. Social democracy's program was shaped not only by the state but also by its own social base. Social-policy demands reflected the needs and concerns of urban industrial workers and journeymen, who could neither return to the land nor aspire to inde-

[77] Werner Conze and Dieter Groh, *Die Arbeiterbewegung in der nationalen Bewegung* (Stuttgart: Klett, 1966), pp. 48, 80-81, 104-105, 114-16; Lidtke, *Outlawed Party*, pp. 51, 321.
[78] See Höhn, *Vaterlandslosen Gesellen*, passim.

pendence and who faced structural change and cyclical crisis simultaneously. Finally, the shift from the free people's state to social policy was reenforced (but not caused) by the SPD's much more explicit advocacy of Marxism in the late 1880s.

If the demands of Social Democratic workers distanced them from the Bismarckian state and signified a rejection of it, so too did their language. Social Democrats stressed class rather than estate (*Stand*), conflict rather than harmony. At least rhetorically they abandoned the prevailing nationalism in favor of a vague internationalism that was combined with a sentiment of loyalty to the German people but not the existing state. It is difficult to know how far internationalism penetrated into the ranks of the socialist movement. On the one hand, workers were exposed to the dominant nationalistic values in school, the army, and the press. On the other hand, workers had been excluded from the bourgeois nationalist movement after 1848. Of equal importance, the mere critique of nationalism and militarism led the state and dominant parties to label the Social Democrats "enemies of the Reich" and "bums without a fatherland." At the very least, socialist workers had a more distant and conflicted relationship with the nation than did those classes and parties who were defined as its core.

Although the Social Democrats abandoned their emphasis on the free people's state, they criticized the existing order. Indeed, after the early 1870s the SPD was the only party in Germany to espouse democracy, for Conservatives endorsed authoritarianism, Liberals embraced conservative nationalism, and Catholics clung to corporatism. On particular issues as well as in general rhetoric, the Social Democrats spoke a language of their own. They blamed the economic crisis, for example, on capitalism and not, as other groups did, on liberalism, the Jews, or foreign competition. They insisted that capital and the Junker aristocracy were Germany's "enemy within." In short, the values, assumptions, and vocabulary of the Social Democratic working class developed outside of and in opposition to those of the dominant society.[79]

Although the tactics of the Social Democrats varied somewhat with the legal situation of the movement, there is remarkable continuity from the early 1870s onward. The primacy of organization and education, the practice of "ambivalent parliamentarism,"[80] and a policy of nonalliance became the enduring hallmarks of social democracy's political practice.

[79] Conze and Groh, *Arbeiterbewegung in der nationalen Bewegung*, pp. 116, 123; *Geschichtliche Grundbegriffe*, 1:842; Rudolf Walther, ". . . aber nach der Sündflut kommen wir und nur wir": *Zusammenbruchstheorie, Marxismus und politisches Defizit in der SPD* (Frankfurt: Ullstein, 1981), p. 40.
[80] The term is Lidtke's, *Outlawed Party*.

For the Social Democrats building a movement was their foremost task. Organization and education were carried on through speeches and in the press, at party and trade union meetings and open rallies, as well as informally on the shop floor and in neighborhoods. If possible this work was done openly, if necessary covertly. Indeed, repression scarcely curbed these efforts, for the Anti-Socialist laws had loopholes, the Social Democratic underground functioned remarkably well, especially in smuggling in illegal literature and working through unions, and the expulsion of leading Social Democrats from major party strongholds merely spread the movement to new areas. But organization and education only recruited the soldiers who were to fight. They did not determine the nature of the battle.

On the grounds of both expedience and theory, the Social Democrats explicitly rejected the use of force, whether in the form of sabotage, terror, or open rebellion. They were equally adamant in their rejection of alliances with other political parties, alliances that were in any case impossible during this period.[81] The Social Democrats chose instead to exploit the electoral and parliamentary channels that were open to them even under the Anti-Socialist laws. As a result, Reichstag elections became the major focus of Social Democratic activity and the party's parliamentary delegation became the de facto head of the party. This tactic was riddled with contradictions. Although the Social Democratic electorate grew astonishingly, the party could wield no power in an unreformed German parliament and parliamentary reform became less and less possible the stronger the Social Democrats became. Equally important, the Social Democrats themselves were profoundly ambivalent about parliamentarism if not hostile to it, for their theoretical reorientation in the 1880s led them to dismiss the parliament as a vehicle for fundamental social change.[82]

Just as the Social Democrats altered their demands, vocabulary, and tactics, so too they changed their theory. Abandoning the eclecticism and residual Lassalleanism of the 1875 Gotha Program, the Social Democrats of the 1880s embraced Marxism and embodied it in the 1891 Erfurt Program. This compromise between radicals and reformists remained the party's official statement of principle until the 1920s. The Marxism adopted, however, was of a most economistic and deterministic sort. Economic development was increasing the contradictions of capitalism and

---

[81] The break between the liberal middle classes and social democracy occurred more slowly in south Germany. See, for example, Jörg Schadt, *Die sozialdemokratische Partei in Baden* (Hannover: Verlag für Literatur und Zeitgeschehen, 1971).

[82] Lidtke, *Outlawed Party*, pp. 326-29; Walther, pp. 55-56.

building the prerequisites for socialism. The much-desired social revolution, which was defined not as a political event but rather as the economic collapse of capitalism, would and could occur only when those contradictions had ripened—an occurrence most Social Democrats expected in their lifetime. Neither the working class nor the Social Democratic movement could hasten the advent of socialism. Rather, their task was, as Kautsky succinctly put it, to organize for the revolution, not to organize the revolution. To be sure, the Erfurt Program urged Social Democrats to work for short-run reform in social policy, suffrage, and the army. But the relationship of such activity to the achievement of socialism was never elucidated by the party's version of Marxism.[83]

Social democracy's adoption of deterministic Marxism was a direct response to the changes that the Great Depression wrought in German economic, social, and political life and to the altered position of the working class and the Social Democratic movement. Deterministic Marxism offered a reasonable and coherent explanation of recent developments. In the wake of the economic crisis and political repression, theories of increasing class conflict, growing exploitation, falling rates of profit, and intensifying cooperation between capital and the state were more plausible analytical tools than earlier socialist views or those of other parties.[84] Of equal importance, the nature of the Great Depression encouraged the view that the collapse of capitalism would result from economic forces alone and not from the subjective action of a class or party. Deterministic Marxism justified the Social Democrats' disillusionment with the German state and with politics in general—a disillusionment that emerged from experience and not theorizing. Deterministic Marxism did not create the political passivity and caution that characterized German social democracy but rather was symptomatic of the party's inability to develop an active political strategy.[85] Deterministic Marxism was espoused because it offered hope to a working class and a socialist movement that were growing rapidly but could not find a way to translate organizational strength and radical consciousness into political power.[86] It provided the promise of revolution in a nonrevolutionary situation, a theory of revolution in a country without an indigenous revolutionary tradition.

If political change was most striking among skilled Protestant factory

[83] Lidtke, *Outlawed Party*, p. 331.

[84] Dieter Groh, "Revolutionsstrategie und Wirtschaftskonjunktur," in *Sozialgeschichte Heute*, ed. Hans-Ulrich Wehler (Göttingen: Vandenhoeck and Ruprecht, 1974), pp. 358-60.

[85] Walther, ". . . *aber nach der Sündflut*," pp. 27, 40, 56-57.

[86] Guenther Roth, *Social Democrats in Imperial Germany* (Totowa, N.J.: Bedminster, 1963), pp. 167-68.

workers, construction workers, and journeymen, it was by no means absent among Catholic workers, especially those in skilled trades and in the Ruhr mines. As a result of the Kulturkampf of the 1870s, Catholicism was politically mobilized and organized in Germany. As a result of economic crisis and the growing appeal of social democracy, political Catholicism could and did pay increasing attention to workers. It rallied them behind a multiclass movement, centered on the defense of and identification with religion. It spoke a vocabulary of *Stand*, not of class, and argued for the harmony of interests among hierarchically ordered estates. But political Catholicism was also critical of industrial capitalism, if only from a precapitalist corporatist direction. It attacked the Bismarckian state and other political parties and championed social welfare and protective legislation. It organized workers into Catholic religious, cultural, and political organizations, Catholic Workers' Associations, and after 1894, into Christian trade unions.[87]

Political Catholicism thus separated Catholic workers from the emerging working class, gave them a different and more conservative outlook and vocabulary than those of the Social Democrats, and contained their political demands and organizational autonomy.[88] In order to achieve these ends, however, political Catholicism was forced to recognize workers' special needs and interests, to mobilize and organize them as workers. Ironically, Catholicism had to politicize workers in order to contain their politicization. It had to separate them from the predominantly Protestant state and society in order to isolate them from social democracy.

Economic crisis, state policy, and religion thus fundamentally reshaped working-class politics in the era of the Great Depression. These elements defined, radicalized, and isolated a working class of Protestant skilled workers and journeymen. This working class, in turn, looked to social democracy because it defended workers' material interests, created a community within an urban industrial world, and explained German economic and political life as well as offering the hope of transforming it.

If economic and political developments contributed significantly to making social democracy a mass movement, they also limited it as a social movement, a political practice, and a theory of revolutionary transformation. Social democracy reflected and reenforced the internal and external class boundaries that material and cultural conditions had created. It could neither appeal to significant segments of wage labor, such as the unskilled, women, and peasant workers, nor curb the growth of a

[87] Nolan, *Social Democracy*, pp. 42-47.
[88] Tenfelde notes that religious differences were particularly detrimental to working-class formation in the Ruhr (*Sozialgeschichte*, p. 469).

separate Catholic workers' movement. Social democracy's program and practice embodied both a recognition of the limits of politics in Imperial Germany and an inability to challenge those limits, let alone to transcend them, through more innovative demands and tactics. Finally, economic crisis and state policy encouraged the adoption of deterministic Marxism, which simultaneously promoted a radical rejection of existing society and passivity within it.

The legacy of the Great Depression proved powerful and lasting for both the process of working-class formation and the ideology and practice of German social democracy. This continuity, in turn, stemmed in large part from that fact that the world of Wilhelmian Germany did not differ significantly from its Bismarckian predecessor. Depression did give way to prosperity, heavy and new industries gained unchallenged primacy, and technological change, internal migration and urbanization proceeded rapidly. But these developments represented the culmination of previous trends and accentuated uneven development and conservative collective protectionism. On the political front, Bismarck departed, the alliance of heavy industry and Junker agriculture experienced periodic difficulties, and most importantly, social democracy developed into a mass move-ment. But the changes neither pushed the political system in the direction of genuine parliamentarism and social reform nor provided the Social Democrats with political allies. In short, the underlying structures of eco-nomic and political life persisted with only subtle modifications.[89]

Although the wage labor force expanded greatly after the mid-1890s, the location of internal class divisions and external class boundaries, as well as the different identities these embodied, scarcely altered. Skilled workers employed in Handwerk, factories, and construction continued to form the core of those who identified themselves as working class, although their ranks were augmented by some peasant workers, younger miners, skilled migrant male Catholics, and women, who abandoned alternative corporatist or precapitalist identities. In general, however, the vast increase in the number of both skilled and unskilled did not bring the life experiences and expectations of the two groups substantially closer together. Union membership reflected these ongoing divisions. The free trade unions, which had over 2.5 million members by 1913, grew by mining traditional reserves more deeply rather than by reaching new

[89] Varain, *Interessenverbände*, passim; Dieter Groh, "Intensification of Work and Industrial Conflict in Germany, 1896-1914," *Politics & Society* 8, nos. 3-4 (1978):349-65; Kenneth Barkin, *The Controversy over German Industrialization, 1890-1902* (Chi-cago: University of Chicago, 1970); Klaus Saul, *Staat, Industrie und Arbeiterbewegung im Kaiserreich* (Düsseldorf: Bertelsmann, 1974); Nolan, *Social Democracy*, passim.

groups. And the SPD continued to speak most forcefully to the needs of this key group of skilled male workers.[90]

Continuity in the movement's social base was paralleled by continuity in organizational forms and strategies. Social democracy, like the dominant society, remained trapped in attitudes, alliances, and strategies from the Great Depression era. As in the past, Social Democratic actions and ideologies reflected the structural and political realities of Germany. On the union front, for example, labor was thrown on the defensive after 1900 by the power of organized industrial interests, the stagnation of real wages, and the intensification of work. In the face of employer intransigence and the lack of union recognition and collective bargaining, strikes became increasingly risky, expensive, and likely to fail. The organizational fetishism, centralization, and cautious reformism that characterized the union movement after 1900 even more strongly than before thus came neither from Social Democratic ideology nor from working-class integration but from the continued obstacles to working-class economic improvement and organizational power.[91]

On the political front, the ideology and strategy of the 1880s continued to speak to the structural and political realities of the prewar years. Reformist Social Democrats could not find allies, strike bargains, or make piecemeal progress in a system where reform had revolutionary implications and other classes were staunchly antisocialist.[92] But radical Social Democrats had no strategy to confront or circumvent the repressive power of the state, the organized power of capital, and the divisions within the working class. Thus the SPD's leaders and many of its members clung to that mixture of ambivalent parliamentarism, organizational fetishism, isolation, and deterministic Marxism that had emerged in response to the conditions of the Great Depression era.

The successes and limits of pre–World War I social democracy were rooted in those features of German society and politics and those aspects of working-class formation and movement development that had first emerged strongly during the 1870s and 1880s and that were solidified rather than transformed thereafter. If the organizational and electoral

[90] Schröder, *Arbeitergeschichte*, pp. 33-53; Nolan, *Social Democracy*, pp. 113-18; Stephen Hickey, "The Shape of the German Labour Movement: Miners in the Ruhr," in *Society and Politics*, ed. Evans, pp. 215-40; Jean Quartaert, "Feminist Tactics in German Social Democracy, 1890-1914," *Internationale Wissenschaftliche Korrespondenz zur Geschichte der deutschen Arbeiterbewegung* 13, no. 1 (March, 1977):48-65. See Richard Evans, ed., *The German Working Class, 1888-1933* (London: Croom Helm, 1982) for recent work on the unskilled.

[91] Groh, "Intensification," passim.

[92] Mary Nolan and Charles F. Sabel, "Class Conflict and the Social Democratic Reform Cycle," *Political Power and Social Theory* 3 (1982):145-73.

successes that accrued from this legacy were most noticeable in the short run, the debilitating effects ultimately outweighed the beneficial ones. The experience of the Great Depression era left the workers' movement with no effective political and economic strategy save patience, organization, and reliance on the presumed inevitable collapse of capitalism. It imbued many Social Democrats with a dangerous fatalism that prevented them from imagining alternative situations and strategies. Their reaction to structures and political configurations, which were very real, established patterns of thought and action—or more accurately, inaction—that proved paralyzing in 1914 and again after 1918, when those structures had changed and fundamental reform was possible.

Conclusion

9 How Many Exceptionalisms?
• Aristide R. Zolberg

I

Beyond Exceptionalism. If capitalism is of a piece, why is the working class it called into life so disparate? As of the middle of the nineteenth century, when the promethean transformations wrought by the industrial revolution had begun to spread beyond the insular confines of its original locus, it appeared not unreasonable for Marx and Engels to assert—if one accepts their substitution of present tense for future as a rhetorical device—that "modern industrial labor, modern subjugation to capital, the same in England as in France, in America as in Germany, has stripped [the proletarian] of every trace of national character."[1] But on the eve of World War I, the historical moment that is here considered the outcome of class formation, the assertion was obviously invalid; and the range of variation already observable with respect to outlook and organization among the working classes of the leading capitalist countries would become much broader yet under the impact of the forthcoming cataclysm and the revolutionary upheavals that followed it.

In minimalist outline, the overall situation a little more than a century after the emergence of industrial capitalism was as follows. From 1800 to 1900, the world's labor force grew from an estimated 432 million to 770 million; simultaneously, the proportion active in the primary sector declined from 79 to 72.2 percent of the total, while for the secondary it rose from 10.5 to 13 percent.[2] Of an estimated 102 million in the secondary sector in 1900, 39 million lived in the four leading industrial countries—the United States, Germany, the United Kingdom, and France—where they constituted 36 percent of the aggregate labor force, nearly three times the level for the world as a whole.[3] These four countries collectively contained only one-fifth of the earth's population but produced about four-fifths of its total industrial output, to which end they utilized 70 percent of the total capacity of steam engines.[4] Together with a hand-

---

[1] A. Mendel, *Essential Works of Marxism* (New York: Bantam Books, 1961), p. 23.

[2] Paul Bairoch, "Structure de la population active mondiale de 1700 à 1970," *Annales: Economies, sociétés, civilisations* 20 (1971), pp. 960-70.

[3] H. Vander Eycken and P. Frantzen, *De tertiaire sector* (Brussels: Editions de l'Institut de Sociologie, ULB, 1970), pp. 16-23.

[4] Douglass North, *The Economic Growth of the United States, 1790-1860* (New York: Norton, 1966), p. v; David Landes, *The Unbound Prometheus* (Cambridge: Cambridge University Press, 1972), p. 221.

ful of smaller nations, they constituted a unique cluster of economies among which industry accounted for 35 to 40 percent of national product. Taking these various factors into consideration, it is reasonable to suggest that if by "working class" we simply mean people engaged in the manufacturing of goods with the aid of machines and in exchange for wages, then on the eve of World War I, something like two-thirds of the human beings who fell within this category lived in the United States, Germany, the United Kingdom, and France.

There is no gainsaying that the forms of collective action industrial workers engaged in to improve their position in the labor market bore a strong family resemblance to one another across national boundaries. But if unions and strikes were now common features of all industrial and industrializing societies, there was also considerable cross-national variation in the frequency and character of strikes, as well as in the organizational characteristics and outlook of unions. One obvious dimension of variation was that the proportion of the labor force in manufacturing that belonged to trade unions—in the broadest sense of that term—ranged from a high of 30-40 percent in Great Britain to 25-30 percent in Germany, about 20 percent in the United States, and a low of about 15 percent in France.[5] It is further self-evident that the relevant bodies varied considerably in their orientation toward capitalism and the existing political regime in both their organizational objectives and tactical methods.

With respect to action in the political arena, one is similarly struck by a combination of resemblances and disparities. Around 1910, the leading industrial societies—with the singular exception of Germany—were liberal democracies whose governments were accountable to representative institutions; male universal suffrage prevailed, except in Britain. One remarkable feature of the political scene is that nearly all working-class organizations were in effect committed to pursuing their objectives within the framework of established political institutions, even if these objectives included revolutionary change. Of the major organizations among the countries under consideration, the French Confédération Générale du Travail (CGT) alone officially rejected this position; even its doctrinaire principles were mitigated by a flexible practice and, as will be seen, there is considerable doubt whether its antisystem stance was in tune with the orientation of a majority of the membership, who themselves constituted but a minority of the French working class.

The activities of the Second International provide some support for the

[5] Annie Kriegel and Jean-Jacques Becker, *1914: La guerre et le mouvement ouvrier français* (Paris: Armand Colin, 1964), pp. 200-208; Vander Eycken and Frantzen, *De tertiaire sector*.

proposition that at the turn of the twentieth century workers of the capitalist world came closer than ever before or since to sharing a common political doctrine, social democracy, and to collaborating in a common cause.[6] That being said, however, it is also evident that in only one of the four leading industrial countries, Germany, had a socialist party actually succeeded in mobilizing the vast majority of working-class voters; that notwithstanding their formal adherence to a common doctrine, national sections of the Workers' International differed considerably on actual strategy and tactics; and that in two of the leading capitalist countries, very few workers were socialists.

It would seem to make little sense, in the face of such varied situations, to approach the study of working-class formation by positing one national pattern as the theoretic norm in relation to which all others are treated as deviant cases. Yet this "exceptionalist" problematic was established early and remains deeply anchored in our intellectual traditions.

The notion that socialism—in the sense of a mass party committed to fundamental change, inspired by Marxist doctrine, and drawing support from a substantial portion of the working class—was the normal outcome of working-class formation is traceable to the remarkable success of the German Social Democrats, who in 1890 had already captured 19.7 percent of that country's electorate and rose to 34.6 percent of the total in the last prewar election of 1912.[7] A reasonable inference is that the party had by this time mobilized the bulk of German industrial workers, with the exception of the Catholic minority. These achievements clinched the party's paramountcy within the Second International and thereby fostered a crystallization of the "exceptionalist" problematic, as reflected in the title of Werner Sombart's 1905 work, *Why Is There No Socialism in the United States?*[8] It should be noted, however, that the question might have been equally asked of Britain, the homeland of industrial capitalism, where workers at that time still voted mostly Liberal. Labour candidates obtained a mere 1.3 percent of the votes in 1900, a level barely above that achieved by a Socialist presidential candidate in the United States two years later.[9]

Overall, it is not far-fetched to suggest that on the eve of World War I, a detached observer might have justifiably considered the Anglo-

[6] James Joll, *The Second International, 1889-1914* (New York: Harper and Row, 1966).

[7] T. Mackie and Richard Rose, *The International Almanac of Electoral History* (New York: Free Press, 1974), pp. 152-53.

[8] Werner Sombart, *Why Is There No Socialism in the United States?* (White Plains: M. E. Sharpe, 1976).

[9] Mackie and Rose, *International Almanac*, pp. 386-87.

American pattern of a working class organized as labor via craft unions, concerned mostly with the marketplace and exercising some power in the political arena through "catch-all" rather than class-specific parties, as a model adumbrating the future of western working classes under advanced capitalism. In relation to this, it was German social democracy that appeared "exceptionalist," a state of affairs that could be accounted for by the obvious fact that Germany alone of the leading capitalist countries was not yet a liberal democracy. To the extent that the German case appeared to constitute a pattern, this was because of the ability of the Social Democrats to persuade a sufficient number of Continental political entrepreneurs to follow their lead. The most remarkable manifestation of this process occurred in France, whose largely home-grown socialist parties coalesced shortly after the turn of the century into the French Section of the Workers' International (SFIO), and formally subscribed to Social Democratic doctrine concerning nonparticipation in government under capitalism. The party's electoral progress, from 10.4 percent of the votes in 1902 to 16.8 in 1914, was undoubtedly attributable to its success in weaning a segment of the working-class electorate from its traditional allegiance to the Radicals.[10] But one can hardly take these developments as evidence that working-class formation in France resembled the German pattern. From an organizational perspective, the SFIO bore but a faint resemblance to its comprehensive and self-contained German counterpart; the party did not control French syndicates; and most French workers were neither Socialist (SFIO) nor syndicalist.

Mutatis mutandis, the debate over which pattern of working-class formation is the exceptional one has continued down to the present. In the era of the Third International, Sombart's question was in effect updated to read, "Why is there no Communism . . . ?"; this problematic was mirrored by the "end of ideology" school after World War II, in which Communism and other forms of working-class radicalism came to be viewed as an atavistic legacy from the bad old days, which unless artificially maintained would wane of their own accord under the conditions of advanced capitalism.

Alternatively, if one approaches the study of working-class formation from a country-by-country perspective, each state of affairs appears to make sense sui generis as a unique configuration shaped by a particular combination of local factors. The relevant literature is generally historical rather than theoretical but historical studies—particularly if constructed "from below"—collectively lend support to an implicit general theoretical proposition that may be stated as follows: If the advent of

---

[10] Ibid., pp. 132-33.

industrial capitalism in a given country necessarily fostered the emergence of a working class, it did not of itself determine the dynamics of its development and its resulting structure. Viewed from this perspective, the process of working-class formation appears as the gradual crystallization of a limited array of patterns out of a broad spectrum of possibilities.

The "exceptionalist" tradition and its mirror image, the "end of ideology" approach, are so bound up in ideological controversy that they have outlived their usefulness as intellectual frameworks suitable for contemporary research; but the adoption instead of a purely historical approach would result in a mere piling up of information, with a concomitant loss of insight-producing intellectual tension. One way out of this dilemma is to treat each historical situation as a case of working-class formation—that is, as something that is akin to one of several possible states of a dependent variable and that can be accounted for by reference to variation among a set of factors considered, for this purpose, as theoretically grounded independent variables.

Since this generic method, which might be termed comparative historical macroanalysis, is well established in a number of social-scientific subdisciplines, no elaborate theoretical justification is required for its application to the subject under consideration. However, given a common misunderstanding of the strengths and limitations of the method, it should be noted that although it bears a family resemblance to quantitative multivariate analysis, it is hardly identical with it. The process of abstracting configurations from historical reality and their treatment as variables entails a certain degree of intellectual make-believe, which is justified only to the extent that we remain aware that it is make-believe. It is also well to keep in mind that the objective of the exercise is not to achieve generalizations—in the statistical sense—but rather to enhance our general understanding of the process of working-class formation by systematizing the observation of cross-national commonalities and variations; eliminating interpretations founded on a mistaken attribution of uniqueness to certain aspects of national configurations; and identifying the combination of factors that best appears to account for the variation that is found, taking into consideration that structural factors merely determined a range of possibilities within which actual outcomes resulted from constant strategic interactions among a number of players.

Historical Outcomes as a Dependent Variable. The present attempt to provide a comparative analysis of working-class formation by devising a framework within which variation in outcomes can be related systematically to what appear to be explanatory variables is by no means the first of its kind. However, an examination of the literature reveals that most of the effort has been brought to bear on devising explanations and remarkably little on what would appear to be logically prior requirements, a precise identification of what it is that must be explained and the conceptualization of this explicandum in a manner that makes crossnational comparison possible and maximizes the theoretical returns of the undertaking.

This is not easy to accomplish. For example, in his pioneering attempt to apply the comparative method to historical accounts of working-class formation, designed to elucidate "How far has economic development conditioned working-class politics in Western Europe in the last century and a half?"—a question examined in somewhat different form in the next section—Val Lorwin conceptualized the explicandum as involvement of workers in "the politics of protest," varying on a scale ranging from "fundamental protest against the social and political order," to "loyal opposition within the framework of the existing regime," and finally to mere "pressure group politics."[11]

Although Lorwin does not address himself explicitly to the problem of operationalizing the dependent variable, it is evident from his discussion that the assignment of various countries to the above categories reflects his assessment of the situation in the post–World War II era and that the criterion for assigning a national working class to the "fundamental protest" category is simply the presence at that time of a substantial Communist party, as in France and Italy. Lorwin also takes such a party to be an indicator of the prevalence, among the working class of these countries, of a disposition he terms "class hatred." By the same token, the absence of a Communist party denotes an absence of class hatred, and mobilization of the working class into the ranks of a Socialist or Labor party, as in Britain, post–World War II West Germany, Scandinavia, and the Low Countries, provides the basis for locating the case at the mid-point of the protest scale. Finally, the absence altogether of any working-class party results in consignment of the outcome to the lowest protest category, mere "pressure group politics."

This example illustrates four distinct conceptual weaknesses commonly encountered in the literature in this field: (1) An anachronistic retrojection into the early twentieth century of variations in outcome that surfaced only after World War I, the Russian Revolution, the Great Depression, and World War II, and that these awesome historical events undoubtedly contributed to bring about; (2) concomitantly, a lack of

---

[11] Val R. Lorwin, "Working-class Politics and Economic Development in Western Europe," *The American Historical Review* 58 (1958):338-51.

specificity with respect to the time frame of the relevant outcome, which is particularly confusing where the state of affairs changed significantly over time, as in Germany and France; (3) in terms of the analytic levels distinguished by Ira Katznelson in the Introduction, a conflation of Class 3—the outlook and disposition of the working class—and Class 4, its organization, which makes it impossible to explore relationships between these two levels; and (4) a drastic reduction of the considerable variety found at the levels of Class 3 and 4 in each of the countries to some sort of "modal" pattern, merging often-distinct relationships to the market and to the political arena, which is then assigned a single location on a unilinear continuum.

In this respect, it is noteworthy that in the course of his discussion, Lorwin himself demonstrates the inadequacy of a unilinear "protest" scale by making distinctions that amount to the introduction of additional analytic dimensions. One pertains to the organizational strength or weakness of the working class, which varies independently of its degree of "class hatred"; and the other is the extent to which the spheres of economic and political action are "confused" (sic) or differentiated. However, the author offers little guidance on how these new dimensions of variation relate to the earlier ones.

How these conceptual difficulties impinge on research is exemplified by the problems one runs into when attempting to compare the outcome of class formation in France and the United States on the eve of World War I. The American outcome is usually characterized as involving widespread craft unionism with a "business" orientation on one hand, and the casting of working-class votes for one or the other of the two major mainstream parties on the other; the French outcome, by contrast, is usually identified as a combination of revolutionary syndicalism and electoral socialism. But then to focus the analysis on determining why the American working class was "moderate" or even "conservative," while its French counterpart was "radical," would entail a gross distortion of social and political reality. In fact, at this time a higher proportion of American industrial workers belonged to unions than was the case in France, and as indicated by voting patterns at AFL congresses during this period, as many as one-third of the members diverged from the leadership's commitment to "unionism pure and simple" and indicated some preference for socialism. Many of them were undoubtedly among the substantial minority of American workers who did vote Socialist in national and local elections. On the French side, there are reasonable indications that for most of the rank and file, membership in the CGT did not entail a commitment to that organization's revolutionary doctrine. Although the CGT rejected parliamentary action, French workers—including probably many CGT members—did vote; and one can infer from aggregate data that on the eve of World War I about as many workers voted for "bourgeois" parties—mainly the Radicals, but also some that were on the right of the political spectrum—as for the SFIO.

Problems similar to the ones discussed with respect to Lorwin are visible in the analysis of "variations in the strength and structure of the working-class movement" presented by Seymour Martin Lipset and Stein Rokkan in the famous introduction to their co-edited work, *Party Systems and Voter Alignments*, and in Lipset's 1983 presidential address to the American Political Science Association on "Radicalism or Reformism: The Sources of Working-Class Politics," which was dedicated to the memory of Rokkan and which synthesizes Lipset's thinking on the issue of "American exceptionalism" over the past thirty years.[12]

The explicandum for Lipset and Rokkan is "not the emergence of a distinctive working-class movement . . . but the strength and solidarity of any such movement, its capacity to mobilize the underprivileged classes for action and its ability to maintain unity in the face of the many forces making for division and fragmentation."[13] In a slightly different vein, they subsequently refer to variation among movements in terms of "which ones would be strong and which ones weak, which ones unified and which ones split down the middle."[14] Their starting point thus appears to be a two-dimensional categorization combining (1) the density of actual working-class organizations in relation to the potential population—in relation to the framework here, something like the ratio of Class 4 to Class 1; and (2) the degree of unity prevailing at the level of Class 4.

However, in their historical account, Lipset and Rokkan appear to ignore this typology and to adopt instead one that is much closer to Lorwin's unidimensional scale. In effect, they attribute to the Russian Revolution the status of a "critical juncture" that determined what emerges in the final analysis as the most important dimension of variation in the process of working-class formation, namely whether the working class was integrated into the national polity or became committed to an international revolutionary movement. However, matters are confused by Lipset and Rokkan's assertion that the Russian Revolution did not in fact generate new cleavages, but simply accentuated long-established lines of

---

[12] Seymour Martin Lipset and Stein Rokkan, eds., *Party Systems and Voter Alignments* (New York: Free Press, 1967); Seymour Martin Lipset, "Radicalism or Reformism: The Sources of Working-Class Politics," *American Political Science Review* 77 (1983):1-18.

[13] Lipset and Rokkan, *Party Systems*, p. 46.

[14] Ibid., p. 47.

division within what they term the "working-class elite," produced by conditions that emerged well before World War I and varied markedly from country to country. The question of whether the Russian Revolution and its aftermath should be considered as an "intervening variable," deflecting in some cases the process of working-class formation from whatever path might have been anticipated on the basis of some specified first-order factors, is fraught with such great theoretical significance that it does not allow such offhand treatment. Before considering that issue, let it be noted that Lipset and Rokkan end up by conflating the integration-revolution distinction with the earlier one pertaining to degree of working-class unity, so that we get a dichotomous typology, "unified" and "domesticable" working-class movements as against "deeply divided" and "alienated" ones.[15] Again, it is evident that the most significant dimension of variation in the outcome of working-class formation is the presence or absence of a substantial Communist party.

In the more recent work mentioned, Lipset forgoes any attempt to construct a multidimensional typology. His explicandum is now simply the orientation of the working class toward politics, conceptualized as varying along a "reformism-radicalism" scale and operationalized in terms of its organizational manifestations. There are three possible orientations, akin to Lorwin's: (1) radical, denoted by the presence of a substantial Communist party, as in Weimar Germany or in Italy and France since 1920; (2) moderate, indicated by working-class support for a socialist party oriented toward the system, as in Great Britain, Australia, Belgium, West Germany, and so forth; and (3) reformist, of which the hallmark is the absence of a substantial labor party, as in the United States, Canada, and New Zealand.

Where does a case like the French fit, in which on the basis of electoral behavior in the post–World War II era, slightly under half of the working class might be assigned to the "radical" category, with the remainder distributed about evenly among the other two? It is evident from Lipset's account that he views the "radical" segment as characteristic of that country's working class as a whole; his explanation is directed at that aspect of the French outcome alone, thus grossly distorting our perception of social reality, and, by the same token, jeopardizing the validity of any explanation that might be provided. Somewhat ironically, the French Communist party thus achieves in Lipset's conceptual world a triumph it has been denied by history. Arising with respect to other cases as well, this problem is inherent in any attempt to reduce a varied array to a modal pattern.

[15] Ibid., p. 48.

War and Revolution as Intervening Variables. It is evident that if these pitfalls are to be avoided, we must fine tune our conceptualization of the explicandum as an array of multidimensional national configurations that articulates salient variations in the disposition and organization of working classes under industrial capitalism in the years immediately preceding World War I. The choice of this point as the outcome of working-class formation is not meant to suggest that no significant change occurred later on; on the contrary, it is predicated on the proposition that the effects of the ensuing cataclysm were so overwhelming that prewar configurations were profoundly altered. Although it is a truism among historians that World War I constituted one of the great watersheds of western history, social scientists are inclined to minimize such overwhelming "error factors" that wreak havoc with theory construction. Yet even a rapid consideration of the evidence indicates that it is not possible to account for patterns of working-class formation around 1925 or so, and of prevailing class relations in the West more generally, on the basis of a simple projection of pre–World War I trends.

To begin with, the war itself had a profound impact on all the cases under consideration here, both directly, at the level of Class 3 and 4, and indirectly, via important changes at the level of Class 1 and 2. Notwithstanding the International's stalwart efforts on behalf of peace, once war actually broke out, most of the leadership and rank and file of the major French and German working-class organizations joined the consensus in support of their national cause. There was little doubt among French Socialists or even revolutionary-minded syndicalists that their country was the victim of imperialist aggression and that, as a democracy, it was well worth defending; concomitantly, on the German side, the war was defined primarily as a defensive one against the Russian tsar, an objective that was quite acceptable to the Social Democrats. As the conflict wore on, however, serious doubt set in; preexisting differences among working-class leaders over strategy and tactics were exacerbated by disagreements over the issue of war and peace; and these divisions were subsequently sharpened further by the Soviet decision to pull out of the war and the responses of Allied governments to this. In both countries, moreover, wartime mobilization had the effect of enlarging the working class by accelerating the movement from rural areas toward the urban wage market. Most of these migrants were recruited into the war-related sector, characterized by large firms and heavy industry in both France and Germany; consequently, the composition of the working class changed significantly in the course of the war. Concurrently, there were important modifications in the structure of capitalism and in its relations with the state.

The war had significant consequences for working-class formation in Britain and the United States as well. It has been suggested that the effects it generated precipitated the break between the British trade unions and the Liberal party, and hence opened the way for the ascent of Labour to the rank of Britain's second party.[16] For Americans generally, the wisdom of national involvement in the European conflict long remained open to question; Woodrow Wilson was reelected in 1916— with considerable support from labor—on the basis of his successful efforts to keep the United States out of it. Once war was declared, however, there were overwhelming pressures to conform with the new national policy. In sharp contrast with the initial stance of its European counterparts, the American Socialist party adamantly stood out of the national consensus, as did the International Workers of the World (IWW). This stance rendered radical working-class organizations extremely vulnerable to charges of disloyalty and legitimized the unleashing of governmental repression against them in the immediate postwar period. In this manner, processes associated with the war consummated the elimination of socialism as an organized expression of the American working class. These various considerations further justify viewing the war as an intervening variable of such overwhelming significance that it provides a theoretical warrant for periodizing the analysis of working-class formation into distinct pre- and postwar segments.

A consideration of the impact of the outbreak of revolution in Russia on working-class formation in the West weighs very much in the same direction. It matters little for the present purpose whether this event is itself treated as one of the processes unleashed by World War I or as a distinct intervening variable in its own right. The most important point to keep in mind is that after 1917, working-class organizations were placed before an unprecedented choice. Notwithstanding heated debates on the subject, in the age of the Social Democratic International the issue of reform versus revolution was not a highly divisive one within the socialist world; commitment to revolution was generalized, but revolution meant the achievement of fundamental structural change, a long-term objective for which reform was an appropriate means, rather than commitment to speedy change by way of violent action.[17] Contrary to all expectations, however, the revolution in Russia was transformed into the Soviet Revolution, and its leadership was able to persuade some socialists that the experience of Russia was relevant to the West. In effect, the choice between reform and revolution took the form of a choice between

[16] C. T. Husbands, "Introduction," in Sombart, *Why Is There No Socialism*, p. 129.
[17] Adam Przeworski, "Social Democracy as a Historical Phenomenon" (unpublished ms., University of Chicago), p. 43.

rejection or acceptance of the conditions set by the Soviet leadership for joining the Third International; the variation in the outcomes associated with this choice is largely attributable to situational factors associated with World War I, such as divisions over the issue of war and peace. One consequence of all this is to cast very serious doubt on the validity of using the presence or absence of a substantial Communist party in the 1920s or at some time thereafter as the indicator of a "radical" or "moderate" outlook among a given country's working class at the beginning of the twentieth century.

II

This section will briefly review in deliberately comparative perspective the outcome of working-class formation as of approximately 1914 in what were then the world's four leading capitalist countries. An attempt will be made to highlight what appear to be the principal dimensions of variation with respect to Class 3 and Class 4—that is, the disposition and organization of the working class, in relation to the marketplace and the political arena. Given that three of the four cases are covered in previous chapters and that the British case is generally well known, other than filling some descriptive gaps the emphasis will be on problems of historical interpretation that are inherent to any macroanalytic comparative undertaking.

Germany. The German case can be disposed of quickly, as it undoubtedly presents the fewest ambiguities. Both Jürgen Kocka and Mary Nolan emphasize in their essays that what distinguished the German pattern of class formation from all others was the precocious and widespread sharing by workers of a class interpretation of social reality and the extensive mobilization of nearly the entire working class—with the exception of a Catholic minority in certain regions—into a single organizational world that included both party and unions, as well as a comprehensive network of ancillary bodies. The German party system was also more sharply organized along class lines than that of any other country where universal suffrage for males prevailed. In this perspective, one can easily appreciate the dramatic electoral outcome of 1890, when the Social Democratic party triumphed over Bismarck by garnering 1.4 million votes, an outcome that forced the chancellor into political retirement and established the SPD's standing as the largest single electoral formation in the German political arena.

Yet if in the French case we are faced with the somewhat strange combination of a low degree of organizational mobilization and a high degree of militancy among the mobilized minority, the German case presents the strange spectacle of considerable organizational strength, founded on a degree of mobilization approaching saturation, combined with political impotence. As noted by George Bernard Shaw in 1896, "The Germans with their compact Social Democratic Party in the Reichstag are apparently far ahead of us. But then their leader, Herr Liebknecht, is going to prison for a speech which Mr. Arthur Balfour might make to the Primrose League with the approbation of England tomorrow."[18] This was by no means a temporary situation; the SPD continued to grow throughout the prewar period and obtained 34.8 percent of the votes cast in the Reichstag elections in 1912, its maximum up to that time. Since electoral participation reached 84.5 percent, it is likely that the SPD vote at this time represented close to a maximum mobilization of non-Catholic workers.[19] With sixty-seven seats in the Reichstag, about one-fifth of the total, as a parliamentary party the SPD was second only to the Catholic Zentrum. But the Reichstag itself had but limited power over governmental decisions in major spheres of public policy, and whatever power the SPD might wield was contingent upon its willingness and ability to collaborate with other parties.

A consideration of the German case in comparative perspective highlights the uniqueness of the SPD's essentially negative relationship to other political parties, itself a token of what has been termed the "negative integration" of the working class in German society more generally. Although the SPD's stance faithfully reflected the Marxist doctrine to which the leadership was committed, that doctrine itself can be understood largely as a response to specific German political circumstances in the formative decades of the late nineteenth century; there is much less certainty about the extent to which this "negative integration" reflected the orientation of the working class as a whole after the 1890s.

From the time of the founding of the SPD to about 1910, the possibility of political alliances with parties founded on other classes was in effect completely foreclosed. The adoption by the SPD of a strict class strategy was in that sense a choice imposed upon the party from the outside, largely as a consequence of the nature of German liberalism and its relationship to the regime. In other countries liberal parties, drawing much of their support from the middle classes, could be counted on to support liberalization of political conditions—an objective whose realization naturally afforded crucial benefits to those seeking to organize work-

[18] Quoted in Joll, *Second International*, p. 76.
[19] Charles Tilly, Louise Tilly, and Richard Tilly, *The Rebellious Century* (Cambridge: Harvard University Press, 1975), p. 199.

ing-class movements and parties. This was not the case in Germany, where the persistence of absolutism in combination with the introduction of universal suffrage at the level of the Imperial Reichstag (1871) meant that the Liberals were threatened by a nascent working-class party before they had an opportunity to consolidate their own class position by participating in governance. In 1878, the weakened Liberals did not vigorously oppose Bismarck's antisocialist legislation, even though the measure was obviously contrary to their general political principles; at the same time, for tactical reasons, they also embraced agricultural protection, a policy that was equally contrary to their economic principles as well as in opposition to the immediate interests of urban consumers. As late as 1907, at a time when in France and Great Britain "catch-all" governmental parties such as the Radicals and the Liberals were actively seeking working-class support by pursuing reformist policies, in Germany the Liberals—reconstituted as the "Freethinker" party—allowed themselves to be wooed by Chancellor von Bülow into joining his antisocialist and anti-Catholic coalition. Although perennial attempts to reimpose legal disabilities on the SPD and the labor unions came to naught, the net effect of such proposals "was to embitter the working class and to deepen the gulf that had existed between it and the rest of German society since 1878."[20] The possibility of a *coup d'état*, should the parliamentary situation become unmanageable, remained ever present. Under these circumstances, the Erfurt declaration of 1891 is hardly surprising, nor is the SPD's insistence on the acceptance of this doctrine by other European parties purporting to represent workers.[21]

Yet there are some indications that the situation was evolving in the immediate prewar years. Notwithstanding the traditional contempt of skilled workers and Marxist leaders for the lowest stratum of the working class, who were believed to be more interested in bread-and-butter issues than in revolution, in Germany as elsewhere in Europe unions had an organizational interest in expanding into the ranks of the semiskilled and unskilled. Responsive to the outlook and interest of their changing membership, as they gained power within the SPD the unions fed a reformist trend; despite Erfurt, union spokesmen within the SPD increasingly insisted that the interests of the party would best be served by efforts to bring about improvements within the existing social and political order.[22] It is noteworthy that in the course of making this point, Gordon Craig

[20] Gordon Craig, *Germany 1866–1945* (New York: Oxford University Press, 1978), p. 265.
[21] Ibid., pp. 96, 167, 281.
[22] Ibid., pp. 266ff.

remarks that the leaders of German unions "were usually hard-headed and practical men, with little of the political fervour of their counterparts in France."[23] In fact, as will be seen, a very similar trend was observable in France as well, where pressures for the adoption of a reformist stance mounted within the CGT as it expanded into the ranks of the less skilled.

Although German workers who voted for the SPD were still publicly denounced as "comrades without a country" by a sovereign who assessed the performance of his chancellors in terms of their ability to contain the forward march of socialism, the participation of union officials in the operations of a variety of public policy boards at the level of local government and collaboration at that level between Social Democratic deputies and representatives of middle-class parties—even including what was in effect a political coalition in the Baden provincial legislature—were signs of a growing degree of working-class integration.[24]

Viewed as a dynamic trend rather than as a static situation, the outcome of working-class formation in Germany on the eve of World War I thus turns out to be somewhat more ambiguous than it first appears. As noted earlier, by pursuing a purely class strategy, the SPD had managed to secure over one-third of the vote in the 1912 election. This was a spectacular achievement, yet far short of what was required for conquering the state by way of the parliamentary road. As the party came close to mobilizing all but Catholic working-class voters, its achievement of an electoral majority was contingent upon the further expansion of the working class itself, a development that in the light of the dynamic of German capitalism was by no means completely out of the question, but was not yet in the offing.

The alternative, of course, was to engage in the coalition game. Although officially the party held fast to its opposition to participation in government, its posture was evidently evolving, and after the 1912 elections Scheidemann was allowed to stand for election as vice-president of the Reichstag.[25] The SPD victory precipitated panic among the military, the bureaucracy, and court circles, reviving rumors of a preemptive coup in defense of the state. However, in 1913, the Social Democrats voted for a new tax law designed to generate additional revenue made necessary by growing army expenditures. Socialist leaders justified their action on the grounds that establishment of the principle that the federal government had the right to impose a direct tax on private property was more important than defeating the military; but in addition, they were aware

[23] Ibid., p. 266.
[24] Ibid., p. 269.
[25] Joll, *Second International*, p. 89.

that a negative vote would not be understood by large sections of the working class who "were just as patriotic and just as vulnerable to military influence as anyone else, particularly when . . . there seemed to be a real possibility of a war to defend Germany against the menace of Slavdom."[26]

In conclusion, there is little doubt that around this time a very large proportion of German industrial workers shared a strong awareness of themselves as a class and were mobilized under the aegis of the Social Democratic party to act as such in a coordinated manner in both the marketplace and the political arena. The party was firmly committed to democracy—an objective whose realization in Imperial Germany would have been tantamount to a political revolution. But in the light of available evidence, it is not far-fetched to suggest that in the course of its steady expansion to encompass the working class as a whole, social democracy was also undergoing a steady transformation from a revolutionary movement into a mediating organization within capitalism. What if there had been no war? This transformation would have undoubtedly accelerated, and the outcome of class formation in Germany would have been quite similar to what emerged after World War I in the Low Countries and Scandinavia—the institutionalization at the level of the working class as a whole of a comprehensive apparatus linked by its organizational elites to the national politico-economic system.

Great Britain. The British case highlights the problems of interpretation noted earlier. The conventional vision, shared by both Lorwin and Lipset, emphasizes the contrast between the outcome of class formation in Britain and on the Continent generally speaking, as indicated most clearly by the fact that the British working class did not support a Communist party in Britain after World War I, when such parties appeared in France, Germany, and a number of other Continental countries. This is generally taken as a manifestation of the British working class's "moderate" disposition expressed, after the waning of the "hump of radicalism" associated with the decades of the Great Transformation, by the "new model" trade unions, cautious organizations with limited economic objectives. Although the unions eventually supported the formation of a class-based party, this was merely a practical response to changing circumstances and reflected their leadership's instrumental orientation toward action in the political arena rather than a doctrinaire commitment to class politics. In keeping with this, "the British Labour Party has always stood apart from the other European Socialist parties: it has been

[26] Craig, *Germany*, pp. 296-97.

fortunate in that the concept of the class struggle has rarely been applicable to day to day English political life."[27]

Yet it is well established that class affiliation has been, ever since the institutionalization of male universal suffrage immediately after World War I, a weightier determinant of electoral alignments in Britain than in most other industrial democracies and that a strong awareness of class continues to pervade most aspects of British society. Moreover, even if it is true that the concept of class struggle has "rarely been applicable," the period immediately preceding World War I appears to have been one time when it was very much so. In what is generally held to be a very insightful account of the final years of Liberal England, George Dangerfield writes of "the workers' rebellion," beginning in 1910, and explicitly attributes to the trade-union rank and file an explosion of "sudden class hatred."[28]

Although apparently contradictory, both these visions of the British situation make sense when considered within our general analytic framework, in which a distinction is made between the disposition or outlook of the working class and its organization. Given that distinction, it is quite possible for a heightened awareness of class—or even an explosion of "class hatred"—to occur within a world that is dominated by organizations that have little or no commitment to a doctrine of "class struggle" or to revolution. And it is indeed this strange combination of widespread and acute class sentiment and often militant fervor with organizations committed to the pursuit of change within the framework of capitalism that is the most distinctive feature of the British pattern of working-class formation and hence provides the explicandum to which we must address ourselves.

The process by which British workers made themselves into a class in the course of the Great Transformation, culminating in the Chartist episode of the late 1830s, is well known. After the defeat of Chartism, collective action tended to be restricted to the marketplace.[29] Aided by a change in the law, which provided them with the possibility of acquiring legal status as corporations and hence to secure protection against malfeasance by their own officers, the "new model" trade unions took off in the 1850s, initially among skilled craftsmen of manual trades but subsequently among skilled workers of core industries as well. Over the next decades, unions often combined with friendly societies and there was a steady trend toward amalgamation along trade lines at the national level.

[27] Joll, *Second International*, p. 2.

[28] George Dangerfield, *The Strange Death of Liberal England* (New York: Putnam, 1961), p. 231.

[29] Richard K. Webb, *Modern England* (New York: Dodd, Mead, 1968), pp. 282-86.

British unions generally followed a conservative policy, exercising caution to wage strategic strikes only; in this manner, they were able to build up resources to the point that strikers in such rare but long confrontations could be financially supported. The Trades Union Act of 1871 incorporated the recommendations of a Royal Commission, established in the wake of a wave of acute industrial disputes, for full legalization of unions, so long as they did not act restrictively.

In this manner, unique in the world of industrial capitalism, "by the early 1870s trade unionism was officially accepted and recognized, where it had succeeded in establishing itself"; yet these organizations so far encompassed no more than a small segment of the British working class. At the end of a period of rapid expansion, 1871-1873, total membership was on the order of 500,000 out of a secondary sector labor force then estimated at around 5.6 million.[30]

Over the next two decades, unions continued to expand along previously established paths; "but the newness that most impressed the general public was the further extension of agitation to the unskilled workers."[31] Although craft unions remained dominant, "general unions"—equivalent to "industrial" unions in the United States—began to make their appearance at this time; unions were also spreading among the lower ranks of white-collar occupations. By 1900, union membership numbered around two million, approximately one-fourth of the manual labor force, undoubtedly the highest density found anywhere at the time.[32]

In the intervening period, the Second Reform Act (1867) extended the suffrage to most urban industrial workers; the Third (1884) did so with respect to rural areas. As of the latter date, household suffrage prevailed throughout the country; most adult males, except for persons on relief and domestic servants resident with their employers, were now entitled to vote.[33] The 1885 Redistribution Act also established nearly equal-sized electoral districts throughout the country. As a matter of course, most working-class voters cast their ballots for the Liberal party; in the late 1860s, however, union leaders launched the Labour Representation League to obtain more direct and reliable representation of their organizations' interests in Parliament by securing the nomination of workers as Liberal candidates. A handful of such "Lib-Labs" were elected over

---

[30] Eric Hobsbawm, *Industry and Empire* (Baltimore: Penguin, 1969), p. 155; Vander Eycken and Frantzen, *De tertiaire sector*, p. 23.

[31] Webb, *Modern England*, p. 385.

[32] Ibid., p. 386; Vander Eycken and Frantzen, *De tertiaire sector*, p. 23.

[33] Mackie and Rose, *International Almanac*, p. 382.

the next decades, mostly from homogeneous working-class constituencies like those found in the mining districts.

Socialism, in Britain, originated outside the working class altogether. In the 1890s a new generation of union leaders began to respond to the ideas generated by proliferating middle-class socialist groups concerning the desirability of looking beyond immediate economic objectives to broader structural ones, such as the collectivization of industry and land. Concomitantly, unions espoused the Social Democratic class strategy in the political arena. Refusing Liberal support, three independent labor candidates were elected in 1892; in the wake of this success, an Independent Labour party (ILP) with a frankly socialist program was launched the following year. Although every one of the twenty-eight candidates fielded by the ILP in 1895 was defeated, over the next few years "the conversion of the labor movement to socialism proceeded steadily."[34]

This conversion was fostered by the concurrence of critical confrontations in each of the two principal spheres of working-class action, the marketplace and the political arena, which revealed the inherent constraints of the established system. The need to coordinate action on behalf of direct representation of trade union interests, enhanced by the recent organization of combative national employers' associations, was endorsed by the Trade Union Congress (TUC) in 1899, largely under pressure from unions representing the unskilled.[35] It was not yet evident, however, whether this would entail collaboration with existing parties or the launching of a new one. Unions were initially slow to join the movement; however, their reluctance was abruptly overcome in 1901, when the House of Lords, empowered under existing constitutional arrangements to act as a judicial body, decided in the Taff Vale Railway Company case that trade unions were financially liable for injuries employers incurred as a consequence of strikes and picketing, a decision that rendered strike action practically impossible.

By all accounts, this confrontation crystallized a sharpened state of class relations in Britain as a whole. Reconstructing the mood on the workers' side, Dangerfield has suggested, "ever since the collapse of Chartism in 1848, [the unions] had pursued a policy of 'opportunism,' of attempting, that is, to obtain for every man a fair day's pay for a fair day's work. And if the Taff Vale Judgment were to be the reward of such mildness, might they not argue that mildness deserved no less? The conclusion, indeed, was unavoidable. Very well, then; they must show their

---

[34] Webb, *Modern England*, p. 393.

[35] Henry Pelling, *A Short History of the Labour Party* (London: Macmillan, 1961), pp. 6-7.

power."[36] And indeed, the number of workers affiliated with the Labour Representation Committee (LRC) through their unions rose from 376,000 in 1901 to 469,000 the following year, and escalated to 861,000 in 1903, by which time the unions were being asked and agreed to make greater financial contributions to the new organization.[37]

Although in retrospect this development can be seen as a crucial step toward the formation of a distinctive party, in 1906 the LRC's candidates stood for the most part under the Liberal label, thus contributing to that party's sweeping national victory. Thereafter the Liberals demonstrated their commitment to the interests of their working-class clientele by speedily enacting a considerable number of social welfare measures long pending on the TUC's legislative agenda. Yet what Manchesterians might do on behalf of organized labor was of necessity limited. The British version of laissez faire did not foreclose state action in the realm of health, education, and the like to improve conditions; "but to insist that employers should pay for a living wage? That was a frightful impairment of freedom."[38]

The trade unions were faced with another legal blow in 1909, when the House of Lords ruled in the Osborne case that unions could not use membership dues for supporting a political party or assisting Members of Parliament financially. Although the Liberals, still in power, might have altered the rule by parliamentary action, they did not immediately undertake to do so. Mounting grievances thus gathered themselves around the working class's own organizations, the trade unions; though many leaders sought to carry on routinely within the "Lib-Lab" framework, this could not withstand the growing anger of the rank and file. It is in connection with this that Dangerfield refers to an explosion of "sudden class hatred," in the course of which "between 1910 and 1914, against the wishes of their leaders," British workers "plunged into a series of furious strikes which, but for the declaration of war, would have culminated in September, 1914, in a General Strike of extraordinary violence."[39]

Talk of a general strike simultaneously evoked the memory of Chartism and raised the specter of revolutionary syndicalism. But evidence for direct influence among British workers of syndicalist ideas from France or from the United States is scant; and only a couple of union leaders— James Connally and Tom Mann—were committed to producer social-

---

[36] Dangerfield, *The Strange Death*, p. 222.
[37] Pelling, *A Short History*, p. 10.
[38] Dangerfield, *The Strange Death*, p. 226.
[39] Ibid., p. 235.

ism. Nor had British workers suddenly become revolutionary-minded. Dangerfield sums up the situation as follows: "The movement on the surface was not revolutionary but rebellious; it did not *consciously* aim . . . at the overthrow of the wage system and the destruction of parliamentary rule; the only revolution that can be discovered in it is a psychological one."[40] What was at work, evidently, was an abrupt change of sensibility, a *prise de conscience* of the sort I have analyzed in another context as a "moment of madness," when new ideas, modes of action, and organizational networks suddenly take root.[41] Changes in the outlook or disposition of a class are, by their very nature, difficult to verify. Here there is some support from indirect evidence concerning the subsequent behavior of British workers: not only the wave of strikes already indicated, but also a very abrupt increase in union membership, from 2.4 million in 1910 to 3 million the following year and 4 million in 1913, when approximately half of all British male workers in the secondary sector had joined.

Given what we know of the bitter class confrontation of 1926, what might have happened in Britain had a general strike been launched in 1914? As it was, even while class hatred mounted, in 1913 mainstream trade union leaders were able to secure from their Liberal allies legislation that negated the Osborne decision. The possibility of a break was in the air, but it had by no means yet occurred. It was anticipated that by the next general elections, Labour would be able to contest one hundred or more seats; but how would these candidates fare? Given that Independent Labour party candidates mustered no more than half a million votes in either of the two 1910 general elections, about 7 percent of the total, it can be inferred that the overwhelming majority of workers were then still voting along traditional lines.

Here also, the war interfered with whatever trends might be projected on the basis of the previous configuration. Union membership doubled again in the course of the conflict and wartime developments drove major trade unions—and thereby TUC as a whole—toward a more independent stance in the political arena. The war appears to have contributed to the further development of what Dangerfield has dubbed "class hatred" but which might be referred to less dramatically as an acute awareness among British workers of their membership in a class, conceived of as a comprehensive corporate group pertaining to both the marketplace and the political arena. Yet at the same time, while further alienating the Irish, the war seems to have had the effect of fostering greater unity among the three British nations of the United Kingdom. In 1918, the

---

[40] Ibid.

[41] Aristide R. Zolberg, "Moments of Madness," *Politics and Society* 2 (1972):183-207.

Labour party surged forward to replace the Liberals as Britain's second major party; class conflict thereby came to be formally institutionalized in the political arena, but in a manner that did not jeopardize the regime.

France. The French case allows greater interpretive latitude than any of the others considered here. Most accounts of French working-class formation around the turn of the century emphasize the emergence of the Confédération Générale du Travail (CGT), a nationwide federation of unions whose official doctrine was revolutionary syndicalism, as its most characteristic outcome. On that basis, French industrial workers are regarded as having achieved a very high degree of class awareness and as having voted collectively for a separatist stance, the most radical conceivable rejection of capitalism.[42] But it is also the case that around 1910, no more than about one million of France's estimated seven million secondary sector workers belonged to *any* sort of labor organization, the lowest rate encountered among the four cases considered here. Of these, only about 600,000 belonged to the CGT proper; the remainder was distributed among a variety of much less radical unions, including extremely conservative Catholic ones.[43] There are also some indications, to which I shall return, that some of the major component unions of the CGT adopted in practice a much more moderate policy than suggested by the parent organization's doctrine. It is on such grounds that Peter Stearns, questioning the representativity of the CGT, has referred to French revolutionary syndicalism as "a cause without rebels."[44] Although Bernard Moss has in turn attempted to rebut Stearns, ultimately interpretations of the French outcome must address themselves to both features: a substantial minority—more radical than is found in Britain or Germany and relatively larger than its American counterpart, the International Workers of the World—and a larger unmobilized segment than is found in those countries as well.

A second problem of interpretation arises from the disjunction between working-class activity in the marketplace and in the political arena. The distinction itself is not quite applicable to the French case, in that the CGT did not view itself as merely a trade union organization—indeed, it

[42] See, for example, Bernard Moss, *The Origins of the French Labor Movement: The Socialism of Skilled Workers, 1830-1914* (Berkeley: University of California Press, 1976).

[43] Edward Shorter and Charles Tilly, *Strikes in France, 1830-1968* (Cambridge: Cambridge University Press, 1974), p. 147.

[44] Peter Stearns, *Revolutionary Syndicalism and French Labor: A Cause without Rebels* (New Brunswick: Rutgers University Press, 1971).

explicitly rejected what came to be called in France *trade unionisme*—but as a political movement that provided an alternative to electoral socialism. As a consequence, social historians of France have tended to consider the CGT in the context of the "workers' movement" (*mouvement ouvrier*), but have generally relinquished socialism to the realm of political history with which they are not concerned. The crystallization of this historiographic tradition has in turn resulted in a vision that exaggerates the separation between the two realms of organizational activity. In reality, regardless of the negative stand taken by the CGT leadership toward parliamentary socialism, in the years immediately preceding World War I, most French industrial workers were casting their ballots for the SFIO and considered its leader, Jean Jaurès, their national spokesman.

A third problem is that in France, as in the other cases considered, the decade immediately preceding World War I was one of significant change. But whereas in Britain, as we have seen, the working class appeared to be going beyond its traditional trade-unionist goals and embracing more general objectives involving a restructuring of property relations, there are some indications that the opposite was occurring in France. Lorwin has suggested that "even while revolutionary syndicalism was the official doctrine of the CGT, reformist currents were important." Once again, the war figures as a major intervening variable: "If the First World War had not come, if the war had not been so long and costly, if the Russian Revolution had not intervened, the reformist currents might have become the unions' mainstream."[45] Robert Wohl has similarly concluded that by the summer of 1914, "every sign pointed to the fact that the CGT was on its way to becoming more of a union and less of a political party," leaving political leadership in the hands of a Socialist party that was itself "no longer revolutionary."[46] In the same vein, Michelle Perrot concludes her contribution here with the observation that on the eve of the war, the attempts by Jean Jaurès to reconcile the labor movement—that is, the CGT—and republican socialism were verging on success.

At the root of these developments was the precocious emergence among French workers of a distinctive disposition that Moss has labeled "federalist trade socialism." Although elaborated into a formal doctrine by Proudhon, this productivist outlook is best understood as the "folk"

---

[45] Val R. Lorwin, *The French Labor Movement* (Cambridge: Harvard University Press, 1954), p. 30.

[46] Robert Wohl, *French Communism in the Making, 1914-1925* (Stanford: Stanford University Press, 1966), pp. 42-43.

ideology of the French working class that, as William Sewell has shown, surfaced in the late 1830s and provided the foundation for the programs workers advocated in 1848. The institutionalization of some of these programs, albeit temporary, contributed to a further crystallization of federalist trade socialism as the culture of French skilled workers. Notwithstanding the tragic outcome of the revolution of 1848, the tradition survived to inspire the Commune a generation later.

The long-standing prohibition against workers' trade associations was lifted in 1884, only a little more than a decade after unions were legalized in Britain. Under the more liberal climate of the Third Republic, syndicates proliferated among skilled workers. In keeping with the established orientation of French working-class culture, their organizational objectives encompassed the transformation of property relations. This was to be accomplished by the gradual formation of producers' cooperatives, capitalized on the basis of dues, which would eventually be converted into shares. In the political sphere, the syndicates were committed to the achievement of a democratic and social republic that would promote their primary objective by extending to established or prospective cooperatives credit facilities from the public sector and by purchasing the goods they produced. To a limited extent, such support was in fact provided by republican governments after 1879 as a form of political patronage.[47]

Since France had established male universal suffrage in 1848, workers became involved in the arena of electoral politics before class formation had proceeded very far, much as was the case for their American counterparts. When political competition was restored after the fall of Napoleon III, urban workers massively supported Republican parties, and within this camp, naturally favored the reformist-minded Radicals. As in Britain, some distinctively labor candidates ran under the Radical label. However, the very first congress of workers' associations, convened in 1876, already considered launching a labor party of some sort.

The development of cooperative socialism remained perfunctory; the associationist tradition survived mostly in the form of a small apolitical island in the capitalist sea. In the 1880s, many of the syndicates began to evolve into more conventional trade unions, emphasizing wages and seeking to achieve structural reforms within the system—the creation of arbitration boards, regulation of the length of the workday, establishment of a pension system, and so forth. They coalesced into a National Federation of Trade Unions at the end of the decade. Although membership surged forward, reaching approximately 400,000 in 1893, this only

[47] Moss, *Origins*, pp. 5, 66-69.

amounted to about 3 percent of the secondary sector labor force, then estimated at about five million. At this time, the level of organizational density achieved by the French working class was approximately half that of the British.

The initiative for organizing a distinctive working-class party was preempted in 1879 by Marx's French followers, Jules Guesde and Paul Lafargue. In contrast with the producer socialism of the syndicates, the Parti des Travailleurs Socialistes de France aimed at the collectivization of property by a conquest of the state, in keeping with Social Democratic doctrine. Notwithstanding a formal endorsement of this objective by the National Workers' Congress, few unions outside of Paris affiliated with the new party, which itself soon split. Reduced to a minority, the Guesdists evolved over the next decade into the Parti Ouvrier de France (POF). Abandoning workers of the skilled trades to the Radicals, POF sought to mobilize the small but growing factory proletariat of the developing industrial regions who, recently recruited from the rural areas, did not yet possess a class culture and hence offered no resistance to social democratic doctrine.[48] Although the Guesdists gained formal control of the National Federation of Trade Unions in 1886, divisions persisted at the level of the rank and file, and the organization split in 1894 as the result of intensified rivalry among emerging socialist parties.

Competing with the Guesdists for working-class support were two other socialist organizations. The majority of the original party, now led by Paul Brousse, evolved into the Fédération des Travailleurs Socialistes de France, better known as the "Possibilists"; they in turn gave rise to another splinter group, the Parti Ouvrier Socialiste Révolutionnaire led by Jean Allemane. Most "laborist" of the French socialist parties, the latter was the most closely attuned to the strain of working-class culture that emphasized revolution through the producer strategy. Concurrently, however, some reform-minded republicans were also beginning to present themselves as "socialists." Known as "Independents," they too solicited working-class support. As was the case for parties more generally, the framework of French parliamentary institutions provided little incentive for these various formations to unify into a single organization. An electoral breakthrough occurred in 1893, when socialist candidates of all persuasions, including "Socialist Radicals," gained 769,000 votes, approximately 11 percent of the total, and secured forty-one seats in the Chamber of Deputies.[49]

The most significant development at the organizational level around

[48] Ibid., p. 103.
[49] Mackie and Rose, *International Almanac*, p. 126.

this time was the emergence, alongside the trade unions or syndicates, of the *bourses du travail* movement, which has been regarded as the French working class's most original institution.[50] The labor exchange was in effect an employment market under the control of local syndicates, initiated in the mid-1880s by a reformist Paris municipal administration. Conceived of as the working class's counterpart of the capitalists' stock exchange, it enabled workers to overcome their dependency on commercial employment agencies, usually under the thumb of employers. Rapidly spreading throughout the country in the form of confederations of local sydicates, the *bourses* movement was a reincarnation of the old aspiration of French skilled workers for socialism in the form of a free association of producers.

After the National Federation of Trade Unions was captured by the Guesdists, their Allemanist rivals organized a National Federation of Labor Exchanges, which thus provided French workers with a "producer socialism" alternative to Marxist social democracy.[51] However, as determined by F. Pelloutier, secretary-general of the National Federation of Labor Exchanges, this goal was no longer to be achieved by the gradual formation of cooperatives nor by following the Social Democrats' electoral path to revolution; instead, the working class would bring about a structural transformation of capitalist society by wielding the ultimate weapon it possessed by virtue of its very existence, the general strike.

With this objective in mind, it was vital to preserve workers' organizations from the clutches of Guesdist social democracy, as well as from the temptation to collaborate with republican governments in order to secure short-term benefits. Moreover, the strategy required keeping labor exchanges and syndicates separate and distinct: syndicates were designed to deal with ongoing demands, whereas *bourses* were regarded as uniquely suited to educate the proletariat in preparation for its post-revolutionary role. Hence, throughout the 1890s, Pelloutier fought all attempts to establish a national umbrella organization encompassing both, a tactic that ensured the de facto supremacy of the labor exchange movement over the syndicates in the short term but undoubtedly contributed to the relative weakness of French labor organizations around the turn of the century in comparison with other industrial societies.

The various issues considered came to a head around this time because of general developments in the national political arena. Waged in the heat of the Dreyfus affair, the 1898 elections entailed what has been

---

[50] Jacques Julliard, *Fernand Pelloutier et les origines du syndicalisme d'action directe* (Paris: Seuil, 1971), p. 7.
[51] Ibid., pp. 119-33.

termed in the literature on American elections an electoral realignment; together, Radicals and the SFIO obtained over three million votes, nearly 40 percent of the total, and approximately the same proportion of seats. The following year, the Radicals came out of opposition for the first time since the founding of the Third Republic to form a leftist coalition government, the Bloc des Gauches, under the leadership of Waldeck-Rousseau who, as minister of interior in 1884, had been instrumental in legalizing labor unions. Dependent on socialist support in the Chamber of Deputies, the premier invited an Independent, A. Millerand, to join the government as minister of commerce. Was Millerand's acceptance a victory for the French working class, or was it the first of many socialist betrayals? By most accounts, it was perceived as the former by the rank and file and as the latter by Pelloutier and other leaders.[52]

Benefiting from the changing political climate, the various socialist parties continued their ascent and acquired greater bargaining power in relation to the Radicals. In 1902, the Independents and "Possibilists," who had recently coalesced into the Parti Socialiste Français, obtained forty seats, with another eleven going to the Parti Socialiste de France, mostly Guesdists. Concurrently, the ties between parliamentary socialists, now mostly arrayed under the leadership of Jean Jaurès, and the government moved ever closer toward an outright coalition.[53] The counterpart of this rapprochement was the creation in 1905 of a Ministry of Labor, which gave unions coming to negotiate in Paris the impression that they were going to *their* ministry, an impression that "might lead to the thought that the Republican State was not merely the instrument of bourgeois domination."[54] An even more substantial indicator of the changing relationship of the working class to the state is that unions now actively sought government mediation in the settlement of strikes because this contributed, on balance, to favorable outcomes.[55]

But if these trends suggested a further integration of the French working class into the system and some convergence with the British outcomes, other developments were more ambiguous. Pelloutier's resistance notwithstanding, the CGT was established in 1902 as an umbrella organization encompassing both the labor exchanges and the syndicates; although the latter were now its dominant component, the organization as a whole was committed to the doctrine of "direct action," confirming the hegemonic status of "producer socialism" among the organized seg-

[52] Shorter and Tilly, *Strikes in France*, p. 114.
[53] Wohl, *French Communism*, p. 37.
[54] Jean-Pierre Azema and M. Winock, *La IIIe République* (Paris: Calmann-Lévy, 1970), p. 128.
[55] Shorter and Tilly, *Strikes in France*, pp. 29-34.

ment of the French working class at this time. One should not infer from this that French syndicalists were committed to violent action or that they shunned efforts to improve conditions here and now; but one of the consequences of the CGT's formal espousal of revolutionary syndicalism was a minimization of the crucial instruments of collective bargaining, such as regular payment of dues and the accumulation of strike funds. Accordingly, in the course of ordinary confrontations between workers and capitalists, French unions as a whole remained generally weaker than their counterparts elsewhere.

The CGT's doctrinal stand also foreclosed the possibility of formal collaboration between the syndicates and socialist parties; yet it is evident from the steady electoral progress of the latter that more workers were in fact voting for them, undoubtedly including CGT members. The coming to power of a reformist government placed the socialists in a quandary as well: the choice of whether to participate in government under capitalism, which was for the German Social Deomocrats a theoretical one only, was for the French immediate and real. As it was, in 1904-1905 Jaurès opted for nonparticipation in order to maximize the chances of uniting the disparate strands of French socialism into a single party, acknowledged by others as the French Section of the Workers' International (SFIO). The operation was quite successful; the SFIO progressed from 875,532 votes in 1902 (10.4 percent of the total) to 1,413,044 in 1914 (16.8 percent), and from 46 seats to 103. It should be noted, however, that this fell considerably short of total electoral mobilization of the working class. Given a low rate of abstentions and the absence of any party to the left of the SFIO, the relative electoral weakness of French socialism at this time is not attributable to the CGT's doctrinal stand; rather, it is likely that some workers continued to vote Radical, and others—particularly in regions of heavy Catholic practice such as Brittany—for parties on the right of the political spectrum, as about one-third of the French working class were doing still in the third quarter of the twentieth century.[56]

In France as in Britain, class tensions appear to have become exacerbated in the years immediately preceding World War I. In 1906, the CGT orchestrated a wave of strikes on behalf of the eight-hour day, patterned after the movement launched by the American Knights of Labor in 1886; this stimulated a rapid growth in membership, much of it attributable to an influx of less skilled proletarians from the pace-setting indus-

---

[56] G. Adam, F. Bon, J. Capdevielle, and R. Mouriaux, *L'ouvrier français en 1970* (Paris: Armand Colin, 1971), pp. 72-73, 84, 87; Richard DeAngelis, *Blue-collar Workers and Politics: A French Paradox* (London: Croom Helm, 1982).

tries.[57] Concurrently, in deference to the directives of the International, the SFIO distanced itself from the Radicals, leaving its leaders no choice but to seek allies on the parliamentary right. In keeping with this reorientation, the authorities—led by Minister of Interior Clémenceau, the old Radical hero—adopted a more repressive stance toward strikers, leading to a bloody confrontation in 1908.

This showdown was very costly for the CGT, which subsequently retreated to a more moderate stance. It has also been suggested that its retreat reflected the preferences of a changing membership, including many newcomers from the mining, textile, and railroad sectors, organized into industrial federations, more concerned with bread-and-butter issues than with striving on behalf of the producer socialism associated with the crafts tradition. The established doctrine prevailed for the time being because under the CGT constitution all component syndicates had an equal voice regardless of membership size, so that the numerous small craft unions retained the upper hand in decision making; but there were growing demands for proportional representation of the syndicates according to membership size in the CGT's governing bodies.

As noted earlier, the unified socialist party nearly doubled its percentage of the vote between 1906 and 1914. Contrary to Lipset's assertion concerning the French Socialists' inability to foster social legislation because of "the ferocity of bourgeois response"—a point that figures prominently in his explanation of the "radical" French outcome—from 1910 onward, under the leadership of A. Briand, the nonsocialist left sought to achieve a new accommodation with the SFIO.[58] In the parliamentary elections of May 1914, the SFIO for the first time outpolled the Radical Socialists. The new government, headed by the Independent Socialist Viviani, promptly enacted an income tax law—a measure that in France as elsewhere in the capitalist world, including the United States, heralded a major step in the formation of a regime based on compromise between classes. And then the war came.

United States. It has been seen that the historical literature on the German and French cases tends to exaggerate the militancy and revolutionary disposition of the working class in the pre–World War I period because the official doctrine of its leading organizations is taken uncritically as tantamount to the disposition of the workers themselves, and because the effects of World War I and the Russian Revolution as inter-

---

[57] Shorter and Tilly, *Strikes in France*, pp. 118-22; Jacques Julliard, *Clémenceau briseur de grèves* (Paris: Julliard, 1965).
[58] Lipset, "Radicalism or Reformism," p. 10.

vening variables accounting for postwar radicalism have been underestimated. Mirroring this, there has been a tendency to exaggerate the conservatism of the American working class by viewing the policies espoused
in the American Federation of Labor (AFL) era as indicative of the outlook of workers and by anachronistically projecting into the pre–World
War I epoch orientations that owed a great deal to later developments.

There is no denying that the AFL was committed from the very outset
to maximizing the interests of skilled workers by controlling access to
crafts, as well as to a narrowly construed "business unionism"; that its
strategy for achieving political influence entailed avoiding permanent
partisan affiliations; and that it deliberately rejected socialism. But this
does not mean that American "blue-collar" workers, in and out of the
AFL, had no awareness of themselves as a class. On the contrary, there
are many indications that they perceived themselves as being engaged in
a perennial struggle with their employers; the widespread image of "the
bosses," which is still prevalent in the language of the American working
class, is hardly a benevolent one. True, the relevant collectivity was narrowly defined—mostly skilled, white, and male—but this was by and
large the case among European workers as well. American workers were
obviously not revolutionary-minded; but if the criterion of a high degree
of class awareness is a revolutionary disposition, then one is led to the
absurd conclusion that hardly anywhere in the capitalist world of the
early twentieth century was a genuinely aware working class to be found.

Lack of interest in revolution did not mean lack of militancy; many
observers have noted the high incidence of violence in American industrial relations, a phenomenon that stems largely from the ruthlessness of
employers, but to which labor has perennially made contributions of its
own. Much as in Europe, union membership was rapidly expanding in
the prewar period. Rising from 447,000 in 1897 to 1.1 million in 1901,
the level doubled to 2.2 million over the next decade and reached 2.7
million in 1914, approximately one-fourth of the industrial labor force—
a level comparable to what was found in Germany.[59]

Moreover, at the time with which we are concerned, the AFL was by
no means the only working-class organization in America, and a considerable range of outlook was found within its own ranks. The Socialist
Party of America, a social democratic organization founded at the turn
of the century, rapidly gained ground in the ensuing decade and was on
the upswing when Sombart visited the United States in 1904. Its influence within the world of organized labor was by no means negligible. In

---

[59] Gerard Rosenblum, *Immigrant Workers: Their Impact on American Labor Radicalism* (New York: Basic Books, 1973), p. 156.

1902, the Socialist platform was supported by 46 percent of the votes cast at the AFL convention, a level that indicated the rapid spread of socialism among component unions. In 1912, a Socialist candidate for the AFL presidency secured a remarkable one-third of the votes against the incumbent, Samuel Gompers. If these votes were in any way representative of the distribution of opinion among the union rank and file, then it can be estimated that nearly 10 percent of the industrial labor force—and perhaps as many as one-fourth of skilled manual workers—were in some sense socialist-minded, a level not out of keeping with what was found in Britain or France around this time.

Concurrently, socialism was also making a breakthrough in the political arena, in a manner very similar to what was going on in Britain. The first Socialist representative was elected to the U.S. Congress in 1910; Eugene V. Debs received 6 percent of the popular vote in the 1912 presidential election; and there were scattered victories at the municipal and state levels. The high point of Socialist electoral strength was probably reached in 1914, when in addition to the 1,200 incumbent municipal officeholders, 33 Socialist legislators were elected in fourteen states.[60]

The geographical distribution of these votes, as well as circulation patterns of Socialist periodicals, strongly suggests that the largest share of them originated among three specific segments of the working class: skilled operatives of mostly German origin located in the industrial cities of Wisconsin and other midwestern states; miners, often of British origin, in isolated and widely scattered western mining communities, where a native American version of militant producer socialism had recently emerged as the International Workers of the World (IWW); and Jewish immigrants from eastern Europe in the garment trades of the New York metropolitan area. Conspicuously absent, by all accounts, were the Irish Catholics, who, as indicated by Amy Bridges in her essay above, made up a very large proportion of America's older urban working class. Moreover, contrary to widespread belief among those who feared socialism and most ominously for anyone aspiring to a socialist future in the United States, this doctrine appeared to hold little or no appeal for the massive waves of immigrants—with the outstanding exception of the Jews already mentioned—who were at that very time contributing to the rapid expansion of the country's industrial labor force.

When considered in the context of a recognition that American workers did share a sense of class founded on their role as *labor*, the fact that

<hr />

[60] James Weinstein, *The Decline of Socialism in America, 1912-1925* (New York: Monthly Review Press, 1967), pp. 93-117.

only a minority of them acted in class terms within the political arena helps to identify the most distinctive feature of the American outcome: the orientation of workers qua *citizens* overwhelmingly toward the political mainstream.

Martin Shefter has indicated that the critical turning point in this respect occurred in the wake of the great confrontation of 1886, when the launching of a concerted antilabor crusade fostered among the leadership of established working-class organizations profound divisions over how to respond. The Knights of Labor, the leading organization at the time, advocated an escalation of the struggle on the economic front beyond the traditionally narrow objectives of trade unionism "pure and simple," coupled with a more thorough mobilization of the working class by expanding the scope of unions to include the unskilled. Their orientation bears a striking similarity to that of the labor exchange movement in France, with an emphasis on achievement by the working class of control over its own institutions, while deemphasizing—if not rejecting outright—action in the established political arena. One possible alternative to this was social democracy, whose appearance on the American scene has already been discussed. As it was, within a decade of 1886, the Knights were overtaken by the upstart AFL, whose strategy was much more narrowly trade unionist. The AFL set out to consolidate its base in the skilled segment of the working class rather than to mobilize more extensively; to secure acceptance by employers as the sole acceptable antagonist—a role well expressed by the French term *interlocuteur valable*; and to maximize its influence in the political arena by exercising pressure on both the two major political parties to promote policies deemed to be in the interest of labor.

The institutionalization of a practice whereby unions function as mediating organizations between the working class and the state must not be viewed merely as representing a lower degree of protest than the formation of a working-class party, but rather as a genuine alternative to the latter. This appears to have been obvious to the principal contenders at the time. Sombart emphasized the originality of the AFL's political strategy, singling out the "quite special system . . . recently put into operation by those representing the workers' interests," in which unions demanded that candidates put themselves on record with respect to relevant issues by responding to a questionnaire. Known as the "Winnetka System" after the city in Illinois where it originated in the 1890s, the practice was officially taken up by the AFL in 1901 and generalized in 1904. Sombart also reports that the Winnetka system was denounced by Socialists as a "begging policy," but that anti-Socialist trade union leaders "attach a great deal of hope to this system" as a device for "permanently remov[ing] the threat and danger of an independent Socialist workers' party."[61]

Notwithstanding important differences between them, both the Knights of Labor and the AFL were in tune with indigenous working-class traditions going back to the earliest phase of U.S. industrialization in the middle third of the nineteenth century. Once elaborated into a doctrine and institutionalized as the official policy of the AFL, unionism "pure and simple" served as the cultural code that programmed the formation of an outlook among newly arriving waves of industrial workers. Just as they learned to speak English, eat American food, dress in American clothes, and play American games, most immigrants quickly learned that to be an American worker was to be a trade unionist and a Democrat or a Republican, but not a Socialist.

Evidence that socialism was gaining ground in the first decade of the century in no way contradicts the proposition that the trend represented by the AFL was already becoming dominant. Looking forward from about 1912, one might have anticipated that Socialism, in the sense of an organized formation in the political arena committed to structural change, was sufficiently entrenched in certain localities and regions to function as a substantial minority force at the national level, possibly taking advantage of cyclical downturns and the like to mobilize a growing share of the American working class. As it was, however, much of the Socialists' thunder was stolen from them by the Democrats in the course of Woodrow Wilson's first term. The establishment of the U.S. Department of Labor in 1913 gave American workers a place of their own in Washington, much as had occurred in France; and the appointment of a former United Mine Workers official as the first secretary further legitimized organized labor as a component of the American regime. Although U.S. workers had long benefited from more extensive freedom of association than most, unions hitherto operated under many legal handicaps. This explains why the Clayton Antitrust Act (1914), which freed unions from the constraints of antitrust regulations, was hailed by Samuel Gompers as labor's "Magna Carta."[62] In addition, the Democrats were credited with ratification of the sixteenth and seventeenth amendments, pertaining respectively to the income tax and the direct election of senators, reforms that had long been on the agenda of American Socialists as well as of the AFL. In 1916, the Wilson administration

[61] Sombart, *Why Is There No Socialism*, p. 61.
[62] Robert Morris, ed., *Encyclopedia of American History* (New York: Harper and Row, 1976), p. 326.

secured enactment of a long-overdue child labor law as well as an eight-hour day on interstate railroads. James Weinstein, a historian sympathetic to the American socialist tradition, has belittled these reforms on the ground that they "entailed no substantial change in the lives of most workers"; but he admits that "their cumulative impact was sufficient to halt the steady growth which the Socialist Party had enjoyed during the previous four years."[63] Much of the labor vote that had gone to Debs in 1912 went to Wilson four years later.

Whereas in France and Germany, as well as in Britain, prewar trends toward greater integration of workers into the system and toward class accommodation were largely offset by tensions generated by World War I, in the American case these trends were further reinforced. Stimulated by international demand, the American economy experienced a spectacular expansion; the AFL's "business" orientation placed it in a position to take maximum advantage of market conditions favorable to labor, which included a manpower shortage induced by the halt in immigration from Europe; and the fact that it delivered the goods provided tangible incentives for joining. Union membership doubled in the war years, with the bulk of the increment going to AFL-affiliated bodies.[64] Since the first Wilson administration was determined to keep the United States out of the European war, the sphere of foreign policy posed no problems for either the AFL or the Socialists. When war came, it was defined as a defensive one; the AFL behaved as most European socialists had done under equivalent circumstances, and joined the patriotic consensus. In contrast with this, by opposing the war from the very outset, American Socialists were doubly deviant, from their European fellows and from the American mainstream. Casting themselves beyond the pale of national politics, they dwindled into a thoroughly marginal minority, which all but succumbed under the repressive blows meted out in the United States as in Europe to radicals in the counterrevolutionary postwar years.[65]

III

With a better understanding of what is to be explained, the contributions of economic and political structures to working-class formation will now be explored by considering them as distinct independent variables; however, these structures should themselves be understood as interdependent determinants in relation to each other. Generally speaking, through-

[63] Weinstein, Decline of Socialism, p. 105.

[64] Morris, Encyclopedia, p. 768.

[65] Robert Goldstein, Political Repression in Modern America, 1870 to the Present (Cambridge: Shenkman, 1978), pp. 103-64.

out modern western history, national variations in economic organization and development determined different patterns of social stratification, and these in turn contributed to varied outcomes in state and nation formation; but, at the same time, variations in political organization and deliberate actions by political authorities played an important role in patterning economic structures.[66]

It might also be noted that although national economic and political configurations will be treated as indivisible wholes for purposes of the present analysis, constructs such as these hide as much as they reveal. As is apparent from the case studies above, sectoral and regional variations in economic and political organization within each of the countries under consideration were sometimes as wide as variations between countries. The present approach is designed to help explore such questions as, for example, the consequences of the fact that a larger proportion of American workers than French were working in large metallurgical factories around 1880; but we should not thereby lose sight of the fact that some French workers were also working in such factories, while some Americans remained employed in artisanal workshops of the sort considered "modal" with respect to the French case.

The Disparate Incarnations of Industrial Capitalism. Does capitalism matter? One would hardly think so when considering what contemporary political science and sociology have to say about working-class formation. Much greater causal weight is attributed to variations in the character of the state and in the political environment more generally than to economic structures of any sort. For example, in his recent work on the subject, Lipset acknowledges that "economic variables such as the timing of industrialization, the pace of economic growth, the concentration of industry, the occupational structure, the nature of the division of labor, and the wealth of the country" have all been cited as relevant variables in the comparative analysis of working-class movements in western society; but he evidently does not believe that they are sufficiently significant to warrant his further attention.[67] This stance, which Lipset shares with Rokkan, perhaps merely reflects a more general tendency among western political sociologists to avoid explanations that smack of historical materialism.

---

[66] The theoretical justification for this cannot be elaborated here. See Aristide R. Zolberg, "The Origins of the Western System: A Missing Link," *World Politics* 33 (1981):253-81; Zolberg, "'World' and 'System': A Misalliance," in *World System Analysis: Competing Perspectives*, ed. William Thompson (Beverly Hills, Calif.: Sage, 1983).
[67] Lipset, "Radicalism or Reformism," p. 1.

As against this, we have the basic vision of classical Marxism, in which industrial capitalism appears on the historical stage as a universal demiurge, wreaking revolutionary transformations that render all societies very much alike in most important respects. The fundamental insight of this tradition, captured by Jürgen Kuczynski's image of the machine as "the forceps used by society to deliver the working class," remains a powerful one.[68] It is indeed the objective reality of a common outcome, "industrial society," complemented by the perception of many who lived through the transformation that they were being subjected to a common experience, that provides the warrant for a comparative undertaking such as this.

At the time this tradition originated, the universe of industrial capitalism was limited to one fully developed case; it therefore made sense to elaborate theory on the basis of the British experience without much concern for significant variation between countries. Regarding the impact of capitalism on working-class formation, Marx and Engels initially set forth in the *Manifesto* the general proposition that "the development of class antagonism keeps even pace with the development of industry." However, they subsequently qualified their views on the subject in the light of developments in Britain and in the United States. It was quite evident by the latter decades of the century that if the further development of industrial capitalism in Britain fostered an enlargement of the working class and its proletarianization, in the sense that an ever larger share was working in mechanized factories, the process did not lead to an intensification of the class struggle. As is well known, this was explained in part by the formation of a "labor aristocracy" in consequence of Britain's paramount position in the world economy; by a general rise in the standard of living; and also by a steady extension of political participation, which had resulted toward the end of Marx's life, and well before the death of Engels, in a substantial democratization of British political life. Engels went even further with respect to the United States; his remarks on why, despite the spectacular development of industrial capitalism, the American working class showed little inclination toward socialism provided leads that Sombart subsequently followed.

We are thus led back to the problem of "exceptionalism," albeit in a somewhat different guise: the question has now become which form of capitalism is the norm, and which the deviant? The answer, of course, must be the same as for the outcome of working-class formation. Once the fundamental features of industrial capitalism have been delineated

---

[68] Jürgen Kuczynski, *The Rise of the Working Class* (New York: McGraw-Hill, 1967), p. 141.

and we begin to scrutinize the actual historical manifestations of this process, the vision of a singular demiurge rapidly dissipates. Capitalism became flesh in a variety of forms, and each of these disparate incarnations functioned as a distinctive experiential matrix for the workers it called into life. Given the multifarious character of industrial capitalism, it stands to reason that the working class emerged concomitantly as an array of disparate groups subjected to different conditions and hence inclined to respond in different ways. Since differentiation was a key aspect of the process that governed the formation of the western working class, variety was a constitutive element of its eventual character.

An examination of the relevant literature in economic history suggests that the national configuration with which we are concerned might be conceptualized as representing the interaction of two variables: (a) the timing and pace of industrialization, and (b) the structure of the economy. The latter can itself be thought of as a combination of several variables, including especially the *extent* of industrialization; the degree to which the individual sector is capital intensive; and the mechanism for procurement of an industrial labor force.

The most commonly evoked proposition concerning the consequences of the timing and pace of industrialization for working-class formation is drawn from W. W. Rostow's *The Stages of Economic Growth*, long popular among social scientists concerned with economic and social development.[69] Although this work, provocatively subtitled *A Non-Communist Manifesto*, was principally an attempt to formulate a theoretical foundation for the development of American foreign policy toward the Third World in the late 1950s, it did advance some propositions concerning the relationship between economic growth and working-class formation and has inspired others to formulate additional hypotheses to this effect.

Rostow's main contention is that Communism is "a disease of the transition" from agricultural to industrial society.[70] However, the rise of Communism in the twentieth century is for him merely a reenactment of the "hump of radicalism," which early developers experienced in the course of the first two stages of growth, the "take-off" and the "drive to maturity," but which gave way to moderation once this maturity had been achieved and the material benefits of industrial capitalism became more widely distributed within the society. Concomitantly, for Rostow, "one failure of Marx's system" was the rise of industrial real wages in western Europe, "and the perfectly apparent fact that the British and

---

[69] W. W. Rostow, *The Stages of Economic Growth: A Non-Communist Manifesto* (Cambridge: Cambridge University Press, 1967).

[70] Ibid., pp. 162-64.

Western European working classes were inclined to accept ameliorative improvements; accept the terms of democratic capitalism rather than concentrate their efforts on the ultimate bloody show-down, the seizure of property and its turn-over to a State which somehow, in Marx's view, the workers might then control."[71]

In Britain, the decades of the take-off and of the drive to technological maturity—extending respectively in Rostow's reckoning from 1783 to 1802 and from 1802 to 1850—were indeed punctuated by successive waves of radicalization (1790s, 1816-1820, 1835-1840) in the course of which the English working class "made itself";[72] and the 1850s did usher in the "new trade unionism," which in relation to what preceded it can be properly labeled a "moderate" phase. But what are we to make of the development among British workers of a sharper sense of class, expressed in greater militancy, on the eve of World War I? For Rostow, France and Germany completed their "drive to maturity" by 1910;[73] but if one can indeed observe a "hump of radicalism" in the decades of the transition, in both of these cases another such "hump" erupted after "maturity" was achieved, and there is reason to think that the late hump was more radical than the early one. A similar sense of indeterminacy emerges from a consideration of the outlook and organizational behavior of the American working class in relation to the take-off stage (1843-1860) and the drive to maturity (1860-1900).

With respect to timing proper, Britain's take-off preceded all the others by about half a century; then, beginning in 1830, France, the United States, and Germany took off in quick succession within ten years of each other. Britain achieved maturity as early as 1850; the others bunch up around 1900 (U.S.) and 1910 (France and Germany). It will be noted that by this count, the United States and Germany took only forty years to complete the second stage, as against Britain's half-century.

What, if any, is the significance of these matters of time in relation to working-class formation? Britain's precocious industrialization is inextricably linked with its paramount position in the international economy; it has been estimated that as a consequence of this, British per capita income was approximately 25 percent higher throughout the nineteenth century than would have otherwise been the case.[74] This is in keeping with the traditional Marxist explanation concerning the waning of the

---

[71] Ibid., p. 158.

[72] E. P. Thompson, *The Making of the English Working Class* (New York: Vintage, 1963).

[73] Rostow, *Stages*, pp. 38, 59.

[74] Patrick O'Brien and Calgar Keyder, *Economic Growth in Britain and France 1780-1914: Two Paths to the Twentieth Century* (London: Allen and Unwin, 1978).

class struggle in the second half of the nineteenth century and the rise of the "new unionism"—that is, the British working class as a whole turned into an "aristocracy of labor," sharing in the material advantages derived from the exploitation of the world at the hands of British capitalism.

In a somewhat different vein, Britain's lead also meant that the formation of a working-class ideology—in the sense of the production of a map to guide one's steps into unknown territory[75]—was of necessity an almost entirely endogenous process. The British working class was very much inspired by American and French ideas in the age of democratic revolution; but its subsequent experience of the "great transformation" was for the time being unique, and it became much more insular in the decades after 1815. In this light, trade unionism can be seen as something akin to a folk invention, the process of stumbling upon an organizational form that made a great deal of sense in terms of the immediate experience of a working class that had been brutally displaced from its rural roots into rapidly growing urban centers, and where manufacturing was conducted in establishments large enough to make for a clear social differentiation between owners and workers.

Although industrialization occurred later in France and America, working-class responses in both cases were still largely endogenous: in the one case, as Sewell has shown, because as a consequence of popular involvement in revolution, workers had begun to constitute themselves into a class before the onset of industrialization; and in the other, as Bridges has demonstrated, because the political experience of workers was unique and external models were of little interest. In the German case, however, lateness does appear to have mattered, in that reflection on the experience of others played a very important role in shaping working-class doctrine and therefore its organization. Working-class formation in Germany owed a great deal to theory; but it is not necessary to invoke some notion of German national character to account for this. By the onset of industrialization in that country, the British and French experiences were already available to theorize upon; and that is of course precisely what Marx and Engels did. The experience of the German working class was exceptional in that even as it was being born, a language was being designed in anticipation of its needs. It is no wonder that it learned to speak that language so precociously.

A suggestive hypothesis concerning the pace of economic development was set forth by Lorwin in the work cited earlier.[76] He conceptualizes this as a dichotomous variable, "rapid" versus "sluggish" growth. The start-

---

[75] Clifford Geertz, *The Interpretation of Cultures* (New York: Basic Books, 1973).
[76] Lorwin, "Working-class Politics," p. 338.

ing point here is the "hump of radicalism" discussed earlier: "Rapid growth in the early stages of industrialization generates protest by reasons of the bewildering dislocations and (for many) the sacrifices out of current consumption which it imposes." Subsequently, however, the variation mentioned enters into play: "Continued economic growth permits the satisfaction of much of this protest." Although Lorwin cautions that even in such cases "some attitudes of protest persist well beyond the economic conditions which aroused them," he has little doubt about the consequences of the contrasting pattern: "Sluggish economic growth may generate the deepest and longest lasting protest by reason of the society's inability to provide well-being and social justice to match social aspirations and by reason of the economic elite's failure to inspire confidence. Slow growth of cities and slow recruitment of the industrial work force facilitate the carryover of traditions of protest from generation to generation."[77]

For Lorwin, "rapid growth" pertained to Britain and "sluggish" to Latin Europe, particularly France. Unfortunately, there is little or no empirical support for this characterization. One of Rostow's major theoretical concerns was to demonstrate that the length of the transition was quite constant cross-nationally, regardless of whether it occurred in a market economy or under "Communism." Completion of the first two stages of growth took sixty-seven years in the British case and eighty in the French—hardly a persuasive illustration of rapidity versus sluggishness.

Leaving Rostow's questionable periodization aside, other time series are no more conclusive. For the twelve leading western countries as a whole, over the period 1870-1913, the average annual rate of growth of total output was 2.7 percent; individual countries ranged from a high of 4.3 (United States) to a low of 1.4 (Italy); Germany was in the middle (2.9); both Britain and France were decidedly below average (2.2, 1.6).[78] Although this does provide some support for Lorwin's notion concerning "sluggish" Latins, it is evident that since the hypothesis is predicated on the system's ability—or lack of ability—to deliver satisfactions to workers, the better measure would be rate of growth of output per capita. When this is done, the relationship predicted by Lorwin is in fact weakened rather than strengthened. The average for the twelve countries over the period indicated is 1.6 percent; the United States remains significantly higher (2.2) and Germany stays in the middle (1.8); the United Kingdom, which still falls below average (1.3), is now overtaken by

[77] Ibid., p. 350.
[78] Angus Maddison, *Economic Growth in the West* (New York: Norton, 1967), p. 28.

France (1.4).[79] Going beyond the cases under consideration here, it might be noted that the "highs" include, in addition to the United States, Sweden (2.3), Denmark (2.1), and Canada (2.0); the "lows" also include Norway (1.4), Switzerland (1.3), the Netherlands (0.8), and Italy (0.7). With respect to the issues of immediate concern here, the only reliable conclusion one might draw is that, as Sombart and others observed at the time, in the decades immediately preceding World War I, American capitalism did indeed produce a higher level of material welfare in the form of individual goods than most of its European counterparts.

In retrospect, it is quite evident that the "stages of growth" approach, like much of the developmental literature of the 1960s—which was in part inspired by it—rested on a fundamentally flawed assumption of structural uniformity, namely that countries proceeded, at different times but under broadly similar conditions, along the same transitional path leading from an agricultural to a mass consumption economy. There is no need to cite here the vast critical literature that has emphasized that in fact, developmental conditions for the West and for the rest of the world differed fundamentally as a consequence of the West's success in forming a capitalist world-economy.[80]

More directly relevant to the present purpose is the recent literature, which emphasizes structural differences as an inherent feature of western economic development. For example, in their comparative analysis of Britain and France, O'Brien and Keyder reject the conventional approach in which Britain is viewed as a model of normal growth, in relation to which the French economy suffered from "backwardness"; they regard instead these two countries as having followed quite different paths, determined by different configurations of opportunities and constraints at the start.[81] This resulted on the eve of World War I in distinct economies with very different structural configurations, each of which provided approximately the same level of welfare.

The specific implications of the O'Brien and Keyder study for the two cases will be discussed below. On a more general level, the approach it represents suggests that if we are trying to understand how the development of industrial capitalism shaped the formation of national working classes, it is useful to consider from the outset that societies generally considered "industrial" today differ considerably in their degree of industrialness—an awkward term introduced here to distinguish the size of the

[79] Ibid., p. 30.
[80] See especially Immanuel Wallerstein, *The Modern World-System* (New York: Academic Press, 1974).
[81] O'Brien and Keyder, *Economic Growth in Britain and France.*

industrial sector in relation to the total economy from "industrialization"—and have in fact done so all along.

A useful indicator of this is the proportion of active population employed in the secondary sector at each of several points in time. As noted in the essays above, a significant segment of the labor force of western societies was already engaged in manufacturing before the industrial revolution; the baseline level can be established in the range of 15-20 percent.[82] As of the middle of the nineteenth century, the range had become much wider, reflecting Britain's historic lead. The proportion of the labor force engaged in the secondary sector around 1850 was as follows: Great Britain, 48.1 percent; France, 26.9; United States, 17.6 (no estimate is available for Germany at this time). Incidentally, the second highest level was found in Belgium (36.3 percent), reflecting that country's industrial lead on the Continent.[83]

Looking forward from that point, one might have reasonably predicted that the British proportion would continue to grow and that others would eventually follow suit; as noted earlier, this was in fact the assumption made by Marx and Engels. But this projection turned out to be wrong on two quite separate counts, both of which are crucial with respect to working-class formation. First, unbeknownst to contemporary observers, it turned out that the level achieved by Britain at mid-century was already very close to its historical maximum, 51.6 percent in 1911. Second, the British level was attained in only two other cases, Belgium (45.5 percent in 1910, peaking at 48.6 in 1947) and Germany (40.9 percent in 1910, peaking at 48.3 in 1961). Neither in France nor in the United States did the secondary sector work force ever constitute anywhere as high a proportion of the total. In France, the percentage rose slowly from the 26.9 percent level noted for 1850 to 33.1 in 1910, most of the increment occurring after 1880; in the United States, it climbed during the same period from 17.6 to 31.6 percent.

Before discussing the implications of these findings, let us note briefly that "mature" capitalist economies may vary not only in their degree of industrialness but also in the extent to which—quite aside from size—their manufacturing sector is industrialized, properly speaking—i.e., is capital intensive with production concentrated in factories. A useful summary indicator of industrialization in this sense for the period under consideration is variation in the use of steampower, because steam remained the most widely used form of mechanical energy, and because, as opposed

[82] Simon Kuznets, *Modern Economic Growth: Rate, Structure, and Spread* (New Haven: Yale University Press, 1967), pp. 88-89.
[83] Vander Eycken and Frantzen, *De tertiaire sector*, pp. 16-23.

to tools, steam-operated machinery was fixed and hence owned by firms rather than by workers. The ranking of Great Britain, the United States, Germany, and France with respect to horsepower per capita in 1910 merely confirms what we already know from the proportion of the labor force in the secondary sector. However, by controlling for size of the labor force, it becomes possible to use horsepower as an indicator of the degree to which the economy was capital intensive. In this regard, around the turn of the century, the United States ranked highest (index: 2.34). Although Britain was more industrial than the United States, it was less industrialized, ranking second (1.78); France, as expected, has a much lower level (1.09). The surprising case is Germany, which falls slightly below France.[84]

Albeit unrefined, these statistical indicators enable us to sketch out somewhat more systematically and with slightly greater precision some hypotheses concerning the consequences for working-class formation of cross-national variation in the structure of industrial capitalism at the time of its emergence. France and the United States will be used as the major illustrations for this purpose.

Like the United States, France never became an industrial society to the same degree as Britain, Germany, or Belgium. On the eve of World War I, 41 percent of the French labor force was employed in the primary—that is, agricultural—sector, the highest proportion among the four cases considered. This reflected the distinctive path of French economic growth in the nineteenth century, analyzed by O'Brien and Keyder in the work cited above.

The starting point for this is the effect of the French Revolution on land ownership. It is likely that the ownership of land was more concentrated in Great Britain than in France from the early modern period onward; and whereas the industrial revolution in Britain is associated with enclosures and further concentation, resulting in the formation of a "surplus population" pushed from the land and driven into the domestic market for industrial labor or into emigration, the French Revolution was tantamount to a wave of what is now called "land reform": it further deconcentrated the ownership of land and placed a much larger share of it into the hands of the rural middle and lower classes. Subsequently, the French rural population did not expand at the same high rate as was the case in most of the rest of Europe, a phenomenon that may itself have been the result of more widespread land ownership, which provided an incentive to limit family size in order to forestall extreme parcelization.

[84] The index is constructed from information in Landes, *Unbound Prometheus*, p. 220, and Vander Eycken and Frantzen, *De tertiaire sector*.

Consequently, unlike Britain or Germany, France did not experience a "great transformation."[85] Agriculture there remained a viable and nearly self-sufficient way of life. In Britain over the course of the nineteenth century, the share of national product attributable to agriculture declined from 32 percent to 6 and in Germany from some undetermined level to 18; in France the drop was much less marked—from an estimated 50 percent to 35.[86] Concomitantly, France experienced much less urbanization and, most dramatically, produced almost no emigration whatsoever.

Against conventional analyses that suggested that France's low degree of industrialness in comparison with other major western societies at the beginning of the nineteenth century was a sign of "backwardness," O'Brien and Keyder emphasize that the French economy was merely more balanced. In per capita income, as a consequence of revolution and war France lagged behind Britain in the early decades of the nineteenth century: however, as noted earlier, although France's gross national product grew at a slightly lower rate than Britain's over the century as a whole, per capita income was about the same in both countries on the eve of World War I because the French rate of demographic expansion was considerably lower.

Not only was France less industrial, it was also less industrialized. The persistence of an extensive and largely self-sufficient rural societal segment in France meant that the country did not offer to its manufacturers as large a market for mass-produced goods as did highly urbanized and industrialized countries such as Britain and Germany or countries undergoing spectacular demographic expansion such as the United States. French capitalists discovered early that their comparative advantage lay in the production of high quality luxury goods, both for home consumption and for export. Such production, however, required the maintenance of a highly skilled artisanal work force; and in relation to this type of production, the workshop was a more efficient organizational unit than the factory. O'Brien and Keyder have established that French workshops were in fact more productive than British ones, while the reverse was true with respect to factories.

Concomitantly, manufacturing remained largely in the hands of petty capitalists. One indicator of this is that around the first decade of the century, entrepreneurs and self-employed individuals amounted to 33 percent of the French labor force, against only 13 percent in Britain, with Germany and the United States occupying an intermediate rank;

[85] Karl Polanyi, *The Great Transformation* (Boston: Beacon Press, 1957).
[86] Kuznets, *Modern Economic Growth*, pp. 88-89.

although the high French level reflected in part the prominence of rural enterprise and its deconcentrated character, it cannot be accounted for entirely by that factor alone.[87] Another suggestive indicator is that whereas in 1906-1907, 47.6 percent of the German industrial labor force worked in plants with fifty or more employees, the proportion in France was only 29.3 percent.[88]

Considered in this perspective, the "producer socialism" of French skilled craftworkers can be seen as an economically rational and socially realistic response to a particular form of capitalism, much as trade unionism was to another. One can also understand why Michelle Perrot insists that, contrary to much of what has been written on the subject, there is little evidence that French workers resisted indutrialization; the process that for them represented capitalism in its most abhorrent form was *concentration*. Once this orientation was established, it provided the baseline from which change occurred; circumstances might stimulate French workers toward more or less radical action, but the organizational form in which their radicalism or moderation was expressed differed profoundly from that of their British or German fellows.

Given the prominence of the American economy in the world of industrial capitalism as of 1910, the relatively low proportion of its labor force found in the secondary sector can hardly be taken as an indicator of "sluggishness." Rather, it reflected the remarkably capital-intensive character of the American industrial sector, a feature that goes a long way toward accounting for the precocious emergence of what has been termed a "special relationship" between the segment of the working class engaged in such production and the owners of capital.

Moreover, the high productivity of the American industrial labor force went hand in hand with the rapid growth of the labor force employed in the tertiary sector, which included work that came to be called "white collar." Expansion of the latter sector kept pace with that of the secondary throughout the nineteenth century, pulling ahead of it in the first decade of the twentieth; as of 1910, the percentage in the tertiary was 35.3, against 31.6 in the secondary. This was, at the time a unique situation, indicated by the fact that in Britain the size of the tertiary sector labor force lagged significantly behind the secondary until the 1920s and in Germany it did so still in 1961, the endpoint of the time series being used. In short, American industrial workers constituted less of a critical mass in the United States than they did in Britain or Germany; there is

[87] Ibid., p. 168.
[88] Richard Kuisel, *Capitalism and the State in Modern France* (Cambridge: Cambridge University Press, 1981), p. 28.

little doubt that the precocious development of a large segment of white-collar workers also contributed to the formation of a more diffuse sense of class among Americans more generally.

Another distinctive feature of the development of American capitalism was the procurement of a labor supply by immigration rather than by transfers from the rural sector; or, more precisely, by transfers from the rural sectors of non-American economies. As indicated in the work of Bridges, there emerged early on a sharp ethnic segmentation of the labor force, roughly divided between more skilled natives and less skilled immigrants. Immigration itself fluctuated widely in the second half of the nineteenth century, reaching a record level—both in absolute numbers and in proportion to population—in the first decade of the twentieth. As of 1910, approximately one-fourth of the American white male labor force (ten years of age or over) was foreign-born; but the proportion rose to over one-third in manufacturing and mechanical industry, and to over one-half in mining.[89] From another perspective, two thirds of the foreign-born were living in cities and constituted nearly one-fourth of the cities' total population.

Equally important, this foreign population increasingly consisted of migrants rather than of immigrants. Steam navigation and the railroad sharply reduced the time and financial costs of long-distance travel, making it possible for European workers from the 1880s on to engage in a form of trans-Atlantic commuting. In the years 1908-1910, there were 32 recorded departures from the United States for every 100 recorded arrivals, with much higher proportions among some groups. Southern Italians, who constituted approximately one-fifth of all immigrants admitted around this time, were truly "birds of passage," with 56 departures per 100 arrivals.[90] In short, as American industrial capitalism matured, about one-third of the American working class—and undoubtedly well over half of the unskilled—consisted of recent European arrivals who did not intend to stay.

Other capitalist economies relied on migrant labor as well, and two sorts of hypotheses have been set forth concerning the impact of this pattern of labor procurement on working-class formation. One stream is traceable to Marx himself. Britain received substantial numbers of Irish migrants from the mid-eighteenth century on; by the time Marx and Engels observed the British scene, something like one-third the population of the major industrial cities of England and Scotland was Irish.

---

[89] Rosenblum, *Immigrant Workers*, p. 74.
[90] Michael Piore, *Birds of Passage: Migrant Labor and Industrial Societies* (New York: Cambridge University Press, 1979), pp. 151-53.

Marx believed that ethnic hatreds compounded the tensions normally engendered by competition among workers. He asserted that the antagonism between English and Irish proletarians was "the secret of the impotence of the English working-class, despite their organization."[91] But this remains an unverified assertion; the prominent role that the Irish played in the Chartist movement, for example, suggests that Marx may have underestimated the ability of English and Irish workers to surmount their antagonisms. Nevertheless, there is little doubt that the phenomenon of "split labor" does constitute an obstacle to collective action.[92]

In the United States there are many indications, dating to colonial times, that native workers tended to regard the incoming flow as a process induced by employers to lower wages, which was indeed very much the case; such resentment played an important part in the rise of the "Know-Nothing" movement and in the concomitant collapse of the second American party system in the early 1850s.[93] Beginning in the 1860s, American labor unions strove to secure the enactment of legislation restricting and later prohibiting the immigration of Orientals, considered as particularly unfair competition because of their willingness to work for lower wages and under worse conditions than whites. In addition, they sponsored the Foran Act of 1885, which prohibited the entry of workers under contract, a practice associated with strike-breaking.[94]

Charlotte Erickson has suggested further that the organizational efforts of the Knights of Labor were defeated by the massive immigration of the 1880s and that this experience in turn exacerbated the nativism of American craftworkers, thus foreclosing for a very long time the option of incorporating unskilled newcomers into a more comprehensive labor movement. This added to the distinctiveness of the American working class at a time when European unions were beginning to make a transition from craft to industrial organization.

The second line of reasoning pertains to the distinctive outlook of migrants and immigrants. The most comprehensive argument has been

[91] Quoted in Michael Hechter, *Internal Colonialism* (Berkeley: University of California Press, 1975), p. 15.

[92] Edna Bonacich, "Advanced Capitalism and Black/White Relations: A Split Labor Market Interpetation," *American Sociological Review* 41 (1976):34-51.

[93] See in particular the contribution by Amy Bridges to this volume, as well as Aristide R. Zolberg, "Contemporary Transnational Migrations in Historical Perspectives: Patterns and Dilemmas," in *U.S. Immigration and Refugee Policy*, ed. Mary Kritz (Lexington: D. C. Heath, 1983), p. 23.

[94] Charlotte Erickson, *American Industry and the European Immigrant, 1860-1885* (Cambridge: Harvard University Press, 1957); Espen Thorud, "Labor and Immigration Policy: The U.S. Case in Theoretical Perspective" (M.A. paper, Department of Political Science, University of Chicago, 1982).

presented by Gerard Rosenblum, who suggests that in addition to their negative role in muting ongoing mobilization, the newcomers contributed positively to the triumph of business unionism, in that as "target workers" who did not intend to stay—even if in the end many of them did— they were oriented exclusively to the workplace.[95] As Katznelson has pointed out, to the extent that the immigrants were incorporated into the community, this occurred by way of the intermediation of political machines, whose organizational structure contributed to the preservation of ethnic subcultures, or even to their creation de novo.[96] These became primary membership units, quite compatible with the instrumental pursuit of economic objectives. C. T. Husbands and Jerome Karabel have made suggestions to the same effect in the course of commenting on Sombart, who himself surprisingly ignored the impact of immigration.[97]

The ethnic segmentation of the American working class can also be viewed as a feature of economic rather than of social organization—in terms of our general framework, as a feature of Class 1 rather than of Class 2. In this light, it can be seen as an indication of the precocious emergence in the United States of a form of capitalism organized around a segmented labor market.

The distinctive reliance of American capitalism on a large supply of unskilled labor has long been noted by economic historians; Brinley Thomas, for example, has pointed out that big bursts of invention coincided with big waves of immigration, and reasons on this basis that thanks to the steady immigration of cheap labor, "the United States was able to take full advantage of [technical] innovations by 'widening' her capital structure with enormous benefit to her physical productivity and economic power."[98] The capital-intensive nature of technological innovations in turn provided an impetus for the stabilization of output in order to ensure high levels of utilization; this, Alfred Chandler has suggested, in turn accounts for the drive toward industrial consolidation that was so characteristic of American capitalism in the post–Civil War period.[99] Taking the matter one step further, Michael Piore has shown how the consolidation movement "laid the groundwork for a dual eco-

[95] Rosenblum, *Immigrant Workers*, pp. 34-58, 146-58.

[96] Ira Katznelson, *City Trenches: Urban Politics and the Patterning of Class in the United States* (New York: Pantheon, 1981), pp. 45-72.

[97] Husbands, "Introduction," p. xxix; Jerome Karabel, "The Failure of American Socialism Reconsidered," *The Socialist Register* 18 (1979):204-227.

[98] Brinley Thomas, *Migration and Economic Growth: A Study of Great Britain and the Atlantic Economy*, 2d ed. (Cambridge: Cambridge University Press, 1973), p. 172; Rosenblum, *Immigrant Workers*, p. 1.

[99] Alfred D. Chandler, Jr., *The Visible Hand: The Managerial Revolution in American Business* (Cambridge: Harvard University Press, 1977), pp. 50-78.

nomic structure. It divided demand in most major industries into two components: a stable component ... which the newly formed trusts attempted to reserve for themselves, and which was met through modern, capital-intensive production technologies in relatively large-scale productive units, and a fluctuating component, handled by much smaller enterprises, probably in smaller productive units and using more labor-intensive techniques."[100]

Piore hypothesizes that this differentiation fostered a corresponding one between two categories of labor—skilled natives to man the stable component and unskilled immigrants to man the fluctuating one. More generally, though the general tendency in capitalist economies is for capital to be the fixed factor of production and labor the variable one, "there are also cases in which the employer is forced to invest in labor in very much the same way he invests in capital, in order, for example, to have a skilled labor force when workers cannot or will not invest in training themselves. ... The nature of the system creates incentives to organize production so that these workers too have more stable, secure employment opportunities and, in this way, extends the dualism inherent in the distinction between capital and labor to a distinction within the labor market itself."[101]

It will be noted that this analysis provides a structural explanation for the formation of "labor aristocracy" segments within working classes more generally. However, it is likely that immigration contributed to institutionalize segmentation as a particularly pronounced structural feature of American industrial capitalism, and this would go a long way toward accounting for the entente that arose between industrialists and the AFL in the crucial decades around the turn of the century. Notwithstanding the understandable resistance of capitalists to unions, accommodation was more likely to be reached with a segment of the working class that was structurally distinctive in the manner indicated and whose leaders explicitly recognized such distinctiveness at the level of doctrine and organization. As Karabel has suggested, "if the sheer wealth of American society militated against the emergence of a mass-based social movement, it did so less through the *embourgeoisement* of the proletariat as a whole than through facilitating the development of a special relationship between capital and strategic sectors of the working class."[102] Finally, the precocious incorporation of the skilled and mostly native sector of the American working class into the "fixed" segment of the capi-

---

[100] Piore, *Birds of Passage*, pp. 144-45.
[101] Ibid., pp. 36-37.
[102] Karabel, "Failure of American Socialism," p. 209.

talist economy may have been facilitated by the even more precocious achievement by workers of political citizenship.

The last feature of the American economy to be noted is the availability of cheap land. Engels, and after him Sombart, placed considerable emphasis on the frontier phenomenon as a factor accounting for the exceptionalism of the American working class; they also believed that the waning of the frontier would result in a rapid rise of class consciousness.[103] However, given the low incidence of movement by American urban workers into agriculture, more recent analysts have cast doubt on the importance of this factor for working-class formation.

Yet there is another way in which the availability of land in America may have played a determinative role in shaping the outlook and disposition of the country's working class. Given the vast supply of land, the costs of owning real property of any kind, beginning with a family home, have always been much lower in America than in Europe. It will be remembered that the widespread incidence of property ownership among the American populace was already noted in the 1830s by Alexis de Tocqueville, who believed that this contributed significantly to the tempering of democracy. In the same vein, but in a different context, J. Capdevielle and E. Dupoirier have identified the distinctive contribution of real-estate ownership—what they call the *effet patrimoine*—independently of income level, to conservative voting in contemporary France.[104] Even in the absence of appropriate data, there can be little doubt that the incidence of ownership has continued to be much higher among American than European workers, all the way to the present. This provides a possible explanation for Katznelson's crucial observation concerning the tendency of American workers to differentiate sharply between their role as labor and their role as residents or as citizens more generally, which would well be worth investigating on a comparative basis.

The Political Regime as a Conceptual Variable. The consequences of variation in the character of political structures on the patterning of working-class formation have been the object of considerable attention ever since this process first aroused the interest of analysts. It will be remembered that Marx, for example, "went so far as to exclude England and the United States from any postulated necessity of violent overthrow of the state precisely because there was no state as such to overthrow,

---

[103] Ibid., pp. 204-206; Sombart, *Why Is There No Socialism*, pp. 115-16.
[104] Jacques Capdevielle, E. Dupoirier, G. Grunberg, E. Schweisguth, C. Ysmal, *France de gauche, vote à droite* (Paris: Presses de la Fondation Nationale des Sciences Politiques, 1981), pp. 169-227.

because of the essentially transformatory nature of the relevant institutions."[105] However, there is little agreement in the literature on how to conceptualize these variations to make systematic cross-national comparisons more manageable. Two major approaches can be identified. The first focuses on the character of the "state," usually conceptualized as a dichotomous variable, in terms of strength or weakness, or even more drastically—as with Marx in the instance just cited—in terms of whether or not a state exists.[106] The second focuses on the character of the regime more generally—on the society's constitution, in the classic Aristotelian sense—usually expressed as combined variation along two dimensions, the degree of liberalism and the extensiveness of political participation.

What, precisely, does it mean to say that there is a state in France but not in Britain, or that the one is strong and the other weak? What leaps to mind are the differing institutional legacies associated with the success of absolutism in the one case and its failure in the other. For J. P. Nettl, "stateness" is a property of culture, pertaining to different conceptualizations of the focus around which a political collectivity organizes its identity. As he sees it, although the first discussion of the state as a focus of this sort is found in Machiavelli, the real development of the appropriate historical tradition took place in France, whose mode of political organization in the early modern epoch provided a model for organizing the state elsewhere in Europe. Subsequently, however, it was in Germany that stateness was elaborated as a cultural tradition. The word became flesh; wherever established, this cultural orientation gave rise to distinctive legal and administrative institutions. Accordingly, Bertrand Badie and Pierre Birnbaum regard the institutional system as the appropriate analytic focus, emphasizing the degree of structural differentiation of the state in relation to society as the relevant variable. In practice, as used by its proponents, the "stateness" variable appears to collapse two dimensions of variation, the one pertaining to centralization and the other to institutional differentiation of legal and administrative structures. Statist societies such as absolutist France or Prussia are characterized by a high degree of both; but nonstatist societies can have a centralized political system (as in Great Britain) or a decentralized one (as in the United States).

Various hypotheses have been set forth concerning the relationship between stateness and working-class formation. Addressing himself to

[105] J. P. Nettl, "The State as a Conceptual Variable," *World Politics* 20 (1968):560-92.
[106] Ibid.; Wallerstein, *Modern World-System*; Bertrand Badie and Pierre Birnbaum, *The Sociology of the State* (Chicago: University of Chicago Press, 1983).

the influence of a strongly articulated notion of the state on processes and structures of dissent, Nettl argues that "it is no coincidence that anti-system movements have more easily been able to develop in societies with strongly developed states—even though the basis of dissent has been as much religious as merely political," because the process of forming a political identity around the state "appears to provide a convenient and polarizing means of disidentification."[107] Although the instances Nettl cites in support of the proposition are taken from the post–World War I period—Weimar Germany, France, and Italy, buffeted by antisystem oppositions from both right and left in contrast to Britain and the United States—the variation under consideration arose considerably earlier, so that Nettl's proposition should be applicable to our own period as well. Indeed, a decade before Nettl, Lorwin independently formulated a similar hypothesis, addressed more particularly to working-class formation, to the effect that "labor movements most dependent on the state may show greatest hostility to the state."[108] The illustrative cases cited are France and Italy, in contrast with Britain and the United States. More recently, Birnbaum has similarly asserted that France's "stateness" accounts for the tendency of its working class to oppose the state, as indicated by the incidence of anarchosyndicalism and later Marxism, in contrast with the trade unionist orientation of the British.[109]

These various formulations appear to be pointing toward a single generic process that might be identified as follows. Wherever the state had historically emerged as a highly differentiated political actor—that is, where a monarchy succeeded in achieving absolutism—and managed to survive as such into the period of the industrial revolution, liberalization did not lead to a sharp separation of politics and economics into mutually exclusive institutional spheres along the lines of British and especially American development. The resulting configuration also imparts a distinctive character to public policy, whereby any collective action by workers to improve their lot entails of necessity a confrontation with central political authorities as well as with employers. This sort of outcome is rendered even more likely by the fact that the configuration under consideration is usually associated with political centralization, it being well established that wherever the political arena is highly centralized, sectoral or local conflicts are more likely to flow quickly toward the apex. Conversely, the combination of a sharp separation between the

---

[107] Nettl, "The State," p. 571.

[108] Lorwin, "Working-class Politics," p. 351.

[109] Pierre Birnbaum, "Etat, corporatisme, et action de la classe ouvrière" (paper presented at 1980 meeting of the Council for European Studies, Washington, D.C.).

institutional spheres of politics and economics—that is, between the public and private sectors—with institutional decentralization and diffused political power, as in the United States prior to its imperial age, would tend to result in narrowly focused working-class organizations and a tendency to confine their action to the appropriate institutional sector.

Beyond this, much of what is being claimed on behalf of the "stateness" hypothesis amounts to a truism: if in the course of the protracted struggle between capitalists and workers the state steadily intervenes on the side of capitalists, it thereby comes to be identified as the enemy of the working class and this assessment is likely to be reflected in that class's hostile disposition toward the state and in a concomitant organizational strategy. However, it is very difficult to distinguish in this respect between the effects of "stateness" and those of regime more generally.

In terms of the "stateness" variable, the four cases considered here fall into two categories, nonstatist Britain and United States and statist France and Germany. However, it is evident that Britain and the United States differed profoundly with respect to their structures of decision making and of political participation throughout the nineteenth century. And from about 1880 on, when it became a democratic parliamentary republic in which power was largely held by middle-class politicians, France resembled the United States much more than it did its fellow-statist Germany, which was then a modernizing absolutist state, still ruled largely by crown and aristocracy. One would surely expect, on the face of it, that such vast differences in regime would weigh at least as heavily in the determination of patterns of working-class formation as would more limited variation with respect to "stateness."

It is something very much akin to the notion of regime that Lipset appears to have in mind when stating that he has sought to identify "variations in national environment that determined . . . the structure of political alternatives for the working class in different western countries before the First World War."[110] To this effect, he singles out two factors as most significant: (1) the nature of the social class system before industrialization; and (2) responses of economic and political elites to demands of workers for the right to participate in the polity and the economy. Each of them is then conceptualized as a continuum. In short, Lipset argues that the more rigid the first, the more likely was the emergence of radical working-class parties, and that this likelihood was further enhanced where working-class demands were denied. Conversely, where the social class system was not rigid and demands were granted early

[110] Lipset, "Radicalism or Reformism," p. 1.

on—a cell containing most prominently the United States—no working-class party arose at all. Intermediate location on each of the variables or some combination involving rigidity on one dimension and flexibility on the other produces either a mixed or an intermediate outcome—radical unions combined with reformist parties, as in France, or the opposite combination, as in imperial Germany.

Albeit suggestive, Lipset's approach—shared by Rokkan as well—is marred by an attempt to apply multivariate techniques to macroanalytic materials and by the imprecise and questionable character of the variables themselves. The result is a historically ridiculous universe, in which pre–World War I Britain, Germany, France, and Russia are equated as having "rigid" and largely "feudal" patterns of social class, as against "nonrigid" patterns in the United States, the Low Countries, and Switzerland; and in which Britain, where one cannot speak of a mass electorate before 1882, is equated with the United States as having achieved political citizenship "early" while the Low Countries and Russia are equated as having done so "late."[111]

Yet when all is said and done, Lipset's analysis strongly suggests, as do the individual country accounts in the present book, that the single most important determinant of variation in the patterns of working-class politics—combining for the moment Class 3 and 4—is simply whether, at the time this class was being brought into being by the development of capitalism (Class 1), it faced an absolutist or a liberal state. This politically fundamental dichotomy subsumes the social stratification variable set forth by Lipset because the prerequisite for the institutionalization of a liberal regime was the emergence of a significant counterweight to the aristocracy, that is, a gentry or a bourgeoisie.[112]

If we limit ourselves to the western world before World War I, the relevant range of regime variation is defined by the United States at the democratic end of the continuum and imperial Germany at the other, which may be termed "modernizing absolutism." The effects of regime are self-evident in both these cases. In America, where democracy preceded industrialization, mass political parties arose before a working class was formed; competing middle-class political entrepreneurs had a vital interest in securing support from the populace at large, and through their efforts white workers were thoroughly mobilized into the parties. As a consequence, space in the political arena was preempted by trans-class organizations; and established actors, with access to resources through

[111] Ibid., p. 15.
[112] Barrington Moore, Jr., *Social Origins of Dictatorship and Democracy* (Boston: Beacon Press, 1967); Perry Anderson, *Lineages of the Absolutist State* (London: New Left Books, 1974).

the institutional apparatus of the state, held a considerable advantage over subsequent challengers, including class-based parties.

The problems generally faced by third parties have long been noted by students of American politics, and were cited prominently by Sombart in 1905. Husbands, who views the matter of political constraints as Sombart's strongest argument for why no social democratic party had yet emerged in the United States, has updated Sombart's analysis of the situation in the early twentieth century in the light of recent research findings.[113] In short, the political alignments established after the crisis of the mid-nineteenth century remained quite stable until the economic crisis of the 1890s. The latter situation provided an opportunity for a radical movement, unattractive to urban and often Catholic workers. Consequently, when populism captured the Democratic party in 1896, many urban workers drifted toward the Republican camp, notwithstanding that party's more conservative stand on social issues. Viewed in this perspective, the Socialist party's forward surge in 1912 was rendered possible only by a temporary disarray of the electoral system owing to a split in the Republican party. However, the opportunity of capturing a substantial share of the working-class vote was equally apparent to the Wilsonian Democrats and, as indicated earlier, they quickly took appropriate steps to that effect. Husbands suggests further that it is the difference in the configuration of the British and American two-party systems at this particular time, rather than more profound structural differences between the two societies, that accounts for the failure of the Liberals to pull off what the Wilsonian Progressives did and hence for the nearly contemporaneous electoral breakthrough of the Labour party.

In contrast with this, at the time of its industrial development, Germany was not yet even a liberal state, let alone a democratic one. Although the Imperial Reichstag was elected on the basis of universal suffrage, this institution had little or no control over the executive; Germans, including workers, were subjects of the emperor, rather than citizens, and Prussian suffrage remained unequal. It is hardly surprising, under such conditions, that the nascent working class was highly responsive to Marxist political doctrine, tailor-made for precisely these conditions.

Viewed in the light of regime, both the United States and Imperial Germany are appropriately seen as exceptional cases. Most countries that experienced industrialization before World War I were neither democracies nor absolutist states; much more typically, they were constitutional monarchies with some governmental accountability to repre-

[113] Husbands, "Introduction," pp. xxiv-xxvi.

sentative institutions and with limited political participation. The two principal variables considered in this section are interdependent in that the earlier and stronger the thrust of capitalism, the more likely was the emergence of political liberalism; where an industrial bourgeoisie ruled, the middle classes generally followed; and it is a truism that liberal regimes were more likely than others to seek accommodation with the lower classes. Somewhat paradoxically, it was in countries such as Britain and Belgium, where the economic and social impact of capitalism was most brutal, that its alienating effects on the working class were most likely to be mitigated by integrative processes in the political sphere. Therein lies the key to Marx's initial mistake concerning the relationship between the development of capitalism and the intensification of class conflict, an error that he himself eventually rectified.

The process under consideration is well illustrated by the British case. Lipset places Britain in the "rigid" category with respect to preindustrial relations between classes; however, in order to account for the fact that rigidity did not foster radicalization as it did on the Continent, he is obliged to invoke an intervening variable, that is, "the strength of noblesse oblige norms among the aristocracy, who consciously served as a 'protective stratum' for workers by enacting factory reforms and welfare-state legislation."[114] But the explanatory value of this factor would be at best very slight, and in the event the assertion of a higher incidence of noblesse oblige in Britain as against other European countries does not bear serious historical scrutiny.

A much more persuasive explanation can be derived from the dynamics of competition between landed and commercial-industrial interests within the framework of a liberal regime. Notwithstanding the persistence of "aristocratic" elements in British society until well into the twentieth century, the political changes brought about from the late 1820s on, known as the "constitutional revolution," entailed a process whereby—to paraphrase what Adam Przeworski and Michael Wallerstein have said about workers under capitalism—the state institutionalized, coordinated, and enforced compromises reached by a class coalition that encompassed capitalists and the middle classes.[115] The triumphant Whig reformers of the 1830s enacted a legislative program, of which the Municipal Corporations Act of 1835 and the New Poor Law of 1834 were the most substantial elements, aimed at coopting the middle classes into the regime, but which simultaneously alienated their erstwhile working-class

[114] Lipset, "Radicalism or Reformism," p. 4.
[115] Adam Przeworski and Michael Wallerstein, "The Structure of Class Conflict in Democratic Capitalist Societies," *American Political Science Review* 76 (1982): 215.

supporters, who responded with Chartism. However, the cooptation of the middle classes provided the regime with a broader political base and helped it weather the mid-century crisis that elsewhere had revolutionary consequences. Once political life was broadened to include the middle classes, parties moved to the fore as key organizations; the dynamic of party politics in turn led to the realization that working-class voters might provide support for one or the other of the contenders, and hence to giving some attention to the interests of that class even before political participation was formally extended to them. This occurred initially at the level of constituencies; but after 1882 both Tories and Liberals manifestly competed for trade union support as well.

It would thus appear that, among the countries where capitalists constituted a sufficient critical mass to play a major role in shaping political outcomes, the critical factor in the institutionalization of a liberal regime was whether or not, when they began to aspire to political power, capitalists struck an alliance with the more numerous middle classes. Where this occurred—not only in Britain but also in Belgium—the established regime escaped the revolutionary upheavals of 1848; this nonevent facilitated subsequent compromises between the politically established middle classes and leading segments of the emerging working class. There were, however, inherent limits to how far parties representing the interests of capitalists might go. It is noteworthy that despite their early success in securing working-class support, both British and Belgian Liberals eventually lost nearly all of it, whereas in both countries Conservative parties—in Belgium, the Catholics—successfully retained a substantial working-class clientele well into the twentieth century. "Noblesse oblige" may have played a role in this; but a better explanation is probably to be found in the religious outlook of part of the working class in both countries.

The political itinerary of British and Belgian mid-century capitalists makes for an interesting contrast with that of the French bourgeoisie, which, after it rose to power in the 1830 revolution, so adamantly resisted middle-class demands for reform along British and Belgian lines that in 1848 the middle and lower classes coalesced long enough to make a revolution, resulting in the precocious advent of a social democratic republic. But this outcome in turn resulted in an escalation of class conflict quite literally to the level of outright class war and hence drastically altered the formative experience of the French working class. A generation later, middle-class republican leaders once again set out to forge a trans-class alliance on behalf of the restoration of a republic; but the rapprochement was tragically interrupted by the Commune and the subsequent civil war.

In the formative stage of industrial capitalism, no western working class achieved as much as did the French in 1848 and again in 1871; but none was made to pay a heavier penalty for its achievements. It is the violence the French working class suffered at the hands of the state that fostered the persistence of a revolutionary culture in its midst until well into the twentieth century. Yet the institutionalization of a liberal regime in the 1880s generated trends similar to those encountered in the United States and Britain, making for an acutely ambiguous configuration. Much more attention has been given in the literature on French working-class formation to the emergence of revolutionary syndicalism around the turn of the century than to the fact that, at that time, the vast majority of French workers voted for the Radical party, a loose national confederation of local machines led by middle-class politicians who were fully aware that under conditions of universal suffrage support from the working class was a sine qua non for political success. Because the balanced character of the French economy and the wide dispersion of land ownership required that any coalition aspiring to political success under liberal-democratic conditions must be responsive to agrarian interests, there were limits to what the Radicals might do on behalf of their working-class allies. Nevertheless, as the Radicals rose to power, much of the French working class no longer viewed the state as their enemy, and acted accordingly.[116]

SOMEWHAT belatedly, it is coming to be more widely recognized in the various social science disciplines that macroanalytic subjects such as class formation imply a research strategy that is both comparative and historical. It is therefore appropriate to conclude this book with an essay in this vein. Although it is the product of an individual, as the author I wish to emphasize that participation in our collective undertaking from the outset was a sine qua non for its elaboration.

The "exceptionalist" problematic entails a distortion of reality that has long misguided research in this field. Issued from heated controversy over the theory and practice of socialism at the turn of the century and subsequently nurtured by many decades of deadly national and international conflicts, this way of addressing the question gets us off to a bad start because it exaggerates the range of variation in the political orientation of various segments of the working class, within and between countries, in the years immediately preceding World War I.

This is not to say national working classes did not differ at all, as indi-

---

[116] Michelle Perrot and Annie Kriegel, *Le socialisme français et le pouvoir* (Paris: Etudes et Documentation Internationale, 1966), pp. 88-91.

cated in the second section of this essay, which reviews evidence from the country studies. In the third section I have suggested that the variation observed can largely be accounted for by differences in the shape of industrial capitalism and in the character of the regime within each of the countries considered. In that sense, the essay contends that the answer to the question in its title is, "As many as there are cases under consideration." I hope that the absurdity of this will lay the old problematic of class formation to rest and stimulate renewed inquiry along more constructive lines.

Contributors

AMY BRIDGES is Associate Professor of Government at Harvard University. The author of *A City in the Republic: Antebellum New York and the Origins of Machine Politics*, she has also written numerous articles on American and urban politics. She is currently writing a book about the political development of the cities of the southwestern United States.

ALAIN COTTEREAU is Chargé de Recherche at the CNRS, Paris, within the Center for the Study of Social Movements. He has conducted research on the role of transportation in the economic and social development of the Paris region, as well as on urban policy in Paris and London in the late nineteenth and early twentieth centuries. His most recent research has focused on working-class cultures in France and on the relationships between urban development and class formation.

IRA KATZNELSON is Henry A. and Louise Loeb Professor of Political and Social Science and Dean of the Graduate Faculty at the New School for Social Research. The author of *Black Men, White Cities: Race, Politics and Migration in the United States, 1900-1930, and Britain, 1948-1968*, and *City Trenches: Urban Politics and the Patterning of Class in the United States*, Katznelson has recently completed a coauthored book, *Schooling for All: Class, Race, and the Decline of the American Ideal*.

JÜRGEN KOCKA is a member of the Faculty of History at the University of Bielefeld. Best known for his numerous studies of the German working and middle classes in the nineteenth century and for attempts to integrate social theory into the historical craft, his books include *White Collar Workers in America, 1890-1940* and *Facing Total War: German Society, 1914-1918*.

MARY NOLAN is Associate Professor of History at New York University. Her book, *Social Democracy and Society: Working-Class Radicalism in Düsseldorf, 1890-1920* is pathbreaking in its integration of economic analysis, social history, and political studies. At present, she is examining economic rationalization, company social policy, and the reshaping of industrial relations in Germany between 1918 and 1933.

MICHELLE PERROT is Professor of History at the University of Paris VII. One of the founders of modern social and labor history in France, she has explored the history of strikes, the impact of mechanization on the formation of the labor movement, the distinctive role of women in working-class history, and the character of such state institutions as prisons.

WILLIAM H. SEWELL, JR., is Professor of History and Sociology at the University of Michigan. His *Work and Revolution in France: The Language of Labor from the Old Regime to 1848* describes the institutional and intellectual frameworks of labor in France as these were transformed by the French Revolution and the industrial revolution. In *Structure and Mobility: The Men and Women of Marseille, 1820-1870*, he examines patterns of social structure, migration, and social mobility in nineteenth-century Marseille.

MARTIN SHEFTER is Professor of Government at Cornell University. His research on American politics has focused principally on political parties and on cities, and on the ways in which patterns of political conduct, once institutionalized, continue to shape the American regime. He has recently published *Political Crisis/Fiscal Crisis: The Collapse and Revival of New York City*.

ARISTIDE R. ZOLBERG is University-in-Exile Professor of Political Science at the New School for Social Research. He began his scholarly career with a focus on the newly independent states of West Africa; his publications on the subject include *One-Party Government in the Ivory Coast*. His main interests in the past several years have been various aspects of the long-term political transformation of western societies, including the sources and persistence of culturally distinct regions and the changing character of international migrations. He has recently focused again on the Third World in a study of refugees.

Index

ADAV, *see* Allgemeiner Deutscher Arbeiterverein
Addams, Jane, 207
AFL (American Federation of Labor): accommodation with employers/conservatism of, 255, 259, 274-75, 426-27, 445; constituency of, 272; eight-hour-day movement and, 264-65; formation of, 228, 261; immigration policies of, 266; Knights of Labor compared with, 428-30; politics and, 256-57, 264-66, 428-29; purpose of, 225; socialism and, 256-57, 426-27; strikes and, 254; voting patterns and, 403; Winnetka system of, 428-29. *See also* unions (U.S.)
agriculture: in France, 139-42; in Germany, 289, 292, 293, 294, 299, 300-301, 356-57, 378; in U.S., 166, 200, 252, 256-58, 259
Agulhon, Maurice, 87, 99
Allemane, Jean, 421
Allgemeine Arbeiterverbrüderung (General Workers' Brotherhood), 327, 335-36
Allgemeiner Deutscher Arbeiterkongress (General German Workers' Congress), 327, 335
Allgemeiner Deutscher Arbeiterverein (ADAV), 329, 339, 340, 342, 345, 346. *See also* social democracy/SDP
Althusserians, 12, 114*n*3, 194*n*94
American Federation of Labor, *see* AFL
American Railway Union, 254
American Revolution, 165, 264
Aminzade, R., 150*n*62
Anti-Socialist laws (1878) (Germany), 360, 379, 382, 385, 386, 388
apprenticeship: in France, 82; in Germany, 285, 286; in U.S., 169-70, 171
Arbeiter, concept of, 282*n*6, 325-27
architecture, *see* space
artisans (France): dominance of, 49-53; factory workers compared to, 52-53, 67-69, 70; formation of working class and, 28, 33, 49-53; guilds and, 51, 53; industrialization and, 72; production and, 54; protest movements and, 52; working-class consciousness and, 52-53, 93-94. *See*

also skilled workers; *specific crafts*
artisans (Germany): formation of working class and, 29, 40; labor organization and, 331-32, 333; nature of work and, 365-66. *See also* journeymen (Germany); skilled workers
artisans (U.S.): culture and, 194-95; disappearance of, 174; formation of U.S. working class and, 28, 35-37; franchise and, 190-91; leadership of, 194; organization of, 174, 176, 177; political economy of, 157, 161, 163-65; republicanism of, 157, 161, 163-65, 178-79, 190-91; wage laborers and, 171, 173-76; wages and, 176-77. *See also* skilled workers
association/federation: in France, 61-63, 66-67, 93, 95; in Germany, 291, 300, 301, 344-46. *See also* labor organizations *entries*
Augerau, Patrice, 96
authority: in France, 103, 145-46; in Germany, 290-91, 317, 320-21, 322, 330-31, 359-61; in U.S., 216, 227, 236-37, 269-71. *See also* city government (U.S.); state, German; state government (U.S.)

Babeuf, Gracchus, 45
Badie, Bertrand, 447
Balibar, Etienne, 8
Barker, Joel, 188
Bebel, August, 332, 339, 345-46
Belgium, 453
Bendix, Reinhard, 37, 192
Berg, M., 119-20
Bergery, Claude-Lucien, 73
Birnbaum, Pierre, 447, 448
Blanc, Louis, 45, 64, 65-66
Blanqui, Adolphe, 134-35
Blanqui, Louis Auguste, 45, 65
Blissert, Robert, 270-71
Boorstin, Daniel, 35-36
Born, Stephan, 332, 336
Boston Tenement House Survey (1892), 205
Bourdieu, P., 93
Bourgeois, Léon, 103-104
bourses du travail movement, 422
boycotts, 220-21

Library of Congress Cataloging-in-Publication Data

Working-class formation.

Bibliography: p.
Includes index.
1. Labor and laboring classes—France—History—19th century. 2. Labor and laboring
classes—United States—History—19th century. 3. Labor and laboring classes—Germany—
History—19th century. I. Katznelson, Ira, 1944-   . II. Zolberg, Aristide R., 1931-

HD8430.W67 1986   305.5′62′094   86-9494
ISBN 0-691-05485-1 (alk. paper)   ISBN 0-691-10207-4 (pbk.)